CASTRO, THE BLACKS, AND AFRICA

Afro-American Culture and Society
A CAAS Monograph Series
Volume 8

CASTRO, THE BLACKS, AND AFRICA

CARLOS MOORE

CENTER FOR AFRO-AMERICAN STUDIES
UNIVERSITY OF CALIFORNIA, LOS ANGELES

Library of Congress Cataloging in Publication Data

Moore, Carlos
    Castro, The Blacks, and Africa / Carlos Moore.
      p.   cm. — (Afro-American culture and society, ISSN 0882-5297; v. 8)
    Bibliography: p.
    Includes Index.
    ISBN 0-934934-32-0 — ISBN 0-934934-33-9 (pbk.)
    1. Castro, Fidel, 1927- —Political and social views. 2. Cuba—Politics and
government—1959-   3. Cuba—Race relations. 4. Cuba—Relations—Africa.
5. Africa—Realtions—Cuba. I. University of California, Los Angeles. Center for Afro-
American Studies. II. Title. III. Series.
F1788.22.C3M66   1988
972.91'064—dc19   .   88-37460
                                                         CIP

Center for Afro-American Studies
University of California, Los Angeles

All rights reserved
Library of Congress Catalog Card Number: 88-37460
ISBN: 0-934934-32-0
    0-934934-33-9 (pbk.)
ISSN: 0882-5297
Printed in the United States of America

TO

Shawna
Kima
Josy
Mbisin
Marcia

Very little can be understood
about Cuba until it is realized
how ethnically African a country
it is.

Robin Blackburn, "Prologue
to the Cuban Revolution"

CONTENTS

FOREWORD

Carlos Moore's study of the race factor in Cuba's internal history and in the evolution of its foreign policy is a remarkable scholarly endeavor. This is one of the most significant books available on contemporary Cuba. It addresses a classic "'non-topic'" in Cuban history: the race factor within Cuba. It examines a major theme of the past quarter century: Cuban policies toward Africa; and it assesses the significance of the race factor in the formation of those policies. Carlos Moore brings together an enormous amount of information not available anywhere else and explores themes rarely discussed with regard to Cuba, either in or out of that country. He argues his case vigorously.

The tone in this work is vigorous and at times harsh. Its judgments will be unpopular with many defenders and with many opponents of Cuba's revolutionary government. The former will dislike the truth that there is racism in Cuba today; the latter will dislike the truth that there has always been racism in Cuba. So the book will be profoundly unpopular among many Cubans who will deny that racism is a factor in Cuban history; and it will be intensely disliked, both by the Cuban government and by many of its enemies who live outside of Cuba.

Moore's central theme is that racism is an inherent part of the history of Cuba, a history shared by the whites who have ruled Cuba before and since the revolutionary victory in 1959, a history for which Cubans both in and outside of Cuba are responsible. His argument suggests that a revolution was warranted in Cuba to address the racial factor, among others, but that the revolution which prevailed was so consistent with the historic past of domination that it has not done so. Instead, like all Cuban governments since independence, the current one acknowledges that racism was a problem under the rule of its predecessors, but not now.

This is not just a scholarly book, however. It is also an angry book by someone who has lived through many of the experiences that inform the work. At times, there are some harsh judgments about individuals, governments, and large groups of people. Readers need not share this anger or these judgments (although, of course, they may) in order to learn from this book. I personally have learned a great deal

ix

from reading it and discussing it with the author. Although I differ
both with its tone and with its substance in many places, I am convinced that no one has been so able to unmask this hidden tragedy in
Cuban history as Carlos Moore: the denial of racism there and, consequently, the enormous difficulty in confronting it.

It has been a common scholarly and popular argument that slavery
in Cuba was not as harsh as in the United States and that race relations in Cuba were easier after the emancipation of the slaves than
in the United States. This book, to its great credit, is not interested
in the comparative study of such evils. It focuses its full attention on
the evil of racism in Cuba, and it shows in some detail that, on its
own terms, it is evil enough. Four major themes run through the discussion. Moore gives various weights to them; in discussing his approach, my own agreements and disagreements with him will also
surface.[1]

One major theme addresses a historical explanation. The race factor has been present in Cuba since the early days of the Spanish conquest and it remains so today. It shapes the way Cubans think about
each other and the manner in which their governors have ruled.
Nonetheless, Cuban governments and key elites have sought to deny
the existence of racism and have behaved as if the race factor were
generally inconsequential. The dominant ideology has been that there
are no whites and no Blacks—only Cubans. I strongly agree with
Moore that the race factor has been of decisive importance in Cuban
history and that its workings led to a hierarchical system of subordination of Blacks. I also agree that a key to understanding the race factor in Cuba begins with focusing on the efforts of so many, especially
those in power, to deny that it even exists. This pernicious paternalism has made confronting racism more difficult.

Unlike Moore (and unlike Cuba's revolutionary government), I believe there was a gradual process that, by the mid-twentieth century
(after a bloody repression in 1912 and repeated abuses during the
1930s), had blunted the sharpest edges of racism in Cuba and permitted the gradual improvement of the social, economic, and political
condition of Blacks. Part of this useful trend developed from the work
of people who are not universally popular among Cubans (some
would hate to be in each other's company): former dictator Fulgencio
Batista, himself a mulatto who often tried to "pass for white"; the
pre-revolutionary Liberal party; the pre-revolutionary Communist
party; and the labor movement led by Lazaro Peña and Eusebio Mujal.

A second major theme addresses an explanation of the structure of
the revolutionary regime's power. It argues that Blacks have suffered
from the policies of the regime led by President Fidel Castro since the

revolutionary victory in 1959, not necessarily because the regime is anti-Black but because it is authoritarian. A regime that tolerates no formally organized oppositic n from any quarter and over any significant issue certainly does not tolerate it from Blacks over the race factor. The revolutionary regime has repressed efforts to establish movements in Cuba that seek to focus on the race factor; that seek to bring issues of importance to Blacks to the attention of leaders; that question the overwhelming presence of whites in the leadership; or that simply wish to promote social, cultural, or political associations among Blacks, focusing on specifically Afro-Cuban issues. From this perspective, the revolutionary regime is as harsh on Blacks as it is on any other groups wishing to pursue autonomous, and especially oppositional, activities in Cuba. I agree fully.

A third theme is surely the most controversial. The revolutionary regime might be called negrophobic. On cultural and ideological grounds, it is repressive of the culture of Blacks in Cuba. It has sought to extirpate Afro-Cuban religions, by fighting them directly or by seeking to transform them into artistic folklore. It denigrates traditional Afro-Cuban culture as barbaric. It accords no standing—other than as an academic curiosity—to African and Afro-Cuban languages in Cuba. It takes no deliberate actions to include Blacks in positions of authority, permitting the racism long ingrained in the society to keep Blacks in subordinate positions. Most crucially, it is more repressive toward Afro-Cuban religions than toward Roman Catholicism. It is also more repressive toward social, cultural, or intellectual groupings organized around Afro-Cuban issues than around other issues. It considers the associational expression of Afro-Cuban concerns and grievances especially unacceptable culturally, where the regime is radically integrationist, and ideologically, where it does not accept ethno-cultural variations in the homogeneous society it wants to build.

There is reason for ambivalence in assessing this theme. It is correct that the regime has been quite harsh in this way. It is also correct that it has focused on specific beliefs and practices that happen to be especially prevalent among, and significant for, Blacks in Cuba in the social, cultural, religious, and political spheres. I do not think it is correct that the regime is deliberately and consciously anti-Black, nor that it and its leaders are unusually more racist than has been the norm in the country's history. Why, then, is the result so tragic, oppressive, and disturbing?

One hypothesis is that the regime's apparent negrophobia at home results from the combination of the cultural burdens of the past with the authoritarian powers of the present and the peculiarities of

Marxism-Leninism on ethno-racial questions. Cuba's current rulers, like its past rulers, have sought to deny racism and to promote cultural assimilation, often with benevolent intentions—even if Blacks, as a result of both policies, are consigned to the bottom of the social stratification pyramid and deprived of their cultural traditions. Past rulers lacked the full powers needed to implement their policy preferences. With regard to the race factor, this incapacity resulted in much pluralism that permitted the flourishing of Afro-Cuban religions and the germination of Afro-Cuban politics and intellectual life. Cuba's current rulers have the power to impose their preferences and rely on an ideology that considers ethno-cultural variations superstructural phenomena to be overcome. It is this extraordinary combination of the past and the present that has had some negrophobic outcomes, damnable on their own terms, even though, in my judgment, they do not result from deliberately negrophobic intentions or policies.

The fourth theme of the discussion is the most consistent with the revolutionary regime's official policy: there have been improvements in the conditions of life for Blacks in Cuba since the Revolution. Moore accepts this, although he does not dwell on it. The revolutionary government abolished the vestiges of legal race discrimination; that did not amount to much, but it was still right. Moreover, because Blacks had been disproportionately concentrated at the bottom of Cuba's social stratification, government policies that sought to teach the illiterate, improve the health of the indigent, ensure a minimum caloric intake against hunger, and provide jobs for all, were bound to benefit Blacks disproportionately. These things have happened, to the Cuban government's credit, and Blacks have indeed benefited.

However, Blacks benefited because they were poor, and not because they were Black. Apart from the modest steps required to dismantle what remained of legal race discrimination, the Cuban government has not had explicitly "pro-Black" or "affirmative action" policies. And, at the top of the regime, those who rule are still white. This does not deny to the Cuban government the credit it deserves for improving the lot of the poor, but it underlines yet again how difficult it is for this regime to be conscious of the problem of being Black in Cuba and of the legitimate and enduring question of the meaning of Afro-Cuban traditions in Cuba. I think that Carlos Moore would share my criticism of the limits of the Cuban government's policies in this regard.

This book's publication is a milestone in the history of Cuba. It should launch a long-overdue discussion about a central issue in that country's history—a country that has made the world, and especially Africa, an arena for its international activities. It will be a painful discussion because the subject itself is so. It should dispel myths about Cuba and about its revolution, which might enable the country and even the regime, were it to face up forthrightly to the issues raised here, to become the better for it. For those who are neither Cubans nor revolutionaries, the book will shed much light on the intricacies of the race factor in a society and for a government that are surrounded by and enmeshed in it but barely conscious of it. Never before has an author delved so thoroughly into the subject of race in the Cuban experience. This is, in short, a book that explores how a people and a revolution have worked hard to ignore a central fact they should have addressed long ago.

Moore's discussion of Cuban policy toward Africa from 1959 onwards likewise fills an important scholarly void. Most scholars who have described and analyzed this policy have focused on the period after 1975, because that is when the major interventions in Angola and in Ethiopia occurred and when the scope of Cuban policy in Africa became large and visible. Moore's work, in contrast, reaches a climax in 1972, when three major events coincided: Fidel Castro's first trip to Africa, Cuba's establishment of diplomatic and other relations with black English-speaking Caribbean countries, and Cuba's formal entrance into the Soviet-led Council for Mutual Economic Assistance. Thus, 1972 proved to be a turning point in Cuban history, setting the stage for several key Cuban policies in the years to come. Moore argues implicitly that the subsequent unfolding of events in Angola, Ethiopia, and elsewhere are but the consequences of a policy whose roots had been set much earlier. His task is to shed light on that important earlier time.

Moore's first conclusion needs stressing: the subject of a Cuban policy toward Africa does exist. Cuba's Africa policy in the 1960s was not that of a Soviet proxy, or puppet, or surrogate, or appendage. Cuba's Africa policy, above all, was made in Havana. It is not Moore's subject to examine all the intricacies of Soviet-Cuban relations in those years, but he shows the conflicts between those two governments, their jealousies, and their difficulty in collaborating on many policies for most of the 1960s. However, Moore also shows the construction of an effective Soviet-Cuban alliance by the end of the 1960s and beginning of the 1970s—a pattern consistent with other trends in Soviet-Cuban relations.

If Soviet dictates do not explain the origins and evolution of Cuban policy toward Africa, what, then, does? The first answer is strategy.

The Cuban government, and especially Fidel Castro, looked for opportunities abroad to project the influence of the Cuban revolution and to combat the United States and its allies. The search for opportunities is a central feature of Cuba's Africa policy and the surest guide through the maze of conspiracies, commitments, and deals made over the years. This opportunistic approach was also bold. Cuba deployed forces to help Algeria in its war with Morocco in 1963. Cuba deployed forces, led personally by Ernesto Ché Guevara, to help insurgents in the Congo (later renamed Zaire) fight against the Leopoldville government. Cuba made and broke deals with insurgents, such as Pierre Mulele, or government leaders, depending on changing circumstances. Some Cuban forces protected the governments of the Congo (Brazzaville) and of Guinea; other Cuban forces trained insurgents to fight against Portugal's colonial empire. Beyond Moore's argument, the recounting of these intricate, important, and little-known events is itself a fascinating account.

Moore insists that there was more to Cuban policy in Africa, however. One ideological dimension, which overlapped the strategic orientation, was solidarity with revolutionary states and movements seen as compatible with Cuba's vision of the '"good future." But a more significant ideological dimension, in Moore's judgment, is the race factor.

The impact of race on Cuban foreign policy, according to Moore, is not simple. Some black Cuban intellectuals, such as Walterio Carbonell, argued as early as 1959 for an Afrocentric Cuban foreign policy to defend the Revolution against its enemies abroad and to root it in the experience of Cuba's own black people. These ideas probably caught the imagination of the leadership. In fact, Fidel Castro over the years has increasingly made reference to the history Cuba shares with many African countries through the slave trade. He has been conscious of the external uses of Cuban demography as well as the internal uses of Cuban foreign policy. Africans, he may have thought shrewdly, would welcome advisers and troops from a partly black country; black Cubans, especially numerous among Cuban troops, would fight in wars overseas to support black governments. Moore shows the Cuban government's manipulation of racial symbols both in Africa and in Cuba to build support for Cuban government policies.

Moore insists that an additional reason for Cuba's entry into Africa was paternalism and disdain for the capacity of African leaders, governments, and movements to build their own future. Cuba would show them how to make and consolidate revolutions in the face of imperialist enemies. This controversial assertion is drawn from many speeches and interviews and cannot easily be dismissed. It is one of the more troubling features of the story.

Strategy, ideology, and possible prejudice are combined in the person of Fidel Castro, who is the decisive actor in the drama that unfolds in the pages of this book. Ché Guevara also played an important supporting role, as did an increasing number of other Cuban leaders as Cuba's Africa policy became more complex.

The domestic dimension of Cuba's Africa policy is equally complex in its effects. On the one hand, Moore shows that some Cuban Blacks who identified with the revolutionary government rose rapidly through the ranks of government and Party and took charge of the implementation of important aspects of Cuba's Africa policy. On the other hand, Moore also shows that the Cuban government did not change most of its internal policies on matters of race even as it became more involved in Africa. The Cuban government remained intolerant of the independent expression of cultural and political ideas and behavior by Cuban Blacks. An independent Africa abroad did not make for an independent, albeit meta-phorical, Africa at home.

Nonetheless, the results of Cuba's Africa policies have been impressive. Cuba's presence has spread throughout the African continent. There has not been much opposition within Cuba to the support for African revolutionary states and movements. Cuba's insurgent allies in the Portuguese colonies eventually came to power. The presence and availability of Cuban troops has become a major power factor on that continent. In fact, Cuba is at least as significant as the more conventionally defined non-African major powers in Africa.

"Little Cuba," to use a phrase cited often in this book, plays war drums heard clearly and with effect across the oceans and throughout the lands of Africa. It is tragic that other drums that might sing within Cuba of the cultural, political, and religious expression of Afro-Cubans do not vibrate so freely and so joyously. That is the twin drama of the race factor in Cuba's own history and in its foreign policy—a drama painfully, articulately, and powerfully presented in the pages of this book.

Jorge I. Dominguez
Professor of Government
Harvard University

NOTE

1. I have addressed some of these themes in my writings. *Insurrection or Loyalty: The Breakdown of the Spanish American Empire* (Cambridge: Harvard University Press,

1980) deals in part with the race factor in Cuba at a crucial moment in the early nineteenth century. *Cuba: Order and Revolution* (Cambridge: Harvard University Press, 1978) considers in part the condition of Blacks before and after the Revolution. See also my "'Racial and Ethnic Relations in the Cuban Armed Forces: A Non-Topic," *Armed Forces and Society* 2(2):273–290 (February 1976).

ACKNOWLEDGMENTS

I am profoundly indebted to the Ford Foundation, whose grant made the publication of this book possible; to Atlanta's Mayor Andrew Young, for having taken an early interest in this work and for having drawn the Foundation's attention to it; to Dr. Jeffrey Puryear, the Foundation official who facilitated the implementation of the grant. Many friends were instrumental at various stages of the long development of this work, and I wish to thank them dearly: Dr. Edem Kodjo, former secretary-general of the Organization of African Unity; Ambassador Donald Eassum, former U.S. asst. secretary of state for African affairs; Dr. Rex Nettleford, University of the West Indies; Dr. Robert Jaulin, University of Paris-7; British historian Lord Hugh Thomas; Dr. Richard Long, University of Atlanta; writer Alex Haley; Dr. Cheikh Anta Diop, University of Dakar.

Dr. Claudia Mitchell-Kernan, director of the Center for Afro-American Studies, University of California at Los Angeles, directed the long and tedious process of turning the original manuscript into this book. She was ably assisted, successively, by CAAS's publication editors, Marcelle Fortier and Toni Lieteau, both as gentle as they were efficient. Sabrina Gledhill and Jacqueline A. Tasch are responsible for a superb editing. Dr. Jorge I. Dominguez of Harvard University read and criticized the original draft, providing invaluable advice. Dr. Edward Gonzalez at UCLA read the final draft, offering pertinent suggestions.

Special support came from: Fatou Sow, Nicole Littré, Marie-Nelly Privat, Albassa Touré, Scarlet Ozier-Lafontaine, Shirley Bowen, Bobby Weisse, Rolland Girard, and Dr. Betty Shabazz, Malcolm X's widow.

Over the period of ten years that it took to complete this work, my wife, Shawna, assisted as editor, translator, documentalist and also typist. So she occupies a place all her own. No words can give thanks for such companionship.

PART ONE

RACIAL POLITICS IN REVOLUTIONARY CUBA

1 THE COLOR OF POWER

At the start of the massive and spectacular Cuban military intervention in Angola in 1975, President Fidel Castro proclaimed Cubans to be a "Latin-African people" whose duty was to assist in the liberation of black Africa, the ancestral continent of perhaps more than half of the island's population.[1] Could Castro have invoked such a strong popular emotional commitment to the support of African revolution had he led, say, a population of predominantly European extraction?

Since Fidel Castro took power in 1959, there has been a strong and growing link between Cuba's domestic racial dynamics and the overall policies of the Revolution. The Revolution triumphed at a time when race and politics had become inseparable in international relations. The countries of Africa and Asia were asserting their power, amid the Cold War waged by the U.S. and the USSR.

The colored world was on the move, after centuries of humiliating defeats at the hands of white conquerors. The victorious Viet Minh unleashing liberationist hopes in Southeast Asia, Ahmed Sukarno's strident anti-imperialism, Nehru's refusal to rely on either of the two blocs: all of these forces converged with bids by the People's Republic of China and North Korea for independence within the Communist bloc, the very roots of the Sino-Soviet conflict.

In the Middle East, Gamal Abdel Nasser had galvanized tens of millions with his daring confrontationist policies. After nationalizing the Suez Canal in 1956, he led Egypt into a successful war against an Anglo-French-Israeli coalition. In Iraq, Gen. Abdul Karim Kassem had seized power in 1958 and begun to threaten international oil interests. And the first winds of anti-colonial nationalism were sweeping Africa. Kwame Nkrumah, a radical Pan-Africanist, took power in Ghana in 1957. The following year, Sékou Touré, an ardent left-wing nationalist, declared Guinea independent in defiance of France.

The Cuban revolutionary leadership would waste no time in attempting to harness these trends to its own advantage. The danger in doing so was that the Revolution might fall prey to the complex dynamics of international political maneuvering, over which Cuba initially had no control. In order to avoid this fate, the Castro leadership would be forced to extend its political influence, to be resourceful to the point of recklessness, and to become ingeniously

3

manipulative. Cuba succeeded in profiting from the superpowers' rivalry, the Sino-Soviet schism, and Afro-Asian ferment, but also fell victim to the Cold War.

The primary goals of the Revolution since its earliest stage were: emancipation from the economic bondage and political tutelage of the U.S., the promotion of social welfare, and the building of a vigorous state capable of leading all of Latin America. On that basis, Cuba could expect to acquire a strong voice in world affairs. These goals conferred upon Fidel Castro and his followers immediate legitimacy in the eyes of a domestic and international audience, but they also brought on an immediate confrontation with the United States, which still suffered from the hysterical political phobias of the McCarthy era.

The uneven confrontation would force Cuba to compromise its independence through near-total reliance on the Soviet Union. This dependent relationship, in turn, presented the new regime with several seemingly insurmountable problems. A symbiotic affiliation with one of the superpowers irremediably tarnished Castro's nationalist and non-aligned credentials both at home and abroad. A crisis of confidence arose that led to the defection of many who had been in favor of the Revolution; the Castroite movement split into opponents and supporters of the Soviet-Cuban alliance. For Castro himself, the dependent relationship posed the problem of how Cuba could enjoy Soviet military protection and economic aid without becoming a mere Caribbean satellite of the USSR.

The attempt to achieve this apparently contradictory result has been at the core of Cuban foreign policy since 1959. In his quest for political *lebensraum*, black Africa soon came to fall within the range of Castro's strategic purview. Cuba faced the growing aggressiveness of the United States, which found itself beset with increasing racial strife in the 1950s, as the civil rights movement began to draw international attention. Cuba's leaders quickly capitalized on the support they derived from the Afro-Cuban population. That group gained increasing political and tactical importance in the eyes of Havana's policymakers. It is to this dynamic interaction between race and politics that we shall now turn in order to better appreciate certain elusive factors that have helped set the stage for Fidel Castro and Cuba to play an extraordinary role in world politics, particularly on the continent of Africa.

An Ethnic Profile of the Revolution

With Castro's victory, the radical nationalist wing of the Hispanic Cuban middle class, which had been frustrated in the war for independence, ostracized in the early decades of the Republic, and thwarted again in 1933, came into its own. The Cuban revolution was essentially a victory of the anti-imperialist[2] segment of the white Cuban middle class.[3] The Afro-Cuban population, having suffered far deeper frustration—even betrayal—throughout its history, had essentially abrogated its role in domestic power politics. "White middle-class students were the vanguard of the fight against Batista," asserted Carlos Franqui, Castro's biographer and a confidant until he went into exile in 1969. The reason for this was simply that "the Cuban people—particularly the black population, which fought the two wars of independence—had found itself in exactly the same position during the 'independent' Republic as during the old colonial days. The Republic had been born, not under the leadership of the mambi fighters who carried out the independence war, but under the auspices of turncoat generals, the Catholic church, Spanish colonialism and the United States. With such a start, the Cuban people, in particular the black population, sort of retreated from politics."[4]

To complicate things even further, Cuba's dictator Fulgencio Batista y Zaldívar was a *mulato avanzado*, a very fair-skinned mulatto who claimed to be white, but who was chided by the Hispanic Cuban upper classes on account of his "inferior" racial background. Following Cuba's system of *racial* classification, Batista was able to "pass" for white. Yet even as Cuba's president, he was barred on racial grounds from private white upper-class Cuban clubs and associations. Consequently, as dictator, he derived some of his power by courting Black Cuba, and many young Blacks were reluctant to join a white middle-class movement to overthrow a "colored" president.[5] (Henceforth, all Afro-Cubans, including those who are light-skinned or mulatto, will be included in the term black.)

In the first months of 1959, Castro's popularity and multi-class appeal were overwhelming. He appeared as the conciliator between conflicting classes, ethnic communities, and interest groups. Whenever he spoke, it was with reassuring promises and appropriate praises to all sectors. "Victory," he repeated in the early weeks of triumph, "was only possible for us because we united Cubans of all classes and all sectors around a single aspiration shared by all."[6] Power, however, was his alone.

Two weeks after his march into Havana, Castro expressed the conviction that "Latin America would be entirely united in a single force, because we have the same race, language, feelings."[7] (Although the term "Latin America" appears in this book, the author strongly objects to its implicit exclusion of the predominant African and Indian peoples and cultures.) Much later, in an interview with two French journalists, he confided how he "remained loyal to his Western and Latin origins."[8] Indeed, a wide sector of the middle and upper white bourgeoisie greeted Castro's arrival with expectations of maintaining the status quo. Castro had promised democratic elections, a free press, and party politics, encouraging such illusions. Cuba's burgeoning land-owning class was also seduced by the nationalistic free-enterprise undertones of the Castro program. This *colono* elite, Cuban owners of sugar mills and estates, was well-organized and increasingly strong under a policy of protectionism and the search for new markets in its fight against U.S. economic imperialism.[9] In fact, by 1959, most cane-growing land was already in the hands of the *colonos*, who since 1948 had been producing 90 percent of the sugar cane ground by the mills (ibid., 74, 81–82).

To the land-hungry white peasantry, Castro took care to project himself as a native "Robin Hood," with land reform as the magical word. To the mass of predominantly black industrial and agricultural workers, the unemployed, and the "lumpen" proletariat, Castro was a sort of "White Redeemer."[10] His promises of full employment and racial integration were overwhelmingly seductive to the most oppressed and populous sector of Cuban society, which hungered for the most elemental of social and human rights.

The Racial Taboo

The man who assumed power in 1959 had done so without having ever made reference to Cuba's racial situation. Castro's silence on this issue was no mere oversight. On the one hand, it was consistent with a long-standing taboo in Cuban ethno-politics. (The Cuban Communist party was the only political party in that country to consistently denounce racial oppression.) On the other hand, it followed tactical considerations. Once in power, Castro retrospectively justified on tactical grounds his silence on several key issues during the period of struggle. In what could be interpreted as an oblique reference to his silence on the racial issue, he compared his approach to Abraham Lincoln's position on the slave question. "I think that all radical revolutionaries, in certain moments or circumstances," said

Castro, "do not announce programs that might unite all of their enemies on a single front. Throughout history, realistic revolutionaries have always proposed only those things that are attainable. . . . (I)t was only at the end of the Civil War that Lincoln proclaimed the freeing of the slaves."[11]

A fervent admirer of Abraham Lincoln,[12] Castro said he had been touched by an early reading of the "abolitionist" novel, *Uncle Tom's Cabin*.[13] Since it is not inconceivable that Castro already saw himself in the early 1950s as a "neo-abolitionist" in Cuba's ethnic setting, it is plausible that he felt that the freeing of Cuba's slaves would have to await the end of the Cuban civil war against Batista.

One of the most important things to Castro in his quest for power was to reassure Cuba's upper and middle classes that he shared their cultural and ideological prejudices. His steadfast silence on the racial issue was a direct result of that approach. In those days, Castro was deeply concerned with preventing his movement from being labeled Communist, and thus alienating the bourgeoisie.[14]

It is clear that Castro recognized the racial issue as particularly divisive and threatening to the sort of class alliances he needed to reach power. He consequently forbade debate about it. Franqui states, "There was no discussion within the July 26 Movement on the issue of the situation of Blacks in Cuba. There was a purely formal condemnation of racial discrimination, but no more. In practical terms, Fidel was quite opposed to a clear definition of a position on such problems. He always said that one should not limit the scope of the struggle."[15]

The only attempt inside the Castroist movement to lift the taboo on the racial question had come from quarters in the Movimiento not directly subject to Castro's authority—the civilian underground.[16] These independent radicals were eager for a concrete ideological formulation beyond the vague liberal content of the Movimiento's communiqués and position papers.[17] Indeed, the "Manifesto No. 1 to the People of Cuba," issued by Castro from Mexico on August 8, 1955, was a fifteen-point rehashing of his earlier "History Will Absolve Me" program. Almost as an afterthought, point number twelve of the manifesto was a rather conventional assurance that the Castroite movement advocated the "establishment of adequate measures in education and legislation to put an end to every vestige of discrimination for reasons of race, sex, which regrettably still exists in our social and economic life."[18] Such constitutionalist trivia fell far short of the sort of clarifications on the labor, racial, agrarian, cultural, and

ideological questions for which the independent radicals now began
pressuring Castro.

Franqui's treatment of the issue for the *Tésis Programática* was,
despite its shortcomings, more attuned to the realities of Cuban racial
oppression. "Three fundamental phases have marked racial relations
in the history of Cuba: slavery, the independence wars, and the republican era. Three elements have interplayed in the Cuban racial
process: (a) economic exploitation, (b) a cultural and psychological
background purporting to justify the demeaning of, or discrimination
against, the Blacks, and (c) the struggle for Cuban integration opposed
by those anti-Cuban currents which attempt to divide us. The first
two [elements] are discriminatory, while the last is egalitarian and
anti-segregationist."[19]

On the cultural issue, inextricably part of the racial question,
Franqui also went a bit further than Castro might have at the time.
"A culture is colonial," he argued, "when it is dependent on others.
It is not a matter of cultural isolationism, [but] by profoundly sub-
merging ourselves into our own realities and national life, into the
human, geographic, historical, social, artistic and rhythmic environment of our people, we can find the source of our true individual,
collective, universal and national culture. . . . The rhythm and sen-
suality of our people is manifested in music and dance [and] in our
religious beliefs and superstitions, as well as in an unsettled racial
presence not yet psychologically fused into one. . . . The contrasting
disharmony is present in all aspects of our existence, but masked by
the hypocritical saying, 'No problem!' But yet, there are very serious
and deep problems. What needs be done is to expose them fearlessly"
(ibid., 152, 153).

In the rush of the sea expedition that brought the Revolution from
Mexico to the Granma landing and on to a guerrilla stronghold in the
Sierra Maestra mountains of eastern Cuba, the *Tésis* was delayed in
reaching Castro, explained Franqui. "But even afterwards the *Tésis*
was never discussed by him for the simple reason that Fidel was
against an ideological definition of the Movement. He felt that an
ideological definition would obstruct the participation of the greatest
possible number of people in the struggle. He also felt—and rightly
so—that the less one said, the less that was outlined ideologically, the
greater the audience of our Movement."[20] Tactical considerations
aside, Castro's avoidance strategy obeyed a thinly disguised prefer-
ence for one-man-show politics and a taste for the unrestrained power
of a messianic *caudillo*. Even then, who among his close followers
would have dared question him?

The state of mind of the unconditional Fidelistas who joined Castro in the foiled assault on the Moncada military barracks, then followed him to Mexico and home again in the Granma landing, was candidly expressed by Guillermo Garcia in a journalist's interview: "I ask Guillermo if there ever were discussions about political ideology while they were in the mountains. He gives a short, nasty laugh. 'Chico, who had time for that? . . . We let Fidel do our thinking for us.' "[21]

A Challenge to Messianic Caudillismo

The independent radical faction's abortive attempt to arouse a debate on the racial question was part of an offensive by a section of the civilian underground wing of the Movimiento 26 de Julio to force Castro to debate fundamental issues, as well as to curtail Castro's increasingly messianic, omnipersonal leadership. Hardly a month after the failed Granma landing, which forced Castro to resort to a guerrilla approach for the fulfillment of his objective,[22] Carlos Franqui impatiently wrote to Frank País, who was then second in importance to Castro: "From my conversations last year in Mexico and other things you know about, I have the impression—shared by other comrades— that Fidel is not in favor of a written program. This I believe is related to his personality and tactical methods and I know it will be difficult to make him change. Nonetheless, we must continue struggling not so much for the program, but with him, to make him understand that whereas he is the leader, today the Organization, as tomorrow the people, must have an important say."[23]

Since the assault at Moncada, Castro had reintroduced into twentieth-century Cuban politics a very Hispanic conception of power, *caudillismo*, in which the very person and actions of the *Jefe* are identified with the national will.[24]

In July 1957, now writing directly to Castro in the Sierra Maestra, Franqui warned: "Caudillismo is one of the fundamental problems of Latin America. It results from various causes: the Hispanic-Arab-Roman legacy. The Spanish conquest of America took place when Spain had not yet undergone the Renaissance, nor the bourgeois and industrial revolutions, nor the reform and the Republic. . . . If the Movimiento prevails over the people, the military over the civilian, caudillismo will be inevitable. New institutions are created before victory, or they will be swept aside thereafter. If victory is obtained by a heroic, vanguard minority, with the sympathy of the people but without their participation, as has been the case until now, a single chief of a military type will impose himself with all the incalculable consequences inherent to any power which rests on a popular but omnipotent will."[25]

These prophetic lines were supported by a letter to Castro written in that same month by Frank País, stressing that, "In a revolution ASSEMBLIES cannot be organized, but neither can everything be centralized in one man . . ." (ibid., 274, 277). But Castro saw the struggle against Batista in highly personal terms, as his war, much as Moncada had been his personal venture. Shortly after the Granma landing, having reached the safety of the Sierra Maestra mountains, he told his followers, perhaps recalling the Moncada fiasco (ibid., 187): "¡Ahora sí que Batista nunca me gana la guerra!" (This time around Batista will never win the war from me!). A year later, decidedly with a sense of mission, he wrote to Celia Sánchez from the Sierra Maestra: "I have sworn to myself that the Americans will pay dearly for what they are now doing [i.e. providing Batista weapons]. When this war is over, a much bigger and longer war will begin for me: the war that I will launch against them. I realize that that will be my true destiny."[26]

Elitist or Popular Revolution?

País's and Franqui's blueprint[27] for a popular revolution that relied on the predominantly black working class[28] and on general strikes would have drastically reduced the elitist role and glamour of the Sierra Maestra guerrillas. It would also have greatly diminished the preponderant influence of the Hispanic Cuban middle class over the struggle and shifted operational leadership to the world of labor. Castro's own charismatic and messianic posture as a revolutionary caudillo would have suffered irreparably. To have accepted the País/Franqui blueprint[29] would have required the *Jefe* to relinquish all claims to the role of the personal Redeemer of Cuba.

Characteristically, Castro did not respond to either Franqui's or País's undertakings. Only a matter of weeks after writing his letter, País was trapped and killed by the police after a tip-off by a black informer named José Randisch. Vilma Espín, at the time one of the prominent leaders of the underground in Oriente province, where Castro's Sierra Maestra stronghold was located, explained the circumstances: "I spoke to Frank over the phone about eight or ten minutes before he was killed. He did not tell me that he was encircled. . . . Randisch, the blackie who had twice pointed out Frank [to the police], was hanging around, for they had taken him to identify [Frank] again. We executed Randisch later on."[30] (In early 1959, Espín

became Mrs. Raúl Castro, and then president of the National Federation of Cuban Women. Her family was co-owner of the Bacardi Rum
Corporation.)

How Fidel Castro reacted to País's letter has never been disclosed,
"but it is doubtful that he took the underground leader's intentions
calmly. . . . His death brought about an internal crisis within [the
Movimiento], but one of Fidel's pressing problems was over. From
then on, the Oriente underground was subordinated to the guerrillas
and the Sierra thesis began to dominate the movement."[31]

With the demise of the only nationally known personality in the
Movimiento who then rivaled Castro both in popularity and audacity,
power inside the Castroist movement shifted entirely to those sectors
of the Hispanic Cuban middle class that were most removed from
Cuba's homegrown culture.[32] To meet the independent radicals'
challenge, Castro conceivably had reinforced his alliance with the
conservative elements of the anti-Batista opposition and the moderate faction of his own movement.[33] These conservatives issued from
Mexico a Manifiesto-Programa del Movimiento 26 de Julio entitled
"Nuestra razón" (Our Cause). It cryptically reassured the upper crust
of Cuban society that "the ideology of the Cuban revolution must be
born from Cuba's own roots and the condition of the people and of
the race."[34] (There is no record of Castro's reaction to that initiative,
but he could have hardly subscribed to such a statement.)

The authors of "Nuestra razón" did not specify which of Cuba's
two basic roots, or the "condition" of which of the island's two races,
was to provide the essence of the Movimiento's ideology. But the
meaning was implicit in the unspoken language of Cuban ethno-
politics—at least clear enough to incite Batista, who was rapidly
losing ground, to resort belatedly to his ethno-demagogic antics of the
1930s. With decreasing hopes of resolving the situation in his favor,
the dictator made several attempts to deflect the opposition of the
black population. Accordingly, his henchmen set about spreading
rumors to the effect that Castro was leading a white revolution, the
success of which would presumably set back for another generation
the "gains" made by black Cubans since the 1930s.[35] From the Sierra
Maestra, *Radio Rebelde* (Rebel Radio) broadcast nightly, countering
that there were Blacks in the Rebel Army and that one of its highest-
ranking commanders, Maj. Juán Almeida Bosque, a Moncadista, was
black. The latter was repeatedly introduced as the "new Antonio
Macéo" (the black general who had led both the "Guerra Chiquita,"
a failed, black-led war against the Spanish colonists [1880–1883], and
the last war for independence).[36]

Five months before his New Year's Eve flight, Fulgencio Batista was still attempting to stem the revolutionary tide with bombastic, incompetent military offensives, indiscriminate terror, and much ethno-demagogy. Previously, Batista's brother had dispatched a black orderly to consult a *Houangan* (priest) of Haiti and a powerful *Obeahman* in Ocho Rios, Jamaica. The orderly, Adan Jimeno, returned with the worst tidings from both errands: all was lost, and to preserve his life, Batista should exit at once. Late in the summer of 1958, at the urging of his brother Belisario, Batista reportedly poured thousands of dollars into promoting a huge meeting of Afro-Cuban religious leaders from all over the country. They were to summon the gods of Africa to his aid and "to appease the demons of war."[37] Three months later, he was forced to flee as Castro's Revolution moved on Havana.

Batista's inglorious exit from Cuban politics bore a final touch of irony. Refused asylum by the U.S., and enjoying only temporary refuge with Dominican dictator Rafael Leónidas Trujillo, he sought refuge in Africa. Liberia's defense minister, who had stopped in the Dominican Republic while on an official visit to Haiti, received an unusual petition: Batista's request for asylum in Liberia.[38] Liberia apparently rejected the Cuban dictator's overture, as Batista left the Dominican Republic for permanent asylum in Franco's Spain soon afterward. The incident, however, was reported sensationally by the Cuban press. It even merited a front-page historical description of a black African country (ibid.). For the first time in more than half a century, continental Africa briefly surfaced as a factor in domestic Cuban politics. It would not be the last.

The Caudillo Mystique

Castro marched to power in the space of forty-eight months with an army that, seven months before Batista's flight, had not exceeded 300 men. It boasted no more than 3,000 in the early days of January 1959.[39] Such an exploit was both a tribute to Castro's skillful system of tactical alliances and a statement of the corruption and disaffection that undermined Batista's incompetent 20,000-man armed forces. Loyal Fidelistas were apt to give full credit to their caudillo, however. In his first public speech, explaining why the Rebel Army had won, Ché Guevara declared that "if we managed to continue, it was thanks to the faith in the people that animated Fidel Castro in those decisive hours; thanks to the confidence inspired in us by his admirable revolutionary *caudillo personality*."[40]

The Moncada attack, the Granma landing, and his Sierra Maestra exploits, when added to Castro's natural charisma and superb rhetorical gifts, made him the logical choice for the role of revolutionary warlord, or caudillo, as insightful men like Carlos Franqui and Frank País had feared. Not only Movimiento loyalists but also the Cuban people were generally convinced of Castro's greatness. The easy collapse of the Batista regime had endowed him and his Rebel Army with an exclusive claim to popular legitimacy and absolute power.[41]

The elitist and messianic character of *fidelismo* was rooted in Castro's personality. As K. S. Karol states, "All the evidence about Fidel reveals a certain aristocratic mind: the sense of duty of a member of the elite who believed that he knew that he must determine the aims and lead the masses to a happier future."[42] Enjoying total power such as no other Cuban leader had experienced, Castro could easily shape a government that most suited his own personality and particular approach to politics. "Fidel thus developed a personal style of governing that was uniquely fidelista and that imbued the new revolutionary order with a populistic character based on strong personal ties between leader and masses."[43] (The paternalistic character of such ties was patently evident in Castro's early speeches.)[44]

The style and practice of the Caudillo's new government were thus imbued with an intrinsically elitist character from the start. The entire trajectory of revolutionary Castroism, from Moncada to the seizure of power, had incubated and reinforced a tendency that the consolidation of Castro's regime would only accentuate. At the time of the Moncada attack, in theory and practice, "*fidelismo* was premised on the belief that the masses were intrinsically non-revolutionary, thereby requiring the leadership of a select core of intellectually superior and proven revolutionaries."[45] Castro's "revolutionary elitism" was to a great extent the expression of an ingrained ethno-cultural elitism. A haughty political underestimation of Cuba's largely black masses was altogether consistent with the Latin framework of race relations within which all Cuban politics have evolved (see Appendix 1).

Castro's low opinion of the revolutionary potential of the Cuban populace, heightened by his personal estrangement from Cuba's popular world and culture (see chapter 3), is revealed in a statement he made to a journalist during an interview ten years after Batista's overthrow: "Do you know how many real revolutionaries there were in Cuba [in 1959] at the moment of the Revolution? Well, there wasn't even one percent. Note that: not even one percent!"[46] Obviously, the "less than one percent" of "real revolutionaries" were reduced to Castro himself and his loyal guerrilla comandantes. It follows that "Fidel and his proven guerrilla vanguard would remain as the governing elite that would lead and revolutionize society in the post-1959 period."[47] It was this nationalistic white bourgeois elite that would eventually impose its revolutionary philosophy upon the Cuban people, an ideology and a strategy that led to Marxism and a Soviet alliance. The first step, however, was to pacify the conservative, moneyed upper classes that had supported the Revolution, and still had the power to cripple the fledgling regime.

2 CASTRO CONFRONTS THE RACIAL ISSUE

Fidel Castro had assumed mastery over a population estimated at 6,700,000,[1] of which conceivably about 50 percent were of African descent (see Appendix 2).[2] Racial segregation both in public and private establishments was still pervasive when the Revolution overthrew Batista. Some Afro-Cuban soldiers who had risked their lives alongside Castro encountered discrimination at hotels and restaurants where their white counterparts were welcomed.[3] Castro nonetheless pointedly minimized the racial question in Cuba in those early weeks of euphoria. In answer to a foreign journalist's question during a press conference on January 23, he even reiterated standard white Cuban platitudes. "In Cuba we do not have the same problem as, for example, in the South of the United States," he said. "There is racial discrimination in Cuba, but to a much lesser degree. We feel that our Revolution will help to eliminate those prejudices and injustices that remain latent. For the time being, we have given proof in our revolutionary struggle of an absolute identification and brotherhood with men of all skin colors. In that sense, ours are the thoughts of [José] Martí and we would be neither revolutionaries nor democrats if we were not free of all types of discrimination."[4]

However, an opinion survey among Blacks conducted independently in late February by *Revolucion*, the publication of Castro's Movimiento directed by Carlos Franqui, brutally contradicted Castro's appraisal. Racism in Cuba was not a "latent" phenomenon, but a veritable plague on the black population, according to the survey. One of the interviewees, Irene Fernandez, complained: "We colored people have many problems . . . because many things are denied us in Cuba. That's why we are suffering a great deal."[5] The general tone of the sample survey was voiced by Cristobalina Sardinas: "Fidel wants the truth told, since lies are worthless. Well, we want to tell him the truth: The black race has always lived under extreme oppression. It is high time that justice be done. Equal opportunities must be given us to exist. If one goes to rent a home and they see you're Black, they refuse to rent. It's an injustice and *we expect the Revolution to do away with it*" (Italics added.) (ibid).

15

Silence on Black Cuba

Two months after Castro's victory, Black Cuba was still unsure of its status with the regime. The racial question remained perilously unanswered. The predominantly black rural and industrial workers, the unemployed, and the white peasantry were the true social base of the regime. But they continued to have no say in the affairs of the exclusively Hispanic Cuban state.

Grass-roots and middle-class Blacks were uneasy about the still-unstated intentions of the new white men in power regarding the race question. Fidel Castro's icy silence on anything remotely touching the plight of Black Cuba, both before and immediately after 1959, was not reassuring. In those early months of the Revolution there was widespread fear among Afro-Cubans that, as in the past, *la gente de color* (the people of color) would be subtly marginalized by the political establishment.

So far, all Black Cuba had obtained were flattering paeans to the "bravery of our Negro population" (references to such men as Antonio Macéo, Juán Almeida Bosque, and Juán Gualberto Gómez) and posts in the new regime's police and army for loyal black subordinates. No individual occupying any of these posts could be expected to voice demands for power-sharing along ethnic lines, a repugnant concept to most Hispanic Cubans, as this strategem had been the rallying cry of the black insurrection led in 1912.[6] Hispanic Cuban politicos had become veritable masters of the art of racial appeasement through the granting of *botellas* (sinecures).

A good description of the apprehensions that gripped Black Cuba on the eve of what was being heralded as a new start in Cuba's history can be obtained from a significant article published in *Bohemia*, a mass-circulation weekly, in February 1959, entitled "Fidel Castro y la integración nacional." Its author, sociologist Juán René Betancourt Bencomo, had written several polemical works on the black question in Cuba prior to 1959[7] and had been one of the prominent founders in 1949 of the bi-racial University Committee Against Racial Discrimination, to which Fidel Castro had belonged for a time. In 1959, Betancourt was president of the Federación Nacional de Sociedades de Color, the black self-help social clubs which included 500 local branches throughout the island, and which the new regime would soon eliminate.

"The mistakes of 1895 should not and must not be repeated today," warned Betancourt, referring to the year the Spanish colonists were defeated and Cuba's independence secured, but at the cost of the exclusion of Blacks, including insurgent leaders, from the affairs of the new Republic.[8] He went on to state,

> It is impossible that anyone should believe, seriously and in good faith, that by ceasing to refer to "blacks" and "whites" the people will forget their existence, and racial discrimination will thus be liquidated by this miraculous method. The daily spectacle of life, which presents some as the titularies of all the material and moral goods, and others as the repositories of all misery and affiliates of all suffering, influences peoples' minds, creating in the victims an apparent inferiority complex and in the victimizers the absurd belief of racial superiority (ibid.).

Nothing short of an organized, bi-racial drive against racism would be effective:

> If our black brother is to be freed from the centuries-old injustice that he has endured . . . [t]hen Blacks and whites of good faith must be organized to this end, for only a social force, supported by a government of the generosity and prestige of the present one, can realize the heroic task of unleashing a new socioeconomic force . . . arriving once and for all at the long-sought goal of national integration. . . . We harbor no fears that Fidel Castro may forget his black brothers, or that he will stumble into the pitfall of a non-productive and chauvinistic attitude regarding the racial question, for he is moved by the best intentions and is fully cognizant of the nature of this issue (ibid.).

Flattering to Castro as those lines were, they betrayed a widespread fear that the revolutionary dream might not serve Black Cuba's interests. Betancourt warned that "the racial problem cannot be resolved with a handful of more or less prestigious, but nonetheless token posts, nor with flattering proclamations" (ibid.). Cuba's new leader, he cautioned, "cannot fall into such traps . . . nor can Fidel fail to do anything, as History obliges him to carry the torch of the revolution into the remotest, most elusive interstices of our nation" (ibid.). Betancourt concluded by bluntly stating that he was writing in order "to temper the general discontent among the black masses because they were not so much as mentioned" in an important document signed by Felipe Pazos, Raúl Chibas, and Fidel Castro that had recently appeared in *Bohemia* (ibid.).

Conciliatory in tone, in substance Betancourt's statement was a warning that the black middle class was determined to break out of its socio-economic and political ghetto. Grass-roots Black Cuba, too, had to challenge its oppression, and men like Betancourt were already appearing as its spokesmen. The black middle class intended to validate its right to enter the traditionally white chambers of power with the support of a grass-roots black clientele, not as puppets in sinecure positions. However, as subsequent events would demonstrate, the new regime hardly saw things in that light. (Within a year of writing this incisive article, Betancourt was forced into exile.)[9]

The Afro-Cuban elite definitely had a vested interest in the Revolution, which promised to overturn a status quo that insisted on the political marginalization of Blacks. The discontent mentioned by Betancourt was no bluff. Unfulfilled hopes evoked unrest. Demands for justice were being heard everywhere. An incident then occurred that would further shake the confidence of Black Cuba. Though unrelated to race, it involved one of the most visible Blacks around Castro.

The Felix Pena Affair

Maj. Félix Pena Díaz appeared in early 1959 to be the most promising black personality of the Castro movement.[10] Unlike most of the other black comandantes, Pena was an intellectual, more inclined to regard Castro as an equal rather than a Redeemer. During the ongoing trials of Batista's soldiers, Castro made Pena president of the Santiago de Cuba war court. Forty-four *Batistiano* pilots, whom Castro had charged with "genocide" for the alleged bombings of civilian populations in Oriente, were on trial. The charge of genocide had sealed the pilots' fate, but as the trial progressed, their guilt became less evident to Pena. As British historian Hugh Thomas summarized, "The defense had argued that the pilots had not killed civilians but, on the contrary, that some had even dropped their bombs on unpopulated places. They claimed to have falsified their reports to their commanders. The bombings of Sagua de Tánamo were also found not to have occurred."[11] Moreover, Pena found no sound proof that the accused group of pilots was responsible for the attack in question. Finding that the evidence was inadequate to prove the pilots' guilt, and despite speeches on the wireless by the prosecutor, Pena acquitted them (ibid.).

Enraged by Major Pena's disobedience, Castro assembled the press and television on March 3. He termed the scrupulous officer's judgment "unjust," declaring that a new "honest tribunal will judge the facts again."[12] In a merciless character assassination, Castro repeatedly implied that Major Pena was serving the interests of Batista's supporters and of the counter-revolution. "The revolutionary tribunal has made a great mistake by absolving those criminal pilots," he charged, "and that amounts to lending service to Batista and providing mercenary airmen for Trujillo and the enemies of this revolution" (ibid.). Castro instantly deposed Pena as president of the court and summoned him to Havana. Pena emerged from his last and presumably stormy meeting with the Caudillo a broken man, and moments later killed himself.[13]

The Subject of Race Is Opened . . .

Exactly two weeks after the Félix Pena affair, on March 22, Castro apparently felt the need to appease and reassure Black Cuba. In a nationwide televised speech, he now admitted that accumulated injustices and a legacy of prejudices from the slave period severely limited the progress of Blacks in Cuba. The revolutionary regime considered the eradication of racial segregation and the implementation of national integration to be one of its humanitarian duties. The drive for integration, he said, would rank fourth in the order of priorities of the Revolution and would focus on three clearly defined areas, labor, education, and recreation:

> One of the battles which must be increasingly and daily emphasized—what I may call the fourth battle—is that which will end racial discrimination in labor. . . . Of all the forms of racial discrimination, the worst is that which limits Cuban Negroes' access to workplaces. We must admit that certain sectors do practice such a shameful thing in our fatherland. Everyone knows that I'm not a demagogue; everyone knows that I hate demagogy; everyone knows that I never tackle a problem without absolute honesty.[14]

Studiously avoiding the political and cultural implications of the racial question, Castro explained that racial discrimination in Cuba was limited to two forms,

> the one practiced in cultural and recreational resorts and that practiced in workplaces. The first to combat is racial discrimination in workplaces. Whereas the first limits entry into certain circles, the second is a thousand times more cruel, for it limits access to the centers where one earns a living; it limits the possibilities of satisfying basic needs. We are thus committing the crime of refusing the possibility of work to precisely the poorest sector of the population. Colonial society made the Negro work as a slave, demanded more of him than anyone else and gave him no remuneration. Our present society (which some wish to call "democratic") refuses to allow him to earn a living. Thus, while the colonizer worked him to death, beat him to death, we want our black brothers to die of hunger! (ibid., 92–93)

Castro implied that racial segregation in recreational resorts was the result of bourgeois exclusiveness and educational segregation. Once again, racial integration was to be the answer:

> There is exclusivism in recreational centers. Why? Because Negroes and Whites have been educated separately. Yet, in the small public schools Negroes and Whites are not separate. In the small public schools Whites and Negroes learn to live together as brothers. If they are together at school, they can be so afterwards in the recreational centers and everywhere else. But if they are educated separately—and the aristocracy does educate its children apart from the Negro—it is logical that later on Negroes and Whites cannot attend the same cultural and recreational centers together. What is to be done? Simply to unify our public schools; afford our public schools all necessary resources. . . . Recreational centers must be built in public schools where Negroes and Whites play together. . . . In the schools white and black children must be together so that later the white man and the black man will be in a position to earn their living together at the same workplaces (ibid., 95–96).

Castro scolded those whites who believed Blacks were inferior beings. "We all have lighter or darker skin color," he explained, because "lighter skin implies descent from Spaniards who themselves were colonized by Moors that came from Africa. Those who are more or less dark-skinned came directly from Africa. Moreover, nobody can consider himself as being of pure, much less superior, race" (ibid., 93). The fight against racial discrimination depended on ethics, self-evident rights and national goodwill.

> There should be no need to draft a law fixing a right inherent to human beings as members of society. Neither should it be necessary to legislate against an absolute prejudice. What we need is to curse and publicly condemn such men who, because of ancient vices and prejudices, show no scruples in discriminating against and ill-treating Cubans because of their lighter or darker hue. . . . It's unnecessary to decree legal sanctions or draft a law to support a campaign for the consumption by Cubans of national products. By the same token, we are going to put an end to racial discrimination in workplaces by launching a campaign against such an odious and repulsive system. The slogan will be: "Opportunity of work to all Cubans, without discrimination of race or sex." Discrimination must cease in labor centers. Whites and Blacks must agree to that and unite together to put an end to this odious racial discrimination in labor centers. Thus, step by step, we will be forging a new fatherland (ibid., 93–94).

. . . And Quickly Closed

Castro's first major pronouncement on the racial question in Cuba revealed how immutable his outlook had been since the days of Moncada. Implicit throughout his speech was the idea that the only legitimate demands of Black Cuba concerned labor discrimination, educational restrictions, and segregationist offenses. Consistent with his strategy of avoidance, Castro entirely ignored the ethno-political and psycho-cultural ramifications of the Cuban system of white supremacy (see Appendix 1). The racial pronouncements of the revolutionary Caudillo had fallen far short of an effective attack on the system of white supremacy in modern Cuba. Rather, what he proposed was the eradication of its most visible adjunct, racial segregation.

Castro's exclusive emphasis on the goal of racial integration was entirely consistent with the Latin model of race relations. What set him apart from any previous Cuban politician was his determination to implement the ethnic code of that model to its fullest integrationist implications. But "integration" was not on the agenda of the most segregationist Hispanic Cuban factions, who feared that the Caudillo intended to alter the complexion of political and cultural power in Cuba. Castro's speech, therefore, "caused some anxiety among conservatives . . . who saw in it a ghost of a slave revolt of the past."[15] A white backlash was set in motion as René Depestre, an eyewitness, describes:

> [T]he entire white bourgeoisie and most white petit bourgeois, even those who would then have given their lives for the Revolution, were panic-stricken as if the Cuban Prime Minister had announced an atomic attack against the island on the following morning. . . . The whole sinister mythology constructed in the days of slavery resurfaced in men's consciousness along with its imaginary procession of evil instincts, lubricity, physical filth, pillage and rape. . . . The volcano of Negrophobia was in eruption.[16]

"Neither Black, nor Red!" The slogan spread like brushfire among white Cubans (not all bourgeois, as Depestre believed). There was talk about rushing white daughters to Miami, lest Castro "unleashed the *negrada* (Negro hordes)". Supported by the conservative wing of the white middle class—and even by groups of white workers, who benefited most from ethnic salary differences and occupational discrimination—the upper classes issued their first challenge to Castro.[17]

As an analyst remarked, "Restrained as they might have been, Castro's first words on the color problem threatened to have consequences which their author may not have anticipated."[18] Castro was the first to be taken aback by the vigor of the white uproar that followed his statement. At no point had he suggested, as it was now claimed, that Blacks should wield political power in Cuba. (That question had been fixed for good after the bloody repression of Blacks in 1912.) The racial question was to him an issue of humanitarian ethics, civil rights, and national goodwill. Consequently, Castro's personal limitations on the racial question were glaringly evident in his reaction to the white backlash.

While maintaining his moderate stance on the issue—conservative in view of the magnitude and complexity of the situation—Castro now strove to appease the white community. In order to do so, he arranged a televised press conference for March 25, and, as an analyst described,

> the Cuban Premier once again condemned those who call themselves Christians but who are racists, those who claim to be followers of Marti but who are racists, those who believe themselves to be educated but who are racists. Now, however—as if to underline the exclusive emphasis in his previous speech upon the public forms of racism manifested in the "two types" of discrimination—he stressed that the Revolution was not going to force anyone to dance with anyone else against his will. He also spoke at some length about the heroism of Mestre, a black man who had fought in the attack on the Moncada barracks in 1953, and dwelled pointedly upon the merits of the mulatto comandante, Juán Almeida. The "line" was the same but the tone was noticeably more diplomatic (ibid., 156–157).

Much more than adopting a more diplomatic tone, as subsequent events would show, Fidel Castro had beaten a hasty retreat. According to Carlos Franqui, Castro felt the hostile white reaction among his own trusted colleagues, who, despite their verbal commitment to racial equality, were not ready to go beyond certain limits. Loyal Castroite leaders, too, believed in the wisdom of one of white Cuba's most resilient sayings on matters of race: "Juntos pero no revueltos; cada cosa en su lugar!" (Together but not mixed-up, for everything has its place!) In fact, nothing proves that Castro was ready to go beyond certain limits himself, as his televised declaration of March 25, 1959, indicated. Questioned by a journalist as to why he had brought up the racial issue in the first place, Castro responded, "there are problems of a psychological order which for a revolution constitute a more difficult stumbling bloc than what could be constituted by the most powerful self-interest." He described these as, "problems in which we have to find ourselves not only confronting a series of interests and of privileges that gravitated to our nation and our people, but also problems which imply that we have to struggle against ourselves. We have to struggle very strongly against our own selves," Castro said. "I was conscious of that fact and knew that I was touching a difficult problem when I took it on."[19]

Appealing to the Bible for support, Castro said, "There are those who call themselves Christians and are racists. They are capable, in fact, of crucifying someone like Christ because he spoke the truth. . . . Because, as far as Christ was concerned, there were no racial differences. He spoke to both the poor man and the rich man, the Negro and the White." Insisting that avowed Christians could indeed be racists despite the seeming contradiction, Castro made comparisons: "There are those who call themselves revolutionaries yet they are racist. There are those who consider themselves to be good people and are racist. And there are those who consider themselves to be quite cultivated but are still racist" (ibid.).

Castro then restated the essence of his first declaration on the race issue. "First, I am not of those who believe that prejudices can be fought with laws but with logic, with arguments, with persuasion. . . . And I made it quite clear that there were two types of discrimination. One in labor centers and the other, which we can say has a cultural character if you like, is discrimination in recreational centers" (ibid.). Racial prejudice, said Castro in a major departure from his previous statement, "is not only found among the sons of the aristocracy. You have very humble and poor people who also discriminate. You have workers who exhibit the same sort of prejudices that afflict the rich, and that is the most absurd, and also the saddest, aspect of this question. . . . What is absurd, and should force the people to pause, is the fact that a big fuss has been kicked up by people who are neither landowners nor landlords, but by people who have nothing but prejudices in their heads! And that's the most painful part of this" (ibid.).

Castro refuted widespread rumors that his previous speech implied that Blacks could thereafter go into white clubs and seek to dance with white women. (These clubs emigrated to Miami, fused and took the name of "The Big Five." The latter continued to segregate racially three decades after the Revolution.) The Caudillo became indignant. "I never told anyone here that we intended to open up the exclusive clubs for Negroes to go in there to dance or mill around. I never said that," he protested. "Gentlemen, people ought to dance, or stroll about, with whoever they please. They must mingle with whoever they like. Who will force anyone here to dance with someone they dislike? In Cuba the only thing that everyone will be forced to dance with, whether they like it or not, is with this Revolution!" (ibid.)

The Revolution had no intention of interfering with personal preferences since it would be "absurd to try to impose oneself on the free will of individuals concerning their personal acts" (ibid.). One must be quite backward, said Castro, "to believe that the Revolution intends to impose things on people, or that the Revolution will be stupid enough to turn the racial question into something that is pressured on people and not, as it should be, into something which is handled by persuasion" (ibid.). Castro voiced surprise at the way whites had misinterpreted his speech on the banning of racial discrimination. Many "absurd" things were said to him after that speech, he said. For example, "I met a young lady who told me: 'The only thing that I do not agree with is this whole business about discrimination.' I asked her why and she answered: 'Because since then Negroes have been walking around all over Havana getting fresh'" (ibid.). To the contrary, he retorted, Cuban Negroes were now happy, rather than getting uppity or fresh with whites:

> I can personally certify that the Negroes were quite happy the other day; they were not being fresh! I have never seen Negroes that happy! They were happy because someone took up their case; because someone had brought them out of oblivion. They were happy that someone had had the courage to defend them in the very midst of a universal form of cowardice. They were happy that someone had defied all of the prejudices to speak the truth. But I didn't notice any of them being fresh, although it's possible that there were exceptions. There might have been a case or two, but I ask: is it just to seize upon exceptions and make them into the general rule? What do you expect? Throughout their entire lives they have been car washers, shoeshine boys, or people who beg for a living. They couldn't go to school. They couldn't receive a good education. And now you expect them to be more refined than people who went to study in Paris! Gentlemen, perhaps you even want them to be speaking French! (ibid.)

The "black peril" scare, deeply ingrained in Cuban politics from the days of slavery, had no foundation, Castro said.

> There is the fear that by taking up the defense of the Negro the latter will become a threat to the rest of Cubans and that Negroes will no longer be respectful. I say that such fears are false because I know

Cubans. I know how they react when told the truth and I know how they react when it comes to justice. I am perfectly sure that more than ever—precisely because with greater honesty than ever before their call for justice is being defended—Cuban Negroes will be *even more respectful than ever*. They are conscious that *not to be so would give the enemies of the Revolution cause to attack them*. They will be more respectful in order not to give any pretext to those who are saturated with prejudices. They will be even more respectful so as not to give the least pretext to anyone to combat our task, our revolutionary task on their behalf. Negroes will be more respectful than they have ever been, because they will want to give no pretext whatsoever to hinder the work that the Revolution is doing to create a greater fraternity and understanding among all Cubans (Italics added.) (ibid.).

Dangerous ambiguities were contained in Castro's words. The words "fresh" and "respectful" transformed every black Cuban into a hostage of the new regime. Castro was in fact representing himself as being responsible for the good behavior of Black Cuba. His guarantee that Blacks would be "more respectful than ever" betrayed a form of white racial bigotry that would plague Cuba's domestic and foreign policies thereafter. Employing pure Lincolnian, neo-abolitionist rhetoric, he sermonized:

I did not touch this problem to open wounds but to close them; to cure them because these wounds have remained open for centuries in the very heart of our nation. So I am appealing to the ones as well as to the others for respect. I am appealing to the ones as well as to the others for understanding. And added to respect I am also appealing for sacrifice. And those of whom I will ask for the most respect, to be respectful, are precisely Negro Cubans on behalf of whom this battle against discrimination is being waged. For we are fighting to eliminate discrimination! And, gentlemen, this does not entail any foolishness about having people dancing with each other if they don't feel like dancing with that person. We intend to see to it that the most respectful ones will be, precisely, those Cubans who are today being defended by this Revolution (ibid.).

Castro went on to describe himself, in typical white Cuban fashion, as someone "who is as white as any white, but who does not consider himself to be pure and who has no prejudices because I am not bothered by sitting beside a Negro comrade. Why?" he asked.

Well, not only because of my instinct for justice, but because I have been exposed to exceptional circumstances to better understand what is unjust and absurd in racial prejudice. And what comes to mind is the most difficult episode of my life; when I remember the *Granma* landing. Those of us who were on that ship, exposed to being swallowed by

the sea, clinging to the same flag and with the same idea in our minds,
Whites and Blacks. And I remember Mestre, our comrade from
Moncada who died in the Revolution. And I also remember Almeida,
who was my comrade and my assistant. . . . So how can I have racial
prejudices after having had the opportunity to witness such events, and
when I have learned to value other people by their virtues rather than
by the color of their skin? Virtues, personal merits, heroism, generosity,
must be the yardstick by which we judge men, no matter what the color
of their skin (ibid.).

In a perfect reproduction of pre-revolutionary racial demagogy,
the Caudillo pointed out the "outstanding Negroes" of Cuban history (soldiers, boxers, musicians, baseball players . . .). These, he
argued, demonstrated that Cuban Negroes were capable of great
achievements.

Everyone is proud of Macéo. . . . Yet Macéo was a Negro. . . . In Cuba
we all feel proud when we talk about Brindis de Salas, who was a great
violinist. And then we have all of these Negro poets. We are all proud
when we talk of Kid Chocolate, who was a boxing champion. We are
all proud when we talk of Miñoso, who was a great baseball player. And,
truthfully, when we have a good singer, someone outstanding, everyone feels proud. And at such a moment, everybody forgets racial discrimination because what they are looking at is the virtue of the person
in question (ibid.).

Castro recalled previous situations in Cuban history in which the
"black peril" had been sounded whenever there was a political
struggle:

[W]e know that during the independence war we also had reactionaries
who used to say that revolution was not possible because if we had independence it would bring about a Republic governed by Negroes. So
they raised all sorts of fears, the same fears that are surfacing today.
They were trying precisely to bring up the black peril which we are dealing with today. Why? Yesterday, as today, that fear was unfounded and
false. Let no one be afraid or alarmed or preoccupied when the Revolution does a work of justice, when it eliminates injustice. . . . There
is a struggle that all of us must carry on together: all Cubans. The struggle against racial prejudice. Prejudice that exists on one side of the population against the other as much as the prejudice that exists on the other
side of the population against the rest. We must combat all forms of
prejudices among the population (ibid.).

He ended by quoting a phrase by José Martí which thereafter became the slogan of the Revolution concerning race relations: "To be

Cuban is more than being White, more than being Black." Accordingly, he said, "A Cuban is simply someone who belongs to no race in particular!" And thus Castro stumbled into the very "color-blind" pitfall against which Betancourt had cautioned him in his *Bohemia* article. Racial Daltonism, Betancourt had appraised soberly, was part of the strategy of evasion of white Cubans. Castro was now employing it as had all white politicians before him. He had frozen the complex fabric of nearly four centuries of violent and subtle interaction between black and white, Africans and Spaniards in Cuba into a handful of simplistic, when not demagogic, equations and axioms.

A Retreat on Racism

The Caudillo had beaten a retreat on the issue of racism, as opposed to racial discrimination per se. Once in power, Castro was no more ready to confront Cuba's white supremacist structure than he had been before 1959. The white backlash had exposed his own severe limitations on a fundamental issue in Cuba's history. His biographer, Carlos Franqui, would later confirm that such was indeed the case:

> Castro's first pronouncements on the racial issue had a tremendous impact because the problem was monumental. It was one of the Revolution's moments of greatest impact, comparable to the nationalization of the sugar mills and the enactment of the agrarian reform. What's curious is that soon after his speech Castro backpedaled on the issue, although he retreated neither on nationalization nor the agrarian reform. . . . However, he retreated on the "racial reform." Why? In my opinion, the leadership—including Fidel—got frightened at the reaction to his first speech when all of the underground fears of the past resurfaced. Fears that have been part of Cuban society over the centuries stirred even among the leadership. Fidel merely found himself confronted with a situation he could handle neither with rhetoric nor with edicts from the top.[20]

In neither of his two speeches did the Caudillo dare venture into the obscure labyrinths of private, personal racism. Was that, too, an area the Revolution would spare? "Fidel Castro at no point singled out discrimination at the interpersonal and familial levels," an observer noted, "as primary targets for the Revolution. Indeed, it is not impossible to understand his second speech as specifically excluding these areas from inspection by the would-be assailants of pre-revolutionary racism. Either way, the policy pursued to date has in practice neglected to tackle, either directly or indirectly, the problem of modifying behavior patterns in the key 'private' areas of the color-class system."[21]

Essentially, Castro's speeches reconfirmed two permanent features of his approach to race relations: a commitment to an integrationist stance steeped in white liberal paternalism and a firm refusal to allow the racial question to escape that framework. In other words, it was out of the question for Blacks themselves to define the content of their own oppression, or define the terms of their ethnic emancipation. David Booth seems to have grasped that situation when he wrote that "in those two speeches in the early months of 1959 Fidel Castro not only identified the aspirations of his movement in relation to domestic racial discrimination but also established the limits beyond which it could not go. Henceforth he referred to the color problem in his speeches only in passing and implying that, with the campaign to end discrimination in workplaces and social centers completed, there was little if anything that remained to be done."[22]

In other words, the government was intent on banning discrimination based on race or color, while racism itself could remain a sort of discretionary ethical question. Implicit in this policy was that Cuba's new white leadership tacitly condoned white supremacy but frowned on racial segregation.

At no time between March 1959 and the Third Congress of the Cuban Communist party in February 1986, *twenty-seven years later*, did Castro or any of his top lieutenants attempt to open Cuba's racial Pandora's box again. Rather, from that point on, the Castro leadership would resist and even repress attempts by black dissenters to force the issue into the open.[23] "When Fidel approached the racial question in 1959," remarked a Haitian Communist, "his words were received enthusiastically. It would have befitted the situation to have pursued that theme further. . . . What made him come to a halt while in such a good position?"[24] An overview of Fidel Castro's racial attitudes before he came to power is in order to give even a tentative answer to this question.

3 CASTRO'S EARLY ATTITUDES ON RACE

Fought with a predominantly black army, as photographs from the period show, the 1895–1898 independence war against Spain was led by the intellectual radical wing of the nascent Hispanic Cuban middle class. Its symbolic chief was the brilliant nationalist, José Martí, but when the United States intervened in the war, power within the independence movement shifted to the most reactionary sectors of the white creole bourgeoisie. It was this class that inherited command of the neocolonial republic. When the nationalistic black middle class formed its own political party (Partido Independiente de Color, or PIC) and rose in revolt in May 1912, several thousand Afro-Cubans were massacred and lynched throughout the island in the biggest blood-letting in centuries. A blanket of silence has covered that event ever since.

The radical wing of the Hispanic Cuban middle class was to reappear forcefully on the political scene as the intellectual vanguard of the aborted 1933 revolution. Antonio Guiteras Holmes appeared then as the immediate successor to Martí's anti-imperialist position. And just as Martí had been, Guiteras was killed fighting for the ideals of national independence and social reconstruction. Both Martí and Guiteras had seen American imperialism as the chief enemy. Both were first-generation Hispanic Cubans.

Although quenched by then-Colonel Batista's successful political tactics in 1933, the revolution was rekindled in 1952 by Batista's second coup. Again, the Hispanic Cuban middle class found its jefe in a charismatic, nationalistic, first-generation Hispanic Cuban intellectual whose personal outlook, personality, and political style have been the basis of Cuban internal and foreign policy since 1959.

The Redeemer Complex

Just forty years after the abolition of slavery in Cuba, and fourteen years after the savage crushing in 1912 of the black insurrection led by the Partido Independiente de Color, Fidel Castro Rúz was born in the predominantly black and most populous Cuban province of

29

Oriente. "I was born to a family of affluent landowners, considered to be rich in that area and treated as such," he stated in a private interview. "I lived surrounded by the sort of privileges that are those of the son of a landowner; given attention by everyone, pampered and treated differently by everyone. In a sense, I grew accustomed to living in a manner that was different from that of my boyhood playmates."[1] His boyhood heroes were great soldiers: Napoleon, Alexander, Caesar, Hannibal[2] and, like most Cuban youths of that era, Tarzan.[3] In a more direct way, "Africa" was peripherally present in the daily sight of black fieldhands, household servants, and *macheteros* (sugar cane cutters), laboring on the Manacas estate owned by the Castro family.

Manacas was located in the municipality of Biran, in the Mayarí region. Virtually an all-white Hispanic enclave in a chiefly black province, Mayarí was an anomaly. The Castro estate employed several hundred laborers, mostly impoverished black Haitian *macheteros*. In the 1950s these workers were producing 18,000 tons of sugar cane per year for the nearby sugar mills.[4] Conditions had not changed much for these *macheteros* since the slave period, which had ended only four decades earlier. The semi-feudal, paternalistic character of master/laborer and white/black relations at Manacas profoundly influenced Fidel Castro's later views on political and racial relations.[5]

His father, Angel Castro, had come to Cuba as a soldier with the Spanish expeditionary forces to combat the revolutionary *mambi* army of ex-slaves, led by such legendary black generals as Antonio Macéo, Quintín Banderas, Guillermo Moncada, and José Macéo. Despite his bitterness at Spain's defeat, Angel Castro returned to Cuba. Like thousands of other Spaniards, he was enticed by the *blanqueamiento* (whitening) policy of Cuba's new rulers, which offered land and facilities to any foreigner who was white. Angel Castro was reputedly an inveterate hater of the Blacks and a stern, if not brutal, disciplinarian. "When he first started as a planter in Mayarí," recalled a friend of the Castro family, "his favorite pastime was shooting at Negroes as if they were so many rabbits. He terrorized the whole area."[6]

A Sense of Mission

From early youth to university, Fidel Castro's schooling took place in exclusive segregated institutions, including Jesuit boarding schools to which only the sons of the white and rich had access.[7] As Hugh

Thomas notes, "The Jesuit education made a strong impression on Castro. . . . One school contemporary commented: 'The Jesuits were training him to be the white hope of the right.' ' "[8] Castro's deep nostalgia for the long, rigorous years of Jesuit tutelage would surface years later in interviews.[9]

A sense of mission and personal predestination evolved with the self-control and austerity inculcated into Castro by his Spanish Jesuit mentors. The messianic twist in Castro's character has been described as "one of the most striking features of his personality, along with his belief that political leadership is his vocation."[10] Castro himself, looking back on his political career, once candidly explained, "Taking into account the circumstances of not having been born into a family of politicians, nor having grown up in a politicized milieu, I was nonetheless capable of a great revolutionary learning and able to play a revolutionary role in a relatively short time. Such would have been impossible of an individual who lacked a special calling."[11]

Long before coming to power, therefore, Castro was convinced that he was born with a mission and acted accordingly.[12] Reliable accounts by intimate friends, long-time political associates, biographers, and political analysts all stress to various degrees Castro's overwhelming will to power and near-obsessive messianic self-image.[13] Thomas observes, "He revelled in action and in crowds and sometimes seemed to regard politics, even violence, as hunting carried on by other means. . . ."[14]

The Bid for Power

Castro's first serious quest for leadership came in 1945 when he entered the world of political gangsterism that was the University of Havana in the late 1940s and early 1950s. His *personalismo* and heroic, macho conception of politics is evidenced by his account of how he clashed with the "action groups" at the university.[15] Castro's successful bid for political leadership of the University of Havana, a beehive of political agitation and the pivotal base of national political power since the 1930s, finally led him into the reformist, nationalistic Ortodoxo party. Having become a successful lawyer and dramatic orator, he already enjoyed the reputation of a *hueso duro* (tough bone) at the time when the party's charismatic, theatrical, and honest leader, Dr. Eddy Chibas, publicly committed suicide in August 1951. Castro immediately took steps to slip into Chibas' empty boots. "[With] the death of Chibas," he said, "the party was left without a leader. . . . Already I was working with the fervent passion of a revolutionary. For the first time, I conceived a strategy for the revolutionary seizure of power."[16] Castro's strategy for achieving power by electoral means was temporarily thwarted by an event that was to halt the democratic process in Cuba indefinitely.

On March 10, 1952, just three months ahead of the scheduled national elections, Fulgencio Batista y Zaldívar pulled off his second military coup. At the time, Ortodoxo lawyer Fidel Castro Rúz had been feverishly campaigning for a seat in Congress. As he later stated, "When the coup d'etat . . . took place, everything changed radically. My idea then became, not to organize a movement, but to try to unite all the different forces against Batista. . . . At that time, yes, I was thinking of organizing it and directing it myself" (ibid.).

The first step was an armed assault on the army barracks of Moncada and Bayamo in Oriente province on July 26, 1953, during the yearly Afro-Cuban carnival. The date had been purposely chosen to coincide with that festivity. "The Moncada conspirators originally numbered 165 men. . . . Composed mainly of young Ortodoxo militants, the group was predominantly white; it was made up mainly of white-collar employees, workers, and vendors, most of whom had but a limited education. . . . In addition, the Moncadistas were bound to Fidel by personal rather than organizational ties. Indeed, even though the attack was to be made in the name of the Ortodoxo Party, Moncada was purely Fidel's personal venture."[17] The attempt failed, but the incident transformed Castro into a national hero.

The daring nature of the attack reflected Castro's profoundly elitist conception of politics. Edward Gonzalez suggests that not only desperate political ambition and reckless machista courage but also a racist underestimation of his opposition were the basis for Castro's bravado, and his failure, at Moncada. "The expectation that a small, select band of revolutionaries could storm and seize a one-thousand-man garrison with a minimum of struggle," Gonzalez observed, "also suggests a contemptuous view toward Batista's army that was reminiscent of the attitude held by the 1930 generation toward the lowly-born mulatto dictator. Indeed, like his predecessors before him, Fidel may well have underestimated the extent to which many in the regular army continued to identify with Batista on the basis of social and racial considerations. Approximately one-third of the officers in the Cuban army at the time were probably of Afro-Cuban descent, while the noncommissioned and enlisted ranks presumably comprised a still larger percentage. This proportion may have been even greater at Moncada, since the garrison was located in Oriente, which contained the heaviest concentration of Cuba's Negro and mulatto population. Hence, many Moncada soldiers evidently saw the fidelista attack as an 'enterprise of the whites,' which strengthened their resolve to fight and to carry out savage reprisals against their white assailants" (ibid., 82–83).[18]

Feelings of loyalty to a "non-white" dictator on the part of his black officers and soldiers caused what proved to be a major setback for Castro. The fate of those Blacks who had joined the attack against Moncada graphically illustrates the fact that, even prior to Castro's accession, Blacks were expected to be grateful for any advantages handed down by a paternalistic government. The penalty for ingratitude, as during the days of slavery, was severe punishment.

About twelve of the insurgents, or Moncadistas, were Blacks.[19] They were humble, restless men from working-class backgrounds, among them Juán Almeida Bosque, Armando Mestre, three brothers —Angel Ameijeiras, Gustavo Ameijeiras, Juán Manuel Ameijeiras— and Agustín Díaz Cartaya.[20] To these men, Castro was not only El Jefe, but also a sort of savior. Díaz Cartaya recalled, "We saw Fidel as Cuba's Redeemer, the heir of Martí, as a politician whose victory would change the fortunes of us Blacks."[21]

None of the black Moncadistas was personally close to Castro before the assault, nor did any of them have any special relationship with him other than that which was necessary for carrying out the attack.[22] This, however, was accepted as normal, as they had already come to look up to him as their uncontested Jefe and intellectual superior. In this sense, the black Moncadistas were following a well-established pattern of post-1912 Cuban ethno-politics.

Involvement by Blacks in anti-government political agitation had been traditionally viewed as "double treason" by those in power. Black Moncadistas captured in the abortive assault were therefore marked off for selective treatment. As Hugh Thomas relates, "Batista's soldiers openly said that it was a disgrace to follow a white such as Castro against a mestizo such as Batista"[23] and at best regarded the black Moncadistas as *negros descarriados* (misguided Negroes) and *gente engañada* (misled people), but never as men intellectually responsible for their action.[24] In fact, some of the black Moncadistas owed their lives to being regarded in that light,[25] as Batista's soldiery considered the attack on Moncada a "plot by Cuban whites."[26]

Most of the black Moncadistas survived the assault to be vilified and at times severely tortured for having "betrayed" Batista. "Several of [Castro's] black or mulatto followers had been taunted by their black soldier captors at the time of Moncada for following a white leader against Batista, the friend of the Negroes. Some soldiers had shown genuine surprise that there were any 'black revolutionaries.' A Negro brick-layer, Armando Mestre, maltreated by the police at Moncada, was told, 'You a revolutionary, you? You don't know that Negroes can't be revolutionaries? Negroes are either thieves or partisans of Batista, not revolutionaries.' "[27]

Castro's survival immediately after the Moncada assault and his position thereafter as a living national hero were both due to the vagaries of the unfathomable racial question in Cuba. At the time of the assault Castro's father-in-law, Rafael Díaz Balart, Sr., was Batista's minister of transport, and his brother-in-law, Rafaelito Díaz Balart, Jr., was Batista's deputy chief of the interior (ibid., 835, 843). Notwithstanding, the dictator issued stern orders that the rebel lawyer was to be killed on sight.[28] A wide manhunt was launched, forcing Castro and several white colleagues to flee the area of battle into the nearby mountains.

Lt. Col. Pedro Sarría, a very dark Afro-Cuban in his mid-fifties, apparently had good reason to thank Batista. He was the grandson of Claudio Sarría, an ex-slave who had become a legendary figure in the war for independence. A career officer, Pedro Sarría had joined the military after Batista's 1933 coup opened to Blacks the then-racially-segregated army officer corps. His career took a turn for the better when the party of soldiers he led in search of the Moncada escapees stumbled on three white rebels asleep in an abandoned peasant hut in the La Gran Piedra mountains. "When Lieutenant Sarría and his men came upon the sleeping Castro and his two followers, their shout was, 'They are white!' ('Son Blancos'), as if proof that they were revolutionaries, not guajiros or workers," related Hugh Thomas.[29] Sarría instantly recognized the ringleader of the Moncadistas and assured him that his life was safe.[30] "He refused to kill Castro or let him be killed by any of his men, but brought him alive, and Castro lives."[31] To keep Castro alive after his capture, Lieutenant Colonel Sarría swiftly informed the provincial capital's press and the Catholic bishop of Santiago de Cuba, Monsignor Pérez Serantes, that he held Castro and was bringing him in. Sarría's gesture may have been motivated by a number of factors. It seems to indicate that a two-fold process was at work: an erosion of Batista's "friend of the Blacks" image and the strengthening of Castro's messianic appeal. (Sarría was eventually dismissed from the armed forces for his "betrayal." After seizing power, Castro made him chief of the security guards of the presidential palace. He died in 1972.)[32]

Castro's life was soon spared once again by the action of another disobedient black army officer. "While Castro was in prison following his capture . . . the prison command was ordered to poison [him]. Jesús Yanes Pelletier, the military supervisor of Donister Prison, refused to poison Castro and warned [him] of the plot. Yanes was relieved from duty at the prison and was forced out of the army a few weeks later."[33] Risking his life by defying orders issued by Batista himself, Captain Yanes not only smuggled edible food into Castro's cell but also alerted the news media about the assassination plot. The resulting uproar in the press forced Batista to call a halt to any attempts to liquidate Fidel Castro. Yanes then fled into exile, later to join the opposition against Batista. (After Castro's victory, Yanes became the Caudillo's aide de camp and chief of his bodyguards. In 1961, however, Castro ordered his arrest and imprisonment without trial for reasons that were never made public. In the early 1980s, Yanes was reported to be still in prison without trial.)[34]

The "disloyalty" of Blacks in favor of Castro throughout the Moncada affair affected even the Cuban Communist party (Partido Socialista Popular). Initially suspecting the Party of having instigated the Moncada assault, Batista ordered its top leadership, old acquaintances of his, to be arrested.[35] While proclaiming its innocence, the Party roundly denounced both the Moncadistas and Batista. Its newspaper, *Hoy*, stated: "We repudiate the putschist methods, peculiar to bourgeois political factions, of the action in Santiago de Cuba and Bayamo, which was an adventuristic attempt to take both military headquarters. The heroism displayed by the participants in this action is false and sterile, as it is guided by mistaken bourgeois conceptions. . . . The entire country knows who organized, inspired and directed the actions against the barracks and knows that the Communists had nothing to do with it. The line of the [Communist party] and of the mass movement has been to combat the Batista tyranny and to unmask the putschists and adventuristic activities of the bourgeois opposition as being against the interest of the people."[36]

A lone voice emerged from within the Party to challenge that position. At the age of twenty-five, Walterio Carbonell was in 1953 one of the best-informed black intellectuals recruited by the Party since the 1930s.[37] A historian and a sharp theoretician, he was a rising star in the youth wing of the Party, which Raúl Castro had already joined in the summer of that year. A specialist on Cuban slavery and Afro-Cuban religions, Carbonell appears to have been responsible for the Party's renewed interest in the racial question in the early 1950s. At the time of the Moncada assault, however, he was already in trouble with the Party leadership for pursuing with "excessive vigor" issues related to racial matters and for expounding views held to be ethnocentric.[38] He had already broken Party discipline in joining an autonomous offshoot of the Frente Contra la Discriminación Racial (Front Against Racial Discrimination) at the University of Havana and outside of Party control.[39]

Carbonell had met Fidel Castro at the University of Havana in the early 1950s. He was convinced that Castro was no mere putschist, but a dynamic and radical nationalist capable of assembling a good portion of Cuba's youth behind him; a man sympathetic to the aspirations of Cuban Blacks.[40] He was incensed at the Party's opportunistic condemnation of the Moncada action, which he saw as the most revolutionary deed undertaken in Cuba since the revolution of 1933 (ibid.). To underscore his revolt, Carbonell again broke Party discipline and sent a congratulatory telegram to Castro, who was imprisoned at the time for the assault on the Moncada and Bayamo barracks.[41] The Party swiftly expelled the "filthy provocateur," "petit bourgeois adventurer," and "undercover agent" with the customary vilification marking such events.[42]

Lest the unilateral action of an "undisciplined" member be mistaken for Party policy, the Communists issued a statement reiterating that "the party rejects this kind of adventurist action [i.e., the Moncada assault] which serves only to immolate dozens of young people."[43] Alluding to Carbonell, it denounced "those who are attempting to involve the newspaper *Hoy* [the Party paper] with a filthy provocation . . . entangling it in the adventure of Castro and his group" (ibid.).[44]

The white middle-class radicals who, under Castro's leadership and initiative, conceived the first serious insurrectional assault against Batista's dictatorship had vaguely referred to Cuba's need for "new men and new procedures," "welfare and economic prosperity," and "total and definite social justice."[45] However, as much as a pervasive racism made the racial question one of the most crucial in any profound overhauling of Cuban society, Castro and his intimate associates were silent on that point. There was no mention of it in Castro's lengthy statement, "History Will Absolve Me,"[46] nor in his explanations to the court on the social reasons behind his revolt against the

Batista regime.[47] Such blindness to the most glaring sore spot in Cuban society was hardly appropriate for the radical nationalist and well-informed social reformer that Castro was at the time. As Thomas pointed out, Castro "had never had anything yet to say on the problem of the Negro in Cuba. . . . There was as ever lacking any mention of racial intolerance; indeed, it would have been possible to have read 'History Will Absolve Me' without ever knowing there were Negroes at all in Cuba. . . . Castro never mentioned the matter in any of his speeches or programmes before the revolution. To read 'History Will Absolve Me' would suggest that Castro was addressing a racially homogeneous nation."[48]

Castro was undoubtedly an ardent anti-imperialist of advanced social ideas, consumed as much by a desire to challenge the imperialist stranglehold over Cuba as by a messianic will to power. If anything, the Moncada fiasco had strengthened his conviction that history had chosen him for the accomplishment of a great design. He was certainly opposed to racial segregation and discrimination on ethical grounds, as would be expected of a white liberal nationalist reformer operating in such a heavily Africanized environment as Cuba. Equally clear is the fact that at no time had he attempted to understand the racial question in its historical, political, or psychocultural dimensions.

A Paternalistic Superiority Complex

Based on two decades of close political association and personal friendship with Fidel Castro, Carlos Franqui, former propaganda chief of the Movimiento 26 de Julio, recalled Castro's racial myopia. "In all conscience, based on the knowledge I have of Fidel on a personal basis, I must say that Fidel Castro is not a discriminator in a segregationist sense. He is not the type of person who would discriminate against a black man just because his skin is black. By the same token, I do not believe Fidel to be a *machista* in the sense that he would discriminate against a woman because she is female, or against a Chinese because he is Chinese. That is not where Fidel's problem lies. Fidel's limitation—great limitation!—is in his incapacity to understand what it has meant and continues to mean to be black in Cuba. He is equally incapable of understanding what it means to be a worker, to be a peasant, or to be a woman! And this has to do with a profound problem of bourgeois and petit-bourgeois revolutionaries who entertain a deeply paternalistic outlook on revolution. It is the problem of those who, having neither emerged from nor lived among the people, come into positions of leadership and nonetheless believe themselves capable of really identifying with the ordinary man."[49]

Until 1953, Castro had never experienced any sort of concrete relationship of intellectual, social, or racial equality with black Cubans either collectively or as individuals. After 1953, with his growing fame as the potential redeemer of Cuba's oppressed workers, peasants, and Blacks, people whose universe he had never even attempted to fathom, such an eventuality naturally became all the less likely. His approach to those sectors was therefore devoid of any concrete sense of equality, particularly as it concerned Black Cuba.

"To understand Fidel Castro's attitude to the racial question," Carlos Franqui said, "we must grasp something very important about his personality and outlook in general: Fidel has never dealt with *anybody* as an equal. He had always had subordinates. The peasants, workers, servants, women, and Blacks, who worked on his family's estate were not his equals. Fidel has always had subordinates whether growing up as a child in his *finca* [estate]; as a youth in the Jesuit schools; as an adult at the university; and as a political and military leader in the Sierra Maestra. Fidel Castro has never entertained relations of equality with the basic oppressed sectors of the society in which he grew up: Blacks, women, workers and peasants. . . ." (ibid.).

On the racial issue, Castro's position was easy to understand, Franqui believed. "He is not a discriminator on the basis of skin color. He simply does not grasp what being Black has meant to black people. Moreover, Fidel has never been in a position of concrete equality with Blacks; he has never dealt with any black person as an equal" (ibid.). Castro's attitude, Franqui asserted, was "a strictly paternalistic one. He does not understand the internal world of Blacks any more than he does that of women, peasants or workers. His perception of relations between Blacks and whites is profoundly paternalistic. Add to this his thoroughly Spanish outlook on all things, his Spanish orientation in matters of culture, and you will have a picture of Fidel Castro's peculiar approach to the racial question. All of this is embedded in his two major speeches on the racial issue in March 1959; the first announcing the end of discriminatory practices in recreational, educational, public and labor centers; and the second back-pedaling on the wider issues of the racial problem, which is one of the most essential issues in Cuban history" (ibid.).

As a first-generation Hispanic Cuban who grew up in an exclusively white, Catholic and Hispanic social and psycho-cultural environment, Fidel Castro had never come to terms with, nor been influenced by Cuba's profound Africanity. At the time of Moncada and thereafter, Castro's attitude towards the racial question, it can be safely said, remained within the traditional framework of the assimilationist Latin variant of race relations and its heavy emphasis on "protective" benevolent paternalism. Nor could it be said that Castro experienced any more of a personal attachment to Cuba's popular culture after 1953 than he might have had before then. Both before and after Moncada, Castro's psycho-cultural world was exclusively steeped in the traditions and assumptions of the Catholic-Hispanic universe. There is no evidence to suggest that either before or after 1953 he cultivated an attachment to, or understanding of, the Afro-Cuban culture.

Since the second half of the nineteenth century, as some analysts have shown, the chief spokesmen of middle-class nationalism in Cuba have been first-generation[50] white Cubans. Of all Cuban whites, first-generation Hispanic Cubans would seem to be the most attached to Euro-Mediterranean traditions, and the least influenced by the home-grown cultures of Cuba. One may reasonably expect such political spokesmen, regardless of their radicalism, to be the least likely to challenge, let alone reject, Cuba's official Euro-Hispanic power structure and profile.

4 BLACK CUBA RESPONDS TO CASTRO

As far as Fidel Castro could see, he was the author of a Revolution which had "established social equality and *given* the Blacks the right to education; the right to work; the right to go to the beach; and the right to grow up in a free country without being hated and discriminated against."[1]

Craving justice and recognition, Black Cuba, notes René Depestre, had endorsed the "racial reform." Past demagogues had used the racial problem for lowly electoral ends. Now, however, a prestigious leader had arrived and clearly stated that the Revolution was to be for all Cubans or it would not be at all. "In the conversation of Negroes and Mulattoes there was no talk of orgies with white women, noisy parties, the invasion of private clubs nor superhuman erotic competition," Depestre remembered. "We spoke of labor, dignity, justice. . . . We spoke about the end of a nightmare and of the possibility of fully exercising our right to historic initiative. . . . Throughout the island those were the great hopes that stirred humble Negro homes in those days."[2]

As the pacesetter of the Revolution, it was the Caudillo's prerogative to determine the role Black Cuba was to play in it. "Because a large bulk of the Cuban population is Black," claimed biographer Carlos Franqui, "the new government was compelled to confront the problem of racial discrimination soon after assuming power. When a series of measures was taken, quickly abolishing social and racial discrimination, the people embraced the Revolution as their own. . . . [But] all decisions were taken by, and imposed from the top; the people had no say whatsoever in what, where, when, or how any measure affecting them should be applied. Such was the case with the agrarian and labor questions. It was also the case with the leadership's banning of racial discrimination in labor, social services, education and recreation. Those primarily concerned had no voice in it."[3]

Castro's Racial Tokenism

The new regime's neo-abolitionist integrationism was bound to appeal to the majority of Cubans,[4] the marginalized descendants of African slaves. Of all Cubans, the latter were the most rejected sector. Torn by an unresolved conflict between a deep craving for acceptance by, and dissolution into, the dominant group, and a recurring awareness of its distinct ethnic self-interests, Black Cuba was seduced by Castro's integrationist promises. Integration thus became a magic word. As observed by an analyst of U.S. ethnic relations, the social consciousness of Blacks in the Americas "possesses inner qualities of different degrees of nationalism and integrationism."[5] Castro's approach had simply been to fuse both these aspects into the concept of "national integration" and therefore declare all matters closed.

By excluding the areas of political power and cultural dominance from his sketchy overview of the racial question, while concentrating exclusively on its segregationist aspect, Castro could honestly pat himself on the back. Cuba's new white ruler was convinced that he had "given" Blacks their freedom. The breakdown of racial segregation within such a narrow context, however, left only one way open to Cuban Blacks: uncritical adoption of the cultural outlook and lifestyle of the politically dominant Hispanic revolutionary elite. The Afro-Cuban Communist poet Nicolás Guillén Landrián could thus gloat over the most trivial results of desegregation. "You don't know how pleased I was to see, in the first days of the Revolution, a Negro boy playing golf in one of the old aristocratic clubs in Cuba," he said. "I do not know whether it was in the Biltmore Yacht Club or what. The fact is that I approached the little fellow and asked him if he liked that sport. The boy looked at me, his face lit up with joy, and he replied: 'Do I like it? I have become an Eisenhower!' "[6]

Conducting a series of interviews during the earliest stage of Castro's rule, a European journalist recorded characteristic black Cuban responses to the new order. He spoke to a twenty-two-year-old woman, an enthusiastic Castro supporter who had joined the Army:

> "We're proud to serve under Fidel. He's a real leader, a genius, a hero, a fine noble-hearted man." . . . She was gazing at me dreamily. I laughed. "What are you thinking about? Your platoon? The ministry?" "Nothing," she replied abruptly. The next moment she said, quite unexpectedly, "You are a real white. Cuban girls like me, with mixed blood, dream of going out with a white man like you. The Revolution has done away with color prejudice but to marry a white man, one

hundred percent white, that would be great. That's a wonderful thing the Revolution could do. It ought to step up the process of making Cuba white. It wouldn't be difficult. You'd only have to invite white men and women to come and settle here. There's room for plenty of people. In that way the coloreds would soon become absorbed, and there'd be no more Negroes, no more prejudices, no more anything. Isn't that a good idea? If you see Fidel you should suggest it to him."[7]

Another interviewee, a Rebel Army officer's bodyguard, expressed similar feelings, though in different words:

A prosperous-looking villa in Marianao, the good residential quarter of Havana. . . . To one side, a rocking chair. Seated in it, a tall lanky Negro with his tommy gun across his knees. . . . "There is a Comandante who lives in it. . . . Mind, I live here too. Look up there, the window on the left. That's my room. I sleep in it. Yes, sir, in this house built by white men, for white men. And I'm a Negro. What's more, they feed me, do my washing and give me sixty pesos a month. . . . Negroes don't feel like Negroes anymore. They have become white men. . . . Before Fidel, I was a shoeshine boy at the Miami. . . . Then Fidel came along. He said: 'Negroes and white folks are all the same, all of us just men. . . .' When Fidel said: 'Negroes and white folk are all the same, all of us just men,' I believed him. Every Negro believed him. We've got reason to believe Fidel" (ibid., 62, 63, 64).

Social improvement, however slight, was seen as synonymous with the adoption of the dominant Hispanic lifestyle and, in fact, becoming white:

"You know," the sentry went on, "Fidel thought about the women too. He said to the Negro women: 'That's all finished your old life. You're going to live like the white women.' I've got a sister, Rita. Before Fidel, there were only two things she could do, become a maid for white folk or become a whore. . . . Now that's all finished. They gave my sister a job sweeping up in an office. She's quite happy now" (ibid., 65–66).

Deep-seated self-hatred, the desire to escape the black persona and dissolve into whiteness, could now become "revolutionary" qualities:

He searched through his pocket and pulled out a cardboard folder. . . . "Look at this. It's my country club membership card. . . . Negroes in the United States, they can't go to a country club. That's reserved for the white. They couldn't here either, before Fidel. They'd get thrown out. It was reserved for the whitest of the whites. . . . It's hard to say to myself: Pablito, all that's finished. You're not a nigger anymore. Ever since Fidel said, 'Negroes and white folk are all the same,

all just men,' I look myself in the mirror every morning. 'Pablito,' I say,
'Pablito, you're not a nigger anymore. You've become a white man.
Fidel said so and Fidel's always right.' " (ibid., 66–67).

In the thick of the Castroite racial reform, the Movimiento's
mouthpiece, *Revolución*, regularly ran a seemingly innocuous half-
page advertisement that perhaps best symbolized the new spirit: "It
has finally arrived!!! Made in Cuba. Protein-based Allyns Hair-
straightening Cream. Now, after repeated scientific research, Allyns
and Co. has put on the market a totally improved HAIR STRAIGHT-
ENING CREAM WITH PROTEINS. $1.50 per jar."[8] Neo-racism was
rearing its head under the cloak, and with the sanction, of the
Revolution.

The "Gracias Fidel" Syndrome

Fidel Castro found fertile ground for the expansion of his messianic
self-image in the climate of overall oppression that prevailed in Black
Cuba upon his seizing power. "Gracias Fidel" was the universal cry
of thanks with which dispossessed Cubans greeted each granted-from-
the-top reform; these deprived workers and peasants, the unemployed, felt all the more compelled to unrestrained loyalty to the man
who had "freed" them.

In a searing analysis, the black psychologist and revolutionary
theorist from Martinique, Frantz Fanon, described the pathetic
phenomenon of racial overcompensation. The oppressed, racially
humiliated, and culturally alienated, he explained, hunger for even
minimal justice. Blacks were therefore liable to overreact to whatever
personal, social, or political gesture—no matter how trifling—was accomplished on their behalf by a member of the dominant group. "The
native is so starved for anything," wrote Fanon, "anything at all that
will turn him into a human being, any bone of humanity flung to
him, that his hunger is incoercible, and these poor scraps of charity
may here and there overwhelm him. His consciousness is so precarious and dim that it is affected by the slightest spark of friendliness."[9]
Cuba's new white revolutionary leaders would fully exploit this
legacy of black oppression.

Typical of the "Gracias Fidel!" phenomenon was a black house-
wife's reaction to the granting of employment to her husband in the
aftermath of Castro's racial reform:

Mrs. Gomez must have been between forty-five and fifty. She was fat,
with light coffee-colored skin. She was happily excited. . . . Eulogio

was her husband. He worked from seven in the morning till six at night in Sears Roebuck, one of the big American stores Castro nationalized. As far as I could make out from Mrs. Gomez's descriptions, Eulogio must have been a porter. She said vaguely, "He helps, you know. He carries up parcels from the basement. They send for him when they have to move furniture. It's a good job; 110 pesos a month. . . . Fidel is my god, my soul, the light of my life. And that's the truth. When we heard the news about our new house, I said to Eulogio: 'You know, Eulogio, that I've always been a good wife to you, and never deceived you. I've always remained faithful. But if Fidel asked me to go to bed with him, I must admit it to you, I wouldn't hesitate. Don't be angry, that's the way it is. . . .' Fidel, Fidel! *¡Que hombre! ¡Que hombre!* [What a man!] But for Fidel we would still be living like pigs, without hope."[10]

In *Sex and Racism*, the black American scholar Calvin Hernton assessed the phenomenon of overcompensation in terms that both echo and complete Fanon's analysis. "Because the Negro is hated . . . so deeply on the basis of his blackness," he pointed out, "any black [person] who receives kind treatment from a white person is indeed grateful . . . After the depraved self concept that centuries of racism has wrought within the Negro, a simple act of human kindness from a white [person] elicits the most extreme feelings of gratitude from the Negro."[11] In a real sense, it can be said that Black Cuba's compensatory response to Castro's "racial reform" was the passionate offering of an uncritical subordination and unswerving political loyalty to the revolutionary white regime. Castro understood it as such[12] and, given his background, there is no reason to believe he expected otherwise.

The Black Middle Class Wants Power

Revolutions have the effect of arousing the consciousness of slumbering oppressed groups and inciting them to express the interests that unite them. To a greater or lesser extent, those social classes establish and define their objectives within limits set by the regime and support it as long as they are not excluded.[13] There was one sector of Afro-Cuba that tempered its "thanks" to Castro with demands for long-denied political enfranchisement. Desegregation, for this group, was simply not good enough. Access to power, not beaches, was the goal of the black middle class.

The passing of the old political order could hardly dismay a subclass reduced to a subordinate clientele status. As one analyst summarized, "the old Cuban society allowed no leadership to emerge from that 40 percent of the population which was black."[14] The mono-ethnic character of the new revolutionary regime, however, did raise early fears that the complexion of political power would remain unchanged. Seen in that light, Juán René Betancourt Bencomo's piece in *Bohemia* was a veritable position paper. Middle-class Blacks had suffered the most from the unspoken segregation of Cuban politics. Consequently, the black middle class was most keenly interested in the integration of political power. In one word, desegregation of beaches and clubs was good, but desegregation of *the state* was even better!

According to the 1943 Cuban census, there were at least 560 black lawyers; 424 doctors, a fifth of the total in the country, were black, as were 3,500 teachers, compared to about 16,000 white teachers. Blacks were said to be well represented in the arts, dominated laundering, sewing, shoemaking, woodcutting, and tailoring, and were on a level with whites as barbers, bakers, carpenters, coopers, and blacksmiths.[15] The political, economic, and cultural influence of the black middle class was still negligible. Blacks in middle class positions numbered approximately 300,000 in 1959, roughly one-third of their white counterparts. The black middle class was virtually absent from the higher and middle levels of management, business, commerce, the armed forces and from the white preserve of government administration.[16]

Since its armed uprising of 1912, the black middle class had failed to assume any leading role in Black Cuba's continuing fight for enfranchisement. Many middle-class Blacks aped the Hispanic value system to the point of espousing its most aberrant manifestations, and strove for absorption by the dominant group.[17] After 1912, radical middle-class Blacks had aligned themselves with the politics and ideology of the Communist party as an outlet for their nationalism and social concerns. After years of timidly campaigning with minimal success for proportional ethnic representation in the affairs of government, Black Cuba's efforts had been brought to a halt when Batista took control of Cuban politics in 1952. Castro's Revolution bore all the signs of an entirely new era. And the black middle class on the whole endorsed it.

A Movimiento de Orientación e Integración Nacional (Movement of National Orientation and Integration), composed of prominent black and white professionals, was set up following Castro's two speeches on race. Its avowed aim was to assist the revolutionary government in carrying out the "racial reforms." The organization's chairman was Dr. José Elías Entralgo, a Hispanic Cuban university professor and sociologist. Elías Entralgo had studied the racial question since the 1940s and was the proponent of a white Cuban version of eugenics. In a controversial work, *La liberación étnica cubana* (1953), he contended that "mulattoization" was the most viable policy for ending Cuba's racial dilemma. Seeing a cause and effect relationship between "mulattoization" and "national integration," Elías Entralgo had saluted the extensive sexual abuse of African women under the slaveocratic colonial regime for heralding a new, heroic era. "The day . . . when a white slavemaster first had intercourse with a slave Negress in the bush or in the barracoon," he wrote, "was the most luminous for mankind. . . . A vivifying transfusion took place that engendered a fertile and plastic symbiosis. From such miscegenation were to emerge new physical attributes and ascending psychic and moral virtues."[18]

La mulatización cubana was a post-revolutionary follow-up to his thesis. The whitening and Hispanization of the Negro, the darkening and Africanization of the whites, Elías Entralgo argued, "would bring about a new product . . . imbued with its own differentiated essence and which we may call mulattohood. The study of mulattoism may thus be divided into three categories: mulattoship, mulattoness and mulattoization. The first is imbued of inferior qualities; the second encompasses intermediary qualities, while only the third is superior. . . . Through a correct orientation in our country's educational and teaching system, we will perhaps be able to proscribe mulattoship, improve mulattoness and stimulate mulattoization."[19]

The black co-chairman of the Movimiento de Orientación e Integración Nacional, Dr. Salvador García Aguero, had been a top-ranking member of the Cuban Communist party since the 1930s and was also a theorist on the racial question.[20] He had supported the Party's expulsion of black labor leader Sandálio Júnco in the '30s and that of Walterio Carbonell in 1953, both of whom the Communists had come to regard as "black chauvininsts" and "Trotskyites." Both Elías Entralgo and García Aguero were therefore quite representative of the type of policies the new regime intended to follow.[21]

In early April 1959, less than two weeks after Castro's "Declaration of Negro Rights in Cuba," a televised panel discussion took place with the aim of assisting the government's integration drive. One of the panelists, Dr. Eudaldo Gutiérrez Paula, was national chairman of the Association of Cuban Journalists and a respected black political opponent of the overthrown regime. He seemed the most appropriate personality to voice Black Cuba's opinion on the issue. Unexpectedly, he disrupted the televised discussion from the start. He pointed out that revolutionary Blacks were conspicuously absent from Castro's cabinet, and he emphasized that the integrationist drive should have begun at the top. The two other panelists, Dr. Eduardo Corona and Dr. Carlos Olivares, were enraged. Only whites comprised the revolutionary cabinet, agreed Corona, but "these were not instances of discrimination but of selection according to criteria of revolutionary merit."[22] Consequently, he continued, "If the State is found to have discriminated on occasion, it was on the basis of personal revolutionary merit" (ibid.). Gutiérrez Paula was indignant. He had to challenge a statement, he said, which implied that only whites were revolutionaries and only whites had merit. There were in Cuba as many Blacks with revolutionary and administrative and political skills, he contended, as there were white ministers in the cabinet. Dr. Olivares, a black Communist party theorist, countered. "The Revolution," he said "will not combat discrimination by placing a Negro in public view as has been done in the past, but by sincerely struggling against it" (ibid.). Unruffled, Dr. Gutiérrez Paula charged point blank: "The foremost discriminator is the State. . . . The integrationist campaign must be taken into that area just as into all others" (ibid.). On this perilous note, Social Welfare Minister Elena Mederos hastily closed the debate. Soon after, the regime unleashed a veritable campaign of harassment at its potential black competitor. One by one, the most respected black middle-class spokesmen would go into exile.

The Assault on the Black Middle Class

By accusing Castro's all-white regime of discrimination, Gutiérrez Paula had voiced much more than a personal opinion; he had expressed the apprehensions of an entire class. When underscoring that as many competent revolutionary Blacks as whites could be found to occupy any post in the revolutionary cabinet, the issue of proportional ethno-political representation had resurfaced wearing the garments of "integration." The black middle class understood integration to mean inclusion into the State on an equal footing with its white counterpart. Once aware of the extent of the black middle class's autonomous political ambitions, however, the revolutionary regime undertook to destroy its only avenue for independent political action: the self-help, all-Black Sociedades de Color (Colored

Societies). This move was carefully camouflaged as part of the desegregation drive.

Founded in 1890 by Juán Gualberto Gómez, one of the most influential nationalist black politicians in Cuban history, the Directório Central de Sociedades de Color had escaped the ban imposed on black organizations by the 1910 Morúa Law passed to eradicate the Partido Independiente de Color. Conceived to promote the education of black former slaves, the Sociedades de Color increasingly became active forums for the social and political demands of Afro-Cubans. After the black insurrection of 1912, the radically castrated black middle class abandoned the rallying cry of proportional ethnic representation. The Sociedades reflected that change and thereafter alternated timid political demands with the vigorous promotion of assimilationist goals.[23] By the mid-1950s, however, assertive representatives of the black middle class, such as sociologist Dr. Juán René Betancourt Bencomo, had defined a "Doctrina Negra" (Black Doctrine). The latter was a platform of specific political demands that would have ultimately wrested the racial question from the monopoly of the Communist party and asserted the identity of Black Cuba.[24]

A shift in the purely "cultural" orientation of the Sociedades towards political action was already suggested by their effusive statements of support for Castro in the first months of the Revolution. The more it appeared that the revolutionary regime intended to do away with party politics altogether, the more the Sociedades became the black middle class's last refuge for the expression of autonomous political demands. "In the early months of the Revolution," an analyst observed, "an attempt was made by Negro Clubs to strengthen their organization, but this was thwarted by the government."[25]

The first limitation imposed by the Castro regime was the restriction of the Sociedades' functions to parties held on Saturdays and Sundays (ibid.). Then, ominously, the government went on to confiscate the proceeds of these festivities. The Sociedades were thus deprived of their only independent source of income and "were encouraged to wither away by administrative actions that deprived them of their income and office space" (ibid., 80). The coup de grace came when the national federation of these associations was abolished along with their provincial headquarters. In a short time, the previously existing 526 Black Societies had closed (ibid., 97). The handwriting was on the wall; Betancourt, national president of the Sociedades, fled into exile.

The destruction of the Sociedades was in line with the regime's determination to destroy all autonomous bases for dissent or protest. It was intended to be, and indeed was, a crippling blow to the political aspirations of the black middle class. A specialist on Cuban affairs concluded that, ''The intervention procedure, by means of which the Committees of Negro Societies that were devoted to the promotion of racial equality were integrated with the hierarchy of government, in effect took away the right of Negroes to express any corporate opinion except one of wholehearted approval. According to government propaganda perfect freedom had been established by the mere fact of revolution, and therefore, the Societies ceased to have any recognized function'' (ibid., 80).

The destruction of the Sociedades was Castro's unequivocal answer to black middle-class demands for proportional ethnic representation in the new regime. It served notice that integration of Blacks into the new regime would follow the old pattern of selection from the top by the ruling group and at the pace prescribed by it alone.[26] As before, selective incorporation into the government required subordination to the politically dominant Hispanic Cuban elite.[27]

The Black Workers Endorse Castro

In 1953, 60 percent of Cuban Blacks were reported living in cities.[28] Black Cuba was also predominantly working-class; heavily concentrated in the agrarian sector, the sugar mills, and construction work, a high proportion of black workers was unemployed or underemployed; a substantial portion was concentrated in the ''lumpen proletariat'' of newspaper and lottery vendors, shoeshiners, street hustlers.

In 1959, out of a total work force of some 2,500,000 laborers, Blacks accounted for an estimated 64.1 percent. As much as 34.3 percent of the black work force was permanently and/or partially unemployed in 1959. Added to the estimated 11.5 percent of Blacks consigned to the lumpen proletariat, approximately 45.8 percent of employable Blacks were in a state of permanent and/or partial unemployment in 1959. The plight of the black worker in pre-Castro Cuba was certainly grave.[29]

Fidel Castro boasted to a journalist that when he took power ''there wasn't even one percent'' of revolutionaries in Cuba.[30] And yet the Cuban working class as a whole had a long record of militant struggles. Revolutionary politics, noted Maurice Zeitlin, had a venerable tradition in the Cuban working class dating to the very foundation of the Republic itself.[31] "The workers formed the major social base of the Communist-led anti-imperialist movement of the late twenties and early thirties that culminated in the abortive popular revolution of 1933–35," he noted. "Thus, the Cuban revolution and socialist ideology had a significant base in the working class long before the revolution's leaders began to think and speak of themselves and their revolution as 'socialist' " (ibid.).

What was true of the Cuban working class as a whole was all the more so for black workers. Comprising the bulk of the workers in Cuba, Blacks had spearheaded every major struggle against oppression from colony to Republic. Socially excluded and discriminated against, bearing the heaviest brunt of economic and cultural oppression throughout Cuba's history, black laborers stood out as a permanently available force for radical agitation and revolutionary enterprise. From the mid-1920s onwards, the Cuban Communist party found its most receptive, durable, and enthusiastic clientele among Blacks. They formed the backbone of the Party right up to Castro's accession to power. "In fact, some of the most prominent left-wing leaders in Cuba were Negroes, and among leaders of the Communist Party, as well as of the non-Communist labor unions, Negroes were well represented. . . During the revolution of the 1930s the 'soviet' of workers and peasants which withstood the military forces of Batista the longest, *Realengo 18*, right into the early months of 1934, was led by a Negro Communist, Léon Alvarez. Perhaps the most revered labor leader was the martyred Jesús Menéndez, the Negro head of the sugar workers' union who was murdered in 1947. . . ." (ibid. 70).

The radicalism of black Cuban workers can be attributed to their self-perception as victims of a system based on economic exploitation. Their pro-Socialist and even pro-Communist proclivities, however, had a subjective basis. The traumas inherited from the slave/colonial period led black laborers to identify more readily with an ideology that offered a class-only explanation for the oppression of ethnic groups and racial integration as the final solution.[32] Thus, black Cuban workers often identified with class rather than with a racial group,[33] and aligned themselves with radical organizations that purported not to see color, allowing them to regard themselves as "colorless,"[34] and to avoid confronting the painful question of *racial* oppression.[35]

In his 1962 survey on differential ethnic responses to the Revolution, Zeitlin found that "while 80 percent of Negroes favored the revolution, only 67 percent of the whites had the same attitude. The favorable attitude was 91 percent among Negroes who had worked nine months or less before the Revolution. Thus, among the most critically marginal—the black and unemployed—was the strongest support for the revolution."[36] The high concentration of Blacks among the unemployed and underemployed—respectively 75 percent and 85 percent—explains why black workers were the real social base of the Castro regime in 1959 and increasingly so thereafter.

Given the complex blend of black economic insecurity and a rebel tradition, observed Zeitlin, "one would probably surmise that Negroes would be more likely than whites to support the revolution" (ibid., 72). His survey did in fact demonstrate that, "taken as a whole, the Negro workers . . . are more likely to favor the revolution than the white workers" and that "the relationship is essentially the same when viewed among only those who were workers before the revolution" (ibid., 77). The reason for the ethnic differential, Zeitlin found, was in "the connection between the racial situation and the prerevolutionary class structure and economic order which the revolution destroyed" (ibid., 83–84).

The response of black Cuban workers to the Castroite order was essentially ethnic, with subjective factors playing as much a part as the material conditions of deprivation forced upon them by the old order. "Indeed, if we look at the effect of change in employment status since the revolution on Negro and white workers . . . the results are essentially the same as when we looked at prerevolutionary employment status alone. Both among the workers who are working more regularly and those who worked regularly before and since the revolution, Negroes are more likely than whites to favor the revolution. . . , and we might infer that *the social status of the Negro racial group accounts for the Negro-white differences"* [Italics added.] (ibid., 78).

As members of an oppressed racial group, black workers easily related the discrimination they experienced to Cuba's economic domination by the United States. Over the years they had proved their willingness to support political programs and leaders with a marked determination to challenge the U.S. More than any other sector of the population, black workers had suffered the direct, even personal, impact of the white American presence in Cuba—occupation troops, industrialists, gangsters, businessmen, and tourists. They naturally tended to believe that "their fight to win full citizenship in their society, their struggle to enlarge their social and political rights and to improve their conditions of life was in the main directed

against foreign economic interests, essentially those of American cor-
porations" (ibid., 288).

The identification of foreign domination as the source of all their
woes may have provided a psychological escape for a group that shied
away from confronting the domestic causes of its oppression, that is,
the prevalence in Cuba of a home-grown system of white supremacy.
Moreover, the image of the U.S. as a land of anti-black hatred and Jim
Crow segregation (an image skillfully played up by Cuba's white ruling classes) further inflamed an anti-Americanism which, translated
into political terms, was pure anti-imperialism. "Thus, the racial
problem in Cuba was, if anything, a boon to Castro. In the hands of
the revolutionaries, the race issue was extremely useful for discrediting the old social order. Furthermore, because of the 'instant liberation' of the Negro, tens of thousands of disadvantaged Cubans were
recruited into the ranks of revolutionary enthusiasts."[37]

"Although the Cuban government is . . . predominantly white in
character," observed an analyst, "the incorporation of the black
masses proved as important as the destruction of a social class in the
delineation of the revolution."[38] The benevolent paternalism and
elite messianic leadership inherent in Castroism found fertile ground
among the politically radical but culturally alienated black Cuban
workers. Imbued with a sense of superiority over those it designated
as *los humildes* (the humble ones), the white revolutionary regime
could feel entitled to expect the willing subordination and instant
political loyalty of those whom it had generously delivered.

The desegregation drive undertaken by the revolutionary regime
demonstrated perhaps Castro's intuitive grasp of Cuban race politics.
"How clever Fidel Castro was to understand what these sons and
daughters of slavery wanted, what embittered them. He didn't
promise them the earth. He simply said, 'You are no longer pariahs.
You're men!' "[39] remarked a European observer. Few of these born-
again black men and women who saw themselves emancipated by the
"racial reform" would have viewed the revolutionary government's
policy of opening up new employment and educational opportunities
to Blacks as "a belated and only partial compensation for past discrimination in Cuba."[40] Rather, grateful black workers were willing
to overcompensate their new white rulers with an increasingly unflinching loyalty. A spontaneous "racial contract" had emerged between Cuba's domestic Africa and the white revolutionary regime.

PART TWO

RACIAL POLITICS AND FOREIGN POLICY

5 CUBA, THE THIRD WORLD AND THE COMMUNIST BLOC

Toward the end of 1959, Fidel Castro began to resort to the "Negro question" in order to discredit his enemies, both domestic and foreign, and to enhance his messianic hold over Black Cuba.[1] His first major use of the race issue as a weapon was to defeat opposing factions within his own movement and to consolidate himself as the sole arbiter of Cuba's fate.[2] The Huber Matos affair gave the Caudillo an opportunity to resort to race-baiting tactics he would perfect into a veritable weapon.

Major Matos had resigned from the army over the issue of communism. "I do not want to become an obstacle to the revolution," he wrote to Castro, "and believe that, before choosing between adapting myself and resignation to avoid doing harm, it is honest and 'revolutionary' to leave. I think that . . . whoever has had the frankness to speak to you of the Communist problem should do so."[3]

Matos's resignation was interpreted by the Caudillo as a challenge to his personal leadership,[4] a "crime" against which he had warned his subordinates from as early as 1954 when he wrote: "The indispensable preconditions of a genuine civic movement are: ideology, discipline, and leadership [jefatura]. The three are essential but leadership is most fundamental. I do not know if it was Napoleon who said that one bad general in battle counts more than twenty good ones," Castro said. "It is not possible to organize a movement in which everyone believes he has the right to issue public statements without consulting anyone; nor can anything be expected of an organization made up of anarchic men, who, at the first dispute, find the easiest way out, breaking and destroying the machine. The propaganda apparatus, or organization, should be so powerful that it would implacably destroy anyone who tried to create tendencies, cliques, schisms, or who should rebel against the movement."[5]

Dramatically arrested at his home by Castro personally,[6] Matos was tried by a kangaroo court on charges of conspiracy and sentenced to a twenty-year term, which he served in full before he was released at the end of 1979. The entire episode underscored the fact that, for Castro, opposition to Marxism was then tantamount to "high treason," as Matos's "crime" had been no more than that. In a matter of months, in fact, Castro would openly declare: "He who is anti-Communist is a counter-revolutionary."[7] A veritable purge of the armed forces, the government, and the administration was under way, with the Communist party already offering its cadres as replacements.

On October 26, 1959, Castro announced the formation of a militia to crush the "counter-revolution." Speaking to a huge rally, the Caudillo made his first public reference to the racial question since his two speeches in March. He likened men such as Huber Matos to the slaveowners of the past. Anti-communism and opposition to his regime, he inferred, were but attempts to suppress the rights his Revolution had "given" Cuban Blacks, the peasants, the have-nots.

"For the first time in the history of the Cuban nation, which has spanned four centuries and began with the Indians persecuted and murdered by the Conquistadores, and which then continued on to a greater stage of slavery, when men were bought and sold like beasts . . . , has emerged a revolutionary power," he said, "which is dealing a damaging blow to all privileges, all injustices, and which has finally redeemed the tarnished manhood of men who in some cases can trace their origins back more than four centuries."[8] Castro asked the one-million-strong crowd whether or not they agreed "with the fact that the beaches, once the exclusive privilege of a few, have now been opened up to the Cuban people regardless of colour, without stupid prejudices. I ask the people if they are or they are not in agreement with the fact that equal opportunities of employment are open to Cubans of every colour. . . . And that is the explanation for our making the Revolutionary Laws which damage national and foreign privileges; it is for that they attack us, it is for that they call us Communists, it is for that they accuse us" (ibid., 96).

A week before the Matos "trial" began, Castro addressed another large crowd in Santiago de Cuba and again likened his opponents to the slaveowners of the last century. "There are some truths that must be said," he told them. "Do you all know who all of those people really are? They are the same ones who, during the last century, were slave-holders."[9] Taking his cue from the Jefe, Raúl Castro, speaking at another mass rally, asked: "What shall we do with the black-skinned men and women for whom Macéo fought? . . . We know 'what to do' with them, for ours are the commitments of José Martí and Antonio Macéo."[10] Ché Guevara, speaking at the University of Las Villas, echoed the new mobilizing theme: "What words could I address to the university that would underscore its primary function in the new Cuba? Simply, that it must become Negro, it must become mulatto . . ."[11]

The sudden insistence on the racial issue by the foremost leaders of the regime was not unpremeditated. Castro was merely reverting, in an entirely new context, to a time-honored gambit in Cuban race politics, from José Martí to Fulgencio Batista. "In the past, it was a frequent political ploy [in Cuba] to denounce the existence of racial discrimination in appealing for electoral support. . . . ," commented a scholar. "Shortly after the Revolution, Castro began his own propaganda campaign on behalf of racial equality. He has asserted that all Negroes in the country can see the social treatment they deserve. Hotels, beaches and resorts have been opened to all, regardless of race, and tangible evidence of segregation has been eliminated. . . . The regime has given maximum publicity to the role of Juán Almeida, a Negro who held the position of chief of staff of the army, citing him as proof of the willingness of the leaders of the Revolution to accept a Negro colleague."[12]

Race as a Foreign Policy Weapon

As more opposition to Castro mounted in the United States, the existence of a racial problem there developed into one of the most damaging foreign policy weapons in Havana's anti-American arsenal. In mid-November 1959, instructions were given to INIT, the state-run tourist organ, to invite the most prominent black Americans to Cuba, "a land free of racial discrimination," for a New Year's Eve banquet with Castro.[13] In late December 1959, former world heavyweight champion Joe Louis, and black baseball stars Roy Campanella and Jackie Robinson arrived in Havana, heading a party of "prominent American Negroes." The visit was well publicized by the Cuban media. Newspapers printed front page photos of the Caudillo's New Year's dinner with his black American guests.[14] To the delight of Black Cuba, national television rebroadcast several times the images of Castro, flanked by his loyal black aide, Juán Almeida, merrily feting the prominent black americanos. Havana had succeeded in its first conscious attempt to woo American Blacks to its side in a war against a common oppressor.

The racial question had proved to be the one element which thoroughly discredited and isolated the conservative and liberal white

Cuban opposition. The upper classes in Cuba were very much self-consciously white, segregationist, and strongly Negrophobic. They were indeed the product, and modern representatives, of the idelogy and economic class interests of the slave-holders in Cuba's immediate past. The "Negro question" was equally Washington's Achilles' heel. Castro would direct increasingly heavier blows to that soft spot the more both countries squared off for a violent confrontation. "Fearing an American intervention, Cuban leaders attempted to short circuit the U.S. by canvassing the sort of support that could allow their revolution to survive if Washington decided to concretely intervene. Hence, on both sides—particularly on Cuba's—a vast propaganda campaign was set in motion. Denouncing American racism and stressing that racial discrimination was eradicated in Cuba, Castro now redoubled his efforts to canvass the support of American Negroes in his struggle against imperialism."[15]

The Fair Play for Cuba Committee, a U.S.-based pro-Castro organization, was set up in the spring of 1960. The FPCC was to become the chief vehicle through which the Cuban leadership sought access to America's black population. Founded by two American television journalists, Robert Taber, a white, and Richard Gibson, a Black, the FPCC was from the outset an effective organ for conveying Castro's message to the black American community. A well-regarded journalist, Taber was a personal friend of Castro, whom he had interviewed in 1958 during the Sierra Maestra campaign. Taber certainly had been instrumental in creating an early awareness in Havana of the importance of canvassing black American support. Gibson, in contrast, seems to have played more of a window-dressing role.

In May 1960, former heavyweight champion Joe Louis, one of the prominent U.S. Blacks invited to Cuba by Castro the previous year, was named U.S. publicity agent to promote tourism to Cuba.[16] Louis, dancer Josephine Baker, novelists Richard Wright and James Baldwin, and a host of other black American celebrities were on Cuba's invitation list, drawn up by the FPCC. Prominent U.S. black intellectuals, associated with leftist and/or civil rights causes, were also eagerly sought out by the FPCC for projected tours of Cuba.

In July 1960, a group of black U.S. intellectuals finally arrived in Cuba on an organized FPCC tour. Among them were poet Leroi Jones (Amiri Baraka), the historian-sociologist Harold Cruse, writer Julian Mayfield, historian John Henrik Clarke, and civil rights activist Robert Williams, whose fortunes were on the rise. Recalling this second organized trip of American Blacks to revolutionary Cuba,

Harold Cruse wrote about his misgivings: "I noticeably held back all outward exuberance for the Cuban situation." he said. "I was admittedly pro-Castro, but there were too many Communists around acting imperious and important. Moreover, there was *the obvious and unclarified position of the Cuban Negro* to consider. Yet we were all treated with such overwhelming deference, consideration and privilege, it was difficult to be critical" (Italics added.).[17] Others in the second group of guests wrote favorably about the trip upon their return to the U.S.[18]

The visitor who would prove instrumental in Havana's attempts to woo U.S. Blacks to its side was Robert Williams. A former Marine and Korean War veteran, Williams was at the time the most militant civil rights leader in the United States. Head of the Monroe, North Carolina, chapter of the NAACP, he had since 1958 advocated armed self-defense as the only road to obtaining the basic rights of black Americans. He had immediately attracted the attention of Cuban intelligence and of Fidel Castro himself.

Williams was born and raised in the Deep South. Accustomed to a racially segregated environment, he was wonder-struck by his Cuban trip. "A Negro, for example, was head of the Cuban armed forces and no one could hide that fact from us here in America," he marveled.[19] Williams said that in Cuba he was "made to feel that I was a member of the human race for the first time in my life" (ibid.). He thanked "Fidel Castro and Free Cuba [for] granting persons of African descent entrance into the human race" (ibid., 70). Such language could only delight white Cuban leaders, who presumably had already begun to regard themselves as the saviors of black Americans, whom they increasingly described in terms such as "wretched U.S. Negroes."

Williams's exaggerated reactions to Castro's "racial reform" made him the most fervent and influential supporter of the Cuban regime among U.S. Blacks. The full weight of his prestige, he warned would be placed at the service of Castro's cause. "As for my being 'used as a pawn in the struggle of Cuba' against imperialist and racist North America, I prefer to be used as an instrument to convey the truth of a people who respect the rights of man, rather than to be used as an Uncle Tom whitewasher of black oppression and injustice and an apologist for America's hypocrisy" (ibid.). He defended Havana's right to criticize the U.S. racial situation. "Cuba's aversion to America's inhumanity to man is not an interference in a 'native American problem.' . . . . Racism in the U.S.A. is as much a world problem as was Nazism. . . . Yes, wherever there is oppression in the world today, it is the concern of the entire [human] race. My cause is the same . . . as Cuba's against the white supremacist imperialist" (ibid., 70, 71).

A good many of the FPCC's activities on behalf of Cuba centered on propagandizing Castro's "racial reform" and extolling the "perfect racial equality" reigning on the island. "There is full freedom there. Every human being has equal rights to work and education. There is no racism: a Negro is the chief of the army," argued a prominent U.S. Marxist leader.[20] The Federal Bureau of Investigation took an interest in the FPCC from the start, and had infiltrated the pro-Castro organization. (The Cuban leadership would later contend that FBI operatives had been among the FPCC's founding members.) In June 1960 Washington declared two Cuban diplomats persona non grata.[21] Carlos Manuel Sánchez y Basquet and Berta Louis Pla y Badia were charged with "distributing anti-U.S. propaganda . . . to augment racial dissension in the U.S." (Italics added.) (ibid.).[22] Washington had now begun to fear the long-term consequences of Castro's exploitation of the American racial situation to further his own ends.

Maj. Manuel "Red Beard" Piñeiro Losada, Cuba's intelligence chief, knew American society intimately, having once lived in the U.S. He spoke English fluently and was married to a Texan dancer. He headed a department which would soon become famous as the Dirección General de Inteligencia or DGI, Cuba's counterpart of the CIA. Piñeiro's involvement in Havana's attempt to woo the black American population clearly meant that the utility of U.S Blacks to Cuba had outstripped pure propaganda purposes. Robert Williams had attracted Piñeiro's attention, and before the close of that summer, the militant civil rights leader was invited back to Cuba. This time, however, he went as Fidel Castro's personal guest.

In 1960, Cuba's propaganda machine stridently criticized Washington on the "Negro question." Meanwhile, a clandestine effort by Piñeiro's department was under way to recruit American Blacks for sensitive operations within the U.S., not excluding acts of sabotage.[23] Within a year, fifteen of those Blacks had fallen into the FBI's hands; five others reportedly fled to Cuba.

The First Declaration of Havana

The propaganda war between Washington and Havana reached new heights in the summer of 1960. To American charges that Cuba was taking a "pro-Red" direction, Havana countered that the White House was following an "anti-Black" course. Washington's efforts to alienate support from the revolutionary Cuban regime thus seemed to boomerang. Meanwhile, in Cuba itself, Castro's charisma and his revolutionary mystique made him "the man of the hour, the new messiah."[24] Voicing popular sentiment, a Presbyterian minister declared, "Fidel Castro is an instrument in the hands of God for the establishment of His reign among men!"[25] Not averse to such comparisons, the Caudillo proclaimed to a mass rally: "Those who condemn this Revolution are condemning Christ, and they would be capable of crucifying Christ, because He did what we are doing."[26]

By late August 1960, material preparation was well under way in the U.S. for the violent overthrow of the Castro regime. A White Paper was submitted to the Organization of American States, which met in San José, Costa Rica, to legitimize in advance an operation Castro had long anticipated. Charging Cuba, among other things, with having trained "Communist agents and guerrillas to spread the Communist revolution throughout Latin America,"[27] Washington asked the OAS to unequivocally condemn the Castro regime as a threat to hemispheric security.

In two speeches delivered on August 30, 1960, Castro attacked the U.S. and denounced the OAS's Declaration of San José. He told Cubans that his regime was a friend of the Communist bloc (ibid.). Three days later, he countered with his own "Declaration of Havana." Castro lashed out against the "discrimination against Negroes and Indians," and proclaimed "the right of Negroes and Indians to full human dignity" (ibid., 120). Cuba, he said, would "gratefully accept the support of Soviet rockets" if invaded by the United States.[28] Apparently with an eye to mobilizing the Afro-Asian bloc, American Blacks, and all Third World peoples on his behalf, he said that:

By offering friendship to the North American people—that is, to the Negroes who are lynched, the persecuted intellectuals, and the workers who are forced to accept the leadership of mobsters—we underscore our intention to walk "with the entire world and not merely with a section of it. . . ." Democracy is incompatible with financial oligarchies, with discrimination against Negroes, the doings of the Ku Klux Klan, ... The National and General Assembly of the Cuban people demands the right of workers, peasants, students, intellectuals, Negroes and Indians . . . to struggle for their economic, political and social claims; the right of every people to enjoy the solidarity of all oppressed, colonized, aggressed and exploited peoples, irregardless of which corner in the world

64   Racial Politics and Foreign Policy

they may be in, or the geographical distance between them. All peoples
of the world are brothers (ibid., 116–117, 118, 121).

Encapsulated in his words was the irrevocably extra-national
proclivity of the Castro regime. On the one hand, it maintained the
right of nations outside the hemisphere to rush to Cuba's succor.
And, as subsequent events would show, it also assumed Havana's
right to intervene in any part of the world where it was in its own best
interests to do so. Washington had declared its "right of hot pursuit."
Castro had countered by proclaiming his own right of retaliation anywhere on the globe.

Courting the Afro-Asian Bloc

Castro's equation of anti-communism with counter-revolution
marked the end of a purely tactical "anti-Communist" neutrality in
Cuba. Cuba's new posture was that of a non-aligned, pro-Communist
Third World state. That policy profile reflected decisive domestic
changes, as described by Hugh Thomas. "Already the Communists
had some positions in the Cuban State; already they were Castro's
followers, though he was not yet their leader. More positively. . .
after years without a clear creed, Castro seems . . . to have felt increasingly drawn towards the idea of a complete explanation of
politics. . . ."[29]

In mid-summer 1959, the Caudillo had reshuffled his government.
Manuel Urrútia y Lleo, the vocally anti-Communist president, was
jettisoned and replaced with Osvaldo Dorticós Torrado, whose links
to the Cuban Communist party dated back to the 1940s. Cuba's new
head of state was a wealthy lawyer, descended from a founding family
of Cienfuegos, one of Cuba's most staunchly segregationist cities. He
was distantly related to nineteenth-century millionaire planter and
slave trader Tomas Terry (ibid., 98, 1085ff). For a time he was the personal secretary to Communist party President Juán Marinello, but he
was also commodore of the Cienfuegos Yacht Club, one of the
racially segregated private white clubs (ibid., 1234). Dorticós had also
been president of the elite National College of Lawyers. Besides his
sound credentials as the descendant of an aristocratic family, Dorticós
possessed the one quality most prized by Castro: unswerving loyalty
and submission to the Caudillo. (Dorticós remained Cuba's president
until the end of 1976, when Castro himself took that title; he committed suicide in 1983.)

Guevara Tours the Afro-Asian Bloc

Assiduously courted by the rival eastern and western camps, the Afro-Asian bloc seemed the most apt to lend Castro the diplomatic protection he sorely needed. Afro-Asian states appeared to be the most logical allies of a revolutionary regime that had eagerly proclaimed itself neutral and anti-colonial. Thus, even while seriously contemplating the option of binding the fate of the Revolution to an alliance with the Soviet bloc, Castro "continued to feel closer to the neutralist Third World leaders than to those of the Communist world, and thought it would be enough to cultivate the former's friendship and be incorporated into their midst to have nothing more to fear from the imperialist powers."[30]

In early June 1959, within weeks of Castro's promulgation of agrarian reform in Cuba, Ché Guevara set out with three aides for a three-month Afro-Asian tour. He arrived in Cairo on June 16 on the first leg of his tour. He became the first Castroite leader to set foot on the African continent, but his visit was devoid of any African significance.[31] His hosts were Pan-Arabists, and Guevara's primary goal was to meet Gamal Abdel Nasser, chief of the non-aligned bloc. Guevara's mission was to woo the non-aligned Afro-Asian states, enlist their backing for the Castroite regime, and procure the advantages of their protective political umbrella.

Whatever interests Havana had in Africa at that juncture were confined to the Arab North, not only because Egypt was then the most prestigious Afro-Asian state, but also because a national liberation struggle similar to Castro's campaign in Cuba was under way to wrench Algeria from French rule. The Castroites viewed the Algerian struggle as the closest reflection in the Third World of their Sierra Maestra experience, and immediately identified with it (ibid.). As for Egypt, Castro was quick to establish parallels between himself and Nasser, the fiery colonel who had successfully defied British imperialism and repulsed a Franco-Israeli-British intervention. Like the Egyptian Rais, Cuba's Caudillo intended to fashion a non-aligned, anti-imperialist, independent foreign policy for his Revolution. And Havana's leadership also anticipated a Caribbean reenactment of the sort of conflict that followed nationalization of the Suez Canal.

Guevara opened his talks with Nasser with appropriate flattery. Egypt's resistance at Suez during the tripartite attack in 1956, Ché told the Rais, had encouraged Castro to launch his own Sierra Maestra campaign. Egypt's leader had always been a "source of moral strength" to the Castroites.[32] In short, Castroism was but a Latin American version of Nasserism. But Nasser was nonetheless suspicious of Castro and his followers. He doubted their revolutionary sincerity (ibid., 311), suspecting Castro to be an opportunist. As their conversation waned, Guevara inquired how many Egyptian landowners had fled the country as a result of Nasser's agrarian reform. Nasser explained that only a few had fled, mostly "white Egyptians," naturalized foreigners (ibid., 312). Guevara was dismayed. "That means," he said, "that nothing much happened in your revolution. I measure the depth of the social transformation by the number of people who are affected by it and who feel that they have no place in the new society" (ibid.). Nasser calmly replied that he had intended liquidating the *privileges* of a class, *not individuals* of that class (ibid.). Now the distrust became mutual.

A lightning visit to the Sudan left Guevara disappointed. That country, he felt, was simply too backward to be of help to Havana. Morocco, then under the rule of the strongly nationalist monarch Mohamed V, lifted Che's spirits: the first important encounter between leaders of the Algerian FLN and a leader of the Cuban revolution took place there.[33] Morocco, Egypt, and Tunisia were then serving as rearguard bases for the FLN. Hence, Castro's decision to set up his first diplomatic missions on the continent in Rabat, Tunis, and Cairo. Walterio Carbonell, the black Cuban who had been expelled from the Communist party in 1953 because he supported Castro, became the ambassador to Tunisia.

Guevara toured Yugoslavia, Indonesia, India, Burma, Ceylon, Japan, and Pakistan, returning to Cuba in early September, dismayed at the poor prospects for trade with the Afro-Asian bloc. Having concluded only two "rather unprofitable treaties with Egypt and Ceylon,"[34] he had discovered the limitations of partnership with nations he felt were much less developed structurally, and perhaps politically, than Cuba. A good measure of his disillusionment could be inferred from the report of his tour he delivered on nationwide television.[35] Somehow he felt compelled to apologize for not having ventured south of the Sahara while on the black continent. "Lack of time forced us to leave out Iraq and other countries from our planned itinerary. . . ," he said. "Nor were we able to visit Ghana—a new African republic we had intended to visit—because the trip was too long" (ibid.).

Black Africa could hardly have figured high on the list of priorities of the Castroite regime at the time. Omission from Guevara's itinerary of black countries headed by the two most radical exponents of non-aligned anti-imperialism in sub-Saharan Africa—Kwame Nkrumah's Ghana and Sékou Touré's Guinea—served to underscore that point. Possibly Nasser had also apprised Guevara of his own misgivings about Nkrumah, with whom he was embroiled in a bitter feud over continental leadership.[36] When Guevara arrived in Cairo, Nasser's dual claim to leadership over Africa and the Arab world was being hotly contested by Gen. Abdel Karim Kassem in the Middle East and by Nkrumah in Africa.

Ever since Ghana had become independent in 1957, Nkrumah had resisted Nasser's hegemonic ambitions over the African continent (ibid.). In fact, while Guevara was in Cairo from July 16 to 19, Nkrumah, Sékou Touré of Guinea, and William Tubman of Liberia met at Sanniquelli and announced the formation of a tripartite Pan-African union. Nasser correctly saw the project as directed against Egyptian hegemony over black Africa. A year before, the Ghana-Guinea union of November 1958 was equally interpreted by the Egyptian president as another of Nkrumah's schemes to undercut Cairo's continental leadership ambitions (ibid., 46).

It is conceivable that in order to cultivate Nasser's friendship, Guevara delayed the opportunity to establish direct ties with black Africa's two most dynamic states. After all, Nkrumah was also regarded as a founding father of the Afro-Asian bloc. Another eloquent indication of the priority Havana afforded Arab North Africa over black Africa was Guevara's suggestion, upon returning to Cuba, that Egypt should become Cuba's diplomatic base for future contact with sub-Saharan Africa.[37]

Guevara's statement that India's development was being stunted by "cows and religion" might have been more than a passing comment.[38] Obsession with religion had characterized all of the Afro-Asian states he visited. Guevara was an atheist, anti-imperialist revolutionary steeped in the western rationalist tradition. Most likely, Guevara returned from the Castro regime's first probe into the non-white world even more firmly convinced of Cuba's political and intellectual advancement over these Afro-Asian countries. However, for tactical reasons, Havana would have to keep up the pretense of advocating a non-aligned anti-imperialism of the Afro-Asian type.

Within three weeks of Guevara's tour, Cuba began a campaign stressing the extra-national vocation of the Revolution and identifying its fate with that of the Afro-Asian bloc. Foreign Minister Raúl Roa García made that point before the U.N. General Assembly. "It is unfortunately evident that the world finds itself divided nowadays into two major groups respectively led by the United States of North America and the Union of Soviet Socialist Republics . . . and a third group which purports to bridge the gap between them but whose strength is more moral than material," he said. "By virtue of its historical position, geographic location and internal obligations Cuba is included in the group of countries designated as 'western.' But the revolutionary government of Cuba will not accept such prearranged options. . . . Concretely, this simply means that we will not accept being forced to choose between the capitalist and communist solutions. There are other roads and solutions."[39] Cuba, said Roa, had already "found its own road to the original solution of its own problems—a road which it shares in common with the other Latin American peoples . . . that road and solution is what links [the Latin American people] . . . to the undeveloped peoples of Africa and Asia in their courageous search for self-expression" (ibid.). For that reason, Roa said, Cuba "can count on the moral support of all the un-developed peoples of America, Africa and Asia, because it is a known fact that defeat of the Cuban revolution would be a great setback as well in the inexorable liberation process of these nations" (ibid.).

Speaking at a mass rally a few weeks after Roa's U.N. declaration, the Caudillo himself proclaimed for the first time that Cubans had a sort of historical mission to fulfill. "Today, the eyes of the whole world are on Cuba," he said. "Cuba elicits the admiration of the whole world and nothing can lower the esteem the peoples of America and the whole world feel for her."[40] Now asserting the uniqueness of the Revolution and of Cubans, Castro struck a heroic, messianic note: "Our revolution has been possible only because of the sort of people Cubans are. . . . The people of Cuba have *a mission to fulfill* and we will fulfill it, because the people of Cuba are the kind with whom a revolution like this can be carried out. . . ." (Italics added.) (ibid.).

The extra-national nature of this mission could be gleaned from a declaration by the Confederation of Cuban Workers (CTC), by then fully under Castroite control. "The Cuban revolution is the guide of the countries of Latin America for the attainment of economic and political liberty," said the document. "Our labour movement, in order to march as the vanguard of the revolution, must also be a guide to the Latin American labour movement."[41] The same tone pervaded a note from Foreign Minister Roa to the U.S. government, underscoring that "in accord with their historical traditions and the idea they entertain of the Nation, their mission in America and *their role in the world*, the Cuban people . . . have now found their own avenues of political, economic, social and cultural expression" (Italics added.). [42]

Castroism and World Communism Converge

Quite plausibly the results of Guevara's Afro-Asian foray motivated Castro to quickly seek the closest possible ties with the Communist bloc. A firm advocate of that course himself, Guevara had returned with strong arguments to buttress that position. For one, all of the non-aligned states he had visited shared a common denominator: they had special economic and trade ties with the USSR, from whom they received considerable military and technological assistance. From Nasser to Nehru, Nkrumah to Sukarno, all neutralist Afro-Asian leaders were close friends of Moscow and Peking, and none seemed unhappy about being the recipient of substantial Communist-bloc aid.

At the same time hostility and fear of the U.S. were driving Castro closer to the Communist bloc, the ranks of world communism were undergoing the greatest split of their history. In the course of the summer of 1959, the Kremlin destroyed agreements to help China develop nuclear weapons, reneged on commitments to help modernize Chinese industry and technology, and imposed a blockade on its former ally.[43] In the meantime, Castro had become convinced that a small underdeveloped country could only escape the clutches of a superpower by relying on another superpower. Unquestionably, Castro was aware of the dangers that such a reliance implied: satellization, loss of sovereignty, and dependency. In that context the growing Sino-Soviet schism was perceived by Havana as a safeguard for Cuba's political independence as it drew closer to the Kremlin.

By showing sympathy for China, believes Cheng Ying-Hsiang, Havana was indicating its readiness to tactically exploit the split. "What made Fidel Castro and Ché Guevara discover at the end of the summer of 1959 that Peking's support could be much more valuable than initially foreseen? Simply, the realization that however strong a sympathy they evoked among Third World neutralists, their support would remain disquietingly passive. They foresaw that once the viciousness of the capitalist camp was unleashed, Cuba would have no other recourse but to hitch itself onto the socialist camp, whereupon Havana's only chance to escape becoming a mere pawn of the Kremlin was to play Peking against it" (ibid., 52).

Guevara's tactical sinophilia quite probably had to contend with Castro's own reportedly ingrained sinophobia. Since the days of slavery, anti-Chinese prejudices had been commonplace in Cuba. Sino-Cubans have been stereotyped as crafty, treacherous, lecherous, and inscrutable. The popular saying, "Vale mas un muerto que un Chino" (A corpse is worth more than a Chinaman), reflects that racist contempt. Castro's former confidant, Carlos Franqui, recalled Castro's dislike of the Chinese as obsessive. "I have spoken many times with Fidel about the Chinese. He feels a great antipathy for Chinese as such. To my surprise, his attitude towards them was visceral: he detests them. His attacks against Mao Tse-tung bore the imprints of that astounding personal prejudice of his."[44]

Prejudices against the Chinese might indeed have played no small part in Castro's open hostility toward China in the mid-1960s, when the ideological Moscow-Peking feud had degenerated into racial innuendos and mudslinging. Did Castro's reported disdain for the Chinese also cause him to resist Peking's strenuous efforts to enlist Cuba's support against Moscow in the early 1960s, even when Havana had good cause to condemn the Kremlin's behavior? In any event, between 1959 and 1969, the Sino-Soviet rift certainly offered Havana not only the leverage to deal with the mighty USSR practically as an equal but even to intimidate Moscow's cautious leadership into committing itself to guaranteeing the survival of the Castroite regime. Castro was to play Peking against Moscow to his own economic, political, and military advantage; displeased but passive, the USSR was forced to dance to his tune.[45]

6   CASTRO DISCOVERS BLACK AFRICA

At the end of 1959, it was evident to close observers that the domestic rapprochement between Castroism and communism was but a prelude to Havana's convergence with the Soviet bloc. Second only to Castro, the most interested participant in a Soviet-Cuban entente was certainly the Cuban Communist party. The inescapable consequences of such an event were perceived forebodingly by many independent radical Castroites. "We knew," explained Carlos Franqui, "that if the Cuban Communist party got hold of the Revolution, Cuba would enter the dark ages politically and that to get her out of it would be worse than fighting a hundred Batistas together."[1] But because of the enthusiastic popular support enjoyed by the Caudillo, radical non-Communist Castroites were increasingly impotent. The most they could do was to use their personal ties with Castro to offer foreign and domestic policy alternatives to the drift towards the Soviet bloc and the Cuban Communist party.

An Afrocentric Foreign Policy Proposal

Perhaps only someone of the ethnic and political background of the Afro-Cuban diplomat, Walterio Carbonell, could have elaborated, at such an early date and with such a keen sense of future events, the sort of *Afrocentric* foreign policy alternative he presented Castro toward the end of 1959. The former Cuban ambassador to Tunisia was the first to alert the revolutionary leadership to the importance of a black African connection. He had urged Castro to adopt a resolutely pro-African stance. Carbonell perceived Africa as the key to a network of Third World alliances that could be a powerful factor in Cuba's negotiations with the USSR. If the Revolution was to resist absorption by the Soviet bloc, it was imperative that the momentum of the Cuban revolution converge with the radical mainstream of African nationalism and decolonization.

Cuba's colorful entry into the arena of world politics in 1959 had coincided with that of the African continent. Between 1956 and 1959,

Castro's fight against Batista and the struggle for independence in Africa shared the headlines. Gamal Abdel Nasser stood up to the western powers at Suez in 1956; Ghana became independent in 1957; Guinea followed suit in 1958, and the Algerian FLN was on the offensive in 1959. Africa was definitely on the move. Yet Castro and his associates seemed totally oblivious of the black continent at that time. "At the beginning of the revolution," stated Franqui, "Fidel and the others had never really spoken about Africa, and it is difficult to say exactly at what point their interest in Africa began. There was, of course, the situation in Algeria, because the war being waged there was so similar to the one we ourselves had fought. In fact, the Algerians had sent some of their people to contact us in Cuba. . . . But there was never, to my knowledge, any discussion or reference to black Africa specifically at this period either by Fidel or anyone else" (ibid.).

Africa came up for discussion only toward the end of Castro's first year in power, Franqui recalled. "After the triumph of the Revolution, the whole question of the relationship between Cuba and the African continent—black Africa particularly—was initially raised by Walterio Carbonell when he proposed, for the first time, the idea of convening a tricontinental conference," Franqui recalled. "Generally speaking, people are ignorant of the facts, but it was Carbonell who first advocated the idea of a tricontinental conference and of establishing special links with black Africa. In fact, he perceived Africa as playing a pivotal role in his tricontinental proposal. That idea took form while he was ambassador to Tunisia in 1959. Tunis was then harboring Algerian guerrilla leaders, was frequently visited by Frantz Fanon, and was a meeting point for African radicals. . . . Personally, it was from Carbonell that I heard the first references to Africa and I know for a fact that it was he who brought up the subject with Fidel" (ibid.).

Barely three months after having been appointed Havana's first ambassador to an African country, Walterio Carbonell was back in Cuba, his diplomatic career cut short by an accident. The car he was reportedly driving accidentally killed a pedestrian in the streets of Tunis, whereupon Carbonell immediately resigned his post.

Four years of exile in Paris, during Batista's regime, had brought him into contact with the exponents of radical African nationalism, grouped around the Fédération des Etudiants d'Afrique Noire en France (FEANF), and with the works of anti-colonialists such as Martiniquans Aimé Césaire and Frantz Fanon, Senegalese Alioune Diop and Cheikh Anta Diop, Haitian Marxist René Depestre, and black American novelist Richard Wright.[2] Carbonell was familiar with the convenors of the Second World Congress of Black Artists and Writers, held in Rome in 1959, and apparently met with Frantz Fanon while in Tunis.[3] He was easily the most Africa-conscious and best-informed Castroite official on the Third World, particularly African affairs. A historian and ethnologist, during his years with the Cuban Communist party, he had also become the most incisive specialist on the race question in Cuba.

Carbonell attempted to impress on the revolutionary leadership the potential strategic importance of the African continent in terms of Cuba's relationship with the two rival superpowers. But at the time, as Carlos Franqui admits, Cuba's new white rulers were ill-prepared for such visionary reasoning. "In 1959 the ignorance of Cuba's leaders, including Fidel and the others, was practically total on Africa," he recalled. "There was in fact an attitude of contempt for Cuba's own Africanity by a leadership which was conspicuously composed of white Cubans. Moreover, at that time Cuba was entirely cut off from the black world. Carbonell's attempts to change that state of affairs therefore ran into strong resistance" (ibid.).

Carbonell, however, was intent on taking advantage of the environment created by Castro's new approach to the racial question as a foreign policy device, the key link being the recognition of Cuba's racial kinship with continental Africa. To this end, he published a series of theoretical articles in *Revolución* challenging the prevalent assumptions about the historical position of what he termed the "African-Cuban population,"[4] taking care to stress the overwhelming Africanity of Cuba's national psychology and home-grown cultures.

Apparently at first Fidel Castro remained aloof. Carbonell then resorted to a public forum. A seemingly innocuous article he published in *Revolución* in early December 1959 was actually a synthesis of the comprehensive proposals he had presented to Castro.[5] In this article, he outlined a strategy that, among other moves, called for the convening in Cuba of a Third World tricontinental congress. He urged the rejection of alliances with either superpower in favor of establishing a third bloc composed of Asia, Africa, the Caribbean, and Latin America.

The example of the African and Asian leaders who had met in Bandung, Indonesia, in 1955, he explained, held important lessons for the Cuban revolution. The strategy of militant Afro-Asian states was geared towards strengthening their independence against western imperialism while keeping the Soviet bloc at a comfortable distance. This was a course that Carbonell felt all Third World countries would do well to follow. The independence of Ghana and Guinea, the anti-imperialist revolution in Iraq, and the upsurge of a strong anti-colonial movement in Asia and Africa could all be traced in one way or another to the "spirit of Bandung" (ibid.). Bandung had laid the foundation for a strategic power bloc independent of the two rival powers that so far dominated world politics. "No matter how powerful a country," Carbonell argued, "it will be incapable of imposing its policies on another if not backed by other states. The United States would not dare impose its policy on Cuba through the OAS were it not for the support it musters from a group of 'democratic' and tyrannical states" (ibid.). Nasserite Egypt was able to resist western imperialism without, at the same time, surrendering its sovereignty to the USSR, because it could rely on its own strategic powerbase—the Afro-Asian bloc (ibid.).

It was impossible for a modern state to survive outside of the context of power bloc arrangements, let alone successfully defend its national sovereignty. "The world is divided into blocs: the bloc of western capitalist countries, and the bloc formed by Russia and the other Socialist states. Outside of 'blocs' no country can exercise any real influence on international affairs. . . . For that reason, Afro-Asian governments have felt obliged to seek unity in order to form a third bloc to defend their national sovereignty much more successfully and exert their influence on world events" (ibid.). Communist Yugoslavia, Carbonell explained, offered a good example of the impotence of a state that attempted on its own to be independent of the two superpowers (ibid.). The only solution left open to the Cuban revolution, he surmised, was the formation of its own powerbase through the transformation of the Afro-Asian bloc into a *tricontinental* power bloc that included Latin America and the Caribbean.

"Like Africa and Asia, Latin America is underdeveloped and needs to defend its national independence" (ibid.), Carbonell argued. The strategic advantage of such a union seemed equally clear: "The day a South American-Afro-Asian bloc comes into being, no power whatsoever could attempt, directly or indirectly, to aggress any of the members of such a Solidarity Community of Underdeveloped Countries. By sheer weight of votes at the United Nations, such an entity would become the predominant diplomatic world force, tipping the international scale in its favor" (ibid.).

Arguing that "geographic distance never deterred the great powers from hooking up their metropoles to the colonies by way of monopolies and supranational arrangements such as the Baghdad Pact,

CENTO, and the OAS," Carbonell emphasized the necessity for the Cuban revolution to promote the building of a tricontinental power-base. "Such a union is possible. As a start, the next meeting of underdeveloped countries should be made to take place in Cuba, which has seized the diplomatic leadership of all Latin America" (ibid.). He listed five immediate benefits to be derived from the convening, under the Cuban aegis, of a tricontinental conference in Havana:

1. Cuba's diplomatic position would be enormously strengthened.
2. The OAS, where only "the most spurious interests" then prevailed, would receive a fatal blow.
3. The basis for a Latin American-Afro-Asian entente at the United Nations would have been laid.
4. The superpowers would be forced to negotiate on an equal footing with revolutionary governments and have to renounce their aggressive designs against them.
5. The possibility for trade, cultural, and even military relations among Third World countries would increase (ibid.).

While perceiving Africa as the most dynamic component of the Afro-Asian bloc—precisely because of its singular history of intense oppression—Carbonell saw Latin America as politically the most experienced of the continents.[6] "The countries of Latin America had the good fortune of achieving their independence one hundred years before Asia, Africa, and the Middle East. Today, however, Latin America happens to be less free than the Afro-Asian states taken as a whole."[7] Through a partnership with the Afro-Asian world, Latin America could retrieve its vanguard role and reassert its independence. "Latin America can recover the leading role it played during the nineteenth century because from an industrial standpoint it is better equipped than the states of Asia, the Middle East, and Africa. Moreover, it is less bound to tradition, and the conflict between archaic and modern social structures is less sharp. Additionally, Latin America enjoys a greater linguistic unity than the underdeveloped countries of the other continents" (ibid.).

By putting up the most radical challenge to American domination in the history of the hemisphere,[8] Castro's revolution had placed Cuba squarely at the vanguard of revolution in Latin America. The Castroite government should, therefore, initiate the ties with Africa:

> *The historic credit of linking Africa and Latin America* must belong to the revolutionary government of Cuba. Through such a union, Cuba herself would be in a position to wield its diplomatic influence at the

United Nations to the fullest extent. . . . Cuba could then become a
world diplomatic center, staking out for itself a role of the highest order
in the diplomatic history of this twentieth century. Because of the
radicalism of our Revolution, and of its chief, Fidel Castro, the underdeveloped peoples would look up to Cuba and its government as their
guide (Italics added.).[9]

Cuba's population of African descent was, in the eyes of Carbonell,
the greatest single asset the revolutionary regime possessed in order
to build a special relationship with the black continent, though,
as Franqui recalls, "the ingrained contempt then reigning in Cuba
for anything African, added to the prevailing ignorance about the
African continent itself, provided a bad climate for the adoption of
[Carbonell's] project."[10] Not to be excluded is the possibility that the
regime might have also felt uneasy about considering policies which
could have the long-term effect of awakening a sort of dormant ethnic nationalism among Afro-Cubans.[11] Be that as it may, and to the
utter consternation of Walterio Carbonell, Fidel Castro did eventually co-opt his proposals. However, as will be seen, Castro went about
implementing them in the context of a Communist state irrevocably
allied to the Soviet Union. An Afrocentric foreign policy strategy
designed to prevent Cuba from being pulled into the Soviet orbit was
turned on its head. The "Carbonell Plan," in due course, became the
"Castro Doctrine" on Africa.

Cuba and the Congo

Throughout the summer of 1960, Patrice Lumumba, the fiery
prime minister of a recently independent Congo, attempted to fend
off a legion of plots to unseat his nationalist government. The Congo
crisis forced Africa even more to the forefront of international
politics. The Congo's independence, on June 30, 1960, had coincided
with Castro's first major nationalizations. Subsequently, the Congolese and Cuban crises evolved in parallel, each culminating dramatically in Lumumba's murder and the October missile crisis. Both
issues concurrently monopolized the debates of the memorable
fifteenth General Assembly of the United Nations in September 1960.

The events surrounding Lumumba's first four months in power had
riveted Castro's attention to the black continent.[12] Threatened by the
merciless intrigues of the major western colonial powers and the
U.S., that defenseless newborn African country was an important test
in the eyes of Havana. At stake was the Kremlin's willingness, determination, and ability to succor a geographically distant, weak,

progressive government threatened with overthrow through direct military intervention by the western imperialist countries.[13] No situation better illustrated Castro's own position vis-à-vis Yankee imperialism than Lumumba's predicament before the western powers. Havana's identification with the cause of the Lumumbists was therefore immediate. Since much of what occurred in the Congo bore direct relevance to Cuba's developing crisis with the U.S., when the Kremlin declared its intention of militarily supporting Lumumba's government in the event of western intervention, Cuba applauded. The Soviet's pledge received prominent exposure in the Cuban media, no doubt reflecting the hope that it also held true for Castro's regime. In a full-page article, *Revolución* warmly commended the Soviets. The carefully worded text bore the distinct hyperbolic language of the Caudillo. "The Soviet Union has played a preeminent role in the Congolese problem. The Soviet government's offer of military aid to the Republic of the Congo has certainly brought the Belgian interventionists and their NATO accomplices to a screeching halt. . . . This is the first time in the history of the USSR that she has played such an important role—and what a role!—in black Africa. These are novel events which will go down in posterity in the history of world diplomacy."[14]

A few weeks prior to Havana's announcement on September 13 that Castro intended to be present at the U.N.'s General Assembly, the Cuban leader instructed his foreign ministry to set up an ad hoc commission on Africa, Asia, and Oceania and report back to him on the major problems of these regions.[15] The commission's hastily drafted report was to form the basis of Castro's foreign policy pronouncements before the U.N. The report inaugurated an era of ever-growing Castroite concern for the black continent's affairs. On September 14, *Revolución*'s headline read: "Topics to be treated at the U.N.: ALGERIA, CHINA, CONGO and CUBA. Fidel Will Speak to the General Assembly."[16]

Fidel Castro landed in wintry New York City with a huge delegation, igniting controversy from the airport to his luxurious hotel. He had come with a carefully thought-out plan of how to wrestle the Afro-Asian bloc to his side by presenting Cuba's case as a typical colonial and neocolonial situation.[17] He intended to define Cuba as a strictly non-aligned nation whose position before the U.S. was no different from those of Egypt and Ghana vis-à-vis Great Britain, Algeria and Guinea vis-à-vis France, or the Congo in respect to Belgium. Personal contact with the Afro-Asian leaders would overcome their hesitation and secure their active backing beyond the traditional assurances of moral support.

Havana was readying itself for a military confrontation with the U.S. Castro now wanted to know exactly what action the non-aligned leaders intended to take when the rapidly approaching hour arrived. To force their hands, the Cuban premier intended to invite them to Cuba en masse for a tricontinental Third World summit. The proposal, of which only Castro's most intimate aides were apprised, had stemmed from the "Carbonell Plan."

The Harlem Show

It seems that the U.S. was misled into believing Cuban President Osvaldo Dorticós Torrado would be heading Cuba's delegation to the U.N. until a few days before Castro himself arrived.[18] Washington was apparently caught without a plan for countering the shock waves the Cuban leader would set off. As would be the case over and over again in Cuban-American relations with Castro, initiative gave him a clear advantage, which the Cuban leader came prepared to fully exploit. Washington's arrogant ineptitude provided him ample room to do so.

Castro's first opportunity was handed to him immediately after his arrival: Washington had restricted the movements of the Cuban delegation to Manhattan. A hostile management of the plush Shelbourne Hotel, where Cuban diplomats usually stayed, demanded advance payment for the Cuban delegation's sojourn. The American press published lurid stories that portrayed the Cuban premier and his men as orgiastic primitives, plucking chickens in their luxurious suites, throwing lit cigars on expensive carpets, and cooking their own food on camp stoves in the bathrooms of their suites. Everything indicated a concerted effort to humiliate, harass, and discredit Castro and his delegation.

On the morning of September 19, Castro personally lodged a protest with U.N. Secretary General Dag Hammarskjold, who offered the Cuban delegation the use of the U.N.'s accommodation facilities. The Cuban premier refused. Castro had a more dramatic move in mind, which he disclosed to his immediate aides, among them Carlos Franqui: he and the entire Cuban delegation would pitch tents in New York's Central Park.[19] This was intended to embarrass Washington beyond measure, as well as vividly dramatize Cuba's global position as a victim of North American discriminatory treatment and aggression. When Castro apprised Robert Taber and Richard Gibson of his intentions, however, the FPCC leaders had a still more outrageous idea: to lodge Castro and his retinue in America's largest black ghetto . . . Harlem![20] Castro seized upon the plan enthusiastically. "¡Vamos a darle un grán golpe a los Americanos!" (We will deal the Americans a strong blow!) he is reported to have told his entourage.[21]

As soon as the U.S. State Department heard of Castro's intentions, the secretary of state hurriedly stepped in to prevent him from exploiting the U.S. racial situation. The elegant Commodore Hotel suddenly offered free lodging to the entire Cuban delegation. It was too late.[22] "Fidel and his men packed their bags and moved to Harlem, at the same time issuing incendiary declarations against racial discrimination in the United States."[23]

Knowledge of Castro's presence in Harlem, once the cultural capital of black America, spread like wildfire among its residents. In a matter of hours, hundreds of Blacks surrounded the Hotel Theresa in swelling throngs, effectively blocking traffic in the area. Castro's success in defying and mortifying the American colossus, wrote an observer, "made him a hero . . . to much larger numbers of Negroes ready to cheer any challenger of white American power. Great crowds turned out to greet the white Cuban Castro when, in pursuit of his own shrewd exploitation of the racial tensions in the United States, he came to Harlem."[24] America's neglected "little Africa," delighted at suddenly being thrust into the world's spotlight, was bursting with excitement.

As soon as Castro and his retinue had moved to Harlem, Havana's propaganda machinery went into full gear. "Cuban propaganda emphasized the racial integration of the revolutionary island, and the contrast with previous regimes, under which Negroes had been effectively excluded from the smarter tourist regions—except, of course, for entertainers or servants—so as not to upset white visitors from the United States. Negro newspapers in the United States noted and approved, while throughout the Americas, leaders of the dark-skinned poor relayed the message."[25]

Mass rallies were convened throughout Cuba by the labor unions, the Cuban Communist party, and the Movimiento 26 de Julio to denounce the Ku Klux Klan and American racism. Cuban radio, television, and newspapers produced stories of the New York police beating Blacks near the Hotel Theresa for shouting, "We want Castro!" A rally of one million Cubans was called together in Havana to protest "the discrimination against Fidel," which was likened to that practiced against U.S. Blacks and black Cubans prior to the Revolution.[26] Maj. Raúl Castro, who was deputizing for Fidel as premier, told his cheering audience: "A victorious enemy gave orders to close the doors of the hotels but must now watch impotently as the heroic population of Harlem opens its doors to our prime minister. . . . The truth, the justice and the logic of the Cuban revolution have pierced the walls of lies . . . winning over the hearts of twenty million oppressed Blacks in the United States."[27]

To the delight of the predominantly black crowd, Raúl Castro skillfully brought to mind the opening of hotels, one of the first achievements of Castro's desegregation drive. Encouraged by the shouts of the crowd ("Fidel, free American Negroes too!" 'Fidel, turn Harlem into another Sierra Maestra!" 'Fidel, *si*, Ku Klux Klan, *no*!"), Raúl Castro went on to compare the racial question in Cuba with that in the U.S., and to link both to the struggle being waged in the Congo:

> To our black brothers of the North, and to those who, led by the patriot Patrice Lumumba, are at this very moment struggling in the Congo, we extend our grateful greetings to the one and fraternal solidarity to the other. The Cuban nation knows that among its people there flows a fraternity based on blood kinship and identity with those who are their brothers and who are fighting European colonialism and imperialism in revolutionary Africa. The people of Cuba today unite in grateful solidarity with the entire American people whose friendship they want to develop, but especially with our tw nty million black American brethren who are the most exploited and humiliated of all. To them go out our friendship and solidarity (ibid.).

Raúl Castro's words signaled an entirely new direction in Castroite foreign policy. The "linkage" proposed in the "Carbonell Plan" had now become a fact: Cuba's domestic Africa, the U.S.'s "little Africa," and continental Africa were now interconnected ethno-political factors in Havana's thinking. In that light, Castro's Harlem performance was not merely a propaganda stunt, but a major tactical victory on three fronts. Cuban Blacks had been made to feel that their Máximo Lider was being subjected by the Yankees to the same segregationist treatment they themselves had experienced for centuries. U.S. Blacks began to consider the bearded Hispanic from Havana as their personal liberator. And the leaders of the newly independent African states massed in New York for the Assembly meeting looked upon Castro with new eyes. The short- and long-term political gains for the Cuban revolution from Castro's Harlem performance were therefore incalculable.

Castro's political cunning, his penchant for effective theatrics, and his capable handling of the racial weapon were abundantly illustrated throughout his stay in the U.S. At first he refused to appear before immense crowds chanting "FI-DEL, FI-DEL, FI-DEL!" below his hotel window. Castro prolonged the suspense for an entire day.[28] In the meantime, he had put through a call to his brother in Havana requesting that Maj. Juán Almeida Bosque—black chief of the army and Castro's most loyal follower since the days of Moncada—be sent immediately to New York.[29] Almeida, in the easternmost part of Cuba at the time, was hurriedly taken to Havana and sent off to New York to join the until-then all-white Cuban delegation (ibid.).

No sooner had Almeida arrived in Harlem on September 21 than Castro, bowing at last to the "will of the masses," appeared at his balcony window smiling and waving, his right arm over the shoulders of his trusted black aide. The sight brought a veritable explosion of joy from the huge crowd of Blacks.[30] To maximize the effect of Almeida's presence, Castro urged him to take a walk in the streets of Harlem and mix with the crowd in the company of Agrarian Reform Institute chief Capt. Antonio Nuñez Jiménez.[31] Delighted, the crowd cheered Almeida and waved signs that read: "U.S. Jim Crows Fidel Just Like U.S. Jim Crows Us Negroes!" Next day, the Cuban press headlined: "Thousands of Americans Cheered Almeida While He Walked Around Harlem," "Brother!' Was the Shout of the People to Almeida."[32] In an evocative front-page photo, *Revolución* depicted Cuba's white foreign minister, Raúl Roa García, lunching at what it described as a Blacks-only Harlem cafeteria (ibid.).

On September 20, the day after his move into Harlem, Castro received a visit from the man who had pledged to keep him in power with nuclear missiles. Stepping out of his black limousine into Castro's open arms, Nikita Khrushchev, all smiles, warmly hugged the Cuban leader on the sidewalk in front of the Theresa Hotel. Cheers and prolonged applause came from the huge crowd of black Americans gathered around the hotel. That an encounter sealing the Soviet-Cuban marriage had taken place in America's "little Africa" was symbolic of things to come. Khrushchev was certainly just as aware as Castro of the impression their rendezvous in the heart of Afro-America would have on the leaders of the Afro-Asian bloc.[33]

Revealingly, Castro's first encounter with official Africa took place on September 22 in the impersonal U.N. building rather than in Harlem—America's grassroots Africa—as Castro would have evidently preferred. Only Nasser and Indian Premier Jawaharlal Nehru followed Khrushchev's example and journeyed up to Harlem to meet the Cuban leader.[34] (The U.N. building was also the site for Castro's meetings with Marshal Tito, Ahmed Sukarno, and the other leaders of the non-aligned movement.)

News of these meetings was unwelcome in Washington, where plans for the Bay of Pigs invasion were already in progress.[35] Perhaps in an attempt to recoup some of the terrain lost to Castro, President Eisenhower threw a lavish luncheon at the Waldorf Astoria for Third World representatives. Shunning the event, Castro organized his own. "I will have lunch with the humble people," Castro told the press, and he invited the entire black staff of the Theresa Hotel to eat with him.

The previous day, he had met with a group of prominent American radicals, including Robert Williams, and been visited by Black Muslim leader Malcolm X. Suspecting that Castro sought to use the plight of U.S. Blacks to score a "psychological coup over the U.S. State Department," Malcolm X remained noncommittal during their meeting.[36] Questioned by journalists on his impressions of the reception given him by black America, Castro replied: "Before coming to the United States we already enjoyed great sympathy among American Negroes because we have always fought against racial discrimination and for equality. We enjoyed that sympathy before coming, but now it has increased even more. American Negroes have grasped one great human truth: that everyone is happy in Cuba."[37]

On September 25, the eve of Castro's marathon five-hour speech to the General Assembly, the FPCC organized a reception for him at the Theresa Hotel, to which only the cream of the left-wing black intellectual community was invited. As one author described this event, "Fidel Castro arrived rather late, and was immediately surrounded by a group of Negroes, each as imposing in stature as Fidel himself. They flung themselves into his open arms. Everyone else then wanted to follow their example, and there were a few moments of pandemonium."[38] Foremost among the black celebrities at the reception was Robert Williams. Already on good terms with Castro, Williams's name would thereafter become inextricably linked with Havana's drive to exploit the American racial situation to its advantage.

Flanked by Major Almeida and an imposing retinue of bodyguards, Castro called Theresa Hotel manager Love B. Woods to his side and presented him with a bust of José Martí inscribed, "He who incites and propagates racial hatred and opposition is sinning against mankind." Amid thunderous applause, the black FPCC executive, Richard Gibson, then offered Castro a bust of Abraham Lincoln with the words "From one liberator to another liberator."[39]

Castro Upstages African Leaders

The Fifteenth General Assembly was taking place at a time when American Blacks were increasingly Africa-conscious, demanding their basic human rights and reclaiming their African cultural heritage. By moving into Harlem, Castro had usurped the Africans' eminence in the eyes of U.S. Blacks. Safely ensconced in their luxurious Manhattan hotel suites, most of Africa's new leaders seemed intent on impressing the western world with their sophisticated, political behavior. Africa's leaders had confined their Afro-American contacts to the elite, while Castro had plunged into the heart of America's largest and most effervescent black "ghetto." Cuba's Caudillo was not hampered by a sense of inferiority to western society, of which he was a highly born member, nor was he bound to be politic vis-à-vis the U.S. His main objective in coming to New York had been to undermine the foundations of American foreign and domestic policy, thereby beating the Yankees at their own game of innuendo, half-truth, and propaganda.

By capitalizing on the U.S.'s racial situation Castro had psychologically outflanked Africa's most politically radical leaders on their own terrain. Acute awareness of this fact may have prevented men like Nkrumah and Touré from meeting Castro in Harlem, which had become stolen ground. More than any other African leader, Nkrumah would have been painfully aware that Castro had put him at a severe disadvantage.[40] Ghana's president had done most of his higher studies in black U.S. universities. He had a long history of close friendship with prominent New World Blacks (e.g., George Padmore, W. E. B. Du Bois, Richard Wright, Alpheus Hunton). Nkrumah naturally had intended his first visit to the U.S. as head of state of black Africa's first independent country to be a sort of homecoming (ibid.). But Castro's theatrics had effectively upstaged his anticipated triumph.

Castro's political pyrotechnics and seductive charisma succeeded in impressing the Afro-Asian leaders as well as U.S. Blacks. Initially, Nasser's "suspicion of Castro's theatricality and his own preoccupation with events in the Middle East made [him] shy away from involvement with Castro."[41] However, the Cuban Caudillo's ability to muster the support of black America strongly impressed the de facto chief of the non-aligned movement. Nasser's importance to Castro was underscored by the fact that he was the first non-aligned leader contacted by the Cuban revolution through Ché Guevara. In addition, three months prior to the General Assembly, Raúl Castro himself had

Surrounded by eagle-eyed bodyguards, author then 18 years old, acts as an impromptu interpreter between Castro and Hotel Theresa manager, Love B. Woods.

Author speaking to a towering Castro. Hotel Theresa manager, Woods, is to the left of author.

Author chats with one of Castro's chief military aides.

Author with Cuban Army Chief, Major Juan Almeida. On the far right is ''Fair Play for Cuba Committee'' founder, Robert Taber.

led the Cuban delegation attending the anniversary celebrations of the Nasserite revolution (ibid., 312).

At their meeting in Harlem on September 23, Castro's courtship of Nasser bore fruit. "Nasser met Fidel Castro for the first time in New York. . . . Castro repeated what Guevara had said about the encouragement given them in 1956 by the way Egypt had stood up to the British, French and Israelis over Suez and had come out on top. . . . Nasser went to visit him up there in the New York black ghetto and he wanted to propose that if the Americans made it impossible for Castro to attend the United Nations then the United Nations would have to be moved to some other country" (ibid., 313, 314). The fact that both Nasser and Nehru journeyed uptown to Harlem could be seen as a victory in Castro's campaign for protection by the Afro-Asian bloc, though the proposal to convene a tricontinental non-aligned summit in Havana did not go down well.

Foreign Minister Raúl Roa had even traveled to Belgrade earlier in 1960 to convince Marshal Tito to convene a "Conference of Hungry Nations" in Havana. Had it materialized, such a summit would have transformed Havana into the Latin American pole of non-alignment—a tremendous psychological and diplomatic blow to Washington. Afro-Asian leaders, however, were unwilling to accept such a proposal. In New York, the Caudillo insisted on the idea, was turned down, and grudgingly left matters at that. (Six years later, he convened a Tricontinental congress in Havana but that, too was stillborn.)

The "Castro Doctrine" on Africa

In a private interview with leftist French journalist K. S. Karol, Castro revealed his strategy for the following day. His speech to the U.N., he told Karol, would link Cuba's predicament to those of the Congo and Algeria. "With a somber expression and in a confidential tone of voice," Karol later wrote, "he informed us that his speech to the United Nations the next day would be very hard to put across. 'Cuba's case is almost identical with that of the Congo and Algeria,' he said."[42]

When Fidel Castro addressed the U.N. General Assembly on the afternoon of September 26, he was assured of an overwhelmingly positive reception. As one analyst pointed out, "Between the Bandung Conference and its successor, the Belgrade Conference of 1961, in which Cuba participated and obtained significant support, twenty-one new independent states were carved out of British and French colonial possessions in Africa. . . . In all circumstances . . . sovereignty was a word to take seriously. Thus when Fidel Castro's Cuba appeared on the scene in the United Nations, there were scores of Afro-Asian countries prepared to give it a sympathetic hearing."[43]

Castro began disarmingly by detailing the harassment that had forced his delegation to seek refuge in "a modest hotel, a Negro hotel in Harlem."[44] The Cuban premier said he was aware that "to some gentlemen, a modest hotel in Harlem, where the Negroes of the United States live, could not be anything but a brothel" (ibid.). After a long historical review of Cuban-U.S. relations, Castro concluded that his country's position was not exceptional. "Cuba's is not an isolated case. It would be a mistake to think so. Cuba's case is that of all the underdeveloped countries; it resembles that of the Congo, of Egypt, Algeria. . . . In short, although we have not referred specifically to the rest, the case of Cuba is that of all the underdeveloped and colonial countries" (ibid., 130).

Establishing a parallel between Col. Joseph Mobutu, who had just deposed the legitimate Lumumba government, and dictator Batista, Castro condemned foreign intervention in the Congo and pledged Havana's backing for the Lumumbists. Cuba would also support the Algerian and South African revolutionary struggles. "We are, therefore, on the side of the Algerian people, as we are on the side of the remaining colonial peoples in Africa and on the side of the Negroes against whom discrimination is exercised in the Union of South Africa" (ibid., 132).

Alternately speaking as the authoritative, self-confident leader of a major power, then as a plaintive representative of a poor, beleaguered Third World nation victimized by the bullying tactics of a superpower, Castro repeatedly drove his point home: Cuba was an American colony. "The difficulties which the people of Cuba have had with the imperialist Government of the United States are the same difficulties as Saudi Arabia, or Iran or Iraq, would encounter if they nationalized their oil. The same difficulties were encountered by Egypt when it, quite rightly, nationalized the Suez Canal. . . . Instances of the nature of these difficulties are provided by the surprise attack upon Egypt, and the surprise invasion of the Congo" (ibid., 131).

The revolutionary process unfolding in Cuba, according to Castro, was an integral part of the general movement towards decolonization in Africa. Cuba was a non-aligned state, struggling to recover its national sovereignty. Cuba was opposed to military and ideological blocs. Cuba was opposed to colonialism, imperialism, and apartheid.

The attention of African leaders focused less on the historical background of Cuban-U.S. relations and their present conflict than on Castro's pointed insistence on establishing a parallel between Africa and Cuba. In fact, the Cuban premier had devoted about one hour of his U.N. address to stress that point. Self-confidently, Castro singled out for flattery those African leaders who met with his approval. He praised their continent as "that Africa which we are beginning to know today, not the Africa pictured on the map or in novels and Hollywood films, not the Africa of semi-naked tribesmen armed with spears, ready to run away at the first clash with the white hero, that white hero who became more heroic the more African natives he killed" (ibid., 133).

The neo-abolitionist imagery that had endeared Castro to Black Cuba surfaced once again as he spoke to his U.N. audience of the New Africa. Adopting a fatherly tone,[45] while African leaders listened intently, Castro now proclaimed,

> [T]he Africa we see represented here by leaders like Kwame Nkrumah and Sékou Touré, the Africa of Nasser's Arab world [is] the true Africa, the oppressed continent, the exploited continent, the continent which was the birthplace of millions of slaves, this Africa whose past is so full of anguish. To this Africa we have a duty: *we must save it* from the danger of destruction (Italics added.).[46]

Cuba supported the proposal made by Ghana "that Africa should be cleared of military bases and thus of nuclear weapon bases; in other words the proposal to free Africa from the perils of atomic war" (ibid.). Castro asked: "Why should we not also go forward toward freeing certain parts of the world from the danger of nuclear war?" (ibid.) That much the world owed Africa, he said.

> Let the other countries make some recompense! Let the West make up a little for what it has made Africa suffer, by preserving it from the danger of atomic war and declaring it a free zone as far as this peril is concerned. Let no atomic bases be established there! Even if we can do nothing else, let this continent at least remain a sanctuary where human life may be preserved! (ibid.)

Castro's insistence that Africa be "saved" from destruction betrayed the sense of mission that would thereafter characterize Havana's growing involvement in African affairs. And one cannot avoid drawing parallels between his protective concern for the black continent and his paternalistic approach to Cuba's domestic Africa.

He seemed imbued with the same "sense of duty of a member of the elite who believed that he knew that he must determine the aims and lead the masses to a happier future."[47] Despite his lavish praise of those African leaders who met with his approval (Lumumba, Nkrumah, Touré), it is questionable whether Castro considered them to be his equals.

The Cuban leader's first major policy statement of the "Castro Doctrine" on Africa can be summarized in three main points. Cuba and Africa are linked by historical bonds (the slave trade) and by common contemporary realities (underdevelopment and decolonization). Cuba supports those forces on the black continent whose anti-imperialism qualifies them as the most representative voices of the "New Africa." Finally, Cuba has a *duty* to perform towards Africa: *to protect* her from the manifold dangers of imperialism.

Castro's was an impressive showing at the U.N. He proved his ability to galvanize black America, to put Washington on the defensive, and to influence the very Third World leaders Moscow was so assiduously courting. These factors bore great tactical importance to Soviet policy makers. Castro's triumph in America's "little Africa," his newly formed connections with continental Africa, signaled the sort of latitude Cuba could enjoy on the black continent.

The penetration of Africa and the Arab Middle East were the Kremlin's top strategic priorities in the Third World. Castro's clear ascendancy over the chief Afro-Asian leaders—particularly those of Africa—must have given Moscow much pause. On the other hand, for all his talk of "colorblindness," the white leader of revolutionary Cuba already had his eyes riveted on a goal to which he would assign a growing priority and increased resources: the extension of Cuba's political influence to black Africa. To this end, Fidel Castro would thereafter strain his rhetorical ingenuity to the breaking point to define and project an Afrophilic foreign policy profile.

7 THE NEW AFRICAN POLICY AT HOME

It would take some years for the full political impact and African repercussions of his Harlem performance to be assessed, but Fidel Castro's first major victory in his courtship of black Africa was certainly his visit to Harlem. The Cuban leader returned from his U.N. expedition in triumph and immediately addressed a mass rally, threatening to seize the American-owned Nicaro nickel mines, excoriating American racism, the Ku Klux Klan, and the colonial domination of Africa.[1] Castro's message was clear: his regime was fighting the same enemy which oppressed black Africa and kept American Blacks at bay. "There are in the very entrails of the U.S. empire," he said, "twenty million oppressed and exploited Negroes whose aspirations cannot be met with a fistful of dollars. It is a much more serious problem because such aspirations can only be satisfied with justice!" (ibid.). He then announced that two of Africa's most prestigious leaders—Gamal Abdel Nasser and Kwame Nkrumah—would be visiting Cuba within the next few months.[2] (However, neither was ever to show up in Cuba.)

Indeed, Castro had pulled off a great coup with long-lasting effects and implications. He had diplomatically defeated the world's foremost superpower, politically dwarfed the most radical Afro-Asian leaders, and, psychologically, begun to cast a protective shadow on a most strategic zone in the Third World. Havana's self-proclaimed duty to "save Africa" from imperialism appears to be a subtle transfer onto the black continent of the ethno-political strategy Castro had successfully applied to Cuba's domestic Africa. Yet at the historic U.N. meeting in September 1960, Kwame Nkrumah had outlined a sort of "Hands-off Doctrine" for Africa. Guinean President Sékou Touré had warned that "Africa has ceased becoming a prey to become herself."[3] (As Touré spoke before the U.N., the world press was headlining uprisings by and massacres of Blacks in Rhodesia, the fierce struggle in the Congo, and the widening offensive of the FLN forces in Algeria.[4])

The day following the Guinean leader's U.N. address, the Democratic party candidate for the U.S. presidency, John F. Kennedy—a personal friend of Touré and the man Castro had called "an illiterate millionaire" during his U.N. speech—echoed Touré's stand. Employing the "neglect-of-Africa" theme in his campaign against Republican rival Richard Nixon, Kennedy had declared, "We must ally ourselves with the surging tide of nationalism in Africa."[5] Both Castro and Kennedy had decided on strategies which depended on alliance with Africa. The coincidence of the strategies of the aspiring American president and the embattled Caudillo even extended to their choice of Sékou Touré as the African leader who was most suitable for such purposes. Assiduously courted by both Washington and Havana, Touré's ambivalent loyalties would thereafter color his relationship with both governments. They would eventually become a major obstacle to Castro's first attempt to create an African bridgehead.

"Africa, Finally!"

Castro's African strategy seemed to have begun to yield results in early October of 1960 when an Egyptian delegation, headed by Egypt's Minister of Economy Abdel Mounem Kaysouni arrived in Havana.[6] Then, on October 8, the Cuban leadership announced the imminent arrival of Sékou Touré. (Revolución devoted a full page to reproducing the most significant portions of the Guinean leader's speech to the U.N.[7]) The prospect of Touré's visit to Cuba naturally caused concern in Washington. Perhaps seeking to placate the U.S. by deemphasizing a visit that for Castro was yet another grand psychological and political coup, Touré told a press conference that Cuba was merely one stop in a tour that would take him to the U.S. South, Canada, and Haiti. He pointedly remarked that the tour had been planned long in advance.[8]

With Havana threatening daily to take drastic steps against all remaining American economic interests in Cuba, both Washington and Touré may have reasonably feared that Castro would seize the occasion of his visit to dramatically announce a Cuban-style Suez coup. And, indeed, on October 14, immediately after the Guinean leader had arrived in Cuba, the Council of Ministers adopted a law nationalizing all banks, sugar refineries, railroads, building firms, and other American-owned interests in Cuba.[9] Phillip Bonsal, the U.S. ambassador to Cuba, was promptly recalled for "prolonged consultations."[10]

Castro had succeeded in making his first African ally an unwilling eyewitness to his escalating conflict with the most powerful super-power. It is not unlikely that both Nasser and Nkrumah, whom Castro had invited to Cuba at the same time as Touré, demurred out of fear of being manipulated into just such a highly embarrassing situation. But exactly two years later—at the height of the October missile crisis—Touré would categorically refuse to take the next step, from witness to accomplice.

Touré's two-day stay in Cuba was emotionally charged for the majority of Cuba's population of West African origin. Coming from the farthest corners, black Cubans had poured into Havana hoping for a glimpse of the African leader. The throngs that lined Touré's route from the airport to the capital could be heard shouting "Africa! Africa! Africa!"[11] *Revolución* reported that a black woman broke down, crying, "Africa, finally! . . ."[12] For the occasion, the newspaper recalled the slave trade that had transplanted hundreds of thousands of West Africans to Cuba, emphasizing that a good many of them had come from Guinea (ibid.). Touré thus appeared to be the living embodiment of a new phase in the historical process that had linked Cuba to Africa since the sixteenth century.

For black Cubans, Touré's visit was cause for ethnic pride, for it was the first time they had seen a black head of state. "When I saw Touré," explained one Cuban Black, "I had to fight back tears. For the first time in my life I felt proud to be Black. . . . I was brought up to think of Africans as naked savages living in trees. But here was an African who was a president! Now I am dying to go over there and see what it's really like."[13]

Black Cuba's pride in Touré's visit provided all the more reason for solidifying its bonds of gratitude with the regime and the man who had made such a thing possible, as Castro had most likely banked on. The Caudillo's intention to fully capitalize on Touré's visit, both for domestic and external purposes, was evident from the start. On hand at the airport to welcome the Guinean president and flanking the Castro brothers and Ché Guevara were Cuba's black army chief, Maj. Juán Almeida Bosque, and the black deputy foreign minister, Dr. Carlos Olivares, who was suddenly removed from his high-ranking post some months after Touré's visit and sent to Moscow as ambassador. (A lawyer, well-versed in international affairs, and a veteran member of the Cuban Communist party, Olivares had been instrumental in Castro's earlier "racial reform" drive. He fought the idea of proportional ethnic representation in the revolutionary cabinet as a "reactionary" black demand. He eventually fell from favor with Castro, and was summarily recalled from Moscow and consigned to obscurity in the early sixties.)

Saluting Touré's arrival, Odón Alvarez de la Campa, secretary general for foreign affairs of the powerful Confederation of Cuban Workers, said, "Today we host the liberator of a territory from whence a long time ago another abominable imperialism took slaves and brought them to our land. Thanks to the January revolution and the abolition of an archaic and unjust system of racial discrimination, these [former slaves] have now become our brothers!"[14] *Revolución* devoted full pages to the history of Guinea and to a biography of Touré that compared him favorably to Cuba's own Liberador (ibid., 16). "With Sékou Touré and Fidel Castro," proclaimed one article, "Africa and Latin America, which share a great many common traditions, have met again" (ibid.). *Lunes de Revolución*, the weekly voice of the Castroite intelligentsia, transformed an entire fifteen-page issue into a supplement entitled "Africa Today."[15]

Touré ended his visit with much fanfare. Cuba and Guinea had signed cooperation agreements that included scholarships granted by Havana for training Guinean students in Cuba. It is not insignificant that in the first accord between the Castroite regime and an African country, Cuba appeared as the donor and Guinea as the recipient. The terms of that relationship were never to be reversed. The political and intellectual initiative of Cuban/African relations that Castro had taken at the fifteenth General Assembly was being consolidated in concrete terms.

Havana's desire to quickly consolidate its first African connection was evident in the deliberate speed with which a Cuban ambassador was sent to Conakry less than two months after Touré's visit. The man chosen for the post, Dr. Salvador García Aguero, was a veteran Communist party theoretician on the racial question, and, appropriately, black. Conakry's own envoy, Ambassador Soumah Naby Issa, arrived in Havana one year later. This may well have been another indication of Touré's cautiousness in not wanting to be implicated any further in an already complex situation.

"Blood Links" vs. Realpolitik

The Castroite leadership may have underestimated the full emotional and ethnic impact of Touré's visit on Black Cuba. As Carbonell had insisted, Africa lay powerfully dormant in the psyche of most Cubans despite centuries of adverse propaganda and degrading stereotypes. Touré's arrival in Cuba had unquestionably awakened a sleeping giant that Castro had intended to keep indefinitely at rest with his integrationist racial reform drive of the previous year. Latent in Black Cuba's response to the Guinean president was evidence of a strong, clandestine ethno-cultural nationalism. Men like Carlos Franqui, who had criticized Castro's cavalier approach to Black Cuba, saw the full implications of the event. "Sékou Touré's visit to Cuba in 1960 was that year's most important event for Cuba, viewed from the angle of the ethnic and cultural structure of Cuban society," he said. The Cuban population was basically derived from two original cradles, Africa and Spain. "But while white Cubans had found a powerful and emotional theme of identification with Spain, the other Cuba, which originated in Africa—black Cuba—continued to be ignored and despised. The real beginning of a rediscovery of Africa and of the black world as such began in 1960 and was highlighted by Sékou Touré's visit to Cuba. . . . In a concrete sense, Touré's visit brought to the surface the question of what I may call 'clandestine Cuba'—black Cuba!"[16]

Taking full advantage of Sékou Touré's visit, the man who had provided Castro with the first Afrocentric foreign policy strategy went on the offensive. Increasingly pessimistic about the regime's handling of the ethnic question in Cuba, Walterio Carbonell grew apprehensive of the motives behind Castro's courtship of the black continent. An Afrocentric foreign policy, in his opinion, was either inseparable from the revalorization of Cuba's domestic Africa or it was a political fraud.[17] In a provocative essay published by *Revolución* while Touré was still on Cuban soil, Carbonell reminded the Cuban leadership that it was chiefly Africans from the Guinean Gulf who had built Cuba's prosperity during the eighteenth and nineteenth centuries.[18] These very slaves, he insisted, had also freed Cuba from the Spanish yoke. Moreover, their relentless struggle against slavery and colonialism had been the incubator of Cuban national consciousness (ibid.). The underlying message seemed clear: the regime's desegregationist emphasis fell far below the accumulated exigencies of centuries of ethnic, economic, and cultural oppression. Access to the beaches, hotels, restaurants, and work centers was no substitute for the ethnic democratization of Cuba's new cultural and socio-political structures.

Carbonell hailed Touré's visit as a landmark for Black Cuba. He reminded that it was "Spanish colonialism [which] severed the relations of kinship and friendship between Cuban Blacks and the Blacks of Africa."

We must have the courage to say it: in Cuba *only the Blacks have kept alive the old religions* of Africa. They were severely persecuted for it by Spanish colonial domination as well as by the so-called "Cuban" governments that bowed and scraped to American imperialism. Blacks are the only ones to have upheld the living memory of the motherland: Africa! Up till today, Africa continues to be a taboo continent in Cuba. Till now no one has shown an interest in Africa's cultures or its political currents, whether reformist or radical. It was felt that being a black continent, the cultures or political aspirations of Blacks were unworthy of consideration. Only a revolutionary government such as that led by Fidel Castro could have shown interest in Africa and invited to Cuba the most radical of its leaders: Sékou Touré. Many rains have had to fall on Cuba and Guinea for these two peoples, united by blood, cultural traditions, music, customs and psychology, to have reunited (Italics added.) (ibid.).

Despite its laudatory tone for the Castroite regime, Carbonell's article implied clear warnings: the revolutionary government's sudden interest in black Africa should not be utilitarian; the attitude adopted towards Cuba's predominant Africanity would be the test of its sincerity; the revalorization of Black Cuba had to go hand-in-hand with a political concern over continental Africa. In this regard, the Castro government's position on Afro-Cuban religions, the repository of Cuba's most powerful cultural distinctiveness, was fundamental.

Domestic Repercussions

The domestic implications of Carbonell's essay could not have escaped Castro's attention. The Caudillo's reaction to the trend awakened by Touré's visit came less than six months afterward, when Carbonell amplified his criticism of the regime's attitude towards Afro-Cuban culture in a highly controversial book, *Crítica: Cómo surgió la cultura nacional.* Cuba's home-grown cultures, it claimed, were essentially African culture in another dynamic setting; Cuba's national consciousness was forged in the slave insurrections of the eighteenth and nineteenth centuries; the still prevalent official history of Cuba was anti-Black; the whole edifice of white supremacy remained standing despite the Revolution's racial reform. Pointing an accusing finger at "those who are revolutionaries and have contributed to liberating our country from the domination of the bourgeoisie, but are incapable of liberating themselves from the ideological power of the bourgeoisie,"[19] Carbonell found it ominous that the regime still refused to take a stand on Afro-Cuban religions. Afro-Cuban religions, he pointed out, were the marrow of Cuban popular culture. The government's refusal to see them in that light could only open the doors to reactionary and racist cultural policies within the new revolutionary setting. For Afro-Cubans, wrote Carbonell, African religions "prevented Spanish colonialism from destroying their rich ancestral experience."

> Thanks to the vitality of these religions, black music could survive: the rhythms and music that gave birth to Cuban music, the highest expression of our culture. I have said that these religious organizations have played a politically and culturally progressive role in the forging of our nationality. This statement may surprise many, because up till now the contrary thesis has prevailed, that is, that black religions are a manifestation of savagery. That was precisely the view upheld by the ideologues of Spanish colonialism and their progenitor, the reactionary bourgeoisie. . . . As a matter of fact, the silence of certain revolutionary writers concerning the political and cultural role of these cults of African origin is becoming highly suspect (ibid., 108).

Less than three months after publication, Carbonell's book was withdrawn from circulation, then banned on Castro's orders. Carbonell was subsequently removed from the Cuban foreign ministry, attacked as a "provocateur" by high-ranking officials, and consigned to obscurity. The man who had awakened Castro's interest in Africa would be made to pay dearly for that very Pan-Africanism. The Castro regime, simply, was developing divergent policies towards Afro-Cuba and continental Africa.[20]

The official birth of Cuba's African policy, dramatized by Sékou Touré's visit in October 1960, coincided with the resumption of a silent, protracted, and relentless war against Afro-Cuban religions and also against any autonomous ethno-cultural manifestations by Cuban Blacks.[21] Three weeks after Touré's visit, a six-month long seminar on ethnology, "folklore," and culture was convened by the Cuban government's cultural and educational affiliates. The seminar led to the organization of an Instituto Nacional de Etnología y Folklore in December 1961.[22] Headed by two Hispanic Cubans, Dr. Argeliers Léon and Isaac Barreal, the Institute's role was to research the full impact of Afro-Cuban music, dance, mannerisms, national psychology, and traditions.

From the outset, the study of Afro-Cuban religions and brotherhoods (Mayombé, Lucumí, Arará, Abacuá) was one of the Institute's priorities. To judge by the pressing tone with which the beginning of such studies was announced, ulterior motives underlay this sudden interest: "Religious sects of African origin will be continuously researched. Studies will be centered on those sects which have come into conflict with the Revolution.''[23] Actually, what was being announced was a frontal assault on Afro-Cuban religions reminiscent of the destruction in the previous year of the Sociedades de Color (Colored Societies.) The first step in that direction was a concerted effort to represent Cuba's African heritage as being "exotic" and "folkloric."

Derogatorily termed "sects" in pre-revolutionary days, Afro-Cuban religious fraternities had been systematically portrayed as "atavistic," 'primitive," and even "criminal." They were accused of being a major hindrance to Cuba's "modernization." Castro himself had come to power with these opinions.[24] He even considered abolishing Afro-Cuban carnivals, replacing them with Spanish *corridas*, or bull-fights (ibid.). Out of his personal distaste for drums, Castro restricted drumming in public places.[25] The growing restrictions imposed on Afro-Cuban religions and festivities as of 1961 were perhaps as much the result of Castro's negative view of black Cuban culture as they were of the apprehensions aroused by Sékou Touré's visit.[26]

The regime's struggle to stamp out Afro-Cuban religious fraternities became a permanent feature of Castroite policy towards Cuba's domestic Africa. Religious leaders began suffering arrest and at times imprisonment in the mid-sixties, and at least one case of execution by firing squad was reported by the end of the decade.[27] Sacred rituals were converted into "folkloric" ballets, and rigid discrimination was exercised against cult members in employment. In 1976, a Lucumí leader was to tell an African journalist, "After the Revolution—in 1972 to be exact—the leadership of the Communist party informed us that thereafter we would have to secure authorization from the CDR before celebrating any of our ceremonies. The CDR is an adjunct of the State Police and we have been refused permission over and again."[28] The Yoruba religion is, however, one of the most important African belief systems in Cuba. About 75 percent of the Afro-Cuban population belongs to it, as well as an ever-growing number of whites. "Catholics do not need permission from the CDR to celebrate their mass," explained the religious leader. "My own son was refused membership in the Communist party because to become a member one has to 'lead a clean life,' be a 'good worker' and have a good 'Marxist-Leninist conscience.' I have come to suspect that my own activities [as a religious leader] caused him to be refused membership" (ibid. 44–45).

The journalist also interviewed a black Cuban couple, the wife a gynecologist, the husband an engineer, who described their predicament as "cult" members: "As far as we Blacks are concerned, there have indeed been changes. My father was a cult leader. When he died I took his place. The cults are what keep us permanently in touch with the Africa of our ancestors. That's all we now have left. At any rate, that's all we had left of our African origins. The change is that even that is being taken away from us. . . . The question we now ask ourselves is: did Cuban Blacks originate in a Spanish province?" (ibid., 44–45)

Summing up his interviews, the journalist remarked that "Adepts of the various Afro-Cuban religions have been arrested for having organized ceremonies outside of the days specifically stipulated by the government. The ceremonies of certain Afro-Cuban cults have been declared incompatible with a Socialist society. Of note is the use of the term sect by the Institute of Folklore to designate African religions in Cuba. The term is in itself significant. Moreover, the dances, music, and sacred ceremonials of the cults, all of which have profound religious meaning, have been mounted as 'folkloric spectacles' for the amusement and distraction of visiting foreign delegations to Cuba, as well as for Cuban audiences. . . . What I was witnessing was an attempt to destroy the values of an entire culture" (ibid., 45).

Anthropologist William Bascom, who studied Afro-Cuban religions for many years, underlined their power just prior to Fidel Castro's seizure of power in 1959. "The worship of African deities, as it is practiced in Cuba today, is known as *santería*," he explained. "Santería is a vital, growing institution, practiced throughout the entire length of the island, in both rural and urban areas; in the latter, in fact, it is probably the strongest. In recent years it seems to have been expanding, recruiting additional members from the Negro, the mixed, and even the white population,"[29] Bascom noted.

> The African elements of santería are predominantly Yoruba, or Lucumí, as the Yoruba of Nigeria are called in Cuba. . . . The Yoruba influence is also recognizable throughout Cuba, despite regional variations, in the names of the Yoruba deities, in similarities to Yoruba ritual, in the Yoruba cities named by Cuban Negroes as homes of their ancestors, and in individuals who can still speak the Yoruba language. On a quick trip in the summer of 1948, more than eighty years after slavery, it was possible to find Cuban Negroes in towns from one end of the island to the other, and in Havana itself, with whom I could talk in Yoruba. (ibid.)

By the end of the 1960s, and in a way reminiscent of the days of Spanish domination, Afro-Cuban religions were "characterized by government officials as prone toward criminal activity."[30] The final declaration of the first National Congress on Education and Culture in 1971 stated: "The Congress considers that juvenile delinquency in its distinctive manifestations forms part of the social pathology which must be observed, controlled and repressed on a national scale . . . , and following a preliminary study of the causes and factors which produce it, the following points were examined: The importance of mental backwardness and school retardation in the development of this phenomenon. . . . The incidence of problems arising from some religious sects, especially some of African origin (ñáñigo and abacuá)."[31] This statement, notes Jorge I. Domínguez, is reminiscent of those made by Cuban anthropoligist Fernando Ortiz in his *Hampa afrocubana* (1910), where he stressed the "criminality" of Afro-Cuban religions.[32]

After conducting a series of interviews with religious leaders in Cuba during the summer of 1976, Michel Legré, an African journalist from Ivory Coast, wrote that Afro-Cuban religious meetings had to be conducted clandestinely, with official approval secured in advance. "My informants, all black Cubans who supported the Revolution, told me that African religious cults were definitely being repressed," he wrote. "However, when I inquired of the officials—all white— they claimed that all religions were respected by the Revolution. Nevertheless, I kept running into a large number of black Cubans who claimed that the government was repressing black African religions. At any rate, what is for sure is that those who practice the African cults in Cuba—an impressive amount of Blacks, as I found out—did live in fear of professing their faith and were reticent to discuss the issue with a foreigner."[33] (As an analyst has pointed out, "Even the term 'Afro-Cuban' [i.e. Cuban blacks as separate and distinct] was officially discouraged."[34])

The repressive policies inaugurated by the government against Afro-Cuban religions may have been indicative of the regime's failure to understand that black Cubans were indeed the embodiment of a distinct culture. "Whatever their origins," one analyst observed, "the various elements of the black population evolved a cohesive Afro-Cuban tradition that permeated not only the artistic and intellectual spheres of Cuban life but also the social and religious aspects, even after the Revolution. . . . In addition, the survival of African spiritualism and the existence of hundreds of societies devoted to a syncretic worship of African saints has greatly influenced the religious life of the island. . . . [S]ome observers agreed that there might be a trend not only toward the integration but toward the assimilation of Cuban Blacks into a white-dominated society. Black intellectuals in Cuba have resisted this absorption, claiming that their culture has the right to be fully expressed—not just as an obscure, quaint, folkloric expression lacking sophistication or meaning for all Cubans."[35]

The regime's assault on the very source of Cuba's Africanity at a time when Havana was forging its first political ties with black Africa indicates that pragmatic exigencies, not sentiment, had led Castro to seek an African alliance. Cuban affairs specialist Jorge Dominguez sustains, not without reason, that the new black revolutionary elite bore a heavy responsibility for such an aberrant situation. "The policy toward Africa," he remarked, "could please enough black leaders to get them to support the Cuban government without insisting too much on changes in internal race relations: this policy toward Africa could co-opt internal support and require the least change in internal policies."[36]

It would seem all the same paradoxical that a white revolutionary regime such as Castro's, determined to play its African cards, would continue maintaining an Afrophobic stance domestically. This is not so, contended Carlos Franqui. "The white Cuban leadership is the product of an entirely different culture and outlook from that of the bulk of the Cuban people," Franqui said.

The leadership really does not understand the way of life of that people. Where is the contradiction? First of all, in the outlook dominated by the notions of happiness and *fiesta* [enjoyment], and the outlook wherein Sparta stands as the prototypical model. The spirit of pachanga [festival]—the term itself sounds African—was an important thing in the Cuban revolution. The opposing spirit was that of the Spartan revolution. Fidel Castro's outlook is dominated by the idea of a Spartan, obedient, laboring, and heroic revolution based on sacrifice. His idea is that of a moralistic revolution. That view is inextricably bound up with the Catholic, Hispanic, and caudillista outlook. . . . The problem is not one of either "good" or "bad," but of mental structures. . . . those young men who acted as the vanguard in that revolution and became its top leaders were both white and middle class.[37]

8 THE BAY OF PIGS

By the end of 1960 Fidel Castro had permanently committed the Revolution to an ideological, military, and economic alliance with the Soviet Union. Anticipating Castro, Ché Guevara had pronounced the Revolution Marxist in August of that year. Addressing the left-wing First Congress of Latin American Youth held in Havana in July and August, he said: "If this revolution is Marxist—and bear in mind I say Marxist—it is because through its own methods it discovered the path pointed out by Marx."[1] Two months later, he would add: "By initiating our struggle, we practical revolutionaries merely fulfill laws foreseen by Marx the scientist."[2]

When Castro met Tito and Nasser in New York in September 1960, they advised him to stay clear of the Cold War and alignment with the Soviet bloc.[3] However, the strategy Castro had already decided upon was the exact opposite. Cuba would force her entry into the Communist camp and align itself against the U.S. By making the Revolution Marxist at breakneck speed, he intended to present Moscow with a fait accompli, thereby hoping to guarantee his regime's survival against the American threat. Havana's continued claims throughout the first months of 1961 that the Revolution was not Communist and that its foreign policy was non-aligned can only be seen as a tactical ploy directed at the Afro-Asian bloc.

Sékou Touré's visit strengthened Castro's determination to adhere closely to the radical Afro-Asian leaders though straining at the same time to weave symbiotic ties with the Soviet bloc. Cuba could perhaps be expected to exploit the sympathy of U.S. President-elect John F. Kennedy for men like Nasser, Nkrumah, and Touré. A few days after Touré's departure, the Caudillo hinted at the soundness of such a strategy when he praised "the important group of neutralist countries that is presently playing such a crucial role in the world and with whom we have established close economic ties and friendly relations. The help of those countries, as well as the prevailing international situation, must be regarded as factors which militate in our favor, counterbalancing the disadvantage we suffer from being surrounded by the forces of imperialism."[4]

Although Castro denied in the same speech that the Revolution was Communist, at that point not only was the Soviet-Cuban bond cemented but also the Cuban Communist party had gained ascendancy within the revolutionary regime. Nonetheless, Cuba's foreign minister, Raúl Roa, in his address to the General Assembly, heatedly insisted that the Revolution was strictly nationalist, democratic, and populist. "The revolutionary government of Cuba is not Communist," he declared, "although it is not afraid of being branded as such. The Cuban revolution knows from whence it came, what it strives for and where it is heading. It did not arise from the works of Rousseau, Jefferson, or Karl Marx, but from the bosom of the Cuban people. . . . Considering its origins, its goals and the prevailing circumstances, it is . . . a nationalist, popular and democratic revolution."[5]

While Roa was busy proclaiming Havana's commitment to a non-Communist course, Castro announced to a mass rally the possibility of an "imminent invasion" by the U.S.[6] The trade embargo imposed by Washington on October 19, the recall of its ambassador on October 22, and intelligence information that a task force of Cuban exiles was being assembled to invade the island lent much credence to his claim. The Cuban government seemed convinced that the last act of the Eisenhower/Nixon administration would be the invasion of Cuba. In an urgent letter to the U.N., Havana warned that "any act of direct or indirect military aggression by the American government against the Cuban government and people could be the spark to set off a conflagration of unsuspected magnitude and consequence for the whole of mankind."[7] This allusion to Soviet nuclear rocket support apparently signified Castro's conviction that the Kremlin would risk a nuclear war to support his regime.[8]

As Havana prepared to repulse an invasion, the break between China and the Soviet Union became final. Nikita Khrushchev had taken advantage of the Conference of Communist and Workers Parties held in Moscow that November to attack China directly and made no bones about the Kremlin's intention to excommunicate the Maoists from the ranks of international communism. From then on, the Sino-Soviet schism would weigh heavily on Soviet-Cuban relations, becoming Castro's strongest lever for forcing Cuba's admission into the Soviet bloc.

The same day Castro forecast an imminent U.S. invasion, Washington announced the conclusion of wide-ranging agreements on economic and technical aid with Guinea.[9] The news must have been received with mixed emotions in Havana; Castro had considered

President Sékou Touré as an ally against Yankee imperialism. On the other hand, it gave the Caudillo hope that his regime could still gain some sympathy and credibility in Washington. By identifying his country's revolution with the new left-wing African regimes, Castro could show up the inconsistency of the U.S.'s Cuban policy. On what grounds could Washington justify its hostility to a regime that advocated a foreign policy akin to those proclaimed by Nasser, Nkrumah, Touré, Tito, and Sukarno? How could Washington take measures against Cuba for enacting economic and political reforms similar to those undertaken in African countries whose newly acquired sovereignty the U.S. seemingly applauded and whose leaders were received with much pomp and ceremony by the American president? Speaking to the General Assembly, Raúl Roa seemed to be driving that point home. "The pretext invoked [by the U.S.]" said Roa, "is that the revolutionary government of Cuba is a pawn of international communism; that it is infiltrated by Communists, or that it is purely and simply a Communist regime, besides being a threat to the peace, security and solidarity of the hemisphere. That same pretext has already been invoked against . . . the United Arab Republic, India, Guinea and Ghana. It is also now being used against the Congo [Leopoldville]. Patrice Lumumba has equally been accused of being a Communist."[10]

In order to more closely associate Cuba's case with those of the newly independent African states, it was essential for Havana to pose as a staunch ally of Africa's liberationist aspirations. "We can reasonably claim," Raúl Roa told the General Assembly, "that this is Africa's year. Indeed, during this period sixteen African countries have achieved their independence. . . . It should also have been the year when independence was proclaimed for all colonial peoples. Most of those who are still under the yoke of colonialism happen to be found in Africa."[11] Havana's interest in Africa's welfare, inferred Roa, was motivated by the fact that Cuba was partly African herself. "Although Cuba is geographically located in the Western hemisphere, and is a Spanish-speaking country," he said, "it is proud of the African blood which has lent color to its folklore, its arts, its culture, its religion and national development" (ibid., 1241).[12]

Castro began his third year in power a calculated step ahead of the U.S. On January 2, 1961, he precipitated a full break with Washington, dramatically ordering the American embassy in Havana to reduce its diplomatic staff from eighty-seven to eleven within forty-eight hours. The following day, Washington broke off diplomatic relations with Havana. Castro's hands were now free. Significantly, no sooner had the break taken place than Czechoslovakia announced it would take charge of all Cuban interests in the U.S. Three days later, Castro mobilized the Cuban armed forces as tons of heavy Soviet military hardware poured into Cuban ports.

The Congo: Havana's War By Proxy

From January through June 1960, Cuba and the Congo concurrently monopolized the attention of the world's media and debates of the U.N. Security Council.[13] Washington's support for the anti-Lumumbist factions and backing of the Belgian interventionists afforded Havana a unique occasion to discredit Yankee imperialism before radical African opinion while validating its own case. The Congo affair paved the way for an even more ambitious rapprochement between Havana and the radical leaders of the New Africa who stood behind Lumumba. In denouncing American plans to overthrow the Castroite regime, Cuban U.N. representatives could effortlessly establish credible parallels between Cuba's situation and the brazen interventionism of the West to unseat the nationalist regime in the Congo. In fact, the Security Council, under the temporary chairmanship of Czechoslovakia, decided on April 10 to treat both questions jointly.[14]

The assassination of Congolese Premier Patrice Lumumba, announced on February 13, 1961, set off an explosion of painful ire throughout the Afro-Asian world. A step ahead of African leaders themselves, the Cuban government immediately dispatched a lengthy message to the Security Council. The assassination of Lumumba, it read, "is the premeditated culmination of an international conspiracy . . . instigated by the Belgian and United States monopolies . . . to continue the economic exploitation of the Congolese people, with the obvious complicity of the colonial powers controlling the Security Council, the tacit cooperation of the Secretary-General of the United Nations and the manifest support of American imperialism, which is the propelling force behind neo-colonialism in Africa and Asia."[15] Cuba's U.N. delegates then unleashed a barrage of attacks against Yankee imperialism, which they held wholly responsible for the Congolese drama.

Of all the Third World countries, Havana seemed to have made the most of Lumumba's murder. Mass rallies were held throughout the island;[16] the media mounted an around-the-clock campaign detailing every aspect of American involvement in the crisis;[17] a three-day period of national mourning, with flags flying at half-mast, was declared. The Castroite leadership undoubtedly shared the worldwide shock and indignation at the internationally televised abuse that preceded the beating, torture, and eventual assassination of the Congolese prime minister. On the other hand, Castro was using the Congo crisis to psychologically prepare the entire Cuban nation for war.

Havana's concern over the tragic events in the Congo primarily reflected Castro's own awareness that Cuba was the next victim on the list of Yankee aggression. News of the unfolding drama in the Congo reached Cuba's leadership concurrently with information that a task force of Cuban counter-revolutionary exiles, assembled in Guatemala, Nicaragua, and Honduras, was poised for a surprise invasion of the island with U.S. military support.[18]

The non-aligned bloc's unanimous condemnation of the U.S. role in the Congo and the worldwide uproar provoked by Lumumba's murder—even in the U.S., where throngs of black Americans broke into the Security Council and interrupted its sittings[19]—could only have encouraged Castro. By standing with those Afro-Asian states which fully supported Lumumba's cause and were enraged by his murder, Havana was preparing the ground for its own hour of reckoning.

Lumumba's martyrdom could only consolidate domestic support for Castro. Cuba's black population regarded Lumumba as a hero and identified with him both on political and racial grounds.[20] The brutal treatment of Lumumba was bound to evoke painful memories in a population still traumatized by its own history of unspeakable brutalities against Blacks. Castro underscored precisely that point when he addressed a mass rally in Havana; he stigmatized the Congolese leader's murder as yet another horrendous crime of Yankee imperialism. He reminded Cubans that "There was a time when all we had here were American magazines, Yankee boots, Yankee news agencies, Yankee comic books, Yankee music . . . and Yankee films. And what did we learn from those films? We learned that the white American is a hero who kills Indians; that in Africa the white American is again a hero who murders African Negroes. Everyone remembers those films. . . . Imperialism was popularizing its own philosophy by depicting Africa as a conglomerate of naked and savage tribes, armed with bows and arrows. And the more savages the Yankee hero killed, the more of a hero he was!"[21]

Drawing a parallel between nineteenth century slavers and modern-day opponents of his regime, Castro asserted that the same forces trying to overthrow his regime had murdered Lumumba. "Today we are horrified by the fact that human beings were torn away from their countries, separated from their families and snatched from one continent to another where they, their children and great-grandchildren were condemned to live as slaves," he said. "Although we are horrified nowadays to know such things happened . . . we should not forget that those crimes of centuries ago had their apologists. . . . Just as those apologists tried massacring and enslaving the Indians a long time ago, and actually did so with the Africans, they are still today trying to defend their social privileges with the same methods used in committing their past crimes. . . . Today it is Yankee imperialism that is vainly attempting to block revolution in Latin America. . . . It is they . . . who murdered Lumumba. It is they who go about murdering revolutionaries everywhere" (ibid., 9–10, 17, 18).

In view of what was happening in the Congo, the revolutionary leadership was duty-bound to save the Cuban people from a renewal of slavery, racism, exploitation, and wanton murder à la Lumumba. In other words, Castro considered it his mission to save the Cuban people from another Congo. "Our duty is to lead the people to victory!" he proclaimed. "Our duty is to save the people from a return of exploitation and crime! Our duty is to spare our people the tragedy of having to fall back into the claws of imperialism. . . . Those are the most sacred duties of the Revolution and of the men who lead it. We must always discharge our duty in such a way as to make the people understand. We must try to make ourselves fully understood by the people. But if while discharging our duty, a section of the people, still in the grip of ignorance and lies, fails to understand, it doesn't matter, we will still go ahead and carry out our duty!" (ibid., 11, 12)

The last phrase in Castro's speech might seem enigmatic, but it was merely the Caudillo's way of actually hinting at his intention of announcing to Cubans that the Revolution was indeed Communist! The mobilization of Cubans around Lumumba's murder, and widespread fear of an invasion, acted as the best psychological background for such a step. Also, Castro sorely needed to proclaim the Revolution Communist in order to gain the full Soviet military backing he was desperate for. To protect Cubans from a counter-revolutionary restoration, and "save" Cubans from being delivered into the hands of the Ku Klux Klan, however, the Caudillo was counting on the assistance of a protector whose performance in the Congo crisis was far from conclusive. As assessed by an analyst, "Soviet support for Lumumba was overwhelmingly verbal. When he was ousted, jailed, and finally murdered, Moscow failed to act. Having earlier failed to give his forces military support, it now refrained from intervening; instead, it concentrated on vicious attacks on the United Nations. . . . On the other hand, the Congo crisis exposed the U.S.S.R. to the African peoples as a power claiming to be their friend in words, prepared to praise Lumumba posthumously as a hero, but ultimately failing to act on behalf of the African revolution it claimed to champion."[22]

The inconsistency of Soviet policy in the Congo, where the Kremlin began by threatening direct military intervention on behalf of Lumumba only to retreat hastily in the face of American military counter-threats, must have given Castro much cause for concern. If anything, Soviet conduct in the Congo reinforced his conviction— shared by Ché Guevara, Raúl Castro, and the Communist Party—that only an avowedly Marxist regime (which Lumumba's was far from being) could expect to enjoy full Soviet military backing. As hinted in his March 27 speech, Castro was anxious to make that commitment at the first available opportunity; it came within a matter of weeks when a task force of Cuban counter-revolutionary exiles, trained and equipped by the CIA, launched its long-awaited attack.

The Bay of Pigs: Washington's War by Proxy

On April 3, 1961, the State Department issued a White Paper that, given the circumstances, was the equivalent of a casus belli. Not only was Castro accused of having "betrayed the Cuban revolution," having "established a Communist bridgehead" and having "delivered the revolution to the Sino-Soviet bloc," but also of having mounted an "assault on the hemisphere."[23] On April 15, two days before the landing of a 1,400-man brigade of counter-revolutionary exiles, Cuban airfields were bombed. But Castro was prepared. Quickly summoning one million Cubans to a mass rally in Havana, he told the throngs, "This is not a country whose ruling system allows the greater majority of people . . . to toil for an exploitative and privileged minority of millionaires, this is not a country whose ruling system allows a sizable segment of its population to be discriminated against and relegated to oblivion as is the case with the Negro masses in the United States."[24] And for the first time, he admitted to the Marxist character of the Revolution. He proclaimed Cuba Socialist. "What they cannot forgive," he shouted defiantly, "is that right here under the very noses of the United States, we have made a Socialist revolution! A Socialist revolution to be defended with our rifles. . . . Comrades, workers and peasants, this is the Socialist and democratic revolution of the humble and for the humble. . . . Yesterday's attack was the prelude to aggression by mercenaries. All units must now go to their batallions" (ibid., 75, 76).

The following day the counter-revolutionary brigade landed and engaged the Cuban forces in battle. Castro's War Communiqué No. 1 "To the People of Cuba," broadcast over loudspeakers throughout the island, declared: "[W]e are now fighting to defend the sacred motherland and the revolution. . . . Onward, Cubans! Let iron and fire answer those who disdain us and want to put us back into slavery. They come to take away the land that the revolution has given to the peasants. . . . They come to take away the dignity restored to the black man and woman by the revolution, whereas we are fighting to uphold that supreme dignity. . . . Onward, Cubans!"[25]

While Castro's 20,000-man regular army, supported by militia forces, made short work of the CIA-backed, practically all-white counter-revolutionary invaders, Raúl Roa was conducting an equally effective offensive before the U.N. Security Council. Exposing Washington's bare-faced lies and discrediting the United States before Afro-Asian opinion, he challenged U.S. Ambassador to the U.N. Adlai Stevenson's assertion that Washington was merely interested in the restoration of democracy to Cuba. "I would like to ask Mr. Stevenson," he said angrily, "what would happen if the government of the United States, which claims to be the champion of democracy, dared arm not only the Negroes of the cotton-fields of the South, but the Negroes right here in Harlem? I dare you: arm them and let's see if they exercise the right to vote or the right to pull the trigger to liquidate existing racial discrimination in the United States. I dare you: arm them!"[26]

The FPCC meanwhile mounted around-the-clock protest marches throughout the United States, surrounding the U.N. building with thousands of primarily black pro-Castro sympathizers.[27] At the FPCC's behest, an impressive group of well-known black American intellectuals issued a widely publicized "Declaration of Conscience." The document, which appeared in the *New York Times*, supported Castro's charge that Washington wanted to destroy a revolution that had freed Cuban Blacks from racial oppression. In it, they declared:

> Because we have known oppression, because we have suffered more than other Americans, because we are still fighting for our own liberation from tyranny, we Afro-Americans have the right and the duty to raise our voices in protest against those forces of oppression that now seek to crush a free people linked to us by bonds of blood and a common heritage. One-third of Cuba's people are Afro-Cubans, of the same

African descent as we. . . . Today, thanks to a social revolution which they helped make, Afro-Cubans are first-class citizens . . . of their country where all racial barriers crumbled in a matter of weeks following the victory of Fidel Castro. . . . This criminal aggression against a peaceful and progressive people must not be allowed to happen. But if it does, we are determined to do all we possibly can to hinder the success of this crime. . . . Afro-Americans, don't be fooled—the enemies of the Cubans are our enemies, the Jim Crow bosses of this land where we are still denied our rights. The Cubans are our friends, the enemies of our enemies.[28]

Never before had leading black American intellectuals and civil rights spokesmen issued such a statement on behalf of a foreign nation. The most important signatory of the black "Declaration" was Robert Williams, who had been personally in touch with Castro. The radical civil rights leader had become Castro's staunchest advocate among American Blacks. His popularity among U.S. Blacks at its peak, Williams summoned black America to Castro's rescue in a series of mass rallies organized by the FPCC. He went on to turn Washington into a laughing-stock internationally by sending a telegram to Raúl Roa and to the U.N. requesting the "immediate landing of Cuban troops in the U.S. South to liberate American Negroes from the Ku Klux Klan!" With obvious delight, Roa read out Williams's message to the Security Council, saying:

When this debate started, I reminded you that Cuba was not alone. Cuba is neither alone in here nor outside of here. . . . Even in the United States she is not alone. As proof of this, and to further teach the U.S. representative a well-deserved lesson, I will read the telegram I have just received: "To the Cuban delegation at the United Nations. Please forward this message to Mr. Adlai Stevenson. Since the United States has proclaimed that it will militarily aid all peoples who rebel against oppression, the oppressed Negroes of the South urgently request the dispatch of tanks, artillery, and bombs, and also request that American airfields, funds, and white mercenaries be made available to destroy those racist tyrants who have betrayed the American revolution. . . . Robert F. Williams, president of the National Association for the Advancement of Colored People in the United States."[29]

Williams followed through with a telegram to President Kennedy. American Blacks, he wrote the president, request the same assistance given Cuban exiles in terms of "tanks, airplanes, artillery, machine guns, and mercenary troops to fight the Ku Klux Klan in North Carolina."[30] The roaring laughter of Afro-Asian delegates and the embarrassed lividness of Adlai Stevenson indicated that Castro had also won the diplomatic war at the U.N.[31] Politically, Washington had received a severe trouncing.

At the height of the crisis, Nkrumah, Modibo Keita, Touré, and Nasser joined Tito, Nehru, Sukarno, and Khrushchev in sending highly supportive messages of solidarity to Castro, prompting Roa's ironic remark to the Security Council that "never before in the history of the world, has a 'government of bandits and traitors' [as Stevenson had termed Castro's regime] had such a universal backing."[32] Indeed, none of the twenty newly independent black African states overtly sided with the U.S. at the United Nations. Half of them either strongly supported Castro's position or voted for resolutions favorable to Havana (Ghana, Guinea, Mali, Egypt, Sudan, Nigeria, Senegal, Somalia, Upper Volta, Ethiopia).[33] The other half, comprised of openly pro-western governments, generally abstained and remained silent throughout the debates (Togo, Central African Republic, Chad, Dahomey, Liberia, Madagascar, Cameroon, Ivory Coast, Congo [Brazzaville], Niger, Congo-Leopoldville). Apartheid South Africa surfaced as the only state in Africa to strongly back Washington's case against Cuba, setting a pattern that would thereafter characterize the triangle of American-African-Cuban relations. Raúl Roa was to make much of this coincidence of interests between the "hyenas of apartheid and the jackals of the Ku Klux Klan."[34]

Even conservative African governments such as Nigeria felt compelled to speak out in favor of Cuba, attentive no doubt to the militantly pro-Castro sentiment of black Americans. Nigeria's U.N. representative, Jaja Wachuku, told the Security Council that Nigeria, "which has just obtained its independence, cannot remain indifferent before the Cuban events. And whereas she recognizes that all peoples have the right, if they so desire, to change their government through legitimate means, she is nonetheless opposed to any outside attempt to overthrow existing institutions."[35] Mali, Guinea, and Ghana came forth, in that order, as Castro's most vigorous African advocates at the U.N.

Mali's representative, Abdoulaye Ly, seemed the most impassioned and also the worst informed. "The existence of the Republic of Cuba," he said "is threatened because that country, it is claimed, is a Communist bridgehead in the western hemisphere. The Malian people are well acquainted with that sort of pretext, invoked each time Mali herself has been forced to defend herself against those interests which threatened her independence. . . . Whatever the case, reference to communism is nothing but a pretext: the Cuban authorities themselves have repeatedly affirmed that their policy was an independent one with no links whatsoever to any ideology."[36]

While unequivocally defending Havana, Guinea and Ghana were by comparison more circumspect. Said Guinea's U.N. delegate, Maurice Camara: "Guinea entertains the best relations with both the United States and Cuba, and that's why she hopes for a reconciliation that will guarantee peace and security in the western hemisphere."[37] Ghana's representative, Alex Quaison-Sackey, took care to note that Accra "has followed with great admiration the efforts deployed by the Cuban government and people to transform the political, economic, social and cultural life of Cuba. . . . On the other hand, Ghana attaches a high price to the friendship that unites her to the United States. . . . The Ghanaian delegation consequently takes part in this debate as [the] friend of both parties concerned, seeking to be agreeable to neither."[38]

Although they were Havana's diplomatic allies, Touré and Nkrumah were loath to plunge head-on into a situation that only Castro seemed to understand completely. Their reluctance to merely parrot the Soviet bloc's arguments in favor of Havana reflected more than the personal ties President Kennedy had formed with them. Having become, with Mali, the USSR's first clients in black Africa, and suspected of being "communistic" themselves, Conakry and Accra were anxious to avoid a stance that Washington could interpret as an abandonment of their non-aligned policy. Moreover, Castro's April 15 pronouncement admitting to the Socialist character of the Revolution could be interpreted as indicating that Cuba had finally chosen her ideological camp. Havana's displeasure at Nkrumah's and Touré's circumspect support would be reflected soon after in the increasing friction that marred her relations with Conakry and Accra.

Black Exile Troops: "Double Traitors"

Castro's armed forces routed the invaders in no more than forty-eight hours.[39] There were fifty-odd Blacks among the exile troops, including Erneido Oliva, the second-in-command (ibid., 1360). Of the four leaders of the "Cuban Revolutionary Council" organized by the CIA to replace Castro's government, there was a token Black. Dr. Antonio Macéo, grandson of Cuba's greatest hero in the War of Independence against Spain, was obviously nothing other than a figurehead. The counter-revolutionaries, naturally, were as eager as Castro himself to resort to traditional Cuban racial demagoguery to gain Black Cuba's support.

Few in number, black counter-revolutionary prisoners were singled out for abuse and severe ill-treatment, as "double-traitors," by Castro's soldiers. Mirroring Batista's handling of the black Moncadistas, the Revolution's white soldiery assaulted and humiliated these black prisoners, accusing them of being "ungrateful" to Castro. "Of all the prisoners," a historian of the invasion recounted, "Negroes received the worst treatment. Their presence in the invasion force infuriated Castro."[40] Contrasting with the treatment received by their white colleagues, the black prisoners were made to feel pretty much like recaptured runaway slaves:

> Quintana, twenty-three years old, small and so black that he was nicknamed "Lumumba" in the Brigade, was captured with two others, one of them white, after eleven days in the swamps. The white man was brought back to Girón, but Quintana and the other Negro were tied to an orange tree with thistles. Their tongues were so swollen from drinking urine and from lack of food that they could hardly speak. For nearly three hours they were kept tied to the tree in the heat of the day while the militia shouted insults and called them "niggers." "Niggers. Why do you come? Why do you come with the Yankees when they treat the Negro no good?" Finally, they were taken to Girón where Castro himself questioned them. Angrily Castro told them they were guilty of treason on two counts: they had betrayed their country and betrayed their race. After Castro left, Osmany Cienfuegos said they were going to be shot. Quintana and two other Negroes were taken aside, lined up and told: "We're going to shoot you now, niggers, then we're going to make soap out of you." After more curses and more pointing of rifles, they were taken back inside. Throughout their imprisonment, the Negroes in the Brigade suffered most at the hands of their captors. (ibid.)

Manuel Arozarena "was pulled from the line and made to jump and run up and down on the wooden floor while guards threw their bayonets at [his] feet. . . . They called Arozarena a traitor and a dirty Negro and said, 'The only thing you are good for is to be a cook or to be cooked' " (ibid., 296). Black Cuban militiamen who fought at the Bay of Pigs heard Osmány Cienfuegos repeatedly heap racial abuse on the black captives.[41] (As Castro's chief executive for the conduct of Third World affairs, Cienfuegos increasingly surfaced as a key figure in Havana's grand African strategy of the 1970s to liberate the black continent from imperialism, neo-colonialism, and white minority rule.)

Fidel Castro assembled the prisoners in Havana's sports arena for a five-hour televised free-for-all propaganda show. "In a matter of minutes the ice was broken and the atmosphere quickly became that of a teach-in, with good-natured student-prisoners and Professor Castro debating a wide range of social, political, and ideological issues."[42] Castro's humor turned sour, however, when he caught sight of one of the black invaders. "At one point Castro singled out Tomás Cruz, of the paratroop battalion. 'You, Negro, what are you doing here?' Castro outlined the gains Negroes had made under his regime and said that Negroes were even permitted to go swimming with white men. Cruz quietly replied, 'I don't have any complex about my color or my race. . . . And I did not come here to go swimming.' "[43]

Castro's unsettling exchange with Cruz, if anything, served to illustrate the extent to which the regime's racial politics conformed to pre-revolutionary patterns:

> *Prisoner*: When Dr. Castro came in here his first remark to me was, "And what are you doing here? . . ." I am aware that your question "And what are you doing here?" is perhaps a reference to my color, considering that since I was captured that has been the chief reproach for which I have been incriminated. . . . I admit that Negroes here in Cuba experienced certain differences according to their social strata; but I can also say that in Cuba I grew up with whites and that I got along with them as a brother. The differences that existed in Cuba between Blacks and whites were attributable to economic reasons. Coming back to Cuba, I now realize that these have been overcome. That is all I wanted to explain.[44]

The Caudillo's cross-examination of the black prisoner was patently demeaning. By some of his remarks and the overall condescending tone he adopted, Castro appeared to view the black captive more as an ungrateful runaway Negro than as a political opponent:

> *Dr. Castro*: Do you feel that there was racial discrimination in our country, yes or no?
> *Prisoner*: To a certain degree, yes.
> *Dr. Castro*: Well, we do not feel that it was "to a certain degree." For instance, were you allowed into the club to which that gentleman who just spoke belongs? . . . Were you allowed entry? . . . Let me now ask you over there a question. [Castro turns to a white prisoner] What club did you belong to?
> *Prisoner*: The Nautical Club.
> *Dr. Castro*: The Nautical Club! Did they let Negroes in there?
> *Prisoner*: No.
> *Dr. Castro*: Now then, sir, why did you not come to fight for the rights of that discriminated fellow, for the undoing of that odious discrimination which was going on since the times of slavery? You were incapable of bearing arms to put an end to that injustice, but you were

capable of coming here to talk on behalf of "ideals," to fight against this revolution which has established social equality, and which has given the Negro the right to education, the right to work, the right to go to a beach, and the right to grow up in a free country, without being hated or discriminated against (ibid.).

Filled to capacity with his supporters, the sports stadium intermittently shook with cries of "¡Parédon! ¡Parédon! ¡Parédon!" (The Firing Squad!). Castro turned again to the black prisoner, Tomás Cruz:

> *Dr. Castro*: Could you have gotten into the Nautical Club?
> *Prisoner*: (Shakes his head negatively.)
> *Dr. Castro*: Yet, you had the audacity to team up here to fight the Revolution along with that other gentleman, with whom you were not allowed to bathe. You could land here on the beaches of Playa Giron to fight the Revolution, but you were not allowed on the beaches for recreation. Nevertheless, you came together with that gentleman who never cared whether or not you were let into his club to bathe, as if the seawater could be stained by your color!
> *Prisoner*: The fact is that I did not come to Cuba out of considerations of whether or not I would be allowed to bathe at a beach. . . .
> *Dr. Castro*: Very well; that's not the point. The fact nonetheless remains that there was racial discrimination in this country; it was not only a matter of being able to bathe in the aristocratic clubs, since Negroes were also discriminated against in the schools. . . . Did you know that in most department stores where the aristocracy used to buy, black men and women could not be employed? It was feared their color would "stain" the neatly wrapped gift packages. . . . Moreover, Negroes were discriminated against at work centers, in the schools, on the beaches. Those are true facts. The Revolution has now put an end to that (ibid.).

Castro's fury at the presence of Blacks in the invading brigade reportedly led to the imposition of stiffer restrictions on black Cubans desiring to emigrate. Castro is said to have personally stormed into the foreign ministry one day and torn up a heap of passports for black Cubans who had requested exit visas.[45] At any rate, it was not until the 1980 Mariel exodus that Cuban Blacks managed to leave Cuba in any sizeable numbers.

The Black American Gamble

Immediately after the Bay of Pigs, Castro's attacks on Washington's weakest flank intensified. Speaking at a mass victory rally on May Day, the Cuban leader compared the lot of American Blacks to that of Afro-Cubans. Black Cubans, he said, had willingly done battle to defend a Socialist motherland, knowing "that he may fall, but never in vain, and that the cause for which he falls will serve for millions of his brothers."[46] American Blacks, in contrast, were forced to die on behalf of white millionaires: "[W]hen a Yankee monopolist . . . talks about the motherland, he is thinking about sending the Blacks of the South, the workers, to be killed to defend the motherland of monopolies. What kind of morality, what reason and what right does he have to make a black man die to defend the monopolies, the factories and the mines of the ruling classes? What right does he have to send the Puerto Rican of Latin blood and Latin tradition to the battlefields?" (ibid.).

Speaking before a Latin American conference in Mexico, Vilma Espín, president of the Cuban Federation of Women and wife of Raúl Castro, echoed: "We know that in the United States 20 million Negroes are the foremost victims of the unjust social system that oppresses us, and that there are many alert men and women among them who have been roused to the righteousness of our cause *and who are ready to struggle on its behalf.*"[47] Addressing an international students congress in June, the Caudillo again excoriated the treatment of American Blacks. "You should not think," he said, "that discrimination is an accident. Why can't the United States end it? . . . Simply because the millionaires do not agree to have a Negro sit at their table, enter the same movie houses or restaurants they do, nor attend the same universities with them."[48]

Before the international seminar on education held in Havana in late June, Armando Hart Davalos, minister of education, charged that "discrimination in education . . . is best exemplified in the United States as racial discrimination. The doors of schools are barred to Negroes who, for years, have been forced to live in a state of ignorance that stunts their cultural growth. . . . The arrogant and uncouth magnates of the South then turn around and justify racial discrimination by invoking the very ignorance they have forced upon the Negro."[49]

To a mass rally assembled to commemorate the eighth anniversary of the Moncada assault, Castro castigated the "superior Yankee race," which meted out the same treatment to Latins as they did to American Negroes.[50] In mid-August, addressing an inter-American economic conference at Punta del Este, Uruguay, Cuban President Osvaldo Dorticos Torrado contrasted the treatment of Cuban Blacks to that of Blacks in the United States, where "human rights are being violated, . . . where millions of Negroes are treated as less than human beings. . . . It is in Cuba that the Negro is *protected*, not only by legal principles, but by true opportunities for work, education and participation in the life of the country without discrimination. . . . In Cuba all men are equal."[51]

Cuban intelligence made new attempts during the summer of 1961 to secure concrete support from black American organizations. Havana had directed its attention to those militant black groups that might eventually take concrete action on behalf of the threatened Revolution. Cuban intelligence was then interested in a U.S. Southern group called the Armed Deacons for Self-Defense (ADSD) and sought to curry favors with the Nation of Islam (Black Muslims). Since Castro's 1960 meeting in New York with Malcolm X, the leader of the Black Muslims, Havana had kept a close watch on that movement. Malcolm X was insistently contacted by Cuba's U.N. mission and invited to visit Cuba. But he remained leery of Havana's motives.[52] *Muhammad Speaks*, the weekly publication of the Black Muslims, had taken up the defense of revolutionary Cuba. However, Malcolm X would later ground his misgivings on the fact that "not even in your so-called Socialist, Marxist, and other type societies have they ever had a black man on the top."[53] The most Havana got from the Black Muslims, besides editorial support, was a visit two years later by Herbert Muhammad, son of the organization's founder and spiritual leader, Elijah Muhammad.[54]

Cuba's hopes for comradeship with black commando groups capable of undertaking "kamikaze" action on behalf of the Revolution in the event of a U.S. invasion remained pinned on Robert Williams. Through Williams, members of the Armed Deacons for Self-Defense and individual activists began to visit Cuba in 1961, traveling via Canada. A Korean War veteran, Williams had already set up and trained several "Self-Defense Committees" in North Carolina and accumulated a small arsenal of firearms.[55] His experiment was threatening to spread to other areas of the Deep South in 1961 when a shoot-out erupted between his units and police troopers in Monroe, North Carolina. The FBI immediately issued a warrant for his arrest and undertook the dismantling of his movement in August 1961. Williams's successful campaign on behalf of Castro and his determination to defend the Cuban revolution with arms inside the U.S. were not unrelated to the large-scale witch-hunt the FBI had for years conducted against his movement.

Thwarting a nationwide FBI dragnet, Williams fled to Canada and on to Cuba in early September. He was sought on charges of "kidnapping." An advocate of the overthrow of the U.S. government by force of arms, Williams swiftly received asylum in Cuba. Although his exile paralyzed Havana's efforts to utilize militant black American groups on its behalf, Castro was to make the best of Williams's presence, not only to intensify his propaganda offensive among black Americans but also to influence African opinion on Cuba's behalf.

The civil rights leader was turned into an international revolutionary celebrity. Interviewed on radio and television, he shared the podium with Cuba's revolutionary leadership on the grand occasions of Castro's monster rallies. The Castroite leadership more than welcomed Williams's vivid descriptions of the horrors of Yankee racism. Before impassioned audiences, the Caudillo himself would often refer to Williams as he taunted and challenged Washington to "allow representatives of the Negro civil rights organizations in the United States to visit Cuba so that they can see how . . . racial discrimination has disappeared in our country once and for all. . . . , [and see how] some leaders, like Robert Williams, who were brutally persecuted there found asylum in this land. And like Williams, all those who are persecuted by reactionaries and exploiters can find asylum here."[56]

Williams's propaganda value soon exceeded the psychological impact that his much-publicized flight to the "island of freedom" would have on both American and Cuban Blacks. He arrived in Cuba in the same year as the first contingent of African diplomats, students, and representatives of liberation movements. In no time, his residential suite at the plush Capri hotel became a choice meeting place for Havana's growing African colony. He met frequently with Ghana's newly appointed chargé d'affaires, Ebenezer Akuete, and with Guinean Ambassador Soumah Issah.[57] Through the Cuban Friendship Institute (ICAP)—covertly a dependency of Cuban counterintelligence—he was brought into close contact with the two African liberation groups that had set up shop in Havana: the African National Congress (ANC), and the UMMA party of Zanzibar. Ambrose Makiwane headed the ANC's representation in Havana. The UMMA's office was staffed by Ali Mahfoudh Mohammed, Salim Salim (later to become Tanzania's prime minister), and Mohammed Foum, who later became Tanzania's deputy foreign minister.

Alternately acting as chief prosecutor of Yankee racism and defense attorney for Cuba's "racial democracy," Williams stood in the good graces of Maj. Manuel Piñeiro ("Red Beard") Losada, Castro's counter-intelligence chief. Piñeiro had received instructions from Castro to look after Williams and acted as liaison with the Caudillo.

Through ICAP, Piñeiro's office made certain that every visiting African delegation conferred with the celebrated American black leader. Williams, however, had trouble from the start with ICAP's leading officials—Giraldo Mazola and Ramón Calcines—who monitored his every movement, including his intimate escapades.

In a matter of months, Williams was broadcasting twice weekly to the American South over *Radio progreso* in what became Havana's most daring "deliberate counter-subversion attempt to have seriously worried the government in Washington."[58] His "Radio Free Dixie" programs, monitored as far as Canada,[59] and his monthly newsletter "The Crusader," widely distributed in the U.S. and Africa, drove home the same message: American Blacks must convert the U.S. South into another Sierra Maestra; black Africa must stand behind a regime that is the friend and protector of the world's oppressed black peoples. Havana could hardly have found a better emissary to convey its redemptionist message to the black continent.[60]

9   THE OCTOBER MISSILE CRISIS

The Castroite regime had proven that Cuba could defend herself against any small-scale attack.[1] Havana's ability to build "socialism in one island" under the very nose of Yankee imperialism, as Castro had proclaimed, was another matter. Cuba's self-proclaimed socialism was another calculated attempt to stay one step ahead of the U.S. Cuban leaders "seemed to believe it would suffice to proclaim that they had taken the Socialist path to be admitted into the 'Great Family' with open arms. They were therefore quite surprised when throughout the summer of 1961, the Eastern bloc countries remained deaf to Castro's speeches proclaiming Cuba a Socialist state on April 16 and May 1 1961."[2]

China's deafness to Castro's Socialist pronouncements seemed more ideologically motivated than anything else. In Peking's eyes, a Socialist country implied a Communist party at the head of the state, and therefore Cuba qualified only as a "national democratic state." Moscow, however, had more practical reasons for withholding recognition of Cuba's self-proclaimed socialism. The island's geopolitical position posed almost insoluble strategic problems for Kremlin planners.[3] The USSR was unwilling to irrevocably commit itself to the defense of a country so vulnerable to American attack. Castro's move thus caught the Soviets by surprise and infuriated them. Years later, Soviet Premier Khrushchev would confide to an American journalist: "Before the forces of invasion had been crushed, Castro came out with a declaration that Cuba would follow a socialist course. We had trouble understanding this statement. . . . [F]rom a tactical standpoint it didn't make much sense."[4]

Moscow's reluctance to embrace "Cuban socialism" was matched by Castro's insistence. On May Day, the international holiday of radical labor, and an important day in the Soviet calendar, the Caudillo confirmed the Socialist character of his regime: "This revolution . . . is a Socialist revolution. . . . [Our new] constitution will therefore be a Socialist constitution. . . . This is a Socialist regime, yes! Yes, this is a Socialist regime."[5]

Castro told the huge crowd that Cuba, as a Socialist state, would hold no more elections. "A revolution expressing the will of the people is an election every day. . . . Do the people have time for elections? No! The revolution has no time to waste in such foolishness. . . . The people know that the revolution expressed their will" (ibid.). Elections, said Castro, would only afford former exploiters and discriminators a chance to stage a comeback to the detriment "of the peasants who do not want to lose their land, the blacks who do not want discrimination" (ibid., 124, 128, 129).

Throughout the summer of 1961 Cuban leaders used every occasion to warn that "the events that will be unleashed as a consequence of an aggression against Cuba will definitely not end in Cuba."[6] In his May Day speech, Castro had been explicit: "We are not interested in having imperialism commit suicide at our expense. They do not care about the death of blacks, Puerto Ricans, or Americans. But we do care about the life of every Cuban."[7] The reference to a nuclear holocaust resulting from aggression against Cuba was clear enough. Nevertheless, the Kremlin was at that moment trying to avoid such a commitment, and Castro knew it.

A Persistent Suitor

As the latter half of 1961 passed, Havana sought to comply with the doctrinal requirements for inclusion into the Communist bloc. In late July, Castro announced the formation of a proto-Communist party—the Integrated Revolutionary Organizations (ORI)—which would rule the state.[8] Staffed with bona fide Marxist cadres, the ORI's secretary, Aníbal Escalante, was the leading theoretician and boss of the old Communist party.

In his attempts to force the gates of the Communist bloc, Castro was even ready to renege on his earlier protestations of "nonalignment." Addressing the first non-aligned summit in Belgrade that September, President Osvaldo Dorticós Torrado went out of his way to underscore the abrupt reorientation in Havana's foreign policy. "When the revolutionary government of Cuba was invited to participate in the preparatory meeting of this conference, it did not hesitate to answer positively," said Dorticós.[9] However, he warned that although "Cuba participates in meetings or deliberations with countries of other continents who are unattached to bloc politics through military and other sorts of pacts. . . . [this] does not mean that we are non-aligned. We are aligned with our own principles and, as the most legitimate representatives of our people, we . . . are determined to answer their fundamental aspirations and live by those principles" (ibid.).

Dorticós's statement was meant to establish Havana's distance from a movement whose titular leader, Marshal Tito, was regarded by Moscow as a "renegade." From Belgrade Dorticós proceeded to Moscow, apparently hoping to reap the benefits of Cuba's first public disavowal of non-alignment. But the joint communiqué published with Soviet leaders at the end of his visit showed no signs that the Kremlin had yielded to Havana's demand for admittance into the bloc.[10] Extending his tour to China, Dorticós proved equally unable to convince Chinese leaders that Cuba was a Socialist state (ibid., 138–139). This was cause for despair in Havana, for Castro had taken care to have Blás Roca, chairman of the old Communist party, accompany Dorticós on his trips to Moscow and Peking. "Osvaldo Dorticós returned to Cuba, therefore, without being able to hear much more than that he was the head of a 'national democratic State' " (ibid., 142).

On December 2, Castro abruptly changed his strategy. He would no longer wait for Moscow and Peking to approve his Socialist credentials. In his customary theatrical style, the Cuban premier said that he had already been won over to Marxism at the time of Moncada but had had to conceal his beliefs for tactical reasons. Thus, upon seizure of power in 1959, he had been a convinced Marxist and would always remain so. "As a student I studied the *Communist Manifesto* and the *Selected Works* of Marx, Engels and Lenin. . . . Do I believe in Marxism? Yes, I absolutely believe in Marxism. Did I believe in it on January 1st [1959]? Yes, I did. Did I believe in it on July 26th [1953]? Yes, I did. . . . Do I harbor any doubts about Marxism, or feel that some of its analyses are erroneous or in need of revision? No, I harbor no such doubts," Castro said. "With great satisfaction and total confidence, I proclaim myself a Marxist-Leninist, and will remain a Marxist-Leninist until I die."[11]

In an obvious attack on the chief proponents of non-alignment (Marshal Tito and Gamal Abdel Nasser), he then denounced as cowardly opportunists those who sought to steer a middle course between two blocs. "We must understand that there is no middle ground between capitalism and socialism. Those who are determined to seek a third course have fallen into an erroneous and utopian position which amounts to . . . complicity with imperialism. . . . Some people—believing themselves very wise—feel that the Cuban revolution should, as they say, take money from both the Americans and the Russians. In other words, there are people who are propounding this type of repugnant, cowardly, vile and mean thesis. . . . There are those who propound a thesis of blackmail" (ibid., 205, 206).

Castro announced the formation of a United Party of the Socialist Revolution (PURS) whose task would be to lead the nation in building first socialism, then communism (ibid., 210). Henceforth, Cuba would be considered as being under the "dictatorship of the proletariat" and on the path of Socialist construction (ibid., 216). The new party and the revolutionary government represented the vanguard elite who would speak on behalf of the workers and peasants (ibid., 218–220, 227–230). Socialist Cuba, under its new Marxist-Leninist leadership, was then declared indissolubly linked to the Communist bloc:

> Imperialism must know, once and for all, that it will never have relations with us. It must know that whatever our difficulties, whatever the sacrifices to build our country and its future . . . it should not harbor any hopes as far as we are concerned. . . . Socialism is triumphant. The epoch of socialism is overcoming the epoch of capitalism and imperialism. The era of socialism is here, to be followed by the era of communism (ibid., 209–210).

China to Castro's Rescue

Had it merely been for doctrinal reasons that Kremlin theoreticians refused to accept Cuba into the Communist fold, Castro's professions of faith on December 2 would have been more than sufficient. Due to eminently strategic motives, however, Moscow's refusal to recognize Cuba's Marxist-Leninist credentials persisted after Castro's speech, to Havana's great surprise and annoyance.

Meanwhile, the Sino-Soviet split had seriously escalated. At the twenty-second Party Congress, held in October, Nikita Khrushchev finally brought the Sino-Soviet schism out into the open by directly attacking Albania, Peking's unconditional ally. Moscow's failure to ratify Cuba as a Socialist state left it open to charges by Peking of "abandoning" the Caribbean nation to imperialist attack. Furthermore, there was the risk that, out of sheer desperation, Castro would accept China's advances to the discredit of the Kremlin. Yet, to recognize Cuba as part of the Soviet bloc would bear equally disagreeable consequences: not only would the USSR find itself committed to nuclear war in the event of an American invasion but also a highly volatile partner would have been introduced into the Communist bloc. Both prospects filled the Kremlin with dread.

On January 2, 1962, exactly one month after Castro had proclaimed Cuba a Marxist-Leninist state under the "dictatorship of the proletariat," China recognized Cuba as a Socialist state. The recognition came in a declaration by Marshal Chen Yi, China's foreign minister, to the effect that, "At present, the Cuban people are pursuing their forward march along the path they have chosen: the path of Socialist development."[12] Castro's Cuba had entered the Communist camp, but through the Great Wall of China. Peking had played its cards well, and Castro would soon follow suit.

China's loud endorsement of Cuban socialism encouraged Castro in his defiance. The Caudillo now had a clear case to defend and additional cause for pressuring the Kremlin. Castro was aware that Washington would certainly act in face of the open, irrevocably Marxist-Leninist character of his regime. Adopting wholesale the Chinese call for instant revolutions throughout the Third World, Havana summoned revolutionaries in South America to action on February 4, 1962, presenting itself as the legitimate revolutionary and anti-imperialist vanguard of South America.

Before a rally of one million supporters, Castro took the rostrum in Havana's Revolutionary Plaza to read a carefully drafted document known as the "Second Declaration of Havana." The document summoned the South American continent to revolution against Yankee imperialism and denounced those who called themselves revolutionaries but who nonetheless preached "peaceful coexistence" with their imperialist neighbor. With accents that were definitely "Chinese," Castro declared that Latin America was ripe for revolution. "The anxiety felt today," he said, "is an unmistakeable symptom of rebellion. The very depths of a continent are profoundly moved, a continent which has witnessed four centuries of slave, semi-slave and feudal exploitation, beginning with its aboriginal inhabitants and the slaves brought from Africa, up to the national nuclei which emerged later: white, black, mulatto, mestizo, and Indian. Today they are made brothers by scorn, humiliation and the Yankee yoke, and are brothers in their hope for a better tomorrow."[13]

The duty of a revolutionary, said Castro, was revolution. In Latin America the Revolution would be based on the peasantry, led by an enlightened vanguard of urban intellectuals, with Cuba acting as the example. "To the accusation that Cuba wants to export its revolution, we reply: Revolutions are not exported, they are made by the people. . . . What Cuba can give to the people, and has already given, is its example" (ibid., 154). Contrasting Cuba's example to the U.S. Alliance for Progress, Castro asked: "How—under what oath—could anyone believe in any benefit, in any 'Alliance for Progress' with imperialism, when under its saintly protection, its killings, its persecutions, the natives of the South of the continent . . . still live . . . as did their ancestors at the time the discoverers came almost 500 years ago?" (ibid., 160–161).

Pitying the lot of "these primitive, melancholy races, brutalized by alcohol and narcotics," Castro reiterated:

> Yes, all these thirty million Indians . . . and the forty-five million mestizos, who for the most part differ little from the Indians; all these natives, this formidable reservoir of labour, whose rights have been trampled on, yes, what can imperialism offer them? . . . Entire tribes which live unclothed; others which are supposed to be cannibalistic; others whose members die like flies upon first contact with the conquering civilization. . . . In what "alliance'—other than one for their own rapid extermination—are these native races going to believe? (ibid., 155)

"[The] nightmare which torments America, from one end to the other," Castro continued, "is that on this continent of almost 200 million human beings, two-thirds are Indians, mestizos, and Blacks—the 'discriminated against' " (ibid., 159). Apart from further discrimination, what did Yankee imperialism have to offer the majority masses of South America, particularly the Blacks? Castro leveled his prime weapon against the U.S.:

> And to the Black. What "alliance" can the system of lynching and brutal exclusion of the Black offer to the fifteen million Negroes and fourteen million mulattoes of Latin America, who know with horror and rage that their brothers in the North cannot ride in the same vehicles as their white compatriots, nor attend the same schools, nor even die in the same hospitals? How are these disinherited racial groups going to believe in this imperialism, in its benefits or in any "alliance" with it which is not for lynching and exploiting them as slaves? Those masses who have not been permitted even modestly to enjoy any cultural, social, or professional benefits, who—even when they are in the majority or number in millions—are persecuted by the imperialists in Ku Klux Klan costumes, are ghettoed in the most unsanitary neighborhoods. . . . They cannot presume to reach the universities, advanced academies and private schools.
>
> What "Alliance for Progress" can serve as encouragement to those 107 million men and women of our America . . . whose dark skin— Black, mestizo, mulatto, Indian—inspires scorn in the new colonialists? (ibid., 156)

With its insistent call for immediate revolution from the countryside, based among the peasants, and scorn for "peaceful coexistence" with imperialism or the local bourgeoisie, the "Second Declaration of Havana" won the approval of the Chinese leadership. Not unexpectedly, Peking gave wide publicity to the document, while the Kremlin passed it over in silence.

A month and a half after the "Second Declaration of Havana," the Kremlin still refused to endorse Cuba's claim to membership in the Communist bloc. Moscow's persistent indifference and outright stubbornness forced Castro to take another decisive step, resorting to open blackmail. On March 26, the Caudillo made a radio-television announcement that he had uncovered a virtual coup d'état by veteran Party leader Aníbal Escalante. In a savage attack on the old-line, pro-Soviet Cuban Communists, Castro accused them of such crimes as trying to sabotage the Revolution, opposing the insurrectional line spelled out in the "Second Declaration of Havana," and attempting to wrest control of the Revolution from him and his die-hard Moncadista supporters.[14] Escalante, who six months earlier had been made organizational secretary of the new Marxist party, was mercilessly attacked by Castro as a sort of lesser Stalin and exiled to Czechoslovakia. Communist party stalwarts were purged by the hundreds from the new Marxist party and replaced with bona fide Moncadistas.

By liquidating the old Party in one sweep and imposing himself as the only source of Marxist legitimacy in Cuba, Castro's position vis-à-vis the Kremlin had changed drastically. Moscow was now being held to ransom. The Sino-Soviet split, which had created two Communist blocs, had set the stage for just such an action. Peking reacted swiftly, applauding the decapitation of the pro-Soviet Cuban Communist party, which it saw as a great victory against "revisionism."[15] Castro's implicit threat was clear: if Moscow continued to close its doors, the Cuban regime would walk through the welcoming portals of Peking. Worse, Castro might even start his own independent Marxist camp outside the authority of either Moscow or Peking. Its back now firmly to the wall, the Kremlin gave in. On April 11, 1962, two weeks after the Escalante affair, *Pravda* announced that Cuba was a Socialist state.[16]

Frictions with Guinea and Ghana

Moscow's acceptance of Cuba's Marxist legitimacy had immediate effects on Cuba's foreign policy. In a way, Castro's triumph reinforced the Castroite leadership's ingrained arrogance towards the Afro-Asian world. Havana grew increasingly exigent as to the ideological conduct of its African partners. Both of the liberation movements represented in Cuba—the ANC of South Africa and UMMA party of Zanzibar—were Marxist and pro-Soviet in orientation. Havana now seemed to believe that its two official partners in Africa—Ghana and Guinea—should also be unequivocally so committed.

In the summer of 1961, Ghana's U.N. ambassador Alex Quaison-Sackey had traveled to Havana to present his credentials as ambassador to Cuba but swiftly returned to New York, leaving day-to-day business in the hands of charge d'affaires Ebenezer Akuete. This was taken as an affront by the Castroite government, which now saw itself as being a leader in world affairs. The fact that Ghana's ambassador to revolutionary Cuba was resident in enemy territory and furthermore was concurrently ambassador to Mexico made matters worse.

Ebenezer Akuete's mission in Cuba was fraught with difficulties from the start. Deliberately snubbed by Cuban authorities and subjected to petty harassments, the Ghanaian chargé d'affaires soon developed an intense dislike for Cuba's revolutionary leadership.[17] A young and inquiring intellectual, Akuete aggravated government hostility by developing a keen interest in the conditions of Blacks in Cuba under the Revolution. Several months after having assumed his post, Akuete no longer hesitated to share his thoughts on the subject, particularly with Robert Williams (ibid.).

To Akuete, the glaring absence of Blacks in the government and leading bodies of the regime was eloquent enough. He considered the trend of race relations under the Revolution as not much different than it had been in pre-revolutionary days, with the exception of the banning of racial discrimination (ibid.). He viewed Castro's posture on Africa as patronizing. Akuete's turbulent relations with the Cuban authorities widened the gap that already existed between Castro and Nkrumah.

Castro's self-proclaimed Marxism-Leninism and declaration of unswerving allegiance to the Kremlin in December 1961 coincided with Guinea's expulsion of Soviet ambassador Daniel Solod, accused of no less than "subversion." Leftist Guinea and Marxist Cuba were manifestly adopting conflicting lines in their relations with the USSR. There are grounds to believe that Castro had even expected President Sékou Touré to follow his lead and declare Guinea's unambiguous attachment to Marxism-Leninism and the USSR.

When Conakry's long-awaited envoy appeared in Havana in early 1962, relations between Conakry and Havana had perceptibly cooled.

Ambassador Soumah Naby Issa was made to wait for several months before being allotted an embassy. He was also greeted with disquieting news by the nineteen Guinean students who had arrived in Cuba the previous October.[18] As a whole, the group's impressions of conditions in Cuba were negative. The students felt that the Cuban authorities strongly resented their attempts to establish personal contacts with black Cubans. They felt that white Cubans, including high-ranking authorities, were patently "racist" in their treatment of Blacks.[19] Two of the students complained that while "we never had any real contact with white Cubans—particularly white females, who would flee from us—obstacles were placed in the way of our relations with black Cubans" (ibid.). In one specific case, a black family traveled all the way from the easternmost part of the island to visit them. They succeeded with much difficulty, only to disappear immediately afterward without leaving a trace.

The students' grievances included the authorities' refusal to allow them to attend Afro-Cuban religious ceremonies. They were bitter.

> We were made to understand that Afro-Cuban religions were not recognized as such. For instance, we had been invited to the outskirts of Havana to attend a Santería meeting. Our whole group was glad to go and when we arrived we found a table had been laid out with food for all nineteen of us. We had been taken there by Proscopio, our Afro-Cuban guide. But no sooner had we started to eat bread than three white men, claiming to be from the Ministry of Education, came in and took our guide aside. The table and food were quickly removed. The atmosphere was heavy and we were greatly embarrassed. We couldn't understand. Nonetheless, we all wanted to stay and follow the ceremony which, we were told, much resembled ceremonies in Africa. But nothing took place and we had to leave. We all concluded that the authorities disapproved of our presence at an Afro-Cuban cult meeting. We guessed that they did not want our presence to lend legitimacy to Afro-Cuban Santería. We were all shocked at that discovery (ibid.).

In sum, the students explained, "We arrived believing the Revolution was homogeneous, for all and with all. But little by little we discovered the racial cleavage. It was Black and white, subtly divided in a thousand different ways and with the latter having the upper hand" (ibid.).

As for Ambassador Soumah Naby Issa, after several months of duty in Cuba, he gave the impression of being a besieged man. He kept out of public view most of the time, entertaining low-key relations with Cuban officials and occasionally issuing short, carefully worded statements of Conakry's support for its Caribbean "friend." In private, his impressions about Cuba began to echo those of the Ghanaian Akuete.[20]

It was apparent that relations had deteriorated between Castro's Cuba and Sékou Touré's Guinea (ibid.). No doubt, Conakry's stern handling of the Soviet Union had irked Havana, while the latter's unconditional alliance with the Kremlin had put Touré on his guard. What could have angered Conakry the most was Havana's increasing tendency to resort to ideological extortion. That year, the Castroite leadership had indeed revealed its contempt for leaders like Touré and Nkrumah who, while professing to be unswerving anti-imperialists, still considered neutrality a valid political platform.

Cuba on Top of the World

In the fall of 1962, Havana's language had come to resemble that of a great power. Seizing every available opportunity to issue stern warnings to the U.S. and regularly reaffirming its irrevocable bonds with the Soviet Union, revolutionary Cuba summoned South America to rise. The day of reckoning with Yankee imperialism was at hand, Havana declared.

In early September, 1962, Castro himself announced, "Cuba is now ready to wage the decisive battle against the U.S."[21] Two weeks later, in a speech to the Committees to Defend the Revolution (CDR), the Caudillo proclaimed Cuba's right to avail herself of whatever weapons she wanted.[22] Behind Castro's big-power posturing was an agreement reached with the Kremlin that summer to arm Cuba with nuclear weapons.[23] Cuban Defense Minister Raúl Castro had traveled to the USSR in early July to conclude negotiations, and the nuclear missiles began arriving in Cuba by early September.[24]

Through placing nuclear weapons in Cuba, the Kremlin sought simultaneously to overturn its strategic military inferiority vis-à-vis the U.S., recover from its defeat over Berlin the previous year,[25] reassert its authority over the Communist bloc, and establish itself as the leading world superpower.[26] For its part, the Castroite leadership could only welcome a decision that had the effect of suddenly turning Cuba into the only Third World nuclear power. Despite Castro's later claims that he had accepted the missiles in the name of "international proletarian solidarity,"[27] it is certain that he engaged in that adventure with the view of finally becoming a major decision maker in world politics.[28] Cuba would henceforth rank as a great power. An earlier statement by Ché Guevara now perfectly reflected the Caudillo's state of mind. "By force of circumstances," said Che, "we are today practically the arbiters of world peace."[29]

The most dangerous international crisis since World War II erupted on October 22 when the U.S. revealed the presence of nuclear missiles and heavy IL-28 bombers in Cuba. There were already twenty to thirty thousand Soviet military troops on the island, and besides the missiles and bombers, the quantity and quality of weaponry that had been transferred there transformed Cuba into the most militarily powerful country in the Third World.[30] Feeling secure at last, Castro was at his cockiest.

On October 23, the day following President Kennedy's grave declaration in Washington, Castro spoke to the Cuban nation, now as the leader of a great power. Havana scornfully dismissed Kennedy's announced military blockade. Scoffing at any attempt to dictate what sort of weapons Cuba could possess, Castro declared that he would squash any attempted U.S. military invasion. He warned:

> We will never be the easy victims of an aggression. . . . [W]e have taken the necessary steps to resist and also—listen carefully, listen carefully—to *crush* any direct aggression coming from the United States. . . . *Cuba is not the Congo.* . . . Cuba is not the Congo! That's why no one will ever come to inspect our country, either under the [U.N.] flag or any other flag. We know what we are doing, and we know how to defend our integrity and sovereignty (Italics added.).[31]

Following Castro's statement, giant posters went up throughout the island bearing the pathetic last photograph of Patrice Lumumba, his hands tied behind his back, brutally manhandled and seized by the hair by a Congolese soldier. The caption echoed Castro's assertion: "Cuba Is Not the Congo!"[32] Almost unanimously, students and diplomats alike, the small African community in Havana resented both the posters and the words of Castro's speech that had inspired them.[33] The general feeling was that Africans were being portrayed as incapable of defending themselves without outside protection,[34] in contrast to Cuba's leaders who, as Castro boasted, did "know what they were doing"!

The parallels Castro had drawn between Cuba and the Congo were not merely rhetorical. By evoking the Congo he meant to revive in the minds of African leaders such as Sékou Touré and Kwame Nkrumah a painful memory of their incapacity to act when a regime they supported was being torn asunder by the brazen interventionism of the West. In the context of the October crisis, Castro's evocation of the Congo was therefore a concrete attempt to involve Africa's two most anti-imperialist states in the conflict. Guinea's support was vital, for once the military blockade of Cuba went into effect, Havana and the Kremlin had to find a safe airbridge to convey the missiles' warheads to the island via Africa. Earlier that year, Soviet technicians had lengthened Guinea's Gbessia airport landing strips precisely for that purpose.[35]

On October 24, according to U.S. Ambassador in Conakry William Attwood, "the Acting Foreign Minister, Alpha Diallo, confirmed to me that the Russians had requested landing rights in Conakry for long-range jets. But he told me not to worry; the government agreed with our stand on the missile build-up, and [President Sékou] Touré had made the decision to refuse the Soviet request."[36] The Kremlin had not only asked Conakry for landing rights but also requested that Gbessia airport be closed to international traffic while Soviet aircraft were en route to Cuba.

Implicitly condemning the installation of missile bases in Cuba, the national political bureau of the Parti Démocratique de Guinée (PDG) denounced the presence of all foreign bases on Cuban soil, whatever their nature, on November 6 (ibid.). Through his ambassador in Havana, Touré reminded the Cuban government of Castro's 1960 U.N. speech advocating the total denuclearization of Africa and his call for the dismantling of atomic bases on foreign soil.

Crucial as it was in blocking a further buildup of nuclear missiles in Cuba,[37] Touré's decision placed severe strains on Guinea-Cuban relations. To Havana, Touré's action amounted to a betrayal, although Conakry had not been consulted beforehand by either Moscow or Havana. Worse still, from Touré's point of view, the earlier lengthening of Gbessia's landing strips could now be regarded as a premeditated Soviet-Cuban step. Most of all, the Guinean leader was outraged at the thought that, once presented with the fait accompli of Soviet missile bases in Cuba, Castro and Khrushchev had expected him to meekly comply with their subsequent initiatives.[38]

Castro's falling-out with black Africa's most militantly anti-imperialist state took place in an atmosphere of mutual distrust and recrimination that would take years to dissipate. Less than a year after taking up his post, Ambassador Soumah Naby Issa quietly returned to Conakry following the October crisis. His last significant action was to have ordered the Guinean students in Havana to refrain from taking part in the military mobilization of the island during the crisis. As a gesture of solidarity, the students had at the height of the crisis donned military uniforms and taken up guard duties behind sandbags until their ambassador informed them that their act ran counter to Conakry's position in the affair.[39] In the summer of 1963,

Ambassador Issa was replaced by Seydou Diallo, a tough former trade union leader who stood up to the Cuban authorities as perhaps no other African diplomat would thereafter.

While American reconnaissance craft continually overflew Cuba, Algerian President Ahmed Ben Bella arrived in Havana, coming directly from the U.S. Ben Bella's visit was greeted by Castro in a welcoming speech as a supreme "act of courage" and solidarity with his regime.[40]

The Algerian president's gesture greatly endeared him to the Castroite leadership. From then on, Castro would not only view Ben Bella as his closest comrade-in-arms in the Third World, but also consider Algeria to be the de facto leader of all Africa, north and south of the Sahara. It was due to the obligations of this militant friendship, and to rescue Ben Bella, that exactly a year later Castro would first commit his powerful forces to armed intervention outside the American hemisphere.

The Rise of a Caribbean Sparta

The October crisis was born out of the USSR's world strategic ambitions and Castro's own messianic, big-power drives through the midwifery of American imperial pretensions. The most far-reaching consequence of the crisis was the aggravation of the Sino-Soviet conflict.[41] Moscow's humiliating capitulation served to validate Peking's denunciations of the USSR. Castro, however, had obtained an American non-invasion pledge, a net gain. From then on, the Cuban revolution would be allowed to run its course without fear of external intervention. Nevertheless, Castro did not emerge unscathed.

In its precipitous retreat the Kremlin had seriously trampled on Cuba's sovereignty. Reduced to being an unwilling spectator while the two superpowers resolved the crisis, the Caudillo had also been humiliated. Moscow had removed its missiles and other "offensive" weapons with Cuba's grudging consent. Worse, the Soviets had unilaterally accepted U.S. demands for an inspection of Cuban territory. "Cuba's security was achieved at the price of a serious deterioration of Soviet-Cuban relations and an increase of Peking's influence in Havana."[42]

After the crisis, conceded Premier Khrushchev, "[O]ur relations with Cuba . . . took a sudden turn for the worse. Castro even stopped receiving our ambassador. It seemed that by removing our missiles we had suffered a moral defeat in the eyes of the Cubans. Our shares in Cuba instead of going up, went down. . . . All the while, the

Chinese were making a lot of noise publicly as well as buzzing in Castro's ear. . . . In other words, the Chinese exploited the episode to discredit us in the eyes of the Cubans."[43]

The October crisis had afforded Peking a perfect occasion to demonstrate its main theses against Moscow: the Soviet "revisionists" stood ready to betray and sacrifice their closest allies on the altar of accommodation with world imperialism; Kremlin leaders were not only unscrupulous "adventurists," but cowardly "capitulationists" as well; the USSR had become an enemy to the Third World.[44]

Castro was no doubt genuinely furious at the Soviet withdrawal.[45] Attentive to the best interests of the Cuban government, however, he was not ready to risk a break with Moscow for an unprofitable alliance with Peking. Now that he considered Cuba as a state whose "security was totally guaranteed," he was anxious for the USSR to continue, even to expand, its economic and technical assistance.[46] Having suddenly lost its strategic relevance to the Kremlin, Cuba was in danger of being discarded, for at that point, the island had become a burden for the USSR.[47] Once again, the Sino-Soviet conflict afforded Castro the best insurance against Soviet economic abandonment. It was only in the context of the Kremlin's struggle with Peking and its efforts to expand its influence over the Third World that Havana continued to be of any use to the USSR.[48]

As a consequence of the October crisis, both Moscow and Havana were forced to reassess their foreign policies, which only increased the tension between the two countries.[49] Moscow had decided on a military hands-off policy in Latin America while seeking to establish close diplomatic and trade relations. Moreover, wide avenues of dialogue and cooperation had opened between the Kremlin and Washington in every sphere from disarmament to technological aid. Toward China, Moscow's policy became highly aggressive, no longer excluding the possibility of open war. The main thrust of Soviet diplomatic and strategic efforts would be geared toward the African continent and the Arab Middle East.[50]

Castro had adopted a diametrically opposite attitude on all these issues. With virtual immunity from North American interference, Castro was bent on pursuing confrontation with the U.S. by exporting the Revolution to Latin America. On the ideological plain, Havana hinted at its neutrality in the Sino-Soviet conflict by rejecting "peaceful coexistence" with the U.S. and attacking the Kremlin's "appeasement" of Yankee imperialism.[51] On the Third World front,

Castro reverted to his initial policy of autonomously seeking the closest links possible with the neutral and non-aligned states that, one year previously, he had castigated as "opportunistic" and "cowardly" for attempting to play Moscow against Washington. The reason for this *volte-face* was evident: the Soviet-American accords over Cuba had "sanctuarized" the island, making Moscow directly responsible for Havana's conduct, a situation Fidel Castro decided to reject.

One of the most far-reaching consequences of the Soviets' decision to admit Cuba into the Communist bloc and to set up missile bases there was the island's transformation into a powerful military installation. When the crisis ended, Cuba had some 30,000 Soviet military personnel on its soil (most were removed by 1963). Its armed forces (FAR) were rapidly rising toward the peak level of 300,000 men they would attain in the mid-1960s.[52] By early 1964, Washington had to concede that the FAR constituted the most powerful and modern military force in Latin America,[53] and that Cuba was a formidable small power. Although deprived of nuclear missiles and heavy bombers, Havana had been bountifully provided with the most sophisticated weapons systems of any Third World country, along with the technicians to instruct Cubans in their maintenance and use.

Cuba's problem of national security had been resolved by the non-interference pledge extracted from Kennedy during the crisis, although CIA-inspired assassination plots and sabotage still continued. Coupled to immunity from external attack, the enormous power of its armed forces enabled Cuba to pursue its long-standing goals by military means. Not only would military considerations dominate Havana's foreign policy but they would also characterize Castro's attempts to gain an extra-national and extra-hemispheric foothold. The militarization of Cuban society, already part of the messianic role Castro had assigned both to himself and the Revolution, was the precursor of Cuba's interventionist approach.[54]

For Castro, the October crisis had "provided the object lesson that Cuba was after all only a pawn in the global chess game between East and West, that to protect her sovereignty she must look outside the great power blocs for alliances."[55] The relevance of the tricontinental strategy outlined two years before by Walterio Carbonell would now become apparent and, in the long run, become the core of Cuban foreign policy. So, while the October crisis ended Cuba's quest for national security, it inaugurated her more enduring quest for political equality with the big powers of the world.

PART THREE

THE PLUNGE INTO AFRICA

10 SUPERPOWER POLITICS AND CASTRO'S "THIRD FORCE"

October 1962 went down in history as the date of the Missile Crisis: two unbearable weeks when most of mankind cowered under the prospect of planetary suicide. At the very threshold, the metallic voices of threats, counter-threats, quieted down. Humankind had retreated from its first walk ever to the precipice. Castroite Cuba had acted as a catalyst for that unparalleled moment of world reckoning. Were it only for such a gruesome achievement, Fidel Castro, the dauntless political strategist, still would have secured his own niche in twentieth century history.

As it was, the solution to the October crisis implied trampling on Cuban sovereignty. The bruises to Cuba's national ego notwithstanding, Castro's brand-new Marxist-Leninist regime had emerged a clear winner from a confrontation which sanctioned its existence. The island's diminutive size and proximity to a neighboring superpower, once sources of deep concern for the Revolution's leaders, were transformed into assets.

Little Cuba had become the only state to force herself into the Communist bloc, despite and against the better judgment of the Kremlin; the only regime to proclaim itself Marxist-Leninist while disregarding a local Communist party and even supplanting it; the only Marxist state wherein the legitimacy of power lay not in institutions such as a Communist party, politburo, central committee, national assembly, or constitution, but in the person of an uncontested supreme leader.

Little Cuba's uniqueness extended to being the only Marxist regime in the western hemisphere, and the only Soviet bloc member to belong to the non-aligned movement. Her exceptional position made Cuba the only Communist state the USSR could neither pressure nor intimidate without risking the alienation of the Third World or an even greater split within the ranks of international communism. Havana was, therefore, the only Communist capital in a position to proclaim its neutrality in the Sino-Soviet schism while continuing to enjoy the full benefits of a clientele relationship with the USSR and of "ideological" courtship with Peking.

Now immune from American invasion, Little Cuba had become the only Communist state capable of defying the U.S. with total impunity. Washington could no longer unleash its full fury against Cuba without risking a major superpower conflagration or the universal condemnation of the Third World. World opinion, Soviet missiles, and Washington's pledge of non-interference combined to form a virtually impenetrable shield behind which the "sanctuarized" Castro government could maneuver. America's demonstrations of hostility were reduced thereafter to botched-up assassination attempts and the ineffectual infiltration of saboteurs.

Little Cuba had shown its willingness to play the game of brinksmanship to the fullest possible extent. Castro's moral and political ascendancy over the Third World had become incontestable as was evidenced by his open, unsanctioned breaches of the non-aligned code of conduct: a de facto military alliance with a superpower; the acceptance, by invitation or concession, of the installation of foreign military bases, nuclear weapons, and foreign troops on her soil; and the loud proclamation of her ideological alignment with a superpower in the Cold War. By overlooking such inconsistent conduct on the part of a member of the non-aligned bloc, the founders of that movement opened the doors wide for the concept of "non-aligned alignment." Championed by Havana at the first non-aligned summit in Belgrade, this sophism seriously impaired what had been effectively developing into an international third force.

Cuba as the Example

As Castro's fourth year in power drew to a close, Cuba enjoyed a truly unique position in the world at large. There was indeed a cause for the Caudillo to regard his work as the unfolding of the "mission" he obliquely spoke of during his guerrilla experience. More than likely, Castro regarded the Marxist Sparta he had created as being the lightning and thunderbolt of history. If anything, his conversion to an ideology predicated upon determinism had provided fertile ground for his messianic proclivities. Cuba's daring foreign policy would now be rationalized in terms of historical laws according to Marxist doctrine.

As an astute analyst of Cuban affairs has observed, Fidel Castro "has always had sufficiently strong and genuine messianic convictions to which he could attribute . . . his political behavior."[1] That he would consequently seek "to make Cuba the Sierra Maestra of the globe and the Cuban Revolution its guerrilla foco" is understandable.[2] However, just as the revolutionary struggle in Cuba was Castro's means of achieving a greater ambition—the conquest of political power—his efforts to widen the front line of struggle against Yankee imperialism would also be in Havana's geopolitical interests.

"Of course we engage in subversion, the training of guerrillas, propaganda! Why not? This is exactly what you are doing to us," explained Castro to an American journalist in November 1963.[3] The exportation of the Revolution was thus a tactical weapon. "With his aim fixed on reaching an agreement with the United States, Cuban subversion in Latin America, he hoped, would give him bargaining power. . . . It would be another powerful element of pressure with which to exact concessions. In other words . . . the export of subversion was something he was prepared to give up—for a price."[4]

The policy of exporting the Revolution was the product of Cuba's accurate assessment of the very narrow margin for maneuver it enjoyed between the superpowers. While Washington and Moscow were continually improving their entente, there was no end in sight to American hostility towards Cuba. That situation was perceived by the Cuban leadership as quite unfair. Castro complained, "The United States continue the Cold War with us whereas they better their relations with the Soviet Union. . . . Cuba simply seeks to entertain with the United States the same relations that the latter entertain with the rest of the Socialist camp."[5]

In order to be treated as an equal by the U.S., the USSR, and the other world powers, Cuba would have to convert its liabilities as a small, sparsely populated, and as yet underdeveloped country into psychological and political assets.[6] The Castroite leadership could take optimum advantage of Cuba's geographic, economic, and demographic limitations by setting itself up as the unique model for guiding the revolutionary destiny of the "underdeveloped" world, while proclaiming itself a "third force" within the Communist world (ibid.). Cuba could thereby create for itself a tricontinental role—one in which both Russia and China would be denied much say—that would establish the Castroite regime as the leading force in the Third World.

Upon assuming power, Castro declared that the Cuban revolution was destined to "take its place as one of the greatest political events in history."[7] His statement betrayed another well-anchored conviction: those Third World leaders who adopted the Cuban model were guaranteed success. The Cuban leadership tirelessly drove home the point that "the Cuban example will be imitated."[8] In fact, Castro himself asked the Cuban nation to pledge that it would uphold Cuba as "the example that will turn the Andes into the Sierra Maestra of the American continent."[9] In 1963, Ché Guevara declared, "We are a showcase, a mirror in which the peoples of America look at themselves."[10] Even that geographic limitation soon began to fade, however. "Cuba," asserted Oscar Pinos Santos, "stands as an example for *all* peoples of the world, especially those in Latin America. Although territorially and demographically small, Cuba symbolizes the way that will most certainly be followed by the peoples of Latin America. . . . Little Cuba is today the guide of the Americas."[11] Not only does 1963 stand out as a year when Cuba's economic, political, and ideological guidelines were being redefined, but also as the critical period during which the influence of the Cuban model was restyled as "internationalist." The more defined the policy of exporting the Revolution became, the wider grew the sphere in which the Cuban model was deemed applicable. Castro described his nation's new status thus: "What is Cuba? Cuba is the example. Cuba is the idea. . . . And since when can ideas be isolated?"[12]

Castro's definition of the Cuban model as the "idea," the intellectual force for revolution in the Third World, was consistent with the elitist and messianic nature of Castroism. The leadership of Cuba seemed to have begun projecting itself as the vanguard of a backward Third World. "Our country," stated Castro, "is of course not a nuclear power, but it is a moral power."[13] Cuba, and Cuba alone, was the only valid model for the peoples of that zone to follow. Castro declared this repeatedly: "We are the first Socialist revolution of this continent. The first and we're proud of it! We are the vanguard of this continent. . . . We are, and will continue to be the example."[14] By representing Cuba as "a moral power," the "idea," and "the example," Havana was subtly declaring the Third World off limits to the two warring giants of the Communist bloc. This claim would later clash irremediably with the assertions of Cuba's foremost rival for the allegiance of the Afro-Asian bloc, the People's Republic of China.

Playing Chess With the Soviets

The Kremlin's retreat during the missile crisis of October 1962 resulted in still greater bargaining power for Havana vis-à-vis the Soviet Union. A "betrayed" Castro could extort concessions while enjoying the privileges of subsidized political autonomy and ideological dilettantism. The Kremlin could not abandon "little Cuba" without incurring the enduring enmity of the Third World and validating Chinese charges that the Soviets were traitors and capitulationists. The USSR was therefore forced to adopt a single, grudging attitude towards the redoubtable Caribbean island: support, support, and more support, no matter what the cost. Conscious of his advantage, Castro undertook to exploit Cuba's unique position to the fullest.

At the beginning of 1963, the Soviets were openly attempting to expel Peking from the ranks of the international Communist movement and to ostracize China from the Third World. Fidel Castro served notice that he would remain neutral in the Sino-Soviet quarrel. Casting himself more and more in the role of arbiter, Castro asserted that "unity should prevail" at all costs within the Socialist community.[15] In a much-publicized interview with Claude Julien of *Le Monde*, published in March 1963, the Cuban leader severely criticized Soviet Premier Nikita Khrushchev's behavior during the October crisis, stating that the USSR should not have removed the missiles without consulting Havana. Castro affirmed that Cuba did not want to be "a pawn on the world's chessboard," and daringly asserted, "The Chinese are right in saying one should not yield to imperialism."[16] Never before had the Cuban leader expressed open support for Peking's ideological position against the USSR. Presumably, his statement was primarily motivated by opportunism.

Within a month of the publication of his statement to *Le Monde*, Castro was in Moscow for a month-long maiden official visit, showering lavish praises upon the Soviet Union.[17] The Kremlin had obviously acceded to his demands and agreed to stretch its military and financial largesse even further. "Were it not for the Soviet Union," said Castro at a Red Square rally, "the imperialists would not hesitate to launch a direct attack on our country" (ibid.). Now absolving Moscow for its capitulation in the October crisis, he asserted that "it was precisely the might of the Soviet Union and the entire Socialist camp that deterred an imperialist aggression against our homeland" (ibid.). Upon returning home, Castro announced a wide range of bilateral agreements on trade, military, and technical assistance, which could make Cuba look hopefully towards the future.[18] A few months later, he confidently announced that by 1970 Cuba would produce a record ten million tons of sugar.[19]

In January 1964, Castro returned to Moscow to sign a still broader range of agreements.[20] He was even more lavish in his demonstrations of gratitude, friendship, and loyalty to the Kremlin on this occasion.[21] All references to China, even of the "neutral" variety, had disappeared. The fact that the Cuban premier had not even attempted to follow his lengthy stays in the USSR with a visit to the People's Republic of China spoke loudly enough about the nature of Havana's "neutrality" in the conflict ravaging the Communist bloc. It was clear—at least to the Chinese—that, while being solidly aligned with its Russian patron, Havana was keeping the Chinese option open in order to extort the maximum concessions from the Kremlin. It didn't take much time for Chinese officials to privately confide that Castro was merely an "opportunist."[22]

Castro's two visits to the USSR were closely related to Havana's decision to shelve its ambitious industrialization program, to rely heavily on sugar and agricultural diversification, and to depend even more on massive Soviet aid.[23] The Sino-Soviet conflict "favored Cuba in that it increased her capacity to negotiate with the USSR. Its existence was one of the political considerations which . . . influenced the Soviet decision to assist Cuban industrialization and to enter into a long-term sugar agreement."[24] This did not mean that all was well between Moscow and Havana. On the contrary, the broad Soviet concessions encouraged Castro further along the independent path that he had already chosen. In August 1964, Havana refused to sign the treaty banning atmospheric nuclear tests. Tension between the USSR and Cuba would mount in direct proportion to the increase in Soviet aid. It was during this period, while the Soviet Union was doing its best to satisfy all of Castro's demands, that Havana was planning an ambitious militaristic foreign policy based on exporting the Revolution to Latin America and even Africa.

The Soviet-American agreements on Cuba arising from the October crisis had turned the USSR into a sort of watchdog over Cuba. Although it secured military immunity for the Castroite regime, that arrangement threatened the political and ideological autonomy that Castro was bent on preserving. Whereas Khrushchev lost no occasion to express the "total solidarity" of the USSR with Cuba and to caution that "Soviet rockets can reach American territory in thirty minutes,"[25] Havana was determined to use its military immunity, both to escape Soviet control and to secure an independent entente with the United States. This goal had to be met while Cuba was still a political and military asset for the USSR in the Soviets' relations with the U.S., China, and the Third World. The maximum time limit for Cuba's realization of such an ambitious objective was set by Soviet Premier Khrushchev himself in early November, when he publicly declared, "We will give the capitalist countries seven years at maximum, and within seven years we will become the first country" (ibid.). There is ample reason to believe that during his first two visits to the USSR, Castro was apprised by Khrushchev of the Kremlin's intention to launch an all-out drive to turn the Soviet Union into the foremost military superpower by 1969 at the latest. The Soviet leader must have realized that such an assurance would deter Cuba from throwing in its lot with pre-nuclear China. On the other hand, there was the implicit prospect, at least inferred by Castro, that Cuba would lose its strategic value once the USSR had achieved strategic parity with, or superiority over, the United States.

But the event that would permanently set Castro on his chosen tactical path was the 1963 assassination of John F. Kennedy. Since Castro's first trip to the USSR early that year, Havana had sent out earnest probes to Washington. Just before leaving for Moscow, Castro had secretly suggested Switzerland as the location for Cuban-American negotiations to arrive at a modus vivendi.[26] That summer, both countries had actually seemed ready to take decisive steps in that direction.[27] In a major concession, Castro announced that he was ready to compensate Americans whose holdings in Cuba had been nationalized (ibid., 143).[28] By September, William Attwood, a member of the American delegation to the U.N., was already meeting secretly with Cuba's envoy, Carlos Lechuga, at Havana's request.[29] President Kennedy had begun to seriously reconsider Washington's Cuban policy and to lend credence to Castro's declarations of good intent.[30] In fact, the Cuban premier had begun to make it clear that, except for his ties to the USSR and Cuba's ideological option, everything else was negotiable, including his new policy of exporting the Revolution.[31]

As Kennedy's assassination had come at a moment when Washington was seriously considering a rapprochement, Castro was understandably upset by it. Speaking to the Cuban nation, he said: "[W]e Cubans, as Latins and Hispanic-Americans, are a people forged in a mixture of races but enjoying a common outlook. Hence, before death—even that of an enemy—our belligerence comes to a halt."[32] Kennedy's assassination, he said, was the work of racist elements. "Inside the United States there are very reactionary currents, racist currents; that is, currents which run counter to the demands for the social and civil rights of the black population: people of the Ku Klux Klan, people who lynch, exterminate, use dogs, and ferociously hate the black citizens of the United States" (ibid., 7–8).

The Interventionist Rationale

Castro forcefully renewed his overtures with Kennedy's successor, asking for Spanish caudillo Francisco Franco's mediation.[33] In an ultimate concession, Havana let it be known that it was ready to "abandon all attempts at subversion in Latin America," provided Washington and its allies would agree to a reciprocal gesture towards Cuba (ibid., 161). But the new administration of Lyndon B. Johnson turned a deaf ear to all of Castro's overtures, shelved Kennedy's accommodationist plans, and reestablished the status quo ante (ibid., 163–170).

The Johnson administration had immediately exhibited its anti-Castro credentials: new raids against the island by exile forces; attempts by the CIA to assassinate Cuban officials (Castro being the prime target); tightening of trade sanctions against Cuba; provocative violations of Cuba's airspace; and utilization of the Guantanamo base for all sorts of harassments (ibid., 152-156). In July 1965, the U.S. prompted the OAS to vote for even more stringent measures for isolating the "red" island and letting it "brew in its own stew." That seemed the essence of the "Johnson Doctrine." Washington calculatedly ignored, or rebuffed, all of Fidel Castro's conciliatory overtures (ibid., 160–163).

Johnson's subsequent election as president in November 1964 (two months after he had unleashed the full force of America's B-52 strategic bombers against North Vietnam) was therefore an ominous sign for Havana. Further, a CIA-promoted coup in Brazil had overthrown the government of Joao Goulart, leaving Mexico as the last of Cuba's friends in the hemisphere. The sudden American invasion of the Dominican Republic in 1965 added to Castro's alarm: it was the first landing of U.S. Marines in Latin America in over thirty years. By July 1965, Fidel Castro had drawn an inescapable conclusion: American-Cuban relations would remain at a hostile impasse for the foreseeable future.

A policy of exporting the Revolution to Latin America seemed the only means left to Cuba for pressuring Washington. Havana's strategic reasoning was simple: if Cuba could light enough brushfires in the Third World, then the U.S., by exhausting itself in an attempt to extinguish them, would be in a weak enough position to negotiate coexistence on Castro's terms. It is hard to refute Blanca Tórres Ramirez's interpretation of the goals Havana pursued through this policy. "As a consequence of the October crisis," she explained,

"Cuban leaders became acutely aware of their precarious situation. The Soviet Union was not ready to risk a war with the United States in Cuba's defense. There was therefore no country which could militarily guarantee [Cuba's] territorial integrity. Alliance with Third World countries and seizing the leadership of the Latin American Communist movement were means of confronting the U.S. with a unified movement. Such a union would have two goals, one military and the other peaceful. The military aspect was to create many armed fronts in order to weaken and divide the forces of the United States. This would have the effect of easing the strain on an isolated Cuba by forcing U.S. attention onto other regions. . . . The peaceful goal was to secure the support of world opinion. For if Cuba was the focus of world attention it would make it all the more difficult for the U.S. to risk its prestige in a direct intervention against that country."[34]

Activism in Latin America and elsewhere also helped to whet domestic Cuban enthusiasm which could further stimulate productivity and help sustain a high level of political commitment towards the regime (ibid., 91).[35] As Edward Gonzalez notes, Castro's combative posture abroad has never stemmed from purely ideological motives: "To the contrary, Fidel is vitally concerned with disparities in world power relationships, and he employs various leverage strategies as the principal means by which to obtain security, economic development, and global influence for his small and vulnerable island."[36]

Cuba's "big push" in Latin America, begun in 1964, was most definitely related to its own national security concerns. In a speech marking the end of Cuba's first week of solidarity with Vietnam, Ché Guevara declared, "The forces that one day will come to repress our own guerrillas throughout the American continent are being trained in South Vietnam. . . . At this moment, South Vietnam is the great laboratory of Yankee imperialism for preparing all of its equipment for a contest which, once begun, may even be of greater importance since it would take place in their very colonial backyard, the American continent."[37] Some months later, calling the U.S. the "chief enemy of mankind," Fidel Castro stated, "The enemy is threatening us and will continue to do so for some time to come . . . [and is] attacking other peoples, as is criminally the case with the people of North Vietnam and also the revolutionary people of South Vietnam."[38] The U.S., he said, "intervenes in the Congo . . . sends its warships, its marines, its aircraft to any place in the world" (ibid.). Therefore, he concluded, "it will be necessary to cut off the hands of these imperialists somewhere in the world, *whether in Vietnam or somewhere else!''* (Italics added.) (ibid., 355).

Both Ché Guevara and Fidel Castro were fully cognizant, as Guevara himself reportedly said, that "the stability of the Cuban regime depended, to a great extent, on the worldwide interplay of forces, in which Cuba could not change a thing without the risk of national suicide."[39] Hence, the strategy of all-around confrontation and overseas interventionism in which Havana was progressively engaging was suicidal in appearance only. The real shortcut to national suicide, as seen by Castro, Guevara, and the top ranks of the Cuban leadership, was confinement of the Revolution to Cuba's shores.[40] It was to precisely such a fate that Soviet leaders were inviting the Castroites by encouraging "peaceful coexistence."

The "Cuban Model" Gains Tricontinental Status

French journalist Claude Julien wrote in 1961 that the Cuban revolution was the "prototype" of the social and political transformations that would take place in Asia and Africa in the decades to come.[41] By 1965 the Castroite leadership was so thoroughly convinced of this that it could announce its tricontinental vocation in most explicit language, contrasting with the precautions formerly observed.[42] Opening the year 1965 with a speech on January 2, Fidel Castro proclaimed that Cuba "has *the right to serve as the example* to all small countries of the world and to all underdeveloped peoples of the world dominated by imperialism and colonialism *wherever they may be''* (Italics added.).[43]

Havana's universalization of the Cuban model as exemplary for all Third World peoples went hand in hand with turning its chief opponent, Yankee imperialism, into the universal enemy. American imperialism, Castro declared on April 19, was the chief foe of the peoples of Asia, Africa, and Latin America, and consequently all forces should be marshaled against it.[44] It followed that if Cuba's chief enemy was also the major enemy of everyone else, then Cuba's "internationalist" actions overseas could be legitimized as acts of solidarity. In his 1965 May Day speech, Premier Castro not only denounced the aggressive actions of American imperialism in the Congo, but also hinted at his regime's willingness to aid the Vietnamese.[45] Two months later, on July 26, the Máximo Lider took another step by proclaiming Cuba to be "the principal foxhole in the battle against imperialism."[46] Castro explained that, if several countries simultaneously engaged the U.S. in battle in various parts of the globe, "they wouldn't have enough airplanes and troops to crush the revolution in Asia, Africa and Latin America all at the same time. . . . To stifle that kind of revolution they would have to repress two-thirds of the planet's people" (ibid.). In Latin America alone, he declared, American troops "will be forced one day to intervene all over this continent. They will then perish in its mountains, its plains, its rivers and cities" (ibid.). As for Cuba, Castro would say some months later, "we want no type of peace whatsoever with imperialism! As long as imperialism exists . . . and there are people fighting against it, their cause will be ours in whichever corner of the world that may be!"[47]

As the front line of the struggle against imperialism—which to Havana was essentially American—Cuba naturally stood as the trailblazer for the rest of the Third World. It is true, admitted Castro, "that with or without Cuba the revolution in Africa and Asia . . . and Latin America is inevitable."[48] However, he added, "it goes without saying that the Cuban revolution served to stimulate that revolutionary process and stood as its example in the first place" (ibid.). The world situation compelled little Cuba to take giant steps in international relations and to open up the way for the rest of the Third World. "This country . . . will serve as the example for others who resemble us, an example in the struggle against imperialism, an example in solving economic as well as social problems. . . . Our country . . . is called upon to play an important moral role in the contemporary world" (ibid.). In Havana's coded language, to play a leading "moral role" in the world was synonymous with the military intervention of Cuban forces abroad. Not surprisingly, Raúl Castro Ruz, Cuba's minister of defense, would gloat: "We have created an army that is stronger than all of the armies of Latin America put together."[49]

Rhetoric designed for internal consumption aside, Havana was most certainly aware of the limits of its margin of maneuverability in Asia, where it could play no more than an active diplomatic role. It was not geographic distance that imposed such a constraint. To begin with, Asia was culturally out of reach. It was also rife with bona fide Communist and/or "progressive" states aspiring to play supranational roles of their own, both in Asia and abroad. Four Asian countries were long-standing members of the Communist bloc (China, Mongolia, North Korea, and North Vietnam). All of the national liberation movements in the area were led by recognized Communist parties.

Regimes like Ahmed Sukarno's in Indonesia, Norodom Sihanouk's in Cambodia, Ne Win's in Burma, Jawaharlal Nehru's in India, and

Sirimavo Bandaranaike's in Ceylon (now Sri Lanka), were vigorously opposed to western colonialism and imperialism. They generally sided with the Communist bloc on all major international issues. Sukarno's Indonesia was the most vociferously anti-imperialist and virulently anti-American. In early January 1965, Djakarta had announced its withdrawal from the U.N. to protest against the policies of western imperialism.

Moving into China's Backyard

Cuba's Minister of Education Armando Hart Davalos appeared in Djakarta in May 1965 at the head of an important delegation. The subject of his discussions with Bung Karno was scarcely related to educational programs. The Indonesian chief was busy promoting a world conference of what he termed the "New Emergent Forces" (CONEFO), to be held in Djakarta in 1966. Fidel Castro wanted to persuade Bung Karno to merge his project with Havana's tricontinental conference, slated for early 1966. The Cuban minister, a man known to be close to the Castro brothers, pleaded against a dispersal of forces and argued in favor of a unified and global response to "the bombings against the cities of the Democratic Republic of Vietnam and the dropping of paratroopers . . . in the Congo."[50] The American imperialists, said Hart, "are accusing us Cubans of engaging in extracontinental penetration on the American continent, whereas they are trying to impose their criteria on other continents by means of force" (ibid.).

Havana considered North Vietnam, North Korea, and the NLF of South Vietnam as its most potentially reliable allies in Asia. Like Cuba, North Vietnam and North Korea were small Communist states, fiercely jealous of their ideological and political independence, and all were engaged in direct confrontation with the United States. Havana, Hanoi, Pyongyang, and the NLF were also anxious to avoid taking sides in the Sino-Soviet quarrel while receiving assistance from both. "None of the three countries," observed Daniel Tretiak, "has been satisfied with the kind of leadership offered by either the Soviet Union or China."[51] Furthermore, Cuba, North Vietnam, and North Korea were decidedly "more willing to take higher risks to expand the boundaries of the Communist system than the USSR or even China. By supporting one another, however, they hope to keep the major powers from interfering excessively in the affairs of the smaller party-states, and they also hope to influence the major powers to provide them with more aid and support" (ibid.). There was ample common ground for a Havana-Hanoi-Pyongyang axis that could strengthen Cuba's bid to become a third force in the Communist world.

In Cuba's relations with its three Asian Communist allies, Havana had the upper hand. At one point, in fact, Havana's opinion carried more weight with them than the sententious, militant pronouncements of Communist China, or the empty proletarian rhetoric of the USSR. Neither Hanoi, Pyongyang, nor the NLF enjoyed the glamour that the Castroite leadership had for the Third World. Despite their long-standing membership in the Communist bloc, orthodox Marxist states like North Vietnam and North Korea also lacked the type of immunity from direct U.S. military aggression that Cuba enjoyed. The most recent and in fact least orthodox member of the Soviet bloc, little Cuba could defy the military might of Yankee imperialism with relative impunity. North Korea had paid heavily in the early fifties for defying that power. In 1965 it was still in constant danger of having its cities, countryside, and industries demolished by the type of devastating raids American strategic bombers were inflicting on North Vietnam.

It was no surprise that, as of 1965, Cuban delegations of all sorts would pay militant solidarity visits to Havana's Asian Communist allies. To dramatize the strength of the Havana-Hanoi-Pyongyang axis, in 1966, a delegation of the highest possible rank, led by President Osvaldo Dorticós Torrado, Minister of Defense Raúl Castro Ruz, and Chief of the General Staff of the Revolutionary Armed Forces Sergio del Valle Jiménez, paid a much-publicized visit to North Vietnam and North Korea and held important talks with the leadership of the NLF of South Vietnam. Characteristic of the entente was the joint communique published in Pyongyang stating "the struggle against American imperialism is at present the principal international obligation of the progressive peoples of the entire world," and that the strategy to be followed was to "harass American imperialism on all points of the globe, on all fronts where it attacks."[52] It is not surprising that Cuba became the first country in the world to recognize the NLF Provisional Revolutionary Government of South Vietnam and to send a full-fledged ambassador, Raúl Valdés Vivo, there in 1970.[53]

The undoubted sincerity of Cuba's condemnations of U.S. aggression in Southeast Asia and the Korean peninsula and proclamations of unswerving solidarity with the Asian liberation movement did not preclude self-serving intentions. At the peak of Cuba's intensive diplomatic activism in Asia, the Castroite leadership paid hardly any attention to Mongolia, a staunch Soviet ally-protectorate, or to the half-dozen pro-Chinese guerrilla movements and Communist parties in Thailand, Burma, the Philippines, Laos, the Malay Peninsula, and Indonesia. By closely adhering to North Korea, North Vietnam, and the NLF while working towards an informal political alliance with the "progressive" regimes of Asia, Havana was securing allies for itself right in China's backyard. The tactical value of the approach was far from negligible at a time of growing competition between Cuba and Peking in Africa, where pro-Chinese sentiments were at a record high, as well as in South America, where pro-Chinese splinter Communist parties were proliferating and becoming an irritant to local Castroite guerrilla movements. Havana was already preparing favorable terrain for the inevitable moment of reckoning with Peking on the issue of mastery over the Third World. With the friends and allies it secured in Asia, little Cuba could cut gigantic China down to size, when the time came, with the same impunity with which it had already tongue-lashed the USSR.[54]

Cuban Expansion Overseas: A Necessity

On March 6, 1965, Moscow was the scene of an angry Afro-Asian student demonstration that did much to discredit the USSR in the eyes of the colored nations it was attempting to woo.[55] The first successful lunar landing by a U.S. spacecraft on March 24—a feat that seemed to confirm the technological superiority of the U.S.—did not boost Moscow's image either. Nor did the whirlwind official visit that Chinese Premier Chou En-lai paid to the African continent in early June. The fact that the Chinese premier concentrated his attention on Tanzania was significant. Like Cuba, Peking was embroiled in the Congo, providing political and military aid to the pro-Chinese faction of the insurgent movement, led by Laurent Kabila in the Kivu area and Pierre Mulele in the Kwilu region.

Sino-Cuban competition in Africa for the favors of the national liberation movements and "progressive" regimes there was an open secret by 1965. In a thinly veiled attack on China, Fidel Castro stated on January 2 that the Cuban leadership would not substitute the intelligence or the heroism of any other Communist party for its own.[56] On March 13 he went even further, stating that while imperialism was intervening in the Congo and attacking Vietnam, the split within the Communist bloc was dangerous "for us, small countries that do not base ourselves on the strength of armies of millions of men, or on the strength of atomic power."[57] Castro then declared: "Division in the face of the enemy was never a correct strategy, it was never a revolutionary, was never an intelligent strategy!" (ibid., 172).

Deprecating the Sino-Soviet dispute as "Byzantine disagreements and academic charlatanry," Castro warned that he hoped neither of the two Communist giants would underestimate Cuba because of its small size (ibid., 176). Yankee imperialism, he said, "has committed great, colossal errors of underestimation in respect of our revolutionary people. It would be regrettable if others committed similar errors. . . . [W]e are not and will never be satellites of anyone" (ibid., 175). Cuba harbored no other ambition than to selflessly assist the liberation of the world's peoples, said Castro, "because we are a small country that does not aspire to become the navel of the world; because we are a small country that does not aspire to become the revolutionary center of the world" (ibid., 173).

Yet, it was precisely because his regime was desperately seeking to establish its hegemony over the international Communist movement and over the Third World as a whole that Castro had embarked on a policy of all-around confrontation and the exportation of the Revolution to Latin America. By giving lessons on revolutionary conduct to the two giants of international communism while disdainfully belittling their rivalry, Castro was attempting to establish "little Cuba" as the true guardian of the revolutionary faith and exemplar of internationalism, even within the Communist bloc. Thus, when Ché Guevara told the Afro-Asian Seminar that "there are no frontiers in the fight to the death" against imperialism and that consequently, Cuba "cannot remain indifferent to what goes on in any part of the globe," he was stating much more than an ideology.[58] "The enaction of proletarian internationalism," Ché added, "is not only a duty of struggling peoples . . . but equally an inescapable necessity" (ibid.).

It was indeed essential for Cuba to break out of the political ghetto to which Washington had confined it as well as to escape the heavy shackles of economic dependence which tied it to Moscow. To do so without being deprived of Moscow's military protection or bowing to Washington's dictates, the Castroite regime had only one recourse, which it was more than predisposed to take: the simultaneous exportation of the "Cuban model" to Latin America and black Africa, the only two zones where, for geopolitical and ethno-cultural reasons, Cuba could expect to exert an influence disproportionate to its size, resources, or military might.

11 USING ETHNICITY AS A BRIDGE TO AFRICA

Havana and Peking viewed one another as potential rivals from the start. Reciprocal utilitarianism had appeared to be the chief trademark of their relations. At war with the USSR for leadership of the world Communist movement and the Third World, Peking sought to associate itself closely with Cuba. The Cuban revolution was the most prestigious revolutionary event that had as yet taken place in the developing world. Association with Cuba could be used as an ideological weapon against the Soviet Union. At war with the U.S., the Castroite regime needed a strong lever to force the USSR into a permanent commitment that would not only guarantee Cuba's economic survival, but also provide the military wherewithal for Havana's pursuit of its goals.

Cuba and China shared identical ambitions for leadership of the Third World. They were therefore bound to establish a relationship based more on rivalry than pragmatic partnership. Moreover, the similarity of some of the primary Maoist and Castroite positions on modern revolutionary politics would oblige Peking to emphasize greatly its theoretical preeminence over the Cuban upstart. For its part, Havana would be forced to prove that it was not merely mouthing or arrogating Maoist formulas.

Castro never showed any inclination or desire to embroil himself in an unprofitable alliance with China, which could deliver neither the type nor the quantity of economic and military goods that Havana required. The strong personal prejudice Castro reportedly harbored against the Chinese as a people may have played no small part in quickly exacerbating beyond all proportion the frictions that had begun to be noticeable in Sino-Cuban relations from the end of 1963. Relations with China cooled increasingly the more it became clear that Havana intended to set itself up as the guardian of revolutionary conduct in the Third World, and as a sort of ideological and political third force. Moreover, Peking had openly called for a decisive split within the world's Communist party precisely at a time when Castro was doing his best to bring the whole of the Marxist movement in Latin America under his aegis. To Peking's anger and discomfiture, Castro denounced as "fractious" the pro-Chinese factions that had broken off from the major Latin American Communist parties in order to set themselves up as the only authentic Marxist-Leninist movements. They were rigorously excluded from the secret meeting of Latin American Communist parties that convened in Havana in November 1964 at Castro's behest.[1]

The fact that Castro barred the Latin American disciples of Mao Tse-tung from the first meeting of Marxist parties to be held in the hemisphere since 1929 was ample indication of what Havana thought of Maoism at that time. Holding the meeting under the aegis of the Cuban Communist party was in itself a partial validation of Havana's self-proclaimed leadership over the Marxist and non-Marxist revolutionary movements in the hemisphere, and the Castroite leaders could not but be "very satisfied with the regional leadership conferred on them by coordinating such a meeting in Havana."[2] Still more vexing to the Chinese was the fact that they were implicitly denounced in the final communiqué of the conference, which not only called for unity within the ranks of the Communist movement (a rejection of the Chinese call for a split between "true" and "false" Marxists), but also bluntly stated that "whatever factional activity, whatever its source or nature, must be categorically condemned."[3] The slap could not have been more resounding.

Why would Castro deliberately antagonize the Chinese at a time when he had embarked on a policy of confrontation with the U.S. and political belligerency with the Soviet Union?[4]

Africa's View of the Sino-Soviet Split

Both in Africa and Asia, the Chinese could count on real support from those who empathized with an underdeveloped, colored country formerly victimized by the western powers and presently being attacked by the white Soviet Union. Well aware of the ethnic underpinnings of the sympathy it could depend on in the Afro-Asian world, the Chinese leadership began shifting its propaganda war against the Soviet Union from the ideological onto ethnic and cultural terrain. Peking's task was greatly facilitated by the Soviets' openly racist postures and practices. (Strobe Talbott notes, "The hatred between the Soviets and the Chinese seems deep-rooted and irreconcilable. Each truly hates the other. The Russians' animus, at least in part, stems from unreconstructed racism—'We white men must stick together' is a common theme voiced by Soviets in private conversations with Americans. . . . The Soviets try to camouflage their dislike as an ideological dispute but it is really visceral."]⁵

Basking in the success of his policy of "peaceful coexistence" on his first state visit to France in 1960, Nikita Khrushchev greeted General Charles de Gaulle with the surprising statement, "Both you and I are whites."⁶ That statement seemed to lend credence to the view expressed by General David M. Shoup, commander of the U.S. Marines, that "fear that a nuclear war between the U.S.A. and the USSR might mean the end of the white race" had prompted the Kremlin and the West to seek detente.⁷

Racial disorders erupted in the Soviet Union, provoked by the fatal stabbing in December 1963 of a Ghanaian medical student by a Russian who opposed interracial dating.⁸ This revived the furor caused earlier that year when the Soviet ambassador to Guinea tried to kidnap Svetlana Oklaova, a Soviet math teacher, to prevent her from marrying a Haitian writer who also worked in Guinea.⁹ The latter incident prompted President Sékou Touré to call in the Soviet ambassador and deliver a stern warning.¹⁰ In 1966, Kenyan students at Baku, in Azerbaijan on the Caspian Sea, went on strike and camped out at the railway station in protest at their treatment and the killing of a Ghanaian student who reportedly had been dating a Soviet colleague despite several racist threats. Their spokesman claimed that Russians had "shown themselves contemptuous of Africans, that in restaurants waiters had refused to serve them, that they had been forbidden to dance with white women in the town, and that several of them had been ambushed and attacked by Russian gangs with sticks and clubs."¹¹

Such incidents were highly embarrassing to the Kremlin. They appeared to confirm reports, long circulating in the non-aligned world and eagerly seized by the West, that color prejudice was common in the homeland of socialism. If such matters had been confined to the USSR, they might have been attributed to a national idiosyncracy; however, the record of incidents, not only in the Soviet Union but in Bulgaria, Czechoslovakia, Poland, and Romania demonstrated the contrary.¹²

The racially based ill-treatment of Africans in the Eastern European Communist countries had incalculably damaging results for the USSR and its allies.¹³ Kwame Nkrumah was among the most appalled of the African leaders, as at least three Ghanaian students had met violent deaths in such circumstances.¹⁴ At one point, he seems to have contemplated withdrawing his nation's students from the USSR altogether (ibid.). Moreover, Ghana's first president was in possession of a document that proved beyond a doubt that Blacks were oppressed within the Soviet borders. A petition by black Soviet citizens is said to have been handed to Nkrumah by Dr. W. E. B. Du Bois, who had visited the USSR in 1959. The petitioners reportedly requested permission to emigrate to Ghana in order to escape racial persecution in the USSR, while asking Nkrumah to intercede with the Soviet government on their behalf (ibid.).[15]

As for Sékou Touré, already sensitive to the ill-treatment of Guinean students—the first to have gone in considerable numbers for training in the USSR—his ingrained suspicion of the Soviet Union could only have grown. Tanzanian President Julius Nyerere stated that these events "proved to me that even among those countries which call themselves Socialist and Marxist there is dislike for black skin."[16] (A Tanzanian student was killed in Romania in circumstances where racial hatred was charged.[17])

African officials were also finding much to be desired in the behavior of Soviet diplomatic and technical personnel towards local populations.[18] The Soviets were charged with smuggling diamonds out of Guinea,[19] using crude racist language in the presence of their African friends,[20] and exhibiting a most contemptuous attitude to their host countries.[21] The USSR eventually came to be seen as just another white power,[22] as some African states, such as leftist Guinea, had been forced to expel their Soviet ambassadors in order to command respect.[23] It did not require any great stretch of the imagination for Africans to start viewing the Sino-Soviet rift through the prism of their own experience with the Soviets. "If the thousands of Chinese who studied here were treated the way we are being treated by our Russian hosts," said a black student in Moscow, "then I can understand very well why there is a rift between the two countries."[24]

China Courts Africa

China's success in translating its claims against the USSR into ethnic and cultural terms had become the Kremlin's biggest problem in the Third World in the early 1960s.[25] Most disquieting to the Soviets was the growing tendency of even its closest African friends to echo Chinese criticism of its policies and agree with China that the USSR was a European state, to be excluded from the Afro-Asian movement (ibid.). At a preparatory meeting in Djakarta for the second Afro-Asian Conference, Guinean Foreign Minister Louis Lansana Beavogui told the assembly that despite the Soviet Union's "excellent relations with Africa," it was nonetheless a European country. Adding salt to the wound, he contended, "If it were said that part of the Soviet Union lay in Asia, the same might be said of the USA with Hawaii, Puerto Rico, etc."[26]

At the third Afro-Asian People's Solidarity Conference in Moshi, Tanganyika, the Chinese openly campaigned for the barring of the USSR and the Eastern European Communist countries on the grounds that they were "white."[27] Julius Nyerere, the host president, openly attacked the USSR, which he accused of taking part in "a second invasion of Africa . . . more dangerous than the first," and attempting to divide the African peoples.[28] By May 1963, the Kremlin had come to the conclusion that it might have to write off the Afro-Asian movement altogether,[29] admitting that some African leaders "would like to direct the solidarity movement not against imperialism, colonialism and its agents, but against all white people."[30] Thus, speaking before an assembly of Third World students at Patrice Lumumba University in Moscow, Soviet Prime Minister Aleksei Kosygin, while attacking western racism, colonialism, and imperialism, cautioned that "any attempt to replace internationalism by an international racism [is] contrary to the spirit of Marxism-Leninism."[31] Preceding Kosygin, high-ranking party theoretician Mikhail Suslov had openly accused China of "greatly fanning nationalist and even racist sentiments amongst the peoples struggling against colonialism."[32]

Moscow's response to Peking's overwhelming racial onslaught was unable to undo the damage. The Kremlin was fighting a losing battle, alternating clumsy flattery of African leaders ("The leaders of African liberation movements are often neither bourgeois nor feudal . . . but rather, as it were, 'Negro Democrats' ")[33] with warnings against ideologies advocating "unity between the negroid peoples of Africa and America's Negroes."[34] On a note of defeat, the Soviet government organ *Izvestia* claimed that Peking's racial policy was building a "Chinese wall between white, yellow and black nations," while comparing the Maoist regime to Hitler's Third Reich.[35] In August 1967, Mao Tse-tung broke his Olympian silence to issue the first of two well-publicized declarations. His "Statement Supporting the Afro-Americans in their Just Struggle against Racial Discrimination by U.S. Imperialism" aroused enthusiasm both in black Africa and among Blacks in the New World. "The evil system of colonialism and imperialism arose and throve with the enslavement of Negroes and the trade in Negroes," Mao said, "and it will surely come to its end with the complete emancipation of the Black people."[36] Four months later, Premier Chou En-lai undertook the first visit by a Chinese leader to black Africa.

Castro Invades China's Racial Turf

Castroite Cuba had decided to dramatically expand its influence on the black continent precisely at a moment when Soviet policy in that area was in hot water. The only Marxist, revolutionary, and non-white country that could attract the attention of African nationalists and successfully compete with China for African favors was precisely little Cuba. Unlike China, Cuba could boast not merely a distant kinship, but direct cultural, historical, and blood links with Africans. A small country, Cuba could appear to be totally altruistic in its declarations of unfailing support for African emancipation. Most important, the Castroite leadership had long since perfected the "racial weapon" and could handle it far better than the relatively unskilled Chinese.

Havana had begun well in Africa by appointing predominantly Afro-Cuban ambassadors to the black African states in which Cuba was accredited. Havana also took care to include black Cubans in official delegations visiting the continent. There was a widespread assumption, therefore, that the heroic island was also in the vanguard of ethnic relations and coexistence. At the Afro-Asian Conference in Moshi, the man who spoke out successfully in favor of expanding the Afro-Asian movement so as to convene a "conference of the three continents" in Havana was the Afro-Cuban ambassador to Mali, José Carrillo, who headed the Cuban delegation. Black Cuban poet Nicolás Guillén Landrián had led the Cuban delegation to the second Congress of Afro-Asian Writers, held in Cairo the previous year. Afro-Cuban journalist Ernesto Vera represented Cuba at the second Conference of Afro-Asian Journalists in Bandung, Indonesia, in 1963. Black faces were therefore increasingly behind the convincing Cuban voices that challenged Maoist delegations at the various Afro-Asian meetings.

China had sensed the trap laid at Moshi when Havana called for the "expansion" of the Afro-Asian movement to incorporate Latin America and its revolutionary movements, which were dominated mainly by Castroite and pro-Soviet parties and groups. But rejection of that apparently logical geographic expansion would have incurred the bewildered reproach of the Africans. How could Peking reject a proposal jointly espoused by Algeria and Cuba, the two most prestigious and authoritative revolutionary governments in the Third World? Actively supported by Ahmed Ben Bella, Castro had won what would turn out to be a major victory against the Chinese. The emergence of a new tricontinental organization on Cuban soil, with Havana as its probable permanent headquarters, would preclude a strictly African and Asian movement. Any Chinese attempt to exclude the Soviets from the new tricontinental movement on geo-ethno-cultural grounds could no longer prevail.

The same tendency that made Africans support a poor, weak, and righteous China against the powerful, industrialized, and calculating Soviet Union began working in favor of little Cuba as it increasingly challenged the Chinese colossus in various Third World forums. Havana consequently pressed down hard on its racial accelerator. As of 1964, the theme of race began to gain wider promotion in the propaganda literature of Cuba's foreign ministry. Typical of that trend was Eloy Merino Brito's contribution to *Política Internacional*, the Cuban foreign ministry's organ, entitled "Racial Discrimination and the Policy of Apartheid."[37] There followed a series of official foreign ministry statements and brochures which, while denouncing apartheid in South Africa and Rhodesia, extolled Cuba as a "genuine racial democracy."[38] One of these propaganda brochures, "Cuba: Country Free of Segregation,"[39] was widely distributed by Cuba's embassies in black Africa.[40]

Castro was bent on preventing the Chinese from capitalizing on the racial issue in a zone already marked out by Cuba as a potential sphere of influence. Cuba's leadership also had to beware of the danger of being berated as "racist" by China, much as the Soviets had been. After all, the political leadership of the Revolution, Cuba's predominantly non-white population notwithstanding, continued to be dominated by white Cubans of Spanish descent.[41] There was no telling what would become of Havana's glittering image as the Mecca of interracial harmony were this anomaly to become the cutting edge of Peking's Africa-oriented propaganda.[42]

Havana's still unchallenged racial credibility allowed Cuba's white foreign minister, Raúl Roa García, to posture at the U.N. as the Don Quixote of anti-racism. "The policy of apartheid imposed in South Africa by a minority of white settlers is one of the most abominable expressions of colonialism," he lectured to the U.N. General Assembly. "The delegation of Cuba, a country in which a Socialist revolution liquidated all vestiges of racial discrimination, stretches out its

fraternal hand to all of those men and women who suffer and struggle for their rights in South Africa."[43] Cuba, he assured, "shares the
repulsion of African states for any sort of unilateral declaration of independence by the white minority exploiting and oppressing the
black majority [in Rhodesia]" (ibid., 259).

Since 1960, whenever the occasion arose, the Castroite leaders had
made a point of peppering their speeches with references to Socialist
Cuba as an exemplar of ethnic harmony. As of 1963, however, that
point was no longer intended solely to discredit the enemy in Washington in the eyes of the colored Third World, but more importantly,
to facilitate Cuba's easy entrance into black Africa through the door
of ethnicity. What more reliable ally of African peoples still fighting
racial oppression and colonial domination could there be than a
former colony whose majority population of African origin had been
freed from the nightmare of racial discrimination?

Castro himself seems to have set the new racial ball rolling when,
on July 26, 1963, he spoke at length before a rally of one million
Cubans on the oppression of Blacks in the United States. "Wasn't
there also racial discrimination here? Who introduced it here but
them [the Americans]? But when exploitation of man by man ceased
here, racial discrimination also ceased! That is why they [the U.S.]
do not want people to come to Cuba. They do not want others to see
what there is in Cuba. . . . Let the Negro leaders of the United States
come here. Allow them to come and visit Cuba so they may see a
society without discrimination, so that they may understand which
road leads towards the elimination of discrimination."[44]

Two months after Mao Tse-tung's blistering public statement in
August 1967 supporting black Americans, Castro was once again on
the racial warpath. "Here, for example," he told a mass rally, "you
do not see the racial problems they have in the United States. And I
ask those visitors presently here, who've come from all corners of the
world . . . whether or not it is an interesting thing that among our
people, among the masses in the schools, hospitals, theaters, beaches,
recreational centers, workplaces, and cultural centers—there is not
even a single trace of that discrimination which was once rampant in
our country?"[45] The Cuban premier warned that the U.S. would continue to be racist so long as it was capitalist. "It is therefore logical
that the [U.S.] State Department is not interested in having American youth, American workers, and American Negroes go to see
[what's happening in Cuba] and begin asking themselves questions"
(ibid., 126). Five days later, the Cuban leader charged the U.S. with

having a high per-capita income for its citizens, but a low "moral per capita" in its treatment of Blacks.[46]

In 1964, the first of the long series of "hot summers" that shook the U.S. afforded Havana another opportunity to widen its racial appeal. Cuban newspaper headlines screamed about racial unrest in the United States. American Blacks were portrayed in the media as being "at the mercy of the Ku Klux Klan, the police, and police dogs, or as poverty-stricken, illiterate souls begging to be fed, employed, and educated by whites."[47] Speaking to a huge crowd in Havana, Castro upheld Cuba as an exemplary racial democracy. The peoples of Africa and Asia, he said, were inspired by the "genuine racial equality"[48] that reigned in Cuba.

Exiled black American leader Robert Williams and a sizeable group of African guests were on hand in Santiago de Cuba, Oriente province, for the mass rally commemorating the eleventh anniversary of Castro's Moncada assault. On that occasion, Castro delivered a lengthy speech defending Cuba's right to export the Revolution. "In the face of the imperialists' call on behalf of counter-revolution, there's the call of the Cuban revolution on behalf of the Latin American revolution: call against call! And we shall see who is right, they or us!"[49] Then, turning to his now favorite theme, Castro denounced the Ku Klux Klan, lynchings, and racial discrimination in the U.S. The world could see, he said, "that [in Cuba] nothing happens like what occurs in New York, South Carolina, Miami . . . lynchings . . . of citizens of the United States because of the color of their skins. Everyone can verify that here we have no racial problems. There were racial problems left us by the imperialists, because we had . . . stores which refused employment to Negro girls" (ibid.). Cuban Negroes, he assured his audience, were experiencing a new dawn.

"I remember when I was a boy I used to go to see Tarzan movies," Castro went on. "What did I see? The white man was always stronger. . . . The white man was intelligent. The white man always persecuted the Negro. The Negro was always uncivilized. . . . What kind of mentality does all of this create in people? . . . It created the idea of racial superiority, of the superiority of the White over the Black" (ibid.). In the new Cuba, said Castro, "there are no white gangs persecuting the Negroes. . . . Here, on the beaches, on our streets, in our theaters or restaurants—everywhere—we live together as brothers. We, Negroes and Whites, live together enjoying equal rights! We, Negroes and Whites, are ready to give our lives for our country" (ibid.). The huge crowd responded in unison with a familiar chant: "Fidel! Fidel! *Gracias*, Fidel!" (Thank you, Fidel!).

Boosting Cuba's Afrophilic Profile

Pushed by events totally unrelated to African affairs, in 1964 Havana resolved to expand its influence in black Africa. As a result, Cuba's foreign policy would shift from merely moral support for the liberation movements and "progressive" regimes in Africa to a more dynamic stance.

The Johnson administration's undeclared war on North Vietnam and the Kremlin's passive response made Castro uneasy, though the Caudillo had good cause to believe that Washington would not attempt an invasion of Cuba. U.S. air raids on Hanoi, however, instilled fears of an air war of attrition against Cuba. With that in mind, Castro lamented that "the presence of nuclear missiles in Cuba would have kept us protected . . . against the danger of a local war [which] . . . for a small country can mean almost as much destruction and death as that caused by a nuclear war."[50] Deprived of nuclear missiles, Cuba was prompted to devise an "internationalist" politico-military defense strategy. In that context, the distant black continent rapidly achieved the status of a zone of vital national security interests, in the eyes of Cuban leaders.

Cuban President Osvaldo Dorticós Torrado arrived in Cairo at the head of a large delegation to attend the second Non-Aligned Summit in October 1964. At that gathering, Havana first emphasized its determination to play a new role in Africa, a continent where the forces of progress and revolution were steadily on the rise. Several territories were engaged in the sort of insurrectional struggle that the "Declaration of Havana" had proclaimed was the only road for the oppressed. Guerrilla wars were being fought on an increasing scale in the three Portuguese colonies (Angola, Guinea-Bissau, and Mozambique), while insurgents in the independent Congo were holding extensive territory. In the Cameroons, guerrillas of the openly Marxist Union des Populations du Cameroun (UPC) were actively reorganizing. Another Marxist group, the SAWABA of Niger, and the Senegalese Communist party (Parti Africain pour l'Independence, or PAI) were also on the verge of launching guerrilla wars against independent states. In every case, Havana's contributions were increasingly available, particularly for the training of military cadres.

Cuba had also gained a new ally in black Africa following the 1963 revolution in Congo-Brazzaville that brought an avowedly Marxist-inspired government to power, led by Alphonse Massemba-Debat. Congo-Brazzaville and six other hard-core "progressive" African states (Ghana, Guinea, Mali, Tanzania, Algeria, and Egypt) were hosts to bustling Cuban diplomatic posts. The Castroite regime could therefore speak of African affairs before the Cairo summit with some authority, even as early as 1964. "It is profoundly moving for a Latin American, in particular a Cuban, to take to the rostrum in Africa, for we know that one can speak to Africans in a firm and straightforward language,"[51] President Dorticós said. The struggle against oppression, subjection, and centuries-old discrimination, he asserted, was "the common denominator for all African peoples" (ibid.). He then launched into a strong condemnation of South African apartheid. Having forever eliminated all forms of racial strife from its soil, Dorticós said, "Cuba has the moral authority to proclaim at this conference the need to raise a very vigorous protest against all manifestations of racial discrimination, whatever their forms and wherever they are practiced" (ibid., 150).

Dorticós aligned Washington, "Cuba's arch-enemy," with Pretoria, "the arch-enemy of all Africans," thus establishing a common racist profile for the respective enemies of Cuban and African emancipation (ibid.). He went on to skillfully implicate neutralist non-alignment with neutrality in the face of racial oppression: "We reject a neutral position in face of the dilemma of genuine equality among all men and the practice of racial discrimination. This conference must take a stand alongside the forces struggling for the equality of man and against the forces which sustain, encourage and accept discriminatory practices" (ibid., 152).

Turning to the situation in Congo-Leopoldville, Cuba's president roundly denounced the utilization of white mercenaries there, "among whom are to be found, in fact, counter-revolutionaries from my own country" (ibid., 147). To some delegates this was a sensational revelation. Congolese Prime Minister Moise Tshombé, who had been refused admission to the Cairo summit, had recruited white Cuban exiles to pilot aircraft that had been bombing and strafing rebel-held areas for two months in a covert CIA operation. The link between Africa's struggle for emancipation from white racist domination and Cuba's defeat of the same enemy at home could not have been clearer, adding credibility to Dorticós's pledge of "solidarity and backing for the liberation movements of the peoples of Angola, Mozambique, so-called Portuguese Guinea . . . and all other African peoples engaged in the liberation struggle." (As Dorticós spoke, Congolese military cadres had already arrived in Cuba for training.) The people of Cuba, Dorticós proclaimed, "will always be at the vanguard of that struggle, whatever the risks or difficulties" (Italics added.)

(ibid., 152). Never before had a Cuban leader made such a statement regarding Africa.

Dorticós's unequivocal proclamation had placed Cuba at the forefront of the African struggle for liberation, a favorable position from which to compete with China's widespread influence. Moreover, by claiming total success in defeating racial segregation and oppression, which Africans still fought to achieve, Havana could also claim to be qualified to show Africans "how things are done." That such thoughts were not far from the minds of Cuba's white leadership was evidenced by Foreign Minister Raúl Roa García's televised press conferences immediately after returning from the Cairo summit. After glowingly depicting "the prestige and authority enjoyed by the Cuban revolution among the underdeveloped countries, especially those in Africa," Roa pointedly remarked, "You must bear in mind that the Conference was held in Africa, a continent in full eruption which is today a focal point of rebellion against colonialist, imperialist and neo-colonialist domination."[52]

What could a small island, thousands of miles from that gigantic "focal point of rebellion," possibly offer Africa? Roa's answer: "This little country, heroically resisting an infinitely superior enemy, is undoubtedly a lighthouse for those African countries present at that conference. Especially so for those countries that have yet to achieve their independence" (ibid., 50). There was no room for doubt, he assured, that "[t]he new African states, as they are called, and the national liberation movements feel a profound sympathy for the Cuban revolution. This sympathy is not of the conventional type, but rather one that was born, grows, and is nurtured by ideals and interests we share in common" (ibid., 49). The unstated bottom line was that Cuba was consequently duty-bound to provide equally unconventional forms of assistance.

Washington's Inept Responses

The Cuban regime's success in establishing close links with the Afro-Asian and non-aligned countries had already caused grave concern in Washington. In 1961 and 1962, the Central Intelligence Agency funded an important African tour by the "Cuban Revolutionary Council," the chief organization of Cuban exiles headed by José Miró Cardona, Cuba's first prime minister after the overthrow of Batista. The tour included most of the newly independent countries of Africa. Never before had any of the anti-Castro exile organizations shown the least interest in Africa. Obviously, the tour was intended to counteract the inroads the Castro regime had steadily made in Africa. The Revolutionary Council's visit to Africa was an indication of the importance that Africa was gaining for Cuba. It also betrayed Washington's fears that Castro might outflank it on the black continent.

Lourdes Casal, the only black member of the CIA-sponsored team, wrote a summary of the trip.[53] Entitled "Africa Before the Cuban Problem," the report stated rather boldly:

> For us Cubans in particular, Africa is of great importance for a variety of reasons. In the first place, our short-term fate is linked to the general course of events in those countries that are called Third World—the world of under-developed countries—because whether we like it or not we belong to that world. Secondly, within the present context of work through which we are trying to retrieve our own revolution—as the only way for Cuba to be capable of assuming her legitimate role in the Third World—the Afro-Asian bloc in general acquires an extraordinary importance. To a great extent, our hopes of victory will depend on a series of very complex international interconnections. If we could canvass the moral support of the African peoples for our struggle, we would by so doing take an important step forward towards the liberation of our own motherland. However, up till now *we have underestimated Africa.* Our whole attention has been concentrated on Latin America, an area which no doubt must occupy a preeminent position in our interest. But what we may call our "hemispheric priority" should not become something exclusive, because the Cuban question has already gone beyond the limits of the Americas so as to become an issue of importance to the whole world. For its part, the Castroite regime has shown that it is very conscious of the importance of Africa, and therefore it is making a sustained effort to cultivate the support of the new African states, maintaining active diplomatic missions in these countries (Italics added.) (ibid.).

Casal admitted that the anti-Castro Cubans had failed to take Africa into account because, "a) there had been no consciousness of Africa's importance, b) we had exaggerated the difficulties of communication, and c) we had not understood the Africans' mentality and considered it useless to lobby them and to ask for support from their countries . . . . Nonetheless, Africa continued to be an active battlefield where we Cubans have up till now refused to engage in the battle. . . . However, an adequate understanding of the major concerns of Africans and of purely African problems will enormously facilitate our task on that continent" (ibid.).

The belated interest in Africa taken by the Cuban Revolutionary Council was to no avail. Not only was this exile group composed primarily of upper-class white Cubans who looked down on Africa, but Havana had already made outstanding advances in the newly independent African states. Of particular interest, however, is the fact that two Cuban Blacks on opposite ends of the political spectrum, Lourdes Casal and Walterio Carbonell, were proposing the adoption of Afrocentric policies to their respective political camps for diametrically opposite reasons. (Casal eventually changed camps, converted to Marxism in the 1970s, and returned to Cuba).

Cuban-Soviet Relations Deteriorate

Havana was unaware that a great change had been taking place in the Kremlin while President Dorticós was vigorously establishing Cuba's African credentials in Cairo. Cuba's president had expressed the measure of Castro's growing impatience with Soviet irresolution in the face of U.S. aggression against Socialist countries. Speaking for Castro, Dorticós had bluntly warned the Cairo summit, ''We want peace, but with dignity. . . . There can be no peaceful coexistence while imperialist aggressions are being simultaneously unleashed against small countries.''[54] This was clearly a reference to North Vietnam, whose position vis-à-vis the U.S. and the USSR most closely reflected Cuba's own. It was precisely to clarify such matters that President Dorticos had scheduled a trip to the USSR immediately following the Cairo summit. With the added weight of Cuba's resounding success in Cairo, Dorticos could have expected to extract even broader Soviet concessions than Fidel Castro himself had obtained during his second visit to the USSR earlier that year.

En route to Moscow, Dorticós made a stop in Algeria where, at a welcoming ceremony at the airport, he praised ''brother Ben Bella.'' Addressing a mass rally the following day, Cuba's president again showered lavish praises on his host and lyrically depicted the growth of a new solidarity between Africa and Cuba: ''Above the oceans, African and American hands will clasp one another . . . the future belongs to socialism!''[55]

Upon his arrival at the Soviet airport of Vnoukovo, Dorticós was hit with the bad news. The man whose largess had helped the ''heroic island'' to survive had just been unceremoniously sacked and replaced with a stone-faced troika. The elimination of Nikita Khrushchev was unquestionably a serious blow to the Cuban leadership. Tight personal bonds of friendship had developed between Castro and Khrushchev over the years, despite residual acrimony over the October crisis.

Their relationship had provided the type of understanding whereby the Soviet leader could agree to dole out millions of dollars of additional aid to Russia's Caribbean ally without having to seek prior clearance from his Kremlin colleagues. Khrushchev's penchant for boisterous joviality, boastful adventurism, and iconoclastic behavior squared perfectly with Castro's own freewheeling machista style.

The good old times of the opportunistic generosity of "Comrade Nikita" (for whom every Third World leader seems to have had an exact price in money or prestige projects) had come to an end. Suddenly Havana had lost a good deal of its blackmailing powers in its relationship with the USSR.[56] Cuba's national security interests demanded the rapid restoration of its bargaining capability through a novel strategy of leverage.

12 EXPORTING THE REVOLUTION

Within months of its independence in July, 1962, Algeria was being courted by the major powers. Cuba, too, had taken the Algerian revolution very seriously. The Algerian revolution appeared to be the closest reflection of the "Cuban model" anywhere in the Third World. More important, from Havana's vantage point, the North African Arab state was another gateway into black Africa. Algeria's flamboyant leader, Ahmed Ben Bella, had made no secret of his intention to transform his country into the springboard of the "African revolution."[1] Ben Bella made this abundantly clear in May 1963 at the inaugural conference of the Organization of African Unity (OAU) in Addis Ababa. Before the assembled heads of state, the Algerian president delivered a short, impassioned speech that was both militantly African and resolutely anti-imperialistic. In one stroke, Ben Bella not only won over the continent's "freedom fighters,"[2] but also established himself as the leader of the entire continent, eclipsing such luminaries as Nasser, Nkrumah, and Touré. Marxist and nationalist African revolutionaries alike began deserting Cairo and Accra for Algiers.

Algeria exhibited all the trappings of a modern Socialist state—a constitution, a national assembly, and a single party with its politburo, central committee and ideological program based on "scientific socialism."[3] This form of socialism sounded as attractive as Cuba's, and Ben Bella himself described it as "Castro-style socialism."[4] The distant Caribbean island seemed close to the heart of the Algerian president. By vowing "we will never accept a piece of bread in exchange for the freedom of others, and above all [for] that of Cuba," Ben Bella had taken the clearest stand in favor of Cuba made by any non-aligned Afro-Asian leader.[5]

Ben Bella's Algeria

The amity engendered by Ben Bella's visit to Cuba at the beginning of the October crisis swiftly took the form of an informal pact. (Outside of the Soviet leadership, Ben Bella was the only leader to have been made aware that the Kremlin had transferred nuclear weapons to Cuba.[6]) Ben Bella obviously regarded Cuba and Algeria as the two vanguard revolutions marked out for continental leadership in Latin America and Africa respectively. To that end, he sought to expand the Afro-Asian People's Solidarity Organization to include Cuba and the Latin American revolutionary movements.[7] To radical Africans, the similarities between Ben Bellism and Castroism were very clear.[8] The popularity of revolutionary Algeria in black Africa resulted in Havana's effortless accumulation of political capital.

The responsibility of turning Havana's eagerness to play a role in the black continent into reality could not have fallen on a better choice. The man selected in 1963 was black, affable, self-confident,[9] and above all supremely competent in the field that would absorb most of his time as Cuba's first ambassador to Algeria: military and intelligence affairs. A hero of the Sierra Maestra campaign, where he served as Raúl Castro's aide in the Sierra Cristal, Maj. Jorge Serguera had been the military commander of Matanzas, one of Cuba's six provinces. A top-ranking official of the army's intelligence apparatus (DIER), which in turn was subordinate to the General Directorate of Intelligence (DGI), Serguera quickly transformed the Cuban embassy into a virtual overseas branch of the Cuban counter-intelligence and armed forces.[10]

Havana's delegation in Algiers came to rank second in importance only to its embassy in Moscow, even surpassing the latter in terms of almost around-the-clock activity. Both the embassy and Serguera's private residence were open houses where Africa's "freedom fighters" could present their credentials to the Cuban revolution and seek concrete help for their revolutionary projects. Havana had definitely come in through the front door. Algiers was not only the political Mecca to the nationalist "one-man-one-vote" variety of freedom fighters (ZANU, ZAPU, SWANU, PAC, SWAPO, FNLA), but even more so to the much more radical liberation movements (MPLA, PAIGC, ANC, FRELIMO) and the avowedly Marxist parties struggling to overthrow established, pro-western regimes (the PAI of Senegal, the FROLINAT of Chad, the IPC of the Cameroons, the SAWABA of Niger, and the UMMA of Zanzibar).

Nasser, Nkrumah Are Wary

One of the immediate effects of the Castro-Ben Bella alliance was to reduce the fierce rivalry between Egypt's Nasser and Ghana's Nkrumah over leadership of the continent. Practically overnight, Ben Bella had credibly staked out such a claim with the one force in the Third World that seemed to have mastered the secret of political success, Castroism. Backed by Havana, Ben Bella had suddenly come to weigh more on the African scale than Nkrumah and Nasser together. And as his influence grew in Africa, so did Cuba's.

Gabriel Garcia Marquez, Colombian novelist and occasional spokesman for the Castroite leadership, stated in an assessment of Cuba's influence in Africa in the early 1960s that, "at that epoch there was no African liberation movement which did not rely on Cuban solidarity either by way of civilian or military hardware, or by way of technical training."[11] Algiers had become an open house for more than a dozen Cubans who were not official diplomats. One of these, Carlos Franqui, who lived for nearly a year in Algiers, shuttled back and forth between the Algerian and Cuban capitals bearing ultra-confidential personal letters between Castro and Ben Bella.[12] In one of these, the Cuban leader warned Ben Bella to "be very careful of [Houari] Boumedienne!" (ibid.).[13] (The latter's coup eventually toppled the Ben Bella regime in 1965.)

"Be very careful of Castro!" could very well have summarized the impressions both Nkrumah and Nasser came to share by mid-summer of 1963. Evidence from Accra and Cairo indicates that both leaders took strong exception to the growing influence, at their expense, of the Castro-Ben Bella tandem.[14] Since the Congo affair, when Egypt led the states that had attempted to keep the Lumumbist regime in power, Nasser had been forced to take a back seat vis-à-vis sub-Saharan Africa, leaving all major initiatives to Nkrumah.[15] Reports reaching Nasser during the summer and winter of 1963, as the result of two prolonged fact-finding visits to Cuba by senior foreign ministry counselor for African affairs Mohammed Abdel Aziz Iss-Hak, indicated that Havana intended to play not a supportive but a leadership role in African affairs.[16] In fact, Aziz Iss-Hak had returned to Egypt convinced that, in the long run, Castro posed a more serious threat to Cairo's leadership ambitions in Africa than Kwame Nkrumah (ibid.). Ben Bella, the Egyptian suspected, was unwittingly acting as Cuba's Trojan horse in Africa. (ibid.). Nasser himself had begun to think along these lines.

Prompted by similar suspicions, Kwame Nkrumah is reported to have resented Ben Bella's self-appointed role as Africa's messiah.[17] Unlike Nasser, however, he seems to have progressively adopted a policy of seeking closer ties with Cuba as a means of counteracting Algeria. If the Castroite luster could rub off on Ben Bella and vice versa, why couldn't it work in the same way for Ghana? That seems to have been Nkrumah's reasoning. At any rate, when Armando Entralgo Gonzalez, Cuba's first ambassador to Ghana, arrived in Accra in August 1963, Nkrumah's rhetoric already betrayed a drastic shift toward "scientific socialism." The tilt of Ghana's foreign policy and external trade in favor of the "fatherland of socialism" was equally evident that year.[18] "In foreign affairs Ghana's voice became steadily more radical; in domestic matters state intervention in the economy and rapid industrialisation were the watchwords, and an attempt was made to transform the C.P.P. from a mass party into a vanguard party. . . . The growing radicalism of [Nkrumah's] foreign policy pronouncements owed much to increasing competition in Africa" (ibid., 112).

Partly in response to the serious rivalry for leadership threatened by Ben Bella, who was assiduously courted by both China and the USSR, Accra joined the radical bandwagon. Droves of Africa's "freedom fighters" had deserted the Ghanaian capital to seek arms, training, material support, and shelter in Algiers. Some of the more radical African movements, such as the PAI of Senegal and the UMMA of Zanzibar, had been sending cadres to Cuba for military training since the previous year. Thus, shortly after Ambassador Entralgo arrived in Accra, he was apprised of Nkrumah's intention to seek the assistance of "brother" Socialist countries in setting up a continental freedom fighters' training center in Ghana.[19] Nkrumah was intent on regaining the initiative seized by Algiers.

The very personality of the man Cuba sent to Accra as its first ambassador demonstrated that, although a newcomer to African politics, the Castroite regime had started out with a clear advantage; the "African mentality" was no secret to the Castroite leadership. Unlike the Cuban ambassadors to neighboring Mali, Guinea, and Algeria, who were all Blacks (Jose Carrillo, the Cuban ambassador to Mali, was a "mulatto," or light-skinned Black), Havana's envoy to Accra was a white Cuban. Until the summer of 1963, he had been deputy chief of the Cuban Foreign Ministry's Departamento de Africa Negra (Black Africa Department).

Entralgo's appointment emphasized the value Havana attached to establishing a firm connection with Ghana, as well as its intention to take Nkrumah's susceptibilities into account. The Cuban government seemed to be aware of Nkrumah's deep resentment when Washington had contemplated appointing a black American ambassador to Accra a year earlier. According to a top Nkrumah aide, the incident revealed how much "Africans had swallowed lock, stock, and barrel the concept that black Americans were third-class citizens. . . . The most glaring instance of this attitude was the question of appointing black diplomats to Ghana. Here Washington had really been given to understand that 'whoever you are thinking of sending, don't send us any black diplomats, because if you do, that will mean that you aren't recognizing Ghana as a real nation; you don't send third-rate citizens to an important nation.' "[20] As a matter of fact, less than one percent of Cuba's diplomatic corps at the time were black, a fact of which Nkrumah was presumably aware.[21]

The First Military Intervention

On October 15, 1963, Cuba's government mouthpiece, *Revolución*, headlined: "Moroccan Troops Invade Algeria."[22] In pure Castro style, Ben Bella called together a mass rally that same night and proclaimed Algeria's will to repel the invaders.[23] When the attack began, Algeria was already "training 1,000 guerrillas from Angola, Mozambique and South Africa, and giving funds and advice to many liberation movements,"[24] twenty-one of which had set up offices in Algiers. Ben Bella was determined to portray the war with Morocco as a matter concerning the whole of Africa.

The parallels between the Moroccan invasion against the young Socialist revolution and the Bay of Pigs landing against Castro's regime two years earlier were too tempting for either Havana or Algiers to ignore. Nor could Cuba miss this chance to display fraternal solidarity with its closest Third World ally. Besides repaying a debt of gratitude contracted during the October crisis, a spectacular Cuban action would dramatically enhance Castro's position as a sure ally, protector, and benefactor of the African revolution. Rushing ahead of Nasser, Castro ordered the first intervention by Cuban armed forces outside of its national boundaries.

Prior to Havana's decision to commit its soldiers and military hardware in a theater of war thousands of kilometers away, several significant indicators had pointed to the predominantly military character of the Cuban-Algerian connection. The Algerian training camps for African "freedom fighters" reportedly counted a number of black Cuban military instructors.[25] Algerian military missions had begun arriving in Cuba since May 1963 and Ché Guevara had appeared in Algiers in July, heading a Cuban delegation including military specialists.[26] The following month, Algeria's defense chief, Col. Houari Boumedienne, made a much-publicized visit to the island. In mid-September, another top-level Cuban military mission was reported to be in Algiers (ibid., 276), followed closely by yet another, which arrived on the eve of Cuba's announcement of the Moroccan invasion.

"The chances are," commented Maurice Halperin, "that Fidel had been informed of the impending confrontation in advance. In any event, he boasted later that Cuban military support was the first foreign aid to reach Algeria" (ibid., 277). In fact, the best proof that Cuba's military involvement had been pre-planned is that Cuban aid, dispatched by sea, managed to reach Algeria only a few days after the invasion was announced. Carlos Franqui, then in Algiers as Castro's personal contact with Ben Bella, recalls that "Cuba sent tanks, heavy equipment and a complete military detachment of about 2,000 men under the command of Maj. Efigenio Ameijeiras and Maj. Aldo Santamaría."[27]

Cuba's "internationalist" assistance took the form of three ships carrying the troops, 40 Soviet T-34 tanks, 4 jet fighters, trucks, and more than 800 tons of light arms, ammunition, and artillery.[28] Most of the soldiers of the brigade were black, as was one of its two military chiefs.[29] The latter, Major Ameijeiras, had been appointed head of the Cuban police when Castro took power. With a reputation for heavy-handedness, Ameijeiras was one of the two surviving leading black figures of the Castroite movement. A veteran of the Granma landing, his loyalty to the Castro brothers was unswerving. (Less than three years after his performance in Algeria, however, Castro expelled him from the Communist party and the armed forces, on charges of corruption.)

After the fighting in Algeria had died down, Havana could count its gains. Despite perhaps a few Cuban casualties and Morocco's severance of diplomatic relations with Cuba, Castro had come out a clear winner. He had indeed taken chances. "At the time, the shipment of men and arms was unpublicized, although the news spread in the upper levels of Havana's bureaucracy where it caused considerable excitement. There must have been excitement in the Kremlin also. Fidel was again taking large risks. If a real war should develop, no one could tell what the consequences for Cuba would be."[30] The political rewards, however, were worth the risks. Africans were impressed that Cuba's assistance had reached Algeria even ahead of Nasser's 1,000-man contingent. That fact alone would make Castro boast thereafter that "men and weapons from our country crossed the Atlantic in record time, reaching Algeria ready to fight alongside Algerian revolutionaries. . . . At the time, distance was no obstacle to our arriving first on the scene. It was proletarian internationalism in deeds, not cheap wordmongering [palabrería]."[31]

Washington's mild reaction to the Cuban intervention—coming exactly one year after the October crisis—must have both surprised and delighted Havana. Through a conspicuously low-ranking State Department official, Washington merely declared that "the government of the United States had received no precise information concerning the presence of Cuban or Egyptian military personnel in Algeria."[32] Under the spell of the Ben Bellist and Castroite mystique, few African leaders took note of the significant precedent Havana had established by sending men and weapons to a war zone many thousands of kilometers away. Castro's first military intervention in Africa had either passed without adverse criticism or been received with admiring awe. Thereafter, that pattern would become invariable.

Exporting "Revolution" to Africa

The Castroite "big push" in Latin America actually began in the early months of 1964, preceded by the institution of compulsory military service in Cuba in November 1963. Weapons and men, including Cuban soldiers and officers, were infiltrating Venezuela and Colombia at a rate high enough for those two governments to accuse Havana of conducting an undeclared war against them. In secluded mountainous areas of eastern Cuba, guerrilla apprentices from half a dozen Latin American countries were undergoing special training under Cuban instructors with a view to opening *frentes* (fronts) at home.

A special training base, set apart from those servicing Latin Americans, emphasized the fact that Havana was intent on "exporting the Revolution" not only to the other side of the Caribbean but also across the Atlantic. A group of African trainees from the island of Zanzibar had quietly arrived in Cuba in the spring of 1963. They were followed eight months later by a batch of Senegalese recruits from Majhemout Diop's Parti Africain de l'Independance or PAI. The Zanzibaris were all members of the left-wing UMMA party of Abdul Rahman Mohammed Babu, which had operated an information office in Havana since 1962. Proud to identify themselves as Marxists, they indeed represented the left-wing element within the clove-producing island's Arabized community.[33] In command of the Zanzibari trainees were three men who were ostensibly in charge of the UMMA Information Office. Ali Mahfoudh Mohammed, the leader of the group, was of Omani Arab origin; his deputy, Mohammed Ali Foum, was of Comoro-Arab origin; Salim Ahmed Salim, the youngest and most Africa-oriented of the three, was officially the secretary of the office.

Their idols were Fidel Castro, Gamal Abdel Nasser, and Joseph Stalin; their goal was to set up a Cuban-style Socialist regime in their own country. Still, the Zanzibaris encountered trouble in Cuba. They began to excite the unwarranted suspicion of the authorities due to their almost exclusive fraternization with black Cuban families, to whom they had been introduced by Afro-Cuban students.[34] The Zanzibaris had several run-ins with the Instituto Cubano de Amistad con los Pueblos (ICAP), which catered to the foreign black and African community at the time. (ICAP was responsible for providing "guides" and "interpreters" to supervise these black foreign guests of the regime.)

ICAP officials had resented the fact that these visitors were making unguided visits to private homes and striking up unauthorized friendships with ordinary black Cubans.[35] Ramón Calcines Gordillo, president of ICAP, and his deputy, Giraldo Mazola, were quickly identified by expatriate Blacks, students and freedom fighters alike, as "inveterate racists."[36] (In 1986, Giraldo Mazola was upgraded to the post of deputy foreign minister.)

When ICAP officials leveled charges of "homosexuality" against the Zanzibaris before Cuban Minister of the Interior Maj. Ramiro Valdéz,[37] it proved to be a most effective way of blocking further contact between these Africans and private Afro-Cuban citizens. Cuba was then in the midst of its first massive anti-homosexual drive, ordered by Castro. A climate of resentment, suspicion, and tension thereafter marred relations between the Cuban authorities and the first African cadres to be trained by the Castroite regime. The antagonism was to last at least until the Zanzibaris left Cuba in late 1963. Within a few months, they would become the undisputed masters of the strategically located East African island.[38]

Although the Zanzibaris were badly treated in Cuba, Abdul Rahman Mohammed Babu, head of their UMMA party, was unconditionally pro-Castro. The Zanzibaris who were ill-treated in Cuba (Salim Salim, Mohammed Foum, Ali Mahfoudh Mohammed) were staunch Marxists and blamed everything they suffered on middle-ranking officials, but absolved Fidel Castro and his retinue from any blame. When they returned home and took power, they were full of praise for Cuba, which they saw as their best ally.[39]

Taking advantage of a grass-roots uprising led by John Okello that deposed the Sultan of Zanzibar in mid-January 1964, the leftist UMMA party took power in alliance with Abeid Karume's Afro-Shirazy party. Together, they proclaimed a "Socialist" regime. Within two days of the coup, Cuban political and military advisers arrived in a glaringly obvious effort to secure their first springboard in black Africa.[40]

Although it seemed for a time that the island was destined to become a Castroite enclave in black Africa, Cuba's advances in Zanzibar were short-lived. Reportedly "uneasy about the general leftward drift of the islands, about the openly expressed Marxist views of the UMMA and their impact on Zanzibari policy, and about the possibility of a disruptive clash on the islands, which were of some strategic sensitivity to Tanganyika,"[41] Julius Nyerere stepped in. The Tanganyikan president's misgivings were reinforced by the fact that the UMMA party was culturally and politically appended to the Arab world. Deeply suspicious of Arab pretensions to the leadership of black Africa, Nyerere sympathized with Abeid Karume's attempts to keep Zanzibar free of the control of the UMMA which, no matter how much to the left it might be, continued to be essentially the representative of Zanzibar's Arab minority. In a secretly prepared move, announced to the press in April (while UMMA leader Babu was on an Asian tour), Nyerere and Karume agreed to unite Tanganyika and Zanzibar. The birth of what was to be called Tanzania marked the end of the left-wing, Arab-Castroite attempt to convert Zanzibar into a Cuban political protectorate on the eastern flank of Africa.

Displaying his vaunted skills as a political tactician, Nyerere quickly integrated the former UMMA leadership into the Tanzanian administration on the mainland. Abdul Rahman Babu became Tanzania's Development Minister; Ali Mahfoudh Mohammed was appointed chief of operations in the Tanzanian People's Defense Force; Salim Ahmed Salim and Mohammed Foum were given ambassadorial posts. (Salim Salim became Tanzania's prime minister in 1985.) Towards Cuba, Nyerere adopted a conciliatory attitude similar to Nkrumah's. The newly installed Cuban embassy in Zanzibar was transferred to Dar es Salaam, and the Cubans treated as virtual allies. Thus, while losing an unconditional ideological ally and military protege, Havana had gained a much more powerful friend strategically located alongside the Congo and Mozambique, two prize territories where the storm of insurrection had already begun.

Assistance to Senegal

Havana's direct approach to the question of African liberation was manifested again that year, this time in West Africa. Cuba maintained diplomatic missions in only three West African states, Ghana, Guinea, and Mali. It was in the latter country, which Havana considered an ideological ally, that Cuba became embroiled in yet another move to establish an African beachhead by supporting a political party struggling against an established pro-western regime. In 1964, Bamako, Mali's capital, harbored two exiled radical political leaders who dreamed of seizing power in the aftermath of a lightning guerrilla war and setting up two more Marxist states alongside Socialist Mali. Both Djibo Bakary, leader of the Marxist SAWABA party of Niger, and Majhemout Diop, secretary general of the equally Marxist PAI of Senegal, were assiduous visitors to Cuba's embassy in Bamako.[42] Diop had already made several trips to Havana in 1962, during which he had arranged with the Cuban authorities to have some of his men trained in guerrilla warfare.

Between thirty and sixty Senegalese arrived in Cuba via Prague in January 1964 for an eight-month training period.[43] Their presence in Cuba coincided with the arrival that summer of another group of African guerrilla candidates from Congo-Leopoldville, headed by Casimir Mbaguira, Albert Kissonga, and Placide Kitunga.[44] These were supporters of the Council for National Liberation (CNL) of Gaston Soumialot, then struggling to topple the openly neo-colonial regime of Moise Tshombé in the Congo. The two groups were kept apart from each other, however, as Castro presumably did not want to advertise his support for the PAI, particularly at a time when the USSR was courting the Senegalese regime.[45] It also seems that the Cuban authorities became disappointed in the behavior of the PAI comrades who, in their moments of leisure, showed a strong predilection for white Cuban women and fun.[46]

The well-trained PAI guerrilla contingent was back in Mali towards the beginning of October, 1964. Reportedly accompanied by three black Cuban military advisers, the group filtered across the Malian-Senegalese border.[47] But the hilly forests of eastern Senegal did not provide the Sierra Maestra conditions which the PAI had counted on for Cuba's first test of the Castro-Guevarist *foquista* strategy in Africa. After operating without success for three months, the PAI's contingent disintegrated. As S. Max Madher Malick, a captain in this "Armée Révolutionnaire" would later explain, the guerrillas were "suddenly condemned to an existence of expediency and misery, an adventurous existence in a countryside which offers no possibility whatsoever of material subsistence; an existence of flight and famine."[48]

The Cuban-backed PAI adventure had taken place in an atmosphere of revolutionary agitation in Africa that allowed it to pass virtually unnoticed. The headlines of the world's newspapers were occupied with the fierce struggle being waged in Congo-Leopoldville by the guerrillas of Gaston Soumaliot against the troops and white mercenaries of Moise Tshombe. The fact that the insurgents were holding 2,000 white hostages in Stanleyville (now Kisangani) commanded sensationalist worldwide attention, obscuring the abortive Marxist attempt to overthrow the government of Léopold Sédar Senghor in Senegal.

The November 24 assault on Stanleyville by Belgian paratroopers transported by U.S. Air Force planes, while aircraft piloted by white Cuban exiles strafed rebel positions, greatly improved Havana's standing in Africa. The sheer racism and blatant gunboat colonialism displayed in this "mercy rescue operation" helped convince nationalist African opinion of the need for efficient outside help in fighting the western powers and their white mercenaries. The assault on Stanleyville thus provided an appropriate psychological climate for the expansion of Cuba's role in black Africa on a scale that would make the Algerian, Zanzibarian, and PAI episodes seem to be no more than the first hesitant steps in Castro's escalating African interventionism.[49]

13 CASTRO CO-OPTS BLACK AMERICA/BLACK AFRICA LINKAGE

The Cuban revolution coincided with another important historical event, which was also intimately linked to the African awakening: grass-roots political, cultural, and social militancy among twenty-five million black Americans suffering what many would call a species of "internal colonialism."[1] Castro, Guevara, and their colleagues were all aware of the vital growing links between Africa and this mass upsurge of an oppressed community bent on reclaiming its cultural roots and establishing the closest political links with what many termed "progressive Africa." In the early 1960s, one man virtually symbolized that new mood and militancy of black America, Black Muslim leader, Malcolm X.

Malcolm X had already attracted Havana's attention some years back when, during Castro's visit to New York to address the U.N., the Caudillo had engaged him in a long conversation at the Theresa Hotel. Since then, however, all attempts to lure the Black Muslim leader to Havana had failed. Malcolm first visited Africa in the fall of 1963, and was warmly received by such leaders as Nasser, Nkrumah, Nyerere, Touré, Kenyatta, and Milton Obote. This tour inspired Malcolm to form the Organization of Afro-American Unity (OAAU), patterned after the Organization of African Unity.

A month after founding the OAAU in June 1964,[2] he returned to Africa to attend the second Summit Meeting of African Heads of States and Governments in Cairo. He was granted observer status and permitted to submit a memorandum denouncing U.S. policies towards the Afro-American community. (The fact that a serious "riot" erupted in Harlem while the OAU was in session served to strengthen Malcolm's position immeasurably.)

The Malcolm X Plan

The Afro-American leader followed this triumph with an extensive tour of black Africa to confer with its top leaders once again. His aim was to internationalize the plight of U.S. Blacks and thereby force Washington to effect concrete solutions to the most urgent problems of Afro-America. He proposed that African leaders support a collective document by black American organizations accusing the U.S. of serious violations of black human rights, to be presented at the United Nations. Malcolm X's success in securing support for this project in Africa was a source of serious concern to the U.S., particularly as the proposed "black paper" was scheduled to be submitted at that year's General Assembly.[3] By the end of his African tour, Malcolm X could count on the support of half a dozen of Africa's nationalist states (ibid.). And it was in Accra, Ghana, that he unexpectedly found the most enthusiastic sponsor of his plan to group the U.S. with South Africa and Rhodesia, as prototypes of white-dominated states practicing ethnic repression against black peoples.

Malcolm X was approached by the Cuban ambassador to Ghana, Armando Entralgo González, through two leading members of the large black American expatriate community that had gathered in Ghana, attracted by the great Pan-African vision of Nkrumahism. In their informal first encounter, Entralgo let Malcolm know that Cuba's Máximo Lider still remembered their meeting in New York. Malcolm X was impressed by Entralgo. The Hispanic Cuban ambassador seemed to be most sympathetic to the plight of Blacks around the world (ibid.). Still more impressive was Entralgo's assurance that Cuba would not only support any attempt by black Americans to put the U.S. on trial for its racial crimes at the forthcoming General Assembly meeting, but would also secure the support of the Communist bloc (ibid.). Moreover, if the black American leader did not find an African state ready to sponsor such an initiative, revolutionary Cuba, a country that had already wiped out racism, would be most happy to introduce the question, along with the issue of independence for Puerto Rico (ibid.).

Armando Entralgo González was well-liked by the African liberation movements represented in Ghana.[4] A specialist in African affairs, he seemed to know the American racial situation well. The ambassador was surprised that Malcolm X had not yet visited Cuba, a country that had given asylum to Robert Williams. A meeting between Malcolm X and Robert Williams in Havana would impress black Americans, but Malcolm was in a hurry to return to the United States.[5] For Malcolm X's last night in Ghana, the Cuban ambassador hosted one of the most glittering send-off parties that the black expatriate community in Accra had witnessed in honor of a black guest.[6]

Malcolm X had evolved quite original ideas for strengthening the bonds between the black struggle in the United States and the war for emancipation going on in their ancestral continent. Malcolm X had confided to the Cuban ambassador that Nkrumah had approved the recruitment of highly trained black Americans to serve in Africa in various capacities.[7] The Ghanaian president was naturally interested in black technicians who could lessen Ghana's dependence on white expatriates. Malcolm X, however, was interested in sealing the Afro-American-African alliance with much more than technological skills. ''We have spilt our blood in World War I, in World War II, in Korea, and we are now spilling it in Vietnam. Why can't some of us do some of the spilling of blood in defense of our own brothers and sisters on the continent of Africa?'' (ibid.).[8] That theme became his leitmotif.

Malcolm X's idea of an ''Afro-American freedom brigade'' composed of Diaspora Blacks to assist in the concrete tasks of African liberation[9] caught Entralgo's attention. Washington was using white Cuban exiles to repress the insurgent struggle in the Congo at that very moment. And it was precisely the Congo that Malcolm X had in mind. The concordance of views between the black American leader and the amiable Hispanic Cuban ambassador seemed total. As events would show in less than six months, there was indeed parallelism between Malcolm's idea and Havana's intention to significantly expand its assistance to the black continent.

Fundamentally, Malcolm X was a black nationalist. However glowing the Cuban ambassador's report to Havana on his conversations with the black American leader might have been, the latter was as leery of Cuba's intentions then as he had been after meeting Castro for the first time in 1960. His ingrained suspicion of ''progressive'' white liberals could not be easily overcome. During a stopover in Paris on his way back to the U.S., he eagerly read a long article critical of the situation of Cuban Blacks since Castro's advent to power. This reinforced his conviction that there was much more than political sympathy behind Castro's open-arms policy towards the black struggle in Africa and the United States. How to respond to Havana's embrace, however, posed a dilemma.

Malcolm X was a political pragmatist. If Cuba wanted to help Africans shake off the yoke of colonialism, then it should. It was up to Africans to erect effective safeguards against the eventual co-optation of their struggles. ''I know that not even in Cuba have the whites let the black man get to the top,'' he said. ''I know Castro has something in mind, but we are weak and need whatever help we can [obtain] to get the white mercenaries and colonialists off our backs'' (ibid.).[10] He also felt that ultimately Cuba's involvement in Africa could prove beneficial for Cuban Blacks.[11] ''Castro is offering help. I say, let's take it; which doesn't keep us from asking what's going on with the black man in Cuba. . . We must know how to use Castro without Castro using us!'' (ibid.). The aim of his new organization was precisely to organize the Blacks in the New World, ''so that the Afro-Americans in the United States will be working in conjunction, in [a] coordinated program with those . . . in Cuba and those in Brazil and those in Venezuela, and those throughout the Caribbean, in Haiti and in the West Indian islands.''[12]

The Congo as Catalyst

Malcolm X returned to New York from a second African tour on November 24, 1964. On that same day, the world media announced that the U.S. and Belgium had intervened in the Congolese civil war against the rebel forces entrenched in Stanleyville. Under the cover of a rescue mission designed to free some two thousand whites held hostage by the insurgents, Washington sided openly with the most hated and discredited black leader then ruling an African state. In and out of Africa, Moise Tshombé was regarded as a blood-stained puppet of western interests.

Rallies to support the Congolese insurgents were organized in America's ghettos in an atmosphere reminiscent of the demonstrations by Blacks throughout the U.S. upon the murder of Patrice Lumumba. Addressing one such rally on November 29, Malcolm X denounced the American intervention. It was an act of ''international banditry and racism,'' he said, which called for the assembly of a brigade of black volunteers to fight alongside the Congolese against the white mercenaries leading Tshombé's army.[13] If the western powers could send anti-Castro Cubans to pilot the planes bombing African populations, or white mercenaries from South Africa and elsewhere to fight the Congolese insurgents, he pointed out, then Afro-Americans had the right and duty to assist their African kindred. (ibid.).

Daily newspaper reports spoke of mass killings in the Congo as the result of the western ''rescue mission.'' The insurgents charged that ten thousand civilians had been massacred by the Belgian-American forces of intervention. At the United Nations, the most racially charged debates in the history of the organization took place. One after another, the African delegates accused the western powers of massacring thousands of black women and children under the pretext of saving two thousand whites. The assault on Stanleyville by Belgian paratroopers airlifted in American transport aircraft had been murderous indeed. The ensuing mass slaughter of civilians had painfully reminded Africans of their helplessness in face of western intervention. Moreover, the Congolese drama seemed a reenactment of the events that led to the tragic end of Patrice Lumumba, whom most Africans revered as a hero and martyr. Cuba would now enter the picture.

photo: John Taylor

Author conferring with Malcolm X in Paris during the 1964 Congo Crisis.

On December 9, in an atmosphere charged with ethnic tension, the man considered number two in the Castroite hierarchy arrived in New York at the head of a large Cuban U.N. delegation. As Castro had done in 1960, Ché Guevara struck the racial chord from the outset. He held long discussions with Malcolm X.[14] Then during a televised interview, in a curious twist of reasoning, he said that inasmuch as Cuba had not imposed the end of racial discrimination in the U.S. as a precondition for dialogue, it was unreasonable for Washington to demand that Havana break its ties with the USSR.[15]

Guevara was to address a mass rally in the heart of Harlem. Organized by Malcolm's OAAU, the meeting was to denounce the intervention in the Congo. However, Ché changed his mind at the last minute, seemingly on Castro's orders. (The latter reportedly feared an attempt on Guevara's life in the midst of Harlem by white Cuban counter-revolutionaries.) Instead, Abdul Rahman Mohammed Babu, Tanzania's Marxist minister of commerce and cooperatives, brought a message from Guevara to the rally. Malcolm X read it to a wildly cheering audience. "Dear brothers and sisters of Harlem," Guevara wrote, "I would have liked to have been with you and Brother Babu, but the actual conditions are not good for this meeting. Receive the warm salutations of the Cuban people and especially those of Fidel, who remembers enthusiastically his visit to Harlem a few years ago. United we will win. [signed] Ché."[16]

It was precisely as a "brother" of black Africans that Ché Guevara addressed the General Assembly of the United Nations on December 11. There was no surprise in his reiteration of Havana's "solidarity with the colonial peoples of so-called Portuguese Guinea, Angola and Mozambique, who have been massacred for the crime of demanding their freedom."[17] This merely reflected Cuba's standard position on the colonial question. Nor would Guevara shock his audience with the assurance that Cubans were "prepared to help [colonized African peoples] to the extent of our ability" (ibid.). However, as he focused his speech on the situation in the Congo, it became clear that the éminence grise of the Castroite regime intended to establish Cuba once and for all as the most efficient protector that the black continent could rely on.

Guevara had already vigorously denounced the U.S.-Belgian intervention in a speech he delivered in Santiago de Cuba shortly before leaving for New York. There, he had emphasized the role being played in the Congo by white mercenaries and Cuban counter-revolutionary exiles. Before the General Assembly, he was to venture further than any other Castroite leader had till then by identifying the Cuban revolution with the black African struggle against white domination, western imperialism, colonial arrogance, apartheid, and white mercenaries.

"The brutal policy of 'apartheid,' " said Guevara, "is being carried out before the eyes of the whole world. The people of Africa are being compelled to tolerate in that continent the concept, still official, of the superiority of one race over another. . . . Can the United Nations do nothing to prevent this?" (ibid., 115). Then he turned to the "painful case of the Congo, unique in the history of the modern world, which shows how, with absolute impunity, with the most insolent cynicism, the rights of peoples can be flouted" (ibid.).

Guevara described the suffering that had been inflicted on the former Belgian colony since its independence. Guevara exalted the memory and patriotism of Patrice Lumumba, and recalled his heinous murder by the very Tshombé who was now the Congo's prime minister. He had touched very sensitive chords. The very name of Moise Tshombé conjured up deep feelings of revulsion in the hearts of African nationalists. Guevara lashed out, "And if this were not enough, we now have flung in our faces recent events which have filled the world with horror and indignation. Who are the perpetrators? Belgian paratroopers, transported by United States' planes, who took off from British bases" (ibid., 116).

Recalling the "small country in Europe, a civilized and industrious country, the Kingdom of Belgium, invaded by the hordes of Hitler," Guevara wondered aloud whether "the sons of Belgian patriots who died defending their country are not assassinating thousands of Congolese in the name of the white race, just as they suffered under the German heel because their blood was not purely Aryan" (ibid.). To an intensely attentive audience, Guevara then declared:

> [T]he scales have fallen from our eyes and they are now open upon new horizons and we can see what yesterday, in our conditions of colonial servitude, we could not observe—that "Western civilization" disguises under its showy front a scene of hyenas and jackals. That is the only name that can be applied to those who have gone to fulfill "humanitarian" tasks in the Congo. Bloodthirsty butchers who feed on helpless people! That is what imperialism does to men; that is what marks the "white" imperialists. The free men of the world must be prepared to avenge the crime committed in the Congo (ibid., 116-117).

The thunderous applause by the African representatives for those words of solidarity was an expression of gratitude to a world leader who had the courage, honesty, and decency to show the Congo events for what they were: blatant racism, interventionism, and aggression. There before the General Assembly stood a white man whose earnest outrage at the patently racist Belgo-American "rescue mission" had conveyed a condemnation that was as sharp as those by Africans themselves. Guevara's words were couched in the same terms that had made the western U.N. representatives and mass media bellow against supposed black racism. Here was a white man who was different from all the others in that he not only understood but obviously shared the gut reactions of black men, the victims of unending suffering at the hands of white tyranny. Ché Guevara, the guerrilla theorist, the purist, the "moral conscience of the Cuban revolution" as some would say, had risen to new heights in the estimation of Africans.

Guevara's implacable logic had controverted the empty rhetoric of Adlai Stevenson, who deemed the Belgo-American operation to have been necessitated by the Congolese insurgents' "violation of international law and standards of civilized behavior."[18] How could the United States speak of "standards of civilized behavior," Guevara asked, when its southern states were still the strongholds of lynching, prowling bands of Klansmen? "How can they presume to be the 'guardians of liberty' when they kill their own children and discriminate daily against people because of the color of their skin; when they not only free the murderers of the colored people, but even protect them, while punishing the Negro population because they demand their legitimate rights as free men?" (ibid., 124).

Rather than being seen as the guardian of democracy, the U.S. now appeared rather as the leader of a motley band of white tyrants comprised most conspicuously of the Afrikaaner regime in South Africa and the white minority dictatorship in Rhodesia. Guevara was firing no blanks. "We understand that today the Assembly is not in the position to ask for explanations of these acts," he remarked, "but it must be clearly established that the government of the United States is not the gendarme of freedom, but rather the perpetrator of exploitation and oppression of the peoples of the world and of a large part of its own population" (ibid.).

Malcolm X's proposal to take the case of racial oppression in the U.S. before the General Assembly surfaced when Guevara warned that "The time will come when this Assembly will acquire greater maturity and *demand guarantees* from the United States government *for the lives* of the Negro . . . population . . . in this country" (Italics added.) (ibid.). With his eyes most certainly on the Afro-Asian bloc, Guevara reminded that "those peoples whose skins are darkened by a different sun, colored by different pigments, constitute the majority" within the United Nations and the world (ibid. 117). Revolutionary Marxist Cuba had implicitly thrown in its lot with that colored majority.

Guevara's outrage at the atrocities committed in the Congo by "white imperialism" was doubtlessly sincere. Behind his indignation at the slaughter of defenseless civilian populations there was much more than sentiment, however; there was also a plan specifically designed to serve Cuban strategic interests. Cuba's gambit lay couched in a key phrase of Guevara's stirring peroration that was possibly drowned out by the applause of African representatives. "The free men of the world," said Guevara, "must be prepared to *avenge* the crime committed in the Congo." Addressing the U.N. General Assembly four years earlier, Fidel Castro had also invoked the Congo as an example of the destructiveness of western imperialism, declaring, "To this Africa we have a duty: we must save it from the danger of destruction."[19] Was Cuba's African mission to "save," "protect," and "avenge" Africa?

The Castroite leadership was very serious about its self-appointed role as protector and benefactor. Cuba, not China, would become the revolutionary guardian angel of the despised and defenseless black continent. Ché Guevara seemingly harbored no doubt whatsoever as to who was best qualified to avenge the centuries of unspeakable crimes inflicted upon Africa, and most recently in the Congo. (Hereafter this former Belgian colony will be referred to by its new name, Zaire.)

Guevara Goes to Africa

Ché Guevara left New York in triumph. He arrived in Algeria on December 18, 1964, on what was his first tour of black Africa.[20] Guevara's assessment was that Africa was the "ripest" zone of the Third World for a revolutionary upheaval of cataclysmic proportions. President Ahmed Ben Bella warmly endorsed Guevara's initiative, which he considered an ideal opportunity for "sounding out the African governments on the possibility of a political union under the leadership of Algiers."[21] To a great extent, Havana depended on the complicity of Algiers in the bold step it was about to take. Ben Bella therefore would be the first foreign head of state to be party to a secret known only by a few top men of the Castroite leadership.

The Cuban revolution had already gained enormous prestige in black Africa. Guevara's performance at the United Nations had dramatically enhanced it. Castro's alter ego was assured of being received as a hero and treated as a potential savior wherever he went on the continent. Moreover, the road for his first incursion into sub-Saharan Africa had already been paved by Cuba's black ambassador to Algiers. Maj. Jorge Serguera had forged the closest of links with all the African liberation movements based in the Algerian capital.[22] It was with one of Serguera's closest friends, Malian ambassador to Algeria Tidiani Guisse, that Guevara and his entourage left Algiers for Bamako, Mali, just after Christmas (ibid.).

Guevara spent a week discussing the state of African affairs with Malian President Modibo Keita and left for Congo-Brazzaville, whose leftist president, Alphonse Massemba-Debat, was now also a Cuban ally. This small West African country was much more strategically important for Havana than huge, impoverished Mali, as it bordered on the huge and turbulent Zaire, where a general insurrection was in progress. And it was precisely on Zaire that Cuba's attention was riveted.

The Council for National Liberation (CNL) had been formed by Christophe Gbenye, Gaston Soumialot, and Egide Bocheley-Davidson. Originally it was headquartered in Brazzaville and enjoyed the full backing of both China and the USSR.[23] Brazzaville was a conduit for the trickle of Peking's aid for the Zairian guerrillas led by pro-Chinese insurgent leader Pierre Mulele and based in the Kwilu region adjacent to Congo-Brazzaville. In addition, Brazzaville was the permanent headquarters for the Marxist MPLA, which was then conducting small-scale guerrilla operations in the enclave of Cabinda.

Ché, Massemba-Debat and Touré

President Massemba-Debat was all too glad of the opportunity to have his self-proclaimed Marxist credentials validated by Ernesto Ché Guevara, one of the most flamboyant figures of the international revolutionary movement. Massemba-Debat's regime, a floppy conglomerate of left-wing ideologues each vying for the presidential chair, could only gain from being associated with Cuba in a highly confidential venture. It was therefore in Brazzaville that Guevara met with one of the top officials of the CNL, Abdulay Yerodia, accompanied by Mandungu Bula Nyati, who had just returned from a long stay in the USSR.[24] Yerodia, who doubled as political adviser to Massemba-Debat, arranged for the first rendezvous between Guevara and Gaston Soumialot, the titular leader of the Zairian insurgents (ibid.).

Guevara's meetings with Angola's Agostinho Neto and the MPLA leadership were overshadowed by his overwhelming interest in the situation evolving in Zaire. The MPLA was then a weak movement with very limited prospects for spectacular growth. It was rivaled by another guerrilla movement, the FNLA of Holden Roberto, supported by the OAU. (UNITA, a more recent splinter group, emerged in 1966, led by Jonas Savimbi, at that time a self-styled pro-Chinese Guevarist.[25]) Nevertheless, it was agreed that Agostinho Neto would pay a secret visit to Cuba that year to discuss concrete means of assistance for his movement.

When Guevara arrived in Guinea on January 8, 1965, he had a delicate mission to perform. The lines between Havana and Conakry, which had been damaged since the October missile crisis, had to be reopened. Cuba's black ambassador to Guinea, Sergio Aguirre del Cristo, had been forced since the crisis to keep a very low profile. President Sékou Touré was as proud and haughty as Cuba's Caudillo, who had offended him during the October affair. The direct Cuban military intervention in African affairs that Ché Guevara had in mind demanded the abatement of Havana's rancor against Sékou Touré. Nor could the Guinean leader remain indifferent to the arguments of one of the most prestigious leaders of the Cuban revolutionary regime. When Guevara and his delegation left for Ghana after a week-long stay in Guinea, Touré was once again in the camp of those African leaders whom Cuba considered "firm anti-imperialist fighters."[26]

Ché and Nkrumah

Guevara chose Ghana as the site of an outspoken and carefully timed campaign stressing Cuba's Africanity. Before his daring "ethnic" speech at the United Nations, Ché had never shown the least public interest in anything related to Africa. On the contrary, he and Raúl Castro had been the chief opponents of the Afrocentric foreign policy blueprint Walterio Carbonell presented to Castro in 1959.

On January 18, two days after arriving in Accra, Guevara met with Kwame Nkrumah. In one important respect, Nkrumah differed from Sékou Touré, Modibo Keita, and the other "progressive" African leaders whom Guevara had already contacted. More than merely regarding himself as the *Osagyefo* (redeemer) of his small state, Nkrumah considered himself as the de facto leader of the entire continent. Nkrumahism was so tightly intertwined with the ideal of a Pan-African union of states that it was hard to tell where the personalistic aspect left off and continentalism began. His continental leadership ambitions had brought the Ghanaian president into sharp conflict with Nasser.[27] Nkrumah was also wary of Ben Bella's rivalry.[28]

Ben Bella could not have failed to warn Guevara that the Ghanaian president was someone to be handled with special care. As his favorite title indicated, Ghana's president saw himself as no mere mortal. Of all of Africa's "progressives," the Osagyefo was one for whom racial sensitivity had more than purely nationalistic value. Nkrumah's concern for what he called "overseas Africans," that is, New World Blacks, was real. His early acquaintance with the Afro-American world while studying in the United States saw to that. And the influence of Pan-African thinkers and activists of the diaspora, such as Marcus Garvey, George Padmore, W. E. B. Du Bois, C. L. R. James, and Ras Makonnen, had shaped his political thinking. Reciprocally, the Ghanaian leader was easily the best-known, most respected African head of state among New World Blacks, who idolized him. When Ghana became the first independent black African state in 1957, it was seen as the torch-bearer for the whole continent. Consequently, a substantial community of New World Blacks had gathered in Ghana since the early 1960s to help realize Nkrumah's dream of a United States of Africa.[29] Mostly black Americans, these Blacks were firm supporters of Malcolm X,[30] in whom both Nkrumah and Guevara had invested great confidence for divergent reasons.

Very little of what Guevara and Nkrumah discussed has filtered out. However, Guevara fully apprised Nkrumah of Havana's decision to take an active part in the struggle in Zaire. It would have been to Guevara's advantage to play up his Afro-American connections by way of Malcolm X. It was also advantageous to point out, as he did, that "Cuba is essentially an *African* country."[31] After all, it was widely known that the Tshombé regime was using white Cuban exiles to combat the insurrection. As one of the most fervent supporters of the Lumumbist cause, Nkrumah's personal revulsion for Tshombé was intense enough to guarantee his support for Cuba's intervention.

Speaking before the Ghana Association of Journalists and Writers, Guevara expressed aloud the conclusion he drew from his discussion with Kwame Nkrumah. "If the imperialists succeed in implanting themselves in the Congo and in operating from there," he warned, "then a number of progressive governments in Africa will be under a serious threat. For that reason, the situation in the Congo is a problem that we all have to consider in common."[32] Guevara hardly needed to elaborate. Nkrumah had always identified the Congo as the key to Africa.[33] In an interview with the Ghanaian organ, *The Spark*, Guevara struck a particularly responsive chord by stressing the common ethnic and cultural links binding Cuba and Africa.[34] "We also see this identity in the influence of African culture upon Cuban culture, as witnessed by the identical musical themes and the obvious popularity of Cuban music here" (ibid.).

Ambassador Armando Entralgo González privately introduced certain members of the Diaspora community of Accra to Guevara. Black American journalist William Gardner Smith was among them. He was the head of the Ghana School of Journalism at the time and was close to Shirley Du Bois, widow of the celebrated Pan-African theorist who, in turn, had been an intimate confidant of Nkrumah. Unlike the other black expatriates working for the Nkrumah regime, Smith was a long-standing Marxist.

Guevara was an avid listener. Concretely, he wanted to know about Nkrumah, Ghana's position in relation to the other African states, and the possible role Cuba could come to play in the struggle against colonialism, imperialism, and white supremacy on the black continent.[35] Smith admired Guevara immensely. He felt honored that the internationally known revolutionary idol should seek his opinions on such important matters. However, he felt that Guevara "had a tendency to simplify things too much,"[36] regarding revolution in general and Africa in particular.

Guevara was particularly curious about Africans' reactions to New World Blacks in Africa.[37] "Because of the number of African descendants in Cuba, we even qualify for membership in the Organization of African Unity," he said, half jokingly. Guevara asked, point-blank, "How do you think Africans would react to an internationalist brigade made up of black Cubans and black Americans fighting alongside liberation movements in Africa to defeat colonialism, imperialism and apartheid?" Without the least hesitation, Smith declared, "Very positively. Definitely so!" Then, as an afterthought, he added jokingly, "Especially if it were led by the great Ché Guevara!" Both men laughed, but only Smith was joking (ibid.).

Guevara's lightning two-day visit to Dahomey was perhaps the most perplexing stop on his itinerary. Dahomey was then a member of the ultra-conservative Conseil de l'Entente. A month after Guevara's visit, it became one of the founding countries of OCAM, which is generally considered to be an attempt by Africa's conservative regimes to counterbalance the radical Casablanca Group (Ghana, Guinea, Algeria, Egypt, Congo-Brazzaville, Mali, Tanzania). Sourou Migan Apithy had been president of Dahomey for exactly one year when Guevara arrived in late January. There were some indications that this regime might be veering closer to the camp of "progressive" African states.[38] And his deputy foreign minister, Stanislas Spiro Adotevi, was a brilliant left-wing intellectual. Adotevi was a long-standing admirer of Ché. "We spent a whole night conferring in my home at Porto Novo," he recalls. "I felt he was a sincere man and someone who was very serious. He was merely discovering Africa and he looked at the continent with sympathy. He was very sensitive to the problems facing the continent. At the time, great leaders were still at the head of the continent and he was very impressed upon meeting them."[39] Adotevi found Guevara "intellectually seductive," but doubted his efficiency (ibid.). Like William Gardner Smith, he felt that Guevara tended to simplify things to the extreme. Politics in Africa was much more of a complex affair than what Ché seemed to believe.

Either Nkrumah or Ben Bella might have suggested Guevara's visit to Dahomey as a means of neutralizing the conservative bloc of African states in relation to Havana's unfolding strategy on the continent. A first step in that direction had been taken during the Cairo Non-Aligned Summit of October 1964, when President Osvaldo Dorticós Torrado met with Apithy and other avowedly moderate leaders to assure them of Cuba's good will towards African peoples.[40] Guevara's quick foray into Dahomey was therefore a costless gesture.

Ché and Ben Bella

From Cotonou and Accra, Guevara returned to Algiers and compared notes with Ben Bella.[41] They also discussed Algeria's boiling internal situation, which had become a source of preoccupation for the Cuban leadership. Shortly before Guevara's arrival, Castro had warned Ben Bella, "Be very careful of [Houari] Boumedienne," with the added suggestion that a preemptive strike against the latter might be in order.[42] Ben Bella replied, "I am well aware [of this threat], but if it is I who must commit an injustice, then I would rather run the risk of being its victim. How could I do such a thing to a comrade, a friend, merely as a precaution?"[43] Castro and Ben Bella clearly did not see power politics in the same light. For Castro, a potential opponent was an actual enemy to be eliminated without hesitation. At that juncture, both Guevara and Castro were bound to see any threat to Ben Bella's absolute leadership of Algeria as a direct threat to Havana's strategic interests. Keeping Ben Bella in power was vital; Algeria had become Cuba's launching pad into black Africa.

Particularly significant to the Hispanic Cuban leadership was the fact that Ben Bella had "developed close personal ties with most of [Africa's leaders], overcoming the hostility of Black Africans towards the Arabs, something Nasser had been unable to do. Ben Bella called these leaders his 'brothers' because like him they were committed to socialism, to the liberation of the remaining African colonies, and to the struggle against western 'imperialism.' "[44]

Relations between Algiers and Accra were not the best at the time of Guevara's tour, however, because of Nkrumah's suspicion that Ben Bella had aligned himself with Nasser to usurp the leadership of black Africa. A few weeks after Guevara's second visit to Algeria, Ben Bella and Nkrumah met in Bamako, along with Sékou Touré and Modibo Keita, in an attempt to coordinate their revolutionary policies on the continent. The mini-summit was broken up by the abrupt departure of Nkrumah "after an argument between him and Ben Bella, and ended without the publication of a joint communiqué" (ibid.). Later that year, Nasser was forced to pay a state visit to Ghana to try and dissipate bad feelings between Accra and Cairo because Algeria and Egypt had become jointly involved in the Zairian civil war. By collaborating closely in an airlift to provide the insurgents with considerable quantities of Soviet weapons in November 1964, Cairo and Algiers appeared to the "Revolutionary Government of the Congo" as bastions of the "African revolution" (ibid., 168, 171). All of this had been done at the expense of Nkrumah's prestige and, apparently, without his being consulted.

Egypt was directly involved in the Zairian affair, providing money and supplies to the insurgents and lending Cairo as a site for the external activities of the revolutionary Lumumbist government. One of the latter's emissaries, Anicet Kashamura, former minister of information in Lumumba's cabinet, met with Guevara in Algiers.[45] The Zairian insurgents were anxious for help after the severe losses brought about by the western intervention in November 1964. It was no longer weapons and money that revolutionary leaders Gaston Soumialot, Christophe Gbenye, and Egide Bocheley-Davidson sought; they wanted the men who could help them seize power. That is precisely what Havana had to offer (ibid.).

In an interview with an Algerian newspaper published on January 30, 1965, Guevara expressed how much he was impressed by the situation in Africa, emphasizing the racial links between Cuba and the continent. "We have always been conscious of the African character of our culture," he said, but conceded his ignorance about Africa till then. "Cuba is Africa's relative and that kinship is the most visible in the Congo where we can detect ethnic, cultural and even physical similarities."[46] (Advanced elements of two black Cuban battalions had already arrived and were furtively poised for action in Zaire.)

Ché Guevara arrived in Egypt on February 11, and met with Nasser on the following day.[47] He concealed from the Egyptian leader what he really had up his sleeve. Guevara merely said he would be continuing to Tanzania to see about a revolutionary committee that had been set up in Dar es Salaam, with the objective of furthering the revolutionary cause in Africa. Guevara also failed to tell Nasser about the two Cuban battalions, entirely composed of Blacks, that had already crossed the Tanzanian border into Zaire to aid the insurgents. Nasser, however, reportedly contacted Ben Bella to find out what was in the making.

Ché and Nyerere

In Dar es Salaam, Guevara met with the man who was perhaps his closest associate in Africa after Ben Bella. Abdul Rahman Mohammed Babu, Tanzanian minister of commerce and cooperatives, was a party to Guevara's entire scenario. Babu's personal ties with Malcolm X had served to give Guevara's plan an Afro-American linkage. Babu was then the avowed leader of the Zanzibari Marxists who, prior to the fusion of Tanganyika and Zanzibar, had dominated the spice island through the UMMA party. Julius Nyerere had absorbed into his regime what were then perhaps the most doctrinaire Castroite Marxist cadres in Africa (these Zanzibaris were even dubbed "the

Cubans"). By so doing, he had not only removed the threat of a turbulent ultra-Marxist Zanzibar on Tanganyika's flank, but had managed to give his regime a much-needed "progressive" luster.

Nyerere's regime had at first been widely regarded with suspicion by the "progressive" hard-core regimes, especially Ghana. To Nkrumah, Nyerere was an English-speaking version of the Ivory Coast's Félix Houphouet-Boigny. Nyerere, in turn, suspected the Osagyefo of Napoleonic ambitions. The conflict never found a truly happy outcome, even when Nyerere began showing signs that he wished to leave the "moderate" camp of African leaders. The soft-spoken *Mwalimu* (Teacher) was particularly in need of a "progressive" face-lift after he had called upon British troops in January 1964 to quell an insurrection within his armed forces. The British intervention in Nyerere's favor had only served to confirm the suspicions nourished by the Casablanca Group towards his reputedly conservative regime. Union with the leftist government of Zanzibar, the incorporation into his government of the Zanzibari "Cubans," and the opening in Dar es Salaam of a Cuban embassy, all enhanced the prestige of the Mwalimu.

Pablo Rivalta Pérez, a black Cuban, had no knowledge of diplomacy or of Africa when he was appointed as Cuba's first ambassador to Tanzania in 1964. A former leader of the Cigar Workers' Union and a member of the old Cuban Communist party, he was a faithful Marxist bureaucrat with longstanding credentials of docility. With the help of the Zanzibari "Cubans," one of whom, Ali Mahfoudh Mohammed, was then a high officer in Tanzania's armed forces, Rivalta Pérez had no trouble gaining Nyerere's confidence. The Mwalimu was delighted by Cuba's selection of Tanzania as a base for the first direct act of Castroite "internationalism" in black Africa. In aiding Cuba, Tanzania was being catapulted into the select ranks of those "progressive" states that could validly claim to be following the Socialist path of development and thus qualify for massive infusions of Soviet and Chinese aid. Moreover, Nyerere could now credibly project himself as a peer of the foremost leaders of the New Africa.

After several meetings with the Mwalimu and Babu, Guevara paid a brief visit to the bases of the two Cuban battalions. When he returned to Dar es Salaam, Ché's confidence in Africa's revolutionary potential seemed limitless. In an interview in Dar es Salaam on February 18, he told the Cuban news agency *Prensa Latina* that, before coming to Africa, he was apprehensive that its leaders were not sufficiently aware of the dangers of Yankee imperialism. However, once having met with Africa's most prestigious spokesmen, he said,

"I can now say that these African countries are quite clear on this question."[48] The tone of Ché's statement suited the role the Cuban leadership had assigned itself vis-à-vis the black continent.

Guevara returned to Cairo on February 19 for a meeting with Gaston Soumialot, who was eager for any foreign intervention that would catapult the CNL to power. In fact, during the height of the fighting in Stanleyville and Paulis in November and December 1964, the insurgents had clamored in vain for Egyptian, Algerian, Ghanaian, and Guinean troops to help them fight off the Belgo-American forces. "I inform Your Excellencies that the responsibility for the loss of Africa is shared between you and me," Gbenye had pleaded in a radio message to Nasser, Ben Bella, Nkrumah, Touré, and Modibo Keita. "I have done that which I could to safeguard the honor of Africa and you have left me alone under the American and Belgian bombardments. I ask you in a final appeal, in the name of Lumumba; if you don't intervene I will adopt a scorched-earth policy."[49]

Despite a desperate visit paid to Nasser at the end of January 1965 by Christophe Gbenye and his foreign minister Thomas Kanza, the UAR was unwilling to send troops to the Congo (ibid., 225).[50] Nasser's armed forces were in fact bogged down in a war in Yemen to maintain the republican regime that had overthrown the monarchy. Nasser apparently felt that the UAR's previous aid to the Zairian insurgents had failed to enhance Cairo's position in black Africa. If anything, the Algerian-Egyptian airlift had created a great deal of antagonism with men like Nyerere and Nkrumah, each of whom had his own reason to fear an Arab monopoly over black African affairs. (Nyerere was fiercely opposed to Nasser, whom he suspected of fanning subversion among the pro-Arab factions in Zanzibar.)

Nyerere's and Nkrumah's suspicions regarding Arab ambitions in sub-Saharan Africa provided fertile ground for Cuba's growing and rather easy assertiveness in Africa. Geographically distant, "little Cuba" was not perceived as a threat by Dar es Salaam, Accra, or any other of the hard-core "progressive" African governments. In fact, not even the conservative African nations perceived Cuba's growing activity as specifically threatening. If anything, leaders such as Nkrumah and Nyerere preferred that distant Cuba become the Mecca of the African liberation movements rather than Algiers or Cairo.

Ché and Nasser

When Guevara and Gaston Soumialot met in Cairo in mid-February 1965, conditions were ripe from all points of view for

Havana to play a leading role in Africa's most potentially explosive and strategic country. The insurgent leadership thought it had found in Ché the magic formula to be catapulted to power. "We felt Ché was a sort of Messiah who would help us overthrow the Congolese government and guarantee our triumph against imperialism," recalled former Lumumba aide Anicet Kashamura.[51] On Guevara's side, too, there was a total predisposition to play the role of the messianic avenger of black Africa. "Since he himself was facing difficulties in Cuba," said Kashamura, "he reacted enthusiastically when our people asked him to join the struggle" (ibid.).[52]

Now, Guevara finally decided to confide his plans to Nasser. The latter's personal adviser and confidant, Mohammed Heikal, recounted what took place. "He [Ché] returned after ten days during which time he had been into the Congo. He told the President that he was distressed by what he had seen there. He had been visiting the forces of two battalions of black Cubans which had been raised and sent from Cuba to fight . . . and he said to Nasser that he was thinking of going to join the struggle and taking over command of the black Cubans. Nasser was astonished. Guevara, who was accompanied by the Cuban ambassador to Tanzania, Señor Rivalta, . . . said, 'I spent all night pacing my hotel room in Shepheards [sic] trying to decide if I ought to come and tell you.'"[53] Nasser, however, was by then fully aware of what Cuba was up to.

Guevara explained his feeling to Nasser that "we must do more for the revolution in the world and I thought I would come and do something in Africa. I have experience in revolutionary activities and organization and I think the situation is ripe in Africa. And I think I will go to the Congo because it is the hottest spot in the world now. With the help of the Africans through the committee in Tanzania and with the two battalions of Cubans, I think we can hurt the imperialists at the core of their interest in Katanga" (ibid., 316). Guevara wanted to know whether Nasser could contribute at least one Egyptian battalion to his big push in Zaire. Nasser flatly refused. "You astonish me," he said. "What happened to all that you were doing in Cuba? Have you quarreled with Castro? I don't want to interfere, but if you want to become another Tarzan, a white man coming among black men, leading them and protecting them. . . , it can't be done" (ibid.).

Nasser stood firm. The UAR would not engage any forces in Zaire. "First of all," he told Guevara, "you must forget all about this idea of going to the Congo. It won't succeed. You will be easily detected, being a white man, and if we got other white men to go with you, you would be giving the imperialists the chance to say that there is no difference between you and the mercenaries (ibid., 319)." The Egyptian Rais was speaking from experience, as he had already had his fingers burned in Zaire. "I believe the Revolution is a world-wide phenomenon which makes no distinction between different colors and races," Nasser continued, "but there are certain things that must be taken into consideration. What we should do is to help the Africans, try to give each people the right to do what it feels is correct. But if you go into the Congo with two Cuban battalions and I send an Egyptian battalion with you, it will be called foreign interference and it will do more harm than good" (ibid.).

Nasser's reaction merely served to confirm Guevara's lingering reservations about the UAR; had it not been for Ben Bella's insistence, the Rais might not have been drawn into the picture at all. It is significant that Guevara had taken care to speak to the Rais of his direct involvement in the Zairian struggle in terms of an *intention*. However, since the summer of 1964, three top CNL officials, Casimir Mbaguira, Albert Kissonga, and Placide Kitunga, had traveled to Havana for military training.[54] A CNL delegation had also arrived in Cuba on January 5, while Guevara was touring Africa, and two hundred hand-picked Afro-Cuban soldiers had been secretly dispatched to Tanzania. The movement of Cuban intelligence officers between Havana and Dar es Salaam was already intense.

Malcolm's Death Changes Plan

Ché Guevara had returned to Algiers for the third time in less than two months. There he learned the shocking news of Malcolm X's assassination in New York on February 21, 1965, an event widely commented upon by the news media throughout Africa. To Africans, Malcolm X's murder meant that the American ruling circles were just as determined to block the redemptionist aspirations of Americans of African descent as they were to thwart those of continental Africans. Kwame Nkrumah, Julius Nyerere, and Sékou Touré were not alone in comparing his assassination to the killing of Patrice Lumumba four years earlier. Malcolm was slain in circumstances that clearly suggested involvement by the CIA.[55]

Until the very moment of his death, Malcolm X was deeply involved in mobilizing support for the struggle in Zaire.[56] Two weeks before his assassination, he had denounced Moise Tshombé as "the only African who was criminal enough to participate in the scheme that the Western powers had of sending in Western troops." He stated that, "if the United States justifies its entry into the Congo with its military forces simply because the Head of State asks them, then Castro, who is the legal Head of Cuba, was well within his rights to ask Russia to put missiles in Cuba" (ibid., 236). American Blacks, he warned prematurely, would not remain with their arms folded before the sending of white Cuban exile mercenaries to kill Blacks in Zaire. "American planes, anti-Castro Cuban pilots, dropping bombs on African villages . . . and blowing black women to bits. . . . The anti-Castro Cuban pilots, what are they? Mercenaries, hired killers. Who hired them? The United States. Who hired the killers from South Africa? The United States; they just used Tshombe to do it" (ibid., 102, 103).

At the time of Malcolm X's murder, about one hundred militant black Americans had already been recruited[57] by the OAAU for direct participation in what Malcolm had termed the "African revolution." But whatever hopes Guevara may have pinned on incorporating these volunteers into the "internationalist brigade" he was in the process of assembling perished with Malcolm X.[58] And though rival Muslim factions were hastily blamed for his assassination, both Cuba and the U.S. had good reason to know better.

Malcolm's assasination did upset Ché's plans to a certain degree, but Guevara pushed along, undaunted, with his scheme to "diasporize" his contingent to the maximum. He sought out recruits among the pool of Afro-Dominicans and Afro-Haitians who for years had received, in Cuba, the best training in irregular warfare. Major Dreke Crúz, the Afro-Cuban military man in charge of the recruiting process, included Adrien Sansaricq among the "internationalists" who were to follow Guevara into Zaire. Sansaricq was at the time one of the chief leaders of the Cuban-based Communist Party of Haiti (PUCH). He would survive the fiasco in Zaire only to perish two years later, in 1969, in an attempt to overthrow Haiti's dictator, François Duvalier.

Officially, Ché Guevara had arrived in Algeria to head Cuba's delegation to the second Afro-Asian Economic Seminar held in Algiers from February 22 to 27. In 1960, Guevara had evoked the need for unity among the peoples of Africa, Asia, and South America, but he had warned that tricontinental solidarity could not be based on "religion, tradition, racial affinities or differences."[59] Yet, throughout his tour of Africa, Guevara now consistently attempted to project Cuba as a sort of Caribbean extension of the African world on the basis of its black population. "It is not accidental that our delegation is allowed to voice its opinion amidst the peoples of Africa and Asia," he pointed out to the delegates of the Afro-Asian Seminar. "A common aspiration—the defeat of imperialism—unites us in our march towards our future, while a common past of struggle against the same enemy has united us all along."[60]

Guevara's attempt to identify Cuba's cause with that of the Afro-Asian bloc took on surprising dimensions as he attacked Soviet trading and political policies towards the Third World. The Communist bloc, he said, had to put an end to its practice of "unequal exchange" with the underdeveloped countries, which made it as exploitative as the capitalist countries (ibid., 5). By engaging in the same economic practices of trade and commerce as the capitalists, said Guevara, "the Socialist states become, in a certain way, the accomplices of imperialist exploitation" (ibid.). Soviet trade with the Third World was consequently an "immoral type of exchange," and it was incumbent upon the Soviet bloc "to liquidate their tacit complicity with the exploiter countries of the West" (ibid.).

Guevara had concrete proposals for the establishment of a new economic order for the Third World and the Communist bloc, based on the principle of "international proletarian solidarity." The Communist bloc should not only underwrite the cost of the industrialization of the underdeveloped countries, but also provide the necessary technical cadres and technological knowledge free of charge. In sum, Guevara declared, "the development of those countries which are engaged along the path of liberation must be underwritten by the Socialist countries" (ibid., 4).

It seemed equally immoral to Guevara that the Communist countries should expect to sell weapons to the peoples and countries struggling against western imperialism and colonialism. "Weapons cannot be a merchandise among us; they must be delivered free of charge, and in whatever quantity is possible and necessary, to those people who need them to strike our common enemy" (ibid., 11). Hence, "the criminal attacks of North American imperialism against North Vietnam and the Congo must be answered by providing all of the instruments of defense these two brother countries require, and by affording them our unconditional solidarity" (ibid.).

The number-two man of the most prestigious Communist state in the Third World had publicly denounced the mercantile, profiteering, immoral conduct of the Soviet bloc with respect to the poor countries of Asia and Africa. Guevara's blunt affirmation that the development of the underdeveloped must be underwritten by the Socialist countries could only have further endeared Cuba to the bloc led by Nasser, Sukarno, Nkrumah, Ben Bella, and Touré (ibid., 7). In an international environment increasingly dominated by self-interest and power politics, the call of Little Cuba in Algiers was for revolutionary ethics, internationalist solidarity, and anti-imperialist fraternity.

Guevara drew the attention of his audience to the situation prevailing in the Congo. He pointed out that it was crucial to the fate of the entire black continent. Who could suspect Ché of any but the purest, most unselfish, and revolutionary intentions? (ibid., 8-9). Still, much was going on behind the smoke screen of the Afro-Asian Economic Seminar that had nothing to do with economics, ethics, or sentimental fraternity, and a great deal to do with the realpolitik of two regimes whose extra-national ambitions were being best served through intensive collaboration and a close alliance.

The Algiers seminar's endorsement of a proposal formulated at the Afro-Asian meeting in Moshi the previous year to hold a tricontinental summit of revolutionary movements and regimes in 1966 was the direct result of intense preparations by Havana with the backing of Algiers. Moroccan Marxist Mehdi Ben Barka, who was deeply involved in Guevara's covert activities, was the chief go-between and coordinator for this most important event. Since the meeting in Moshi he had shuttled back and forth between Cuba and Algeria. (Like Malcolm X, he was also assassinated in the most mysterious circumstances within months of the Algiers Afro-Asian Seminar.)

For his last round of discussions with Ben Bella, Ché Guevara had beside him the very man who would become the secretary-general of the tricontinental movement and who, in that capacity, would assume responsibility for coordinating all of Havana's projected "internationalist" actions in the Third World. Till then, however, Capt. Osmány Cienfuegos Gorriarán had shown no particular predisposition to playing any significant international role. He was mainly a protegé of the Castro brothers. Known by the cognoscenti to be the inconspicuous right-hand man of the Cuban intelligence chief, Maj. Manuel Piñeiro Losada, his presence at the side of Guevara in Algiers augured the leading role he would thereafter play as organizer of the secret services in Africa, and subsequently as overall supervisor of Cuba's military ventures there.[61]

A careful reading of one of Guevara's key statements to the Algerian newspaper *Revolution Africaine* gives a clear picture of where his attention was focused at the time. "Africa is one of the most, if not the most, important battlefields today against all forms of oppression," he told Josie Fanon in an interview.[62] His mind was not in the least upon Latin America, where he would ultimately lose his life, but on Africa's very heartland, where he could hope to write his best pages as a revolutionary crusader. From Algiers Ché returned to Cairo once more. He spent two weeks further coordinating his plans with the Zairian insurgent leadership,[63] then flew back to Havana on March 14 to a discreet reception, and thereafter disappeared.

14   THE "BIG PUSH" IN THE CONGO

On March 16, within two days of Guevara's return to Cuba, Havana Radio detailed an informal summary Ché had given his staff at the Ministry of Industry on his recent African tour. He frankly admitted to his previous ignorance of the real situation on that continent. He also implied that he was not alone in his former underestimation of the black continent. "Ignorance about Africa is a serious thing for us," he said. "[T]here is an extraordinary ignorance prevailing on our part about Africa."[1]

"Ché Guevara returned from his African tour frankly impressed," said Carlos Franqui, "and he relayed his optimism to the entire leadership as to the immediate possibility for Cuba to play an important role in Africa."[2] Throughout his trip, Guevara had expressed surprise at the numerous ethno-cultural and psychological correspondences between the African peoples and the bulk of Cuba's own population. The extent of Ché's surprise was perhaps proportional to his ignorance of Cuba's domestic Africa. Remarking at one point that, "It is no accident that Cuban music is so popular in Africa," Guevara concluded that "Congolese music certainly determined our own, which would therefore explain why our rhythms are quite at home there."[3] Guevara was not known to be addicted to either dancing or drumming. His aversion to Afro-Cuban fiestas and rhythms (of West African origin, and not just Congolese) was perhaps as strong as Castro's.

The Castroite leadership had come to agree with Chinese Premier Chou En-lai, who stated during his first visit to the black continent in 1963 that "Africa is ripe for revolution!" As attested by the two Communist giants' fierce struggle to gain a foothold there, the "dark continent" seemed to provide the key to mastery over the Third World. Where else but on the continents of Africa and South America could Castroite Cuba hope to play a major role in influencing the course of events at minimal material expense and strategic risk to itself? The basically sound Castro-Guevarist strategy consisted of creating a tricontinental lever by building a solid network of alliances in Asia and exporting the "Cuban model" of revolution to South America and Africa. As Guevara explained to Ciro Bustos, a personal friend, that pivotal strategy was militarily applicable only in South

America and Africa. "He believed," said Bustos, "that his thesis could be applied in two continents: Africa and South America, with *the advantage in favor of Africa* because of its greater distance from the United States and its greater logistic possibilities (Soviet Union, China, United Arab Republic, Algeria)" (Italics added.).[4] Therein, and nowhere else, lie the roots of the Afrocentric metamorphosis that Havana's foreign policy had increasingly undergone since the October missile crisis.

A Carefully Planned Operation

Ché Guevara's severe condemnation of the Soviet Union, pronounced on behalf of Cuba at the Afro-Asian Seminar in Algiers, had fully represented the views of Castro himself. His complaints about the Soviets' behavior during his private conversations with Nasser, Ben Bella, Nkrumah, Touré, Massemba-Debat, and Nyerere further reinforced Havana's image as an independent Third World country. For its own reasons, Havana found it advantageous to establish that, despite its symbiotic military and economic dependence on the USSR, Cuba was politically and ideologically aligned with the small, underdeveloped colored countries. But Guevara's castigation of the Soviet Union was so harsh that some of the leftist leaders of African liberation movements heavily dependent on Soviet aid (Eduardo Mondlane, Amilcar Cabral, Agostinho Neto) were reportedly upset.[5] Still more upset was the USSR.[6]

Castroite "anti-Sovietism" was a calculated risk. Although it was politically advantageous for Havana to adopt a critical stance vis-à-vis Moscow, that policy invited a serious deterioration of Cuban-Soviet relations. If we consider Cuba's position in world politics, the Soviet-baiting tactic was neither gratuitous nor illogical. Guevara explained the essence of Cuba's dilemma: "The real question is: Must Cuba give up its sovereignty to the Russians? Is it possible that they don't understand that this country has had too many kinds of paternalism from the great powers to accept a new one silently?"[7] He contended that, "If there is no understanding of national peculiarities within international socialism, we might as well give up; the Socialist nations will feel that they are being treated as small countries by big powers to whom being big is more important than being Socialist" (ibid.).

Ricardo Rojo asserts that Guevara was also "afraid that Soviet protection might stand in the way of Cuba's development as an autonomous nation" (ibid., 135). Due to Soviet pressure, all plans for rapid industrialization, of which Guevara was the chief advocate,[8] had been abandoned in favor of a return to sugar monoculture and heavy reliance on agriculture. However, the Cuban leadership was now ready to embark on an operation that would allow it to outflank both superpowers and restore Havana's diminishing national autonomy.

Ché Becomes "Tatu"

It was indeed a grave decision for the Cuban leadership to make. The second most important personage in the Castroite hierarchy was to assume personal responsibility for the victory of a faltering insurrection in the heart of black Africa. If successful, that venture would place the most strategically relevant country in Africa squarely within Havana's political sphere of influence. Only the promise of such a prize could have justified the decision of the Cuban leadership to take two risky steps: direct military intervention by regular Cuban forces on behalf of the Supreme Council of the Revolution insurgents, and the personal participation of Ché Guevara in the Zairian civil war. Ché would even acquire a "nom de guerre" assigned by the insurgent leadership: "Tatu," which in Swahili means number two.

"Ché Guevara's eight-month stay in the Congo . . . constitutes the most enigmatic part of his life," Gabriel García Marquez, a personal friend and confidant of Fidel Castro, was to observe as late as 1977. "Ten years after his death, the details concerning that brief period still remain scanty, despite the fact that more than a thousand people were in on the secret. However, what is still the strangest aspect are the personal and political reasons that compelled him to undertake a crusade which at the time seemed so alien to his cultural formation. . . ."[9]

Guevara's departure for the jungles of Zaire, however, was no hasty improvisation. Rather, as Ricardo Rojo explained, it was "a maneuver carefully planned by the Cuban political security service, run by Maj. Manuel Piñeiro."[10] Ché's departure was prepared with extreme care, said García Marquez, considering the "difficult problem of rendering unrecognizable a man whose photos were plastered on the walls of half the world."[11] Among the select few who knew of the maneuver was Edouard Sumbu. A top aide of CNL leader Gaston Soumialot, Sumbu had been sent to Cuba to act as a liaison between Havana and the Zairian insurgent leadership. He was to accompany Guevara to safe port once he had reached Algiers undetected. Another insider was D. H. Mansur. Officially, Mansur was a journalist for Tanzania's daily, *Uhuru*. He had arrived in Havana that spring with a discreet military delegation led by Tanzania's deputy minister of defense. The low-profile visit was connected with the intense preparations being made by Maj. Manuel Piñeiro Losada and his right-hand man, Capt. Osmány Cienfuegos Gorriarán, plans known only to the highest echelon of the Cuban bureaucracy.

While in Cuba, Mansur was constantly in the company of Major Piñeiro himself, or the latter's closest aides.[12] Despite such precautions, however, Mansur's addiction to boasting and flaunting his authority would eventually prove disastrous to the DGI's attempts to mask Cuba's "internationalist" action in Zaire (ibid., 8-13). He was, it seems, the "Deep Throat" who eventually blew Guevara's cover.

The camouflage by Cuban intelligence notwithstanding, the possibility that Guevara's presence in the former Belgian Congo at the head of Cuban fighting units might be discovered could not be ignored. That eventuality might trigger the sort of adverse, hysterical propaganda that Nasser feared. The western powers would by no means pass up such an opportunity. The Stanleyville "rescue mission" would be legitimized a posteriori, and there would be a chorus of condemnation by the West and its African allies at the U.N. against "outside Communist intervention."

Havana's original scenario for "Operation Congo" included the integration of token forces from various African countries, such as Egypt, Algeria, and Ghana. The Castroite leadership needed to make its intervention look as African as possible. Accordingly, the two Cuban army battalions that were to be the core of Guevara's forces were entirely composed of Afro-Cubans. These soldiers had entered Zaire disguised as native Africans (ibid., 8). If worst came to worst, Havana could fall back on the argument that these "overseas Africans" were acting in solidarity with their African kindred.

The assassination of Malcolm X a few weeks before Guevara's return to Cuba had seemed to rule out including a sizeable number of black Americans among the "diasporized" forces Ché planned to command. Havana may not have abandoned that idea altogether; another popular revolutionary hero of the U.S. black community, Robert Williams, was living in Cuba as an exile. In fact, his supporters in the U.S. had just formed the Revolutionary Action Movement (RAM), a clandestine militant group advocating the "violent revolutionary overthrow of the racist and exploitative American system of oppression."[13] That year, Williams had drafted a widely circulated blueprint for armed black uprisings in the U.S. in what he termed a "minority revolution."[14]

Cuban officials were aware of Williams's great popularity among radical black Americans. His pamphlets on conducting urban guerrilla warfare from the U.S. ghettos were preferred reading material for many militant black American youths. So, on March 31, 1965, the day before Guevara supposedly handed his famous farewell letter to Fidel Castro renouncing his Cuban citizenship, ministerial post, membership in the Cuban Communist party, and his rank of major, Ché summoned Williams to his office at the Ministry of Industry.[15] Williams did not have the faintest idea of why he was suddenly brought to see Guevara. In fact, he got it all wrong.

Guevara found Williams bitter about his experience as a black exile in Cuba. He had come to suspect that the Castroite regime was supporting the struggle of American Blacks for propaganda reasons;[16] that the highest-ranking officials of the Cuban leadership were conspiring to "sabotage the Afro-American struggle"; and that these officials were "racists" and acting as "counter-revolutionaries." Williams believed Major Pineiro and his chief aide were responsible for his woes (ibid., 5, 13–14).

"After our long conversation about my problems and the world situation," Williams recalls, "Ché said that he was assigning an official to help me with my immediate problems. . . . He said that he was going to the interior of Cuba for a period of one month, after which he would return to Havana and personally assume responsibility for helping me. He said that as soon as he returned he would call me by telephone so that we could take up where we left off. It was already dark and the building was deserted with the exception of the armed guards assigned to guard the Ministry of Industry and his own guards. That was the last I heard of revolutionary 'Ché' Guevara."[17]

If Guevara had summoned Williams to his office for several hours of discussion on the eve of his disappearance from public view, it was for something other than hearing out Williams's complaints. In fact, Guevara was most likely taken back by such an outpouring of bitterness. Had Williams totally misinterpreted the object of that audience? Had the black American leader unwittingly written himself out of what might have been the most exciting chapter of his life as a militant revolutionary? In all probability, yes.

A Disastrous Beginning

Guevara was in his last weeks of seclusion, preparing for his involvement in Castro's biggest overseas gamble, when Cuba received the terrible news. On June 20, 1965, a military coup led by Col.

Houari Boumedienne overthrew Ahmed Ben Bella, "the man on whom the Cubans had pinned their hopes for an African revolution."[18] Castro reportedly received the news with greater shock than he had learned of President Kennedy's assassination two years earlier.[19] The event enraged the Cuban leader.

Castro's strong reaction to the coup was in direct proportion to the serious blow it dealt to Havana's vital interests in Africa. The symbiotic ties between the Cuban and Algerian leaders were inextricable from those interests. Hence, Cuba's Máximo Lider was not interfering in the internal affairs of another country when he declared to a solemn audience that "the military *pronunciamiento* that overthrew the revolutionary government of Ben Bella is not and cannot be qualified by anyone as a revolutionary *pronunciamiento*."[20] The coup could only have been counter-revolutionary, as it was carried out "against he who unquestionably represented the majority will of the [Algerian] people" (ibid., 315).

Castro vilified the coup as "treacherous," "inglorious," "ignominious," and reminiscent of Batista's (ibid., 316, 321). He singled out Algerian Foreign Minister Abdel Aziz Bouteflika as "the one who undoubtedly masterminded the *cuartelazo*," accusing him of being "not a revolutionary, but a right-winger, known as such by the whole world and by the Algerian people; an enemy of socialism; in short, an enemy of the Algerian revolution . . . ; a reactionary" (ibid., 320).

It is remarkable that the Cuban premier placed all of the blame on Bouteflika while sparing Colonel Boumedienne, who had actually carried out the coup. It was also significant that Cuba waited a full week after the coup before making an official statement. There is good reason to believe that Castro's realpolitik was to keep an option on Colonel Boumedienne and the new junta in power. "Of immediate concern [to Castro], which he could not mention, was that Ché Guevara was on the verge of taking off for Algiers, which was to be the base from which a Cuban guerrilla force was to proceed to the Congo."[21] Hence, Castro was conciliatory towards Boumedienne, a man whom he personally detested and had distrusted from the outset.[22] The Congo operation was vital to Cuba's global strategy, and Havana was ready to compromise so long as it could proceed as planned.

It is impossible to conceive that Colonel Boumedienne, as head of the Algerian armed forces, was ignorant of the Zaire operation or the agreements Ben Bella had concluded with Guevara, namely the dispatching of Algerian forces to serve under Ché's command. In the purest tradition of Castroite pragmatism, the Cuban premier took care to signal to the new man in power that Havana was ready to come to terms under certain conditions. Referring to the Algerian junta, he said,

> Our attitude will be determined by deeds and will be based on principles. . . . [O]ur wish is that they may have the courage to prove with deeds that they are more revolutionary than the man they overthrew. . . . Our own position will be determined by what they will do in spite of what they have done now. . . . If those who engineered the coup prove by their deeds that they are against imperialism; prove with deeds that they are wholeheartedly with the Algerian revolution and body and soul with the revolution of the oppressed peoples of Africa and the world, then we will neither deny them support nor backing. And should the day come when imperialism turns against them because they are revolutionaries and threatens Algeria, we would not deny them either our moral support or our own blood to help.[23]

The message was clear: Havana would accommodate and in fact protect the new regime in the event of external aggression, provided that it carried through the elaborate operation already under way. Boumedienne's priorities did not extend south of the Sahara, however. "The most significant change in Algerian foreign policy after the overthrow of Ben Bella," explained David and Marina Ottaway, "was the shift in emphasis from Africa to the Arab world. . . . Because of his character and education, Boumedienne was more attracted to the Arab world than to Africa. He accused Ben Bella of having tried to suppress Algeria's identity as an Arab nation in order to make himself more acceptable as a Pan-African leader."[24]

Algeria's new boss spoke little but clearly. In reference to Ben Bella's African strategy, Boumedienne said: "He once talked to us in this manner: 'We must not act in Africa as Arabs because Arabism is hated there, but only as Moslem Africans leaving aside any idea of Arabism.' . . . We reacted violently, declaring that this was an opportunistic policy. We are at once Arabs and Africans, and we must remain deeply attached to our Arabism in the sense of civilization and progress."[25]

There was not the slightest indication that the new regime would honor the stratagem developed by Castro, Ben Bella, and Guevara, let alone dispatch Algerian forces to Zaire. On the contrary, Boumedienne's regime did everything but break diplomatic relations with Cuba, ordering the closing of the well-staffed *Prensa Latina* agency in Algiers and expelling its ostensible journalists. Both countries recalled their ambassadors. Within a year of the coup, Cuban-Algerian trade had dropped to $200,000 from over $3 million in 1965.[26]

The Algerian coup sowed real panic among Africa's "progressive" states, which were much weaker politically and more fragile militarily than the Ben Bellist regime. The fact that Boumedienne had toppled Ben Bella so easily made leftist leaders aware of the possibility of a military putsch in their own countries.[27] Gamal Abdel Nasser ordered several security measures that were carried out by his military boss, Field Marshal Abdel Hakim Amer. Kwame Nkrumah "was so shaken that he did not allow the news of the coup to be made public in Ghana for four days" (ibid.). Sékou Touré accurately reflected the apprehensions of Modibo Keita, Alphonse Massemba-Debat, and Julius Nyerere when he declared that "the coup d'état cannot leave us indifferent because our fate is closely tied to that of Algeria" (ibid.).

Guevara, according to some reports, had secured the promise of token units for his operation from Ghana, Guinea, Mali, and Congo-Brazzaville. The Algerian coup ended that expectation, too. None of these hard-core "progressive" leaders could spare even a symbolic batallion from their minuscule armies. Ben Bella's fall, consequently, "instigated an urgent revision of the entire diplomacy of African alliances which Guevara had built up in his fiery tour at the beginning of the year. As the Cubans saw it, the African revolution was going under, torpedoed by neocolonialism and anarchy."[28]

The success of Havana's intended "big push" in Zaire was intricately linked to complex logistical support from Algeria. The dramatic change introduced by Boumedienne's coup would have been reason enough to call off the whole operation. But the architect of Cuba's world strategy was famed for engaging in maximum-risk, virtually impossible enterprises that ended in what seemed miraculous victories: the attack on Moncada barracks; the disastrous Granma landing; the overthrow of Fulgencio Batista by a force of fewer than one thousand guerrillas; the victory at the Bay of Pigs. Cuba had even profited from the dangerous October missile crisis. Castro and his loyal followers had always prevailed. So rather than jettison the mission, "a hasty revision of logistic arrangements was required; and when Ché left Cuba the following month, Cairo instead of Algiers was his first stop."[29] Cuba would go it alone.

Mission Impossible[30]

Guevara set out for Zaire at the end of July. "He traveled with only one person, a huge, imposing Negro who was both his bodyguard and military aide," wrote Gabriel García Marquez. "The man was so conspicuous and attracted so much attention that 'Ché' Guevara kiddingly advised him to paint himself white so as to be less noticeable along the way."[31] Placide Kitunga and Albert Kissonga, the two insurgent leaders who had been undergoing training in Cuba, had left for Cairo ahead of Guevara.

Ché was received in the Egyptian capital by Sebastian Ramazani, a top military insurgent leader who operated in Kivu. He then left by air for Bujumbura, bearing an Egyptian passport and disguised as an Arab in full djellaba, fingering Koranic prayer beads all the way. This Arab trader was greeted in Burundi's capital by the leftist director-general of the foreign ministry, Evariste Bankamwabo, the only member of the government of Burundi to know of this operation.[32] Guevara left almost immediately for Uvira, then Fizi and Albertville (now Calima) in Zaire.

Three different sets of problems imperiled Guevara's mission from the outset. First, the political leadership of the insurrection was unstable. Soumialot was not on the best of terms with the two other insurgent groups in the field, led by Laurent Kabila in the Kivu region, where Ché was to be based, and by Pierre Mulele in the Kwilu area. Kabila's headquarters at Kigoma, on the eastern bank of Lake Tanganyika, was the command post of the entire zone under his authority, which was known as Zone D.[33] This area was the most important, as it was the main port of entry for weapons and provisions from China and Cuba en route to the rebel-held areas.

The second problem facing Guevara was the effect of the Sino-Soviet schism on the ranks of the insurgent leadership. Kabila and Mulele were pro-Chinese, the latter having been militarily trained in China. However, Kabila was the chief recipient of Peking's aid, which entered through the port of Dar es Salaam. According to the insurgent leadership's minister of justice and the interior, Kasmarlot Kassongo, Kabila suspected from the outset that the presence of Guevara's Cuban force in Zone D was an attempt by the pro-Soviet Soumialot faction to establish its authority (ibid.). Kabila, it seems, did not agree with, nor had he been previously consulted about, the integration of Guevara into his zone (ibid.).

The third problem sprang from Guevara's character, cultural background, and the role he was supposed to play in the Congolese struggle (see Appendix 3). This last point seems to have been ambiguous and the source of much friction. According to García Marquez, "Ché's mission was to train guerrilla groups for the National Revolutionary Council of the Congo."[34] But it is highly unlikely that the second most important personage of the Cuban revolution had made such elaborate arrangements merely to serve as a guerrilla instructor. For months, Cuban instructors had been training Zairian insurgents at special camps in Tanzania. The two army battalions under Ché's command were made up of hardened, hand-picked shock troops, solidly grounded in the techniques of irregular warfare. Ché had gone to Zaire to fulfill a mission of which even Soumaliot perhaps was unaware.

Guevara's outlook and personality were completely at variance with the general conditions in which he would be operating. His was a stern, Spartan, and imperious nature, and he had little, if any, fondness for merriment. Guevara was "very hard; very rough. . . . He was rough a majority of the time, but sometimes, with some people, he was very tender. . . . I think he had two personalities," recalled Regis Debray. "Ché was also a very authoritarian man. In the guerrilla camp he would simply say, 'This is the way it will be.' Ché did not tolerate discussion. . . . [He] was a very introverted person . . . was often alone. He was glad to speak to somebody, but he didn't find men able to converse with him, so he preferred to be alone. . . . He was a very bitter man."[35]

Guevara was also haunted by a characteristically Hispanic obsession: heroic death. "The turning point in each man's life," he had told Nasser during their last conversation, "is the moment when he decides to face death. If he decides to face death, then he is a hero whether he becomes a success or not. He can be a good or bad politician but if he cannot face death he will never be anything more than a politician." The Egyptian Rais asked, "Why do you always talk about death? You are a young man. If necessary we should die for the Revolution, but it would be much better if we could live for the Revolution."[36] It appears that he never received an answer.

Guevara's attitude towards life and death, his weltanschauung, is encapsulated in *Socialism and Man in Cuba*, which he wrote while touring black Africa. In this work, he outlined a "Brave New World" and the coming of a "New Man." The New Man, he said, eschewed "vulgar pastimes" and gaiety for a solitary life governed by Spartan discipline. The New Man must be heroic at all times and, consequently, seek "posts of greater responsibility, of greater danger, with the fulfillment of . . . duty as the only satisfaction." The New Man is characterized by "assiduity and sacrifice," and an aptitude for "mobilization and leadership." He must "combine an impassioned spirit with a cold mind and make painful decisions without flinching." The New Man must also have a strong capacity for burning hatred. "Hatred is an element of struggle; relentless hatred of the enemy that impels us over and beyond the natural limitations of man and *transforms us into effective, violent, selective and cold killing machines.* Our soldiers must be thus; a people without hatred cannot vanquish a brutal enemy" (Italics added.).[37]

When Guevara entered Zaire, he already knew of the manifold problems afflicting the insurrection at the time. Among these were political infighting, military setbacks, ideological schisms, and ethnic divisions. His critical remarks to Nasser during their last conversations in Cairo attest to his awareness of these weaknesses.[38] His presence indicated Havana's conviction that the Zairian leaders could not overcome their problems without significant foreign intervention, but Castro may have underestimated the extent of the divisions among the insurgent leadership.[39] Moreover, according to Anicet Kashamura, "the leaders of the insurrection had no true knowledge of Marxism. He [Guevara] was shocked by this and appalled at the extent of their internal divisions, even on the battlefield."[40]

At least five different factions were vying for leadership of the Zairian insurrectional movement in 1965. Of these, only two could credibly claim to have troops on the battlefield inside the country. One faction, led by Christophe Gbenye and Thomas Kanza, respectively the president and foreign minister of the ephemeral Popular Republic of the Congo, had been scattered after the Belgo-American "rescue mission." Gbenye had been minister of the interior in Patrice Lumumba's cabinet in 1960, and Kanza was the Lumumbists' permanent representative to the U.N., with ministerial rank.[41]

Another faction, which included such personages as Etienne-Richard Mbaya, Abdulay Yerodia, Kasmarlot Kassongo, and Egide Bocheley-Davidson, had given rise to the CNL in Brazzaville. A third group, formed in Cairo under the leadership of Gaston Soumialot, the former minister of defense in Gbenye's Popular Republic of the Congo, called itself the Supreme Council of the Revolution. It was intended to be both the political organ and external wing of the strong guerrilla movement of eastern Congo.

Of lesser importance, but still a factor in Congolese politics at the time, was the faction led by Antoine Gizenga, the former vice-prime minister in Lumumba's cabinet, who had gone into exile in the USSR. Pierre Mulele, former minister of education in Lumumba's cabinet, represented the fifth faction with his guerrilla army in Kwilu.

The Mulelists were considered the most leftist of all these factions vying for power. Pierre Mulele had slipped back into his native Kwilu region from Congo-Brazzaville after a year of guerrilla training in

China. The self-proclaimed Marxist regime of Alphonse Massemba-Debat had allowed Mulele to operate a training base in Gamboma on the Congo-Brazzaville side of the River Congo. Mulele had begun the armed struggle in Kwilu in 1963 with the small cadre of arms and men he had gathered at the Gamboma base.[42] Unlike the other factions, the Mulelists were receiving neither weapons nor funds from the outside.[43]

Gaston Soumialot sought Mulele's allegiance by offering him the office of first vice-president of the Supreme Council of the Revolution. Mulele swiftly declined. He rejected all of these leaders whose only common denominator was the claim to being the heir to Lumumba's mantle. Mulele saw them as being no more than opportunists and arm-chair revolutionaries, hungry for personal power.[44] He particularly loathed Soumialot's pretension to being the new Lumumba. "Lumumba said that someone stronger than himself would come to complete his work. That man is me. . . . I have come to Stanleyville. I will soon come to Leopoldville," Soumialot had once boasted in a radio broadcast.[45] Coming from a man who belonged to the same ethnic group and region as the martyred prime minister, such a claim had to be taken seriously.

Separated from Mulele's Kwilu by some 1500 kilometers of thick equatorial forest, the region of Kivu and Northern Katanga was the other fief of the Zairian insurgency. Designated as the Eastern Zone, or Zone D, this huge region was the domain of three powerful ethnic nations: Atetelas, Babembes, and Balubas of Northern Katanga (Balubakat). The dominant languages were Swahili, Kitetela, and Kibembe. Kabila's *simbas*, or lions, as the insurgent guerrillas called themselves, were mainly Atetelas. Gaston Soumialot was himself an Atetela from the Bakussu group, and Laurent Kabila was a Baluba from Northern Katanga. Both were the recognized leaders of the insurgent movement in Zone D, but each operated from his own ethnic and cultural constituency.[46]

The Soumialot-Kabila alliance was a marriage of convenience. Kabila saw the Supreme Council of the Revolution as an important external voice for Zairian insurgents, but no more. Although logistically instrumental, providing such essentials as weapons and funds, the Supreme Council was totally inefficient politically. Kabila allowed Soumialot to monopolize the international limelight, aware that ultimate power rested in Kigoma and the thousands of simbas under his command. Most of the simbas, however, belonged to Soumialot's ethnic group. Consequently, Kabila had staffed his headquarters with loyal officers from Northern Katanga.

Negotiations in Zone D

Ché Guevara's entry into Zone D came at a time when the struggle for leadership of the Zairian insurgent movement was at its fiercest. Colonel Pakassa and another Congolese had just been assassinated in Cairo. Etienne-Richard Mbaya had narrowly escaped an attack that killed one of his followers. The mysterious assassinations and disappearances of several Cairo-based Zairian leaders were officially represented as the work of "imperialist agents," however, most of those crimes were directly linked to the infighting in which Soumialot seemed to have the upper hand. It was therefore with misgivings that Kabila and his deputy greeted Guevara's arrival.[47]

Relations between Soumialot and Kabila were strained. The Cairo-based Supréme Council appeared to be a fief for the Atetelas, Soumialot's ethnic community. Kabila suspected important Supreme Council members, such as Kasmarlot Kassongo, the minister of justice and of the interior, of attempting to infiltrate assassins into Zone D in order to eliminate him. Indeed, Soumialot had made repeated attempts to curtail Kabila's powers in Zone D.

Guevara had made his first contact with Kabila earlier that year when he went to Kigoma to visit the Cuban forces and directly appraise the situation. Kabila had been amiable. This time, however, Guevara had not come as a guest. It was Soumialot who had requested troops from Havana and offered Guevara a position of command. Obviously, Soumialot was seeking a short-cut to power. He was reportedly fearful of the military successes of Pierre Mulele's Kwilu guerrillas. By relying on Cuban troops, Soumialot could count on a staunch external ally against a rival guerrilla movement. (This scenario would be repeated ten years later in Angola.)

Guevara's dealings with Kabila took place in a climate of contrived friendliness that would constantly deteriorate. Both had very definite ideas about what the Zairian revolution should be and how it should be carried out. Guevara had come with a blueprint all his own, which presumably enjoyed Soumialot's full endorsement. For the sake of efficiency, Ché wanted a single operational command to supersede both the eastern and western wings of the insurrection. The forces under Mulele and Kabila should be brought under one military umbrella, with operational instructions and coordination emanating from a single command post, he thought. Kabila and Mulele would still act as zonal commanders, but their immense areas would be split into sub-zones, each having a unit of Cuban officers and troops. Mulele and Kabila would keep their titles of commanders-in-chief; their respective zones would be called "fronts." The eastern and western fronts would have a purely military connotation rather than an ethno-geographic one.

The command structure Guevara outlined to Kabila was an exact replica of the one used in the Sierra Maestra campaign against Batista. Dar es Salaam would continue to be a port of entry for military supplies into the eastern "front." Pointe Noire on the Atlantic seaboard, some 2500 kilometers away from Kigoma, would become a second port of entry for supplies shipped directly from Cuba across the Atlantic to Congo-Brazzaville, then on to the western front. Tanzania and Congo-Brazzaville were to be the rear bases of the movement, linked to the operational center by a powerful radio network run by Cuban military technicians. The radio system would be the chief instrument for the operational coordination and unification of the insurrection's two wings.

Havana would not only provide the requisite equipment, technicians, and weapons, but would also send in additional units of elite black Cuban troops and officers. As witnessed by the adaptability of the Afro-Cuban soldiers already in Zaire, these troops would be psychologically and culturally at home. Their presence was justified in advance by the participation on the other side of counter-revolutionary white Cuban exiles and other white mercenaries from South Africa, Rhodesia, France, Belgium, Britain, and Germany. Havana was ready to raise the military level of the struggle from sporadic guerrilla ambushes to sustained conventional warfare.

As Guevara sought to persuade Kabila, news reached them of the outbreak of the most serious uprising by Blacks in the modern history of the U.S. The explosion had begun in the Watts area of Los Angeles, California, on August 18, a few weeks after Guevara had entered Zone D. This time it was no "riot"; the U.S. Army and the National Guard had made their appearance on the streets of America in armored vehicles. Black Americans were rebelling violently in the citadel of world imperialism; the importance of that black uprising to the struggle in Zaire was obvious. Kabila told Guevara that many of the U.S. soldiers in the Congo were black Americans.

If Kabila was uncommitted to the major aspects of Guevara's plan, he never gave this away. But Guevara's plan unquestionably endangered his own position. Ché's overwhelming presence was another factor. Kabila was unmoved by Guevara's arguments that the "tribal" tensions and personality quarrels that plagued the struggle in the Zaire could find a temporary solution if a "neutral" party became the commander-in-chief. Guevara had been polite but firm on that score. The problem of overall military command had to be settled. The solution he proposed was to be temporary; the important thing was to seize power. Ché believed that those destined to march in the vanguard and lead the Zairian people to a new future would emerge from the ranks of the insurgents in the course of the struggle. The insurgency, however, required a single military chief during the interim.

Guevara did not have to stress the fact that he was by far the most experienced in insurrectional and modern warfare. On the contrary, as reported by Abdulay Yerodia, he maintained a remarkably low profile, so as to avoid offending either Mulele or Kabila. Yet, it was clear that Ché's entrance into the picture potentially threatened both men's political authority and military credibility as seasoned guerrilla warlords. Until then, both Kabila and Mulele had reigned unchallenged over their respective zones.

Kabila's response to Guevara's proposals clearly indicated the grounds on which he intended to base his cooperation with Ché and the "internationalist" forces sent in by Cuba at Soumialot's request. Ché was to limit his military authority to the two Cuban battalions. He would operate in the Fizi-Baraka-Elizabethville region, directly under the control of Idelphonse Massengo, Kabila's right-hand man. That situation, Kabila in turn stressed, was "temporary." Pierre Mulele would have to be contacted; his agreement to Guevara's proposals would have to be secured; a meeting between Guevara, Kabila and Mulele would have to be arranged.

Kabila entrusted the delicate mission of contacting Pierre Mulele, some 1,000 kilometers away in the jungles of Kwilu, to one of his most trusted officers: Major Mitudidi. In the best of situations, it would take Mitudidi three months to get to Kwilu and back. Meanwhile, Guevara would remain under Massengo's jurisdiction. In short, Kabila's "temporary" solution had the same ring as Guevara's own bid for a "temporary" role as the unchallenged military leader of the Zairian revolution.

15 "OPERATION CONGO" BACKFIRES

The Cuban operation in Zaire was considerably hampered by the growing divergences among China, Cuba and the USSR. The weapons entering the port of Dar es Salaam and transported more than a thousand kilometers overland to Kigoma were Chinese. But Moscow retained an option on the insurgents by providing Soumialot's Supreme Council of the Revolution with substantial funds. The propaganda generated by both countries for the favor of the various Zairian factions was intense. The latter perceived themselves as being "pro-Chinese" (Mulelists, Kabilists), or "pro-Soviet" (Gizengists, Gbenyists). Gaston Soumialot, who pretended to play a centrist role, was widely suspected of attempting to accommodate Cuba, the Soviets, and the Chinese all at once.

Towards the end of 1965, China's dominant influence over the Zairian insurgency had to be reckoned with. Peking's diplomatic missions in Bujumbura and Dar es Salaam were nerve centers for the network of direct contacts that China maintained with the various factions. The introduction of a Cuban factor into the equation was therefore most disturbing to the Chinese. Peking had come to regard the Castroite regime as the Soviet Union's Trojan horse. Havana, in turn, saw the role being played by the Chinese in the Third World as the greatest stumbling block to Cuba's own political aims in that zone. Zaire thus became the scene of a fierce and silent tug-of-war between anti-"revisionist" China and messianic Communist Cuba. The USSR stood on the sidelines, keeping Antoine Gizenga and his exiled cohorts in reserve in Moscow. The Kremlin hoped for Peking's defeat at the hands of the Castroites, even if it meant greater leverage for Cuba in its dealings with the USSR.

Cuban and Chinese Pressures

In August 1965, Gaston Soumialot made an important tour which took him to China, the USSR, and then Cuba. While in Moscow, he attempted to bolster his position through a tactical alliance with Antoine Gizenga. Soviet planners knew the strategic importance of

Zaire in the international power struggle, and Gizenga was their main asset. The Kremlin was only too happy to foster an alliance that could afford it some leverage in any Zairian revolutionary government.

In Peking, Soumialot tried to persuade the Chinese that, once in power, he could serve their interests in Africa better than Kabila or Mulele. China was known to support the Mulelists and Kabilists and consider the other factions as "pro-Soviet," or simply "pro-imperialist." Peking had one concrete complaint: Cuban forces had been brought into a struggle that had survived the Stanleyville debacle due to China's unflagging assistance. As far as Peking was concerned, Cuba had thrown off its neutralist mask and was merely a front for Soviet revisionism. The Chinese wanted Guevara and the Cuban troops out. China could accept Soumialot's claim to be Lumumba's successor, but politely reminded him that the Zairian martyr had been "betrayed" by the Soviet revisionists, for which Cuba was but a surrogate.

Soumialot reached Havana in mid-September, 1965. His position was now quite complicated. In Moscow, he had accepted an alliance that did not satisfy the Chinese. In Peking, he had made concessions that ran counter to his Cuban obligations. Presumably, he had gone to Cuba to try to arrive at an arrangement that would be acceptable to all. However, Havana had gone into Zaire in pursuit of its own aims, which the pervasive dissensions among the Zairian insurgents were obstructing. According to Anicet Kashamura, Soumialot had come to reconsider Cuba's "internationalist" assistance, which he had so eagerly sought since the end of 1964. Cuba suspected Chinese pressures, besides his own opportunism, behind Soumialot's wavering position. Until Guevara could gain the upper hand within the insurgent movement in the field, however, Havana needed Soumialot.

The Cuban leadership had little confidence that any of the Zairian factions vying for power could win the sort of revolution Castro and Guevara apparently had in mind.[1] Consequently, Guevara's mission was not only to ensure that the Zairian revolution succeeded militarily, but also to guarantee its political success over the very men who claimed to be its representatives. Havana was in no way disposed to withdraw. Moreover, if the Chinese had their way in the Congo, it would be difficult for Cuba to regain lost ground.

The feuds within the Zairian insurrectional movement had escalated to the point where they were also putting strains on Tanzania. The pro-Marxist faction within Tanzania's government, composed of the ex-UMMA party Zanzibaris, was openly siding with Kabila. Soumialot's Cairo-based faction accused Kabila of hoarding the war materiel moving through Dar es Salaam to Kigoma and of withholding arms from guerrillas who were loyal to the Supreme Council. Julius Nyerere, who was on very good terms with Peking, was certainly aware of China's hostility toward the Cuban presence. Caught between these various conflicting interests, the Tanzanian president suspended the transit of all military supplies from Dar es Salaam into Zaire in September 1965.

When the news of Nyerere's decision reached him, Soumialot rushed to Tanzania. His arrival was timely. Dar es Salaam was preparing to host the second Conference of Nationalist Organizations from the Portuguese Colonies (CONCP) from October 3 to 8. Soumialot's words to the inaugural session of that meeting reflected the strain he was under as well as the decision he had arrived at after examining all of the pieces of the Zairian puzzle. He pointedly evoked Lumumba's memory and said that the total liberation of Zaire "would automatically bring about that of the Portuguese colonies and the rest of Africa."[2] Victory in the Congo was therefore a matter of life or death and was a concern for all of Africa. The struggle was "confronting enormous difficulties," he complained, compounded by the "feeble means placed at its disposal today" (ibid., 103). The Zairian fighters were nonetheless "ready to accept all of the sacrifices, all of the misery, all sorts of deprivations . . . and live this war through with all of its consequences until we are able to liquidate the shame [i.e. Moise Tshombé] from the face of the world" (ibid., 104).

Soumialot had chosen this meeting to make a veiled disclosure: the Supreme Council had decided to narrow its objectives to the ouster of Tshombé. In other words, Soumialot was implying his willingness to come to an understanding with a "national" government, so long as Moise Tshombé was excluded. "We have never been alone in this struggle," Soumialot told the gathering, "as the independent and progressive countries of the world are beside us and are our rear base. Their participation in our struggle is active and clear-cut" (ibid.). Less clear-cut was the reason behind Soumialot's sudden decision to reduce the goals of the insurrection to the ouster of one man rather than the overthrow of the entire neo-colonial machinery put in place by the Belgians in 1960 and propped up since then by regular western interventions. Notwithstanding his shower of praises for "brother Mwalimu Nyerere," and tirade against "colonialism, neo-colonialism and imperialism headed by the USA," Soumialot was already preparing the terrain for what Havana would consider a "non-revolutionary" and "superficial" solution to the civil war in the Congo (ibid.).

Havana Against Soumialot

Castro's concern over developments in Zaire may be ascertained from the speech delivered by the black Cuban ambassador to Tanzania, Pablo Rivalta Pérez, before the eighteen leftist and Marxist delegations at the CONCP summit meeting. Key passages presumably emanated directly from Castro himself.

Rivalta Pérez addressed the assembly on its final day. He was reportedly the only foreign diplomat to participate in the secret sessions in which the MPLA, FRELIMO, PAIGC, and CLSTP (Sao Tome and Principe) mapped out a strategy for military cooperation. A common destiny and a common enemy, said Rivalta Pérez, linked Cuba to the African freedom fighters.[3] Cuba was aware, he said, that "wherever there exists the struggle against colonialism, neocolonialism and imperialism, we are in solidarity with and are responsible for our struggling brothers" (ibid., 174–175). Better still, Cubans "could never remain with folded arms and enjoy the benefits of our revolution without sharing them with our brothers from the oppressed countries" (ibid., 175).

With the exception of FRELIMO, the other three movements in the Portuguese territories were Marxist and pro-Soviet. Even within FRELIMO, the man considered as its chief theoretician, Marcelino Dos Santos, was an avowed pro-Soviet Marxist. Therefore, China did not enjoy much elbow-room at the CONCP gathering. Representing the Chinese Afro-Asian Solidarity Committee, Liang Keng had timidly told the gathering that China understood their struggle because "the Chinese people . . . has suffered from imperialist domination and oppression. . . . We are comrades in arms and brothers."[4] Cuba had a stronger claim to advance, however.

Rivalta Pérez, who wore suits à la Nyerere and whose dark skin and tightly curled hair made him indistinguishable from the African delegates, had stressed Cuba's special kinship with black Africa. "Our people understand the struggle of the Portuguese colonies and African people in general," said the ambassador. "Our African ancestors were taken to Cuba as slaves, but today their descendants, the people of Socialist Cuba, are ready to come back and spill their blood with the people of the Portuguese colonies of Africa in their struggle for national independence against exploiters. And *they will do so* to accomplish their internationalist duty!" (Italics added.)[5] The conference hall resounded with applause as Agostinho Neto, Eduardo Mondlane, Marcelino Dos Santos, Amilcar Cabral, Mario de Andrade,

Tomás Medeiros, and other leaders of the guerrilla movements in the Portuguese colonies sprang to their feet. The two Soviet observers, Nikolai Basanov and Peter Ivfloukov, were all smiles. Expressionless, China's Liang Keng applauded politely.

Cuba's "overseas Africans" would return to shed their blood in the struggle going on to liberate their motherland. That language was definitely new. Ambassador Rivalta Pérez also denounced those who were attempting to sow dissension among the revolutionaries of Zaire. "We have seized the occasion of these past days of friendship to sound the alarm and condemn the maneuver of Yankee imperialists in the Congo," he said (ibid., 173). After intervening militarily, imperialism was now in the process of "intriguing to provoke and deepen divisions in the ranks of our Congolese brothers and to sow confusion among the independent states of Africa who are morally and materially assisting the national liberation movement of the Congo. This is being done to create schisms and block the development of the struggle" (ibid.). Yankee imperialism, said Rivalta Pérez, was "looking around for a neo-colonialist agent capable of bringing about right now a superficial solution to the Congo rather than a radical one which would endanger their neo-colonial interests in the Congo" (ibid., 173–174).

Rivalta Pérez's references to intriguers attempting to create "divisions in the ranks" of the Zairian fighters and to "sow confusion" among the progressive African states then aiding the insurgents were barely camouflaged allusions to China. The warning against the appearance of a "neo-colonialist agent" capable of setting Zaire along a reformist, rather than a revolutionary, path clearly condemned Soumialot. Indeed, the latter had just informed Castro in Havana of his intention to seek a negotiated settlement of the civil war. By calling only for Tshombé's ouster before the CONCP summit, Soumialot had revealed the only precondition for what Havana now condemned as a "superficial solution."

Steps to Reconciliation

A "national" government in which the troopless Gizenga faction could share power with the others was not at all a disagreeable solution to the USSR. Peking was inclined to accept an arrangement that would not only include the pro-Chinese factions, but also halt Cuba's lightning progress in black Africa. Only Havana stood to be a clear loser.

At the beginning of August, the major rival Zairian factions and personalities had met in Cairo to settle their leadership squabble and define a platform of cooperation.[6] Nasser supported that move for he was opposed to all foreign intervention in the Zairian civil war, including Cuba's. The various factions had agreed on two preconditions for a negotiated settlement. First, the ouster of Moise Tshombe from power along with his men. Second, the withdrawal of all foreign military and paramilitary personnel from Zaire. The latter proviso pertained to white mercenaries, U.S. military advisers, and Belgian troops, but also included any outside forces fighting on the side of the insurgents. Once these two conditions were met, a National Reconciliation Government including all of the representative personalities of the opposition would be proclaimed in agreement with Joseph Kasavubu, who would retain the presidency.

The Cairo agreements were quickly communicated to Nkrumah by Christophe Gbenye and immediately endorsed by the Osagyefo (ibid.), who was anxious to diminish Nyerere's increasing stature as a progressive leader of international repute. To widen its own base among the African states, Ghana was feverishly preparing to host the third OAU summit, slated to take place in Accra from October 22 to 27, 1965. The French-speaking "moderate" states had decided to boycott the summit. They accused Nkrumah of actively interfering in their internal affairs and seeking their overthrow by violent means. They also blamed him for the civil war in Zaire. Their absence would destroy the OAU summit, and Nkrumah was ready to do almost anything to ensure their participation. As Zaire was one of the bones of contention between the "progressive" and "conservative" African states, both Nkrumah and Nasser undertook to reassure the latter that they supported a negotiated settlement.

Nasser was particularly concerned. Continued warfare in Zaire could destabilize the Sudan, which was then combatting the Anya-Anya rebels in its south.[7] The Egyptian president, whose feud with Nkrumah had greatly abated since the Algerian coup, fully agreed that the Zairian civil war had to end.[8]

On October 13, 1965, Joseph Kasavubu summarily dismissed Moise Tshombe as premier. Calling for the withdrawal of white mercenaries from Zaire, Kasavubu's was the voice of "national reconciliation." There was much excitement among the leaders of the Supreme Council in Cairo and Christophe Gbenye and his followers in Uganda. Gizenga hastily announced his intention of returning to Zaire from

Moscow. Kasavubu had vowed to attend the OAU summit in Accra, forcing the other French-speaking African "conservative" leaders to soften their stand. The Osagyefo was happy.

When the Zairian president arrived in Ghana, Nkrumah recalled, "we were all glad to welcome him."[9] At the OAU summit, Kasavubu fully played his leading role. He spoke out against white mercenaries turning Zaire into a battlefield. He also said he opposed outside intervention in the affairs of sovereign African states and that he was determined to start from zero. All mercenaries would be expelled without delay; there would be a National Reconciliation Government that included "all of the children of the Congo." In a reconversion typical of African politics at the time, Kasavubu told his audience, "While the Congo needs Africa . . . Africa needs the Congo" (ibid.).

As Nkrumah would admit years later, the prevalent feeling was that "the future of the Congo appeared brighter than it had been for a long time" (ibid., 287). National reconciliation in Zaire became a catchword. Five years of political turmoil, insurrection, and foreign intervention had killed an estimated number of more than one million people (ibid., 278).

"The Cubans Must Leave"

In serving as the rear base of the Zairian insurrection and as the port of entry for "internationalist" assistance in men and weapons that came into the eastern zone, Tanzania had been guided by sound Pan-African considerations.[10] Like Nkrumah, Nyerere considered Zaire to be the key to Africa's destiny. The whole of southern Africa was under white rule, and in Southern Rhodesia there were clear signs that a declaration of independence by the white minority was imminent. There was a growing peril in the form of a constellation of white minority regimes ruling South Africa, Southern Rhodesia, South West Africa, and the Portuguese colonies of Mozambique and Angola.

The situation south of his borders alarmed Nyerere, who was convinced that once the white minority in Rhodesia proclaimed its so-called independence, its counterparts in Mozambique and Angola would soon follow suit (ibid.). These concerns had impelled Tanzania to aid the Zairian insurgents, FRELIMO and the other liberation movements in the Portuguese colonies. The CONCP summit in Dar es Salaam reflected these perceived threats. Nyerere's fears equally explain his agreement that Tanzania should become the transit point for Cuban and Chinese aid to the Zairian insurgents.

Nyerere's fears were realized on November 11, 1965, when Ian Smith unilaterally proclaimed the independence of Southern Rhodesia under minority white rule. A second South Africa was born. This move made Zaire all the more relevant. The "progressive" leaders of the continent clamored for a nationalist solution in Zaire that would pull Leopoldville away from the influence of the white-dominated states of the south. The rapid installation of a nationalist regime representative of all Lumumbist factions was imperative.

Cuba's leadership could not have been totally surprised when, in early November, Gaston Soumialot requested the withdrawal of the Cuban forces. Naturally, Lumumba's heirs would never forget Cuba's supreme act of "internationalist" solidarity, he said. (The bodies of the Afro-Cuban soldiers reported to have perished in Zaire were never brought home, nor did Havana ever admit to have suffered severe losses.) However, in order to facilitate a reconciliation of all of the parties concerned, and so form a truly nationalist and progressive government in Leopoldville, the Cuban forces in the eastern zone had to be withdrawn as quickly as possible. Ché Guevara was kindly requested to leave with them.

Pierre Mulele had not been a party to the negotiations that led to the Cairo agreements. He was now unwilling to rally to the reconciliation formula worked out without him.[11] It was difficult to conceive of the Mulelists continuing an armed struggle against a government that would include such prominent Lumumbists as Gbenye, Soumialot, Bocheley-Davidson, and Gizenga. But Mulele gave no sign that he was ready to emerge from his Kwilu bastion or integrate his simbas into the forces of a revamped central government.

Laurent Kabila, commander in chief of the eastern zone, was not a party to the Cairo negotiations either. His attitude paralleled that of Mulele, though Tanzania's decision to stop the inflow of war materiel into Zone D diminished his chances of continuing to oppose the Cairo decisions. Like Mulele, Kabila was to adopt a wait-and-see attitude, refusing either to leave his bastion or to dissolve his forces.

The one satisfaction Kabila had out of the new situation was the sudden rift between Soumialot and the Cubans. Understandably, Guevara was bitter. He had spent nearly six months in the eastern zone in a futile attempt to bring Kabila and Massengo around to his views. He had participated in only minor encounters and led insignificant battles against the forces of Leopoldville. He had waited patiently, stoically enduring the alien conditions, customs, and environment in which he was forced to operate. Now, before his plan could be put into action, he was simply asked to pack up and return to Cuba. The Cairo agreements were tantamount to treason. The opportunism of a gang of pseudo-revolutionary leaders was destroying the prospects of a true revolution in Zaire. Guevara would not be a party to any such maneuver.

Ché met with Kabila in mid-November, 1965, and he found him much more amenable to the Cuban proposals. Soumialot's hasty dash for power had exposed him to the progressive and revolutionary camp for what he really was: an opportunist and a demagogue. Conditions now seemed favorable in both insurgent quarters for the implementation of the plan Guevara had proposed from the outset. Kabila and Mulele could now join in a common front of opposition to the treacherous agreements of Cairo-based politicians. Kabila and Guevara reportedly agreed on a maneuver: the Cuban troops would make a show of preparing their withdrawal while stalling for time. Meanwhile, Mulele would be contacted. Unknown to Guevara or Kabila at the time was that Major Mitudidi, Kabila's trusted envoy, had been executed by Mulele upon his arrival in Kwilu, after engaging in a heated argument with the Kwilu chieftain.

By the end of November, Soumialot had become anxious about Guevara's continued presence in the area. He again contacted Havana and requested Tatu's rapid repatriation with the black Cuban troops. Castro and Guevara had exchanged several important messages. Guevara was to feign withdrawal from Zaire, redeploy the two Cuban battalions in Congo-Brazzaville, and establish contact with Mulele's forces. Kabila and Mulele now appeared as the vanguard of the Zairian revolution.

Guevara Discovered

The reconciliation laboriously achieved between Joseph Kasavubu and the nationalist opposition was destroyed on November 25 by a coup d'état. Col. Joseph Mobutu had again moved to the forefront of Zairian politics. The bloodless coup was followed by a bloody general offensive against the insurgent bastion in eastern Zaire. The strength and efficacy of the attacks by a once incompetent Zairian army betrayed new guidance. The onslaught was directed at the area under the control of Massengo, precisely where the Cuban troops and Guevara were operating.[12] Several black Cubans were reported killed in fierce fighting.[13] Guevara was quick to suspect that Leopoldville troops were being directed by American counter-insurgency experts, and that the identity of the Afro-Cuban forces had been discovered.[14]

In early December, deadly commando operations were carried out in the very area where Guevara was encamped. Tatu himself fell into two near-fatal ambushes,[15] which dispelled whatever doubts he might have had that American intelligence was fully aware of his presence in Zaire. The CIA had pinpointed the exact area where he was located. Conceivably, such discoveries had prompted Mobutu's coup. Strong evidence pointed to D. H. Mansur of Tanzania, who was a party to the secret Cuban operation in the Congo from the start, as the most likely source of the leak that led to the discovery of the Cuban forces in Zone D.[16]

Less than a month after the ambushes that nearly cost Guevara his life, Mansur arrived in Havana. No longer his self-confident self, Mansur had something on his mind; he was worried and distraught when he spoke with Robert Williams. Confidentially, he now revealed to an incredulous Williams that Cuban forces were fighting in Zaire. "Mansur . . . stated to me that the Cuban government . . . had sent many black troops there disguised as Congolese," reported Williams, "and that . . . [they] fought in the Congo and had a base in Tanzania where they received their food and supplies and often came for rest. . . . He went on to say that the Cuban government was using these black troops in Africa to engender political influence on behalf of the Soviet Union and that most of these troops were massacred, slaughtered because the imperialists discovered their presence" (ibid.).

The serious racial unrest besetting the United States at the time may well explain why there was no U.S. outcry at the U.N. against the intervention of black Cuban troops in Zaire. Given the circumstances, such a revelation could only enhance the prestige of the Castroite regime among black Americans and give Castro added luster. Still, Williams was shocked by the revelations of the Tanzanian intelligence officer. "I asked Mansur why he had turned against the Cubans since his last visit and he said it was because he found out that the Cubans were no good after working with them directly through the Embassy of Cuba in Dar es Salaam. He claimed that Cuba had a black Cuban there as ambassador who had to take orders from a white Cuban who was the first secretary and that this proved the Cubans . . . were using black puppets to further their own political interests, and those of the Soviet Union. . . . He told me that the director of Radio Havana asked him what could Cuba do to counteract the Chinese influence in Africa and that he should work for them in trying to do so" (ibid.).

A Tricontinental Backdrop

Guevara's tenacity, as well as Havana's resolve to hang onto Zaire, apparently made Castro persist in the belief that a master stroke could suddenly reverse the string of misfortunes that had beset "Operation Congo" since the start. Cuba's obstinacy indicated the importance it attached to bringing that huge country into its sphere of influence. The relevance of that goal to Cuba's vital interests justified any efforts expended to achieve it. The departure of Cuban forces from Zone D by January 1966 was consequently a redeployment rather than a retreat. Guevara would now take his chances in the western zone of Zaire. But while redeploying its forces in Congo-Brazzaville, Cuba was feverishly preparing the most important international gathering it had ever hosted. The Tricontinental conference was due to open on January 6, 1966. On January 2, Fidel Castro disclosed in a speech that Cuba was facing serious "trade problems" with China over the volume of rice exports.[17]

The timing could not have been better to bring the silent Sino-Cuban conflict into the open. Castro had chosen the proper place and circumstances for the showdown and his case was clear. Gigantic China was twisting the arm of little Cuba as punishment for its refusal to take China's side in the Sino-Soviet conflict. Peking was using a drastic reduction in the volume of rice exports to starve the brave Cuban people into submission. In short, the Chinese were instituting a food blockade against Cuba that resembled the Yankee imperialist embargo. Few could suspect the real motives behind the violent anti-Chinese bitterness vented by Fidel Castro during and after the famous tricontinental meeting. Yet these outbursts had nothing to do with Chinese rice. Simply, the Castroite regime held China directly responsible for the near disaster facing "Operation Congo" at that very moment.

When Premier Chou En-lai had visited Tanzania in June 1965, the situation in Zaire and the convening of the second summit of the Afro-Asian Peoples Solidarity Organization (AAPSO) were the chief topics of his discussions with President Nyerere. The AAPSO summit was slated to be held in Algiers on November 5 of that year. (The meeting should have taken place in mid-June, but was postponed because of Boumedienne's coup, which took place a week before the conference was to open.) For China, it was essential that the AAPSO summit take place.

Considered the direct descendant of the Bandung conference, the AAPSO had become China's chief propaganda instrument against the USSR. Control of AAPSO gave Peking the type of leverage that it sought to deny the Kremlin in the Third World. "The Afro-Asian Conference, whose name is already indicative of its character," said an official Chinese declaration, "is a summit conference of Asian and African countries. It is neither an international meeting . . . nor a summit involving other continents. Least of all is it a United Nations gathering. Consequently, participants to the Second Afro-Asian Conference must necessarily be countries of Asia and Africa, or national liberation organizations from those two continents. . . . According to that principle, the Soviet Union is not qualified to participate in the Afro-Asian Conference."[18] Only countries enjoying Soviet economic largess (Cuba, Egypt, Ghana) opposed this view.[19]

China had good reason to fear that the tricontinental conference was a Soviet-Cuban stratagem for swallowing up AAPSO. Top-ranking Cuban officials had spent a good part of 1965 traversing the Third World in order to secure massive participation in the Tricontinental, while seeking to prevent the holding of the AAPSO summit. Havana's rationale was that all forces should be marshaled behind one single Third World summit; the AAPSO meeting should be abandoned in favor of the Tricontinental, which included Latin America and was thus more representative. According to the Cubans, the Tricontinental would be the unifying agency for all anti-imperialist organizations on all three continents. But Peking saw through the Cuban and Soviet ruse and steadfastly refused to discuss a postponement of the AAPSO summit, let alone consider AAPSO's eventual merger with the projected Organization for the Solidarity of the Peoples of Africa, Asia, and Latin America (OSPAAAL).

The Algerian coup had eliminated the chief co-sponsor of the Cuban-inspired Tricontinental. However, Peking also suffered its own loss that year when a military coup sharply curtailed the powers of Ahmed Sukarno. An abortive coup by leftist Indonesian officers led by Colonel Untung and backed by the Partei Kommunis Indonesia (PKI) had provoked a right-wing counter-coup by the most reactionary elements of Indonesia's military establishment in September 1965. The rise to power of General Suharto in a reign of terror that claimed the lives of hundreds of thousands of PKI members, including its secretary-general, Dipa N. Aidit, put an end to the regime China considered its best ally in the Third World.

The demise of the bombastic regime of Bung Karno removed all hopes for the convening of a second Bandung Conference. Meanwhile, Havana was successfully rallying all of the "progressive" forces of the Third World to its position. Capt. Osmány Cienfuegos Gorriarán was the Cuban intelligence official in charge of the preparations. Moroccan pro-Soviet Marxist leader Mehdi Ben Barka was the general coordinator. Both had managed to convince even the firmest of Peking's supporters that the only solution was to hold a single meeting.

Speaking for Havana in what might as well have been AAPSO's funeral oration, Ben Barka proclaimed Cuba the country most suitable for serving as headquarters for the militantly anti-imperialist organization that the OSPAAAL was intended to be. The Tricontinental summit, he said, would be an historic event, "since both of the two currents of the world revolution will be represented: that of the Socialist revolution originating in the October revolution, and that of national liberation. . . . The Cuban revolution is the concretization of both of these currents . . . [and Cuba] is the best qualified country to hold such a gathering."[20] In October, 1965, China meekly acknowledged that "conditions were not ripe" for convening the AAPSO.

Publicly, Peking blamed Soviet revisionism, but in practice, China was now bent on making Havana pay for its tacit defeat. China was to increase pressure on both Tanzania and the Zairian insurgents for the ouster of all Cuban military personnel from Zaire. Havana felt the pinch. On October 3, 1965, in a public speech announcing the metamorphosis of the United Party of the Cuban Socialist Revolution (PURSC) into the Communist party of Cuba, Fidel Castro took China to task without naming her. He also ended several months of suspense and rumors about Ché Guevara's disappearance. He publicly read Ché's farewell letter, which proclaimed: "Other nations of the world call for my modest efforts. I can do that which is denied you because of your responsibility at the head of Cuba. . . . I have always been identified with the foreign policy of our Revolution and I will continue to be."[21]

Among the foreign guests sharing the rostrum with Fidel Castro, only Ben Barka knew that the words "other nations" referred to Zaire.[22] Ben Barka also knew to whom Castro was referring when he vehemently warned that Cuba had no lessons to learn from anyone else; that the ideological education of Cubans would be carried out by the Cuban Communist party and none other. "Our Party will educate the masses. Our Party will educate its militants. Understand this well!! Our Party! No other party except our Party and its Central Committee!"[23] Even more explicitly, Castro shouted, "We could never say that those who have helped us defeat the imperialists are accomplices of the imperialists" (ibid., 26).

Castro warned that he would not allow the divisions reigning within the Communist bloc to influence Cuban politics (ibid., 24). Cuba would develop its own ideas, its own methods, and its own Communist system (ibid., 21); Cuba aspired "to a Communist world in which all nations have equal rights . . . in which no nation has a veto. . . . We hope for a free society of free nations in which all the countries—large and small—have equal rights" (ibid., 26). Logically, Cuba needed no leave to be present in any part of the globe. "We shall never ask permission of anyone to do anything. We shall never ask anyone permission to go any place. We shall never ask permission of anyone" (ibid.).

The first salvo Castro launched against China on January 2, 1966, was followed up during the Tricontinental conference with open attacks on the whole range of Peking's policies. To begin with, the pro-Chinese movements were not invited to Cuba. Those who managed to get to Havana were prevented from participating in the summit. Lodged in distant hotels, they were forbidden to enter the conference hall, and treated as simple tourists. The Castroites even applied pressure on some African delegations to adopt an anti-China stance, according to Karamoko Keita of Mali.[24] Peking's delegation wisely kept a low profile. The Chinese delegates were virtually reduced to silence, hardly given the floor by Cienfuegos, who chaired the sessions and was appointed secretary-general of the OSPAAAL.

Addressing the closing session of the Tricontinental summit on January 15, 1966, Castro triumphantly likened the meeting to the first International held by Karl Marx and Friedrich Engels. He lectured the assembly on revolutionary principles. He praised those who met his approval and castigated those whose conduct he judged incorrect. He classed the PAIGC in the first category, designating it "one of the most serious revolutionary movements of Africa," while terming its chairman, Amilcar Cabral, "one of the most brilliant and clairvoyant leaders of Africa."[25] He reserved his attacks for men like the pro-Chinese leader of the guerrilla movement in Guatemala, Yon Sosa. He accused Sosa, who was Chinese, of being a tool of "international Trotskyism" (ibid., 3-4). Castro announced that the new leader of the Guatemalan guerrillas would be Turcios Lima (ibid.).

Castro also declared that little Cuba stood ready to dispatch forces to Asia. Although Cuba was "but a small state and enormously distant from Cambodia," said Castro, "we' are ready to contribute as much as our means allow to reinforcing Cambodia's defense. All they need do is ask for our help. Whenever they judge that the situation requires our help, then they only need ask, for we are ready to support them" (ibid., 2). Cuba was also ready to assist the other Southeast Asian countries fighting Yankee imperialism, including Laos, North Vietnam and South Vietnam. "We are a small state very close to the coasts of the metropolis of imperialism," Castro said, "but our men, our revolutionary fighters, our militants are wholeheartedly ready to fight imperialists in any part of the globe. . . . The world is big and the imperialists are everywhere, and as far as Cuban revolutionaries are concerned the whole world is their battlefield against imperialism!" (ibid.).

Zaire was foremost in Castro's mind in every word of his speech before the Tricontinental. Yet, not once did he specifically mention it. Instead, he legitimized the presence of Cuban forces there by claiming the whole world as Cuba's battlefield. He spoke at length about Guevara and, in rather vague terms, depicted Africa as a zone "where imperialism is making frantic efforts to strengthen its domination" (ibid., 3). The struggle on that continent, he said, was decisive. Cryptically, he called for African revolutionaries to "close their ranks," to act with a "sense of responsibility," and to be "serious." Still more cryptic were his references to the "weaknesses and errors" exhibited by African liberation movements which he did not name.

The revolutionary movement in Africa had "suffered serious blows and setbacks," continued Castro, but they had to surmount their difficulties and learn from their mistakes (ibid.). "Their setbacks should not discourage them; they must serve as lessons and lead to the appropriate measures and steps necessary to surmount their present difficulties, and to overcome the weaknesses of the revolutionary movement" (ibid.).

In a final stab at the Chinese leadership, Castro closed by denigrating those "who exhibit a mentality of superiority and even a delirium of insolent superiority."[26] Cuba would honor its obligations and be worthy of the confidence shown in its leadership by the Third World when it chose Havana as the headquarters of OSPAAAL and Capt. Cienfuegos as its secretary-general (ibid., 4).[27] What country was better qualified than Cuba to serve as a bridge for the three continents?

"Our country, our people, as everybody has been able to see, has a varied ethnic composition, which is the result of a mixture between peoples originating from different continents. This is what makes us profoundly close to Latin America, profoundly close to Africa, and profoundly close to all of the peoples of the other continents" (ibid.).

A Feigned Departure

Much that dealt with Zaire went on behind the scenes of the tricontinental conference. Castro was worried; "Operation Congo" was going under. Among the hundreds of African delegates attending the two-week gathering, hardly anyone took notice of two Tanzanians. Constantly in the company of Captain Cienfuegos and his boss, Maj. Manuel Piñeiro Losada, they were hardly interested in the sessions of the meeting.[28] One of these men was the chief of intelligence of Tanzania, who was "on a secret mission" (ibid., 7). His companion was D. H. Mansur. Dar es Salaam could not risk its good relations with China any further; Tanzania would remain neutral in the Sino-Cuban conflict.[29] The Tanzanian counterpart of Major Piñeiro had come to Cuba primarily to arrange the repatriation of Guevara and his forces. The situation had also become untenable for Nyerere.

"The crisis in the relations between Peking and Havana," explained Ricardo Rojo, "had an immediate effect on Guevara's stay in the Congo. It is difficult to establish the sequence of events, since virtually no one in a position to shed light on the affair has done so. According to one version, the Chinese pressured the Cubans to leave."[30]

Guevara left Dar es Salaam by air for Cairo and then apparently went on to Paris some time in January 1966.[31] According to one report, he stayed in the Paris apartment of a Frenchman of Slavic origin, Haroun Tazieff, who was one of the select few to know of Guevara's true identity and whereabouts (ibid.). From Paris, Guevara apparently flew directly to Brazzaville, where the two Cuban battalions had been secretly redeployed.[32]

The Brazzaville authorities were fully in agreement with Havana's refusal to abandon Zaire either to imperialist stooges such as Colonel Mobutu, or to such "demagogues" and "opportunists" as Gaston Soumialot and his cronies. Guevara now intended to use his troops in support of Pierre Mulele.

Ange Diawara, a young Marxist stalwart, was chief political commissar of the Congo-Brazzaville army at the time. He was designated by Alphonse Massemba-Debat to coordinate the linkage of Mulele's and Guevara's forces.[33] Congo-Brazzaville was to become the base for an operation that would bring arms, men, and supplies into the Kwilu area, where Guevara now expected to operate.[34] According to Diawara, Guevara intended to make a supply line that was not dependent on Tanzania but on Congo-Brazzaville to assist the forces of Pierre Mulele.[35] But Diawara needed time to establish contact with Pierre Mulele. Deeply entrenched in the jungles of Kwilu, the legendary guerrilla chieftain had not even approached the border with Congo-Brazzaville in over a year.

Mulele did not depend on Brazzaville either for weapons or supplies. His contacts with Massemba-Debat's government were very irregular and made through intermediaries. In fact, since evacuating the Gamboma training base in 1963, Mulele seemed not to have crossed the River Congo. Such revolutionary autonomy implied a long wait for the impatient Guevara. However, Ché was impressed by the Spartan aspects of Mulele's self-sufficiency and the reputed efficiency of his forces.

Besides Diawara, Massemba-Debat, and a few of the latter's closest aides, the only other person in Brazzaville to be aware of what was going on was the black Cuban ambassador to that country, Antonio ("Ñico") García. Another black Cuban, Teófilo Acosta, had arrived in Brazzaville at about the same time as Guevara. Officially, Acosta represented Cuba's news agency, *Prensa Latina*.[36] Outside of a very small circle in Brazzaville and Havana, no one could have been aware of what was in the making.[37] This time, Nasser, Nyerere, and Soumialot had been kept out of the picture altogether (ibid.).

According to Diawara, Guevara was supposed to "lead a column charged with opening up a rear supply line stretching from Congo [Brazzaville] to Mulele's forces in the jungles of [Kwilu] Province."[38] But as Ricardo Rojo points out, "Although on February 15, 1966, Guevara thought that he would remain in the Congo 'a long time,' his stay there would be over in another month."[39] Misfortune continued to plague Cuba's covert operation, even though Diawara had "received Guevara in top secrecy upon his initial arrival in the Congo" and handled subsequent arrangements in the same manner.[40]

Despite these great precautions, Castro received a surprising message from Gaston Soumialot. Another serious leak had taken place. Initially, Soumialot had believed that the Cuban forces and Guevara had withdrawn and returned to Cuba as he had requested. Somehow he discovered that he had been double-crossed. Castro had merely shifted his rifle from one shoulder to another. Cuba was now assisting forces the Supreme Council president considered to be more than a small threat. He thought Cuba was now on the side of the Mulelists, whereas Guevara had not yet been able to enter the Kwilu, explained Anicet Kashamura.[41] "In fact, as far as we know, Mulele himself distrusted Ché. Being a Marxist and definitely pro-Chinese, he considered Guevara to be an adventurer at best" (ibid.).[42]

Soumialot and his colleagues were convinced that Cuba had betrayed them.[43] He urgently contacted Havana from Cairo and "informed Castro that he must order Guevara to leave Brazzaville immediately, or Soumialot would publicly denounce his presence there, setting off an international scandal."[44] Havana was now in a bad position. Cuba had continued its operation behind the backs of Nasser, Nyerere, Nkrumah, Touré, and Modibo Keita. All of the good will patiently cultivated in black Africa was now at risk. Castro quickly acquiesced.

Havana was unable to ascertain the origin of the leak that had led to the discovery of Guevara's presence in Congo-Brazzaville. Castro reportedly suspected that Chinese intelligence was involved. One cannot exclude the possibility that the CIA had been aware of Guevara's whereabouts all along.[45] More than likely, however, Castro's suspicions that Soumialot got wind of the new situation through Peking were correct. Ricardo Rojo seems to imply this when he affirms that the end of Guevara's mission in Brazzaville was undoubtedly linked to "tensions between Moscow and Peking and a reflection of this tension among the guerrilla commandos in the Congo."[46]

Castro was anxious for Guevara to pull out. A series of messages to that effect were exchanged between Havana and Brazzaville. Guevara, however, insisted on staying. As much of a Promethean voluntarist revolutionary as the Máximo Lider himself, Ché was convinced he could pull off "Operation Congo" in extremis. He would stay and accomplish his mission, even against Castro's best judgment.[47]

Guevara Goes Home

Guevara apparently pleaded for time. "But Soumialot applied more pressure," revealed Rojo, "and at the end of February two men who had Fidel Castro's full confidence and were close friends of Ché's traveled to Cairo, and from there to Brazzaville: Major Emilio Aragonés, a figure of the first rank in the Cuban hierarchy, and Major Drake [sic], an officer of the army."[48]

A member of the tight circle of Castro's personal confidants and long-standing intimate friends, Major Aragonés was a high-ranking official of the Cuban government. His fellow traveler, Maj. Victor Dreke Crúz, was then one of the three highest ranking Blacks in the Cuban armed forces, along with Maj. Juán Almeida Bosque and Maj. José Causse Pérez. Dreke had fought under Guevara in the Sierra Maestra. He was the man Castro appointed to select the black Cuban troops and officers sent to Zaire. Their stopover in Cairo may have been intended both to persuade Soumialot not to cause a scandal and to give him tangible evidence that, this time, Castro intended to honor his word. (A member of the 100-strong Central Committee of the Cuban Communist party in 1966, Major Dreke was dropped from that post a year later and relieved of his army command without explanation and has not been heard of since. It seems that a similar fate befell Major Causse at about the same time.)

Guevara needed no confirmation that imperialism was in the process of launching a large-scale assault on the black continent. That part of the world was quickly becoming the chief arena for an apocalyptic clash between the forces of reaction and those of progress, just as he had envisioned. But the news that reached him on February 24, 1966, was a shock all the same. A bloody military coup led by an obscure figure, General Ankrah, had toppled the iron-fisted government of the greatest visionary of "progressive" Africa. The regime of Kwame Nkrumah had fallen easily, despite the dogged resistance of the thousand-man guard officered by Soviet and East German military advisers that had protected the Osagyefo.

Aragonés and Dreke arrived in Brazzaville and found Guevara in a most warlike mood. The coup in Ghana was merely fuel in the fire. It proved that if a revolutionary bastion was not secured in Africa in a short time, the "progressive" regimes of that continent would tumble one after the other. The already unstable regime of Massemba-Debat could not agree more with that view, as Aragonés and Dreke would find. Brazzaville's position was well summarized by Ange Diawara, for whom "the hopes of the African revolution were riding on the success of the Guevara-Mulele link-up."[49] And it was precisely, he claimed, "on the eve of that successful link-up between Guevara's column and Mulele [that] Fidel Castro sent a team of special messengers to pull Ché out of the Congo" (ibid.).

Ché clearly did not read the African situation in the same way as Castro. The special envoys reportedly handed him a coded message that Fidel and Ché had agreed upon beforehand, "only to be used in

the most urgent circumstances and which was therefore to be responded to immediately" (ibid.). Castro was adamant. Guevara must
depart right away but leave behind the two black Cuban battalions.
Havana had an entirely new plan. "Aragonés and Dreke explained the
situation and stressed the need to obey Havana's orders at once
without arguing."[50] Guevara was reluctant. However, he was a
soldier; the man in Havana was still his commander-in-chief.

In the first half of March, 1966, Guevara, his black bodyguards, and
a few Afro-Cuban officers departed from Brazzaville for Cuba. Ché
had spent almost nine months in Zaire and left as secretly as he had
come. His actions in Zaire had been a drastic departure from Cuba's
usual tactful policy of restricting its involvement to anti-colonial
national liberation movements. In the case of Zaire, Cuba had attempted to help overthrow the government of an independent state,
a mistake Castro would not repeat.

Saving Africa from Itself?

Far too many things had gone wrong in too short a time for Havana
not to see the need for reassessing its Africa strategy. With the demise
of Ahmed Ben Bella and Kwame Nkrumah, Cuba had lost its two
most solid allies in Africa. Nkrumah's overthrow particularly had
"forced the Cubans to face up to a reality: the utter frailty of those
African states which swore by the name of socialism and anti-
imperialism but whose base of support was shaky."[51] That this had
to be taken into account was one thing; what to do about it was quite
another. This dilemma apparently divided Cuba's foremost
policymakers into two diametrically opposed camps. Guevara considered the "loose," "immature," and "undisciplined" African revolutionaries as the major stumbling block to revolution. Fidel Castro felt
that the disarray of revolutionary African circles offered Cuba even
greater possibilities of maneuvering on that continent. The confusion
reigning among the progressive forces in Africa, Castro reportedly told
Angolan leader Agostinho Neto, made Cuba's internationalist assistance all the more necessary.[52]

Guevara's disappointment had been too great for him to agree, and
his bitterness was too strong to believe in Africans anymore. He attributed his failure in Zaire to the "irresponsibility" of African revolutionaries, their irresolution in face of imperialism. In his opinion, it
was the subjective factor that acted as a serious impediment to the
development of the African revolution. Black Africans were just not

ready; Cuba's future on the black continent was therefore bleak. The African revolution, Ché seems to have concluded, would have to be incubated outside of Africa. African children, brought up in Cuba in a "Marxist culture" and a "detribalized" environment, were his answer to the need for a Spartan revolutionary vanguard. For the time being, the human material was just not ready.

Before leaving Zaire, "Guevara suggested that as a last resort, we send hand-picked groups of simbas to Cuba specifically for Marxist ideological training," recounted Anicet Kashamura. "He told us bluntly, 'At least that way you will be laying the groundwork for revolution in Africa fifty years hence. But for the time being, you people don't even have an army to speak of.' "[53] Abdulay Yerodia confirmed the substance of that statement. "That was certainly an unjust assessment," he said, "which had particularly offended and further antagonized guerrilla leader Laurent Kabila."[54]

Mario de Andrade, one of the former leaders of the MPLA, also reported disagreements between Guevara and the leaders of Mozambique's FRELIMO guerrilla movement.[55] The latter refused to yield to Ché's insistence that they abandon their plans for launching guerrilla war in Mozambique and instead concentrate all their forces in Zaire. "The way he saw it," said Andrade, "was that victory in the Congo was essential and everything had to be subordinated to that aim . . . [H]e regarded the Congo as a sort of continental vanguard" (ibid.).

The "Mitudidi affair," in which one of Kabila's top military and political leaders was executed in Kwilu while on a mission to persuade Pierre Mulele to form an operational linkage between both guerrilla forces, further increased the tensions between the Cubans and their would-be proteges in Zaire.[56] According to Ciro Bustos, who later participated in and survived Ché's Bolivian debacle, Guevara told him that his experience in Africa had proven negative because the human element was not up to par.[57] There was no fighting spirit, no Spartan army, no trustworthy leadership; in short, it was just a big mess.[58]

At the outset, Guevara had been convinced that only through Cuba's assistance could Africa be protected from both the voracious imperialism of the West and the mercantile dishonesty of the Eastern Europeans. After his Congo campaign, Ché openly predicted that African emancipation was going to take "a very, very long time."[59] Nothing would happen, he felt, until a "new kind of African" emerged. In the meantime, he is reported to have said, "Let's hope that the Russians never latch onto these lands, for if they do, these poor Blacks are going to be colonized a second time."[60]

Ché's "African pessimism" resurfaced in the last important document he wrote from Bolivia. His famous message to OSPAAAL, urging the creation of "One, two, many Vietnams," reduced Africa to an insignificant role in the battle. In terms of neo-colonial invasion, he stated, Africa was still a virgin land. And although "American imperialism certainly had designs on Africa, in the long run, it didn't yet have major interests there to defend."[61] This meant that "we have to ask ourselves serious questions about the possibilities of the liberation struggle of Africans in the coming decades. Right now there is a rather intense struggle going on in the Portuguese colonies. . . . However, the political and social evolution of Africa doesn't point to a continental revolutionary situation. The liberation struggles against the Portuguese will most likely end victoriously. But Portugal is but a lesser lackey of imperialism whereas the only true revolutionary battles are those which bring the entire imperialist apparatus to its knees" (ibid., 157–160).

The conclusions Guevara drew from his prolonged stay in the heart of the black continent were Eurocentric and even racist.[62] According to one of his biographers, Guevara "did very little to hide his arrogant disdain towards black Africans who had refused his leadership" (ibid.). In this regard it is disquieting that more than twenty years after his death, Ché's African journal remains unpublished, though the document is known to be in the hands of the Cuban authorities. "I think that book will be published," Regis Debray assured in 1968, because "there is no reason to keep it a secret."[63] But time has not proved Debray right. "It was in the notebooks on his Congo campaign that Ché recorded his personal appraisal of Africa and the Africans," noted Anicet Kashamura. "It is significant that the Cuban authorities have never published them."[64]

Fidel Castro may have shared many of Guevara's conclusions on Africa. But unlike Ché's fatalism, Castro held a dynamic, Promethean overview: Africa could be saved in spite of itself. Hence, though Cuba suspended its aid to Zairian guerrillas in June, 1966, its troops remained permanently based in neighboring Congo-Brazzaville. Conceivably Castro considered the Zaire fiasco to be a temporary setback rather than a policy failure; a setback due in large part to the pernicious actions of the Chinese. This might explain why Cuba moved to expand its military presence in Africa precisely after this serious blow.

The Shift to the Portuguese Colonies

Guevara had failed to appreciate the importance of the liberation movements in the Portuguese colonies. Fidel Castro was not as short-sighted. Agostinho Neto, president of the MPLA, arrived secretly in Havana in June or July of 1966, with a small delegation headed by Major Endo, military chief of the movement. (The first batch of about one hundred MPLA military recruits arrived in Cuba in October 1966.) Castro and Neto reportedly took to one another immediately. The Angolan leader's credentials were impeccable. A hard-core Marxist, the culturally westernized Neto seemed in every respect to be the kind of reliable partner Cuba sought in Africa.

Men such as Agostinho Neto, Amilcar Cabral, and Marcelinho dos Santos were part of a predominantly "mulatto" urban elite. They were ignorant of African languages, coming from a de-Africanized middle class whose origins dated back to the nineteenth century. These "Luso-Africans" were the product of Portuguese colonization and became known as the *asimilados* (assimilated ones),[65] whether Catholics, Protestants, or Marxists. Cuba's Hispanic Cuban leadership conceivably felt more at ease with these "Latin-African" comrades than with leaders from less familiar cultural backgrounds.[66]

The most immediate outcome of Neto's trip to Cuba was a diversification of functions for the contingent of primarily black Cuban troops stationed in Congo-Brazzaville. Within two years their numbers were to rise from about two hundred to one thousand.[67] This indicated Cuba's growing interest in the feeble Angolan Marxist guerrillas rather than in the self-styled Socialist government of Congo-Brazzaville. The survival of the fragile "Marxist" regime of Massemba-Debat in Congo-Brazzaville, however, became even more important, as that country was the rear base for the MPLA. The Cuban troops there would play a triple role: protection of the Brazzaville regime, training of MPLA and PAIGC military cadres, and direct participation in the anti-Portuguese guerrilla war.[68]

By 1970, about one hundred black Cuban soldiers were reportedly in active combat with the MPLA.[69] No longer confined to the Cabinda enclave, Cuban-trained MPLA soldiers were also operating in the Dembos-Nambuangongo region, deep inside Angola.[70] (One of these units was named the "Camilo Cienfuegos Column," in honor of one of the heroes of the Cuban revolution.)

Once Cuba was convinced that it could no longer strike a spectacular blow in Zaire, Fidel Castro immediately lost interest in the outcome of the "Congolese revolution." Until June, 1966,[71] when Fidel

Castro ordered the suspension of any assistance to the Lumumbist forces, Havana had regularly praised the Zairian insurgents. By 1968, rumors were rife in certain Zairian circles that their struggle had been "sacrificed." At one point, the information leaked that Leopoldville, Brazzaville, and the MPLA had agreed that the latter, which till then had operated only in the Cabinda enclave, would gain a "right of passage" into Angola.[72]

An agreement was indeed entered into between the Soviet-backed MPLA and the U.S.-supported FNLA of Holden Roberto in Kinshasa on December 13, 1972, six years after Cuba had disengaged itself from Zaire. This agreement allowed the MPLA forces (and their Cuban officers?) to cross over the borders of both Congos into Angola. In return, the MPLA had reportedly promised the Brazzaville leaders some sort of "sharing" of the Cabinda enclave once Angola was independent.

Did Cuba back up such an agreement with a pledge of "non-interference" to the Zairian leaders? Whatever the case, the last chapter of Cuba's Zairian episode was closed when a very ill Pierre Mulele appeared unexpectedly in Brazzaville in July 1968. Accompanied by his chief spokesman there, Mibamba Zenon, Mulele may have sought asylum in the Cuban embassy,[73] according to one of many contradictory accounts. What transpired thereafter is also unclear.[74] Two weeks after his sudden appearance in Brazzaville, the legendary leader of the Kwilu guerrillas was executed by a firing squad in Leopoldville.[75] According to the Brazzaville authorities, by shooting Pierre Mulele, General Mobutu had violated certain "agreements" that have never been made public.

Cuba's role in this affair was also ambiguous. Immediately after Mulele's execution, *Granma*, the official organ of the Cuban Communist party, began a vigorous denigration campaign against the guerrilla leader. "When the Congo (K) revolutionaries sweep away the oppressors and bring the traitors to judgment," *Granma* gravely editorialized, "the name of Pierre Mulele should figure at the top of the list of traitors, both during his lifetime and after his death."[76]

PART FOUR

THE POLITICS OF
"AFROCASTROISM"
AT HOME AND ABROAD

16 BLACK POWER AND CASTRO

Coherent in its formulation, the "Castro Doctrine" on Africa was also elastic in its applications. It was credible because it stood on sound premises, of which Cuba's undeniable Africanity was the most stirring emotionally. This aspect created as many friends for Castro as the political rhetoric of the Revolution.

Emerging from several centuries of colonial and racial domination, black Africa was weak and defenseless, as witnessed by the Congo crisis in 1961 and the murder of Patrice Lumumba. The newly independent African states, particularly those which had chosen the "Socialist path," felt constantly threatened by their former colonizers and by the superpowers. They were eager for some form of external assistance to promote their national goals. Cuba's defiant bid for independence from the mighty U.S. was admired by most Africans. In turn, Cuba resorted to explicit racial arguments to buttress its growing role in black Africa.

During the OSPAAAL conference in January 1966, Fidel Castro lobbied friendly African leaders, seeking sponsorship for Cuba's admission into the OAU. Was not Cuba an "overseas African country?"[1] (Later, Fidel Castro would use the term "Latin-African" to describe Cuba and its population.) Castro therefore still felt the need to legitimize Cuba's military presence in Africa. "Why not accept Cuba as a member of the Organization of African Unity?" he asked during a meeting with the Afro-Asian press on January 28, 1966. "We have been expelled from the Organization of American States," he argued, "and we would be happy to be part of the OAU, all the more so since African blood flows in the veins of half of the Cuban people."[2]

By rushing to the aid of the motherland of half of Cuba's population, the Revolution was therefore performing its historic and "internationalist" duty. The successful integration of Afro-Cuban troops in both Zaire and Congo-Brazzaville seemed to prove the Cuban leader correct. Afro-Cubans had suffered no rejection phenomenon on the black continent. So when Amilcar Cabral, leader of the PAIGC, addressed the tricontinental assembly of revolutionaries, he endorsed Fidel Castro's claim. "We consider the people of Cuba as Africans," he stated. "It suffices to know Cuba intimately and to watch how Cubans behave to be convinced of this. It is also enough to refer to

251

our historical blood-links and to the political options that unite us. We are therefore certain that Cuba, despite its own difficulties, will not cease increasing its aid to our heroic liberation struggle."[3]

The PAIGC leader was visibly moved when he emphasized Cuba's commitment to redressing the wrongs engendered by slavery. "By retracing the old, painful and tragic path of our ancestors who were transplanted as slaves from Guinea and Angola to Cuba," he said, "we return today as free men to strengthen the historical blood-links and culture which unite our people and the Cuban people."[4]

After four years of incessant racial propaganda aimed at the black continent, had its "progressive" leaders finally taken the hook? To judge by Cabral's speech favoring the expansion of Cuba's "internationalist" role in Africa, the answer is yes.

To Massemba-Debat's Rescue

Cuba's entry into the OAU would have been a monumental victory for Castro, reinforcing his position before the U.S. and the USSR. The "progressive" leaders of African liberation movements, themselves increasingly dependent on Soviet aid, would have applauded the event. It was indeed less embarrassing to depend militarily and politically on a small Third World ally—which, in addition, was "African"—than on Eastern bloc countries. Save for Congo-Brazzaville, however, none of the independent African states agreed to open the doors of the OAU to Cuba. Neither Julius Nyerere, Sékou Touré, or Gamal Abdel Nasser were anxious to see Cuba overspread its influence in Africa. And though Kwame Nkrumah was an ardent Pan-Africanist, he could hardly have agreed to endorse a Cuban petition for membership.

Castro's overall Africa policy, as well as his debt of gratitude for Congo-Brazzaville's backing at the OAU, gave Cuba a big stake in maintaining the regime of Massemba-Debat, whose domestic power base consisted solely of support by the southern Lari-Bakongo ethnic group.[5] This precarious situation eventually required the permanent stationing of one thousand regular Cuban troops at the Dolisie military base (now Loubomo).

The Cuban ambassador to Brazzaville, "Ñico" García, a black Cuban, prided himself on having around-the-clock access to the presidential palace.[6] The Congolese themselves saw the Cuban troops as Massemba-Debat's private army. Even his bodyguards were hand-picked black Cubans. Massemba-Debat had good reason to seek shelter behind such a screen. His army was officered mainly by men of the majority northern Bangala-Mbochi ethnic groups; a member, Marien Ngouabi, finally ousted Massemba-Debat in 1968.

Official rhetoric overflowed with Marxist references to the "class struggle," the "dictatorship of the proletariat," the "power of the people," and the "building of scientific socialism." But as far as the Bangala-Mbochi populations were concerned, Socialist Congo was nothing but a monopoly of the southern ethnic groups.[7] Massemba-Debat knew well that his regime rested solely on support from two quarters: the Lari-Bakongo and the Cuban military.

Ambroise Noumazalay was named prime minister in May 1966, conceivably to ease tensions in the restless country, but this further polarized latent conflicts. Within a month, the much-dreaded revolt took place, when two senior officers, Marien Ngouabi and Jean-Jacques Poignet, attempted to seize power in a coup. Rebel troops subdued the nerve centers of Brazzaville, seized the Voice of the Congolese Revolution, and encircled the presidential palace. Massemba-Debat had already taken refuge in the Dolisie military camp, entirely controlled by Cuban troops. From there, he ingloriously appealed to Havana for help.

It took the Cuban forces no more than forty-eight hours to put their unseated client back into the saddle. In the process, Ambassador García demonstrated his own extra-diplomatic power as Havana's virtual proconsul. García had not acted on an explicit order from his superiors to respond to Massemba-Debat's anguished appeal. He enjoyed full powers to act. It was therefore on the orders of a diplomat that the Cuban troops, to the surprise of the putschists, moved into action. The black Cuban troops encircled and recaptured every strategic point that had fallen into the hands of the Congolese army.[8] That operation marked the third time Cuban forces had gone into action on the African continent. But again, the event went largely unnoticed.

Disquiet Among Africans at Home

The number of African students in Cuba on scholarships of all sorts rose steadily during the 1960s. From barely thirty students in 1964, there were five hundred from several African countries in 1966, and their numbers continued to increase at a rapid pace. (Congo-Brazzaville alone accounted for eighty students.) It was from this group of privileged, specially selected Africans that accusations repeatedly emerged which disconcerted the Cuban authorities. Many students claimed that Socialist Cuba remained a racist society.[9]

Especially embarrassing was the claim that racism was a source of friction between these African students and their hosts, including their teachers and white fellow students (ibid.).

Every so often, the Cuban authorities spoke of "provocations" and "troublemakers." The latter, according to reports, generally would be spirited back to their homelands. (Such was the case with Samuel London, a Guyanese engineering student arrested and deported for being "racially divisive.") African students kept finding new grounds for their indignation, however. It was a time when Cuba's official anthropologist, José Luciano Franco, still took such liberties with Africa's history as to claim that, "From a prehistoric point of view, we have not found any trace of the Negro [in Africa] beyond the Neolithic age."[10]

John Clytus, a black American then working for the Cuban government, witnessed the growing conflict. "From such diverse countries as Guinea, the Sudan, Kenya, Rhodesia, South Africa, the Congo and Angola, they shared a common view on Communist Cuba," he remarked. "To a man they were angry about the racial prejudice there. . . . [In 1966] . . . ninety Congolese students had demanded to be sent back to the Congo, after some members of their group had fought with Cuban 'revolutionary' soldiers over some racist remark that the latter had made to them. I had only found out about it from another student. The newspaper [Granma] didn't dare print it."[11]

Onesimo Silveira, formerly a PAIGC representative in Europe, reported that students sent to Cuba from Guinea-Bissau had complained about racism. They told Amilcar Cabral of "rather unpleasant incidents which involved the trainees from Guinea-Bissau and which they attributed to a latent racism in Cuba."[12] Havana's embarrassment was all the more serious, considering its rivalry with China, an impoverished colored nation that also felt an historic call to aid the black world.[13] Cuba could not afford the sort of scandals involving black students that plagued the Eastern bloc countries. The decision to isolate all foreign students on the Island of Youth may have been a consequence of such considerations.

Black Power Backfires

The Cuban authorities had allowed the mass exodus of the Congolese students so as not to lose face. Robert Williams's discreet exit a few months later, in August 1966, did snowball into a scandal, however. Williams chose to live in faraway China with his family because of his disappointment with Cuba, and he said so in an "Open

Letter to Fidel Castro."[14] Havana and Peking were by then in a state of open ideological war. Cuba was pouring out a torrent of invective against the Maoists, with the latter reciprocating handsomely.

In a newsletter with international distribution from Peking, Williams now painted a disquieting picture of Cuban "racial democracy." Power in Cuba, he said, was in the hands of a "white petit bourgeoisie," while Afro-Cubans were feeling the pinch of a fast-returning, subtle racism.[15] Was this the same man who, upon arriving there in 1961, had instantly become Cuba's most famous guest in exile, and who had showered lavish praises on Castro? "Cuba is the mirror of the future," Williams had declared then, "for it is here that one can truly see and experience the spirit of brotherhood which will prevail in the world of tomorrow, among peoples of all colors."[16]

Williams's charges against the Castro regime were damaging; they came from an internationally known left-wing black American militant whom none could ignore. Williams's defection was not only a great blow to Castro's self-made racial image, but also served to exacerbate Sino-Cuban tensions. After all, Williams's accusations were disseminated from China, and the Chinese also aided him in publishing *The Crusader* and distributing it worldwide.[17]

Williams's falling-out with Castro, described in his biography, *Black Crusader*, attests to his having become a thorn in the flesh of Cuba's white leadership. According to Williams's biographer, Robert Carl Cohen, a rumor began circulating in January 1965 that Fidel Castro had said, "Williams is getting too big for his pants. We are going to have to cut him down to size. . . ."[18] As Cohen detailed it,

> It was around this time that the chairman of the Communist Party in Havana called him into his office and declared, "Williams, we want you to know that the Revolution doesn't support Black Nationalism. We believe in integration, in White and Black workers struggling together to change capitalism into Socialism. Black Nationalism is just another form of racism. Cuba has solved her race problem, but if we went along with your ideas about black self-determination in the United States, it wouldn't be long before somebody would start demanding that our Oriente province should become a separate Black state and we are not going to let that happen" (ibid., 289, 290).

Cohen explains that Williams finally felt he'd "discovered one of the keys to his problem: the Party was afraid of Black Nationalist concepts spreading to the more than one-third of the Cuban population of African ancestry. This wasn't because they really suspected the Afro-Cubans of harboring separatist sentiments. . . . Instead, Williams believes that the Havana Communist Party, which was predominantly White, knew that, compared to the Black and mixed elements in the central and eastern areas, it enjoyed a disproportionately large voice in the government, and feared that an awakening of Black self-consciousness might lead to demands for a more equitable distribution of power" (ibid., 290).

Fidel Castro had always gone beyond the limit to attract black Americans, their movements, and their leaders. He had represented Cuba as a "racial democracy," keenly aware that winning and maintaining Afro-American support had practical value for any country in conflict with the U.S. Thus, when the violent racial explosions erupted in the U.S. in 1967, Cuba's media had a field day. The Black Power movement was at its strongest, and Stokely Carmichael, at the height of his popularity, was perceived as its spokesman. Havana was anxious for the latter's endorsement, chiefly to blunt Williams's attacks. Castro not only wanted to invite Carmichael to Cuba, but was reportedly eager to persuade him to stay.

The "hottest summer" known to the U.S. in terms of race relations coincided with Cuba's "big push" into Latin America by guerrilla proxy. When the newly created Organization for Latin American Solidarity (OLAS) convened in Havana in August 1967, Fidel Castro produced Stokely Carmichael at a mass rally and shouted: ". . . Stokely, ésta as tu casa!" (. . . Stokely, this is your house!) Castro introduced Carmichael warmly, told him he could remain in Cuba if he so desired (presumably to "replace" Robert Williams), and threatened to expand the revolutionary struggle right into the "bastion of world imperialism" through black America.[19]

Carmichael's participation as a special guest in a conclave reserved to the leaders of the insurrectional movements of Latin America, where Ché Guevara was attempting then to gain a foothold in Bolivia, could have had only one possible interpretation. Cuba was clearly attempting, as it always did in a situation of crisis, to use the racial unrest in the U.S. to its own advantage. The insurrectionist atmosphere created by the black American revolts at the time—the burning of cities, mass confrontations with the National Guard, urban guerrilla snipers, and the encirclement of black communities by armored vehicles and steel-helmeted "army" personnel—indeed gave the impression that Washington was facing an internal Vietnam. Castro said as much. Carmichael's presence at the OLAS meeting, he warned, should be interpreted as a sign of "the rapprochement between the revolutionary movement in Latin America and the revolutionary movement inside the United States" (ibid.).

Osvaldo Dorticós Torrado scarcely concealed Cuba's purely tactical interest in the Black Power revolt. In his opening speech to the OLAS, the Cuban president declared that "racial violence [has] been triggered in the United States [and] several North American cities [are] prey to this convulsion."[20] That situation, said Dorticós, bore witness to the "internal contradictions which, on the one hand inhibit the combat capacity of [American] imperialism to combat revolutionary movements by its having to be concerned over its own domestic front, and which reveals on the other hand its incapacity to guarantee . . . the survival of national oligarchies" (ibid.). Indeed, the violent racial explosions in the U.S. had drawn the attention of the two major Communist powers, which also hoped that the outbursts would weaken the U.S. global position.[21]

According to Cuba's media, the wave of violent "race riots" which swept through the U.S. in the summer of 1967 announced the beginning of the end of Yankee imperialism.[22] Whether or not Castro would so delude himself was another question. What seems to have preoccupied Cuban leaders, however, was how to vaccinate black Cubans against the Black Power concept. For although it encouraged the Black Power movement in the U.S., Castro was also concerned that the movement might infect Cuba. Still reeling under the effects of the conflict with Robert Williams, Cuban authorities saw the need to make certain fine distinctions. "It is from the black segment of the American population that the revolutionary movement in the United States and its revolutionary vanguard will emerge. This is so because it is the black sector which is the most exploited, the most oppressed and the most brutally mistreated in the United States," Fidel Castro explained. "It is not because of racial problems that this movement has emerged," Castro clarified, "but because of a social problem, that of exploitation and oppression."[23]

Even more instructive was the series of "clarifying" articles which appeared in *Granma* concerning the Black Power movement. Novelist Edmundo Desnoes, a Hispanic Cuban intellectual and not a mere Party hack, was called upon. He started by drawing subtle distinctions between "our" Negroes and those of the U.S. Desnoes explained that even as far back as slavery, Blacks in Cuba had fared better than those in the United States. "American society is fundamentally racist," he wrote, "which explains why the situation of black Americans increasingly compares with those of colonial societies in Latin America, Africa and Asia. It is true that our Negro population in Latin America suffered from the double alienation of being slaves in a colonial situation. However, that difference has attenuated in view of the basic confrontation between imperialism and all underdeveloped countries. In the context of this struggle, racial discrimination in Latin American countries against Indians, Negroes, or mulattoes has a lesser importance" (Italics added.).[24]

The difference between the situation of "our" Blacks in Latin America and U.S. Blacks was also manifested in the purely socioeconomic demands of the former and the more "emotional" claims of the latter. As inferred by Desnoes, Latin American Blacks (Afro-Cubans being regarded as "latins") enjoyed a sort of intellectual advantage over their U.S. kindred. "The black American movement," he stressed, "has emotional and even religious roots and is fueled by factors of humiliation and shame. Black Americans have neither the training nor the conditioning required for a well-thought-out intellectual response, for they are protesting and struggling under the accumulated weight of several centuries of exploitation and loss of identity" (ibid.).

Also writing in the Party organ, Juana Carrasco stressed that "although in recent years there has been a tendency among North American Negroes to turn towards African history and culture (clothing, languages, African names, non-straightened hair, and other external signs of identification with their roots), . . . this desire to idealize negritude also has its negative side."[25] Carrasco specified negative and even dangerous aspects of ethnic identification with black Africa. The Black Power movement, she said, could only ward off such dangers by attracting white support. She concluded that "it is more necessary than ever to achieve unity among Negroes and then obtain the support of whites in the struggle to overthrow capitalism. That's the only realistic way towards a veritable solution to the problem of racism in the United States or anywhere else in the world" (ibid.).

The government's concern came out clearly in a long essay on Black Power by writer Alberto Pedro, which was published by the important review, Casa. Pedro first repeated the distinction, past and present, "between Latin American Blacks and Blacks from Anglo-Saxon cultures," specifying that the latter had never possessed anything at all. "To the contrary, they have been denied their most elementary civil rights,"[26] and their peculiar situation had engendered an equally unique political movement. There was definitely a risk that Latin American Blacks might mistakenly identify with the Black Power doctrine and even adopt it as their own. "To say that all

Blacks are brothers," Pedro warned, "is equivalent to saying that all Blacks are equal, a premise we all know to be strictly racist. The alleged fraternity between Blacks is a trap. On the basis of such a mystification, one is easily led to establish affinities with such oppressors as Duvalier in the Americas and Tshombe in Africa" (ibid.).

With a note of sarcasm, Pedro said that, "It would be interesting to carry out the cruel experiment of shipping off an honest Cuban Negro with bags and all to, say, Haiti or Congo-Kinshasa, for blissful vacations among his 'race brothers' over there, in defiance of class interests and national borders" (ibid., 140). One ought to study Africa as one would study any other part of the world (ibid.). There was a need to consider "the ever-present risks of idealizing [Africa] or falling prey to the fetishistic belief that the world's racial problems can be solved by the mere fact of donning African tribal garments— regardless of their beauty—or by importing a traditional god, like Shango, from Bahia or the Guinea Coast" (ibid.). Pedro ended on a note of alarm:

> The problem is even more serious since *oppression has practically emptied the Negro's head*; where there ought to be a clear understanding of the most complex problems of the contemporary world, we are instead faced with an idiotic, puerile and inconsistent reasoning. We have noticed with alarm that all too frequently such a narrow reasoning affects not only the mass of Blacks, but their leaders and intellectuals as well. It is useless to adopt an ostrich-like attitude when what is at stake is the very dignity of the Negro. Black intellectuals must be cautioned: no one has the right *to replenish the empty brains of the Negro masses* with new imbecilities! (Italics added.) (ibid.).

Thus, while encouraging the violent aspects of Black Power activism, the Cuban authorities looked upon its cultural manifestations as being negative. As of 1967, the authorities took firm, humiliating measures against those black Cubans who dared wear their hair naturally in an "Afro," or who wore "odd" clothing reminiscent of African dashikis and boubous. The Black Power movement had set these trends in motion as symbolic steps away from inferiority complexes and toward a retrieval of identity. In Cuba, however, the Ministry of the Interior and the Central Committee of the Party considered it at best "eccentric strangeness," or at worst acts of "racial provocation" leading to the division of the Cuban people.[27]

There were reports of black men and women being summoned to the nearest police station and at times to the dreaded Ministry of the Interior itself, where they were urged to cut their Afros and exchange their "odd" clothing for "Cuban" apparel. (ibid.). According to official doctrine, only "deviants" (i.e., homosexuals) and other anti-social elements would engage in extravagant behavior such as the wearing of Afros and dashikis, especially when that behavior included listening to rhythm and blues, jazz, and funk, which the Party condemned as "imperialistic music" (ibid.).

Fidel Castro had done everything he could to impress Stokely Carmichael. The latter had even addressed the closing session of the OLAS as a respected American revolutionary leader, greatly impressing the would-be revolutionary guerrilla caudillos of Latin America. In a speech to more than a million of the faithful, Fidel Castro virtually sanctified Carmichael. "We would be more than honored if he chose to live here," said Castro, "but he doesn't wish to stay in Cuba because he considers the struggle at home to be his fundamental duty. Whatever the case, I would like him to know that this country is and will always be his home in any circumstances."[28]

Seven years earlier, Fidel Castro had welcomed Robert Williams in equally enthusiastic terms. While Castro was praising Carmichael, however, Williams was issuing scathing denunciations of the "deplorable racial situation" reigning in Cuba,[29] which the regime countered with the less credible charge that Williams was a "CIA agent."

Castro did not hide his interest in extending a protective arm to the black insurrectional movement developing in the United States. "[I]t must be said," he stated, "that the imperialists are . . . especially angry about the visit of such a black leader [as Stokely Carmichael], who represents the most exploited and oppressed sector in the United States. They are also angry because of the rapprochement between the revolutionary movements in Latin America and the revolutionary movement inside of the United States."[30]

Persona Non Grata

When Carmichael left Havana at the end of August 1967 for a tour of Africa and Europe, Castro had cause to believe that the black leader was firmly in his camp.[31] Among the personal gifts the Caudillo gave Carmichael were a bulletproof vest and the "loan" of two black bodyguards (ibid.). However, on a stopover in Paris, Carmichael confided the serious doubts he harbored about the racial democracy that had been flaunted by Cuban officials during his visit (ibid.). He was disturbed over the fact that Cuba's top leadership was exclusively white, and that Blacks were nowhere to be seen in positions of real power (ibid.). He dismissed as a "pack of lies" Cuba's assertion that Williams was a CIA agent. (Carmichael met and conferred with Williams while in Peking.) Carmichael felt that though Castro had accomplished a great deal in revamping Cuba, Blacks were no closer to being in power than they were before the Revolution. The color of power in Cuba hadn't changed with the Revolution; one was still dealing with White Power in Cuba, Socialist or not (ibid.).

While Carmichael was still conferring with Fidel Castro in Havana, Rap Brown—the second most important personality in the Black Power movement—expressed distrust of Castro's intentions.[32] And within months of Carmichael's return to the U.S., he openly asserted the irrelevancy of communism to Blacks in general. In the strongest attack on communism by any of the radical Black Power leaders, he said:

> Now then, that brings us to the point of this thing about communism and socialism. Let's get to that once and for all. Communism is not an ideology suited for black people, period. Period! Socialism is not an ideology fitted for black people, period. Period! The ideologies of communism and socialism speak to class struggle. We are not just facing exploitation. We are facing something much more important, because we are the victims of racism. [Neither] Communism nor socialism . . . speak to the problem of racism. And racism, for black people in this country, is far more important than exploitation. So that for us, the question of racism becomes uppermost in our minds. . . . We must therefore consciously strive for an ideology which deals with racism first. . . . That's what we recognize. . . . It is our humanity that is at stake. It is not a question of dollars and cents.[33]

After this speech, Carmichael was declared persona non grata in Cuba, and an officially inspired rumor began circulating that the Black Power leader had been "co-opted by the CIA."[34] The rapprochement between the Black Power movement and Cuba had been brief. Havana was now ready to throw in its lot with a rival faction, the Black Panther movement, which fancied itself Marxist-Leninist. The Black Panthers emphasized guns rather than "black cultural nationalism," urban guerrilla war rather than mass rallies, and secrecy based on tightly knit cells similar to the structure of Communist parties. Their doctrine of "class struggle" and their desire for an alliance with "white progressives," made the Black Panthers altogether acceptable to Havana.

On December 25, 1968, Eldridge Cleaver, the de facto spokesman and theorist of the Black Panthers, arrived secretly in Cuba, while daily shootouts were occurring across the U.S. between armed Panthers and the police. He was kept out of public view by Cuban intelligence. Once again, however, things went wrong between Cuban officials and their revolutionary black guest, who also began complaining of "racism."[35] Within five months of his arrival, Cleaver boarded an airliner headed for Algeria, a meteoric fall from "comrade" to yet another black persona non grata.[36]

17 THE TURNING POINT

The period from 1966 to 1969 is one of the most intriguing in the history of revolutionary Cuba's foreign policy. The fiasco in Zaire—an episode so bizarre that, two decades after, it remained cloaked in mystery—was followed by a string of setbacks and baffling international quarrels. On the surface, it seemed that Fidel Castro had decided to take on the whole world.

Cuba was in conflict with the USSR, the People's Republic of China and, of course, with the "hereditary enemy" and its allies in Latin America (all governments of the area save Mexico). It was also at odds with the Latin American Communist parties and Trotskyist movements. Independent-minded guerrilla leaders, like MR-13 leader Yon Sosa in Guatemala, refused to be dictated to by Havana. The leaders of the Guatemalan revolution were chosen in armed struggle in the streets and mountains of Guatemala, he had warned, not in the Hotel Habana Libre. Fidel Castro was accused of having attempted to apply to MR-13 the same big-power policy the Soviet Union had exercised on Cuba.[1]

Castro's confrontationism was actually the outcome of an ingenious and coherent foreign policy strategy based on political brinksmanship. When that policy began to backfire from all directions, an over-confident Cuban leadership—trapped by overestimating of its own manipulative prowess—was left dangerously exposed. What else could explain Cuba's stunning foreign policy turnabout in mid-1968 and subsequent swift re-accommodation with the Kremlin?[2]

For the black continent, these events presaged a sharp escalation in Cuba's military-political role there. In fact, the end of Fidel Castro's all-around confrontationism allowed Cuba, with Soviet urging and blessings, to selectively direct the brunt of its "internationalist" efforts towards black Africa, dealing a lethal blow to Chinese influence in passing. All of this occurred in a swift succession of highly dramatic events.

Confronting China

The convening in Havana of the Tricontinental conference in January 1966 had been the occasion of open confrontation between

Cuba and China. No sooner was the gathering over than Havana unleashed its full fury on the People's Republic of China, accusing it of
having incited Cuban military cadres and officials to engage in
treasonable acts.[3] On March 13, 1966—exactly a week after Guevara
had returned from Africa—Fidel Castro assaulted the Chinese with
a fierceness that surprised many. Speaking to a mass rally, in what
some observers termed "a vulgar and unbridled attack,"[4] he said that
Chinese leaders were "incompetent" and "senile" old men and
likened China to an "absolute monarchy."[5] In contrast, he said,
Cubans had "the chance of being ruled by young men" whose only
concern was to "administer" power on behalf of the people. "Power
is neither mine nor vested in a group of ten or twenty people,"
claimed Castro. In Cuba, power was "not even in the hands of the
Party's Central Committee," but belonged to the masses, he insisted.
"Power is in the hands of the people, whereas our duty is merely to
administer it. We are but the administrators of the people's power!"
(ibid.) Maoism, explained the Caudillo, was but "fascism flying under
the banner of Marxism-Leninism." As for the Chinese who followed
their government—masses whom Castro likened to a "herd that
moved by conditioned reflex"—he said he cared little what those
"millions of Chinese" might think about Cuba (ibid.).

"The violence of such language," noted Jacques Levesque, "was as
painfully insulting, if not more so, as the diatribes China had up till
then directed at the USSR, a fact which must have caused great shock
in Peking."[6] Some analysts were quick to detect much more than
mere political rivalry in the virulence of Castro's attacks. The Sino-
Cuban quarrel, ventured Lee Lockwood, was "probably more the
result of ethnic and cultural differences than theoretical distinctions."[7] That belief was more than a probability to French agronomist
René Dumont, former technical adviser to Fidel Castro, who has
documented some of the Caudillo's private anti-Asian outbursts.[8]
Castro's biographer Carlos Franqui was convinced that the Sino-
Cuban feud achieved the intensity it did because of Castro's initial
dislike for Chinese as such, compounded by Peking's attempt to woo
the Sino-Cuban community. "Fidel was enraged when he learned that
the Chinese embassy was working up Cuban Chinese and considered
such actions as no less than subversion,"[9] Franqui recalled.

It would be surprising if China had failed to note the Cuban government's shutting down of all Chinese-language newspapers and
reviews. These publications, which had existed in Cuba prior to the
Revolution, were channels through which Peking might have hoped
to rekindle historical ties. Chinese diplomats in Cuba quite early sus-

pected the Caudillo's dislike, all politics aside, for the Chinese as a people.[10] They were also conscious of the deep sympathy—rooted in Black-Chinese amity in Cuba dating back to the days of slavery—that China could expect from a broad section of Afro-Cubans. Chinese embassy officials were equally cognizant of the ill repute which the conspicuously racist, arrogant *rusos* (Russians) had earned themselves in an essentially non-white country.[11] As an analyst has noted, the large Soviet presence in Cuba "is more tolerated than welcomed by most Cubans . . . [as] the Russians also have a reputation for showing ill-disguised contempt toward Cuba's large black and mulatto population."[12]

Some black Cuban intellectuals had expressed sympathy for China in its conflict with the USSR.[13] Similar sympathies seem to have brewed within the armed forces, leading to insistent reports of the sudden fall from grace of a certain number of black army officers.[14] Some of them, like Maj. Victor Dreke Crúz, were personal friends of Robert Williams, who left Cuba in July 1966 to air his accusations against its white hierarchy from China. Dreke was dropped from the Party's Central Committee in 1966 and relieved of his duties. Maj. José Causse Pérez, who only the year before had been lecturing Cuban soldiery on the role of the Party within the armed forces, also slipped into obscurity in 1966. Apart from Maj. Juán Almeida Bosque, Dreke and Causse had been the highest-ranking Blacks in the military.

Throughout Havana's mud-slinging campaign, China observed a strict silence, while giving Williams free reign to expose the treatment he'd experienced during his long Cuban exile. The highest officials of the Castroite establishment thus came under fire, among them Maj. Manuel Piñeiro Losada, chief of intelligence at the time; Capt. Osmány Cienfuegos Gorriarán, secretary-general of the Tricontinental and director of the "Liberation Committee"; Capt. Emilio Aragonés, personal aide to Fidel Castro and an important secret service figure; and Maj. René Vallejo, the Caudillo's personal physician and confidant. Williams accused them all of being nothing less than a "gang of unscrupulous vipers" who openly engaged in "counter-revolutionary activity, graft, piracy and all manner of subversion. . . . Their nefarious handiwork is covered by officials of the security police whose loyalty extends only to themselves."[15] Williams said that the black Cuban was "again becoming a pathetic victim of race prejudice and discrimination . . . while the face of the Cuban government was becoming whiter and whiter" (ibid., 8).

Going beyond its claim that Robert Williams had become a "CIA agent," Havana countered with ruthless efficiency. In May 1967, tens of thousands of forged copies of Williams's publication, *The Crusader*, were mailed from Havana to the U.S., Africa, and the Caribbean, provoking considerable confusion. Bearing Williams's signature and masthead, these forgeries denounced Mao Tse-tung and his "arrogant, power-mad underlings" and "thugs," for having "betrayed the Cuban Revolution."[16] Racist "chauvinism" and "ethnocentric fanaticism," charged *The Crusader*, led to the systematic practice of "discrimination against Africans" and other black peoples throughout China.[17]

Williams issued indignant press releases from Peking to denounce this forgery, which "beyond the shadow of a doubt was done under the auspices of Cuban G-2 . . . [and by] a high official of the Cuban Commission of the Tricontinental Organization."[18] (Though unnamed, Capt. Cienfuegos, one of Williams's most outspoken foes, was thus fingered as a major culprit.) Cuba, however, had already turned its attention to another vicious fight with a former ally, the USSR.

One, Two, Three Vietnams!

Strains between Cuba and the Soviet Union had been escalating since 1964. Their divergent policies toward Latin America had set the two countries on a collision course. Havana's audacious "adventurism" in the U.S.'s very backyard had contrasted sharply with Moscow's strategic caution in that area.[19] As Cuba was now openly at war with China, however, the Kremlin could stiffen its opposition to a policy it considered to be recklessly provocative. In 1966, however, Havana was confident of imminent revolutionary victories in Latin America. That optimism came through in a speech Fidel Castro delivered on December 18, 1966, in which he prophesied that the U.S. "will be defeated when instead of one Vietnam there will be in the world two Vietnams, three Vietnams, four Vietnams, five Vietnams."[20] Ché Guevara had again left Cuba some months earlier, with the assignment of igniting these Vietnams on a continental scale. "With Fidel there will be neither marriage nor divorce and I have no intention of becoming another Trotsky," he had told Carlos Franqui.[21]

The OLAS was set up in July and August 1966 under tight Cuban control to act as a sort of general headquarters to coordinate and monitor the actions of the guerrilla movements in Latin America. "OLAS is the interpreter of tomorrow's history," said Castro at its first meeting, "because OLAS is a wave of the future, symbol of the revolutionary waves sweeping a continent of 250 million . . . pregnant with revolution."[22] (*Ola* is Spanish for "wave.")

The only problem—a major one—was that the delivery of the continent's nascent revolutions seemed impossible without Cuban forceps. Ché Guevara, who had slipped undetected into Bolivia in September or October 1966, had brought along a staff of no fewer than fifteen senior Cuban military men, ranking from captains to majors. Some of them were even members of the Cuban Communist party's Central Committee. In Venezuela alone, several hundred Cuban soldiers were reported to be operating with local guerrillas.[23] Equipped with light artillery, anti-aircraft guns, and heavy mortars, these troops were reportedly under the command of the Cuban armed forces' Maj. Raúl Menéndez Tomasevich. (Promoted to general, Tomasevich was chief of staff for operations in Angola from 1976 to 1978.)

The Venezuelan Communist party protested such "flagrant interference" in a letter to Castro, but the Caudillo accused it of being a "gang of detractors and slanderers" of Cuba who were part of an international conspiracy against his Revolution. Castro said that his guerrilla followers could forgo the aid of local Communists. Seemingly to intimidate the latter, and to establish Cuba's continental leadership beyond question, the Caudillo heaped truculent insults upon Venezuela's Communist party leaders in a series of public speeches. He called them "liars," "renegade Communists," "rightists," "deceitful," "cowards," "pseudo-revolutionaries," "defeatists," "charlatans," "immoral," "treacherous," "the enemy of revolutionaries," and "instruments of imperialism" and "servants of the oligarchy."[24] He then warned ominously, "We have some unfinished business with that group of traitors" (ibid., 231).

Making Enemies Everywhere

While taking on all of the continent's pro-Soviet Communist parties—an indirect attack on the USSR itself—Castro also surprisingly accused Yugoslavia's party of failing to assist the world revolution and of being agents of American imperialism. As for the Soviet Union, in a speech on March 13, 1967, Castro made it clear that, "This Revolution that sprang from a tiny group of men . . . will maintain its independence. We proclaim to the world: this Revolution will hold true to its path; this Revolution will follow its own line; this Revolution will never be anybody's satellite or yes-man. It will never ask anybody's permission to maintain its own position either in matters of ideology, or in domestic or foreign affairs" (ibid., 205).

That "proclamation to the world" was primarily intended to be heard in capitalist Western Europe. Increasingly isolated, the Cuban regime had begun courting the West in 1967. Speaking to a huge crowd in early January that year, Castro declared that the success of revolution in Latin America would actually benefit western financial interests. "We must tell Europeans this: don't be fooled by imperialism and don't be frightened by revolutions in Latin America," Castro said. "If revolutions occur in Latin America, Europeans will have little to lose and very much to gain. Yankee imperialism's economic empire is based on that zone of the world, hence revolutions in Latin America will only affect American monopolies."[25]

The Soviets came under increasing attack for having established, or maintaining, diplomatic and trade relations with "oligarchic" regimes that Cuba was actively attempting to topple. "If solidarity is a word worthy of respect," Castro said, "the least that we can expect of any state of the Socialist camp is that it will lend no financial or technical assistance of any type to those governments."[26] Trading with and giving loans to "oligarchic governments," said Castro, was tantamount to "repressing . . . persecuting and assassinating guerrillas." Such "unprincipled" conduct amounted to "helping to suppress revolution" in Latin America (ibid., 203, 204).

Angered by Havana's stinging attacks, several Latin American Communist parties in turn questioned Castro's double-standard code of ethics (ibid., 235, 236). Cuba, they pointed out, maintained active trade and diplomatic relations with, among others, Franco's dictatorship in Spain, Salazar's colonialist regime in Portugal, and Zionist Israel, all of them regimes fighting revolutionary guerrillas. Was Cuba above the moral laws it sought to impose on others? Castro, evidently embarrassed, merely dismissed the issue as a "repugnant" attack on Cuba (ibid., 234, 235).

The counter-charges by Latin American Communist parties, pro-Soviet to the core, were the Kremlin's first move in seriously dealing with its ungrateful Caribbean protege. A new situation had emerged that made such punitive action possible without the risk of a world outcry on behalf of the heroic David of international politics. Through his unbridled, self-righteous attacks on non-aligned Yugoslavia, China, Latin American Communists (pro-Chinese, pro-Soviet, and Trotskyist), and the USSR, Fidel Castro had isolated Cuba within its own ideological universe. Gamal Abdel Nasser—who had refrained from visiting Cuba and long opposed expansion of Castro's role in Africa—was suspicious of Cuban-Israeli diplomatic, economic, and trade relations.

Even in the Caribbean, in which Cuba had shown no interest, Castro managed to create enmities. In September 1967, he attacked Trinidad and Tobago in unwarrantedly sarcastic terms for having supported Venezuela's denunciation of Havana's attempt to topple the Caracas government. Implying that Trinidad and Tobago—a primarily black, non-Latin country—had no right whatsoever to pass judgment on Cuba's actions in the hemisphere, Castro remarked haughtily,

> Isn't it ridiculous that even the spokesman of an English colony had the right to attack Cuba! What are the merits of this colony except to have passed from British hands to those of the Yankees? Yet, this spokesman of a so-called "Republic" named Trinidad-Tobago—a British colony until a few days ago, and a Yankee colony today—set himself up as a judge and condemned Cuba during an OAS meeting. Isn't that just ridiculous? What a shame![27]

The Caudillo was now burning even potential bridges. But Castro did not care. He spoke only of the imminent revolutionary holocaust that was about to befall Latin America. The war would be "total," he told a mass rally in April 1967. "Of course [the U.S.] won't have too many experts to send, because the Vietnamese have put many of the 'Green Beret' experts out of commission. And if the imperialists send increasing numbers of 'Green Berets' against the guerrilla movements, so much the worse for the 'Green Berets'! . . . [The] revolutionaries are going to settle accounts with them."[28] As for Ché Guevara, Castro said, "The imperialists are wondering where Ché is. . . . They would pay anything to find out. But . . . if they really care for the good health of their 'Green Berets,' then they had better do their best not to meet up with Ché!"[29]

Operation Bolivia Explodes

In May 1967, several officers of the Cuban Armed Forces were captured upon landing on the coast of Venezuela. When this was exposed in the press, Havana could no longer deny its hemispheric military interventionism. Characteristically, however, a declaration by the Central Committee of the Communist party of Cuba, admitting for the first time that members of its armed forces were indeed participating in the "liberation struggles" in Latin America, asserted Cuba's "right" to help the continent's "patriotic forces."[30]

Castro was convinced of the inevitable success of "Operation Bolivia," still a secret to all but the highest-ranking members of the armed forces and intelligence organs. The Cuban government was therefore at the peak of its cockiness. Before a mass rally, Castro spoke in terms worthy of a medieval warlord. He dismissed all of the "oligarchic" armed forces of Latin America and lamented being shackled by his obligations as prime minister at a moment when the whole continent was on the verge of explosion. To the roar of approving cries of "¡P'alante, Caballo! ¡P'alante!" (Forward, War-horse! Forward!), Castro boasted:

> I just read a news dispatch in which the gorilla Castelo Branco—that specimen who is president of Brazil—has defied me to start up a revolution over there. All I can say in situations such as this is that I sorely regret not being a Brazilian. Even so, I am ready to forego all of my official duties—my post as prime minister, or rather my "burden" as prime minister, if you wish—so as to become an ordinary Brazilian citizen. And then, I am absolutely sure, Castelo Branco and all of those other gorillas over there would hastily take to their heels, as was the case right here in Cuba with Batista![31]

More than revolutionary bravado, this was true Spanish, caudillistic machismo, marching under the banner of Marxism and proletarian internationalism. But the Castroite leadership did not stop there. "Not even twenty million Yankee marines can manage to crush the revolution unfolding in Latin America," asserted Castro.[32] Armando Hart Davalos echoed: "American imperialism has mobilized four hundred thousand men against a small country like Vietnam, and still cannot win. So it would have to multiply that number of soldiers by fifty to deal with the revolutionary movements in Latin America. In other words, it would take twenty million men to confront the onslaught of the masses in Brazil, Colombia, Venezuela, Peru, Guatemala and the other Latin American countries."[33]

Fidel Castro's fiery speeches were encouraging; so were the victorious "war communiqués" the Cuban media issued daily, monitoring the progress of the guerrilla fronts in Venezuela, Guatemala, Colombia, Peru, Brazil, Nicaragua, Bolivia, and elsewhere. Therefore, no one was prepared for the shock. On October 15, 1967, the Caudillo solemnly announced that Ché Guevara had died in Bolivia on October 9. A minor skirmish with Bolivian soldiers had felled the heroic figure whom Castro had said he would willingly pit against all the troops of imperialism.

The Bolivian fiasco marked the utter failure of Cuba's policy of exporting the Revolution. Guevara's death demoralized nearly all of the continent's guerrilla *focos*. One after the other, they ceased operations under various pretexts. More important, however, it revealed the utter bankruptcy of a Cuban-fostered myth, which Regis Debray had codified in *Revolution in the Revolution?*:[34] the invincibility of white, middle-class macho guerrilla bands headed by iron-fisted, visionary caudillos, dedicated to the self-appointed task of "liberating the people."

Save for the predominantly white countries of Argentina, Chile, Uruguay, and, perhaps, Costa Rica, "the people" in "Latin" America were primarily Blacks and Indians. The people, therefore, had been conspicuously absent from the leaderships of these Castroite liberation movements. As Gerard Challiand has aptly pointed out,

> Rhetorical excesses were the trademark of these [guerrilla] movements, whereas most were comprised of but a few dozen warriors, or a few hundred men at best, lacking any real popular base. . . . Their out-of-proportion notoriety [in Europe] was no doubt due to Eurocentric reflexes, as these revolutionaries were whites, therefore closer to [Europeans], even culturally speaking. . . . We are accustomed to viewing Latin American societies as non-racist only because of our ignorance about them and because they are analyzed according to wholly inadequate criteria.[35]

Castro's "exportationist" policy contrasted sharply with Cuba's tactical restraint in the Caribbean, despite the existence next-door in Haiti of one of the most tyrannical of regimes. The "two, three, many Vietnams" that Fidel Castro clamored for were politically convenient only so long as they flared up at a good distance from Cuba's borders. The Caudillo's ambitious strategy of war with the U.S. by proxy[36] had failed, notwithstanding Castro's angry warning that Guevara's "battle cry will reach not just one receptive ear, but millions of receptive ears. And not one hand but millions of hands will stretch out to take up arms!"

The Cuban leadership knew the game was up.[37] In March 1968, Castro turned his rage inward and unleashed on Cuba a so-called *ofensiva revolucionária* (revolutionary offensive). Puritanical and repressive, the operation turned out to be an onslaught on all remaining private retail trade and on "parasitism." The police were summoned to "crush the scoundrels, . . . [the] softies, the weaklings, the cowards, and the traitors."[38] Castro declared that money would soon be abolished; moral incentives would soon replace salaries; Cubans would start building communism right away, alongside socialism.[39] Cuba was said to be on the verge of making the biggest jump in agricultural development ever witnessed in history.[40] According to Castro, the island could produce gigantic sugar crops. A new goal, to be achieved within two years, was therefore set: "Ten million tons of sugar, at least, but not a single ton less," ordered the Caudillo, "whether there's drought or not!"[41] For that purpose, Cuban society would be militarized: "We will all become soldiers, though remaining workers or students" (ibid., 5).

Confronting the USSR

The massive disruption of the Cuban economy brought about by the *ofensiva revolucionária* was accompanied by a new round of attacks on the Soviet Union, held partly responsible for Guevara's failure. The pro-Moscow Bolivian Communist party had refused to be involved in Ché's guerrilla action. Its leadership had also rejected Guevara's demand that total leadership of the struggle in that country be vested in him alone.[42] Cuba, however, had hardly any more cards left to support its successful Soviet-baiting antics.

In 1967 the USSR was faced with serious problems of its own, which made the Kremlin even less likely to yield to Cuba's continued taunting and insults. Soviet foreign policy had suffered a major blow in the Middle East as a result of the Arab-Israeli Six-Day War in June of that year. The USSR had been unable to prevent the defeat of its Arab clients. Israel's lightning victory over the heavily Soviet-armed Egyptian forces heralded the decline of Soviet influence in the oil-rich Arab world, an area which the Kremlin had painstakingly cultivated and into which it had poured billions of rubles since the early 1950s.[43] Thus, less than three months before Cuba's debacle in Bolivia, the Kremlin had suffered its own diplomatic and political Waterloo.[44] As a result, the Soviets were eager to reach an agreement with the U.S. on the whole range of issues causing tension between them.

Within two weeks of the Six-Day War's end, Soviet Prime Minister Aleksei Kosygin arrived in the U.S. for a summit meeting with President Lyndon B. Johnson. A wave of race "riots" was taking place at the time, but the Soviet press, unwilling to antagonize the U.S., was silent about them. On the very eve of the Glassborough summit, the People's Republic of China tested her first thermonuclear device, a grim reminder to all that the Sino-Soviet dispute might not remain restricted to ideological arguments.

Kosygin seems to have reached sound agreements with Johnson, and the Soviet premier went directly to Havana with a stern message for Castro: exportation of Revolution to Latin America had to stop. Cuba could continue to send weapons, advisers, and other assistance to Africa, but the guerrilla struggles in Latin America had to be frozen.[45] Castro's reaction, no doubt influenced by his overconfidence that Guevara would succeed in Bolivia, can be gleaned from the high point of his speech on July 26, 1967. "We Cubans," he warned solemnly, "must become accustomed to the idea that [in the event of a U.S. attack] we will be going into battle alone!"[46]

Understandably, the Bolivian disaster three months later only served to fuel Havana's bitterness at Soviet-American detente, a policy which, as Castro had said on May 5, 1966, only worked for the big powers but meant nothing to small countries like Cuba and North Vietnam. However true, the Soviets gave an idea of what was in the making for Cuba in late December 1967 when *Pravda* prominently published an article entitled "Oil Bridge Across the Ocean." Of all Socialist countries, stated the article, "Cuba is currently the largest consumer of Soviet oil."[47] A few days later, in January 1968, Fidel Castro announced a severe and immediate rationing of gasoline and the adoption of war-time conservation measures. These were called for, he explained curtly, "to preserve the Cuban people's dignity."[48] Calling for self-reliance, the Caudillo announced a cutback in Cuba's petroleum supply, due to a sharp reduction in Soviet shipments. Cuba, he warned, was readying itself for any eventuality, "including the most unimaginable" (ibid.), in order to uphold its dignity. The rationing affected all areas. "In early 1968, as a result of Soviet economic sanctions against Cuba [and consequent] delays in the delivery of oil," reported a specialist, "the Cuban armed forces are reported to have been forced to turn over 30 percent of their fuel reserves for use in agriculture."[49]

Castro's retaliation was swift and direct. It took the form of the well-publicized arrest, expulsion from the Cuban Communist party and trial by a war court of a group of pro-Soviet Cuban Communists.[50] The charges leveled against them were, as usual, extravagant: conspiracy, subversion, defamation of the Revolution, "perfidious criticism" of Fidel Castro, treachery, "clandestine circulation of documents" contrary to the Revolution's line, collusion with the Czech and Venezuelan Communists, "secret meetings" with members of the Soviet embassy in Cuba, circulation of rumors intended to "undermine the credibility and prestige" of the Revolution and its Máximo Líder, "identity of goals between the micro-faction and the CIA."[51]

The scandal generated by the so-called micro-faction trial encouraged public belief that Cuban intelligence had actually smashed a Soviet plot to overthrow Castro. The thirty-odd defendants received lengthy prison sentences, from two to a maximum of twenty years, and bolas (rumors) spread of an impending break in diplomatic relations between Cuba and the USSR. Even the French daily, Le Monde, feared that Castro had gone too far. "By liquidating its pro-Soviet elements, the Cuban Communist party has pushed its relations with the Soviet party to the brink," said the newspaper. "Western observers now feel that such aggressiveness on the part of the Cubans will make it extremely difficult, if not impossible, for Soviet leaders to maintain an accommodating attitude towards Havana and that they may very well be forced to reassess the whole range of relations between the two countries."[52]

Everything pointed to an unstoppable escalation of the conflict. Some Soviet diplomats and KGB advisers had been requested to leave Cuba in the aftermath of the micro-faction trial. With befitting solemnity, Cuba announced its refusal to attend the preparatory meeting, in Budapest, of the following year's World Congress of Communist parties.[53] Cuban-Soviet relations stood at the brink. The steady weakening of Cuba's military potential, as a consequence of Soviet oil cutbacks, was a nightmare that Cuba's leaders now had to contend with. A full Soviet embargo would bring Cuba to her knees, crippling its industry, economy, and armed forces. Castro's next unexpected step was most likely taken in anticipation of that event.

In July 1968, at Cuba's request, secret parleys began in Mexico City between U.S. and Cuban government representatives,[54] the first such talks since both governments had severed diplomatic ties in 1961. Three years before, Fidel Castro had declared emphatically that Cuba "wants no peace of any sort with [U.S.] imperialism."[55] On May 23, 1966, armed forces chief Raúl Castro had sworn on Cuba's revolutionary honor, "Never shall we seek reconciliation with [American] imperialism; not even—as Fidel already stated—within the framework of a so-called regional peace in the Caribbean."[56] Suddenly, Cuba was desperately seeking, if not reconciliation, then at least a truce. But Castro had absolutely nothing to offer in return for peace—even if transitory—with Yankee imperialism.

Observers agree as to the Kremlin's determination to resolve its Cuban dilemma swiftly, particularly as the USSR was beset by foreign policy worries and setbacks. The Kremlin had lost face in North Vietnam; was embroiled in an intractable conflict with Albania; was facing a growing military challenge from China and North Korea's open defiance. The USSR's influence in the Middle East had eroded. Closer to home, disquieting events were taking place in Czechoslovakia. The Soviets were confronted with a serious undermining of their authority within what they considered to be their own security perimeter. The "democratization" process launched with wide popular support by the new Czech leadership, dubbed the "Spring of Prague," could be contagious. "Socialism with a human face"—the slogan of the new Czech leadership—sounded ominous. If it were left unchecked, it could lead to the "dismemberment" of the Socialist camp. The Kremlin then pronounced its "Brezhnev Doctrine," which asserted that the USSR could not remain indifferent to the fate of socialism in other countries. In other words, none who entered the Communist bloc would be allowed to leave it thereafter.

A Surprising Turn

On August 20, 1968, while Cuban and American negotiators were meeting in Mexico City, Warsaw Pact forces invaded and occupied Czechoslovakia. Even Moscow's long-standing allies (such as the Communist parties in the West, particularly in France) hastily condemned the Soviet action. North Vietnam remained prudently silent. China, Albania, and North Korea denounced it as a "wanton imperialistic invasion." In the eyes of the Third World, the USSR now appeared as she had often been portrayed: a brutal, dangerous, deceitful superpower bent on expansionism and world domination at all costs. The Soviet Union stood condemned before the entire world.

On August 23, 1968, to the astonishment of all, a lone voice broke the chorus of Communist, non-aligned, and capitalist condemnations. Fidel Castro declared that the Soviet invasion of Czechoslovakia, although hardly legal, had put a halt to a "dangerous evolution towards counter-revolution."[57] The threat of a "dislocation of the Socialist camp" in Czechoslovakia had been halted. The USSR had discharged her "internationalist proletarian duty." The "Brezhnev Doctrine" should be extended to include Cuba.

The Caudillo's pronouncement to a stunned Cuban and international audience, was another masterful coup of realpolitik. More isolated than ever, Cuba had been driven to seek a truce with its "hereditary enemy" from the weakest possible position. The sudden collapse of the guerrilla movement in Latin America deprived Havana of even that dubious bargaining card. And, as the "micro-faction" trial demonstrated, there were men right in the Cuban Communist party who gleefully toyed with the idea of getting rid of their "inefficient," "capricious" Caudillo along with his handful of faithful "petit-bourgeois" sycophants.

Under fire from both Communist giants, its daring all-around confrontationist policy in shambles, its economy drifting towards disaster, the "heroic island" had reached a veritable impasse. For the first time, there was nothing ahead but defeat. The first person to grasp Cuba's new predicament, despite, or due to the masterful antics and politics of its Máximo Lider, was the Caudillo himself. It was no longer a matter of changing gears, but direction, and he did so at the first available opportunity: the Soviet invasion of Czechoslovakia.

What better strategy, aimed at rapidly getting back into the good graces of the powerful Kremlin, than to support its universally condemned invasion? As the USSR began showing its gratitude for such timely, if totally unexpected help, Fidel Castro quietly surrendered. Cuban President Osvaldo Dorticós Torrado was received in Moscow, at Havana's request, from October 14 through 17, 1968—less than two months after the Soviet invasion of Czechoslovakia. The talks seem to have proceeded quickly. Cuba, as could be expected, agreed straight down the line with the Kremlin's outlook on world politics, and a thaw in Soviet-Cuban relations followed almost immediately.[58] Moscow abandoned its belligerent plans, and Cuba just as promptly proclaimed its "unfailing friendship" for the mighty "fatherland of socialism."

It was in the course of these fence-mending talks, observers believe, that Cuba agreed to the key proposal Aleksei Kosygin had unsuccessfully made to Fidel Castro exactly a year before: that Cuba should leave Latin America alone and concentrate its military and political efforts on Africa instead.[59] For Havana, it was a painless switch.

Fast losing ground in the Middle East, which heretofore had been its only zone of influence in the Third World, since 1967 the Soviets had been progressively turning their attention to the black continent once again. Cuba, in turn, having lost ground entirely in Latin America, needed no persuasion to devote its full attention to a continent where it already wielded considerable political clout.

Cuba's remorseless about-face was evident when Fidel Castro totally omitted any reference to guerrilla struggles in Latin America during his tenth anniversary speech in January 1969. A few months later, he further startled his followers by showering lavish praise on the military junta of General Alvarado in Peru.[60] Adding insult to injury (no doubt for the benefit of the guerrilla movements still holding out in the mountains), he proclaimed: "If I were a Peruvian, I would be on the side of the military [junta]!"[61] Finally, during his visit to Chile in December 1971, Castro declared for the first time: "The Cuban Revolution is not a model that can be exported."[62]

By August 1969, Radio Havana had already ceased broadcasting its habitual incendiary appeals for armed struggle.[63] Silence fell over the continuing guerrilla operations of those who had remained faithful to Guevara's credo. The most prominent of these, Venezuelan guerrilla leader Douglas Bravo, openly accused Fidel Castro of having "betrayed" the revolutionary cause in Latin America in favor of an unprincipled alliance with the USSR.[64] Castro didn't even reply.

Cuba was decidedly in a forgiving mood after President Dorticós's pilgrimage to Moscow. In November 1968, Algerian Foreign Minister Abdelaziz Bouteflika—whom three years earlier Castro had lambasted as a "rightist" and "counter-revolutionary'—was warmly welcomed in Havana. Everybody concerned conveniently forgot Fidel Castro's vituperative insults,[65] as well as the fact that Ben Bella, Cuba's loyal friend, still languished in an Algerian jail. Cuba's rapid fence-mending with Algeria was, it seems reasonable to conclude, connected to Havana's new agreement with Moscow on a concerted drive into the black continent.

Cuba's leadership went all the way in its new direction. "We think that a serious study of the experience of the first proletarian state in history, the Soviet Union, is quite indispensable," Armando Hart Davalos said meekly on September 24, 1969. "We go even further than that, and assert that this experience is a decisive element in teaching us what we ourselves have to do."[66]

Carlos Rafael Rodríguez, number-three man in the Castroite hierarchy, arrived in Moscow in June 1969, at the head of a strong delegation. The Cubans had decided to participate after all in the world summit meeting of Communist parties, an event which, a year earlier, Cuba had promised not to attend. Some weeks before the conference, the Soviets had discreetly sounded out their Warsaw Pact allies, as well as the United States, on their reaction to a "surgical" nuclear strike against China.[67] This World Congress of Communist Parties was, therefore, much more than the usual exercise of expressions of ideological allegiance to the fatherland of socialism. Rather, it was meant to be a forum for the collective endorsement by the world Communist movement of Moscow's lethal plans for China.

There is little wonder that, alarmed at such a project, the Communist parties of China, North Vietnam, North Korea, and others that were "non-aligned," refrained from attending what was virtually a war council.

The Kremlin was in a hurry. Even while the conference was in progress, reported K. S. Karol, the Soviets "tried to sound out the delegates' reactions to a possible preemptive strike against China's nuclear installations in Sinkiang. Anti-Chinese hysteria had reached such heights in Moscow that many Communist parties much closer to the USSR than the Cuban had carefully avoided declaring their 'unflinching' solidarity with the Soviet Union. No wonder, therefore, that the world press treated the presence and declaration of Carlos Rafael Rodríguez as the USSR's chief political success during the conference."[68]

Cuba went far beyond any other delegation at that conference, not only by endorsing any future military action taken against the Chinese, but by clearly implying that it stood ready to join the fight alongside the mighty USSR. "We declare from this tribune," said a belligerent Rodríguez, "that in any decisive confrontation, whether it be an act by the Soviet Union to avert threats of dislocation or provocation to the Socialist system, or an act of aggression by anyone against the Soviet people, Cuba will stand unflinchingly by the USSR."[69]

Rodríguez's proclamation was not merely an innocent expression of renewed friendship with the Kremlin. Carefully worded, the statement reflected Cuba's fierce anti-China saber-rattling and Fidel Castro's own repugnance for the Chinese, combined opportunistically to give Cuba the appearance, and thereafter the status, of the Soviets' most loyal accomplice.

A consummate political strategist, Castro had come to accept the cynical conclusion Kremlin leaders had spelled out a year ahead of their Czech invasion: world politico-military bipolarity was an accomplished and unchallengeable fact of contemporary international relations. "In our times," a high-ranking Soviet leader told a western strategist, "there can be no longer an authentic Third Force on the world scene. Those who try to become such a force have simply arrived too late in history, when there is not any room left."[70]

After spending eleven years conceiving foreign policy stratagems specifically designed to make Cuba a "third force" in world politics, could Castro totally abandon that goal without endangering the stability of his hybrid regime, which thrived on political high-wire tactics, diplomatic acrobatics, and which was accustomed to feeling safe only in situations of permanent tension, domestically and internationally? Could a Cuban population schooled to expect the worst easily accommodate to a situation of peace on all fronts without dangerously turning its attention to demands for social, political, economic, and ethnic freedoms?

Reaccommodation with the USSR thus posed new problems for Cuban leaders. In a way, President Osvaldo Dorticós Torrado had addressed the question in his opening speech to the World Congress of Intellectuals held in Havana from January 4 through 12, 1968. "An underdeveloped country such as ours," he said, "has but one alternative for successful revolutionary construction: impressive economic achievements, feats of epic scope and heroic exploits; or inertia, disaster, defeat and paralysis of the revolutionary process!"[71] In plain words, to galvanize Cuban workers' productivity in the midst of sacrifice and scarcity, overambitious goals had to be set and endless drama sustained with such gambits as sudden military mobilizations, bombastic "internationalist" operations, and breathtaking domestic coups de theatre. Without new worlds to fashion, new frontiers to push back, and continuous political Russian roulette to play, the internal dynamics of the Cuban revolution would grind to a halt.

In 1968, Cuba was on the brink of economic disaster. Fidel Castro had lost his strategic gamble right in his own geopolitical fief. Cuba had virtually isolated herself. Where in the world could Havana turn to accomplish the heroic exploits and feats of epic scope needed to maintain the sacrificial commitment of a disenchanted population? What "virgin" ground was left to conquer? Only on the gigantic black continent did the Castroites indeed still have unfinished business.

18 THE SOVIET-CUBAN ALLIANCE IN BLACK AFRICA

In Cuba, 1970 could have appropriately been dubbed "The Year of Sovietization." For eleven years under the unchallenged, charismatic power of its Caudillo, Cuba's revolutionary process had relied on spontaneity and defied labels. Now Cuba, as Gilles Martinet observed sadly, had finally succumbed to the general rule: adoption of structures for which the USSR furnished the blueprint.[1] It followed that whatever "internationalist" efforts Cuba would carry out thereafter had to represent an automatic extension of the Soviet model. Did this imply Havana's abandonment of its long-standing quest for a voice in the affairs of the big powers? Had Fidel Castro given up his ambition to become the spokesman for the Third World, whose population accounted for three-quarters of mankind?

Africa as a Lever

Castro's Cuba had already built up its own political constituency in black Africa. Relying only on itself, and long before a suitable climate existed for a coordinated policy with the USSR, Havana had gained a foothold in Africa. As for the USSR, repeatedly held at bay in Africa, it could hardly have failed to weigh the advantages of following in the wake of a small, still romanticized, Third-World Communist power. Moreover, unlike any of its allies or clients, Socialist Cuba was a country with abundant, disciplined manpower of African origin. To secure a strong foothold in an area where the USSR would have to rely on Little Cuba to achieve its aims had been worth the cost of the "internationalist" ventures that Cuba had undertaken in Africa since 1964. The idea was to place the Kremlin in a state of political dependence on Cuba in Africa. If successful, Cuba could effectively reverse its economic and military dependence on the USSR.

The agreement to "swap" Latin America for Africa, and to become the willing accomplice of global Soviet expansive efforts, was therefore in line with traditional Castroite realpolitik. By becoming indispensable to the Kremlin in black Africa, Cuba could again bargain for its independence. As the Kremlin's armed proxy there, Cuba could hope to simultaneously avail itself of the political, military, and logistical means it needed to become a real middle power.

The Soviet-American agreements of 1962 barred Cuba from possession of "strategic weapons." It is not unthinkable that, by unconditionally allying itself with the Kremlin, Cuba sought to force the Soviets' hand even on this issue. Up till then, the USSR had cautiously avoided accepting Cuba into the Warsaw Pact. "A vital issue facing Castro since his seizure of power in 1959," noted Leon Goure, a specialist on Soviet-Cuban military relations, "has been to secure a binding Soviet commitment to come to Cuba's defense in the event of a domestic uprising or U.S. intervention in Cuba. While Soviet leaders have given Cuba repeated verbal assurances that the Soviet Union would come to its aid in the event of an attack, no formal defense or alliance treaty has been signed. Nor is Cuba a member of the Warsaw Pact. Castro has repeatedly fished for such a treaty, which would not only assure Cuba's security but also possibly increase his ability to regain some initiative in Latin America."[2]

Havana has never accepted this disadvantage as permanent; twice in 1970, Fidel Castro publicly pressured the USSR on the matter. "We will never break our political ties with the Soviet Union," he said on April 22, "let alone what they term our military ties. To the contrary! As far as we are concerned, we stand ready to broaden our military ties to the Soviet Union."[3] A few months later, on August 23, Castro went further: "Once again I repeat: far from seeking to loosen our military ties with the Soviet Union, our goal is to broaden them to the extent feasible. . . . Our policy is clear . . . : We will reinforce our ties with the Soviet Union as much as we can!"[4]

It was precisely Soviet reluctance to "broaden" its military ties with Cuba that incited the latter to envision an ambitious, wholly autonomous military program geared at producing its own short-range rockets and, ultimately, nuclear weapons.[5] In the mid-1970s, Cuba began to receive Soviet assistance in developing nuclear energy.[6] If anything, Castro's intention to achieve a military nuclear capability (at the level, perhaps, of Israel or South Africa) is but another indication of the Caudillo's ultimate quest for strategic, as well as political autonomy. (In the mid-1970s, Fidel Castro, Jr., a Soviet-trained nuclear physicist, was appointed head of Cuba's Atomic Energy Agency by his father.)

Another element of importance must be evoked when considering the metamorphosis of Soviet-Cuban relations in the period from 1966 to 1970: the attainment by the USSR, for the first time, of strategic parity with the West. *Pravda* did not exaggerate when it declared, on July 7, 1968, with a solemnity befitting the occasion, that the world had entered "one of those rare instances in history where two antagonist parties admit to having attained a full balance of power in every sense of the term."[7] In its April 1969 report, the London Institute of Strategic Studies had announced that the USSR had "seemingly" caught up with the U.S. in numerical missile strength, and that "probably" towards mid-1969 the Soviet Union would have surpassed the United States in absolute numbers of operational ICBMs.[8] By 1970, western strategic analysts were admitting to nuclear parity between the USSR and the West.[9] This knowledge must have heavily influenced Fidel Castro's decision to throw in his lot entirely with the Soviet Union.

A new confidence seems to have flowered in the shadow of the Soviets' ICBMs. In July 1969, a Soviet naval task force entered Caribbean waters—for the first time—to render Cuba a "courtesy" visit.[10] Four months later, Soviet Minister of Defense Marshal Gretchko, commander-in-chief of the Warsaw Pact forces, arrived in Cuba, also for the first time, on yet another "courtesy" visit (ibid.). In April 1970, two Soviet spy planes (similar to the U.S.'s U-2 aircraft) landed in Cuba for the first time. And, in May 1970, an entire fleet of conventionally and nuclear-powered Soviet submarines and missile-launching surface warships arrived for its inaugural two-week "courtesy" sojourn at the port of Cienfuegos.

On January 4, 1971, President Richard Nixon denounced, in a televised declaration, this "reinforcing of Soviet military presence" in Cuba. He announced that both superpowers had "widened" the 1962 Soviet-American agreements on Cuba to preclude the building of naval bases on the island.[11] That new proviso, however, did not change the essential facts: long gone were the days when the U.S. Navy would close Caribbean waters to the Kremlin's warships. For Castroite Cuba, a new era was at hand.

Soviet Pressure Shifts to Black Africa

The USSR had made a powerful friend and wielded great influence in the Arab Middle East through its stern 1956 ultimatum to the West at the height of the Suez Crisis. Rais Gamal Abdel Nasser, undisputed and adored leader of the Arab world, savored his victory and repaid the USSR handsomely. The United Arab Republic was the Kremlin's first Third World ally. To the Soviets, Nasser was doubly useful. Not only did he open the Middle East to the USSR's influence, but Cairo also pretended to hold the keys to the "dark continent." ("Africa will be freed by the United Arab Republic," Nasser had, in fact, stated.)[12] The Kremlin believed him. As Nikita Khrushchev explained in his memoirs, "it was in our interest to support Nasser's bourgeois leadership because it promised to weaken the influence of English colonialism in the Near East, and that was in the interest of the Soviet Union."[13] The building of the costly Aswan Dam, he confessed, was a way of winning over not only the Egyptians, but the entire Third World—Arabs and black Africans in particular (ibid., 440).

Ten years after Suez, Soviet policy in the Middle East was in shambles. Nasser's own image in that zone had seriously eroded by the time he died of a cardiac arrest in 1970. Accustomed, perhaps, to a scornful underestimation of the Egyptians,[14] the Soviets presumably did not expect the heavy blows Nasser's seemingly tame successor, former National Assembly President Anwar al-Sadat, had in store for them: the massive purge, arrest, and imprisonment of the entire pro-Soviet Nasser leadership; the swift expulsion of hundreds of Soviet military advisers; the abrogation of UAR-Soviet "naval facilities" agreements; rapid rapprochement with the U.S. and a correspondingly hysterical media campaign against the USSR. Biting the hand that, for over a decade, had fed Egypt with billions of rubles' worth of military, economic, and civilian assistance could only accelerate the Kremlin's disaffection with the most powerful state in the region. A Soviet shift to black Africa was the only logical next move.

In 1960 and 1961, the Kremlin had attempted to enter the black continent in a major way. The USSR had rushed to the aid of the threatened populist government of Patrice Lumumba. American counter-threats, however, had forced the Soviets to back down. The Kremlin had watched helplessly as Lumumba's promising anti-colonialist regime was torn to pieces by both western-inspired and local intrigues, culminating in Lumumba's ouster and murder. For the Kremlin, which was stigmatized among its black clients as a white power, a cascade of setbacks followed with friendly "progressive" African regimes such as Guinea, Ghana, Mali, Congo-Brazzaville, and Tanzania.[15]

The closure of the Suez Canal in 1967 as a result of the Six-Day War suddenly heightened the strategic relevance of the black continent for both power blocs.[16] Control of the Cape route, access to the Indian Ocean, and the concomitant quest by the U.S. and USSR for naval facilities in coastal African states, became urgent priorities in the early 1970s.[17] The strategic importance of such countries as Guinea, Somalia, Nigeria, Equatorial Guinea, Angola, Mozambique, and Madagascar was enhanced threefold, and both superpowers acted accordingly, courting, enticing, seducing, or threatening in order to obtain the coveted naval facilities.

It was FRELIMO's Marxist leader, Marcelino dos Santos, who first drew attention to the tactical importance of liberation movements in former Portuguese colonies like his own Mozambique, where victory would confer decisive strategic advantages. Modern sea transportaion, he said, "relies on the use of huge tankers and so confers a preeminent role on the 'Cape Route.' This fact puts the struggles of the Portuguese colonies of Angola, Guinea-Bissau, Cape Verde, and Mozambique in the light of as many strategic points needed for the conquest of these sea lanes. The archipelago of Cape Verde continues to be an ideal strategic area from which to control communication's flow from Europe to the South Atlantic and to Latin America."[18]

While worried that an ever-expanding Soviet navy might take control of vital sea lanes, many in the West were also haunted by an age-old fear: being cut off from access to Africa's minerals. Black Africa had a monopoly over twenty-three of the thirty-six materials classed by the United States as militarily or industrially "strategic." If a number of these African states were to fall under the ideological sway of the Kremlin, U.S. strategists reasoned, the Soviets would then gain control over ninety percent of the strategic materials essential to the western world.[19]

What such preoccupations on the part of both superpowers and their surrogate allies clearly indicated was their consistent view of the black continent as merely an expedient objective in the Cold War. Specifically African problems such as apartheid, famine and disease were of little if any concern.

Naval Maneuvers

The USSR obtained initial and substantial advantages by enlisting Cuba's aid in Africa. Strong-arm regimes eager for Soviet military aid seized power in Equatorial Guinea (October 1968); Libya (September 1969); Somalia (October 1969); Dahomey (December 1969); Congo-Brazzaville (1970); and Uganda (January 1971). Massive military aid to Nigeria, Somalia, and Guinea obtained the first permanent naval facilities for the Soviet fleet on the black continent while the U.S. was still caught in its Vietnamese quagmire.

The federal military regime in Lagos, fast losing its contest with Biafra, eagerly sought military assistance from any available quarter, and received it from the Kremlin. On November 22, 1968, Lagos and Moscow signed a military and economic cooperation agreement. The Soviet-Nigerian treaty provided for generous arms supplies and a cadre of military advisers for the Nigerian armed forces. In March 1969, scarcely four months after the treaty was signed, a Soviet naval squadron entered the port of Lagos. "Four Soviet warships, including two missile-launching destroyers and a submarine," reported *Le Monde*, "will, starting on March 5, pay the first-ever visit to this country [Nigeria]. Government circles in Lagos are mute on the visit, except to describe it as a 'courtesy visit. . . .' But Lagos diplomatic circles believe the USSR is seeking a long-term agreement with the Nigerian government for the use of Lagos—in due consideration for its strategic position—as a relay for the Soviets' military and civilian fleet."[20]

In October, 1969, a pro-Soviet junta seized power in Somalia. It swiftly ceded the port of Berbera to the USSR and, in record time, the Kremlin installed there the first Soviet military base on African soil. The price of the Berbera naval station was the reorganization, training, equipping, and advising of Somalia's armed forces by four thousand Soviet military experts.[21]

Still with an eye to obtaining as many naval facilities as possible along the coasts of the black continent, in 1970 Moscow succeeded in signing agreements with the island states of Equatorial Guinea and Mauritius. Sékou Touré's Guinea, the Kremlin's first "Marxist" ally in Africa, was reportedly sounded out in that year for the concession of a Berbera-type base on Africa's Atlantic seaboard. A self-styled Marxist, in 1961 Touré had expelled a "seditious" Soviet ambassador, and, in 1962, had refused landing rights to Soviet craft headed for Cuba at the height of the missile crisis. Old grievances were now shelved, however, in favor of security interests.

"Already from April 14 to May 4," reported analyst Babacar Fall, "two large-scale Soviet war maneuvers code-named 'OKEAN' were carried out along Guinea's coast. Commanded from Moscow by Soviet naval chief Admiral Gorchkov, a total of two hundred warships of all types had participated in that war exercise."[22] Touré's fear of being overthrown had spurred a cooperative understanding among Guinea, the USSR, and Cuba. Black Cuban units, stationed permanently in Guinea since 1966, fluctuated from a low of some three hundred men to a peak of one thousand.[23] They played a decisive role in repelling a raid on Conakry by a band of Portuguese soldiery and allied Guinean exiles on November 22, 1970, and took credit for saving Touré's life. Touré's suspicion that top members of his armed forces had colluded with the invaders led to the bloody so-called Fifth Column trials, and to the disarming of large sections of the army, whose top leadership was decimated.

By 1971, Guinea's reliance on Soviet-Cuban protection was nearly total. The national militia, the only body to command Touré's confidence, was trained by black Cuban officers in Guinea; its chief, Capt. Mamadi Bayo (who would become minister of youth upon Touré's death in 1984), was trained in Cuba.[24] But no written record is available of a trilateral "cooperation agreement" believed to have been reached in 1971 by Guinea, the USSR, and Cuba, whereby Touré agreed to Soviet and Cuban use of Guinean waters, ports, air space, airport, and territory to further the cause of what Conakry termed "the African Revolution."[25]

The USSR's new position of military parity had immediately translated itself in a burst of multi-pronged offensives in the Third World, with the black continent as nerve center. Soviet diplomacy, many believed, was irrevocably headed towards the "aggressive" determination that had marked the Khrushchev era. The Kremlin could afford to forge ahead with the knowledge that, in a major crisis, it had the means to make others back down.

It would have been naive of the Soviets to have expected their chief adversary to fold its arms and let them advance, unopposed, into the only zone of the globe untouched by the Yalta agreements. Perhaps, the USSR and its close allies underestimated the adaptive faculties of "Yankee imperialism," in contrast to the rigidity of what Maoists termed "social imperialism." Precisely because of its strategic inferiority to the Soviets, Washington would take the least expected of steps under an administration—Richard Nixon's—held to be the most anti-Communist since the days of Harry S Truman. In a masterful stroke of realpolitik, calling to mind the old proverb that "states have no permanent friends, only permanent interests," the U.S. entered into a spectacular reconciliation-alliance with the People's Republic of China. The latter, under the administration of Mao Tse-tung, Ling Piao, and other "anti-imperialist" hard-liners, was also under the threat of a devastating surprise nuclear attack by the Soviets.

President Nixon's arrival in Peking in late February, 1972, sealed the de facto alliance of a growing big power with what was still the world's most grimly determined superpower. The Soviet Union was now faced with a suddenly narrowed strategic gap between the super-powers. The very situation the USSR had tried to prevent—a strong China on her borders—had now become an inescapable certainty. A new tactical situation had arisen, and to counter it, the Soviet Union—ejected from the Middle East, cautious in Latin America, de-terred in Europe, and also losing ground in the Indian sub-continent where the "friendly" regime of Indira Gandhi was battling a wave of unpopularity[26]—had no alternative but to considerably step up its African offensive, which was already under way.

Castro Visits Africa

On May 1, 1972, during the traditional military parade where new types of weapons were first shown, Castro mentioned that he planned an imminent trip to Guinea. It would be his first to black Africa. Within twenty-four hours of the May Day parade, Fidel Castro left Cuba from José Martí International Airport on a direct flight to Conakry. The Cuban media covered the event in unusually minute detail. The Caudillo had not been able to sleep; he had feverishly studied files regarding Guinean and African affairs; he had kept up the Guinean ambassador to Cuba, René Loua Fassou (who had succeeded Mami Kouyate, now Touré's presidential aide), with a barrage of questions about Guinea.[27] Since its independence, Castro had con-cluded, Guinea had "made a leap of two thousand years that made it one of the most advanced African countries."[28] Sékou Touré and Guinea had now become the "pillars of revolution" on the African continent (ibid.).

The Caudillo's first visit to Africa was a momentous occasion for most Cubans. Centuries-old memories now resurfaced in the popu-lar mind. Castro had crossed the middle passage, the infamous sea-lane that had linked Cuba to the Gulf of Guinea throughout more than three centuries of slave trade. The Caudillo himself had calcu-lated the full impact of such a trip on the population. According to *Granma*'s special correspondent, Rudy Casals, Castro hardly repressed his feelings. "He's beaming with joy," reported Casals. "He's smiling, talking, joking, and said, gleefully: 'We are about to cross the Atlantic!'" (ibid.).

As photographs published by the media showed, the entire top echelon of the Cuban establishment had converged on José Martí air-port to bid godspeed to "querido compañero Fidel" (dear Comrade Fidel) (ibid.). The atmosphere brought to mind the eve of each icon-like moment of the Castroite saga: the Moncada attack; the *Granma* landing; Batista's flight; Comandante Castro's triumphal entry into Havana; the Bay of Pigs invasion and the declaration of Cuba as "Socialist"; the October missile crisis.

They did not appear in the photographs that *Granma* published of the departure from José Martí, nor in those of the arrival at Gbessia airport in Guinea; the media neither mentioned their names nor showed them. But upon his arrival at Guinea's airport, which was sealed off for the event by Cuban soldiers who had been stationed in Guinea since 1966 and loyal forces of Touré's Cuban-trained Milices Nationales, Castro was accompanied by an unusually large number of Cuba's top military personnel.[29] (The international press was barred from the airport, and not even *Horoya*'s reporters were allowed to photograph the arriving party.) About one hundred military men were believed to have landed with Fidel Castro.

Mami Kouyate spoke Spanish fluently, having been, from 1961 to 1968, Guinea's chargé d'affaires and then ambassador to Cuba. At the time of Castro's visit, he was presidential aide to Touré and chief specialist on Cuban affairs. He interpreted for Touré with Dabo Bengaly, who was also Cuban trained. As Kouyate explained, however,

> Castro came with his own interpreter, a military man who spoke French perfectly, slept near Castro in Touré's private residence, and who took over whenever Touré and Fidel discussed sensitive matters. We only translated the "folkloric" conversations between the two leaders. When it came to military matters, we were asked to leave, and Castro's interpreter (we never even managed to know his name) took over. Neither of the two leaders wanted Guineans in on their strategic conversations, no matter how close we were to the President. In fact, not even Bea [Guinean Prime Minister Lansana Beavogui] was allowed to sit in on the secret sessions (ibid.).

The reasons for all of the secrecy would only become apparent some time after Castro's visit. Almost to a man, the most senior leaders of Cuba's intelligence and Revolutionary Armed Forces (FAR) had landed with Castro. Maj. Manuel Piñeiro Losada, then director of the DGI, was never seen in public while he was in Guinea. Nor was Capt. Osmány Cienfuegos Gorriarán, director of the "Liberation Committee," the organ of the secret services in charge of African guerrilla movements, secretary-general of the OSPAAAL, and president of the Party's Commission on Foreign Relations.

Other discreet members of Castro's delegation were the top five soon-to-be generals who, four years later, would lead the Cuban armed forces' wars in Angola and Ethiopia: Maj. Zenen Casas Regueiro, first deputy minister of the FAR and head of FAR's Joint Chiefs of Staff; Maj. Rigoberto García Fernández, deputy minister of the FAR and chief of its Department of Combat Readiness; Maj. Julio Casas Regueiro, deputy minister of the FAR and its head of services; Maj. Arnaldo Ochoa Sánchez, rising star of the FAR, chief of the army of Havana, and reputed even then to be one of the most redoubtable of Cuba's military strategists (he is credited with having defeated the Somalian army during the Ogaden war); Maj. Raúl Menéndez Tomasevich, chief of the army of Havana and chief of the FAR's Department of Operations (in 1976, he headed the Cuban expeditionary force to Angola).

Enjoying high visibility alongside Castro, however, was Maj. Juán Almeida Bosque, the black first deputy minister of the Cuban armed forces. For Almeida, this was his second trip out of Cuba accompanying Fidel Castro. (The first was his trip to New York in 1960, when Castro set up headquarters in Harlem's Theresa Hotel.) Many observers were puzzled by the fact that, no sooner had Castro ended the African leg of his trip in Algeria than Juán Almeida returned to Cuba directly. At that point, Carlos Rafael Rodríguez, who was white and perhaps already the third most important Castroite leader, replaced Almeida for the East-European portion of the tour. (Since then, Fidel Castro has noticeably made it a point to receive visiting black dignitaries with Almeida at his side.)

Accompanied by their respective aides and bodyguards, Cuba's top men of war made an impressive sight. When he saw the Cubans emerge from the huge Soviet plane, Prime Minister Lansana Beavogui is said to have whispered, in jest, "*Bilahi* [My God], Castro brought over the whole Cuban army!" Dressed alike in khaki uniforms, the Cubans could have passed for bodyguards or military aides. However, eight years spent in service in Cuba had allowed Mami Kouyate to identify them, as well as their ranks and their positions in the Party. There was room for all sorts of conjecture as to the reasons for their arrival, for, secretive as ever, Touré had only briefed his closest collaborators on Castro's impending visit. It was intended, he is reported to have told a small gathering of insiders, to strengthen Guinea's defensive potential, reinforce the struggle of African liberation movements, and to help the progressive African states to protect themselves from coups d'etat (ibid.).

In Cuba, the media treated the event as though the first man had set foot on the moon. Radio, press, and television informed the Cuban population of the most insignificant details of the trip, starting with the landing. "It was 10h50 in Conakry and 6h50 in Havana," reported *Granma*, "when Fidel's feet touched African ground for the first time. He then warmly embraced Guinea's President Sékou Touré. Thus began an incontestably historic trip."[30] At a huge rally at the "September 28" Stadium, Castro called Touré "my comrade and brother" and declared Cubans and Guineans to be "brothers in terms of culture, but also in terms of blood-links."[31] In an impassioned speech, Sékou Touré proposed an "anti-imperialist pact" of progressive forces for which Guinean territory would become the "operational base."[32] To that end, said Touré, his government "stood ready to take all of the necessary measures" (ibid.) and face whatever concomittant dangers.

Babacar Fall argues credibly that, by the time Castro had arrived, the Guinean regime was already under the military protection of Cuba and the USSR.[33] In the previous year, some 300 Cuban troops had helped to save Touré's regime. Nevertheless, Touré remained fearful of a large-scale land, air, and marine invasion by the Portuguese forces stationed in neighboring Guinea-Bissau. Amilcar Cabral's PAIGC, which was headquartered in Conakry, received military supplies through Guinea and had a great many troops stationed in Guinean territory. When all this is taken into account, explains Fall, direct Cuban military assistance was vital to Sékou Touré. Through the Ideological Institute, set up and manned by Cubans since 1968, wrote Fall, "Cubans took charge of the tasks of political and ideological formation besides that of military training. . . . Top-echelon officers perfected their training in Havana. Cuba shaped the paramilitary force called the 'Guinean Militia,' and Cubans officered the army and police, whose combined force was 30,000 men." All in all, by 1972, Guinea had already turned into "a political as well as military stronghold and key position of the Soviets' South Atlantic defense system" (ibid.).

The first of a series of Cuban "security bases" was reportedly stationed at "Km 33," and was described by Guinean officers as a veritable "security bolt which barred any army advance from the interior into the capital." Moreover, Castro had surrounded Sékou Touré with Cuban bodyguards. Wherever the Guinean army was garrisoned, according to the Guinean officers, "you will find a strong military Cuban contingent whose mission is to watch us and, if the case arose, neutralize us."[34] That was reportedly the situation in Kindia, Labe, Kankan, and other cities, "so that even if the Cuban troops are no more than several hundred well-trained men, armed to the teeth, the entire Guinean army is impotent for, as everybody knows, it is barred from having its own ammunition" (ibid.).

The "Máximo Protector"

Surrounded by a phalanx of bodyguards, some wearing civilian clothes, Fidel Castro began his public visit to Guinea flanked by Major Almeida and another unsmiling black Cuban wearing dark sunglasses, Oscar Oramas. Newly appointed as ambassador to Guinea, the latter was a man of action. Then in his early thirties, he reportedly went straight into the foreign service after years of ladder-climbing in the secret service. He was intensely feared by the embassy staff. Even after a year's service as a diplomat, he was still identified, in whispers, as the "mascot of 'Barba Roja'" (the nickname of intelligence boss Piñeiro). Oramas's extraordinary career includes the role of ambassador-proconsul to Angola during the most critical phase of the Cuban military intervention there, and then that of chief of the Department of African Affairs at the Foreign Ministry in Havana. (At the time of writing, he is Cuba's ambassador to the U.N.)

Traditional fidelista showmanship, mixed in with sound public-relations support for Sékou Touré, made up a great deal of Castro's week-long stay. The Cuban leader addressed huge rallies, through interpreter Dabo Bengaly, in a country-wide tour. Castro harangued workers to work more, and militias to redouble their vigilance against the plots to "eliminate our comrade Touré."[35] He called upon the youth to show themselves worthy of their leader by vowing "the most absolute loyalty and fidelity" to President Touré.[36] "The first duty of all Guineans," said Castro, "is to express a constant loyalty, gratitude and obedience towards comrade Sékou Touré" (ibid.). Guineans would be "ungrateful" if they did not follow Touré unflinchingly, for no one else but Touré "gave them independence, freedom and well-being."[37]

To Castro's description of him as the descendant of the greatest warriors in Guinea's history, the supreme commander of the Guinean revolution replied: "Fidel Castro and the Cuban revolution are one. The people are in power. Racial discrimination, which still is a scourge here in Africa and in the U.S., has totally vanished in Cuba. . . . Before, people spoke of 'little Cuba.' But nowadays everyone has come to admit the fact that we're dealing with a 'Big Cuba'!"[38]

At the height of the excitement, Castro—perhaps for the first time since coming to power—abandoned his green fatigues to don full African garments. He was enchanted by his first contact with Africa, reported *Granma*'s correspondent. Castro's enchantment was such that he effusively praised the very drumming that he intensely disliked in Cuba. "Everything is so beautiful here, so united and homogeneous," said Castro rapturously. "It is just as if everything was endowed with a soul. . . . But what strikes me most is to discover that a Guinean culture, an African culture, does exist. You can feel it everywhere: in the music, the dances and songs. . . . Guineans even speak with their drums, with their hands, their gestures, dances and smiles."[39]

Less "folkloric" in content and tone, the final communiqué signed by both parties on May 8, 1972, stated that Castro had "recalled that throughout several centuries, African and American peoples shared the same fate. . . . Africans were present in the struggle against Spanish colonialism and they influenced the formation of Cuban national culture. . . . Guinea can henceforth count on Cuba, morally and materially, whatever the circumstances."[40] The document in itself was banal, as tradition demanded. However, the agreements which Touré and Castro are believed to have reached during their airborne conversations, with supporting documents reportedly only on the Cuban side, were not. "Guinea had formalized its agreement to become the staging base for Soviet-Cuban military and political influence in Africa," explained Mami Kouyate, "but years later we would discover that the results of Guinean-Cuban cooperation, as far as Guinea was concerned, could be summarized in one word: zero."[41]

In practical terms, Guinea had become Cuba's new gateway into black Africa, and its virtual protectorate. The way the Caudillo spoke and carried himself tended to highlight that fact. "The imperialists have been wanting to eliminate comrade Sékou Touré," Castro told a mass rally in Kankan, "but comrade Touré will never be liquidated."[42] Whereas, Castro continued, "in the past, your forefathers . . . were forced to fight almost weaponless for decades, armed with mere bows and arrows,"[43] the world situation had radically changed. Today, he promised, "you will no longer stand alone. You will always be able to count on the total, absolute and unflinching support . . . of our fighters who stand by ready to go anywhere, to help a fraternal revolutionary people."[44]

In a last public speech to cadres of the Parti Democratique de Guinée (PDG), the Caudillo, in full battle dress, unsmilingly alluded to "important agreements" he had concluded with Touré and warned:

If those mercenaries [who attacked Conakry on November 22, 1970]
were not even capable of holding the docks of Conakry, who could vanquish well-armed, well-trained and properly officered Guinean armed
forces? . . . From now on we will be united, as in one struggle, in peace
as in war, and whatever the circumstances. . . . Our peoples stand
united as one. Henceforth, Guinea will be able to count on Cuba, as
Cuba on Guinea. . . . And if imperialism dares commit other criminal
attacks against Guinea, then our weapons and soldiers, if need be, will
be coming over to assist the Guinean soldiers. Let the imperialists be
advised of this![45]

The Search For Airports

On May 7, 1972, Fidel Castro unexpectedly left Conakry and flew
to Sierra Leone. Flanked by half-a-dozen senior secret service and
military officials, including Juan Almeida, Castro was also accompanied by Guinean Prime Minister Lansana Beavogui. His six-hour visit
was described as a "courtesy." It was discovered some time afterwards, however, that the move won Cuba access to Robertsfield airport in exchange for Cuban military advisers for President Siaka
Stevens's small army. Sierra Leone and its dictator depended on
Guinea for survival. A year before Castro's arrival, Stevens had called
in Guinean troops to put down a military coup. On March 26, 1971,
he hastily signed a "mutual defense pact" with Conakry that
legitimized the permanent stationing of Guinean forces in Sierra
Leone.

Just ten days before the Caudillo's trip to Guinea, Sierra Leone and
Cuba had simultaneously announced the establishment of diplomatic
ties in what could be interpreted as a shotgun marriage. Understandably, there had been no time for a Cuban envoy to be on hand in
Freetown to await Castro, who arrived to an uneasy welcome. Occupying Guinean troops had taken over security operations and lined
the avenue leading to the presidential palace. Speeches were brief and
devoid of the warmth expected of newlyweds.

In a single public statement, Castro praised the "courage" of Sierra
Leone, a dictatorship Cuba had just added to its list of "anti-
imperialist" African allies. "We sympathize with Sierra Leone," he
stated, "for our peoples have a lot in common. How can we forget
that, centuries back, men and women were violently torn away from
these coasts, reduced to slavery and taken to the island of Cuba?"[46]
As a result of "such monstrous crimes," Castro told Stevens, "we are
brothers today, not solely because of our common ideals, but because

of our blood-links. . . . We are two fraternal countries in the broadest sense of the word. . . . And I can guarantee that you can rely on your . . . loyal and trustworthy Cuban brothers" (ibid.).

Some months after Castro's visit, Sierra Leone's foreign minister, Desmond Luke, was received in Havana to formalize mutual cooperation agreements.[47] Stevens had agreed to give landing rights to Cuba's Compañía Cubana de Aviación (Cuban Aviation Company), and was eager to tighten his friendship with such a powerful ally. Theoretically, the Guinea/Sierra-Leone "mutual assistance pact" placed Freetown under Cuba's military aegis, too. Technically, then, following Castro's visit, Sierra Leone's international airport was already open to Cuban aircraft. The inaugural flights of Cubana de Aviación began towards the end of the year, bringing to Sierra Leone the first batch of black Cuban military advisers, bodyguards, and diplomatic personnel. (The Cuban military staff there is believed to have numbered 125 men in 1977, and 500 in 1983.) Havana's ambassador to Freetown, Alfonso Herrera, was appropriately black. Up till then, he had been Cuba's consul to Jamaica.

Within two months of his African tour, on July 26, 1972, Castro again slammed shut the doors to any possible entente with the U.S. "No need to launch diplomatic offensives, or send out feelers to the Cuban Revolution," he warned. "Cuba's doors will remain firmly closed to Mr. Nixon's politicking and gimmicks."[48] That pledge would soon evaporate, however, as the search for airport facilities became an acute preoccupation for the Cuban military. Within four months of Castro's speech, the announcement that the Cuban government had proposed to the U.S. an anti-hijacking agreement came as a double surprise.[49] The U.S. promptly accepted amid widespread rumors that a Cuban-American rapprochement was, perhaps, in the making.[50] Rather than seeking "rapprochement" with the U.S., however, Cuba had other reasons for this unexpected proposal.

Air piracy—mostly to Cuba—had plagued Cuban-American relations throughout the 1960s. American civilian aircraft were constantly being hijacked to Cuba, to Havana's seeming delight. After gaining a major foothold in Guinea and a toehold in Sierra Leone, which opened those countries' airports to Cuban aircraft, the Cuban government apparently became seriously interested in putting a halt to the wave of hijackings. Significantly, Havana began to employ the term "air piracy." This turn of events seems to square with the way Cuban-African relations were developing. One may speculate that this move could have been linked to Cuba's concern with guarantee-ing the safety of air lanes, particularly those over the Atlantic. In 1972, Equatorial Guinea, under dictator Macias Nguema, gave Cuba landing rights for its Bata and Malabo airports, in exchange for Cuban military advisers and bodyguards, and some troops. Making increas-ingly regular runs over the Atlantic, to convey military personnel and weapons to Guinea-Bissau and return with wounded Cubans and PAIGC recruits, Cubana de Aviacion suddenly became vulnerable to "reverse air piracy," or sabotage by terrorist Cuban exile groups. Sig-nificantly, the FAR had prudently entrusted its transatlantic opera-tions to Cuba's civilian airline, rather than to its own aircraft.

The conclusion of the Cuban-American anti-hijacking agreement in early 1973 was the first major accord between the two countries since 1959. To that end, Castro had even dropped his pledge never to negotiate with the U.S. until the latter had lifted its embargo. The ac-cord was to Cuba's advantage, for many reasons. In case of a major crisis in Africa, the eight- to nine-hour nonstop flight to Sierra Leone and Guinea could be perilous for heavily laden aircraft. Landing and refueling facilities were necessary at some intermediary point.

The states of the Caribbean therefore became the next target for the solicitude of Cuban diplomacy. Setting aside its long-standing lack of interest in its neighboring Caribbean islands,[51] Cuban leaders in-cluding the Caudillo himself went to work. By September 1974, agreements for airport use had been reached with Guyana,[52] Jamaica, Trinidad and Tobago,[53] and Barbados.

Within slightly more than twenty-four months of Fidel Castro's "historic" trip to Guinea, Cuba had legally secured landing, transit-ing, and refueling facilities for its aircraft in four Caribbean airports and another three airports on Africa's Atlantic coast (Gbessia, Robertsfield, and Brazzaville). Cuba's FAR could not have wanted more. The military leadership had succeeded in establishing a viable air network—with Cubana de Aviacion as a front—that was already an operational Cuba-Africa military air-bridge.[54] It was the Cuban leader himself who inaugurated that network in September 1973, when, en route to Algiers, he made successive stopovers in Jamaica, Trinidad and Tobago, Guyana, and Guinea.[55] (It was Fidel Castro's second trip to Africa—and to Guinea in particular—within a period of sixteen months.)

On all fronts, Cuba seemed to be moving with deliberate speed. In the space of two years, from 1972 to 1974, Havana did more than its share to bridge the gulf that had up till then separated Cuba from the rest of the Caribbean. That gulf had to a large extent been due to the fact that the predominantly Hispanic revolutionary leadership of Cuba identified exclusively with Spain and its Latin American off-spring. It was also because Havana remained extremely prudent in its own ''backyard.'' Moreover, throughout the 1960s, apart from Guyana's Marxist premier, Cheddi Jagan, Cuba could hardly have found suitable political partners in the area, even if it had sought them.

The new political and logistical importance of the Caribbean island states was inextricably linked to the renewed interest Cuba now shared in black Africa with its Soviet ally. Strictly speaking, Cuba's foreign policy strategy towards the Caribbean can be dated from then on.

19 BLACK CUBA IN THE "AFRICAN DECADE"

Fidel Castro's first trip to Africa inaugurated a veritable "African Decade" politically. Thereafter practically all aspects of African affairs dominated the major speeches made by the Revolution's principal leaders. How did all of this reverberate in the consciousness of Afro-Cubans? What changes in the consciousness of the Hispanic Cuban leadership did an intimate relationship with Africa produce? In his *Retrato de Fidel con Familia*, biographer Carlos Franqui wrote that "Africa is so deep within us, but so ignored, that it's as though it weren't there,"[1] that "the black Cuban world is the popular Cuban world," whereas by contrast, "the Hispanic world is a tragic, . . . flavorless, . . . old, dead and intolerant world" (ibid., 212). Had Fidel Castro himself come to similar conclusions after his first direct contact with the black continent?

In Guinea, the Caudillo had marveled at the way Africans dressed, moved, danced, gesticulated, sang, and laughed. He had admired their colorful costumes and the natural hairstyles of the women. Like Ché Guevara during his first visit to black Africa, Castro had discovered that the peoples of Africa had their own cultures. He marveled to the extent of transgressing the atheism of Marxist ideology: in Africa, he exclaimed, everything seemed to be endowed with a soul. Much of what Cuba's white rulers rejected or repressed at home, or remained absolutely indifferent to, Castro discovered a liking for in Africa.

What impact would this new "Afro-Castroite" vision of Africa and black cultures in general have on the Cuban establishment's domestic racial policy? Marxist Swiss sociologist Jean Ziegler has ventured to provide an answer. He admits, first, that,

> During an initial phase of their revolution, Cuban Communists merely applied the Leninist interpretation of human social evolution. The progressive schooling of the former black sub-proletariat, . . . the installment of a Socialist society—they thought—would necessarily do away with religious, cultural and mystical irrationality among the formerly exploited classes. . . . Particularly zealous Communist party provincial leaders tried to accelerate that process in their fiefs by organizing aggressive, militantly anti-clerical and atheistic repressive

campaigns against the Afro-Cuban cults. . . . But, twenty-three years after the Revolution, . . . the end of racial discrimination, . . . and the radical transformation in every sphere of the lives of the formerly exploited black masses, . . . far from disappearing, the cults, to the contrary, are growing and expanding as never before in the history of that country.[2]

Cuba's new rulers, with the exception of Maj. Juán Almeida Bosque, were "all whites from the haute or petite-bourgeoisie" (ibid.). The Castroite establishment, Ziegler implies, was naturally incapable of understanding Afro-Cuba:

Without exception, men or women, all of them bore deep inside the ideology of their original class. In their collective unconscious, the Blacks, by virtue of their history and birth, were forcibly inferior to whites, so the road to their elevation passed through education and progressive assimilation. In one word, the integration of Blacks into the conceptual universe of the whites. None of these leaders would have challenged the idea of Western rationality as a universal value. And they were absolutely incapable of admitting the irreducible specificity and richness of African cultures, their depth and infra-conceptual wisdom (ibid., 342).

However, according to Ziegler's interpretation, these white, petit-bourgeois, revolutionary rulers went through a profound metamorphosis when they came into direct contact with the African continent, especially when they met with its "progressive" leaders and theorists. Ziegler dates that crucial "change" to the Tricontinental conference, held in Havana in January 1966. He considers that event to have opened a "second phase" in the white Cuban establishment's attitude towards Afro-Cuba (ibid.):

The presence of Amilcar [Cabral], as well as other African heads of state, had an impact and decisive influence on the evolution of the mentality of the Cuban leadership. The latter were attempting at the time to concretely organize a tricontinental anti-imperialist struggle. Hence, Cuban leaders were forced to listen to the analyses of these African leaders; try and understand the particular characteristic of each people; familiarize themselves with the cultural heritage, cosmogony, and symbolic world of the various African nations. The simplistic Leninist vision of the world and of the men inhabiting it gradually began to seem insufficient to grasp the complex tricontinental reality. And it was thanks to Agostinho Neto, Marcelino dos Santos, Mario de Andrade, Amilcar Cabral, Gamal Abdel Nasser, Joseph Ki-Zerbo, and to the ceaseless debates that Cuban leaders held with them as of 1966, that the cultural status of Blacks in Cuba began to change. Progressively, the leaders of the Cuban Communist party became conscious of the particular role played by African civilization in the universal history of mankind. The Cuban interventions in Africa had the effect of accelerating that process even more. . . . And I must insist on this dialectical interplay perceptible since 1966, between the internationalist practice of the revolution and the gradual emergence of a new perception of the history and specific identity of the black Cuban community (ibid., 342, 343).

The year 1972 marked the beginning of an officially approved "African Decade." There was a steady flow of visiting African, Caribbean, and black American leaders, delegations, and cultural groups into Cuba. It started with the arrival, in late August 1972, of African singer Miriam Makeba, with her full consort of African musicians. Her gorgeous African attire, natural, unstraightened hair, and voice that sprang from the very womb of the black continent sent shockwaves through the Afro-Cuban population.[3] Her concerts became moments of trance. Even Makeba was taken aback by the effect of her presence. Mobbed everywhere, she was given tearful *abrazos* (hugs) by black men and women, and repeatedly told "Gracias! Gracias! Gracias!" (ibid.). At first, she thought they were thanking her for finally coming to sing in Cuba, since, she said, "a nasty rumor had been going around for some time in Cuba that I would not go perform there except if paid in American dollars!" (ibid.). (It may be recalled that Makeba was married to Stokely Carmichael, and that the Black Power leader, who then lived in Guinea, was already persona non grata in Cuba.) It was only later, when Carmichael explained the complex Cuban racial situation, that Makeba understood that "Gracias, Makeba!" was a deeply felt statement meaning, "Thanks, my sister, for reminding us of who we are and that Black should be beautiful in Revolutionary Cuba, too" (ibid.).

Makeba's tour across Cuba was an event to which the media devoted considerable time and space. Her every movement was reported on. With Fidel Castro in the lead, Cuba's highest ranking officials appeared at her performances. The Máximo Lider even ordered that Makeba be given immediate Cuban "citizenship." At an official ceremony, held on September 4, 1972, Foreign Minister Raúl Roa García read out the official "citizenship-granting" text, and gave the performer her Cuban passport.[4]

On the heels of Makeba, who spent ten days in Cuba, giving five concerts in Havana alone, came the black Communist *pasionaria*,

Angela Davis, in early October 1972. Her huge, natural "Afro" hair-style challenged centuries of unspoken anti-Black prejudice.[5] It was a silent invitation to all black Cuban women—especially the Party comrades—to throw all their hotcombs into the Caribbean sea.

Davis was first introduced to the people by Fidel Castro, at one of the largest mass rallies ever held in Cuba, an event marking the twelfth anniversary of the Committees to Defend the Revolution. Castro's words, "Dear Comrade Angela Davis," unleashed thunderous applause and shouts that lasted several minutes.[6] Such enthusiasm had rarely been heard since the early days of the Revolution. Castro was troubled by such "tumultuousness," which he said was in contrast to the "disciplined" and "orderly" behavior of mass rallies in Cuba.[7] It reportedly took five minutes before Castro could continue his introductory remarks and introduce the "Dear Comrades of the Central Committee." At one point, visibly irritated, Castro complained to the crowd, "I am embarrassed to think that our guest of honor, Comrade Angela Davis [applause], might have to address us in such conditions. . . . What I am saying is not meant as a criticism; I know you will set things in order by yourselves, and listen attentively, as she deserves, to Comrade Angela Davis [applause]" (ibid.).

The Caudillo had obviously failed to grasp what was really happening. Starved as they had been for over a decade for positive symbols of self-identity, black Cubans had reacted to Angela Davis's beautiful, unstraightened, "Afro" hair. Here was someone everyone could identify with without fearing being tagged as "counter-revolutionary" or as a "black racist." Angela Davis was a Communist, a heroine, a "runaway" Negress, approved of by Cuba. She wore a lovely, "loud"-colored, tight-fitting dress and did not straighten her hair. She was black. She was defiant. She was revolutionary. She was beautiful in a sense that Afro-Cubans understood in their secret code of blackness. She was beautiful, like Makeba, not in spite of her *pelo malo* or bad hair, but because of it.

The stone-faced white leaders of the Revolution fidgeted in their seats. Davis herself seemed bewildered at the commotion she was involuntarily causing. Castro relaxed his approach as the crowd continued chanting and shouting.[8] "I must say," he remarked, "that I have become accustomed to watching you listen attentively every year to the progress reports of the Defense Committees. I am also aware that you have enormous respect and consideration for Comrade Marturelos, who should have been the first speaker . . . "[9] Castro was again interrupted by shouts. The following dialogue ensued:

[Castro] All of the racket is coming from this side, and you may not want to say why, but I know what's happening. [Shouts from the public] What is it that you are trying to say? Is it the heat? [The public: "No!"] It's not the heat? [The public: "No!"] Well, some say that it's because people are tightly pressed against one another. Too many people are here. [The public: "We just want to see Angela Davis."] Oh, so what you want is to see Angela Davis close up? [Applause] So all this is, again, Angela's fault [Applause] (ibid.).

Few guests of the Cuban regime have been given the risky honor of addressing Cubans at a mass rally, as Angela Davis was. It was a moving moment for black Cubans, whether they agreed with the regime or not, to see that beautiful, defiant black woman speaking to a whole people starved for the most elementary symbol of their ethnic worth. It matters little what she said,[10] nor that she was most likely unaware of the great cathartic moment she had produced. Her great contribution has been made. The Ministry of the Interior had been defeated: no black Cuban, woman or man, was reported thereafter to have been arrested for styling his or her hair naturally. One of the elements of contagion which the government had feared would come into Cuba via the Black Power movement had entered legally with Angela Davis, a full-fledged, ardently pro-Soviet black Communist. The "Afro" was no longer illegal in Cuba, although whites and assimilated Blacks may have still disliked it.[11]

The Peruvian troupe Peru Negro (Black Peru) toured Cuba in September 1972, with a repertoire of songs and dances originating in Africa.[12] Other cultural troupes would follow, coming from the Caribbean (Jamaica) and Africa (Guinea). Then began an unending stream of ministerial delegations from African and Caribbean countries, and then of heads of state. From the U.S. came Huey Newton, the founder of the Black Panther party. He arrived in Cuba sometime in 1973 and lived in seclusion there for several years, leaving as secretly as he has come. Cuba was, once again, interested in black Americans.

Teófilo Acosta, the black number-two man at Cuba's U.N. mission in New York until 1976, when he was suddenly expelled (he was later appointed Havana's Ambassador to Zimbabwe), is credited with having created widespread sympathy for Cuba among influential black Americans.[13] These increasingly visited Cuba in the 1970s: Sidney Poitier, Harry Belafonte, Congressman Ronald Dellums, clergymen, civil rights activists, and representatives of professional organizations (Transafrica, *Black Scholar Magazine*, The National Conference of Black Lawyers, The National Council of Black Churches).[14]

These foreign black visitors returned home with glowing reports. Their greatest handicap, of which the Cuban regime took full advantage, was their total ignorance of how Cuban race relations functioned, both before and after the Revolution. None of these visitors had the least knowledge of the terrible occurrences that took place prior to, during, and after their visits. They knew nothing about the silent war going on between a broad section of the Afro-Cuban population and a regime determined to wipe out Africa and blackness from the Cuban landscape.

That war was unremitting. It continued throughout the Sixties, as Castro increasingly used an image of Cuba as a racism-free society to form and deepen ties with Africa's black political progressives. Long after Castro was home from his joyous maiden voyage in black Africa, Black Cuba continued to pay a special price for his domestic policies.

Black Resistance Grows

The First National Congress on Education and Culture took place in Cuba from the 23rd to the 30th of April 1971. Surprisingly, the Congress declared that "the Socialist revolution is in itself the highest expression of Cuban culture."[15] Hence, the Congress felt free to attack the Afro-Cuban Abacuá brotherhood, labelling it a "focus of criminality," and of "juvenile delinquency."[16] The severity of the charge was in proportion to the hatred the government nourished for a prospering underground black organization that it had failed to uproot, neutralize, co-opt, or intimidate. That same year, the Ministry of the Interior internally circulated a pamphlet on the Abacuá with diagrams of its organizational structures. The Cuban secret police was dealing with the Abacuá brotherhood as it would to dismantle a CIA spy ring. The brotherhood was being singled out; the Mayombé and Lucumí followers—though constantly watched—were no longer the objects of intense persecution. The government's strategy had changed from wholesale attack on all Afro-Cuban religions to a combination of tactics aimed at driving a wedge between them. Whenever one was being violently repressed, the others were offered, and given, truces, and were actively courted.

These tactics represented a change from the bulldozer approach employed until the late 1960s, which had only produced the opposite of desired results: Afro-Cuban religions had gone deeper underground and grown in size. They had become veritable parallel societies that gave the harassed worker breathing space and a chance to commune with the comforting deities of Mother Africa. The need to force them back above ground (where they could be monitored and, if need be, pounced on again), forced the regime to offer a de facto truce. The Marxist sociologoist, Jean Ziegler, is closer to the facts on this score than the superficial appraisals of most observers. Writing in 1983, he described the new situation as follows:

> Throughout these last years, Party leaders have done a veritable about face regarding the Cabildo [Afro-Cuban religions], in terms of their conduct as well as perception. But the initiates of the Afro-Cuban cults have also changed: by sheer intelligence and ruse, they have adapted to the successive changes in Party policy towards them. A subtle, complex, dialectical situation, revocable at any time, has developed between both camps. . . . We can summarize the present-day attitude of Cuban Communists towards the Afro-Cuban community's cults as follows: despite decisive mutations which have taken place since 1966, it would be naive to pretend that the present Cuban leaders admire, like, or even understand the Cabildo. The profound meaning of its many mysteries continues to elude most of them. . . . In fact, things are even more complex today than my previous remarks might lead one to believe. Between the Revolutionary leaders and the Cabildo leaders a very tight and subtle game is being played out. Cabildo followers— Yalorixa, Yawo, or Babalao—continue to distrust Marxist militants. But they accommodate to them and make optimum use of official institutions. . . . Cuba's Cabildo is currently playing the role of a class ideology. The Cabildo expresses a demand which is fundamental to all Afro-Cubans: to be taken into account on the basis of their irreducible identity and distinctiveness, as well as in terms of legitimate political ambitions in a nation culturally rooted in three different continents at once.[17]

The regime had evolved a more sophisticated policy towards the Afro-Cuban religions, based on a better structural knowledge of them. The Abacuá brotherhood, most feared and hated by the government, was regarded in only confrontational terms. But, in daily life, who was an Abacuá follower, or Ñañigo? He was none other than the sugar-cane cutter (*machetero*), the stevedore, the construction worker, the dock-worker. Worse, he was the common foot soldier in the army. It was this Ñañigo ubiquity at large that the Party feared. Moreover, as a secret all-male brotherhood based on levels of initiation, the secret society of Abacuá was virtually impenetrable by the state security organs. Contrary to the open, purely religious Mayombé (Regla de Palo) and Lucumí (Anagó) religions, the Abacuá was, has always been, and will presumably always be, a most hermetic secret society of *ecobios* (initiated brothers).

The unrelenting witch-hunt carried out against centuries-old Afro-Cuban religions, which had organized most of the black uprisings during the worst days of slavery, led an impressive number of black workers to flee Cuba during the 1980 Mariel exodus. The result was a strong implantation of these religions in the United States.

Ñañigos have shown their capacity to retaliate powerfully. In late 1969, the regime had a strong warning following the wave of persecutions it unleashed against Abacuá followers in reprisal, it seems, for the uncovering of an all-black underground movement[18] called the Movimiento de Liberacion Nacional (MLN). Although there was no conclusive evidence that the Abacuá as such was involved, the indiscriminate arrests of known Ñañigos were carried out. As the repression continued into 1970, the Abacuá brotherhood took an action that frightened the government even more. For the first time since Fidel Castro came to power, a successful twenty-four-hour strike was carried out, paralyzing the entire port of Havana.[19] It went totally unreported in the state-controlled media.

A Party-like Underground

The MLN was set up by a former soldier and explosives technician, Gilberto "Johnny" Aldama, some time in 1968.[20] Given the conditions of extremely tight security in Cuba, it is remarkable that this movement went undetected for over a year. More surprising still, it was discovered purely by accident in 1969, and most of its members held jobs for which some form of security clearance was required (e.g., bodyguards for white army majors, workers in explosives factories, sentries). Many of the women involved were "household help" for army officials. Others worked in factories connected in some way with national defense. "We consciously screened candidates, precisely in search of Blacks who had some form or another of security clearance," explained Aldama,[21] upon his release from prison in 1981.

How could such a movement emerge in the first place? "It happened naturally," recalled Aldama, "just by sitting around and talking about the situation of Blacks in Cuba. After so many years of revolution, sacrifices, and lives given up to defend it, Blacks continued being despised at the bottom" (ibid.). The organization was loosely patterned after the structure of some of the state security organs. MLN members never held a "pure" meeting. They met only during birthdays, weddings, or some other festivity. They always used the term *compañero* (comrade), and never met in groups of more than half-a-dozen people. Aldama traveled several times across Cuba for a variety of purposes attached to his official duties and set up small cells of people. One of the MLN members, who worked for the Ministry of the Interior, screened prospective candidates by using the ministry's computer files.

By late 1969, Aldama and the others decided that the organization could begin operating. They had amassed considerable explosives and detonators. Their caches were the basements and garages of the comandantes for whom some of them were bodyguards, house sentries, or domestic help. Another reason they had gone undetected was because the MLN was not connected with exile groups abroad. However, a fatal decision, made against Aldama's best instincts ("I wanted escape routes for any 'burned' member," he explained), led to catastrophe. The black secret service officer who accidentally stumbled on the MLN came from abroad. He was picked up at a beach by Aldama and other MLN members and given refuge. This initial blunder triggered a series of investigations which, in the end, corroborated the agent's reports: an all-black underground opposition movement existed. Aldama and an undisclosed number of the organization's leaders in Havana were swiftly arrested.

Gilberto Aldama was nineteen years old when he was arrested and sentenced to death by firing squad. He took full blame for setting up the organization and minimized the roles of those others who had been arrested. None broke, despite heavy interrogations, and more than 80 percent of the MLN members have never been discovered. Aldama convinced his interrogators that the recruitment had never gone beyond Havana. After he had spent two weeks on death row, Aldama's sentence was suddenly commuted to thirty years' imprisonment, of which he served twelve. In 1981, Gilberto Aldama was among some 1500 political prisoners released from Cuban jails and allowed to emigrate. (Fidel Castro promised the newly installed French Socialist government of Francois Mitterand that he would release political prisoners.[22])

The "Black Manifesto Plot"

Sara Gómez, a young black filmmaker, was acknowledged to be one of Cuba's most innovative directors. She was interviewed in Havana in July 1967 by French writer-filmmaker Marguerite Duras. Gómez was then only twenty-four, but spoke like a centuries-old sage. "There are things that one begins by accepting intellectually, but which thereafter bring on terrible, serious emotional conflict," she said, speaking of male-female relations.[23] But Gómez could not have excluded Cuba's racial dilemma from that profound statement. She was too aware, too sensitive, too black, and too much of a rebel. "More than ever," she told Duras, "I put my trust in the role of troublemakers; in those hard-headed people you find in every school, on every farm, in every factory: people who are always ready to bring up an issue that none thought about before, to demand answers, thus forcing the others around them to think a bit further" (ibid., 3).

In 1968, Sarita Gómez was among the group of Afro-Cuban intellectuals the regime had identified as Black "troublemakers." At one point these diehards were called together by Minister of Education José Llanusa Gobels. They met with him privately in a closed room at the Hotel Habana Libre. The meeting took place a few days before the opening of the World Cultural Congress in January 1968. It had been rumored that these black intellectuals were holding private meetings and had drafted a position paper on race and culture in Cuba. They purportedly intended to present it to the Congress. The authorities quickly dubbed it a "Black Manifesto" and went on to baptize it with the name "plot."

Black intellectuals felt rightfully that the primarily white Cuban delegation to the Congress was not representative of Cuba's population and could not but present a false, distorted view of Cuba's complex racial and cultural situation. Carlos Franqui, one of the Congress's sideline organizers, attempted to dissuade them from an action which he thought would be "divisive and make it appear as if there was a racial problem in Cuba."[24] (A year later, Franqui himself went into exile and ultimately conceded that he had been wrong on that occasion [ibid.].)

Minister Llanusa Gobels is said to have told the black intellectuals, some twenty in all, that the government was aware of their initiative and wanted to discuss the matter. He gave the impression the authorities wanted to incorporate their ideas into the general document Cuba would present to the Congress. Everyone was supposed to speak their minds openly. Fidel Castro himself had finally taken an interest in their ideas and complaints. Dissident Afro-Cuban novelist, Esteban Cárdenas, wrote a detailed account of the meeting. He listed those present. The number and intellectual caliber of those black dissenters deserves special attention.

Walterio Carbonell, perhaps Cuba's most innovative historian and ethnologist, was a former diplomat. He was expelled from the old Cuban Communist party (Partido Socialista Popular) in 1953, for having supported Fidel Castro's attack on Moncada. His book on race and culture in Cuba was banned by Castro in 1961. From then on he became the most unrelenting critic of the regime's racial and cultural policies.

Rogelio Martínez Furé, a poet and essayist, was one of the most important Cuban ethnologists. Regarded as one of the most informed Cuban Africanists, he had specialized in studying the ancestral roots of Afro-Cuban religions. Nancy Morejón, poet, journalist, and linguist, had specialized in Afro-Cuban poetry. Nicolás Guillén Landrián and Sara Gómez were among the top ten filmmakers in Cuba. Pedro Deschamps Chapeaux and Alberto Pedro were both ethnologists.[25] Juan Manuél Casanova was a writer and journalist; Eugenio Hernández and Gerardo Fulleda Léon were leading playwrights; Luis M. Saenz was a journalist and fiction writer. Ana Justina, Serafín Quiñones, Manuel Granados, Wichy el Negro, and Pedro Peréz Sarduy were talented novelists and poets.

Cárdenas recounts that, "at first, the most naive of those called in believed that, finally, the revolutionary government had taken an interest in the thoughts coming from Blacks, a people whose different historical background made up for a unique insight on Cuba's cultural personality."[26] For this reason, they spoke their minds. Minister Llanusa listened to the outpouring of ethnic grievances and then it was his turn to speak. He looked around the room stonily, scrutinized everyone, and told the group that they were being virtually "seditious." The Revolution would allow no sort of activity that would "divide" the people along racial lines. The government and the Party were solely authorized to theorize on matters of culture. As for matters of race, only hidden enemies of the Revolution could bring up a subject that had been resolved since 1959. The drafting of any sort of "black manifesto" for presentation to a Congress hosted by Cuba was inconceivable. Even the intention was an act of provocation. They would either have to recant or face the consequences.

"So it was now clear that the government cared nothing about what these black personalities thought," wrote Cárdenas. "The aim of the meeting had been to find out who was who, so as to better perfect repressive methods and conduct reprisals against individuals in different ways. . . . The 'dialogue' had been purely Machiavellian, and all of these black intellectuals were thereafter forced into silence. Of those present, the majority painfully realized that they had been tricked. Their dreams and the reality would never fuse. In the end, each one went his or her own way, some becoming accomplished opportunists, others going mad, some being taken straight to prison, one fleeing into exile in 1980, while others died" (ibid.).

Only Walterio Carbonell dared to defy the minister. When he spoke, he rescued the collective dignity of all those whose heads were now bowed, who sat in silent disbelief, or who trembled in fear.[27] Carbonell, Wichy el Negro, and Nicolás Guillén were immediately placed under arrest. The others remained free but were warned by the authorities to stay clear of the Congress site. Some were reportedly confined to their homes for the Congress's duration. At some point, Carbonell was spirited away to a labor camp in Camaguey. For years, no news was heard from him. He w .s rumored dead. Then, in 1974, he was reported to have been released. Black Cuba had lost one of its most important and defiant spokesmen in this half of the century.

Guillen reportedly lost his mind in jail and was interned in Havana's psychiatric hospital. Manuel Granados apparently attempted suicide, failed, then suffered a nervous breakdown and was interned in Havana's psychiatric hospital. Most of the others were granted the opportunity to "rehabilitate" themselves and given small jobs in various government agencies (Nancy Morejón, Pedro Pérez Sarduy, Rogelio Martínez Furé, Alberto Pedro, Pedro Deschamps Chapeaux, Luis M. Saenz, Serafín Quiñones). A few were reported to have repented to the extent of becoming efficient detectors of the "black virus" for the state's internal security organs.

The World Cultural Congress took place, as scheduled, on January 4-12, 1968. None of the Blacks who attended it could have remotely suspected the terrible blow that had just fallen on the most daring figures of the Afro-Cuban intelligentsia. Few saw anything sinister or strange in the circumstance that the Cuban delegation was all white, except for Nicolás Guillén, Sr. However, all unawares, visiting Trinidadian poet John LaRose and Jamaican novelist Andrew Salkey repeatedly asked the "wrong" questions and sought to meet the "wrong" people. In his *Havana Journal*, Andrew Salkey wrote of his chance meeting with Nancy Morejón at the Writers' Union (UNEAC) headquarters:

> "Will we see you at the Congress?" I asked. "No." "Why not?" "You can come here to meet us, and talk." "Why won't you be at the Congress?" "Space doesn't allow for all of us to attend. We're quite a number, you know." "You're so uncomplaining. I don't understand." "Nothing to complain about." "But you're a writer and you haven't been invited to the Congress in your own city." "We all couldn't be, as I told you a while ago." "And you aren't hurt or upset about it?" "No. In any case, we'll be able to meet the delegates when they visit the Union. You must come as often as you wish. We'll be here to talk to you."[28]

Salkey was amazed that Morejón should accept her exclusion from the Congress so calmly. He could not have known of the painful emotional turmoil that was probably ravaging that sensitive critic and poet. (Although she continued writing, Morejón never again involved herself in ethnic protest.) Salkey continued:

> Took John and Robert [Hill] aside and told them about the situation. They too had come up against the same "limp acceptance" of the Congress matter. Marcos [the guide], who hadn't been around for some time, slipped into the conversation from nowhere. He reminded us that most of the young Union members were inexperienced and a little immature, that the well-known Cuban writers would certainly attend and read their papers, and that for security reasons, for the protection of all the visiting delegates, only authorized persons would be allowed to come into the hotel. He was quite firm about the good sense of the information he had given us. . . . We left the Union abruptly. Marcos became concerned. We told him, rather arrogantly, that we did not want any kind of protection against the young unestablished writers and artists of Cuba. . . . John told us the story of a student he'd heard about who was writing a thesis on the poetry of Aimé Césaire, and who, he thought, might very well not be able to meet the poet at the hotel (ibid., 38).

Looking back on the period when those lines were written (in 1969), a surreal atmosphere creeps into these passages. In re-reading the account by Jamaican writer Barry Reckord of his visit to Cuba that same year, a similar sensation is produced by his question to a black Cuban cadre member as to what the racial situation was really like. She answered:

> "Cuban blacks still complain that we are over-represented in sport and under-represented in the government. Afro-Cubans read *Granma* and there is a big page regularly, in colour, about African culture, but certain Afro-Cubans were excluded from our famous cultural conference because the Government didn't want their reflections on the racial set-up in Cuba." And what is the racial set-up? "Well, we all get the same education but since blacks used to be at the bottom there is still a cultural lag and proportionately more black children drop out. Some Afro-Cubans want a special government effort to push black children, but the Government believes that these things will right themselves. . . . The Government wants no kind of racial issue. They don't want to pass the word that where a black can be promoted he must be given preference. The schools are there for everybody, the hotels. There is no public racism. But a lot of private racism."[29]

British Marxist scholar David Booth has admitted that whatever observable changes occurred among Cuban Blacks during the 1970s were "largely the result of the efforts of a conscious group of young black intellectuals and artists . . . with the assistance of a minimal number of whites who understand the nature and dimensions of the problem. Changes have occurred in the best cases without substantial help from the established authorities in the appropriate agencies and institutions of the state, and in the worst cases despite active obstruction."[30] Gains have been made by black intellectuals, he said, but "without openly challenging the established myths" (ibid.). The "racial revolution" was yet to come, for, he concedes:

> In the end there will be no substitute for a thorough public discussion which explicitly focuses on the manifold dimensions of continuing racism in personal relations between Cubans and which, by the use of the entire apparatus of propaganda and organization at the disposal of the national leadership, is carried on to every level of Cuban political and social life. To date the central leadership has shown little inclination to initiate such a discussion. . . . It is still the case that there is a species of taboo of frank public discussion on the color question. Since, as it has been defined, racial discrimination has been abolished, it is easy to accuse those who insist that there is still a color problem in Cuba of gratuitously creating division in the ranks of the people, of being inverted racists, and even of acting as the conscious or "unconscious" agent of imperialism. It is misleading to suggest . . . that an incipient Black Power movement was stamped out in 1967, but it is true that at least two known attempts during the 1960s to open a debate on some of the more burning issues raised here were firmly rebuffed without explanation (ibid., 170–172).

. . . And Other "Conspiracies"

A so-called "Movimiento Black Power" did emerge autonomously in Cuba in 1969 and spread until it was crushed by the secret police in 1971. It involved another group of Afro-Cuban intellectuals who defied the authorities by wearing their hair in "Afros" and getting together to read and comment on Frantz Fanon's works. Sara Gómez, Manuel Casanova, and Eugenio Hernández were again involved, the only members of the "Black Manifesto" group who continued taking such risks. More than a hundred prominent but as yet unestablished black intellectuals spearheaded this new black protest. Among them were Esteban Cárdenas (poet), Ivan Cesar Martínez (journalist), Abraham Rodríguez (playwright), Ernesto Gonzalez (writer), and R. Fowler (sculptor). In 1971, nearly all of the "ringleaders" of the "Movimiento Black Power" were arrested.

The case of Ivan Cesar Martínez was quite peculiar. He is said to have recanted in jail. When released, he was given a government job. Two years later, he was appointed ambassador to Guyana, and subsequently ambassador to Trinidad and Tobago; and then ambassador to Barbados, a post he still held in 1986. Others, after recanting, were also put to use in areas profitable to the regime.

Esteban Cárdenas managed to flee into exile some years later. (His brother, Osvaldo Cárdenas, was then the top intelligence officer in charge of Caribbean affairs for the Party.) Sarita Gómez continued to make, and to dream, wonderful films until 1972, when, still in her early thirties, she died of heart failure. Manuel Casanova was among the ten thousand Cubans who took refuge en masse in the Peruvian embassy in 1980, and went into exile. Nancy Morejón turned her attention exclusively to literary matters and was thereafter allowed to travel abroad.

Booth's conclusion that, in the long run, "it may very well turn out less easy . . . to bring about the definitive suppression of the heritage of slavery in countries like Brazil and Cuba than in more obviously racist societies such as the U.S., . . . irrespective of the class character of the state," gives an idea of the magnitude of the problem with which black Cuban intellectuals were faced (ibid., 172). The violent breaking up by the secret police of the informal black Afro-Cuban Study Groups in the mid-1970s is another case in point.

What became known as "Afro-Cuban Study Groups" began in 1974, virtually in the same spontaneous fashion as the black Movimiento de Liberación Nacional had in 1968, or as the idea to present a black position paper to the 1968 World Cultural Congress, or as the so-called "Movimiento Black Power."[31] "First, we would just sit around to listen to nice records, dance, and talk a bit," recounted Reinaldo Barroso, one of those ultimately accused of having initiated these all-black group study sessions. "Then someone would say, '*Oye, chico*, I have an *Ebony* magazine with an article on this or that.' And then we just started passing interesting information to each other about black movements around the world, about African cultures, and things like that. We hadn't even realized that by coming together to listen to music—jazz, soul, funk, salsa, Fela's Afro-beat— we unconsciously were fulfilling a need to talk about ourselves as Blacks."[32]

According to Esteban Cárdenas's written account of the events that followed, "In 1974, a group of young Blacks . . . started up the first of a series of study groups. They merely wanted to investigate, analyze and study the history of Cuba, but from the standpoint of its link with black African cultures."[33] They all felt a deep void within themselves, although the state's media and the leaders of Cuba proclaimed that they had all they needed. There was nowhere Blacks could go, no institution, movement, or school in Cuba, said Cárdenas, to satisfy a thirst for ethnic fulfillment (ibid.). "They felt that a supposedly revolutionary country should have some type of structure which could allow Man to get rid of whatever form of historical alienation, derived from the colonization of the mind, was imposed by western culture," he explained. "For instance, they felt it was abnormal for Cuban Blacks, men and women, to continue behaving the way they did, wanting to become physically white, or as close to it as possible, and aping white behavior. Craving to become like the whites resulted from the exploitation and oppression Europe had imposed over several centuries on countries known as the 'Third World,' they felt. In other words, these young Blacks were theorizing heavily on the concept of racial alienation" (ibid.).

Cárdenas further related that the Editorial Ciencias Sociales of the Ministry of Culture had flatly refused, in 1974, to even consider publishing Cheikh Anta Diop's *Blacks in Antiquity*, or any of his other works. "It was argued that Diop was a falsifier of history who had 'Negrified' Greek history and 'Negroized' the ancient Egyptians," Cárdenas recalled. "The young black scholar who had made the proposal that Diop's works be published, Lázaro Rodríguez, was immediately summoned before both the Editorial Board and the base cell Party committee of the publishing outfit. He was asked to explain the reasons behind such a proposal which betrayed 'ideological escapism,' 'black racism' and indicated his 'lack of firmness and loyalty to revolutionary principles' " (ibid.).

The young Afro-Cubans who started the "study groups" simply hungered for knowledge of their historical past—in Cuba as well as in the general history of mankind. They were women and men, all Blacks, their ages ranging from 18 to 25 years. All were born under the Revolution; they had known no other system but socialism. They didn't hide, or try to meet covertly. This was not because they felt that what they were doing was innocent: reading "black" books, commenting on "black" issues, listening to "black" music from various parts of Africa and the world. On the contrary. They were painfully aware of the price they would sooner or later have to pay for their "suspicious" quest, though there was nothing sinister in their undertaking. They were born under the Castro regime, and understood it too well to make the mistake of going about their business in secret. "We grew up under a system where everyone is watched, so we just acted normally," Barroso recalled. "We always met at someone's flat to have fun, dance, play records and, as a part of that whole boisterous commotion, we exchanged knowledge about things Black" (ibid.).

They knew that the secret police would soon infiltrate their groups, so they decided that no name, especially nothing like "study group," which would have really sounded subversive, should be attached to their activities. If anyone ever got curious, the answer was to be simple: "Dancing, singing, and listening to music are enjoyable things, and the Revolution was made to bring joy, not sadness, to the Cuban people." In a word, they were happy Cuban Blacks, happy to be Cubans, happy to be revolutionaries, and only incidentally Blacks. As Cárdenas explains further, "they were all acutely aware that the social situation in Cuba was characterized, particularly at that stage of 1974–75, by extremely repressive methods. But they persisted with their studying and research. And they began to meet more and more frequently, with youthful zeal, as if wanting to show that those black intellectuals who were repressed years before, and were now silent, deserved successors who would break the silence" (ibid.).

There was no leader, for there was no organization. They had no name, for they were not a movement. (The Cuban Constitution forbids any movement but the ruling Communist party.) Success increased their apprehension, however. "Black study groups" were started up by other young Blacks. This snowball effect meant only trouble, and they all knew it. Still, they went ahead, with the feeling that "the black dignity and self-knowledge we were acquiring was worth the risk of the inevitable knock on the door," as Barroso later explained (ibid.).

Cárdenas details the events that followed in rapid succession. "The whole affair blew up quickly. The state security organs had been watching all along what these blacks were up to, right under the noses of the secret police. In 1975, it felt the moment had come to put an end to their activities. (It is likely that agents of the political police branch, and voluntary informers, had begun attending the meetings.) What the police seemed most afraid of was that Cuban blacks in general would end up knowing about the existence of such 'Study Groups' " (ibid.).

In early 1975, the secret police staged a pre-dawn raid of Reinaldo Barroso's home in the Vedado section of Havana. Cárdenas's account concurs with Barroso's. "Barroso was taken by surprise. His Vedado home was entirely surrounded by groups of police. They were armed to the teeth and had lots of special assault rifles. They carried strong flashlights and used bullhorns to summon him out. That's how, one after the other, these young people were taken from their homes, in a way quite reminiscent of what we saw in the newspapers of how the [U.S.] police hunted down, surrounded the homes, and flushed out unarmed Black Panthers during the 1960s" (ibid.).

There is no record of how many were arrested over the following weeks. "None of those arrested was even near thirty years old," said Cárdenas, "but for all of them there began a most harrowing experience." The dramatic "busts" were reserved for those considered to be the ringleaders, but anyone who had ever attended a "meeting," even if only once, was contacted by the secret police. Most were young students, workers, and unestablished artists—writers, musicians, and poets. Summoned by mail, all were extensively interrogated by the political police and threatened with long prison sentences if they withheld any information they had about the *conspiración* (conspiracy).

No fewer than one hundred young black men and women are believed to have been interrogated by the police during 1975 in Havana alone. (The "study groups" were just beginning to catch on in other provinces when the police carried out their dragnet operation.) Barroso himself does not know how many people were arrested, nor how many "study groups" were broken up. The informal gatherings had been under no one's particular control. "The idea came up to do it. We were about five or ten of us at the first 'meeting' if you can call it that—but then others who felt the idea was valid took it up. Soon, I myself was being invited to attend 'meetings,'" Barroso admitted (ibid.)

The "Afro-Cuban Study Groups" had been no more of a "conspiracy" than the 1968 black position paper (so-called "Black Manifesto") was a "plot" or the so-called "Movimiento Black Power" an attempt at "subversion." The "ringleaders" were imprisoned briefly under a variety of charges: illegal association; subversive meetings; "parasitism"; anti-social behavior; and "divisive activities." Again, individual fates varied, not so much according to the nature of the charges, but depending on the attitude of the incriminated person. Some were designated "political criminals;" they underwent multiple interrogations while in prison. Some were sent to "re-education" work camps; others were released, watched for a week or two, and re-arrested on the same charges. (Barroso left Cuba for France in 1981 as a political refugee.)

"Produce as Much as Your Slave Grandfather!"

The Cuban population as a whole was more than entitled to enjoy the exciting events that began with the "Africa Decade" of the 1970s. Between 1968 and Castro's visit to Africa in 1972, Cubans had lived through a veritable purgatory. In the intervening period, their society had been swiftly transformed along the standard Soviet model, with new repressive labor decrees. The *ofensiva revolucionaria* of 1968, in which even small street-side bars and coffeeshops were liquidated, had turned the country into a drab, militarized society. Then, Castro's order to the nation to produce no less than ten million tons of sugar in 1969 had stretched the sacrificial endurance of Cuban workers to breaking point. A definite rupture of the Revolution's "social contract" had ensued when producers and rulers, for the first time since 1959, opposed one another in broad daylight.

"The Year of the Decisive Effort," 1969, was that of the Gran Zafra. Fidel Castro, very much in the manner of a plantation owner, had made a "pledge of honor" that Cuba would produce ten million tons of sugar.[34] "He considers all of Cuba as his personal domain," said French agronomist René Dumont, the Caudillo's one-time adviser. This gigantic mobilization of manpower and resources was targeted at more than doubling Cuba's annual sugar production. which had averaged less than five million tons of sugar annually. But the new Soviet-Cuban reconciliation had included economic agreements wherein the Castroite regime had bowed to the "division of labor" among Socialist countries in which each partner specialized in certain main products.[35] Cuba officially joined the Soviet bloc's economic commonwealth, or COMECON, in July 1972, but the decision to re-orient its economy to that purpose seems to have been taken between the end of 1968 and early 1969. Fidel Castro had meekly accepted a division of labor wherein Cuba became the "sugar bowl" of the Eastern bloc. Among other things, this meant the reinforcement of a one-crop economy—monocultura—which had always been decried as a legacy of Yankee imperialism.[36] More than ever before, Cuba was to live under the "tyranny of sugar" introduced by the colonial slave-holder system. But the despised one-crop economy now had to be lauded as a "victory" for Cuba.[37]

The views of Cuban workers were never solicited. The unified, state-run trade union (CTC) was not their voice. When its chiefs spoke, it was the government and the Party speaking to the workers. Even French Marxist economist Charles Bettelheim, an expert on the

Cuban economy, concluded in 1971 that, "after having followed, for several years, an ascendent course which instilled hope in all Socialist militants, the Cuban Revolution has progressively entered into a degenerative phase."[38] Bettelheim denounced as "dangerously Taylorist" the new system of worker control announced in 1970, with stiff sanctions for "loafers," "laziness," "absenteeism," and "irresponsibility."[39] These were the ills which Fidel Castro held to be responsible for the Gran Zafra's failure (ibid.). Castro's regime was neither by nor for the workers, observed the French economist, since a "new class of privileged rulers" had emerged, whose only function was to administer and issue commands.[40]

At the end of May 1970, in a televised address to the nation, Fidel Castro for the first time called Cuban workers "irresponsible." Thereafter workers were split into two categories: those who were "exemplary," on the one hand, and the "bad," "lazy," "freeloading," "shiftless," on the other. The government announced immediately afterward that Cubans who had not applied for exit visas before May 21, 1970, would henceforth not be allowed to leave the country. Finally, in January 1971, a dreadful, repressive "Law Against Laziness" was promulgated.[41] Some of its provisions were: ablebodied males between the ages of seventeen and sixty years old, discovered to be without a job, students excepted, could be sentenced "to perform forced labor for a period ranging from six months to two years. . . . Workers found to be out of work for fifteen consecutive days, without justification, will be sentenced to one-year periods in re-education camps" (ibid.).

The Cuba that Charles Vanhecke, *Le Monde's* special envoy, observed was a far cry from the "heroic Cuba" of the 1960s. He reported "[a]n omnipresence of state security organs, or felt as such by the people; a conformist press, radio and T.V.; and on each and every block, Committees to Defend the Revolution, or CDRs, which people do not hesitate to call spy rings" (ibid.). As for the workers, he reported little change in the lot of those cane-cutters whose ancestors were shipped to Cuba from Africa precisely to accomplish a brutish form of labor. Of these predominantly black *macheteros*, many of whom are Haitians, he said: "Year after year, to accomplish its Zafra, Cuba needs five hundred thousand men. However, there are only seventy thousand professionals left, . . . wielding the same tool the slaves used: a machete. So one is witness to a repetitive scene: in silent columns, armed with their machetes, these *macheteros* attack sugar-cane stalks as high as a hut. Eight, nine hours per day, and seven days per week, they repeat the same mechanical, precise, boring gestures. They are paid on the basis of what they cut: 1.67 pesos per *arroba* of cane stalks cut" (ibid.).

The machetero's is one of the most degrading forms of work; hence, black African slaves were brought over by the millions to perform that labor in the Caribbean. Nevertheless, for Cuba's white rulers (who sometimes made a point of going to the sugar-cane fields on weekends for a few, televised hours), these sugar-cane cutters were sleeping on their jobs! Was not the failure of the Gran Zafra due in part to their "lazy" refusal to go beyond the last mile? On June 12, 1971, an angry Fidel Castro berated:

> This Revolution will only attain its moral zenith when men who are free will be capable of equaling the production of those who were forced to do so as slaves. . . . Slavery has disappeared, but there is no proof that a rational free man is capable of surpassing the production of a slave society without being coerced to! In the final analysis, that's the problem we're debating now. . . . I am personally convinced that you still have people about the place who need a certain degree of coercion.[42]

The Party's organ, *Granma*, took up the Caudillo's astounding statement to unleash its own campaign. A half-page, unsigned editorial (which meant it was written by a high Party ideologue), was unambiguously entitled, "We Must Make a Free Man Produce More Than When He Was a Slave." In the "battle we're fighting to extirpate from our society the ideological left-overs of our past (of which delinquency, laziness and absenteeism . . . are the sub-products), certain things must be made quite clear," proclaimed the editorial. "For instance, workers must now become conscious of the freedom they enjoy and become aware of the advantages they receive. But above all, they must become aware, also, of the duties conferred on them by virtue of being free men who enjoy these advantages! . . . It is not enough to be a free man. . . . So, we must strengthen our ideological work to make the masses understand what their freedom means. Perhaps, then, we will obtain from a free, non-alienatèd man more labor, more production than what he gave when he was still a slave."[43]

The Cuban regime's bluntly stated position on the productivity of a free worker as compared to that of the island's former slaves had far-reaching implications. Fidel Castro's declared personal conviction that certain workers needed "a certain degree of coercion" to produce, had had no parallel since 1959. Cuban workers needed the whip. Translated into modern language, the "whip" was a series of stringent labor sanctions ceaselessly being added to the new, repressive, all-inclusive Labor Code: anti-vagrancy laws, decrees against "social parasitism," forced, unpaid labor in "rehabilitation" and re-education" camps, and the dreaded, all-encompassing law on "economic sabotage," which could send a worker before a firing squad or to life imprisonment.

The slave labor versus free labor controversy created by the regime in the early 1970s was only conceivable coming from men who had never performed manual labor. Slavery meant nothing to them, save as an intellectual abstraction, an economic category at best. A certain amount of restraint can compensate for a lack of sensitivity. Only sheer arrogance, backed by a tremendously repressive system, could inspire Cuba's bureaucrat-leaders to sermonize to a working population, which had already sacrificed an entire generation to the Revolution, about "making the masses understand what their freedom means'; or how "the duty to produce" was the counterpart of "the freedom and advantages they enjoyed."

All the same, Cuba's white leaders were aware that they were not speaking in a vacuum. They ruled over a society in which the majority of workers had forefathers who had been slave laborers. Throughout 350 years, their brutally extracted productivity had generated the pre-revolutionary fortunes of almost every top leader of the Castroist regime (as well as the white exiles whose privileges and riches had been confiscated by the Revolution). If nothing prevented the Caudillo from ordering a people still laboring under the traumatic legacy of centuries-old racial-economic oppression to produce as much, if not more, as their slave grandparents, it was because the "racial contract" had expired. The mass exodus of Blacks through Mariel in 1980 would prove it beyond dispute.

There was a bottom line to these bluntly repressive declarations by Cuba's Hispanic rulers ("administrators of the people's power," as Castro dubbed his regime). It was simple. For the ruling Hispanic Cuban elite, now a self-righteous aristocracy of revolutionary bureaucrats, racial equality, sexual equality, and social equality had become mere abstractions, obligatory rhetoric. No longer really in tune with the so-called "masses," they could shamelessly revert to, and reactivate, the language of the slave-masters of old, who knew only one command: "Produce! Produce! Produce!"

These were the ex-racist, petit bourgeois leaders metamorphosed into the staunch racial democrats and lovers of Africa that Swiss

Marxist Jean Ziegler spoke of. Their transfiguration, which Ziegler dated from January 1966, was presumably attributable to Fidel Castro's discovery that "intelligent" Blacks existed, and that Africans had made some form of contribution to the general welfare of mankind. These were, also, the same "internationalist" crusaders who were then readying themselves to perform "epic feats" in Africa in order to redeem the black continent from its centuries-long enslavement.[44]

Over and again Cuba's white revolutionary leadership had proved that Afrocentric foreign policy self-interest never ruled out Afrophobic domestic initiatives; all to the contrary. And Castro would fittingly wind up Cuba's "Africa decade" with the strongest possible affirmation of that axiom of Cuban race politics.

20   HEYDAY OF THE CASTRO DOCTRINE

Fidel Castro has shown an extraordinary consistency in his vision of the African continent, from his "We must save Africa" statement to the United Nations in September 1960 right up to the tremendous political and military role he played on that continent during the 1970s. He disagreed with Ché Guevara's "African pessimism" in 1966. He rejoiced at his first personal contact with the black continent in 1972. Ultimately, he found confirmation for what we have already dubbed the "Castro Doctrine" on Africa.

Castro's "Doctrine" was based on the belief that Cuba's leadership was duty-bound to "save" and "protect" tribal African peoples. According to his implied postulate, African peoples could never achieve liberation without the aid of outside forces. While providing that help, Havana would strengthen her own political position in the world. The weaker and more threatened African "progressive" forces were, the wider the doors would open for Havana's fulfillment of her "internationalist" duty. Encoded in ideological jargon, the "Castro Doctrine" on Africa was spelled out in a couple of Marxist cliches: Africa was the weakest link in the chain of world imperialism, and victory there would decide the issue of who would rule the world— the barbaric capitalist bloc, or the benevolent Communist camp. The conquest of Africa could be justified ideologically as a necessary short-cut to world socialism. For the Cuba of 1972, spoiling as it was for an epic internationalist feat to accomplish, the conquest of Africa could only come in the wake of decisive military confrontations.

Interviewed by the editor of the Marxist review *Afrique-Asie*, Fidel Castro voiced, for the first time in public, the ideological premise of his "Doctrine":

> Africa today is the weakest link on the chain of imperialism. It is there that as of late the greatest crimes have been committed against any people. And it is also there that excellent prospects exist for passing practically from tribalism to socialism without having to transit through the various stages other regions of the globe have had to experience. If we are militant revolutionaries, then we are duty-bound to

support the anti-imperialist, anti-racist, and anti-neo-colonialist struggles [in Africa]. Africa is of prime importance today. Imperialist domination is not as strong there as it is in Latin America. Therefore, the possibilities for bringing about a fundamental evolution on the African continent are real. . . . If the struggle is still very tough in Latin America, it is because the bourgeoisie has a grip over the economy, the universities, the press, and all sectors of national life. That phenomenon doesn't really exist in Africa where, properly speaking, there is no bourgeoisie.[1]

It was in Africa that the most forceful blows had to be struck. Contrary to what Ché Guevara had maintained, Africa was ripe for the "jump" from tribalism into communism precisely because of her "backwardness," Castro felt. "If you ask me if all of Africa will one day be Socialist," he further explained. "I could tell you that yes, it will be, . . . they have no other alternative. . . . In Africa, there is a terrible backwardness: sanitation conditions are terrible . . . ; there are no universities, or they have very few students; there are no technicians. . . . If they don't follow the Socialist path, they will never be able to solve their problems."[2] The Máximo Líder was not far from saying, in fact, that Cuba had a "civilizing" role to play on the black continent. Indeed, the Caudillo perceived black Africa in very much the same terms in which he viewed Black Cuba.

The Opening Gambit

The "African Decade," according to a former Cuban official, was the period when Blacks were appointed to positions of greater responsibility with relative ease.[3] For the first time, Blacks were appointed ministers: Nora Frometa (Light Industry), Armando Tórres Santrayl (Justice), and Rafael Francia Mestre (Agriculture). However, the chief beneficiaries were appointees to the secret services, the diplomatic corps, the armed forces, and the police. Black manpower was needed for deployment in Africa and, increasingly, the Caribbean. The Cuban secret services had begun making inroads in Africa in 1968, with a cadre of mostly black secret service officers led, from 1962–1978, by a black Cuban, Ulises Estrada.[4] By 1980, out of twenty-one Cuban ambassadors sent to Africa, more than two-thirds were Black. (There were no black Cuban ambassadors to Europe, Asia, or the Middle East at that time, however.)

In the armed forces, where Blacks were well represented at troop level, their percentage decreased the higher up one went in the military establishment.[5] In fact, there was not a single black general or admiral in the entire Cuban armed forces. It could be argued with great credibility that the Castroite military establishment, an institution as elitist as any other military force, was not looking for black brains, but for black brawn. The Cuban troops sent to Africa, even as far back as Ché Guevara's modest expedition in 1965-66, were overwhelmingly black at the foot-soldier level. When Fidel Castro made his eventful trip to Guinea in 1972, Maj. Juán Almeida Bosque was the only Black among his military retinue. His presence in Guinea was regarded as more linked to his color than to any consideration of military competence.

The "African Decade" did create a small elite of black cadres at the middle-echelon level in the armed forces, the secret services, the diplomatic corps, and the police. It was an "elite" without a base in the population, however. Black promotion in the 1970s was carried out according to the specific requirements and criteria of the ruling bureaucracy. Consequently, it led to the creation of a sort of "lumpen elite," dependent on the Caudillo and his direct subordinates for survival. The role of black cadres under the Revolution followed the same pattern of black promotion in the pre-revolutionary period.

The "African Decade" became by extension a Caribbean decade in which Caribbean ministerial delegations and heads of state visited Cuba with great fanfare. Cuba was anxious to draw certain Caribbean states as close as possible, but some Caribbean leaders proved more difficult than others. Forbes Burnham of Guyana became an ally. So did Michael Manley of Jamaica. But the prime minister of Trinidad and Tobago, Eric Williams, gave Havana trouble.

Both Manley and Williams visited Cuba in July 1975. Manley was warmly welcomed; Williams less so. The latter's conversations with Castro were reportedly tense. The Caudillo apparently was anxious to expand an air services agreement to include non-civilian aircraft. A particularly infuriating session with Williams, during which the Trinidadian leader apparently refused to commit himself further on bilateral agreements, was recounted by a former Cuban official.[6] No sooner had Williams and his delegation left the conference room, he said, than Fidel Castro burst out in a furious tirade of insults against "that shit-eating nigger (¡*El negro come mierda, éste*!)" (ibid.).

The Castro-Williams disagreement broke out into the open five months later with Port-of-Spain's release of a terse statement. "A request has been made by the Cuban government, through its Civil Aviation in Trinidad and Tobago, seeking permission to land Cuban army planes at Piarco International Airport for refuelling," said the document. "The Cabinet has refused the request of the Cuban government. . . . The Cabinet's decision has been passed to the Director of Civil Aviation for transmission to the Cuban government."[7] Having learned that Cuba was transporting soldiers aboard its "civilian" aircraft, Williams decided to tear up the old agreement. Cuban aircraft were to use the airports of Barbados and Guyana instead.

When Castro visited Guinea in 1972, the situation of Cuba's proteges, including the liberation movements, was critical. Eduardo Mondlane, head of FRELIMO, was assassinated in 1969. The Soviet-Cuban choice for a successor, the mulatto Marxist Marcelino dos Santos, was rejected for unknown, dark-skinned Samora Machel, who steered FRELIMO away from the Soviet-Cuban orbit and turned to China instead.

In Congo-Brazzaville, Cuban forces were more than a thousand strong by 1968,[8] not only protecting the quasi-Marxist regime of Alphonse Massemba-Debat, but also assisting the Angolan MPLA, headed by Castro's protege Agostinho Neto. Things were going badly once again for Massemba-Debat, who had been overthrown in 1966 but restored by a Cuban military intervention. Now, in a coup that took the Cubans entirely by surprise, Col. Marien Ngoabi overthrew Massemba-Debat and seized power in 1969. Pragmatically, Castro switched sides and declared for the winner.

In Guinea-Bissau, where Cuba had some troops shouldering Amilcar Cabral's PAIGC, there was dissension between the under-privileged dark-skinned troops and the almost exclusively mulatto leadership. Castro had assigned twenty-five bodyguards for Cabral's personal protection. Nevertheless, within nine months of Castro's visit to Guinea, and despite the Cuban bodyguards, Cabral was killed by his own men in January 1973. His brother, Luiz Cabral, took over and proclaimed Guinea-Bissau independent in September of that year, opening the way for legal intervention by Cuba's FAR to oust the Portuguese and establish Luiz Cabral's government. (That possibility was, indeed, discussed at one point by the PAIGC leadership.)[9]

Agostinho Neto was also in grave trouble throughout 1973. About half of the MPLA openly revolted against him in May 1974, issuing an "appeal" to all MPLA followers.[10] Only a miracle could have saved Neto, Cuba's and the USSR's closest ally in Africa after the assassination of Amilcar Cabral. That miracle came suddenly on April 25, 1974, when a group of left-wing officers seized power in Portugal.

They quickly moved to declare their acceptance of the independence of all of Portugal's colonies. Otelo de Carvalho, the young leader of the coup, paid a surprise visit to an enthusiastic Fidel Castro in July 1974 to hold secret talks. The Caudillo reportedly told Carvalho that Cuba wanted permission to legally dispatch military forces to Angola to shore up the MPLA. An agreement to that effect seems to have been reached before the end of that year.

The "opening" for which the FAR had been laying the logistical groundwork was suddenly there. The door had burst open for the Máximo Lider to perform an "epic feat" of international dimensions. Had Cuba's Caudillo ever missed an opportunity to shape events to his advantage? From Moncada to the Bay of Pigs; from the missile crisis to his fateful visit to Guinea, the answer was, no.[11]

Intervention in Angola

Bold. Bombastic. And wholly unexpected. The Cuban military intervention in Angola, following South Africa's incursion, began in late 1975 and involved 36,000 troops. "Operation Carlota," as it was codenamed, bore the distinct trademark of Fidel Castro's win-or-lose brinksmanship. Far from being the product of Soviet pressures on Cuba, the intervention was rather a dramatic escalation of Cuba's involvement since the early 1960s in African affairs, as aptly appraised by Pamela Falk.[12] Castro had again demonstrated that he slept with only one eye closed. Angola provided the most telling evidence of his consummate skills as an opportunist in pursuit of long-standing goals.

For a small, restless, pugnacious middle power, quarantined by the U.S. and held on a leash by the USSR, Cuba was understandably proud of its feat of arms performed 12,000 kilometers from its shores. Havana relished the action of its Africa corps as much as it did the U.S.'s dumbstruck inaction and impotent anger. In its euphoria, Cuba's Hispanic leadership would revert to the "civilizing messianism" that had pervaded Havana's Afrocentric rhetoric of the 1960s. Cuba went into Angola, Castro told American television interviewer Barbara Walters, in order to "save a black people of Africa"[13] from destruction at the hands of the Nazi-like South African regime. "The African blood that runs through our veins and permeates our culture and history," explained Cuba's ailing foreign minister, Raúl Roa, "weighed heavy in making that decision."[14] Moreover, he continued, one of the chief pillars of Cuban foreign policy rested on the premise that "Africa's destiny is inevitably ours also" (ibid.).

Years later, speaking in Belgrade, Yugoslavia, to the preparatory conference for the 1979 Non-Aligned Summit, Cuba's then Foreign Minister Isodoro Malmierca Peoli passionately defended Havana's controversial intervention as a case of Cubans returning to their ancestral home to assist their kindred. "Cubans returned to the continent of their ancestors, from which they had formerly left as slaves," he declared, "to uphold the struggle of dispossessed (Africans) against colonial oppression and to answer the call of legitimate governments and peoples faced with aggression by racists, annexationists and lackeys of imperialism."[15] Cuban soldiers had not gone to Africa to despoil Africans but rather to "protect them against aggression,"[16] added Malmierca.

Notwithstanding an uproar in the West, Africans were unquestionably impressed by and supportive of the Cuban intervention in Angola (See Appendix 4). Was it not hypocritical that western countries, for whom foreign military intervention was practically a matter of policy, could display outrage at Cuba's own brand of "internationalist" muscle-flexing? Moreover, the Cuban intervention in Angola took place in a highly complex framework of race politics that involved Blacks in Africa, in Cuba, and in the rest of the world. To have opposed Castro's "internationalist" action would have been tantamount to tacitly approving white South Africa's invasion of Angola. The West had underestimated the extent to which Blacks in general, and Africans particularly, abhorred the Nazi-like apartheid regime in South Africa.[17] Welcoming the assistance of expeditionary forces overwhelmingly composed of Afro-Cubans[18] to repel Pretoria's white army was therefore a justifiable option in the eyes of most Africans. The Swiss sociologist, Jean Ziegler, depicted this situation succinctly when he wrote that "in November 1975, Cuban regiments, three-fourths of which were made up of black troops, returned home from across the seas, disembarked at the port of Luanda and pushed the (South African) invaders back . . . . Black Cubans had blocked the way of white South African tanks and paratroopers."[19] Even anti-Castro black Cubans had closed ranks with their African kindred in opposition to the white supremacist regime.[20]

"The success of Cuba's penetration in Africa," underlined a Malian official, "lies, in my opinion, in Cuba being a *small* country that Africans do not fear being swallowed by. The other important factor is that Cuba's military, diplomatic and technical personnel in Africa is primarily composed of Cuban Blacks; people who are culturally very close to Africans in the way they enjoy themselves and in their general outlook."[21] An Ethiopian official said that "when black Cuban troops return to Africa, it is not at all as mercenaries, but as fighters in the struggle to redeem Africa from the clutches of imperialism; we should not forget that more than half of the Cuban population is of African origin on account of their ancestors having been shipped to Cuba as slaves."[22] The MPLA leadership itself was keenly aware that black Cuban forces would considerably soften African hostility to the intervention.[23]

Fidel Castro initially went out of his way to reassure African leaders that they had nothing to fear from his troops. The latter were in Angola solely to protect that country against a South African invasion. But in 1977 that pretense would be challenged by events inside Angola itself. In May 1977, the popular, dark-skinned military leader, Nito Alves (then minister of interior), nearly succeeded in overthrowing the MPLA's mulatto-white leadership headed by Agostinho Neto. Cuban forces unhesitantly went into action against the *nitistas* and helped crush the bloody rebellion. Havana's immediate reaction was to beef up its forces in Angola to over 30,000 men while halting altogether the token troop withdrawal it had just begun as a "gesture" to the U.S.

Few would argue that Neto could have weathered the *nitista* storm had Castro's forces not been in Angola. The MPLA leader would therefore steadfastly resist pressures from other African states to progessively replace Havana's forces with an OAU inter-African force.[24] Nor did Nigeria's discreet attempts to convince Luanda to gradually replace Havana's forces with equivalent Nigerian contigents bear fruit (ibid.). The MPLA leadership, too frightened of the potential consequences, increasingly became a hostage as well as a protege of its overseas ally.

Fidel Castro vowed to pursue his Africa policy, stressing that, "racial discrimination *existed* in our country . . . . In keeping with the duties rooted in our principles, our ideology, our convictions and our very own blood, we shall defend Angola and Africa."[25] But Cuba's second massive military thrust into Africa beginning in December 1977 could hardly be viewed as a matter of blood links or the struggle against apartheid, western colonialism and imperialism. When Cuban tanks began rolling over the flatlands of the Ogaden, it was a tightly coordinated operation of the Soviet Union. Cuba's intervention in Ethiopia implied war against Socialist Somalia, a militantly leftist African state which up till early 1977 was considered an ally of both Cuba and the USSR.

Castro on "Law and Order"

Castro found it necessary to justify his military action in Ethiopia in support of a Marxist African regime against a fellow Socialist African state. Cuba's new line of argument was that it was merely maintaining law and order on a black continent threatened by chaos. Cuban forces were in Ethiopia to prevent the nightmare dreaded by all African heads of state from becoming a reality: the Balkanization or "Biafranization" of their countries as a consequence of ethnic "separatist" uprisings. "On that occasion," explained Fidel Castro, "an invasion from the south—from Somalia—was launched to seize the Ogaden, a huge area of Ethiopian territory, while the (Eritrean) separatist movement in the North was being fanned . . . . It was a difficult moment for Ethiopia. The revolution could have collapsed; the Ethiopian people needed our help and we sent it."[26] And Castro added: "No one could help them (Ethiopians) when they were invaded by Mussolini's troops, but this time they received support from tiny Cuba." (ibid.)

Cuba pumped 25,000 soldiers into Ethiopia, conceivably to uphold a sacred tenet of the OAU's charter: the intangibility of borders inherited from the colonial past. In Ethiopia, Castro was also fighting secessionism, the bogeyman of African leaders. Only incidentally did Havana appear to be shoring up the shaky Marxist regime of strongman Lt.-Col. Mengistu Haile Mariam. Ironically, the reviled Eritrean "separatist" movement was the same one that Havana had trained, aided and abetted throughout the 1970s when Emperor Haile Selassie was in power. Indeed, the two largest Eritrean forces—the EPLF and ELF—were bona fide Marxist movements.

Cuba's second large-scale military undertaking in Africa was again greeted with indulgent approval by African public opinion at large (See Appendix 4). African assent was due not only to Castro's law-and-order explanation but also to Somalia's near-total isolation from the rest of black Africa[27] after it joined the Arab League in the early 1970s. The claim by Somalians that they were an Arab-Semitic rather than Negro-African people had been received as a slap in the face by black Africa. Resentment was fueled by Somalia's reiterated territorial claims against Kenya. Thus, sub-Saharan Africa had a case against Somalia's pro-Arab "expansionism" long before Castro even dreamt of playing such a crucial role in the geopolitics of the Horn.

The invasion of Ethiopia in 1935 by fascist Italy had converted Ethiopia into the symbolic embodiment of black resistance to European colonialism. Ethiopia's cause against Mussolini's Italy had ignited passions among Africans and Blacks on the other side of the

Atlantic, U.S. Blacks and Jamaicans primarily, some of whom went as volunteers to fight alongside the Ethiopian army.[28] Sympathy for Addis Ababa—the OAU's present headquarters—was carried into the 1960s and 1970s by the spread of the Rastafari religious movement in the Caribbean and the popular reggae music that sprang from it. (Emperor Hailie Selassie, who visited Jamaica in the late 1960s, is the highest divine figure in the Rastafari faith.) Furthermore, Africans had welcomed the accession to power of a junta comprised of lowly, dark-skinned officers (Mengistu, Atnafu, Abate, Teferi Banti), which had done away with the haughty, fair-skinned Amharic-speaking aristocracy that often fancied itself Judeo-Semitic rather than Negro-African stock.

Though not as emotionally stirring as the Angolan intervention, Cuba's military offensive in Ethiopia, which smashed the Somalian forces and sent them back across the common border, met with no great adverse reactions in Africa or the rest of the Third World (save for some of Somalia's Arab friends). By and large, African officials espoused the view that whatever Havana's hidden agenda, a case could be made for its military action in Angola and Ethiopia.[29] That consensus strongly influenced the opinion U.S. Ambassador to the United Nations Andrew Young would voice—to the outrage of western public opinion—concerning Cuba's "stabilizing" role in Africa.[30] But as former Assistant Secretary of State for African Affairs Donald B. Eassum remarked, newcomer Young may have been more attuned to then-prevailing African feelings and realities than most of his critics.[31]

Some African officials, such as the former minister of education of Mali, Seydou Badian Kouyate, felt that Cuba's African policy would force upward mobility for Cuban Blacks at home.[32] In other words, Afro-Cubans would ultimately become unintentional beneficiaries of their country's heavy involvement in their ancestral home. "The black Cuban suffers from centuries of alienation as a result of the severance of his cultural ties to Africa," explained Mario de Andrade, founding president of the MPLA. "In that respect," he said, "the large-scale presence of Afro-Cubans in Angola and other African countries as combatants or civilian workers will be a powerful factor of cultural dis-alienation for the black Cuban."[33]

The Impact in Black Cuba

"Operation Carlota" was appropriately named after a black Cuban woman who led a 19th-century slave insurrection. It made a tremendous psychological impact on Afro-Cubans, even those who were opposed to the regime.[34] Fidel Castro's unprecedented proclamation at the height of the intervention that Cuba was a "Latin-African" country produced the desired effect among a population blatantly underrepresented in all areas of domestic as well as international decision-making. "The Angolan intervention," observed an eyewitness, "represented perhaps the one moment in the Revolution when black Cubans felt as if *they* were spearheading the policies of the regime."[35] It seemed indeed to be the sort of opening the "Carbonell Plan" had anticipated as a short-term evolution towards the empowerment of Blacks. It can be argued credibly that Afro-Cubans had come to identify foreign policy as the most conducive arena for fulfillment of their ethnic aspirations.[36]

There was a definite sense of racial pride in being cast by no less than Castro himself in the role of dutiful crusaders: sons and daughters of Africa who had rushed to redeem the motherland from the clutches of vicious white South Africa. There was unmitigated pride in the performance of a heroic feat that amazed world opinion. Domestic rewards in terms of ethnic power-sharing could be reasonably expected.

The Ethiopian intervention shattered that image. The utter complexity of the Horn's geopolitics, the inability to discern clear-cut enemies or espouse an emotionally-stirring cause, broke the spell. In Ethiopia nothing was clear any longer. To the contrary, the enigmatic wheelings and dealings bred confusion. At one point, Fidel Castro in person was playing peacemaker, shuttling between Addis Ababa, Mogadishu and Southern Yemen, attempting to establish a revolutionary federation of Socialist states of the Horn (Ethiopia, Somalia, Djibuti, Eritrea) with Southern Yemen. Within months, Cuban divisions were pouring into Ethiopia to battle the Somalians. The confusion and apprehension generated by this obscure situation coalesced into a mute opposition to a military enterprise in which, as an Afro-Cuban writer explained, "one could no longer draw the line between the good camp and the bad cause."[37]

A young Afro-Cuban woman who left Cuba via Mariel said: "It was the Ethiopian thing that really opened our eyes to the fact of being no more than tools, and our children cannon fodder, to be used by the government in Africa. We were proud to be of African descent, but as women we were also afraid of having our sons, husbands or brothers sent to die over there for nothing!"[38]

The existence of such feelings among the black population seemed to have escaped the regime completely or to have been underestimated. Yet as early as 1978 there was a definite sense, as verbalized by an Afro-Cuban, that black Cuban families were "paying a very high price"[39] in Africa while receiving low dividends in return at home. That conviction, at least in part, motivated the setting up of the all-black, underground opposition, Movimiento de Liberación Nacional, uncovered by the secret police accidentally in 1978 (see chapter 19). "We all had the strong feeling that the government didn't really consider us as human beings but as instruments of policy," explained Gilberto Aldama, the movement's chief organizer. "That's how we came to prefer the prospect of death in Cuba fighting to change our situation as Blacks rather than the glory of shedding our blood and that of other Blacks like us over in Africa."[40]

In March and July 1979, leftist-Marxist revolutionary movements seized power respectively in Grenada and Nicaragua. Cuba played host in September 1979 to the Sixth Summit Conference of Non-Aligned Heads of State and Government; Castro was named president for a two-year period. Shortly after, a military takeover in Surinam, headed by Maj. Desi Bouterse, swept a leftist regime into power. Fidel Castro's international prestige seemed at its apex.

At the time of these events five out of six ambassadorial posts in the Caribbean were filled by black Cuban diplomats. (Ambassador Ulises Estrada's arrogant behavior in Jamaica had earned him unanimous dislike; he was replaced by the more amiable Willy Hodges, also black.) Fifteen of the twenty-one Cuban ambassadors accredited to African states were black. However, there were only five black ministers out of a total of thirty-four: Hector Rodríguez Llompart (State Committee for Economic Cooperation), Armando Tórres Santrayl (Justice), Nora Frometa (Light Industry), Rafaél Francia Mestre (Agriculture), Sergio del Valle Jiménez (Interior).

Only four members of the fourteen-man Political Bureau of the Cuban Communist Party's Central Committee were Afro-Cuban (Juán Almeida Bosque, Blás Roca, Sergio del Valle Jiménez and the non-voting Miguel José Cano Blanco), and of the Central Committee's 146 members, only sixteen were black. An estimated 35 percent of the 481 deputies of the National Assembly of People's Power were Blacks. In the armed forces, the situation was even more dramatic: not a single Black had been elevated to the rank of general or admiral. Cuba's Joint Chiefs of Staff were for all intents and purposes entirely Hispanic,[41] whereas the overwhelming majority of the infantry stationed in Angola and Ethiopia at the time (anywhere between 30,000 and 35,000 men) was comprised of Afro-Cubans. The overall proportion of Blacks occupying leadership positions in the combined structures of power in Cuba in 1979 (Council of Ministers, Council of State, Communist Party Politbureau and Central Committee, FAR, National Assembly) did not exceed 12 percent.[42]

In 1979 the Cuban leadership may have been better informed about what was going on internationally than in Cuba itself. Cuban leaders continued ignoring the serious underrepresentation of black Cubans in all but sports, folkloric troupes, rank-and-file soldiery and the labor force. Continued Cuban silence on the domestic race question, while making a big issue out of it in places like South Africa, Zimbabwe, and the United States, was an uningenious ploy. Such a policy betrayed one fact: the Castroite leadership was completely out of touch with the growing feelings of disenfranchisement rampant among Afro-Cubans.

About 3 percent of Cuba's total population of ten million serve in the Fuerzas Armadas Revoluciónarias (FAR) as active-duty and ready-reserve personnel.[43] Another 1.2 million serve in the Territorial Troop Militia (MTT), which Fidel Castro set up in 1981. (Cuba's civilian "internationalists" totaled 21,000 in 1985, Angola alone absorbing 5,000.[44]) The Angolan operation demonstrated that the FAR had mobilized forces following a racial criterion,[45] explained Jorge I. Domínguez. (Racial selection had already been used, but on an infinitely smaller scale, for Ché Guevara's campaign in Zaire.) Although a logical and astute maneuver by any standard, mobilization along racial lines was precisely what undermined the very premise on which the race politics of the Revolution rested.

Since 1959 the keeping of racial statistics had been frowned upon by the Hispanic leadership. The regime held fast to José Martí's maxim on race: there are no black or white Cubans—just Cubans! However, as Domínguez pointed out, the success of military enterprises such as "Operation Carlota" hinged on troop mobilization along racial lines. (ibid.) The irony was not lost on Afro-Cubans, many of whom would thereafter accuse the regime of practicing "racial hypocrisy rather than racial democracy!"[46] Had the regime taken a calculated risk when, for the sake of expediency and efficiency, it undermined the only cogent argument it had devised to resist black demands for affirmative action programs and proportional ethnic representation? "We felt that if we were good enough to be shipped off to fight wars in Africa *because* we were black-skinned, then we ought to be considered equally fit, as Blacks, to share responsibility in everything affecting the fate of Cuba,"[47] explained Esteban Cárdenas. (Esteban's older brother, Osvaldo Cárdenas, was, until late

1983, one of the highest-ranking black intelligence officials, responsible for the Party's Office for Caribbean Affairs.)

In a significant reversal, Cuban authorities in 1983 released for the first time the racial population statistics resulting from the 1981 census. (Census results relative to race were not released for the 1970 census and were later claimed to have been "lost".[48]) According to the regime, the tally was: 66 percent white, 21.9 percent mulatto and 12 percent black, or a total of 33.9 percent Afro-Cubans. (It must be kept in mind that, in terms of Cuban racial standards, that the Rev. Jesse Jackson qualifies as "mulatto," Adam Clayton Powell Jr. as "white" and Sidney Poitier as "black."). The standard joke among those who felt that the figures released sharply conflicted with visual reality was contained in the ironic question, "¿Y el resto donde esta? ¿En Angola?" (And where are the rest? In Angola?).[49]

From the vantage point of many Cuban Blacks, the 1981 census results could be interpreted in two ways. Socialist census enumerators had continued to rely on old stereotypes to classify the descendants of Africans in Cuba, maintaining traditional attitudes about *blanqueamiento* (whitening). Or the regime had consciously understated the actual size of the Afro-Cuban population to undercut mounting pressures for proportional black representation in government. Whatever the case, the purported Afro-Cuban share of the population (33.9 percent) curiously tallied, almost to a tee, with both the estimated percentage in 1980 of rank-and-file Afro-Cuban membership in the 500,000-strong Communist party of Cuba (34.5 percent)[50] and the estimated black proportion (35 percent) of the 481-member National Assembly of People's Power. If the census figures were correct, therefore, Afro-Cubans would have been "overrepresented" both in the Party, the Council of State and the National Assembly.

A Widening Credibility Gap

As Cuba's "African Decade" drew to a close, faint but perceptible signs suggested that perhaps Fidel Castro had overplayed his hand. For one, there was conflict between his assertion that Cuba was a "Latin-African" nation and the glaring absence of Cuba's African component from decision-making posts. That situation could hardly square with the preponderance of Afro-Cuban soldiers on African battlefields from the Atlantic seaboard to the Indian Ocean. Perhaps the sturdy arrogance of Cuba's white rulers led them to believe that Africans would raise no such questions despite their increasing familiarity with the inner workings of the Cuban regime. After all, as the Cuban saying went, "¡A caballo regalado no se le miran los colmillos!" (You don't look a gift horse in the mouth.) Had Castro not gone into Africa to "save" black peoples from destruction?

Kenyan scholar Ali A. Mazrui was the first to challenge the standard arguments invoked by Cuba and its African allies to legitimize Fidel Castro's Africa policy. In a study that has gained relevance with the passing years—*Cuba's Castro and Africa's Castration: A Case Study in Micro-Dependency*[51]—he raises interesting questions about Cuba's military and political role in Africa.

What were the underlying implications and motivations of Castro's Africa policy? Why the preponderance of Afro-Cuban manpower in war theaters? Did the "Afro-rhetoric" of Cuba's leaders square with the racial profile of their regime? Why had Cubans and Russians intervened militarily in Africa only once the wars in question became internecine struggles "between the natives"?

There is a tendency to forget, said Mazrui, that "there was no Cuban army to help the liberation of Angola for as long as the Portuguese were still in occupation" (ibid., 21), and that "it was only after the Portuguese departed from Angola in 1975, and the war had become primarily one among Africans themselves, that the Cubans were suddenly available for Angola's liberation, and the Soviet Union was at last willing to supply war planes and heavy artillery" (ibid., 21, 22). Neither Cuba nor the USSR, Mazrui believed, wanted to risk confrontation with Portugal, a NATO country, preferring a low-risk, African-vs-African situation (ibid., 22). All of which raised the question as to the real agenda underlying the Cuban role in Africa.

Mazrui dismissed the argument that the utilization of Afro-Cuban forces legitimized Castro's intervention in Africa as a case of Pan-Africanism. "There has been a suggestion in some circles that Cuba's intervention is in fact a kind of renewed validation of Pan-Africanism. After all, Cuba's population is at least forty percent black in one sense or another. . . . (and) in his effort to legitimize Cuba's intervention . . . Castro himself has emphasized the African blood flowing in the veins of many Cubans" (ibid., 23). For consistency, Mazrui tested the inherent logic of that argument with a provocative comparison: "If the United States were to start describing itself as fundamentally an 'Afro-Caucasian' country, would that help to give Washington legitimacy to participate in a future African war? Is the presence of people of African ancestry in a country outside Africa an adequate basis for the intervention by that external country in an internal African conflict?" (ibid., 23).

The inescapable questions that arise regarding Cuba's black troops in Africa, argued Mazrui, were rather that of "who made the decision to intervene; what is the actual structure of political power in Cuba as between black and white; and what was the composition of the actual men who were sent to fight . . . "(ibid., 25). Were the United States to send "an army consisting entirely of black Americans to participate in a conflict in Zaire," said Mazrui, "that would not make the black American intervention a case of Pan-Africanism. One would have to investigate the race of those who made the decision to send those black Americans, the structure within which such decisions were made, and whether or not the motives for the intervention were inspired by a solidarity based on shared African ancestry" (ibid., 25).

Taking for granted the political superiority of the MPLA of Angola over its rivals (FNLA and UNITA), and putting ideological preferences aside, the Cuban intervention in Angola and Ethiopia still posed difficult questions. "The point we are raising," Mazrui points out, "is whether this kind of issue should have been decided ultimately by a Caribbean factor introduced into a delicate balance of forces. Was the Cuban tail once again wagging the Africa dog?"

21 AFROCASTROISM AND THE POLITICS OF MICRODEPENDENCY

On January 1, 1989, the Cuban revolution will have turned thirty. The youngest of the Castroite old guard dating from Moncada will be over 60 years old. More than 50 percent of Cuba's present population was born under the Revolution. Not only age but events have caught up with the Cuban leaders.

The decade of the 1980s appears to be the watershed marking the start of Cuba's seemingly irreversible decline in power at home and abroad. Ten thousand Cubans stormed the Peruvian embassy in Havana in April 1980 seeking refuge. An unprecedented mass exodus of 125,000 fled the island through Mariel seaport from April to September of that year. Fidel Castro unexpectedly lost highly valuable allies. Prime Minister Michael Manley was voted out of power in Jamaica. President Luis Cabral, overthrown by a coup d'état in Guinea-Bissau in November 1980, took up asylum in Cuba. Prime Minister Maurice Bishop was also ousted from power, then assassinated; Grenada was invaded by U.S. forces in October 1983. President Lynden Forbes Burnham of Guyana died in August 1985 during surgery performed by Cuban doctors.

Two symbolic figures of the Revolution committed suicide: the Moncada and Sierra Maestra heroine, Haydee Santamaría (1980) and former President Osvaldo Dorticós Torrado (1983). The regime also suffered its first-ever defections by top-ranking Marxist officials in the military or government: Lt.-Col. Joaquín Mourino Pérez of the FAR (1983); Vice Minister Manuel Sánchez Pérez (1985) of the State Committee for Material and Technical Supply; Air Force Brig. Gen. Rafael del Pino Díaz; Maj. Florentino Aspillaga Lombart, chief of intelligence in Prague (1986).

To compound Havana's worries, the new Soviet leader, Mikhail Gorbachev, in power since March 1985, seemed intent on placing Soviet-Cuban relations on a back-burner.[1] The door to Soviet-Cuban tension was opened once again.

A Black Exodus

The storming of the Peruvian embassy in Havana caught the government unaware. But more shocking was the human flood—

125,000 Cubans—that swept out to sea through the port of Mariel and washed ashore in the United States before the regime hastened to shut off the escape route in September 1980. Some estimated that two million Cubans had hoped to escape through Mariel.[2] The regime's brutal reaction—public beatings, stonings and clubbing to death in an operation called *repudio*—shocked liberal-minded diplomats based in Havana.[3] Judging by the content of a report by the ambassador of Grenada in Cuba at the time,[4] Cuban officials were particularly concerned by the high percentage of Blacks among the Mariel escapees. As many as one-third of the refugees—some 25,000—were reportedly Afro-Cubans.[5] That alone gave credence to long-standing charges on the part of Blacks about the regime's racially discriminatory emigration policy.

The "black exodus" through Mariel—mostly young and working-class Afro-Cubans—was the clearest signal of the widening disaffection of Black Cuba toward the Castro regime. "Because of the regime's essentially white, middle-class Hispanic origins," pointed out Gonzalez and Ronfeldt, "the racial issue has remained a highly sensitive one for Cuba, where Afro-Cubans have been estimated to comprise 50 percent or more of the island's population."[6]

Mariel provided evidence of the degree to which the government was out of touch with "its own" Blacks, and the extent to which the latter had come to reject the regime's racial tokenist window-dressing. The bottom line seemed to be that Castro's "Great White Father" image had seriously eroded among younger generations of Blacks who grew up under the Revolution. Afro-Cuban youth, one may surmise, were more concerned about the prospect of being "volunteered" into wars overseas than about the old bogeyman of pre-1959 segregated beaches.

In the wake of Mariel, wrote Tad Szulc, "Castro appeared to have concluded that the nation required a certain relaxation of tensions—the Mariel experience was a trauma because the regime was taken aback by this manifestation of internal resentments—and must be allowed a degree of consumer freedom."[7] Accordingly, a number of food items were released from rationing; free peasant markets were authorized; new legislation was enacted intended to attract foreign investments (with foreign companies allowed 49 percent ownership in joint ventures with the Cuban state); dialogue with the Cuban Catholic Church was initiated; the repression against Afro-Cuban religions eased, though not their continued folklorization for tourist consumption.[8]

A sizeable number of Blacks who fled Cuba through Mariel were adepts of one or another Afro-Cuban religion. Some Babalawos, Paleros and Abacuá leaders were also to be found among the Marielitos, as they came to be known in the U.S. Through them came direct testimony[9] of the harshness of Castro's repression against African religious faiths. The Miami-based Association of Babalawos had reportedly intended to petition the Nigerian government regarding repression of the Lucumí or Yoruba religion in Cuba.[10]

In 1981, the government began a conciliatory drive towards Afro-Cuban religions and their adepts. Concomittantly, dialogue began with the Catholic hierarchy of Cuba. (In 1985, Castro's bestseller, *Fidel and Religion*, was published in Cuba.) A newly-created Office of Religious Affairs, directly attached to the Central Committee of the Cuban Communist party, was placed under the supervision of the Afro-Cuban Marxist ethnologist, José Felipe Carneado Rodríguez. A member of the original Cuban Communist party, Carneado had been a specialist on Afro-Cuban religions since the 1940s and had produced party position papers on racial discrimination in pre-revolutionary Cuba.

Mariel undoubtedly jolted the government into a hasty review of its standard approach to the race issue in Cuba. In the midst of the crisis, a Cuban review roundly denounced unspecified Blacks "of Cuban origin"[11] who had denounced the regime's racial policy as being a fraud. The euphemism "Blacks of Cuban origin" seemed to imply that any black Cuban who balked at the regime's racial policy was not really Cuban. The review said these Blacks were but "ideologues of imperialism who attempt to put in doubt the historic accomplishment of the Revolution's swift eradication of the racial problem and try to demonstrate that no progress whatsoever has been achieved by the Revolution on the socio-racial plain." (ibid.) Such "reactionary postulates" were only meant to obscure the "phenomenal difference between the situation of full equal rights and absolute respect as citizens enjoyed by the Cuban Negro as compared to the horrors experienced by Negroes and other racial minorities in the United States" (ibid., 21).

Many Blacks who left through Mariel reported that they had been the subject of racist verbal abuse and taunts on the part of white Cubans, soldiers as well as ordinary pro-Castro whites. A woman was told, "*Negrita*, the Ku Klux Klan will certainly have a job for you— washing sheets!" A black *chiste* (joke) circulating at the time portrayed a white soldier sardonically asking a departing Black: "Tell me, negrito, what will you do over there when the yankee calls you *'nigger?'* " (Ironically, in this context, *negrito* is Cuban for *"nigger".*) Answer: "*Chico,* I'll just say 'kiss my black ass!', push a button and roll up the windows of my limousine." The joke suggests that although Afro-Americans may suffer racial slights, they are capable of retaliation and wield far more economic and political clout than Blacks in Socialist Cuba.

The regime lost its only black intellectual of international standing and repute, who up till then had acted as an able apologist on the racial question,[12] when René Depestre tiptoed out of Cuba in 1981 for exile in France. A growing number of scholars, including Marxists like the Swiss Jean Ziegler and the British David Booth, began to express views not unlike those put forward at a 1985 conference on Cuba: "The present state of race relations, if left unattended, will pose a grave challenge to Cuban society . . . . More concretely, racial polarization is advancing. A growing elite of Afro-Cubans, rewarded for their accomplishments but denied access to bureaucratic power, may eventually challenge the regime's legitimacy."[13]

The Grenada debacle in October 1983 marred Castro's celebration in January 1984 of his quarter-century rule over Cuba, by far the longest one-man dictatorship in Cuba's entire history.

Still reeling from its most traumatic foreign policy setback since Ché Guevara's Bolivian fiasco, the regime welcomed the Rev. Jesse Jackson, who was then rising to international prominence. Accompanying Jackson was California Congressman Mervyn M. Dymally, then chairman of the Congressional Black Caucus, a body Cuban intelligence had repeatedly made attempts to influence in the past. Four months before that trip, Dymally had been thoroughly briefed on the prevailing racial situation in Cuba and on the underpinnings of Havana's Africa policy.[14] Upon arrival, therefore, some members of Jackson's delegation were fully aware that a racial problem existed in Cuba, too.

If only because of Jackson's imposing dignity before Fidel Castro, the latter was incapable of extracting racial mileage from the presence of America's first credible black presidential aspirant.[15] Jackson stuck to his own agenda (ibid.) and pointedly refrained from the eulogies to Cuba's "racial democracy" that visiting black dignitaries had once proferred to their white hosts. His impact may be measured by the *chiste* that made the rounds as a consequence of his trip. A young Black, up before the Party's admissions commission, is portrayed sweating out a last question, "What is the difference in how things are run in Cuba and the USA in terms of Negroes?" After some time, he finally answers, "Well, comrades, the difference is that we run in the Olympics for Fidel; they run in the U.S. for President!"

The pacifying gestures undertaken by the regime in the wake of Mariel included the freeing of political prisoners. Imprisoned MLN black dissidents, including Gilberto Aldama, were released. (Aldama had spent twelve years in prison and was thirty years old when he arrived in France in 1981; he subsequently moved to West Africa.) Reinaldo Barroso, one of the founders of the "Afro-Cuban Study Circles" in the mid-1970s, was allowed to emigrate, also to France, in 1981. Black dissident intellectuals, formerly implicated in what the political police had exaggeratedly dubbed the Cuban Black Power "conspiracy," began finding employment.[16] Walterio Carbonell, the most prestigious black dissenter, resurfaced to publish low-key historical articles in minor reviews.

A Suspicious New Policy

The regime's novel policy of vigilant tolerance toward the "atavistic African cults," as the Party had once designated them, was best underscored by the reported visits[17] of the Party's watchdog for religious affairs, the Afro-Cuban scholar José Carneado Rodríguez, to several *plantes* (Afro-Cuban religious initiation ceremonies). Indicative of the new sophistication Carneado brought into the Party's handling of Afro-Cuban religions was the visit in June 1987 of his Majesty Alaiyeluwa Oba Okunade Sijuwade Olubuse II, the *Ooni* of Ife. The Ooni is the paramount spiritual authority of the Yoruba people of Nigeria and of all those in the Americas who worship the Yoruba deities (Shango, Yemanya, Oshun, etc.). Olubuse II is therefore to be regarded as the spiritual leader of the Lucumí religious hierarchy in Cuba, comprised of Babalawos or priests.

Though officially the guest of ICAP, the Ooni was met upon arrival by high-ranking Party officials. Besides Carneado, who masterminded the event, these included Politbureau members Jorge Risquet and Armando Hart Davalos. At the end of a weeklong stay (June 21–26, 1987), the Ooni and his delegation met separately with President Fidel Castro and twenty hand-picked Cuban Babalawos. From the meeting with Castro emerged two important decisions: the Fourth International Congress on Orisha Tradition and Culture, originally slated to take place in Haiti in 1988, would now be hosted by Cuba; a Cuban cultural center—named not after an Afro-Cuban historical figure but after the Hispanic-Cuban José Martí—would be set up in Ife, the spiritual capital of all adepts of the Lucumí faith.

After his visit with Castro, the Ooni, according to *Granma*, "underscored the role played by the Cuban President in creating a society free from racial discrimination . . . ."[18] Dr. Omotoso Eluyemi, the Apena of Ife and the Ooni's adviser for cultural affairs, was also reported by *Granma* to have praised the action of Cuba's Yoruba clergy (Babalawos) and the position of the Lucumí faith in Cuba. Dr. Omotoso is in fact the current chief of the powerful and secret *Ogboni* brotherhood of the Yorubas, hence his authority and proximity to the Ooni. The Apena, who is also chairman of the Department of Archaeology at the University of Ife spent several years studying in the Soviet Union. Describing himself as a socialist, he was reported by *Granma* to have stated that, "In Cuba the solution of racial problems has surpassed what the so-called industrialized countries have done. Cuba is the only country I know of up to now where the color of a person's skin has been totally eradicated from the people's mind and this can only be achieved by means of a socialist society" (ibid.).

As a symbolic gesture of appeasement towards Afro-Cuban religions, the Ooni's visit spoke loudly of the Party's new and sophisticated approach. But then its opposition had demonstrated little impact. In 1985, estimated a high official of the Cuban Catholic clergy,[19] about 85 percent of Cuba's population—working-class Cuban whites included—were followers of one or another of the Afro-Cuban worship systems. "Marxism-Leninism is not satisfying the spiritual and emotional needs of Cuba's increasingly young society," pointed out two specialists, "and to the regime's dismay, black and mulatto 'internationalists' in Angola have returned to Cuba with a renewed interest in santeria and other Afro-Cuban cults. Castro has sought to meet the challenge by establishing the Party's Office of Religious Affairs, meeting with U.S. Catholic bishops, discoursing on religion and engaging in a 'dialogue' with Cuba's Catholic hierarchy in 1985 and 1986."[20]

It is neither improbable nor at odds with the divide-and-rule policies Castro is adept at applying to his opponents that the regime's rapprochement with the Catholic Church is ultimately aimed at counterbalancing the Afro-Cuban religions. As a consequence, the latter may be facing an infinitely more complex and sophisticated strategy of long-term eradication. The regime may indeed be consciously revitalizing Cuban Catholicism, with an estimated peak of 100,000 members island-wide in 1985, in the hopes that the Church will eventually destabilize Afro-Cuban religions with what has already been dubbed "Afro-Christian syncretism." Monsignor Carlos Manuél de Céspedes, secretary general of Cuba's Catholic episcopate, conceded the possibility of such intentions on the part of the government.[21] In that case, the church would have merely resumed its centuries-old practice as a repressive adjunct of the state.

Proportional Ethnic Representation?

In 1985 Fidel Castro began a major "rectification" drive supposedly aimed at halting the regime's deviation to a non-revolutionary course. Major figures of the regime, including former untouchables, were either demoted, dismissed or disgraced. The huge bureaucracy was apparently escaping the Caudillo's grip, and some analysts even came to interpret the creation of the 1.2 million-strong Territorial Troop Militia (MTT) as an attempt to counterbalance the institutionally pro-Soviet FAR.

The beefy, complacent Cuban bureaucracy was accused by Castro of chronic "inefficiency" and even "corruption." The Caudillo threatened to "hurl the masses against those responsible for such irritating deeds,"[22] the threat itself acknowledging the establishment's acquired power. In recent years, Gonzalez and Rondfeldt remarked, "the Cuban elite has become broader, more difficult to manage and control, and more institutionalized, with well-defined organizational interests emerging in both the civilian and military sectors."[23] A new generation of cadres, many issued from the African campaigns, aspired for leadership in both government and the military, they noted. "Among these newer civilian and military officials are Blacks and mulattoes who have yet to gain a share of political power that even begins to approximate their share of the island's population or that reflects their disproportionate participation in the Angolan and Ethiopian military operations." (ibid.)

The "rectification" campaign, reminiscent of Mao Tse-tung's last pitched battle against China's bureaucracy, cast a new light on the regime's overtures to the Afro-Cuban population. Addressing the Third Party Congress in February 1986, Fidel Castro, for the first time since 1959, admitted, without being explicit, that a racial problem existed in Cuba.[24] He promised that thereafter the Party would pursue a conscious, relentless drive to bring Blacks, women and youth into the leadership. The appointments of Estéban Lazo Hernández to the exclusive fourteen-man Politbureau, and of Gladys Robinson Agramonte and Juán Robinson Agramonte to the Central Committee, said Castro, were indicative of a new "injection of Blacks" (ibid.) into the Party.

This shift toward "racial affirmative action," most analysts agreed, was more symbolic than real. The Politbureau still included only two Blacks, while a mere 34 percent of the Central Committee membership was Afro-Cuban. However, the analysts conceded that though "the proportion is still modest, the new emphasis on affirmative action suggests that the regime recognizes it can no longer practice racial discrimination, particularly as Afro-Cubans serving in Africa show signs of having regained a new sense of ethnicity."[25]

Castro's choice of the term "injection" may very well indicate strong resistance on the part of the white bureaucracy to *integrate* its ranks, opening room for a fast-growing Afro-Cuban elite. Thus, the Third Congress's landmark statement on the racial situation in Cuba said more by omission than the Caudillo's breach of twenty-seven years of obdurate silence. "In order for the Party's leadership to duly reflect the ethnic composition of our people," said the document, "it must include those patriots of proven revolutionary merit and talents who in the past have been discriminated against because of their skin color. The promotion of all capable members of our society and their incorporation into the Party and its leadership must not be left to chance."[26] The gist of that terse declaration of intent was nonetheless clear: "Eventually . . . a Castro or post-Castro regime must find ways of sharing political power with the rising expectations of the Afro-Cuban population."[27]

The irony of Castro's late conversion to affirmative action policies was not lost on the population. In no time the country was filled with all sorts of chistes, white racist ones and bitter black ones, such as "Gracias a Diós, Fidel Volvió!" (Thank heavens, Fidel is back!), implying: where has Castro been for the past twenty-seven years that he has just now discovered the existence of racial discrimination against Blacks?

Another chiste portrayed a self-satisfied Castro checking the results of an opinion survey after his Third Congress speech. "So, are our Negroes happy with the posts I've promised them in the Party and the government?" he asked. "Comandante, our samples indicate that they're deeply worried," his chief aide replied. "Worried? About what?," thundered Castro. "Well, Comandante, it's being rumored that you intend to blame Cuba's economic failures on *them* at the next Party Congress!"

In all probability, Fidel Castro's appeal for the "injection" of Blacks, women and youth into the leadership was largely self-serving. Racism, sexism and "youthism," were indeed very potent issues because of their emotional rather than ideological content. Has the

Caudillo set himself up before the unruly white, male and elderly Hispanic-Cuban bureaucracy as the advocate of the "have-nots" in terms of the power structure? "Afrocastroism" may thus be attempting to secure a new lease on life domestically at a time when abroad, it seems to be exhausting its credibility and political possibilities.

A Final Offensive in Southern Africa?

In late December 1979, the Soviets invaded Afghanistan to stem an unpredictable situation of growing tensions and political restlessness that had settled on the USSR's Muslim borders. Convulsed Iran had turned into a volatile neighbor and declared war on Iraq, the Kremlin's most powerful ally in the Middle East. Pakistan, under stern military rule, became the base for anti-Marxist guerillas at war with the pro-Soviet regime in Kabul. The USSR was forced to relent in its drive in Africa to turn its attention to the security of its sensitive borders. Deprived of direct Soviet backing, Cuba's forces in Angola had to fall back in turn on a defensive, peace-keeping role that spelled much frustration for the FAR. Fidel Castro was obliged to subdue his "internationalist" drive on the continent at the precise moment when Cuba seemed headed for a glorious "ofensiva finál" against Pretoria.

In the light of data turned up more than a decade after the 1975 Angolan intervention,[28] there is little doubt today that even had South Africa not invaded Angola, Cuba still would have mounted its military operation to rescue the MPLA and maintain it in power. Castro's biographer, Tad Szulc, admitted that "contrary to Fidel's own assertions, it was not South Africa's armed intervention in the Angolan civil war that forced him to rush his forces to Angola. The truth is that Castro beat everybody to it, entering the conflict in an impressive display of instinct, imagination and daring."[29]

Given the background of Third World repugnance for the white South African regime, the question of who intervened first may seem purely academic. What is increasingly troubling to many Pan-Africanists, however, is the disquieting fact that the initiative in solving the gravest problem currently facing Africa—the liquidation of the white South African regime—continues to be not in the hands of Africans, but in Fidel Castro's.

At the Non-Aligned Summit held in Harare, Zimbabwe, in September 1986, Castro bluntly declared he would not recall his troops until apartheid and white minority rule had ended in South Africa. That statement, signifying Cuba's determination not to let go of its African trump card, was received with mixed emotions in African quarters, including those of Havana's proteges. It was even unclear whether Luanda saw things in that same light. In fact, 1985 saw a revival of Cuba's interest in southern Africa as manifested by Fidel Castro's growing references to the "200,000 Cubans" who had already served in Africa and the "200,000 more" who were ready to go. Escalation of the black struggle in South Africa was invariably offered as the reason for the growing concern about a country that seemed to have become a fixation for Cuba's leaders. "We are the only country which has actually fought the South African racists and fascists—*the only country in the world*—in addition to Angola, of course, which was under attack" (Italics added.).[30] Castro told two visiting black American officials in 1985.

Cuba and South Africa share certain features in common though organically and structurally speaking, their socio-political systems of rule are diametrically opposed. Both regimes have to contend with growing demands of varying intensity for power-sharing from a black majority population. Both states act as arch-enemies in a continent they regard as their sphere of influence. Cuba and South Africa exist in a state of isolation within their natural geographic spaces. Marooned in the Caribbean with enemies for neighbors and distant powers for allies, Cuba's geopolitical predicament is not unlike South Africa's. Both are authoritarian, militarized societies on a permanent war-footing owing to a perceived threat from within and without. A bunker-type outlook, fed by a powerful nationalism, characterizes both systems. The Castroite and Afrikaner states—the latter being of the Nazi type—are end-products of intense protracted struggles against major imperial powers. As a consequence, these regimes enjoy a degree of autonomy that allows them to escape strict superpower control. These features combined tend to heighten rather than lessen the probability of military confrontation between Havana and Pretoria.

Since its debacle in Grenada in 1983, Cuba has been constrained to passivity in Central America, irrelevance in South American, and once again airtight isolation in the Caribbean. Only Africa, particularly the southern region, continues to offer Cuba room for politico-military maneuver in response to shifts in the world's balance of forces. Hence, in late 1985, Havana was reported[31] to be testing the grounds for some spectacular operation in southern Africa, presumably with Angola, Zimbabwe or Mozambique as springboards, whereby Cuba's military offensive could resume in that region.[32]

Castro could justify such a policy, surmised Gonzalez and Rond-feldt, "as a national war of liberation against South Africa's hated apartheid regime. In so doing, he could rally black Africa's support and, at the same time, help legitimize the Soviet foothold in Southern Africa."[33] Cuba reportedly sought Soviet "clearance and support to issue a formal declaration of war against South Africa to try to turn the struggle against the white regime into an international crusade such as that fought against Hitler" (ibid.).

On the strength of statements the *London Observer* attributed to "a senior government official in Havana," Cuban leaders were said to believe that "with enough hardware, they could win a war against South Africa."[34] Such "leaks" may indeed be orchestrated by the Castro regime itself as a warning to the United States of Cuba's potential for further destabilizing the South African situation,[35] or as a subtle reminder to Gorbachev of Cuba's ability to exercise "internationalist" reprisals against eventual reduction of Soviet aid commitments, for example. Cuba's ability to stir up major trouble in a most sensitive area of the globe is, in itself, a negotiable asset, since if Castro unilaterally began a major drive against the white South African regime, the Kremlin would have no alternative but to fall into step. That, precisely, was the scenario of the 1975 military intervention in Angola.

Technically speaking, the option for an "internationalist" action in South Africa is wide open to Havana, though the military and political risks would be high. A humiliating defeat of the FAR could provoke unprecedented popular unrest inside Cuba, particularly among the Blacks who in all probability would have to bear the brunt of the massive fighting. Rebellion by a humiliated Cuban military cannot be entirely discarded either. But the rewards for such a daring operation could outweigh the risks. Castro's regime would be politically reinvigorated. Black enthusiasm would be rekindled domestically, and overwhelming Third World endorsement secured. On a more personal level, Fidel Castro would have secured the perennial historical landmark he has relentlessly sought.

For the seemingly doomed, beleaguered Afrikaner regime, a war with Cuba would be a godsend. Pretoria would also gain a new lease on life and break its increasing isolation by turning the hostilities into an ideological ("the struggle against communism") rather than racial-political battle. That course would allow the white regime to recoup lost ground with traditional allies (the U.S., West Germany, France,

Israel, Great Britain) and sow confusion in African ranks. Inveterately anti-Communist regimes, like those in Zaire, Kenya and the Ivory Coast, would presumably observe neutrality. Owing to his unbroken record of collaboration with the apartheid regime, it is reasonable to expect UNITA leader Jonas Savimbi to directly or indirectly assist Pretoria in a major conflict. (Opportunistically, Savimbi could order his 20,000 irregulars into a generalized offensive against Luanda and the other major cities, for example.)

The white South African military would definitely be more comfortable handling a situation of conventional warfare that would allow it to bring into play bombers, short-range missiles, heavy artillery, and assault tanks, than facing the crippling effects of massive civil insurrection. Military confrontation between Cuba and South Africa would in all probability sharply polarize superpower support behind each of the protagonists at a critical time.

For Africa, however, such a development would entail a definite risk of escalation. Any military operation resulting in the impairment of South Africa's regular forces could very well prompt the wanton retaliatory destruction of several populous, defenseless sub-Saharan capitals by Pretoria's bombers carrying conventional or even atomic weapons. Lagos, Ibadan, Dakar, Abidjan, Nairobi, Dar-es-Salaam, Kinshasa and Luanda would seem the most likely targets. The neo-Nazi regime would not hesitate to attempt genocide on the black peoples of the continent, the Senegalese scientist, Cheikh Anta Diop, believed.[36] Diop monitored Pretoria's advances in nuclear technology uninterruptedly from 1955 to 1985. He estimated that even a limited atomic attack against half a dozen of black Africa's most populous centers would still kill several million Africans, given Africa's unpreparedness for such an eventuality (ibid.).

A "Creeping" Intervention?

As late as 1982, African National Congress leader Oliver Tambo had not ruled out the possibility of "internationalist" help from Cuba to unseat the white minority regime.[37] In 1986, however, the ANC gained further international legitimacy after Tambo held high-level talks with British and American officials in London and Washington. The changing perception of the ANC by the West, from "terrorist gang" to legitimate interlocutor, might indeed have made its leaders less open to the Cuban temptation, though for obvious reasons it is improbable that the ANC would ever publicly renounce the option of Cuban military aid. But would Havana necessarily require ANC approval to conduct an "internationalist" action designed to "save" the black people of South Africa from destruction?

President Fidel Castro has already declared his decision to remain in Angola until apartheid and white minority rule in South Africa have disappeared.[38] "The imperialists perhaps never imagined that our small country, some 10,000 to 12,000 kilometers from Angola," he remarked, "would have such staying power and perserverance, such strength in keeping up its military and civilian cooperation with this country for eleven years."[39] Not only Angola but a future independent Namibia, and presumably all of Africa's frontline states, required the presence of Cuban forces for their protection. "If we withdrew from Angola and they gave formal independence to Namibia," Castro argued, "what security would Namibia have? It would be a virtual bantustan as long as apartheid existed." (ibid.) Havana had never before spelled out in such clear terms the permanent character of its military presence in Angola: some 35,000–40,000 Cubans, as reported *Granma* in 1986 (ibid.). "Two hundred thousand Cubans have been in Angola," Castro boasted, "and if 200,000 more are needed, they will go, too!"[40]

Reliable reports indicated that during 1986-87 the Cuban military began to replace Angola's fifteen garrisons in the battlefields of the south.[41] This change and a reported reshuffling of Cuban officers in Angola in late 1986 are believed to signal the arrival in Angola of increasingly sophisticated Soviet weaponry since 1984. (ibid.) Is Havana again positioning itself to exploit an eventual opening? Analysts have underlined the fact that, unlike other Third World leaders, Fidel Castro "does not hesitate to defy even the prospect of nuclear war."[42] Speaking of Washington's impotence before Cuba, Castro scoffed: "What can they do? Drop three nuclear bombs here? . . . Three nuclear bombs or 100, 1,000 or 10,000 nuclear bombs amount to something if you're afraid of them, but if you aren't, they're chicken excrement, that's all!"[43]

Conceivably, Pretoria's ability to employ atomic weapons against black Africans would not deter Cuba's Caudillo from initiating a conflict in Southern Africa, were it to Havana's advantage. The question African policymakers and scholars may therefore have increasing reason to ponder is under what circumstances Cuba could unilaterally undertake an action that would force all black countries to fall in line.

Any number of situations could prompt Fidel Castro to engage in a diversionary operation abroad: inability to ultimately overcome his bureaucracy in the current "rectification" campaign; widespread manifestations of discontent; aggravation of latent racial tensions; serious trouble within the young, Soviet-trained, technocratic military establishment. In fact, even the Caudillo's contracting an incurable illness, as far-fetched as that may seem, could be the basis for a suicidal but glorious "internationalist" operation to save South African Blacks from their tyrannical white rulers.

Renewed tension with either the USSR or the United States could also force Havana to retaliate where neither superpower has effective control over Cuba's actions. From whatever vantage point it is viewed, the threat of an ofensiva final against Pretoria is already a big international trumpcard in the hands of Cuba's leaders. The 1.2 million-strong MTT, representing 10 percent of Cuba's total population under direct Party command, created "the conditions which enable us to feel that we are invincible,"[44] Castro said in 1985. It is believed the MTT would allow the FAR to dispatch abroad as many as 100,000 regular troops for a major conventional war without weakening Cuba's own defense requirements.

A Cry for Independence

Havana has made a good case for its brushfire-fighting and law-and-order role on a continent which Castro designated as "backward"[45] and which most whites continue to regard as the "Dark Continent." Little Cuba's military might does contrast sharply with the painful impotence of an entire continent before the white South African regime, its chief enemy. But among the continent's Pan-African-oriented intelligentsia there is a growing sense of humiliation as the role of external forces widens in the settling of internal African affairs. This sense of humiliation is reported at its greatest in those frontline states where reliance on the Cuban military has increased over the past decade in direct proportion to Pretoria's threat.

Complaints are growing about the behavior of the Cuban forces,[46] but it is clear that none of the regimes currently being protected by Cuba could last very long without it. Added to the concrete threat from Pretoria, that situation is causing increasing concern in certain African circles, where it is felt that Africans themselves are capable of and must devise strategies geared to finding indigenous solutions to any African problem.[47] "One may not take pride for long in someone else having to put your own house in order,"[48] remarked OAU Secretary General Edem Kodjo, concerning all foreign military interventions Africa has witnessed since independence. The next generation of African leaders, Kodjo felt, would have to be more strategy-conscious than ideology-prone in order to face the growing complexities of a technology-oriented world.[49]

Founding president of the MPLA Mario de Andrade believed that "African solutions to African problems are the only real and durable solutions."[50] The scientist, Cheikh Anta Diop, feared African leaders might be mortgaging the continent's future by becoming excessively reliant on external assistance in order to meet emergencies, such as drought, civil strife, or border wars. Diop was of the conviction that systematically resorting to external "shortcuts" not only delayed the real solutions but risked destroying Africa's innovative faculties.[51]

The "Castro Doctrine" on Africa, formulated as early as 1960, posited Africa's dependency on Castroite Cuba in order for the black continent to realize its emancipation goals (liquidation of white minority regimes, elimination of the remaining colonial holdings, empowerment of black majorities). In turn, Fidel Castro's regime in Cuba became increasingly reliant on Africa in order to regulate its relationship with the major powers and superpowers and to sustain mass political loyalty in Cuba's predominantly African multi-racial society. The initiative of that relationship having come from Cuba, that Caribbean island thereafter increasingly accentuated its lead. Kenyan scholar Ali A. Mazrui calls the Cuban-African relationship one of micro-dependency.[52]

The consequences of World War II, on the one hand, and the decolonization process in Africa and Asia on the other, Mazrui explained, have led to distinctly new modes of dependency. He categorized the two dominant forms as macro-dependency and micro-dependency. The first concerned "variations of dependency between one country in the Northern Hemisphere and another, or between one industrialized state and another . . ." (ibid., 1). Macro-dependency involved "variations in affluence among the affluent or degrees of might among the mighty" (ibid.).

Micro-dependency, on the other hand, was related to increasing "variation of technical development among the underdeveloped, or relative influence among the weak, or degrees of power among those that are basically exploited," Mazrui said. (ibid.). In such a situation, the underdeveloped country became "disproportionately reliant upon another or disproportionately influenced by another" member of the same underdeveloped world (ibid., 6). Mazrui believed that because the black continent was structurally the least developed of the three continents of the Third World, Africa was "particularly susceptible to micro-dependency" (ibid., 7). Thus, Africans in the twentieth century "have been much more often followers than leaders, responsive rather than innovative" (ibid.), he said. Africa's micro-dependency upon the Arab world was economic and to a certain extent cultural; the continent's micro-dependency upon Latin America was "military and to some extent ideological" (ibid., 8). Were Cuba's organizational structure to be transplanted onto Africa soil, "a form of imitative micro-dependency of Africa upon Latin America might re-emerge," Mazrui said (ibid., 17).

The bitter fruit of colonialism created the worst sort of dependency, Mazrui acknowledged, but he cautioned against a simplistic overemphasis of that problem. "It is simply not true," he protested, "that all forms of international dependency concern interactions between industrialism and sources of raw materials" (ibid., 1,2). In any of its guises, Mazrui cautioned, "Dependency is a form of political castration" (ibid.).

Africa's current powerlessness, African scholars concede, is the price black peoples continue to pay for their colonial rape by the West and the Middle East. Her micro-dependency, however, relates to an evolution which began taking place in the 1960s. In this context, African regimes that rely on foreign benefactors—of whatever ideological or political suasion—must bear responsibility for Africa's compounded dependency into the 21st century.

APPENDIX 1 *   THE LATIN MODEL
OF RACE RELATIONS

The profile of race relations that prevails wherever Spaniards or Portuguese established their colonies is present in Cuba in all its complexity. This model's primary characteristic is denial: insistence that Blacks are "well-treated," that on the whole slavery was more benevolent under Iberians than under Anglo-Saxons.[1] The very fact that white slave-owners had intercourse with African women is presented as evidence that, by not enforcing "Jim Crow" and "Heartbreak" laws from the beginning, Latins were showing great open-mindedness and kindness—especially toward their illegitimate "mulatto" offspring. The regular sexual exploitation of black women by their slave masters, especially during the colonial period when white females were scarce, produced a large mixed population. Although it was said they had more noble qualities than their dark-skinned relations because of their white blood, "mulattoes" fared little better than Blacks both socially and economically. (As Appendix 2 illustrates, white officials found "mulattoes" useful in diminishing the perceived numbers of people of African ancestry, thus representing Blacks as a perpetual minority group with a barely perceptible rate of growth.)

Other characteristics of the Latin model of race relations are the beliefs that: integration and miscegenation will "solve" the black "problem"; whitening through miscegenation, increased white immigration, and a ban on "colored" immigrants will eventually eradicate such "bad" traits as curly hair, dark skin, and African features in the general population; Blacks are not discriminated against as a race, but as members of the lower classes, in which they abound (concomitant is the belief that "money whitens"). Political power is arrogated exclusively to whites. Even the lightest-skinned African descendants have difficulty passing into the highest strata of government.

The politics of the Latin variant of race relations are founded on an intrinsically integrationist benevolent paternalism. The emphasis on

---

* Appendix 1 was written by Sabrina Gledhill, M.A. in Latin American Studies, UCLA.

protector/ward relationships on both the interpersonal and political levels is the legacy of the feudal systems of relations prevalent in the Iberian peninsula. When brought to the colonies, this system developed into the distribution of Indians into *encomiendas* under a "protector" (*encomendero*), whose nominal duty was to civilize them. Transferred to master/slave plantation relations, this pattern of tutelage shaped Cuba's development through the post-slavery period. Its effects were manifold, and always malignant. As Eugene Genovese writes in *Roll, Jordan, Roll*: "Wherever paternalism exists, it undermines solidarity among the oppressed by linking them as individuals to their oppressors. A lord (master, *padrone*, *patrón*, *padrón*, *patrão*) functions as a direct provider and protector to each individual or family, as well as to the community as a whole. . . . Paternalism created a tendency for the slaves to identify with a particular community through identification with its master; it reduced the possibilities for identification with each other as a class. Racism undermined the slaves' sense of worth as black people and reinforced their dependence on white masters. . . . Paternalism in any historical setting defines relations of superordination and subordination. Its strength as a prevailing ethos increases as the members of the community accept—or feel compelled to accept—these relations as legitimate."[2]

APPENDIX 2   IS CUBA A BLACK OR
A WHITE COUNTRY?

Census Reports of the Pre-Revolutionary Period

The question of Cuba's past and present racial demographic composition defies any rational solution through combining objective truth and official statistics. In his thorough study *Blacks in Colonial Cuba, 1774–1899*, Kenneth F. Kiple demonstrated the "treacherous" nature of colonial census data, unreliable to the extent that they may "justify almost any position, as was recently demonstrated by two students of Cuban slavery who have used demographic data to 'prove' diametrically opposed arguments."[1] Are the censuses of the Republican, pre-revolutionary period any more credible?

Writing in 1935, Raymond T. Buell et al. observed, "It is estimated that altogether, until the abolition of the slave trade, more than a million Africans were carried to Cuba. . . . Many mulattoes now pass as white Cubans, and it is consequently difficult for the census to make accurate distinctions. Some Cuban observers believe that not more than half of the total population is pure white."[2] Black Cubans have consistently charged that during that period, foreign whites were set down as "Cuban" in the censuses (particularly the populous resident Spanish community) in order to bolster the white category, and that light-skinned Blacks were co-opted as "whites" for the same purpose.

As far back as 1934, noted Afro-Cuban journalist and polemicist Gustavo E. Urrutia explained that situation as the consequence of an unavowed official policy. "In Cuba a pro-white policy is enacted in every field of national life," he remarked, "and one of the methods of such a policy is to classify mulattoes as *white* in censuses and demographic reports. . . . However, the number of Cubans who truly qualify as white is small. . . . Most of those classified as such are neither white in terms of color nor race."[3]

W. E. B. Du Bois, the black American scholar, estimated in 1939 that "the present Negro population in Cuba probably runs to about seventy percent despite official statistics."[4] In his *America South*, Carleton Beals warned against the racial unreliability of Cuban census data, estimating closer to the truth that only 30 percent of Cubans were whites and 70 percent Blacks of various hues.[5]

For the 1943 census, enumerators (presumably whites) left it up to each person to determine if they were "white," "Black," "mulatto," or "yellow." The reported results gave a total black population of 25.2 percent.[6] The preceding census of 1931 had reported Afro-Cubans as comprising 28 percent of the population. Notwithstanding, the 1946 edition of the *Encyclopedia Americana* stated that "About 60 percent of the population is classified as white and 40 percent as Negro and mulatto."[7] Donald W. Bray and Timothy F. Harding estimated that Blacks comprised 50 percent of the population of Cuba in 1953.[8]

If we are to believe the census data of the Republican period, the black Cuban population was 29.7 percent in 1907 and 27.2 percent in 1919, and remained virtually unchanged thereafter. The low credibility of pre-revolutionary census reports is a recurrent theme among Cubanologists of the period. "Other estimates, for example," observed W. MacCaffey and C. R. Barnett, "indicate 30% white, 20% mestizo, 49% Negroid and 1% Oriental."[9] Though Cuba was perhaps the whitest of the Caribbean islands, William R. Bascom emphasized in 1953 that "the official census figures undoubtedly underestimate the number of Negroes and the Negro-white admixtures in Cuba."[10]

Although in the 1950s the black population was described as being under one-third of the total, according to Hugh Thomas, "an accurate figure is hard to give, since in 1953 the identification of this or that individual by the curious and misleading euphemism 'coloured' was left to the enumerators, whereas in previous censuses account was taken of the declarations made by the persons concerned. Presumably, therefore, the identification was inaccurate. At least one other published estimate suggested that as many as half of the total were 'Negroid' and another 20% really mulatto, an estimate with which many intelligent observers would agree."[11]

White Cuban anthropologist Fernando Ortiz is reported by Thomas to have estimated the actual size of the Afro-Cuban population in 1953 at 70 percent (ibid.), whereas Irving L. Horowitz believes it was 40 percent.[12] Boris Goldenberg estimated the black portion of Cuba to have been 60 to 70 percent of the total in 1953.[13]

Even the *Encyclopedia Britannica* guardedly cast a shadow of doubt on the integrity of the racial figures of the 1953 census and suggested that "the proportion of the population with some Negro ancestry is much higher than the figures indicate."[14] In his "Cuba, Color and the Revolution," David Booth conceded that the racial "interpretation of these data is fraught with difficulty. . . . It has frequently been suggested that all the census statistics systematically overstate the 'whiteness' of the total population and one published estimate has gone as far as to suggest that the proportions may have been 30 percent white, 40 percent Negroid, 1 percent oriental and 20 percent mestizo in 1953."[15]

Census Estimates and Reports of the Revolutionary Period

The revolutionary regime that took power in 1959 was even more sensitive to the racial demographic issue than those preceding it. First, it imposed a total ban in which raising the question became "divisive" and therefore "subversive." Then, in 1983, the government surprisingly released the results of the 1981 census in which the Afro-Cuban portion was declared to be about 5 to 6 percent higher than in the pre-revolutionary period: 33.9 percent.

Walterio Carbonell estimated that in 1959 Cuban Blacks comprised at least 50 percent of the population. He claimed that, in private, Fidel Castro and his inner circle believed Cuba had a *"mayoría de color,"* or "colored" majority.[16] There was a tacit agreement to taboo that issue, however, for fear of white disaffection, particularly among the traditionally prejudiced white working class and peasantry, as well as the middle classes (ibid.).

Throughout the 1960s we are faced with a continuing pattern—a carry-over from the pre-revolutionary period—of confusion and conflict between estimates by most foreign (and some Cuban) specialists on the Revolution, and the official line regarding the size of the Afro-Cuban population. For instance during a speech on May 22, 1964, to sugar-cane cutters in Oriente, Defense Minister Raúl Castro spoke of Cuba's "two million dark-skinned Cubans" (*de piel oscura*), but omitted giving corresponding figures regarding light-skinned black Cubans or whites.[17] Two years later, in an interview with foreign journalists (which went unreported in the Cuban press), Prime Minister Fidel Castro went on record as stating that "African blood flows in the veins of half of Cuba's population."[18]

In 1968, Antoine G. Petit, a Marxist economist who worked and lived in Cuba for a decade, reported that "according to very conservative estimates by Cuban officials . . . the black element of the population is held to be 52% of the nation's whole."[19] Officially, however, the blackout was total, and to raise the issue was still "subversive."

Between 1960 and 1970 more than 500,000 Cubans—of whom 96.4% were reported to be white—left Cuba.[20] The Mariel exodus of

1982, of which about 20% were reported to be Blacks, increased the "white hemorrhage" to nearly 700,000. According to certain estimates, had it not been for the stringent measures taken in 1965 by the Cuban authorities to stop the exodus, perhaps between one and three million Cubans might have fled the island by 1982, reducing the white population to irreversibly low proportions. Apparently, the authorities took this into account. The 1981 census results released in 1983 reported that "the white population is suffering a net regression."[21] White emigration alone, therefore, contributed to a sudden proportional increase in the size of the black population. Added to this, a veritable "black demographic boom" is reported by visitors to Cuba. Although the authorities release no figures on differential racial growth rates, Cuban demographer Juán Pérez de la Riva attributed Cuba's population growth partly to "the fertility cult deeply rooted in Africa's traditions."[22]

During a press conference in Paris, American political figure Andrew Young mentioned the white exodus factor as an issue influencing Cuban domestic politics. "In Cuba," he said, "there was a larger proportion of darker-skinned people with Castro's revolution than against it and many anti-Castro whites fled when he won. This produced an abnormal racial balance."[23] In the 1976 edition of the *Area Handbook for Cuba*, one of the most authoritative data sources on all vital aspects of revolutionary Cuba, the authors speculated that the mass exodus of whites since the Revolution, "accounted not only for the greater cultural and ethnic homogeneity, but also for the greater relative number of blacks and mestizos observed in the 1970s. Although Cubans themselves did not speculate on increases, many foreign observers estimated the number of blacks at between 30 and 40 percent, mestizos and whites constituting the remainder."[24]

The first population census conducted under the revolutionary regime, in 1970, was welcomed with an expectation commensurate to the importance of determining the extent of black underrepresentation at all echelons of leadership in the new Cuba. But what emerged from that exercise was an even greater confusion, to which mystery was added: the authorities refrained from releasing the data collected concerning race. The basic form employed by enumerators who carried out the 1970 census included a query (No. 5) about color of the skin and listed four categories to be checked in response: white, Black, mulatto, and yellow.[25] However, without the least explanation, the ethnic data collected regarding the racial categories listed were never released by the Cuban government.

Lourdes Casal, a black Cuban scholar, attempted to solve the ethno-demographic puzzle in her essay "Race Relations in Contemporary Cuba." Publications to date of the data of the 1970 Cuban census, she pointed out, "have not included any breakdowns of the population according to race. . . . However, in spite of the absence of published information on the racial breakdown of the Cuban population as of 1970, it is possible to speculate on the nature of the changes. It is my estimate that the percentage of non-whites in the Cuban population should have increased from 26.9 in the 1953 Census to a figure no less than 40% in 1970."[26]

Casal, a prominent pro-government figure in the U.S. Cuban exile community, is reported to have gone to the National Archives of Cuba on one of her trips to the island in the 1970s, only to find that all racial data collected in the 1970 census had vanished.[27] According to Jorge I. Domínguez, the Cuban authorities claimed subsequently that the racial data of the 1970 census were "lost."[28]

Throughout the 1970s, therefore, we observe a continuing pattern in which Afro-Cubans were unofficially considered to be the bulk of Cuba's population. Left-wing analysts Donald Bray and Timothy F. Harding wrote, "Although official figures list less than one-third of the Cubans as black or mulatto, perhaps half of the population actually has some 'African blood.'"[29] U.S. Communist party leader Joseph North wrote that during his first visit to Cuba, "I discovered what many do not yet know, that more than half of its populace is not white."[30] Similarly, after a first visit to Cuba in 1968, French Marxist theoretician Daniel Guerin wrote, "the descendants of Africans comprise about half of the population and are reproducing at a faster rate than the whites."[31]

After a visit to Cuba in 1977, André Orleans, director of the National Institute on Statistics and Economic Studies (INSEE) of France, reportedly estimated the black population to be 50 percent at that time.[32]

The second census carried out under the Revolution in 1981 widened the credibility gap beyond bridging. This time, the enumerators were the ones to assess the "race" of an individual, even over the latter's protest.[33] The 1981 census results, published in 1983, created quite a stir within Cuba. The two leading official ethnologists, Rogelio Martínez Furé and Miguel Barnet, for example, gave estimates that contradicted the census reports. After conducting a bus census in the capital, in 1974 and 1975, Martínez Furé, who is Black, and by far the most knowledgeable of the regime's intellectuals on the ethnic issue, estimated the Afro-Cuban population to be 66 percent.[34] Miguel Barnet, who is white, said in 1984 that "the majority of the Cuban population is white, but there are 43% of mulattoes whose origins go back to the enslavement of Africans."[35] Barnet is silent about that portion of the population which is neither white nor "mulatto."

In contrast, the 1983 edition of the semi-official French yearbook *Quid* stated: "Cuba. Population 9,706,369: Blacks 55%, Whites 30%, Mulattoes 15%, Orientals 1%."[36] Former Cuban official Juán Benemelis (exiled since 1980) estimated the black population to be "well above 60% in 1985," and mentioned "a veritable black demographic explosion over the past twenty-five years."[37]

In a polemical "Reply to the Cuban Authorities," Spanish author Fernando Arrabal declared: "The authorities of Cuba state that 66% of the island's population is white. But the opinion of specialists is quite different. The 1976 edition of the *Atlas*—published by the left-wing French weekly, *Le Nouvelle Observateur*—states on page 58 as follows: 'The Cuban population is comprised of 30% whites, 55% of Negroes and 15% mulattoes.' As a result of the demographic explosion of the black population, coupled to the exodus of the whites, it is estimated that nowadays, in 1985, whites account for *less* than 20% of the population."[38]

The Marxist Swiss sociologist Jean Ziegler is closer to that belief than to the officially sustained one. Writing in 1983, he stated a more-or-less general consensus among foreign specialists on Cuba, that the proportion of Afro-Cubans "may be well over 65% of the total population of ten million."[39]

The "Majority"/"Minority" Question

Cuba is prototypical of societies which function along the lines of what I loosely call the "Latin model" of race relations. A UNESCO publication, *Introducción a la cultura Africana en América Latina*, took note of the fact that most so-called "Latin" American countries excluded ethnic classifications from census data.[40] Such a practice made it difficult, when not impossible, "to determine the level of participation of Afro-Americans in the various aspects of national life" (ibid.). Similar observations have been made with regard to those Latin American countries with a large or even a majority Indian population.

Italian statistician Giorgio Mortara raised one aspect of the problem, the sheer complexity of defining race anthropologically in certain multi-racial countries:

> Because of the heterogeneous composition, it is quite difficult to neatly discern ethnic group characteristics in most Latin American populations. In several countries the majority population of vast areas are in-

habited by (pure or mixed) aboriginal populations. Such is the case particularly in Mexico, Guatemala, Ecuador, Peru, Bolivia and Paraguay. However, in certain cases, such as Guatemala and Bolivia, census classification which is supposedly ethnic is grounded on *social* rather than on anthropological criteria. . . . Consequently, census data on race or color are necessarily inaccurate. . . . Thus, someone who is dark-skinned—say a mulatto or a mestizo—will often be classified as *white*, if he happens to be a General or a Minister of State, notwithstanding visual evidence to the contrary.[41]

Chilean statistician Adolfo Gaete Darbo raised yet another problem in his "Evaluación de las Estadísticas Vitales in America Latina," admitting that the training of Latin American enumerators is deficient. "Out of fourteen countries, only one (Chile) requires studies in the social sciences and adequate training to become an enumerator. . . . In all of the other countries it is enough to read and write to qualify for such a function. . . . The statistics gathering systems of many countries do not encompass the totality of the population . . . because they exclude parts of the territorial surface and/or certain ethnic groups. . . . As a rule, Latin American countries are unaware of the degree of veracity of their vital statistics."[42]

All of these deficiencies, which are to be found among all so-called developing countries, play their role in establishing the unreliability of statistics in countries of the "Latin model" type. What part does deliberate racism play, however, in societies which glorify whites while Blacks and Indians are systematically denigrated and oppressed, not only socioeconomically and culturally but also racially? "One cannot deny," admitted L. A. Costa Pinto, "that studies regarding the Blacks in Latin America have barely begun . . . [and] that a whole generation of authors . . . tended to underestimate, when not deny altogether, the influence, contributions, and even the physical presence, of Blacks in many countries of Latin America."[43] French anthropologist Alfred Metroux attributed this state of affairs to ingrained racism. "Many intellectuals and politicians" he said, "suffer from what I would call—for want of a better term—'racial pessimism.' I have witnessed in many otherwise intelligent and perceptive individuals a pronounced tendency to attribute whatever is criticizable in their country to the 'heavy legacy of Indian blood.' Such racial pessimism is equally blatant in the embarrassed shame and uneasiness exhibited by these ruling classes regarding the existence of Indians in their countries. When such a presence cannot be denied, an attempt is made to diminish its importance."[44]

Mexican sociologist Rodolfo Stavenhagen pointed out in this regard

It's commonplace to read that from the 19th century onwards all Latin American countries experienced a rapid, and ongoing process of biological and cultural crossbreeding . . . and that the mestizo (considered as a cultural element as well as a social group) has now become the dominant element culturally, socially and politically, besides being in addition the "progressive," 'modernizing" and "nationalist" sector of these nations. In this perspective, Indian communities are presented as mere historical vestiges of an archaic world left behind. As such, they are regarded as "traditional," or marginal societies whose very existence is a stumbling block to socioeconomic development, and which sooner or later will tend to, and will have to disappear for the sake of national integration.[45]

Because of a de facto, deliberate, and unrelenting policy of *blanqueamiento* (whitening), census racial statistics in Latin America are, and will continue to be in the foreseeable future, part of an essentially ethno-political issue imbued with a high emotional charge on both sides of the racial spectrum, even if unavowed.

Brazil, which prides itself on being a "racial democracy," announced in 1970 that race would no longer figure in census statistics.[46] This decision, which has the effect of rendering a statistical study of the status of Afro-Brazilians impossible, was supposedly taken in the name of anti-racism. Using an identical argument, the revolutionary authorities of Cuba have steadfastly refused to release statistics that could allow a comparative study of the basic racial aggregates of Cuba in the various domains of national activity such as the economy, armed forces, government, Communist party, and the National Assembly.

Is there reason to suspect that, after twenty-four years of consistent blindness to race in census-taking and official population estimates, the sudden revelation of census statistics in 1983 following a racial breakdown was meant to reinvigorate the notion of a white Cuba with a black "minority'? Many black Cubans adopt that view. However, although no doubt comforting to those who insist that Cuba is a white country, the census results disclosed in 1983 are afflicted with the same lack of credibility as those of the pre-revolutionary period. Despite a quarter of a century of Revolution, the traditional system of racial categorization, typical of the Latin model of race relations, has remained unchanged: "Black," "White," and "Mulatto."

A last word: I contacted several demographers, including a specialist on ethnic demography at the French National Institute for Demographic Studies (INED). My intention was to find out whether, barring a census, other means were at their disposal to estimate the size of a particular ethnic aggregate with respect to the rest of the population. Dr. Georges Tapinos (INED) and Dr. Georges Zouain (UNDP) were as affirmative as were other U.N. demographers approached. Various methods are widely used by demographers in such cases. The hitch, however, is that relative freedom of movement and tacit official consent are required in order to carry out such probes.

It seems fair to conclude, therefore, that given the closed nature of Marxist Cuba, analysts of all sorts will continue to be obliged to rely on estimates of the Afro-Cuban share of the population—unless, of course, official census results, before or after the Revolution, are to be accepted as the objective, unbiased racial portrait of the population of Cuba. This, as we have seen, is not the case!

APPENDIX 3   CHÉ GUEVARA'S CULTURAL CONFLICTS IN AFRICA

The Ethnocultural Problems

If Ché had expected to find the slightest reflection of his "New Man" among the simbas, he was quickly disappointed. From the outset, he apparently made no attempt to relate to the strange world in which he found himself immersed. Even with the insurgent leaders Guevara was uncommunicative and aloof. It is true that Guevara had to conceal his identity from the curious. On at least one occasion he was mistaken for a white mercenary prisoner. There was much more behind his attitude of total withdrawal and non-communication, however. Although he often sought refuge in the company of the black Cuban soldiers, with whom he could converse in Spanish, he still kept to himself, frequently taking notes.

The Congolese *maquis* was diametrically opposed to the human and cultural milieu that Guevara had known in Cuba's Sierra Maestra. In Cuba, the guerrillas had been in a mountainous environment peopled by poor white peasants, or *guajiros*, who had been brought to Cuba during the Spanish colonial period from the poorest regions of Spain, partly to replace black slave labor in the countryside, and partly in response to an overt policy of *blanqueamiento* (whitening). The Hispanic guajiros clung to the cultural traditions of their native land. Men like Castro and Guevara had felt at home among them.

The density of the population in the area where Guevara operated had nothing in common with the sparse, isolated clusters of *bohios* of the Sierra Maestra. The villages in Zone D were made up of several thousand people, all linked to one another by intricate symbiotic ties. The individualism of the Hispanic Cuban guajiro was unknown there. Moreover, the large villages that provided the simbas with food, recruits, and intelligence information were themselves part of a greater ethnic and cultural reality, the tribe. These ethnic groups were large entities ranging in magnitude from tens to hundreds of thousands. Like the village, the tribe was not a conglomerate of individuals but a tight maze of inter-community relations, deeply rooted in common symbolism and beliefs about animals, plants, and the origins, existence, and destiny of human beings. Another network of ancestral alliances and vows linked these villages, clans, and tribes. The lone individual so prized by Guevara was unknown in that part of the world.

Guerrillas with "Brujería"

The supernatural and magico-religious phenomena that filled the lives of the villages and tribes of the eastern part of the Congo went further than Guevara may have initially suspected. The simbas engaged in the same magico-religious practices as did their natal villages. Guevara could quickly identify these rites with those existing in Cuba and called *brujería* (witchcraft), or *magia negra* (black magic). It would be unthinkable for a simba to go into battle without special anti-bullet charms and amulets (*grisgris*); or without seeking the advice of elderly wise men. (Guevara could not have failed to recognize these men as the equivalent of the Afro-Cuban *santeros*, who were reputed to possess magical powers and the ability to read the future). These powerful magico-religious practitioners advised the insurgent leaders of the probability of success or failure of future battles.

Guevara's assessment of the world in which he found himself was indeed gloomy. Day after day, he would note his views on customs he considered primitive, magico-religious practices he saw as backward, and a general behavior on the part of both the simbas and their leaders which he judged as inefficient and irrational.[1] His mission was to propel the Congo into "scientific communism," but the world that opened before him during the eight months he spent in Zone D belonged to the socioeconomic and cultural realm of what he, as a Marxist, would categorize as "primitive communism."

No matter how cogent the explanations, Guevara could only see certain practices as being atavistic and barbaric.[2] He discovered with utter disgust that the simbas removed some of the vital organs of their slain white mercenary enemies to make charms and amulets as a way of appropriating the courage of the fallen foe. The Congolese fighters were definitely not the "effective, violent, selective and cold killing machines" Guevara considered to be the model of the modern, scientific, revolutionary warrior.[3] Worse, he had come to suspect these warriors and those of their leaders who wore such charms and amulets of engaging in cannibalism.[4]

Intricate war-dances preceded the great battles; victorious encounters were celebrated with all-night dancing and drumming in the villages near the simba encampments. To Guevara, such preparations and celebrations were a pure waste of energy. Simba warriors and leaders alike led lives far removed from that of Guevara's Spartan soldier and model guerrilla. In Guevara's code of conduct, their nightly escapades were seen as indulgences. Practices that made the simbas believe in their own invulnerability to bullets were considered by Guevara as the best way to deplete the ranks of the insurrection. Gabriel García Marquez said that

> Ché had become aware that the warriors were wearing necklaces against mortar shells and bracelets against machine-gun bullets and painting their faces with charcoal to confront the risks of war. He became so engrossed in those absurd cultural traditions that he began an in-depth study of African religions and the Swahili language in an attempt to change things from the inside, for he was acutely aware that a pernicious force can be anchored deep inside men's hearts which not even bullets can uproot.[5]

The Backward Vanguard

The ideological failings of the Congolese revolutionaries could be remedied with proper Marxist training. What was more difficult to deal with for Guevara were the dangerously entrenched residuals of "irrational" notions among the leaders of the revolutionary movement. By the Castro-Guevarist definition, they were to act as the vanguard. Nevertheless, Guevara found them to be just as immersed in "absurd cultural beliefs" and "irrational" religious and magical practices as their followers.

The vanguard was supposed to be on an infinitely higher moral, cultural, and ideological plain than the masses it was destined to lead. But the Congolese guerrilla leaders were, in Guevara's opinion, as backward as their simba troops, despite their western education. How to accommodate the fact that the very group supposed to act as the trailblazer for the continental African revolution was fully in the grip of spiritualistic beliefs, rituals, and "strange ceremonies" so like those which the Cuban revolution was determined to stamp out on its domestic front?

APPENDIX 4 SURVEY: AFRICAN YOUTH AND THE CASTROITE INTERVENTION IN AFRICA[1]

Cuba's popularity in Africa has never been as strong as it was when many of its troops were permanently camped on the black continent. At the peak of Cuba's military and political involvement there, an overwhelming majority, 72.5 percent of the African youth questioned, said they approved of Cuba's military interventions in the conflicts in Angola and Ethiopia; 26 percent said they were totally against them; and only 3 percent were undecided. Given the tremendous uproar over the Cuban military presence in Africa, it was most surprising to see to what extent African young people supported it. For example, at the time when the Cuban military and political intervention was most conspicuous, 66 percent of the youth interviewed said they would like to see a Cuban-type regime in their own countries, against only 11 percent who did not agree and 22 percent who were undecided (1 percent gave no response).

When this survey was carried out, the Cuban military force in Africa had reached 40,000 soldiers as a result of the Cuban intervention in the Somalo-Ethiopian war (December 1977–March 1978), and the continuation of Cuban-Angolan military operations against the South African-supported UNITA rebels in southern Angola.

Young Africans placed Cuba (20%) well after the United States (45%) as the country where they would most like to be scholastically and professionally trained, putting Cuba just ahead of the European countries (17%) and the USSR (17%). The fascination with Cuba increased when the question was where they would most like to spend a holiday. Cuba ranked first (43%), ahead of the United States (26%), all the European countries (18.5%), and the USSR (11%).

What attracted these respondents to Cuba? Cuba's "economic progress" was admired by 27.3 percent, while 16.7 percent cite the "policy of aiding liberation movements," and 16.8 percent mention the political changes that have reportedly resulted in a real "people's democracy" in Cuba. The "installation of racial and social equality" was considered by 15.2 percent to be the greatest Castroite success. Yet a large number of those interviewed (24%) did not reply.

A Warm Welcome—For Afro-Cubans

The African youths questioned were particularly receptive to the Cuban presence in Africa. This is explained in large part by their perception of Cuba as culturally and ethnically similar to Africa. The majority (67.5%) thought that Cuba was composed primarily of Blacks and people of mixed African and Spanish origin. They felt that the Afro-Cubans were "at home in Africa" (62.5%), although 35.5 percent considered them "foreigners" and 2 percent were undecided. None of those interviewed had ever met a Cuban, and the majority (57%) did not know how they would react if they accidentally met one of their transatlantic cousins. Only 1.3 percent admitted they would be mistrustful, whereas 22.2 percent said they would try to strike up a conversation, and 19 percent said they would invite him to their homes.

Not Well-Informed

A striking result of this survey was that only 14 percent gave relatively well-informed answers about the Cuban revolution. Although the Castro regime is very popular with the African youth, they lack information on the economic, political, and social situation of a regime that 66 percent of them would like to import as a model for their own country. A significant percentage (20%), for example, were convinced that 50 percent of the Cuban leadership was of African origin ("Blacks and Mixed"). When asked to state the three greatest accomplishments of the Cuban revolution, a relatively large number did not know what to answer (24%). Those who mentioned "economic progress" as Castro's most impressive success went on to attribute feats to the Cuban revolution that not even Castro himself has suggested, including "nuclear force," "equality of income," and "industrial power."

The contrast between the Anglophone and Francophone African youth was most noticeable on this point. The young Francophones were infinitely better informed about the Cuban revolution and its African extensions than were their Anglophone counterparts. The Anglophones, however, knew more about the problems in South Africa.

Cuba Yes, But . . .

What these African youths liked the most and were the most unanimous about (72.5%) was Havana's "internationalist" policy, precisely what others term its "interventionism." Cuba was seen as the country that forced the champions of apartheid to retreat from Angola (1975–1976); that flew to the aid of an African state threatened with dismemberment (Ethiopia, 1977–1978); and that guarantees the national unity of the African states and the inviolability of their borders.

Nevertheless, there were serious reservations when it came to long-term the Castroite policy in Africa. As a student leader from the Ecole Normale Superieure in Bamako (Mali) explained in June 1979, "We'll be for Cuba as long as they're on our side, but we'll fight against them if we ever discover they're manipulating us." (Yet he was among the 27.5 percent who were convinced that the Cuban intervention in Africa was motivated by altruism.) Although the Cuban presence in Africa was overwhelmingly approved, the majority of these young people were convinced that there were "unavowed ulterior motives" behind Havana's "internationalist" actions. A considerable number (24.5%) were silent on the issue.

Anglophones: Cuba?

I had originally intended to carry out this survey both in an Anglophone African country and a Francophone African country. Senegal and Nigeria were selected.

Only nine out of a hundred questionnaires distributed to students at the University of Lagos (May 1978) were returned, and those were only half completed. The others were returned with "Don't Know" written in various places, or almost entirely covered with question marks. The attempt to substitute Ghana for Nigeria (May 1978) was equally a failure. Only three questionnaires given to the students at the University of Legon were returned entirely completed; fifteen were half filled out. I thus came to the conclusion that the young Anglophone Africans were not interested in Cuba, knew very little about it, and did not feel affected by Cuba's political and military role on their continent.

Appendix 4

The Questionnaire

TABLE I

CUBAN MILITARY INTERVENTION IN AFRICA

1. Do you approve of Cuba's intervention in African conflicts such
as Angola's or Ethiopia's?

MALI		IVORY COAST	
Yes	90%	Yes	55%
No	10%	No	42%

TOTAL:	Yes	72.5%
	No	26 %
	No response	1.5%

2. Do you think that Cuba's actions in Africa have been motivated
by altruism or unavowed ulterior motives?

MALI		IVORY COAST	
Altruism	33%	Altruism	22%
Unavowed ulterior		Unavowed ulterior	
motives	67%	motives	29%

TOTAL:	Altruism	27.5%
	Unavowed ulterior motives	48 %
	No opinion	24.5%

TABLE II

CUBA AS A MODEL

1. Do you think that the kind of society Cuba has would be good or bad for African countries such as your own country?

MALI		IVORY COAST	
Good	84%	Good	48%
Bad	7%	Bad	15%
Undecided	9%	Undecided	35%
		No response	2%

TOTAL: Good 66%
            Bad 11%
            Undecided 22%
            No response 1%

2. In which category would you place the three greatest accomplishments of the Cuban revolution?

MALI		IVORY COAST	
Economic	37 %	Economic	17.7%
International	27 %	International	6.3%
Domestic political	18.7%	Domestic political	15 %
Social, Cultural	17 %	Social, Cultural	13.3%
No answer	0.3%	No answer	47.7%

TOTAL: Economic 27.8%
            Domestic political 16.8%
            International 16.7%
            Social, Cultural 15.2%
            No answer .... 24 %

TABLE III

KNOWLEDGE ABOUT CUBA AND CUBAN SOCIETY

1. In your opinion is Cuba composed of Blacks, whites or people of mixed race?

MALI		IVORY COAST	
Black	31%	Black	29%
White	24%	White	40%
Mixed	45%	Mixed	30%
		No response	1%

TOTAL:	Black	30 %
	White	32 %
	Mixed	37.5%
	No response	0.5%

2. In your opinion are the Cuban leaders Blacks, whites or of mixed race?

MALI		IVORY COAST	
Black	21%	Black	19%
White	37%	White	62%
Mixed	42%	Mixed	18%
		No response	1%

TOTAL:	Black	20 %
	White	49.5%
	Mixed	30 %
	No response	0.5%

TABLE IV

AFRICAN PERCEPTION OF AFRO-CUBANS

1. Do you think that a black Cuban, because of his African origins, is at home in Africa or do you consider him a foreigner?

MALI		IVORY COAST	
At home	68%	At home	57%
A foreigner	32%	A foreigner	39%
		Undecided	4%

	TOTAL:	At home	62.5%
		A foreigner	35.5%
		Undecided	2 %

2. If you accidentally met a black Cuban, would you invite him to your home, strike up a conversation, or would you keep your distance?

MALI		IVORY COAST	
Invite him	17.3%	Invite him	21 %
Talk with him	23.3%	Talk with him	21 %
Keep a distance	1.4%	Keep a distance	1.3%
Undecided	58 %	Undecided	56 %

	TOTAL:	Invite him	19.5%
		Talk with him	22.2%
		Keep a distance	1.3%
		Undecided	57 %

TABLE V

CUBA AS A PLACE TO VISIT

1. Would you prefer a scholarship to study in the U.S., in Europe, in Cuba, or in the USSR?

MALI		IVORY COAST	
US	35%	US	55%
Europe	21%	Europe	13%
Cuba	29%	Cuba	11%
USSR	15%	USSR	19%
		Undecided	2%

TOTAL:		
	US	45%
	Europe	17%
	Cuba	20%
	USSR	17%
	Undecided	1%

2. If you had the choice of a paid vacation to Cuba, Europe, the US, or the USSR, which country would you like to visit?

MALI		IVORY COAST	
Cuba	48%	Cuba	38%
Europe	19%	Europe	18%
US	24%	US	28%
USSR	9%	USSR	13%
		Undecided	3%

TOTAL:		
	Cuba	43 %
	Europe	18.5%
	US	26 %
	USSR	11 %
	Undecided	1.5%

NOTES

All foreign language translations into English are the author's unless otherwise attributed.

CHAPTER 1

1. Fidel Castro, *Angola girón africain* (Havana: Editorial de Ciencias Sociales, 1976), 26.
2. Robert Scheer and Maurice Zeitlin, eds., *Cuba, An American Tragedy* (Harmondsworth, England: Penguin Books, 1964), 61–62.
3. See Lee Lockwood, *Castro's Cuba, Cuba's Fidel* (New York: Vintage Books, 1969).
4. Carlos Franqui, interviews with author, Montecatini, Italy, 15–17 April 1977.
5. Information provided to author by Jorge I. Domínguez, March 1985.
6. Speech at Central Park, New York City, 24 April 1959, in Fidel Castro, *Pan sin terror* (Havana: Ediciones Movimiento, 1959).
7. Press conference of 22 January 1959, Hotel Riviera, Havana. Transcribed in *Revolución*, 23 January 1959, p. 14.
8. Interview with Etienne Lalou and Igor Barrere, April 1961, in *Fidel Castro parle*, ed. Jacques Grignon-Dumoulin (Paris: Maspero, 1961), 253.
9. Juan Martinez-Alier and Verena Martínez-Alier, *Cuba: Economía y sociedad* (Paris: Ruedo Ibérico, 1972), 69.
10. For a reliable study of early attitudinal responses of the various social sectors of the Cuban people to Castro, see Lloyd A. Free and Hadley Cantrill, *Attitudes of the Cuban People toward the Castro Regime in the Late Spring of 1960* (Princeton, N. J.: Institute for International Social Research, 1960).
11. Lockwood, *Castro's Cuba*, 160, 161.
12. Frank Mankiewicz and Kirby Jones, *With Fidel: A Portrait of Castro and Cuba* (New York: Ballantine Books, 1976), 50.
13. See Fidel Castro's televised speech of 24 June 1960, in *Obra revolucionária* 12, 25 July 1960, p. 20.
14. From Mexican exile, Castro indignantly wrote to the Cuban press in July 1956 to deny Batista's charges that his movement was Communist: "What moral right . . . does *Señor* Batista have to speak of communism when he was the presidential candidate of the Communist party in the elections of 1940, when his electoral slogans hid behind the Hammer and Sickle, when his photographs hung next to those of Blas Roca and Lázaro Peña, and when half-a-dozen of his present ministers and confidential collaborators were prominent members of the Communist party?" (Published in *Bohemia*, 15 July 1956, reprinted in Hugh Thomas, *Cuba, or the Pursuit of Freedom*, [London: Eyre and Spottiswoode, 1971], 887.)
15. Franqui, interviews with author.
16. The initiative was the work of a hard core of independent radicals—Frank País, Carlos Franqui, René Ramos Latour, Faustino Pérez, Enrique Oltusky, Armando Hart, and Félix Pena. Of this group, Pérez, Oltusky, and Hart (whites) became ministers after 1959.

17. Franqui, interviews with author.
18. Rolando E. Bonachea and Nelson Valdés, eds., *Revolutionary Struggle 1947-1958. The Selected Works of Fidel Castro*, vol. 1 (Cambridge, Mass.: M.I.T. Press, 1972), 270. See also *Pensamiento Crítico* 21(1968):207-220.
19. Carlos Franqui, *Diario de la revolución cubana* (Paris: Ruedo Ibérico, 1976), 150.
20. Franqui, interviews with author.
21. Lockwood, *Castro's Cuba*, 23.
22. Contrary to popular legend, Castro had intended a repeat performance of the Moncada assault upon landing in December, 1956. See: Yves Lacoste, "Fidel Castro et la Sierra Maestra," *Hérodote* 1, no. 5 (1977):7-33.
23. Franqui, *Diario*, 189.
24. Leslie Manigat, *Evolution et révolutions. L'Amérique latine au XXème siècle, 1889-1929* (Paris: Editions Richelieu, 1973), 136
25. Franqui, *Diario*, 272-73.
26. Letter to Celia Sanchez, 5 June 1958, reprinted in Franqui, *Diario*, 473.
27. Bonachea and Valdes, *Revolutionary Struggle*, 98-99.
28. Franqui, interviews with author.
29. Carlos Nicot and Vicente Cubillas, "Relatos inéditos sobre la accion revolucionaria del líder Frank País," *Revolución*, 30 July 1963, p. 2. See also Bonachea and Valdés, *Revolutionary Struggle*, 99.
30. Franqui, *Diario*, 287, 288. The term Vilma Espin used, "negrito," translates either to "nigger" or "blackie," depending on the context in which it is employed. In any case, it is derogatory. White Cubans claim it's a term connoting affection! Afro-Cubans, much like black Americans, use "niche" (nigger) among themselves as a term of endearment and intimacy, but would react with violence if it were used by whites. The latter, in turn, do *not* use the Kalo term *niche* or *nichardo* but "negrito" or "negro de mierda" (nigger shit), as a racial insult.
31. Bonachea and Valdés, *Revolutionary Struggle*, 98-99, 100-101.
32. The *foquista* conception found its most elaborate elucidation in Ché Guevara's *Reminiscences of the Revolutionary War* (New York: Monthly Review Press, 1968) and Regis Debray's *Revolution in the Revolution?* (New York: Monthly Review Press, 1967).
33. Edward Gonzalez, *Cuba under Castro: The Limits of Charisma* (Boston: Houghton Mifflin Co., 1974), 93-94.
34. As quoted in Thomas, *Cuba*, 952. "Nuestra razón" was actually drafted by Mario Llerena, MR-26-7 international representative.
35. Carlos Moore, "Le peuple noir a-t-il sa place dans la révolution cubaine?" *Présence africaine* 4, no. 52 (1964):202.
36. "During the armed struggle . . . Batista began to propagate rumors that Castro was intending a 'revolution for whites' . . . with the intention of alienating the black masses from the armed struggle. The rebels were quick to point out that they had a Negro in their midst. The rebels lost no time in comparing Almeida to the black general Antonio Maceo and presenting him as the new Maceo" (Moore, "Le peuple noir," 211-12).
37. Thomas, *Cuba*, 1122.
38. *Revolución*, 5 February 1959, pp. 1, 2.
39. Castro's own accounts agree with Hugh Thomas's assessment that, "At the end of 1958 the rebel army was a heterogeneous group of about 3,000 at most, many of them civilian camp followers." (*Cuba*, 1042).

40. Ernesto Ché Guevara, speech to the *Nuestro Tiempo* cultural society, 27 January 1959, in Grignon-Dumoulin, *Fidel Castro parle*, 67.
41. Gonzalez, *Cuba under Castro*, 48.
42. K. S. Karol, "Where Castro Went Wrong," *New Republic* 7 (August 1970).
43. Gonzalez, *Cuba under Castro*, 52.
44. Extolling the "new men governing the destiny of the Cuban people," he remarked that the Cuban people now had

    [L]eaders who are at their service; leaders who live modestly . . . who work. They see leaders who mingle with the people; who meet with the people; who give their hand to the poor Cuban and to the rich Cuban, to the black Cuban and to the white Cuban alike. Hence, there is created a complete identification between leaders and people, and for the first time there is a genuine democracy, for the first time the people can reach the leader and speak with him on equal terms.

    Statement published in *Revolución*, 10 April 1959, p. 2. Translated in Gonzalez, *Cuba under Castro*, 52.
45. Gonzalez, *Cuba under Castro*, 52, 93–94.
46. Karol, "Where Castro Went Wrong."
47. Gonzalez, *Cuba under Castro*, 93.

CHAPTER 2

1. See Fidel Castro, *Bilan de la révolution cubaine* (Paris: Maspero, 1976), 171.
2. The question of how many Blacks there are in Cuba remains highly controversial. In his only public statement on this subject, however, Fidel Castro reported to foreign journalists in 1966 that *half* of Cuba's population was of African descent. (See *Le Monde* 30–31 January 1966, and *Al Ahram*, Cairo, 29 January 1966.) For a full discussion of Cuban racial demographics, see Appendix 2.
3. Moore, "Le peuple noir," 199. This information is based on the author's conversations with two black Rebel Army soldiers in 1962, and with Agustín Diaz Cartaya, one of the black *moncadistas*.
4. Fidel Castro, press conference on 23 January 1959, transcribed in *Revolución*, 23 January 1959, p. 14.
5. Interviews by J. Hernández Artigas, in "¡Negros no . . . ciudadanos!" *Revolución*, 20 February 1959, p. 16.
6. The insurrection of 1912 was an armed black uprising led by the Partido Independiente de Color. U.S. troops were landed, and the insurrection was crushed after three months of fighting. Thousands of Blacks were summarily executed as suspected sympathizers of the revolt. See Rafaél Fermoselle-López, "Black Politics in Cuba: The Race War of 1912" (Ph.D. diss., The American University, 1972); Serafín Portuondo Linares, *Los independientes de color. História del Partido Independiente de Color* (Havana: Publicaciones del Ministerio de Educación, Dirección de Cultura, 1950).
7. See Juán René Betancourt Bencomo, *El negro, ciudadano del futuro* (Havana: Cardenas y Cia., 1957); idem, *Doctrina negra: La única teoría certera contra la discriminación racial* (Havana: P. Fernández y Cia., 1955).
8. Juán René Betancourt Bencomo, "Fidel Castro y la integración nacional," in "Recuento de la grán mentira comunista," recopilación de la revista *Bohemia* 1, no. 2:36 (Hialeah, Fla: Empresa Recuentos, 1959).

9. See Juán René Betancourt Bencomo, "Castro and the Cuban Negro," *Crisis* 68, no. 5 (1961):270–274.

10. Pena was a young university student in Santiago de Cuba, Oriente Province, when he joined the struggle against Batista in the early 1950s. A close companion and schoolmate of Oriente underground leader Frank País, he had cast his lot with the Castroite movement from the start. To coincide with Castro's *Granma* landing, Pena and País organized several attacks on military posts in Oriente in the hope of sparking a national uprising. Following País's death and the abortive April 1958 general strike, Castro summoned Pena to the Sierra Maestra. (Biographical data on Félix Pena Díaz provided by Carlos Franqui in interviews with the author, Italy.)

11. Thomas, *Cuba*, 1202.

12. Fidel Castro, statement to the press, in *Revolución*, 3 March 1959, p. 15.

13. Charismatic and eloquent, Pena was a national revolutionary figure in his own right, more inclined to regard Castro as an equal than as a redeemer, according to Franqui. Interviews with the author, Italy.

14. Fidel Castro, speech on 22 March 1959, in René Dépestre, "Carta de Cuba sobre el imperialismo de la mala fé," *Por la revolución, por la poesía* (Havana: Instituto del Libro, 1969), 92.

15. Thomas, *Cuba*, 1205.

16. Dépestre, "Carta," 96–97.

17. For a study on the resistance of white Cuban workers to the breakdown of segregation in work places, see Geoffrey E. Fox, "Race and Class in Contemporary Cuba," in *Cuban Communism*, 3d ed., ed. Irving Louis Horowitz (New Brunswick, N.J.: Transaction Books, 1977), 421–442.

18. David Booth, "Cuba, Color, and the Revolution," *Science and Society* 40, no. 2 (1976):156.

19. *Revolución*, 26 March 1959, p. 2.

20. Franqui, interviews with author, Italy.

21. Booth, "Cuba, Color," 169-70. See also Martínez-Alier and Martínez-Alier, *Cuba: Economía*, 25–26.

22. Booth, "Cuba, Color," 157.

23. See Thomas, *Cuba*, 1433; Booth, "Cuba, Color," 169-71; Marin Loney, "Social Control in Cuba," in *Politics and Deviance*, ed. Ian Taylor and Laurie Taylor (Harmondsworth: Penguin, 1973), 50; John Clytus, *Black Man in Red Cuba* (Coral Gables, Fla.: University of Miami Press, 1970), 76; Elizabeth Sutherland, *The Youngest Revolution* (New York: Dial Press, 1969).

24. Antoine G. Petit, *Castro, Débray contre le Marxisme-Léninisme* (Paris: Laffont, 1968), 121–22.

CHAPTER 3

1. Fidel Castro, taped interview with Carlos Franqui, in Franqui, *Diario*, 9.

2. Mankiewicz and Jones, *With Fidel*, 50.

3. In several of his earlier speeches, Castro frequently referred to "Tarzan" comics as having provided his early vision of Africa. However, he told Carlos Franqui that his favorite comic book was "El Gorrión" (Franqui, *Diario*, 14).

4. Thomas, *Cuba*, 805.

5. Castro's only intimate relationship with Blacks during his childhood—three black teachers, two of whom raised him for almost two years, and a black Haitian diplomat who became his godfather accidentally—was revealed by him for the first time in Frei Betto, *Fidel y la Religión: Conversaciones con Frei Betto*, (Havana: Oficina

de Publicaciones del Consejo de Estado, 1985) 108–114. For an interesting dialogue between Fidel Castro and one of the black former field hands of the Manacas estate, see Lockwood, *Castro's Cuba*, 13–14, and *Bohemia* 23(4 June 1965):37.

6. Victor Franco, *The Morning After* (London: Pall Mall Press, 1963), 79.

7. "There at the place where we spent the first years of our childhood, we attended schools where we never had a black schoolmate and we enjoyed riches that we had never sweated for," admitted Raúl Castro in a speech given 7 December 1959 at the Capitolio (*Revolución*, 8 December 1959).

8. Thomas, *Cuba*, 807, 808.

9. Franqui, *Diario*, 16—17.

10. Franqui, interviews with author, Italy.

11. Fidel Castro, interview with Franqui, *Diario*, 9.

12. This conviction pervades Fidel's interviews with Carlos Franqui, *Diario*, 9–28.

13. See Lúis Conte Aguero, *Fidel Castro: Psiquiatría y política* (Mexico City: Editorial Jus, 1968); idem, *Los dos rostros de Fidel Castro* (Mexico City: Editorial Jus, 1960); idem, *Fidel Castro; Vida y Obra* (Havana: Editorial LEX, 1959); Teresa Casuso, *Cuba and Castro* (New York: Random House, 1969); Franqui, *Diario*; Robert Merle, *Moncada, Premier combat de Fidel Castro* (Paris: Laffont, 1965); Gerardo Rodríguez Morejón, *Fidel Castro, Biografía* (Havana: P. Fernández, 1959); Herbert L. Matthews, *Fidel Castro* (New York: Simon and Schuster, 1969); Thomas, *Cuba*, 803–844; Gonzalez, *Cuba under Castro*; Andrés Suárez, *Cuba: Castroism and Communism, 1959-1966* (Cambridge, Mass.: M.I.T. Press, 1967); Ernst Halperin, *Fidel Castro's Road to Power*, vol. 1, *Cuban Politics from Machado to Moncada* (Cambridge, Mass.: Center for International Studies, M.I.T., December 1970).

14. Thomas, *Cuba*, 822.

15. Fidel Castro to Gloria Gaitán de Valencia, *América libre* (Bogotá, Colombia), 22–28 May 1961, in Thomas, *Cuba*, 810–11.

16. Lockwood, *Castro's Cuba*, 81.

17. Gonzalez, *Cuba under Castro*, 81.

18. See also Ramón Eduardo Rúiz, *Cuba: The Making of a Revolution* (Amherst: University of Massachusetts Press, 1968), 158.

19. Thomas, *Cuba*, 825, 1122 (see Thomas's Appendix XI, p. 1546, for a social and ethnic breakdown of the Moncadistas).

20. Juán Almeida Bosque survived Moncada, the *Granma* landing, and the Sierra Maestra guerrilla war to become the chief of the army in 1959. Ever since, he has come to typify the position of the handful of acculturated and docile Blacks whose presence in the higher echelons of leadership is strictly dependent on their unflagging personal loyalty to the Castro brothers. Armando Mestre also survived Moncada, but was later killed during the struggle against Batista. Juán Manuel Ameijeiras died at Moncada. His brothers Gustavo and Angel survived, only to be killed in 1958 while fighting under Castro. A fourth brother, Efigenio Ameijeiras, did not participate in the Moncada assault, but landed with Castro from the *Granma* and fought in the Sierra Maestra campaign. He became chief of the national police in 1959, but was arrested in 1966 under accusations of abuse of power and negligence. In the early 1980s, Ameijeiras was put in charge of building a hospital in honor of his brothers (information to author by Jorge I. Domínguez, March 1985). Agustín Díaz Cartaya composed the *Himno del 26 de julio* (*Hymn of the 26th of July*), which became the anthem of Castro's political movement, just four days before the Moncada assault. Díaz Cartaya was part of the group that attacked the Bayamo barracks as a diversion for the main Moncada attack. He survived Moncada and landed from the *Granma* with Castro, being among those who

were immediately dispersed after the landing. He made his way to Havana and continued fighting with the underground. After Castro's victory he remained in obscurity and, in the mid-1960s, totally disappeared from public view.

21. Agustín Díaz Cartaya, interview with author in Havana, September 1963.

22. See Franqui, *Diario*, 70–71, 79.

23. Thomas, *Cuba*, 1122.

24. Díaz Cartaya, interview with author.

25. Thomas, *Cuba*, 1122. Merle, *Moncada*, 264, 268.

26. See Halperin, *Castro's Road to Power*, 88–91; Gonzalez, *Cuba under Castro*, footnote, p. 83.

27. Thomas, *Cuba*, 851.

28. Charles P. Howard, Sr., "The Afro-Cubans," *Freedomways* 4, no. 3:380.

29. Thomas, *Cuba*, 851. For a full account of Castro's capture, see Merle, *Moncada*, 268–269. Castro's own account appeared in *La Calle* (Havana), 30 May 1955.

30. Merle, *Moncada*, 268.

31. Howard, Sr., "The Afro-Cubans," 380.

32. Information to author from private source inside Cuba.

33. Howard, Sr., "The Afro-Cubans," 380. See also Thomas, *Cuba*, 1073.

34. Information to author from private source inside Cuba.

35. These included Blás Roca, Carlos Rafaél Rodriguez, and Lázaro Peña.

36. See *Daily Worker* (New York), 5 August 1953, p. 3, and 10 August 1953, p. 2, in Scheer and Zeitlin, *Cuba, An American Tragedy*, 126, 127.

37. The top Party leadership then included a good number of Blacks, among them, Blás Roca Calderío, Lázaro Peña, Oscar Pinos Santos, Severo Aguirre, Carlos Olivares, and Salvador García Aguero.

38. Walterio Carbonell, interview with author, Havana, September 1963.

39. An opponent of the Frente at the university, Carbonell reported, was Hispanic Cuban writer Roberto Fernández Retamar, who regarded the organization as "black racist." Retamar became in 1969 the secretary-general of UNEAC, then president of Casa de las Américas in the 1980's.

40. Carbonell, interview with author.

41. Thomas, *Cuba*, 887–88.

42. Carbonell, interview with author.

43. Thomas, *Cuba*, 888.

44. After being expelled from the Cuban Communist party and driven into exile by Batista's police, Carbonell represented the Movimiento 26 de Julio in Europe until 1959. In that year he was appointed by Castro as the first Cuban ambassador to an African country, Tunisia. In 1961 he was stripped of all official attributions after airing his views on the "Negro question" in a book, *Crítica: Cómo surgió la cultural nacional* (Havana: Ediciones Yaka, 1961), which was banned on Castro's orders. He was finally arrested and imprisoned without trial in a labor camp from 1969 to 1975.

45. Scheer and Zeitlin, *Cuba, An American Tragedy*, 58.

46. See Fidel Castro, *La História me Absolverá: Autodefensa del Dr. Fidel Castro Rúz ante el Tribunal de Urgéncia de Santiago de Cuba de Octubre de 1953* (Havana: Delegación del Gobierno, Capitolio Nacional, Sección de Impresos, 1960).

47. See Marta Rojas, *La generación del centenario en el Moncada* (Havana: Ediciones R, 1965).

48. Thomas, *Cuba*, 822, 851, 1121.

49. Franqui, interviews with author, Italy.

50. Maurice Halperin, *The Rise and Decline of Fidel Castro* (Berkeley: University of California Press, 1972), 8. See also Bonachea and Valdes, *Revolutionary Struggle*, 4.

CHAPTER 4

1. Fidel Castro, dialogue with the Bay of Pigs captives (*Playa girón* [Havana: Comisión Nacional del Monumento a los Caidos en Playa Girón, 1961], 456–57).
2. Depestre, "Carta de Cuba," 98.
3. Franqui, interviews with author, Italy.
4. Manuela Semidei, *Les Etats-Unis et la révolution cubaine* (Paris: Presses de la Fondation Nationale des Sciences Politiques, 1968), 57–58. See also Maurice Zeitlin, *Revolutionary Politics and the Cuban Working Class* (New York: Harper & Row, 1970), 285–86.
5. Harold Cruse, *Rebellion or Revolution?* (New York: William Morrow, 1968), 154.
6. Nicolás Guillén, interview with Dennis Sardinha, *The Poetry of Nicolás Guillén* (London: New Beacon Books, 1976), 80.
7. Franco, *The Morning After*, 40, 42, 43.
8. *Revolución*, 13 April 1959, p. 6.
9. Frantz Fanon, *The Wretched of the Earth* (Harmondsworth: Penguin Books, 1967), 112.
10. Franco, *The Morning After*, 68, 69, 70.
11. Calvin C. Hernton, *Sex and Racism* (London: Paladin, 1970, 76–77).
12. Fidel Castro, in Lockwood, *Castro's Cuba*, 172.
13. Nelson Amaro Victoria, "Mass and Class in the Origins of the Cuban Revolution," in *Cuban Communism*, ed. Horowitz, 173.
14. Irving Louis Horowitz, "Authenticity and Autonomy in Cuban Communism," in *Cuban Communism*, ed. Horowitz, 120.
15. Thomas, *Cuba*, 1119, 1120.
16. See Thomas, *Cuba*, 1109, 1119–1120; Robert Freeman Smith, ed., *Background to Revolution: The Development of Modern Cuba* (New York: Alfred Knopf, 1966).
17. Thomas, *Cuba*, 1124–25.
18. José Elias Entralgo, *La liberación étnica cubana* (Havana: Imprenta de la Universidad de la Habana, 1953).
19. José Elias Entralgo, "La mulatización cubana," *CASA* (Havana) 36–37(May-August 1966):76–80.
20. See Salvador García Aguero, "Preséncia africana en la música nacional," *Estúdios Afrocubanos* (Havana) (1937): 114–127.
21. Entralgo was appointed dean of the Faculty of Humanities of the University of Havana in 1960. His son, Armando Entralgo, was appointed Cuba's first ambassador to Ghana in 1963. García Aguero became Cuba's first ambassador to Guinea in 1961.
22. See "Campaña contra la discriminación racial," *Revolución*, 8 April 1959, p. 2.
23. The Sociedades split into "mulatto" and "Black" branches, adopting names that reflected the acculturating mood of Black Cuba's upper crust, "Atenas" (Athens) and "Amantes del Progreso" (Lovers of Progress), among them. Nonetheless, they enjoyed great adherence among the mass of black Cubans as the only recreational and political meeting places available to Blacks before the Revolution.
24. See Betancourt Bencomo, *Doctrina negra*; idem, *Preludios de la libertad. La tragédia del negro y la táctica del partido comunista* (Havana: P. Fernandez, 1950); idem, *El negro*.

25. Howard I. Blutstein et al., *Area Handbook for Cuba* (Washington, D.C.: The American University Foreign Area Studies, 1971), 97.
26. For a summary of the defeated black middle class's grievances against the Castro regime, see Betancourt Bencomo, "Castro and the Cuban Negro," 270–74.
27. As of 1960, the Castro regime imposed a defacto ban on ethnic enumeration in all future census accounts, work force statistics, and population data (see Appendix 2).
28. Fox, "Race and Class," 425.
29. "To the extent to which our own data . . . indicate the relative material insecurity and deprivation of Negro and white workers, it is clear that proportionately more Negroes than white workers were unemployed, received low wages, and had only minimal schooling before the revolution, while fewer of them were able to become skilled workers. Insofar as such systematic disadvantages as these could become politically relevant, then, it might be expected that Negro workers would be more amenable to the appeals of racial agitation and more likely to be revolutionaries than white workers" (Zeitlin, *Revolutionary Politics*, 69–70).
30. Karol, "Where Castro Went Wrong."
31. Zeitlin, *Revolutionary Politics*, 3, 4.
32. Abdias do Nascimento, "Afro-Brazilian Ethnicity and International Policy." Paper presented to the first Congress on Black Cultures in the Américas, Cali, Colombia, 24–28 August 1977. Graciously provided to author by Abdias do Nascimento.
33. Fox, "Race and Class," 439.
34. Blutstein et al., *Area Handbook*, 78.
35. Booth, "Cuba, Color," 150.
36. Zeitlin, *Revolutionary Politics*, 53.
37. Richard R. Fagen, "Revolution: For Internal Consumption Only," in *Cuban Communism*, ed. Horowitz, 188.
38. Horowitz, "Authenticity and Autonomy," 120.
39. Franco, *The Morning After*, 64.
40. Fox, "Race and Class," 422.

CHAPTER 5

1. Fidel Castro, "Conferencia de prensa. Dr. Fidel Castro Ruz, 27 de julio de 1959," 3d ed. (Capitolio Nacional), 38. (brochure)
2. Thomas, *Cuba*, 1227.
3. Quoted in Thomas, *Cuba*, 1244. For the entire text of Matos's letter of resignation to Castro, see Yves Guilbert, *Castro l'Infidel* (Paris: La Table Ronde, 1961), 127–128.
4. Thomas, *Cuba*, 1255–57.
5. Fidel Castro, letter of 14 August 1954, in Franqui, *Diario*, 107. My translation closely follows that of Irving L. Horowitz, ed., *Cuban Communism*, 67–68.
6. Franqui, interviews with author, Italy.
7. Fidel Castro, speech of 26 June 1960, *Revolución*, 27 June 1960.
8. Fidel Castro, speech at the Presidential Palace, 26 October 1959, in *Fidel Castro Speaks*, ed. Martin Kenner and James Petras (Harmondsworth: Penguin Books, 1972), 95.
9. Fidel Castro, speech on 30 November 1959 in Santiago de Cuba, *Revolución*, 1 December 1959, p. 8.
10. Raúl Castro, speech at the Capitolio, 7 December 1959, in Baldomero Alvarez Rios, ed., *Cuba: Revolución e imperialismo* (Havana: Instituto del Libro), 426–27.

11. Ché Guevara, speech at the University of Las Villas, *Revolución*, 31 December 1959, p. 2.
12. Blutstein et al., *Area Handbook*, 79–80.
13. Charles Howard, Sr., interview with author, Havana, July 1963.
14. See *Revolución*, 31 December 1959, p. 1.
15. Semidei, *Les Etats-Unis*, 72.
16. Scheer and Zeitlin, *Cuba, An American Tragedy*, 287.
17. Harold Cruse, *The Crisis of the Negro Intellectual* (New York: William Morrow, 1967), 356.
18. See Leroi Jones, "Cuba libre," *Evergreen Review* (November/December 1960):139-159; Harold Cruse, "Cuba y el negro norteamericano," *Casa de las Américas* (Havana) (August/September 1960):65–67.
19. Robert Williams, *Negroes with Guns* (Chicago: Third World Press, 1973), 69.
20. Joseph North, American Communist party executive, testifying before the Eastland Investigating Committee, in Alvarez Rios, *Cuba: Revolución*, 53.
21. Lester A. Sobel, ed., *Cuba, the U.S., and Russia, 1960–1963* (New York: Facts on File, 1964), 9.
22. See also *New York Times*, 19 June 1960. One of the expelled diplomats, Cuban consul in New York Dr. Plá y Badia, had been the chief liaison between Havana and the FPCC.
23. Julio Medina, interviews with author, Havana, September 1963. Medina apparently received instructions from Piñeiro to recruit elements favorable to the Revolution among American Negroes and intensify propaganda work among them. (My best recollection of Medina's words.) The author was taken by Medina to meet Major Moleón, during the summer of 1960. The latter, whom I met and talked with in his hotel suite near the U.N. building, specified that Castro wanted the mobilization of American Blacks to be a top priority of the movement's U.S. activities.
24. Jaime Suchlicki, *University Students and Revolution in Cuba, 1920–1968* (Coral Gables, Fla.: University of Miami Press, 1969), 87.
25. Rafaél Cepeda, "Fidel Castro y el reino de Diós," *Bohemia*, 17 July 1960, p. 110. As quoted in Richard R. Fagen, "Charismatic Authority and the Leadership of Fidel Castro," *Western Political Quarterly* (June 1965):278.
26. Fidel Castro, speech to coordinators of sugar cane cooperatives, Havana, 11 August 1960, in *Revolución*, 12 August 1960.
27. Sobel, *Cuba, the U.S., and Russia*, 17.
28. Fidel Castro, "Declaración de La Habana," in *De Marti a Castro* (Mexico City: Editorial Grijalbo, 1970), 117, 119, 120.
29. Thomas, *Cuba*, 1227.
30. Cheng Ying-Hsiang, *Idylle sino-cubaine, brouille sino-soviétique* (Paris: Armand Colin/Fondation Nationale des Sciences Politiques, 1973), 44.
31. Franqui, interviews with author, Italy.
32. Mohammed Hassanein Heikal, *Nasser. The Cairo Documents* (London: New English Library, 1972), 311–12.
33. Carlos Franqui could not be altogether affirmative on this score (interviews with author, Italy).
34. Thomas, *Cuba*, 1242.
35. Ché Guevera, televised summary of his Afro-Asian tour, transcribed in *Revolución*, 8 September 1959, p. 18.
36. See Tareq Y. Ismail, *The U.A.R. in Africa. Egypt's Policy under Nasser* (Evanston, Ill.: Northwestern University Press, 1971), 42–50.

37. Guevara, televised summary of Afro-Asian tour, p. 18.
38. Thomas, *Cuba*, 1242.
39. Raúl Roa, speech to the U.N. General Assembly, 24 September 1959, in *Revolución*, 25 September 1959, p. 2.
40. Fidel Castro, speech on 26 October 1959, in Louis Constant, ed., *Fidel Castro. Revolution cubaine*, vol. 1 (Paris: Maspero, 1968), 109.
41. See *Notícias de Hoy*, 24 November 1959, p. 3, quoted in Scheer and Zeitlin, *Cuba, An American Tragedy*, 129.
42. Raúl Roa, note to U.S. ambassador to Havana, 13 November 1959, quoted in Grignon-Dumoulin, ed., *Fidel Castro parle*, 135.
43. Ying-Hsiang, *Idylle sino-cubaine*, 49.
44. Franqui, interviews with author, Italy.
45. Ying-Hsiang has documented this interpretation convincingly (*Idylle sino-cubaine*, 61–91).

CHAPTER 6

1. Franqui, interviews with author, Italy.
2. Walterio Carbonell, interviews with author, Havana, September 1963.
3. Carlos Franqui believes such a meeting "most likely" took place, but could not be affirmative (interviews with author, Italy).
4. See Walterio Carbonell, "A propósito de las causas de la revolución de 1895," *Lunes de Revolución* 37(30 November 1959):12–14.
5. Walterio Carbonell, "Congreso mundial de paises sub-desarrollados," *Revolución*, 5 December 1959, p. 2.
6. Carbonell, interviews with author.
7. Carbonell, "Congreso mundial."
8. Carbonell, interviews with author.
9. Carbonell, "Congreso mundial."
10. Franqui, interviews with author, Italy.
11. Carbonell, interviews with author.
12. For a detailed account of the Congo crisis, see Catherine Hoskyns, *The Congo Since Independence, January 1960-December 1961* (London: Oxford University Press, 1965).
13. See *Revolución*, June-November 1960.
14. "The U.N.'s Intervention Aggravated the Congo Crisis," *Revolución*, 11 September 1960.
15. Franqui, interviews with author, Italy.
16. *Revolución*, 14 September 1960.
17. Franqui, interviews with author, Italy.
18. Julio Medina, interviews with the author, Havana.
19. Franqui, interviews with author, Italy.
20. Author's recollections, confirmed by Franqui, interviews, Italy.
21. Franqui, interviews with author, Italy.
22. See Grignon-Dumoulin, *Fidel Castro parle*, 212.
23. K. S. Karol, *Guerrillas in Power* (New York: Hill & Wang, 1970), 7.
24. Harold R. Isaacs, *The New World of Negro Americans* (New York: Viking Press, 1963), 337.
25. Ronald Segal, *The Race War* (London: Jonathan Cape, 1966), 158.
26. M. Halperin, *Rise and Decline*, 80.

27. Raúl Castro, speech to mass rally in Havana, 19 September 1960, *Revolución*, 20 September 1960, p. 8.
28. Author's recollection.
29. Juán Almeida, conversation with author, Theresa Hotel, Harlem, September 1960.
30. Author's recollection. See also Moore, "Le peuple noir," 212.
31. Juán Almeida told the author that Fidel Castro had suggested he mingle with the crowds. Conversation with author, Theresa Hotel.
32. See *Revolución*, 22 September 1960.
33. In fact, one of the reasons for Castro's visit to New York was to seize the opportunity of personally meeting the Afro-Asian leaders he had been courting since the previous summer. This was primarily to invite them en masse to Havana for an informal Third World summit, either immediately after the Assembly's session, or at some time early in the following year.
34. Franqui, interviews with author, Italy.
35. M. Halperin, *Rise and Decline*, 81.
36. Malcolm X, interview with author, Paris, November 23-24, 1964. See also Malcolm X, *The Autobiography of Malcolm X* (New York: Grove Press, 1966), 73.
37. *Revolución*, 23 September 1960, p. 15.
38. Karol, *Guerrillas*, 7.
39. Author's recollection.
40. I am grateful to the late William Gardner Smith, former director of Ghana's School of Journalism under Kwame Nkrumah, for this interpretation (interviews with author, Paris, October 1970).
41. Heikal, *Nasser*, 311.
42. Karol, *Guerrillas*, 8.
43. M. Halperin, *Rise and Decline*, 42.
44. Fidel Castro, speech to the fifteenth session of the U.N. General Assembly, 26 September 1960. In *Official Records of the General Assembly*, part 1, vol. 1 (New York: United Nations, 1960), 118.
45. Author's recollection.
46. Fidel Castro, speech to fifteenth General Assembly, 133.
47. Karol, "Where Castro Went Wrong.'

CHAPTER 7

1. Fidel Castro, speech at the Presidential Palace, 29 September 1960, in Alvarez Ríos, *Cuba: revolución*, 443.
2. See *Le Monde*, 2–3 October 1960, p. 4.
3. See Sékou Touré, speech to the U.N. General Assembly, 10 October 1960, in *Official Records of the General Assembly*.
4. See *Le Monde*, 11 October 1960, pp. 3, 7.
5. See *Le Monde*, 12 October 1960, p. 2.
6. See *Revolución*, 7 October 1960, p. 1.
7. See also *Le Monde*, 8 October 1960, p. 5, and *Revolución*, 11 October 1960, p. 6.
8. See *Le Monde*, 13 October 1960, p. 8.
9. See *Le Monde*, 16-17 October 1960, p. 3.
10. See *Le Monde*, 22 October 1960, p. 16.
11. Information to author during interviews with black Cubans who witnessed the event, Havana, summer 1962.
12. See *Revolución*, 15 October 1960, p. 15.

13. Author's recollections of a conversation with a worker at the Cuban Ministry of Communications, Havana, summer 1962.
14. In *Revolución*, 14 October 1960, p. 12.
15. See "Africa hoy," *Lunes de revolución* 82, 24 October 1960.
16. Franqui, interviews with author, Italy.
17. Carbonell, interview with author, Havana.
18. Walterio Carbonell, "Africa y Cuba," *Lunes de revolución* 82, no. 24 (October 1960) 5.
19. Carbonell, *Crítica*, 20.
20. See Hélène Carrère d'Encausse, "Problème interne, instrument politique: Pouvoir communiste et Islam en Union Soviétique," *Le Monde Diplomatique* 281(August 1977):12–13. The author is particularly grateful to Professor Carrère d'Encausse for having drawn an analogy between Cuba and the USSR in this regard (interview with author, Paris, March 1978).
21. See Pierre Golendorf, *Sept ans à Cuba* (Paris: Belfond, 1976), 44–45; Jan Knippers Black et al., *Area Handbook for Cuba*, 2d ed. (Washington: Foreign Area Studies, 1976), 102–104; Ronald H. Chilcote and Joel C. Edelstein, eds., *Latin America: The Struggle with Dependency and Beyond* (New York: John Wiley & Sons, 1974), 700–702; Sutherland, *Youngest Revolution*, 62–78, 150–155; Thomas, *Cuba*, 1121, 1432–34; Barry Reckord, *Does Fidel Eat More than Your Father?* (London: Andre Deutsch, 1971), 127–28, 135; Booth, "Cuba, Color," 169–72.
22. See "Creación del Instituto de Etnología y Folklore," *Actas del Folklore* 1(10–12):33–35.
23. See *América Latina* 7, no. 2 (Rio de Janeiro).
24. Franqui, interviews with author, Italy.
25. Jorge I. Domínguez has drawn my attention to the fact that Carlos Franqui pointedly asserts that Castro's taste in all "high culture"—including ballet—is, in fact, non-existent. However, ballet was politically useful, whereas drumming was not (comments to author, 7 May 1985).
26. Franqui, interviews with author.
27. Information to author from Dr. Alfredo Melgar, a Spanish physician who graduated from Havana University medical school, lived in Cuba uninterruptedly from 1960 to 1968, was chief of the Cuban Red Cross for Havana, and part of a group of physicians chosen to join Guevara in Bolivia (interviews with author, Geneva, March 18, 1977).
28. Michel Legré, "Les africains à Cuba," *Jeune Afrique*, 18 January 1978, p. 45.
29. William R. Bascom, "The African Heritage and Its Religious Manifestations," in *Background to Revolution*, ed. Smith, 113.
30. Chilcote and Edelstein, *Latin America*, 656. See, for example, "La Sociedad Secreta Abacuá," *Revista Jurídica Militar*, No. 1 (1969):13–24, and "Santería," *Trabajo Político*, December 1968.
31. See "Declaration by the First National Congress on Education and Culture," *Granma* 19, 9 May 1971 (English weekly summary).
32. Jorge I. Domínguez, conversation with author, 7 March 1985.
33. Information to author by Michel Legré, a journalist from the Ivory Coast who conducted a wide range of taped interviews with Cuban Blacks, particularly religious leaders, during a one-month stay on the island in July-August 1976 (interview with author, Paris, 13 March 1977).
34. Flora Mancuso, "The Theater of the Black Diaspora: A Comparative Study of Black Drama in Brazil, Cuba and in the United States" (Ph.D. diss., New York University, 1975), 108. (Graciously provided to author by Dr. Mancuso.)

35. Black et al., *Area Handbook*, 98, 103.
36. Comments to author, 7 March 1985.
37. Franqui, interviews with author, Italy.

CHAPTER 8

1. Ché Guevara, speech to the first Congress of Latin American Youth, 28 July 1960, in Ché Guevara, *Oeuvres révolutionnaires: 1959-1967*, vol. 2 (Paris: Maspero, 1968), 49.
2. Ché Guevara, "Notas para el estudio de la ideología de la revolución cubana," *Verde olivo*, Havana, 8 October 1960.
3. See Jorge Edwards, *Persona Non Grata*, (London: Bodley Head, 1973), 258.
4. Fidel Castro, televised speech on 17 October 1960, in Grignon-Dumoulin, *Fidel Castro parle*, 229.
5. Raúl Roa, speech to the 909 Plenary Session of the U.N. General Assembly, 31 October 1960, in *Documents officiels de l'Assemblée Générale. Quinzième séssion. Première partie*, vol. 1 (New York, 1960), 833.
6. See *Le Monde*, 1 November 1960, p. 16.
7. See *Le Monde*, 21 October 1960, p. 8.
8. See Ché Guevara's blunt statement to that effect to Scheer and Zeitlin, *Cuba, An American Tragedy*, Appendix 5, 339.
9. See *Le Monde*, 1 November 1960, p. 16.
10. Raúl Roa, speech to the 892 Plenary Session of the U.N. General Assembly, 7 October 1960, in *Documents officiels*, 545.
11. Raúl Roa, speech to the 937 Plenary Session of the U.N. General Assembly, 6 December 1960, in *Documents officiels*, 1239.
12. Uninterruptedly serving as foreign minister from 1959 to the end of 1976, Roa was instrumental in ousting Walterio Carbonell from his Foreign Ministry post. Although Roa was the author of several voluminous works on Cuban history and culture, none reflect the pride in Cuba's Africanity that he spoke of to the General Assembly.
13. See *Security Council Official Records. Sixteenth Year*, (Supplement for January, February and March/April, May and June 1961), New York: United Nations, 1962.
14. See *Documents officiels de l'Assemblée Générale. Quinzième séssion (Seconde Partie). Première commission (comptes rendus analytiques des séances, 21 Mars-21 Avril, 1961)* (New York: United Nations, 1961), 19.
15. Raúl Roa, telegram to the U.N. Security Council president, 13 February 1961, in *Security Council Official Records. Sixteenth Year* (Supplement for January, February and March 1961), 108.
16. Author's recollection.
17. See *Revolución* and *El Mundo*, 13-25 February 1961.
18. For a detailed account of the CIA's preparations for the invasion, see Thomas, *Cuba*, 1300-1311.
19. Author's recollection of events to which he was an eyewitness.
20. Franco, *The Morning After*, 232-233.
21. Fidel Castro, speech to the Rebel Youth Organization, 27 March 1961, in "Nuestro Templo: La Patria. Nuestro Culto: La Justícia" (Havana: Editorial en Marcha, 1961, pamphlet), 15-16.
22. Zbigniew Brzezinski, ed., *Africa and the Communist World* (Stanford: Stanford University, 1963), 32, 33. For a detailed review of Soviet reactions to the Congo crisis, see Christopher Stevens, *The Soviet Union and Black Africa* (London: Macmillan, 1976), 11-19.

23. See *Cuba* (Washington: Department of State Publication 7171, Inter-American Series 66, April 1961), 2–10, 11–19, 19–25, 25–33.
24. Fidel Castro, speech on 16 April 1960, in *Playa girón*, vol. 4, 54.
25. Fidel Castro, "Al pueblo de Cuba," in *Playa girón*, vol. 1, 81, 82.
26. Raúl Roa, speech to the Security Council, 18 April 1961, in *Playa girón*, vol. 3, 220.
27. Author's recollection of events to which he was an eyewitness.
28. See "Cuba—Declaration of Conscience," *The Afro-American*, 22 and 29 April 1961; *New York Post*, 25 April 1961. Among those signing were Ossie Davis, Robert Williams, Harold Cruse, Dr. W. E. B. Du Bois, Leroi Jones, Maya Angelou, Julian Mayfield, William Worthy, Daniel Watts, and John Henrik Clarke.
29. Raúl Roa, speech to the Security Council, 20 April 1961, in *Playa girón*, vol. 3, 320–321.
30. See Williams, *Negroes with Guns*, 109.
31. Author's recollection of events to which he was an eyewitness.
32. Raúl Roa, speech to the Security Council, 20 April 1961, 321.
33. See *Documents officiels de l'Assemblée Générale*, 99–100, 104–105.
34. Akhbar Marof, Guinea's U.N. representative, interview with author, New York, April 1961.
35. Jaja Wachuku, Nigeria's U.N. representative, remarks to the Security Council on April 20, 1961, in *Documents officiels*, 97.
36. M. Ly, Mali's U.N. representative, remarks to the Security Council on 18 April 1961, in *Documents officiels*, 69.
37. Maurice Camara, Guinea's U.N. representative, remarks to the Security Council, 17 April 1961, in *Documents officiels*, 60.
38. Alex Quaison-Sackey, Ghana's U.N. representative, remarks to the Security Council on 20 April 1961, in *Documents officiels*, 86.
39. Thomas, *Cuba*, 1361.
40. Haynes Johnson, *The Bay of Pigs* (New York: Norton, 1964), 184–185.
41. Interviews with author, Havana, summer 1962,
42. M. Halperin, *Rise and Decline*, 111.
43. Johnson, *Bay of Pigs*, 296.
44. Fidel Castro, televised dialogue with prisoners at Havana Sports Palace, 26 April 1961. *Playa girón*, vol. 4, 455–59.
45. The author has heard first-hand reports from Afro-Cuban exiles (especially those who left Cuba as a consequence of the 1980 Mariel boatlift) that the authorities do place specific restrictions on the emigration of Blacks. However, the reference to Fidel Castro tearing up passports of Afro-Cubans came from a rightwing publication. (See "La igualdad racial, otro mito comunista en quiebra," *Frente obrero revolucionário democrático cubano*, [Miami], January 1964, p. 3.) The reliability of this information is, therefore, open to question.
46. Fidel Castro, May Day speech, in Kenner and Petras, *Fidel Castro Speaks*, 122,124.
47. Vilma Espín, speech to the "Latin American Conference on National Sovereignty, Economic Emancipation, and Peace," Mexico, March 1961, in Alvarez Rios, *Cuba: Revolución*, 435.
48. Fidel Castro, speech to the International Union of Students, Havana, June 1961, in Alvarez Ríos, *Cuba: Revolución*, 437.
49. Armando Hart, speech to the World Anti-Illiteracy Seminar, Havana, June 1961, in Alvarez Rios, *Cuba: Revolución*, 435.
50. Fidel Castro, speech on 26 July 1961, in Alvarez Rios, *Cuba: Revolución*, 432.
51. Osvaldo Dorticós Torrado, speech to the Inter-American Economic Conference at Punta del Este (Uruguay), 5–17 August 1961.

52. Information from Malcolm X to author, Paris, 23–24 November 1964.
53. Malcolm X, speech at the Maubert Mutualité, Paris, 24 November 1964, in *Présence Africaine* 26(54):24.
54. Herbert Muhammed toured Cuba in the summer of 1963 as part of a group of black American journalists (author's recollection).
55. Williams, *Negroes with Guns*, 95–98.
56. Fidel Castro, speech at the Chaplin Theatre, Havana, 3 October 1965, in *Fidel Castro* (Havana: Instituto del Libro, 1968), 10, 11.
57. Author's recollection of events to which he was an eyewitness as Williams's personal interpreter from 1961 to 1963.
58. Saverio Tutino, *L'Octobre cubain* (Paris: maspero, 1969).
59. From 1962 to 1963, the author was news broadcaster for Williams's bi-weekly "Radio Free Dixie" programs.
60. For an account of Williams's tribulations in Cuba, see *Le Monde*, 21 July 1966; *The New York Times*, 14 November 1966; *The Philadelphia Tribune*, 10 January 1967; *Los Angeles Free Press*, 17 February 1967, pp. 9, 12. Williams's own account is presented in a sixteen-page "Letter to Fidel" (28 August 1966) and in his monthly newsletter *The Crusader* 8, no. 3:6–8, published in Peking.

CHAPTER 9

1. Gonzalez, *Cuba under Castro*, 125.
2. Ying-Hsiang, *Idylle sino-cubaine*, 136.
3. Jacques Levesque, *L'URSS et la révolution cubaine* (Paris: Presses de la Fondation Nationale des Sciences Politiques, 1976), 52, 53, 55.
4. Edward Crankshaw, ed., *Khrushchev Remembers* (Boston: Little, Brown 1970), 492.
5. Fidel Castro, May Day speech, 1961, in Kenner and Petras, *Fidel Castro Speaks*, 130–31, 132.
6. Fidel Castro in Johnson, *Bay of Pigs*, 178.
7. Fidel Castro in Kenner and Petras, *Fidel Castro Speaks*, 133.
8. Fidel Castro, speech on 26 July 1961. See *Revolución*, 28 July 1961, pp. 6–9.
9. Osvaldo Dorticós Torrado, speech to the first Summit Conference of Non-Aligned States, Belgrade, September 1961, in "Cuba devant le 'Tiers-Monde' " (Paris: Cuban Embassy publication, 1961, brochure).
10. Ying-Hsiang, *Idylle sino-cubaine*, 137.
11. Fidel Castro, speech on 2 December 1961, in Constant, *Fidel Castro*, 194, 195, 210.
12. Ying-Hsiang, *Idylle sino-cubaine*, 152.
13. Fidel Castro, Second Declaration of Havana, in Kenner and Petras, *Fidel Castro Speaks*, 146.
14. See Fidel Castro, "Algunos problemas de los métodos y formas de trabajo de las ORI," *Obra revolucionária* (Havana) 10 (1962):7–32.
15. See Ying-Hsiang, *Idylle sino-cubaine*, 174-77.
16. See Levesque, *L'URSS et la révolution*, 57–59.
17. Author's recollection of conversations with Ebenezer Akuete, Havana, July 1962.
18. The Guinean student contingent was made up of Diallo Macki, Camara Manka, Samura Dantili, Camara Momo, Conde Babu, Cissoko Musa, Ulare Musa, Lamine Kaba, Dabo Bengaly, Ba Souleymane, Abdelaziz Hadiri, Salifou Bangoura, Soumah Ansoumany, Dambuya Dauda, Kante Abduraman, Conde Lancey, Yan Diane, and Alpha Barry. In addition, there were Samuel Kinene (Uganda), Henry Niakairo,

John Muzuka, and Charles Chikerema (Zimbabwe), Jules Ngunza (Zaire), and Paul Ngokane (South Africa).

19. Salifou Bangoura and Abdelaziz Hadiri, interviews with author, Paris 14, March 1977.
20. Author's recollection of conversations between Soumah Naby Issa and Robert Williams, during which author acted as interpreter.
21. Fidel Castro; see *Bohemia*, 7 September 1962, pp. 58–59.
22. Fidel Castro, speech on 28 September 1962, in *Obra revolucionária* 27(1962): 5–12.
23. See Crankshaw, *Khrushchev Remembers*, 493.
24. See Levesque *L'URSS et la révolution*, 58.
25. See Robert M. Slusser, *The Berlin Crisis of 1961* (Baltimore: Johns Hopkins University Press, 1973).
26. On the various aspects of the October missile crisis, see particularly Walter Wells Layson, "The Political and Strategic Aspects of the 1962 Cuban Crisis" (Ph.D. diss., University of Virginia, 1969); Alain Joxe, *Socialisme et crise nucléaire* (Paris: Editions de l'Herne, 1973); Elie Abel, *The Missile Crisis* (Philadelphia and New York: Lippincott, 1966); Herbert S. Dinerstein, *The Making of a Missile Crisis: October 1962* (Baltimore: Johns Hopkins University Press, 1976).
27. See Fidel Castro, interview with *Playboy*, December 1966, pp. 59–64.
28. Joxe, *Socialisme et crise*, 219.
29. Ché Guevara, *Hoy*, 12 July 1960, as quoted in Semidei, *Les Etats-Unis*, 123ff.
30. See Thomas, *Cuba*, 1408, Sobel, *Cuba, the U.S.*, 117–21.
31. Fidel Castro, speech on 23 October 1962, in idem, *Cuba et la crise des Caraibes* (Paris: Maspero, 1963), 54.
32. Author's recollection of events to which he was an eyewitness.
33. Author's recollection of the reaction of the African students to Castro's statement at the time.
34. Author's recollection of conversations after the crisis with Ghana's chargé d'affaires Ebenezer Akuete, Guinean ambassador Seydou Diallo (who replaced Naby Issa after the crisis), and Mami Kouyaté, Guinea's cultural attaché.
35. Stevens, *The Soviet Union and Black Africa*, 23.
36. William Attwood, *The Reds and the Blacks* (New York: Harper & Row, 1967), 109.
37. See Robert F. Kennedy, *Thirteen Days. A Memoir of the Cuban Missile Crisis* (New York: W. Norton, 1969), 122-23.
38. Seydou Diallo, Guinean ambassador to Cuba after the October crisis, conversations with author, Havana, summer 1963.
39. Interview with two of the students, Salifou Bangoura and Abdelaziz Hadiri, Paris 14, March 1977.
40. Fidel Castro, speech welcoming Ahmed Ben Bella on 16 October 1962. See *Revolución* 17 October 1962, p. 2.
41. Andre Glucksmann, *Le discours de la guerre* (Paris: U.G.E., coll. 10–18, 1974), 252.
42. Levesque *L'URSS et la révolution*, 65.
43. Crankshaw, *Khrushchev Remembers*, 500, 504.
44. See *Renmin Ribao* (Peking), 15 December 1962, quoted in Sobel, *Cuba, the U.S.and Russia*, 97–98.
45. See Lockwood, *Castro's Cuba*, 223, 225, 226; Fidel Castro, speech at Havana University, *Revolución* 6 November 1962, p. 1; Thomas, *Cuba*, 1414.
46. Suarez, *Cuba: Castroism*, 183. See also Lockwood, *Castro's Cuba*, 229.
47. Blanca Tórres Ramirez, *Las relaciones cubano-soviéticas (1959-1968)* (Mexico: El Colegio de Mexico, 1969), 54–68; Robert S. Walters, ,'Soviet Economic Aid to

Cuba," in *Fidel Castro's Personal Revolution in Cuba: 1959-1973*, ed. James Nelson Goodsell (New York: Knopf, 1975), 169-73.

48. Levesque, *L'URSS et la révolution*, 107.
49. Tórrez Ramirez, *Las relaciones cubano-soviéticas*, 53-54; Levesque, *L'URSS et la révolution*, 108-110.
50. See Robin Edmonds, *Soviet Foreign Policy 1962-73* (London: Oxford University Press, 1975), 53-62; Hélène Carrère d'Encausse, *La politique soviétique au Moyen Orient, 1955-1975* (Paris: Presses de la Fondation Nationale des Sciences Politiques, 1975), 154-181; Stevens, *The Soviet Union and Black Africa*, 21-27.
51. See Fidel Castro, speech of 15 January 1963, in *Revolución*, 16 January 1963, pp. 1, 8-10.
52. Marta San Martín and Ramón L. Bonachea, "The Military Dimension of the Cuban Revolution," in *Cuban Communism*, ed. Horowitz, 410-411.
53. See U. S. Department of State, *U.S. Policy Toward Cuba* (Washington, D.C., 1964), 2.
54. See Irving L. Horowitz, "The Military Origins of the Cuban Revolution," and "Military Outcomes of the Cuban Revolution" in *Cuban Communism*, ed. Horowitz, 66-102; Fidel Castro speech of 26 July 1963, in *Revolución*, 27 July 1963; Raúl Castro, "Millón y medio de hombres al servicio militar obligatario," *Bohemia*, 15 November 1963, pp. 36-47.
55. See Blutstein et al., *Area Handbook*, 478-480; René Dumont, *Is Cuba Socialist?* (London: Andre Deutsch, 1974), 91-111; Fidel Castro, "Estamos creando las bases para la industrialización," speech on 2 October 1963, *Verde olivo*, 13 October 1963, pp. 4-7.

CHAPTER 10

1. M. Halperin, *Rise and Decline*, 3 (note).
2. Lockwood, *Castro's Cuba*, 358. See also Miles D. Wolpin, *Cuban Foreign Policy and Chilean Politics* (Toronto: Lexington Books, 1972), 43-60.
3. Herbert L. Matthews, *Return to Cuba* (Stanford: Bolivar House, 1964), cited in M. Halperin, *Rise and Decline*, 318.
4. M. Halperin, *Rise and Decline*, 318.
5. Tutino, *L'Octobre cubain*, 291.
6. Irving L. Horowitz, "Cuban Communism," in idem, ed., *Cuban Communism*, 35.
7. Speech of 3 April 1959, in *El Mundo* (Havana), 3 April 1959.
8. Interview in *Revolución*, 23 January 1959, p. 1.
9. Speech of 26 July 1959, in *Revolución*, 27 July 1959.
10. Alvarez Ríos, ed., *Cuba: Revolución*, 102.
11. Oscar Pinos Santos, *História de Cuba, Aspectos fundamentales*, 2d ed. (Havana: Editorial Universitaria, 1963), 340.
12. Speech of 22 February 1963, in *Revolución*, 23 February 1963, pp. 3-5.
13. Speech of 28 September 1963, in *Política Internacional* (Havana) 4, no. 4: 123. (MINREX, 1963).
14. Speech of 19 April 1964, in *Politica Internacional* 2, no. 6 (1964): 110-11.
15. Speech of 15 January 1963, in *Revolución*, 16 January 1963, pp. 1, 8-10.
16. See Claude Julien, "Sept heures avec M. Fidel Castro," *Le Monde*, 22 and 23 March 1963.
17. See Fidel Castro's speeches during his first visit to the USSR, in *Revolución*, 2 May 1963, p. 16; 9 May 1963, pp. 1, 5.

396 Notes to pages 145 to 152

18. Speech of 4 June 1963, in *Obra revolucionária* (Havana) 15 (1963): 9–46.
19. Speech of 27 November 1963, in *Politica Internacional* 1, no. 4 (1963):215. Castro repeated the pledge to harvest 10 million tons by 1970 a few months later in a televised speech (see *Obra revolucionária*, 6 February 1964, p. 6).
20. See "Joint Soviet-Cuban Communique on Stay of Fidel Castro in the Soviet Union," *Current Soviet Documents* (New York), 10 February 1964, pp. 19–26.
21. Speech of 23 January 1964, in *Bohemia* (Havana), 31 January 1964, pp. 44–45.
22. Viriato da Cruz, pro-Chinese former secretary general of the MPLA, later exiled in China, conversations with author, Paris, November, 1965.
23. Levesque, *L'URSS et la révolution cubaine*, 114–15.
24. Tórres Ramirez, *Las relaciones*, 70–71.
25. See "Dans sept ans, l'URSS sera la première puissance du monde," *Le Monde*, 9 November 1963, p. 6.
26. See *I. F. Stone's Weekly*, 10 June 1963, p. 3.
27. See Semidei, *Les Etats-Unis*, 140–50.
28. See also, *Le Monde*, 12–13 May 1963.
29. Semidei, *Les Etats-Unis*, 161.
30. See Arthur Schlesinger, Jr., *A Thousand Days: John F. Kennedy in the White House* (New York: Fawcett World Library, 1967); Attwood, *The Reds and the Blacks*; Semidei, *Les Etats-Unis*, 148–51; Jean Daniel, *L'Aventure du vrai* (Paris: Albin Michel, 1979), 355–60.
31. Semidei, *Les Etats-Unis*, 161.
32. Speech of 25 November 1963, in *Obra revolucionária* 31(November 1963): 6.
33. Semidei, *Les Etats-Unis*, 160–161.
34. Tórres Ramirez, *Las relaciones*, 89–90.
35. Gonzalez, *Cuba under Castro*, 146–150.
36. Edward Gonzalez, "Complexities of Cuban Foreign Policy," *Problems of Communism* (Washington, D. C.) 26, no. 6 (November-December 1977):9.
37. Alvarez Rios, ed., *Cuba: Revolución*, 357.
38. Speech of 1 May 1965, in Alvarez Rios, *Cuba: Revolución*, 367.
39. Ricardo Rojo, *My Friend Ché* (New York: Dial Press, 1968), 136.
40. See Ciro Roberto Bustos, "Account by Ciro Bustos of His Stay with Guevara's Guerrillas in Bolivia," in Jay Mallin, ed., *"Ché" Guevara on Revolution* (New York: Delta Books, 1969), 199–200.
41. See Claude Julien, "Un prototype de révolution contre l'impérialisme économique," *Esprit* (Paris) 4(April 1961): 568–569.
42. A careful analysis of the speeches and declarations of the top leaders of the Castroite regime will show that it was not until 1965 that Havana began projecting itself openly as the prototypical model for the entire Third World.
43. Speech of 2 January 1965, in Christine Glucksmann, ed., *Fidel Castro: Discours de la Révolution* (Paris: Union Générale d'Editions, Col. 10/18, 1966), 239.
44. Speech of 19 April 1965, in *Politica Internacional* 3(10): 186 (1965).
45. Speech of 1 May 1965, in Alvarez Ríos, ed., *Cuba: Revolución*, 355.
46. Speech of 26 July 1965, in *Bohemia*, 30 July 1965, pp. 56–73.
47. Speech of 14 November 1965, in Alvarez Rios, ed., *Cuba: Revolución*, 244.
48. Speech of 26 July 1965, in *Bohemia*, 30 July 1965, pp. 56–73.
49. Raúl Castro, speech of July 1967, in Alvarez Rios, ed., *Cuba: Revolución*, 128.
50. Armando Hart Davalos, speech of 15 May 1965, in Alvarez Rios, ed., *Cuba: Revolución*, 405.

51. Daniel Tretiak, *Cuban Relations with the Communist System: The Politics of a Communist Independent, 1967-1970* (Waltham, Mass.: Advanced Studies Group, Monograph 4, June 1970), 39.

52. Tutino, *L'Octobre cubain*, 306. For a detailed analysis of Havana's relationship with North Korea during this period, see Tretiak, *Cuban Relations*, 41-43.

53. Raúl Valdés Vivó, a member of the old Cuban Communist party since the early 1940s, was ambassador to Cambodia in June 1967. Regarding Havana's relations with the NLF of South Vietnam in the 1965-1970 period, see Tretiak, *Cuban Relations*, 40-41.

54. Heikal, *Nasser*. 318.

55. See G. S. P. Freeman-Grenville, *Chronology of African History* (London: Oxford University Press, 1973), 251.

56. Glucksmann, ed., *Castro: Discours*, 142-43.

57. Kenner and Petras, eds., *Fidel Castro Speaks*, 171.

58. Speech to Afro-Asian Seminar, Algiers, 27 February 1965.

CHAPTER 11

1. Daniel Tretiak, "Cuba and the Soviet Union: The Growing Accommodation," *Orbis* (Philadelphia) 11, no. 2 (1967):443; Thomas, *Cuba*, 1477; Levesque, *L'URSS et la révolution*, 125-27.

2. Levesque, *L'URSS et la révolution*, 126.

3. See "Comunicado de la conferencia de los Partidos Comunistas de America Latina," *Cuba socialista* (Havana) 5(February 1965).

4. Gonzalez, "Complexities," 14.

5. Strobe Talbott, "Curious Contrasts in Communism," *Time International*, 10 November 1975, p. 16.

6. See Claude Krief, "De Gaulle à Moscou," *Nouvel Observateur*, 15 June 1966, p. 12. See also "Nous les blancs," *Révolution* (Paris) 9(May 1964): 4.

7. See "End of the White Race?" *Revolution* 1(4-5): 34 (1963).

8. See Segal, *The Race War*, 313; Thomas P. Melady, *The Revolution of Color* (New York: Hawthorn Books, 1966), 98-100; *New York Times*, 19 December 1963. See also David Burg, "The People's Friendship University," *Problems of Communism*, November-December 1961; Priscilla Johnson, "Apartheid U," *Harper's Magazine*, December 1960.

9. See Robert Levgold, *Soviet Policy in West Africa* (Cambridge, Mass.: Harvard University Press, 1970), 158; *New York Herald Tribune*, 7 February 1963; Attwood, *The Reds and the Blacks*, 120-22.

10. See *Daily Telegraph* (London), 14 February 1963.

11. Segal, *The Race War*, 313. The first African student riots in Moscow took place on 6 March 1965.

12. See also "Czech Racism Seen by Africans," *International Herald Tribune*, 23 May 1965; Levgold, *Soviet Policy*, 262; Robert and Elizabeth Bass, "Eastern Europe," in Brzezinski, ed., *Africa and the Communist World*, 102.

13. Alexander Werth, "Fifty Years After: A Portrait of the Soviet Union in Jubilee Year, 1967," *New Statesman* (London), 29 September 1967, p. 390. See also *U.S. News and World Report*, 1 August 1960; Andrew R. Amar, *A Student in Moscow* (London: Ampersand, Ltd., 1961); Michel Ayih, *Ein Afrikaner in Moskau* (Cologne: Verlag

Wissenschaft und Politik, 1961); Aderogba Ajao, *On the Tiger's Back* (London: Allen & Unwin, 1962).

14. William Gardner Smith, interview with author, Paris, October 1970.

15. For a detailed account of the tribulations of the indigenous black Soviet community, see Svetlana Alliluyeva, *Only One Year* (New York: Harper and Row, 1969), 231–236.

16. Julius Nyerere, conversation with author, Dar es Salaam, 20 July 1964. Professor Abdias do Nascimento of Brazil was present.

17. Dr. Oumar Kane, president of the African Student Association in Romania at the time, interview with author, Paris, February 1977. The Tanzanian's body was found in Lake Herastrau in Bucharest in 1973, exhibiting signs of death by beating, not drowning. Exiled Romanian student Popescu Ion, who knew the victim, corroborated Dr. Kane's version in a conversation with the author, Paris, March 1978.

18. Richard Lowenthal, "The Sino-Soviet Split and its Repercussions in Africa," in Sven Hamrell and Carl Gosta Widstrand, eds., *The Soviet Bloc, China and Africa* (Uppsala: The Scandinavian Institute of African Studies, 1964), 143.

19. See David T. Cattell, "Communism and the African Negro," *Problems of Communism*, September-October 1959; Sergius Yakobson, "Russia and Africa," in Ivo Lederer, ed., *Conference on a Century of Russian Foreign Policy* (New Haven, Conn.: Yale University Press, 1962); Levgold, *Soviet Policy*, 124.

20. Alexander Erlich and Christian R. Sonne, "The Soviet Union: Economic Activity," in Brzezinski, ed., *Africa and Communist World*, 69–70; Levgold, *Soviet Policy*, 124–125, 151 (note).

21. See John Barron, *KGB: The Secret Work of Soviet Secret Agents* (London/New York: Bantam Books, 1974), 61; Levgold, *Soviet Policy*, 125.

22. Segal, *Race War*, 315, 316, 317.

23. Dallin, "The Soviet Union," 34; Levgold, *Soviet Policy*, 124–128.

24. Jan Carew, *Moscow Is not my Mecca* (London: Secker and Warburg, 1964), 81. Countering Soviet charges that Guinean workers were "shiftless" and "lazy" while their leaders were "not to be taken seriously" (*France Soir*, 26 October 1961), Peking praised the "hard-working, intelligent Guinean workers," who "mastered their trades surprisingly quickly," and had thus "exploded the lie spread by those upholders of white supremacy that Guinean workers are lazy and stupid" (*New China News Agency* broadcast in English to Asia and Europe, 15:36 GMT, 27 September 1963, in Levgold, *Soviet Policy*, 151ff).

25. Levgold, *Soviet Policy*, 148.

26. See "Proceedings of the Meeting of Ministers in Preparation of the Second African-Asian Conference, 10–14 April 1964" (Djakarta, mimeograph, p. 41), in Levgold, *Soviet Policy*, 154.

27. Dallin, "The Soviet Union," 43.

28. V. Kudryavtsev, "Problems of Afro-Asian Solidarity," *International Affairs* (Moscow) 5(1963): 55.

29. Lowenthal, "Sino-Soviet Split," 141.

30. Kudryavtsev, "Afro-Asian Solidarity," 52.

31. "Le Président du Conseil Soviétique demande aux jeunes nations de s'opposer a l'impérialisme sans faire de racisme," *Le Monde*, 1 July 1965, p. 1.

32. See *Le Monde*, 20 March 1969, p. 2.

33. K. Ivanov, "Present-day Colonialism: Its Socio-economic Aspects," *International Affairs* (Moscow) 10(1960): 20.

34. Levgold, *Soviet Policy*, 260.

35. See Frank Tucker, *The White Conscience* (New York: Ungar, 1968), 231, 232.
36. Mao Tse-tung, "Statement Supporting the Afro-Americans in their Just Struggle against Racial Discrimination by U.S. Imperialism," *Peking Review* 34(18 August 1967): 6.
37. Eloy G. Merino Brito, "Racial Discrimination and the Policy of Apartheid," *Política Internacional* 2, no. 8 (1964):19–35.
38. These brochures were widely disseminated by Cuban embassies around the world in the mid-1960s. In 1979, the author could still find people in Senegal and Mali who had carefully conserved such propaganda material.
39. *Cuba: Country Free of Segregation* (Havana: Ministerio de Relaciones Exteriores, 1965, brochure).
40. Gardner Smith, interviews with author.
41. As of 1963, that fact had already begun to be denounced by black Cuban intellectuals such as Walterio Carbonell. See Thomas, *Cuba*, 1117, 1121, 1432–1433; Black et al., *Area Handbook for Cuba*, 2d ed.; Moore, "Le peuple noir," 208–211.
42. That may not have been too far off from the minds of Chinese leaders for, a few years later, pro-Peking Marxist theoreticians such as Haitian Communist Antoine Pétit would write: "In Cuba, for example, everybody knows that despite the falsification of official statistics, the crushing majority of the population is of black origin or descent. . . . At the beginning of the revolution, [Castro's] government made it a point to send the greatest possible number of black diplomats to African countries. At present, most of the Cuban advisers and technicians in Congo-Brazzaville are reportedly Black, as if by chance. Yet, it is as difficult to find a Negro in the high spheres of the government as a needle in a haystack" (Pétit, *Castro, Débray*, 115, 116).
43. Raúl Roa García, speech of 15 October 1965 to U.N. General Assembly, in *Política International* 3, no. 11–12 (1965):258.
44. Speech of 26 July 1963, in *Obra Revoluciónaria*, 7 August 1963, pp. 25–26.
45. Speech of 28 September 1963, in *Política Internacional* 1, no. 4 (1963):125
46. Speech of 3 October 1963, in *Obra revolucionária*, 9 October 1963, p. 26.
47. Clytus, *Black Man in Red Cuba*, 24.
48. Speech of 3 January 1964, in *Obra revolucionária*, 9 January 1964, p. 13.
49. Speech of 26 July 1964, in *Bohemia*, 31 July 1964, pp. 40–54.
50. Fidel Castro, in Lockwood, *Castro's Cuba*, page 140.
51. Osvaldo Dorticós Torrado, speech to Second Non-Aligned Summit, Cairo, 8 October 1964, in *Política International* 2, no. 4 (1964):145.
52. *Cuba dans la Deuxième Conférence des Pays Non-Alignés* (Havana: Direction de l'Information [MINREX], 1964), 49.
53. In Maria Cristina Herrera and Leonel Antonio de la Cuesta, eds., *Itinerario ideológico. Antología de Lourdes Casal* (Miami: Instituto de Estudios Cubanos, 1982), 49–51.
54. Dorticós Torrado, speech of 8 October 1964, 148.
55. Osvaldo Dorticós Torrado, speech of 12 October 1964, in *Politica Internacional* 2, no. 8):185–186.
56. See Torres Ramirez, *Las Relaciones cubano-soviéticas*, 110–114; Levesque, *L'URSS et la révolution*, 162–166.

CHAPTER 12

1. See David Ottaway and Marina Ottaway, *Algeria: The Politics of a Socialist Revolution* (Berkeley/Los Angeles: University of California Press, 1970), 2.

2. Znedek Cervenka, *The Organisation of African Unity and Its Charter* (London: C. Hurst, 1968), 12.
3. Ottaway and Ottaway, *Algeria*, 4. For a critical analysis of Algerian socialism, see Gerard Challiand, *L'Algérie est-elle Socialiste?* (Paris: Maspero, 1964).
4. Ottaway and Ottaway, *Algeria*, 156.
5. Ahmed Ben Bella, speech of 4 April 1963, in Ottaway and Ottaway, *Algeria*, 155.
6. M. Halperin, *Rise and Decline*, 185.
7. Ottaway and Ottaway, *Algeria*, 156.
8. See Cercle Taleb-Moumié, *Fidel Castro ou Tshombé? La voie algérienne vers le socialisme* (Paris: Maspero, 1962).
9. Alioune Cissé, Senegalese ambassador to Algeria at the time, interview with author, Nouakchott, December 20, 1978; Tidiani Guissé, Malian ambassador to Algeria from 1962 to 1966, interview with author, Dakar, 14 November 1979.
10. Franqui, interviews with author, Geneva, 17–18 March 1977.
11. Gabriel García Marquez, "Opération Charlotte," *Liberation*, 27 January 1977, p. 10.
12. Franqui, interviews with author.
13. See also Carlos Franqui, "Las prisiones de Ben Bella," *Cambio 16* (Madrid), 5 March 1978, p. 61.
14. Smith, interview with author; Mohammed Abdel Aziz Iss-Hak, counselor on African affairs of the Egyptian foreign ministry and former Egyptian ambassador to the Congo (Kinshasa) during Patrice Lumumba's government, interview with author, Cairo, December 1964.
15. Ismael, *The U.A.R. in Africa*, 72–73.
16. Aziz Iss-Hak, interview with author.
17. Smith, interview with author.
18. See Stevens, *The Soviet Union*, 41–42, 101–110, 112.
19. Smith, interview with author.
20. Ras Makonnen, *Pan-Africanism from Within* (London: Oxford University Press, 1973), 278–279.
21. Orlando Blanco, Cuban charge d'affaires to Morocco from 1961 to 1963 and to Switzerland from 1963 to 1966, interview with author, Geneva, 18 March 1977.
22. *Revolución*, 15 October 1963, p. 1.
23. See *Le Monde*, 17 October 1963, p. 5, for fragments of Ben Bella's declarations.
24. See Ottaway and Ottaway, *Algeria*, 163.
25. Information from a Senegalese trainee, former militant of the PAI and of the Fédération d'Etudiants d'Afrique Noire en France (FEANF), who wished to remain anonymous, interview with author, Dakar, July 1978.
26. M. Halperin, *Rise and Decline*, 275.
27. Franqui, interviews with author.
28. Ottaway and Ottaway, *Algeria*, 166, n. 40. See also, *Le Monde*, 1–3 November 1963.
29. Franqui, interviews with author.
30. M. Halperin, *Rise and Decline*, 277.
31. Speech of 26 July 1965, in *Política Internacional* 3, no. 10: 315.
32. Richard Phillips, U.S. State Department spokesperson, quoted in *Le Monde*, 3–4 November 1963, p. 11.
33. Author's recollection of lengthy conversations with Ali Mahfoudh Mohammed, Salim Ahmed Salim, and Mohammed Ali Foum, Havana, during 1962 and 1963.
34. Author's recollection of events to which he was an eyewitness.

35. A cover organization for the DGI, the ICAP was known to conduct around-the-clock spying on the community of foreign black residents in Havana in the early 1960s. Through ICAP's "guides" and "interpreters," Ramón Calcines and Giraldo Mazola kept a close watch on the opinions and lifestyles of these guests of the Cuban revolution. The latter in turn considered Calcines and Mazola to be among the most anti-African and anti-black of the Cuban officials placed in charge of their affairs. (Mazola was appointed deputy foreign minister in 1985).

36. Author's recollection of events to which he was an eyewitness.

37. Author's recollection of a meeting before the Minister of the Interior, Ramiro Valdés, in which Ramón Calcines and Giraldo Mazola leveled the charge against the three Zanzibaris in the summer of 1962.

38. For an appraisal of the background and materialization of the Zanzibari revolution, see Michael Lofchie, *Zanzibar: Background to Revolution* (Princeton: Princeton University Press, 1965); John Middleton and Jane Campbell, *Zanzibar: Its Society and Its Politics* (London: Oxford University Press, 1965); Keith Kyle, "Coup in Zanzibar," *Africa Report*, February 1964, pp. 18–20; idem, "How It Happened," *The Spectator*, 4 February 1964, pp. 202–203.

39. Of the three, Salim Ahmed Salim has had the most remarkable career. He became Tanzania's permanent U.N. representative and chairman of its decolonization committee in 1970. Concurrently, he was also ambassador to Cuba. In 1979, he was elected president of the annual General Assembly of the U.N. In 1985, he became prime minister of Tanzania. Ali Mahfoudh Mohammed, a colonel in the Tanzanian army, was arrested in 1972 and accused of political murder along with Abdul Rahman Mohammed Babu. Mohammed Foum was deputy foreign minister in 1979.

40. John Okello, *Revolution in Zanzibar* (Nairobi: East African Publishing House, 1967), 176.

41. Hank Chase, "Tanzania's Jailed Left" (London: n.p., 1978, pamphlet), 5.

42. Karamoko Keita, former permanent representative of Mali to the World Federation of Democratic Youth in Bucharest, interview with author, Bamako, Mali, 28 December 1976.

43. Information provided by a former PAI cadre trained in Cuba who wishes to remain anonymous, interview with author, Dakar, July 1978.

44. Anicet Kashamura, former Lumumbist minister of information, interview with author, Paris, March 1977.

45. See Levgold, *Soviet Policy*, 161, 336.

46. Information from anonymous PAI cadre, interview with author; confirmed by Senegalese journalist Ibrahima Signaté, interview with author, Dakar, 14 January 1976.

47. Ibrahima Signaté, interview with author. The author was, however, unable to find evidence of the active participation of these three Cubans in the guerrilla movement.

48. S. Max Madher Malick, "La conféssion d'un membre du P.A.I.," in *L'Unité Africaine* (Dakar), 11 March 1965, p. 5. See also *Dakar-Matin*, 26 June 1965.

49. In an interview with French journalist Claude Julien two weeks after Cuba's forces engaged the Moroccans in battle, Ben Bella denied having requested Havana's military assistance. He claimed that "Cuba was sending a sugar cargo to Algeria. It was Fidel Castro himself who had decided to add tanks and intructors to the cargo. Algiers had made no such request but had accepted" (*Le Monde*, 8 November 1963, p. 1).

CHAPTER 13

1. See Cruse, *Rebellion, or Revolution?*
2. For the full text of the OAAU's program, see George Breitman, *The Last Year of Malcolm X* (New York: Merit Publishers, 1967), 105–124.
3. Malcolm X, conversations with author, Paris, 23–24 November 1964.
4. An act that had further enhanced Entralgo's status with the Accra-based freedom fighters was his marriage soon after taking up his post to a light-skinned black Angolan militant of the MPLA.
5. Malcolm X, conversations with author.
6. Smith, interview with author. The occasion was commemorated in Malcolm X's autobiography, in which he noted, "My final Ghanian social event was a beautiful party in my honor given by His Excellency Mr. Armando Entralgo González, the Cuban Ambassador to Ghana" (Malcolm X, *Autobiography*, 359).
7. Malcolm X, conversations with author.
8. The author was one of those to whom Malcolm X turned to request help in the recruitment of qualified Blacks living in Europe.
9. Malcolm X, conversations with author.
10. From notes taken by the author of his conversations with Malcolm X.
11. Malcolm X, conversations with author.
12. Malcolm X, transcript of taped and filmed interview with the author and Lebert Bethune (filmed by John Taylor), 23 November 1964.
13. Malcolm X, speech at the Audubon Ballroom, Harlem, 29 November 1964, as recounted to the author by Peter Bailey, then editor of the OAAU's newspaper, interview, Paris, 1966.
14. Less than two and a half months after the tumultuous U.N. debates on the Congo, Malcolm X was assassinated in New York in circumstances that directly incriminated the CIA. See Eric Norden, "The Murder of Malcolm X," *The Realist* (New York) 73(February 1967), pp. 1, 4–22; and *Ramparts* (New York), June 1969, p. 32.
15. Ché Guevara, televised interview on "Face the Nation," in *Política Internacional* (Havana) 5, no. 20:167.
16. In George Breitman, ed. *Malcolm X Speaks, Selected Speeches and Statements* (New York: Merit Publishers, 1965), 110.
17. Speech to U.N. General Assembly, 11 December 1964, in Mallin, ed., *Guevara on Revolution*, 114.
18. See *Security Council Official Records. Nineteenth Year* (Supplement for October, November, and December 1964) (New York: United Nations, 1966), 197.
19. Speech to Fifteenth General Assembly of the U.N., 26 September 1960, in *Official Records of the General Assembly*, 133.
20. The data concerning Ché's campaign in the Congo in chapters 13 and 14 are derived from extensive conversations with eight Zairians who are either former members of the CSR or were indirectly associated with the insurrection movement. None agreed to be quoted and requested total anonymity. The author personally interviewed Abdulay Yerodia, Anicet Kashamura, Bula Nyati, Misano Ngoie, Kasmarlot Kassongo, and those who requested anonymity. General Nicolas Olenga's version was obtained from him by a fellow detainee, Alix Balin, while he was detained at Ekafera camp. Although not involved in the events described, Hygin Mulele, son of the former leader of the Kwilu guerrillas, gave important evidence. These sources conflicted with one another on major points and interpretations of events. The author merged concording accounts in reconstructing the events which are recounted in this and the following chapter.

21. Rojo, *My Friend Ché*, 168–169.
22. Tidiane Guisse, former Malian ambassador to Algeria (1962–1966), a close friend of Major Serguera at the time, interview with author, Dakar, 14 November 1979.
23. Ismael, *U.A.R. in Africa*, 220–21.
24. Mandungu Bula Nyati, one of the protagonists of the 1963–1965 Congolese insurrectionary struggle who, in 1974, became foreign minister of Zaire, interview with author, Paris, February 10, 1971.
25. Jonas Savimbi was a fervent admirer of Ché Guevara's guerrilla theses and in a general way fancied himself a "Castro-Guevarist" with Trotskyite proclivities (interview with author, Cairo, July 1964).
26. Seydou Diallo, Guinean ambassador to Cuba from 1963 to 1966, interview with author, Bamako, Mali, December 27, 1976.
27. Ismael, *U.A.R. in Africa*, 43–47.
28. See Ottaway and Ottaway, *Algeria*, 2, 170.
29. See Makonnen, *Pan-Africanism*, 168, 278–279; William Gardner Smith, *L'Amérique Noire* (Paris: Casterman Col. PH, 1972), 76–77, 80–83.
30. Smith, interview with author; Leslie Alexander Lacy, "African Responses to Malcolm X," in Leroi Jones and Larry Neal, eds., *Black Fire* (New York: William Morrow, 1968), 32–38; Leslie Alexander Lacy, "Malcolm X in Ghana," in John Henrik Clarke, ed., *Malcolm X. The Man and His Times* (New York: Macmillan, 1969), 217–225.
31. Smith, interview with author.
32. Ché Guevara, speech in Accra, Ghana, 19 January 1965, in Alvarez Rios, *Cuba: Revolución*, 404.
33. See Kwame Nkrumah, *Challenge of the Congo* (New York: International Publishers, 1969).
34. See *Política Internacional* 5(20): 177 (1967).
35. Smith, interview with author; see also Smith, *L'Amérique*, 143–144.
36. Smith, *L'Amérique*, 144.
37. Smith, interview with author.
38. Stanislas S. Adotevi, Deputy Foreign Minister of Dahomey at the time, interview with author, Dakar, 21 December 1979.
39. Adotevi, interview with author.
40. Adotevi, interview with author.
41. Rojo, *My Friend Ché*, 169.
42. Franqui, "Las prisiones," 61.
43. Letter from Ben Bella to Castro, delivered by Carlos Franqui.
44. Ottaway and Ottaway, *Algeria*, 170.
45. Anicet Kashamura, former minister of information in Lumumba's government and one of the external officials of the Congolese insurgency of 1964–1966, interview with author, Paris, 28 February 1977.
46. *Política Internacional* 5, no. 20 (1967):181, 182.
47. Heikal, *Nasser*, 315.
48. *Política internacional* 5, no. 20 (1967):185.
49. Christophe Gbenye, radio message on 1 November 1964, in Ismael, *U.A.R. in Africa*, 222.
50. Kanza was the U.N. representative of Lumumba's government.
51. Kashamura, interview with author.
52. According to Ricardo Rojo, the agreement for Guevara to assume command of the two Afro-Cuban battalions was reached during his meeting with Soumialot in Cairo on 19 February 1965 (*My Friend Ché*, 170, 171).

53. Heikal, *Nasser*, 315.
54. Kashamura, interview with author.
55. Smith, interview with author; see also Clarke, ed., *Malcolm X*, 114–19, 125–27, 235–67. For CIA connection to the assassination, see Norden, "The Murder of Malcolm X," 1, 4–22.
56. See Breitman, ed., *Malcolm X Speaks*, 156–57, 233–34, 235–36.
57. Estimate based on fragmented reports by some of Malcolm X's former aides and followers. Some of the latter went on to found the clandestine Revolutionary Action Movement (RAM), in 1965.
58. The plan to send these black Americans to the Congo collapsed with Malcolm X's death. For security reasons, presumably, Malcolm had centralized the project to the extent that none involved had but a sketchy idea of how it would materialize.
59. Ché Guevara, *Oeuvres I: Textes militaires* (Paris: Maspero, 1968), 121.
60. Ché Guevara, "Une commune aspiration: La defaite de l'impérialisme, unit Cuba à l'Afrique et à l'Asie" (Havana: Ministère des Affaires Etrangères, Direction de L'Information, n.d., pamphlet), 3.
61. Osmany Cienfuegos is best remembered for having argued for the summary executions of the Afro-Cuban exile prisoners who participated in the Bay of Pigs landing in April 1961 (see Johnson, *The Bay of Pigs*, 184–185).
62. *Révolution africaine* (Algiers), 26 December 1964.
63. Rojo, *My Friend Ché*, 171.

CHAPTER 14

1. See *Etnología y folklore* (Havana) 7, January-June 1969, p. 28. To the author's knowledge, no full text of that talk, which was Guevara's final public appearance, has been published to date.
2. Franqui, interviews with author.
3. *Política Internacional* 5, no. 20 (1967):182.
4. Bustos, "Account," 200. Bustos, an Argentinian, was a personal friend of Ché Guevara. He was a prominent member of the embryonic Argentinian guerrilla movement, and was liaison between Guevara and the Argentine guerrillas. Bustos met with Guevara in his Bolivian hideout in 1967 to discuss coordination plans and Guevara confided to him the great deception he had suffered in Africa.
5. See Bruno Crimi, "L'Afrique et la tentation cubaine,' *Jeune Afrique* (Paris), 16 April 1976, p. 11.
6. According to Carlos Franqui, Guevara's speech in Algiers created serious tension with the USSR (interviews with author).
7. Rojo, *My Friend Ché*, 134.
8. See Jorge I. Dominguez, *Cuba: Order and Revolution* (Cambridge, Mass.:Belknap Press of Harvard University Press, 1978), 383–85, 385–400.
9. Gabriel García Marquez, "En Afrique: Les mois de tenèbres," *Afrique-Asie* 147, p. 55 (31 October–13 November 1977). Castro still refrains from including the Congo in his list of Cuban actions in Africa (see interview in *Playboy*, August 1985).
10. Rojo, *My Friend Ché*, 182.
11. García Marquez, "En Afrique," p. 55.
12. Robert Williams, "Open Letter to Fidel Castro," 28 August 1966 (roneotyped), pp. 6–8, communicated to author by Williams.
13. Roneotyped position paper by the RAM, communicated to the author by its founder, Max Stanford, 1965.

14. See Robert F. Williams, "USA: The Potential of a Minority Revolution," *The Crusader* (Havana) 6 and 7, 1965.
15. Ché Guevara's farewell letter to Fidel Castro, which was undated, was delivered to Castro on 1 April 1965. See Fidel Castro, "Nuestro partido representa la historia reciente de la patria" (Havana: Editor en Colores, 1965, pamphlet), p. 18.
16. Williams, "Open Letter," pp. 1, 5, 15.
17. Robert F. Williams, "Cuba: The Tragedy of No Proletarian Cultural Revolution," *The Crusader Newsletter* (Peking) 8, no. 3 (March 1967):9.
18. Suarez, *Cuba: Castroism*, 224.
19. Edwin Tetlow, *Eye on Cuba* (New York: Harcourt, Brace and World Inc., 1966), 249.
20. Castro, speech of 26 June 1965, in *Política Internacional* 3, no. 10 (1965):314.
21. M. Halperin, *Rise and Decline*, 277-78.
22. See Franqui, "Las prisiones.'
23. Castro, speech of 26 June 1965.
24. Ottaway and Ottaway, *Algeria*, 241.
25. Houari Boumedienne, interview in Egyptian daily *Al-Ahram*, 23 October 1965, in Ottaway and Ottaway, *Algeria*, 241-242.
26. M. Halperin, *Rise and Decline*, 279.
27. Ottaway and Ottaway, *Algeria*, 230.
28. Rojo, *My Friend Ché*, 178.
29. M. Halperin, *Rise and Decline*, 278.
30. See note 1, chapter 4.
31. García Marquez, "En Afrique," 56. According to Anicet Kashamura, Guevara went directly from Havana to Prague, and from there to Cairo (interview with author).
32. This and the preceding information in this paragraph from Anicet Kashamura, interview with author.
33. Kasmarlot Kassongo, at the time minister of justice and the interior of the Cairo-based CSR, interview with author, Lagos, Nigeria, 21-22 September 1979.
34. García Marquez, "En Afrique," 56.
35. Marlene Nadle, "Regis Debray Speaks from Prison," *Ramparts*, 24 August 1968, p. 40.
36. Heikal, *Nasser*, 318, 322.
37. Ché Guevara, "Socialism and Man in Cuba," in Mallin, ed., *Guevara on Revolution*, 128-143.
38. This interpretation is suggested by Guevara's distressed comments to Nasser after having briefly visited the Cuban forces based in the Congo in March 1965 (see Heikal, *Nasser*, 315).
39. See note 20, chapter 13.
40. Kashamura, interview with author.
41. Thomas Kanza, whom the author knew personally during the period of 1960-1961, when he was Lumumba's U.N. representative, joined Gbenye's faction in 1964 but left for London two years later and seems to have played no further role in Congolese politics. See Kanza's *Conflict in the Congo* (London: Penguin Books, 1972).
42. Hygin Mulele, son of Pierre Mulele, interview with author, Paris 8-10 March 1979.
43. Entrenched in the Bandundu region of Kwilu bordering on Congo-Brazzaville, the Mulelist insurrectionary movement was based on the two major ethnic communities of the area: the Babundas and Batendes. Reputed to possess magical powers that made him immune to bullets, Mulele, a Babunda, was a legendary figure. By 1965, he was reported to have had as many as 15,000 guerrillas under his command (Nkrumah, *Challenge of the Congo*, 240).

44. Hygin Mulele, interview with author.
45. Nkrumah, *Challenge of the Congo*, 252.
46. Perhaps as many as 25,000 *simbas* were under Kabila's command in 1965. He had risen through the military hierarchy to become the commander-in-chief of Zone D shortly after the debacle in Stanleyville which ended Gbenye's "Popular Republic of the Congo." Kabila was second only to Soumialot in the Cairo-based CSR, and all of the military leaders of the insurrection at that time, including the legendary general Nicolas Olenga, were under his authority. Based in the Fizi-Baraka region, General Olenga was forced to submit to Kabila's authority and took orders from the latter's powerful deputy, Idelphonse Massengo. Like Kabila, Massengo was a Baluba from Northern Katanga. Kabila was unknown outside the area he commanded. He was not among the "historical figures" who had rubbed shoulders with Lumumba and who thereafter shielded themselves by invoking his memory. Kabila was a member of the new generation, a man from the inside who had risen steadily through the ranks to become a politico-military leader in his own right. Assiduously courted by the Chinese at the time, he was reputed to be a Marxist of Maoist proclivities, like Mulele. From his headquarters in Kigoma, on the eastern bank of Lake Tanganyika, Kabila totally controlled the influx of weapons from China entering Zone D via Dar es Salaam.
47. All my informants agreed on this point, particularly Kassongo, Bula Nyati, Kashamura, and Balin.

CHAPTER 15

1. Bula Nyati, interview with author.
2. Gaston Soumialot, speech to the second CONCP conference, 4 October 1965, in *La lutte de libération nationale dans les colonies portugaises* 2d ed. (Algiers: Information CONCP, 1968), 102.
3. Pablo Rivalta Pérez, speech to CONCP conference, 8 October 1965, in *La lutte.*
4. Liang Keng, speech to CONCP conference, 5 October 1965, in *La lutte de liberation nationale.*
5. Rivalta Pérez, speech, in *La lutte.*
6. See Nkrumah, *Challenge of the Congo*, 286.
7. Ismael, *The U.A.R. in Africa*, 202–203.
8. For a well-documented analysis of Egypt's policy in the Congo from 1960 to 1965, see Ismael, *The U.A.R. in Africa*, 202–210.
9. Nkrumah, *Challenge of the Congo*, 286.
10. Abbas K. Sykes, former Tanzanian ambassador to Canada, France, and the Sudan, interviews with author, Paris 14–18 March 1978.
11. Hygin Mulele, interview with author.
12. The *nom de guerre* that the top Congolese insurgent leadership had given Guevara, "Tatu," which in Swahili means "number two," underscored the ambiguity of Guevara's status. Was he "number two" to Kabila, in whose area he was supposed to operate, or to Soumialot himself?
13. Alix Balin, interview with author; Williams, "Open Letter," 6.
14. Balin, interview with author.
15. Ange Diawara, former political commissar of the army of Congo-Brazzaville, as told to the author by one of Diawara's former aides in Dakar, 2 February 1980. My informant requested anonymity.
16. Williams, "Open Letter," 12.

17. See Fidel Castro, "Siete años de revolución," *Cuba socialista*, February 1966, pp. 2–27.

18. *Pekin information*, June 1965. The statement was signed by "The Observer," which generally indicates a high-ranking official in the Chinese Communist party. For a detailed analysis of China and the AAPSO, see Charles Neuhauser, *Third World Politics: China and the Afro-Asian Peoples Solidarity Organization, 1957–1967* (Cambridge, Mass.: Harvard University East Asian Research Center, 1968, monograph).

19. See Ismael, *U.A.R. in Africa*, 92; Heikal, *Nasser*, chapter on Chou En-lai; Ottaway and Ottaway, *Algeria*, 2, 156–158, 158–162.

20. As quoted by Tutino, *L'Octobre cubain*, 297.

21. Castro, *Nuestro partido*, 19.

22. Within a month of his trip to Cuba, Ben Barka was abducted by Moroccan secret agents, reportedly acting in complicity with French and American intelligence, and assassinated in a villa near Paris.

23. Castro, *Nuestro partido*, 24.

24. Karamoko Keita, interview with author.

25. Fidel Castro, speech of 15 January 1966, in *Granma* (special weekly edition in French), 16 January 1966, p. 2.

26. Castro, speech of 15 January 1966.

27. Two months prior to the tricontinental conference, Captain Cienfuegos had been appointed president of the Foreign Relations Commission of the Central Committee of the new Cuban Communist party, with Major Piñeiro Losada as vice-president. Cienfuegos had therefore come to outrank even the chief of Cuba's intelligence apparatus. As secretary-general of the OSPAAAL, he was directly in charge of all of Cuba's "internationalist" actions in the three continents.

28. Williams, "Open Letter," 6.

29. As told to the author by a high-ranking official of Tanzania's foreign ministry, Dar Es Salaam, in June 1974.

30. Rojo, *My Friend Ché*, 185–186.

31. Kashamura, interview with author.

32. Ange Diawara to one of his European aides (anonymous source).

33. Eldridge Cleaver, "Fidel Castro's African Gambit," *Newsweek* (international edition), 3 May 1976, p. 13.

34. Diawara to one of his European aides (anonymous source).

35. "Eldridge Cleaver," interview by Curtice Taylor in *Rolling Stone*, 11 September 1975, p. 44.

36. Acosta remained in the Congo until 1969, when he returned to Havana and joined the foreign ministry.

37. Diawara to one of his European aides (anonymous source).

38. Cleaver, "Castro's Gambit," 13.

39. Rojo, *My Friend Ché*, 185.

40. Cleaver, "Castro's Gambit," 13.

41. Kashamura, interview with author.

42. Hygin Mulele contests this opinion, however. He contends that his father was unaware of the efforts being made by Guevara and Diawara to make contact with him (interview with author).

43. Bula Nyati, interview with author.

44. Rojo, *My Friend Ché*, 185–186.

45. See García Marquez, "En Afrique," 55.

46. Rojo, *My Friend Ché*, 185.
47. Diawara to an European aide (anonymous source).
48. Rojo, *My Friend Ché*, 186.
49. Ange Diawara to Eldridge Cleaver, recounted in Cleaver, "Castro's Gambit," 13.
50. Rojo, *My Friend Che*, 186.
51. Ibrahima Signaté, interview with author, Dakar, 14 January 1977. Signaté's statement was based on extensive discussions he had with Franklyn Alleyne, first secretary of Cuba's embassy in France, in January 1976.
52. Fidel Castro to Agostinho Neto during their first meeting in Havana in 1966, reported to the author by former MPLA envoy to Nigeria Joaquim de Lemus, interview with author, Lagos, October 1975.
53. Anicet Kashamura, interview with author, Paris, 28 February 1977.
54. Abdulay Yerodia, interview with author, Paris, 16 March 1983. Yerodia was a prominent member of the CSR.
55. Mario de Andrade, interview with author, Paris, 18 October 1983.
56. Yerodia, interview with author.
57. Bustos, "Account," 200.
58. Juán Vives, one of the few whites to have participated in "Operation Congo," gave his own version after defecting to the West in 1980:

    The experiment was doomed to absolute failure from the very start since the ideological conditions were not ripe. Ché's very presence in Africa was in itself a mistake. The population did not accept whites. Plus African leaders were somewhat leery about the nature of the role we were playing in the Congo. Despite the fact that Ché did his best not to appear as the boss and that all public relations matters were left in the hands of Major Draque—a man as black as a crow—everything still went wrong (Juán Vives, *Les maitres de Cuba* [Paris: Laffont, 1981], 338–339).
59. Ché Guevara to Anicet Kashamura, during a meeting reportedly held in the Paris home of volcanologist Haroun Tazieff, a personal friend of Guevara. Kashamura to the author, interviews.
60. Ché Guevara to Juán Vives, in Vives, *Les maitres*, 97. This statement is quoted with reservations, however.
61. Ché Guevara, "Message à la Tricontinental," *Oeuvres III: Textes Politiques* (Paris: Maspero, 1977), 303–305.
62. Mallin, ed., *Guevara on Revolution*, 44.
63. Nadle, "Debray Speaks," 41. Debray was one of Guevara's confidants.
64. Kashamura, interviews with author.
65. See Mario da Souza Clington, *Angola libre!* (Paris: Gallimard, 1976).
66. Fidel Castro employed the term "Latin-African" for the first time in public in April 1976 in order to justify Cuba's massive military intervention in Angola.
67. Jorge I. Domínguez provided the information that the Cuban troop level in the Congo was one thousand men in 1968.
68. Onesimo Silveira, former representative of the PAIGC in Europe, interview with author, Dakar, August 14, 1976.
69. Castro Lopo, MPLA military officer trained in North Korea, interview with author, Paris, January 3, 1974. See also Crimi, "La tentation," 12.
70. See García Marquez, "Operation Charlotte," 11.
71. See *Tricontinental* 1, July-August 1966, pp. 63–70.
72. Kashamura, interview with author. In a conversation with the author, Mario de Andrade confirmed that Agostinho Neto had met with the authorities of Congo-

Leopoldville, seeking an agreement that would give the MPLA passage into Angola. Paris, October 18, 1983.
73. H. Mulele, interview with author. Yerodia sustains exactly the opposite, interview with author.
74. Kashamura, interviews with author.
75. See *International Herald Tribune*, 3 October 1968, p. 5, and 9–10 October, 1968; *Le Monde*, 9 October 1968.
76. Teófilo Acosta, "Pierre Mulele: Un traître qui fit confiance a d'autres traîtres," *Granma* (weekly edition in French), 7 October 1968. Yerodia believes that such a vengeful statement must have had a connection to the "Mitudidi affair." Mitudidi, one of Kabila's right-hand men, was sent over to the Mulele-dominated Kwilu area. His mission was to convince Mulele that a link-up between both guerrilla forces, with Cuban backing, was the only way to seize power. Mitudidi, a military man, was supposed to have remained in Kwilu as a representative of Kabila's forces, and as a symbolic second-in-command to Mulele. After a series of heated disagreements, Mulele ordered Mitudidi's execution. This jeopardized Cuba's plans to bring both wings of the Congolese insurgent movement under its control. Mulele, who was pro-Chinese, had mistrusted Guevara and Cuba's plans from the outset and never endorsed them (Yerodia, interview with author).

CHAPTER 16

1. Radio Havana overseas broadcasts, monitored in Africa, reportedly made several references to Cuba being a sort of overseas African state throughout the month of January 1966.
2. Fidel Castro, press conference, 28 January 1966 (see *Al-Ahram*, 29 January 1966; and "M. Fidel Castro souhaiterait que Cuba entre à l'O.A.U.," *Le Monde*, 30–31 January 1966, p.3).
3. Amilcar Cabral, "Decidés à resister," *Tricontinental* 8(1968): 125.
4. Amilcar Cabral, *Unité et lutte 1: L'Armée de la théorie* (Paris: Maspero, 1975), 284.
5. Felicité Tchibindat, former member of the Groupes d'Etudes Revolutionnaires, interview with author, Paris, 10 April 1981.
6. Vincent Ricardou, former French technical assistant to the Congolese government and personal friend of Ambassador García and Ange Diawara, head of the Militia, interview with author, Dakar, 5 June 1979.
7. Tchibindat, interview with author.
8. Ricardou, interview with author.
9. See Clytus, *Black Man in Red Cuba*, 42, 152.
10. See Jose Luciano Franco, "Preséncia de Africa en America," *Tricontinental* 14(1969): 47.
11. Clytus, *Black Man in Red Cuba*, 42, 152.
12. Silveira, interview with author.
13. Bruce D. Larkin, *China and Africa* (Uppsala: The Scandinavian Institute of African Studies, 1964), 206.
14. Williams, "Open Letter'; see also Tom McGrath, "Robert Williams: Racism in Cuba?" *Los Angeles Free Press*, 17 February 1967, p. 9.
15. See Williams, "Cuba: The Tragedy," 8.
16. Robert Williams, speech at the "Clínica la Inmaculada," Havana, 18 June 1962, in *El Mundo*, 19 June 1962, p. 3. The author was Williams's interpreter on that occasion.

17. Tretiak, *Cuban Relations*, 31.
18. See Robert Carl Cohen, *Black Crusader: A Biography of Robert Franklin Williams* (Secaucus, N.J.: Lyle Stuart, 1972), 289, 290.
19. *Granma*, 20 August 1967, p. 2.
20. Alvarez Rios, ed., *Cuba: Revolución*, 435.
21. C. L. Sulzberger, "Race and Revolution," *International Herald Tribune*, 20 September 1967, p. 5.
22. See Clytus, *Black Man in Red Cuba*, 24, 55–56.
23. *Granma*, 20 August 1967, p. 3.
24. Edmundo Desnoes, "El movimiento negro en los Estados Unidos," *Granma*, 31 December 1967, p. 10.
25. Juana Carrásco, "Plus que jamais, l'unité doit se renforcer," *Granma* (French weekly), 24 August 1969.
26. Alberto Pedro, "Poder negro," *CASA* (Havana) 53(March-April 1969): 137.
27. Reinaldo Barroso was part of the group of Afro-Cubans who set up "Afro-Cuban Study Groups" and encouraged natural hair styles among Blacks until his arrest in 1974. He was subsequently allowed to leave for France, where he took up residence as a refugee (interview with author, Paris, May 5, 1981).
28. *Granma*, 20 August 1967, p. 2.
29. Robert Williams, letter to Max Stanford, founder of RAM, August 1967.
30. *Granma*, 20 August 1967, p. 2.
31. Stokely Carmichael, interview with author, Paris, September 1967.
32. Rap Brown to Oriana Fallaci, in *Le Nouvel Observateur* 148(11–17 September 1967).
33. Stokely Carmichael, "A Declaration of War." Speech at the Oakland auditorium (California), 17 February 1968 (brochure), pp. 19–20.
34. Stokely Carmichael, interview with author.
35. See Lee Lockwood, *Conversations with Eldridge Cleaver* (New York: McGraw-Hill, 1970), 19.
36. Eldridge Cleaver, *Soul on Fire* (Waco, Texas: Word Books, 1978), 143–144.

CHAPTER 17

1. Quoted in Adolfo Gilly, "A Conference without Glory and without Program," *Monthly Review* 17, no. 11 (April 1966):26.
2. See, for example, Gonzalez, "Complexities of Cuban Foreign Policy," 1–15.
3. See Fidel Castro, *Le gouvernement chinois a trahi la bonne foi du peuple cubain* (Havana: N.p., 6 February 1966, pamphlet).
4. Leo Huberman and Paul Sweezy, "The Tricontinental and After," *Monthly Review*, 17, no. 11 (April 1966):9.
5. *Granma*, 15 March 1966, p. 3.
6. Levesque, *L'URSS et la Revolution*, 139.
7. Lockwood, *Castro's Cuba*, 355, note.
8. René Dumont relates that, during a private discussion with Fidel Castro, the latter unwarrantedly referred to the Japanese in derogatory terms—as "*couillons*" (assholes)—and did not think highly of them (See Rene Dumont, "Il y a deux Fidel Castro," *L'Exprèss*, 20–26 July 1970, p. 28). Dumont explains elsewhere that, "Castro's disdain for the Japanese may perhaps be a more or less conscious survival of a racism we all have trouble doing away with" (René Dumont, *Cuba est-il Socialiste?* [Paris: Seuil, 1972], 162).

9. Carlos Franqui, interviews with author.

10. Chin Ming Huan, *Sinhua*'s permanent correspondent in Havana, confided to the author as early as 1963 that his diplomatic compatriots were convinced of Fidel Castro's resentment toward them due to race. Three years later, as the Sino-Cuban feud broke into the open, Mai Feng, first secretary of the Chinese embassy in Paris, repeatedly used the term "racist" to characterize Castro's attacks on his country (interview with author, Paris, October 1966).

11. Author's recollection of informal meetings in Havana with Chinese *Sinhua* correspondents and young Afro-Cuban sympathizers held in private apartments in the early 1960s.

12. *Time*, 10 July 1978, p. 10.

13. Walterio Carbonell, like many other Afro-Cubans, sided with China out of a feeling that a racist USSR was attempting to bully a colored country. Pro-Chinese sentiments in Africa during the same period arose from similar considerations. See Larkin, *China and Africa*, 206.

14. Tom McGrath, "Robert Williams," 9; see also Tretiak, *Cuban Relations*, 31.

15. Williams, "Cuba: The Tragedy," 7–8.

16. See *The Crusader* 8, no. 4 (April-May 1966). A copy of this forgery was sent to the author from Peking by Robert Williams. It contains articles entitled, "Cuba Betrays the Cuban Revolution," "Hypocritical Actions of the People's Republic of China," "Chinese Contempt for Small Nations," "Chinese Distribute Anti-Cuban Propaganda in Cuba," "World-Wide Chinese Slander Campaign Against Cuba," "Chinese Blackmail and Strangle Small Nations," and appropriate eulogies for "Cuba Today."

17. *The Crusader* 8, no. 4.

18. Robert Williams, "Crusader Forged Again," 20 May 1967 (Peking, press release).

19. See Stephen Clissold, *Soviet Relations with Latin America, 1918–68* (London, New York: Oxford University Press, 1970), 3–65.

20. *Bohemia*, 23 December 1966.

21. Franqui, interviews with author.

22. Kenner and Petras, eds., *Fidel Castro Speaks*, 224.

23. See Vives, *Les Maîtres*, 341; see also "Seis años de agresión" (Caracas: Ministerio de Relaciones Exteriores de Venezuela, Imprenta Nacional, 1966, document).

24. Kenner and Petras, eds., *Fidel Castro Speaks*, 181, 187, 215, 218, 231, 233.

25. Fidel Castro, speech of 1 January 1967; see "Les Européens ont beaucoup a gagner dans les révolutions latino-américaines," *Le Monde*, 4 January 1967, p. 4.

26. Kenner and Petras, eds., *Fidel Castro Speaks*, 235.

27. Fidel Castro, speech of 28 September 1967, in *Ediciones OR* 22, p. 33. Castro evidently knew that Trinidad and Tobago was no more a "British colony" than Mexico was a Spanish one. The antipathy that Castro created so gratuitously worked greatly to Cuba's detriment during the Angolan civil war, when Eric Williams retracted an agreement to allow Cuban aircraft to refuel at Piarco airport in Trinidad.

28. Kenner and Petras, eds., *Fidel Castro Speaks*, 218.

29. *Granma*, 20 April 1967, p. 7.

30. See Tutino, *L'Octobre cubain*, 308.

31. *Política Internacional* 4(15): 131, 132 (1966).

32. Fidel Castro, in Alvarez Rios, *Cuba: Revolución*, 249.

33. Armando Hart Dávalos, in Alvarez Rios, *Cuba: Revolución*, 270.

34. See Debray, *Révolution dans la Révolution?*.

35. Gerard Challiand, *Mythes révolutionnaires du Tièrs Monde* (Paris: Seuil, 1976), 67, 80.
36. See Rojo, *My Friend Ché*, 191–193.
37. Castro, speech of 18 October 1967, in Kenner and Petras, eds., *Fidel Castro Speaks*, 249.
38. Castro, speech of 13 March 1968, in Kenner and Petras, eds., *Fidel Castro Speaks*, 352, 353.
39. Castro, speech of 26 July 1968, in Kenner and Petras, eds., *Fidel Castro Speaks*, 280–281.
40. Castro, speech of 19 April 1968, in Kenner and Petras, eds., *Fidel Castro Speaks*, 261.
41. *Granma*, 21 April 1968.
42. On the dispute between Ché Guevara and Bolivia's Communist party leader, Mario Monje, See Mallin, ed., *Guevara on Revolution*, 161–184.
43. See Hélène Carrère d'Encausse, *La politique sovietique au Moyen-Orient, 1955-1975* (Paris: Presses de la Fondation Nationale des Sciences Politiques, 1975).
44. Andre Fontaine, *Un seul lit pour deux rêves* (Paris: Fayard, 1981), 114.
45. Vives, *Les Maîtres*, 179.
46. *Granma*, 27 July 1967.
47. See *Le Monde*, 30 December 1967; Daniel Tretiak, "Cuba's Integration into the Communist System," in J. F. Triska, ed., *The World Communist System: International and Comparative Studies* (New York: Bobbs-Merrill, 1960), 17–20.
48. See "Castro Edict Gas Rationing Cooling Anniversary Ardor," *International Herald Tribune*, 6 January 1968.
49. Goure, "Cuba's Military."
50. See *Informe del Comité Central del Partido Comunista de Cuba sobre las actividades de la microfracción* (Havana: Instituto del Libro, 1968).
51. See "Informe del Comandante Raúl Castro ante el Comité Central del Partido," *Granma*, 11 February 1968.
52. "Moscou pourrait reviser ses accords avec La Havane," *Le Monde*, 31 January 1968, p. 3.
53. See "The Meeting of the Central Committee," *Granma*, 4 February 1968, p. 1; see also Tretiak, "Cuba's Integration," 6.
54. See "Des entrétiens secrèts américano-cubains auraient lieu à Mexico," *Le Monde*, 6 August 1968.
55. Fidel Castro, speech of 14 November 1965, in Alvarez Rios, *Cuba: Revolución*, 242.
56. Raúl Castro, speech of 23 May 1966, in Alvarez Rios, *Cuba: Revolución*, 327.
57. *Granma*, 24 August 1968, p. 2.
58. See Tretiak, "Cuba's Integration," 6.
59. See Tretiak, "Cuba's Integration," 6; Vives, *Les Maîtres*, 217–218. The author fully agrees with this view.
60. See "La réforme agraire péruvienne est la plus radicale de toute l'Amérique latine," *Le Monde*, 29–30 June 1969.
61. See Charles Van Hecke, "Virage à droite au Pérou?" *Le Monde*, 7–8 October 1976, p. 7.
62. *Le Monde*, 4 December 1971.
63. See "Cuba Tones Down Overseas Radio," *New York Times*, 24 August 1969, p. 26.
64. Author's recollection of a statement to the press made by Douglas Bravo in those terms. See also Challiand, *Mythes révolutionnaires*, 66–93; Horowitz, ed., *Cuban Communism*, 65. M. Halperin, *Rise and Decline*, 279.

66. K. S. Karol, "The Reckoning: Cuba and the USSR," in Horowitz, ed., *Cuban Communism*, 514.

67. For an idea of the alarming events provoked by the Sino-Soviet military confrontation, see Neville Maxwell, "Le conflit frontalier entre Moscou et Pékin," *Le Monde Diplomatique*, March 1974, p. 5; K. S. Karol, "Nixon et son Judas," *Nouvel Observateur*, 25 February-5 March 1978, p. 43; *Le Monde*, 4, 5, 13, 18 March 1969, 11 April 1969, 13 May 1969, 10 July 1969, 29-31 August 1969, 18 September 1969, 10 December 1969; Andre Fontaine, "Great Temptation," *Survival* 11, no. 11 (November 1969):351; Roderick MacFarquar, "Brinkmanship," *Survival* 11, no. 11:353-355.

68. Karol, "The Reckoning," 531.

69. Carlos Rafaél Rodríguez, quoted in Karol, "The Reckoning," 512. For the entire speech, see Carlos Rafaél Rodríguez, speech to the Conference of Communist and Workers Parties in Moscow, *Política Internacional* 7, no. 25 (1969).

70. Maxwell, "Le conflit frontalier," 5.

71. *Granma*, 5 January 1968. Dorticós Torrado committed suicide in July 1983.

CHAPTER 18

1. See Gilles Martinet, *Les cinq communismes* (Paris: Seuil, 1971), 229.

2. Goure, "Cuba's Military," 73.

3. *Granma* (weekly in French), 3 May 1970.

4. *Ediciones COR*, 24-25.

5. See Vives, *Les Maîtres*, 212-215. Neither Cuba, the U.S., or the USSR have commented on these revelations. Both Edward Gonzalez and Jorge I. Domínguez disbelieve Vives's account (note to author).

6. Domínguez to author.

7. See *Pravda*, 7 July 1969, quoted in Joxe, *Socialisme*, 538).

8. See "L'Union Soviétique pourrait posseder en 1969 d'avantage de missiles nucléaires que les Etats-Unis," *Le Monde*, 12 April 1969.

9. Domínguez to author.

10. Curt Casteyger, "Political and Strategic Implications of Soviet Naval Presence in the Caribbean," in Thebergue, ed., *Soviet Seapower*, 60-61.

11. See Casteyger, "Political and Strategic Implications," 63, and *International Herald Tribune*, 9-10 January 1971.

12. See Ismael, *U.A.R. and Africa*, 93.

13. Nikita Khrushchev, *Nikita Khrushchev Remembers* (London: Andre Deutsch, 1971), 432.

14. Barron, *KGB*, 61. For example, KGB defector Vladimir N. Sakharov described an angry outburst by his station's superior in Egypt—Viktor Birunov, officially the vice-consul—at learning that a Soviet woman had been molested by an Egyptian: " 'You fool! What do you expect me to do?,'" Birunov snapped. 'The Arabs are subhuman and act like animals. You are supposed to be civilized and have sense enough to know that. I have told you not to go to the marketplace at night. You are to blame, not the animal. . . . The Egyptians are Arabs, and the Arabs are all just like niggers,' he declared. 'Subhuman, all of them. I tell you, though, sometimes I don't know who are worse, the subhuman or our stupid women.' The word Sbirunov actually used was the plural of '*chernozphy*,' the term by which Russians popularly refer to black people of all nationalities. Literally translated, it means 'black ass' " (ibid.).

15. See Madan Sauldie, "Moscow's New Hopes in Africa," *Africa* (London) 66(February 1977): 61–63.
16. However, Africa has attracted Russia's strategic attention since the Czarist epoch, as demonstrated by Edward T. Wilson, *Russia and Black Africa Before World War II* (New York and London: Holmes and Meir Publishers, 1974).
17. See Philipe Leymarie, *Océan Indien. Le nouveau coêur dµ monde* (Paris: Karthala, 1981).
18. Marcelino dos Santos, "Une guerre internationale,' *Tricontinental* (Havana), March-April 1971, p. 9.
19. See "The Mineral Crisis," *International Herald Tribune*, 10 November 1980, p. 53.
20. "Visite d'une escadre soviétique à Lagos," *Le Monde*, 6–7 March 1969.
21. See Jean-Claude Guillebaud, "Orages sur la mer rouge,' *Le Monde*, 23 June 1977, p. 5.
22. Babacar Fall, "La croisade cubaine," *Africa* 12 (1978):41.
23. See *Voix d'Afrique* (Abidjan) 23 (6 September–3 October 1976), p. 13; *Jowol Jemma* (Dakar-Abidjan) 17 (October–November 1976); Garcia Marquez, "Opération Charlotte," 10.
24. Ibrahima Kaké, interview with author, Paris, 13 January 1984.
25. Capt. Bayo and Ibrahima Kaké agree on the total absence of any treaty or document whatsoever between Guinea and foreign states throughout the twenty-six-year, iron-fisted rule of Sékou Touré (interviews with author). Touré, nicknamed "Sylli" (elephant), is reputed to have had a prodigious memory to which, out of fear of betrayal, he is said to have consigned all sensitive affairs of state. Personal notes and documents kept in his possession are rumored to now be in a sealed chest in the custody of his close friend, King Hassan II of Morocco.
26. See D. L. Price, "Setbacks for the USSR in the Middle East," *Soviet Analyst* 5(22): 2–3 (28 October 1976).
27. See *Granma* (daily, in Spanish), 3–10 May 1972. Rudy Casals, "Fidel Castro donne ses premieres impréssions sur la Guinée," *Granma* (French weekly), 14 May 1972, p. 3.
28. Fidel Castro, "Interview du Commandant Fidel Castro à l'aéroport," *Granma* (French weekly), 14 May 1972, p. 3.
29. Mami Kouyaté to the author (interview Rome, 29 January 1985). Kouyaté was a faithful insider of Touré's regime until the latter's sudden death in 1984. He occupied a succession of sensitive posts (ambassador to Cuba, political adviser to Touré, ambassador to Angola, among others). When we spoke, he had just arrived in Rome as ambassador to the new military regime, a sharp demotion from his previous posts. Álthough he recounted in detail the events he witnessed during Castro's visit—as presidential aide and translator for both heads of state—he refused to describe the role played by any other Guinean official on that occasion.
30. Rudy Casals, "Huit heures à bord de l'IL-62 qui a conduit Fidel de la Havane à Conakry," *Granma*, 14 May 1972.
31. Fidel Castro, "Discurso en el estadio '28 de septiembre,' " 3 May 1972, in *El futuro es el internacionalismo. Recorrido del Comandante Fidel Castro por países de Africa y Europa Socialista* (Havana: Instituto del Libro), 1972, p. 17.
32. See "M. Sékou Touré accueille M. Fidel Castro à Conakry," *Agence France-Presse*, Bull. Afrique 7786, 4 May 1972, p. 2.
33. Fall, "La croisade cubaine," 41.
34. *Jowol Jemma* 17, October–November 1976. (Given to the author by Alpha Ibrahima Sow.)

35. Fidel Castro, speech of 6 May 1972, in *El futuro es el internacionalismo*, 43.
36. Fidel Castro, speech of 4 May 1972, in *El futuro*, 27.
37. Castro, speech of 6 May 1972, 23.
38. Sékou Touré, speech at Kissidougou, 4 May 1972.
39. Fidel Castro to Rudy Casals, in Casals, "Fidel donne ses premieres impressions," 3; and Fidel Castro, speech of 3 May 1972, 17.
40. See *Comunicado conjunto cubano-guineano* (Conakry), 8 March 1972, in *El futuro*, 51–54.
41. Kouyate to author, interview. Rome, 29 January 1985.
42. Fidel Castro, speech at Kankan, 4 May 1972, in *El futuro*, 23.
43. Castro, speech at Faranah, 4 May 1972, in *El futuro*, 29.
44. Castro, speech at Kankan, 23.
45. Castro, speech of 5 May 1972, in *El futuro*, 42.
46. Castro, speech at the Presidential Palace, Freetown, Sierra Leone, in *El futuro*, 59.
47. Desmond Luke, interview with author, Lagos, October 16, 1976.
48. Fidel Castro, speech of 26 July 1972, in *El futuro*, 474.
49. See "La Havana propose à Washington de negotier 'sous peu' un accord sur la piratérie aérienne," *Le Monde*, 22 November 1972.
50. See *Le Monde*, 16 November 1972; *International Herald Tribune*, 14–19 November 1972, 4 December 1972.
51. See Carlos Moore, "El lugar del Caribe en la política internacional de Cuba a lo largo de veinticinco años de revolución," faculty seminar paper presented at the Universidad Interamericana de Puerto Rico, San Germán, under the sponsorship of CISCLA, 31 October 1984.
52. This agreement was incorporated into the "Basic Agreement on Economic and Scientific-Technical Cooperation Between the Republic of Guyana and the Republic of Cuba," signed by H. D. Hoyte, Guyana's minister of economic development, and by Rene Anillo Capote, Cuba's first deputy minister of foreign affairs, in Havana on 10 November 1975. See especially the "Aide Memoire." (Document obtained through the Institute of International Relations of the West Indies, in 1975.)
53. See "Trinidad and Tobago Signs Air Services Agreement with Cuba," press release 457, Office of the Prime Minister, Public Relations Division, 6 September 1974. (Document obtained through the Institute of International Relations of the West Indies, in 1975).
54. Jorge I. Domínguez correctly states that "another use of Cubana de Aviación was to spread political influence; Cubana was one way to show the flag" (note to author, 9 September 1985).
55. See *Le Monde Diplomatique*, December 1973, p. 44.

CHAPTER 19

1. Franqui, *Retrato de Fidel con Familia* (Madrid: Editorial Seix Barreal, 1981), 84.
2. Jean Ziegler, *Les Rebelles* (Paris: Seuil, 1983), 341.
3. Miriam Makeba, interview with author, Lagos, October 1974. All of the author's Cuban friends agree that Makeba was the most thrilling performer ever to come to Cuba.
4. See *Granma* (French weekly), 10 September 1972, p. 3.
5. In Cuba, natural, unstraightened hair among Blacks is referred to as "pelo malo," or "bad hair."

6. See *Granma* (French weekly), 8 October 1972, p. 2.

7. *Granma*, 8 October 1972, p. 2.

8. As told to the author by participant in mass rally.

9. *Granma*, 8 October 1972, p. 2.

10. See Angela Davis's speech in *Granma*, 8 October 1972, p. 5.

11. See Booth, "Cuba, Color," 170.

12. See *Granma*, 12 September 1972.

13. Teófilo Acosta was at one point the most important black Cuban within the secret service. He began his career as a "journalist" in Congo-Brazzaville, in the service of *Prensa Latina*, the Cuban news agency. His real mission was reportedly to maintain contact with Ché Guevara, then operating in Zaire. From a journalist, Acosta was transformed into ambassador to Congo-Brazzaville. Eventually, he was appointed to the U.N. mission in New York. Expelled from the U.S. on charges of espionage, he went on to other diplomatic posts and in 1982 he became ambassador to Zimbabwe.

14. Harry Belafonte confided to Nester Alméndros, the film photographer and director, about an incident in which, while the singer was on a visit to Cuba, an Afro-Cuban let him know that Blacks were still being discriminated there (Alméndros, interview with author, Paris, April 18, 1983).

15. See *Les chémins de la culture à Cuba* (Havana: Editions Politiques, 1971, pamphlet).

16. See *Granma*, 30 April 1971, for the "Final Declaration of the First National Congress on Education and Culture," or, *Granma* (English weekly), 9 May 1971.

17. See Ziegler, *Les Rebelles*, 339, 341, 342–343, 344, 345, 346, 359.

18. Gilberto Aldama, interview with author.

19. Information to author from several people, including Esteban Cárdenas and Gilberto Aldama.

20. Aldama, interview with author.

21. Aldama, interview with author. The citations in the following pages are from the same source.

22. Aldama, interview with author.

23. See interview with Sara Goméz by Marguerite Duras, "La nouvelle génération cubaine."

24. Carlos Franqui admitted this to the author, interviews. Franqui now accepts that his attitude might have been wrong.

25. Jorge I. Domínguez notes that Deschamps Chapeaux was also "a very good historian of the mid-nineteenth century" (note to author, 9 September 1985).

26. Esteban Cárdenas, written report sent to the author, April 1985. Information and citations from Cárdenas in the following pages are from this source.

27. There are various versions reported of a strong altercation between Minister Llanusa and Walterio Carbonell. It is absolutely false, however, that he threatened to found a "black Communist party." Although this is a widely held belief, I have found no testimony to support it.

28. Salkey, *Havana Journal*, 37-38.

29. Reckord, *Does Fidel Eat More?*, 127.

30. Booth, "Cuba, Color," 170.

31. The "Cárdenas Report."

32. Reinaldo Barroso, interview with author, Paris, May 5, 1982.

33. Barroso, interview with author.

34. Dumont, *Cuba, est-il socialiste?*, 80.

35. See Carmelo Mesa-Lago, *Cuba in the 1970s* (Albuquerque: University of New Mexico Press, 1976).
36. In fact, most of the speeches of the revolutionary leaders, during the early stages of the Revolution, decried *monocultura* as the chief enemy of Cuba's development.
37. See Michel Guttelman, *L'Agriculture socialisée à Cuba* (Paris: Maspero, 1967), 175.
38. Charles Bettelheim, "La Revolution cubaine sur la 'voie soviétique,' " *Le Monde*, 12 May 1971, p. 6.
39. See Fidel Castro, speech of 26 July 1970, in *Bohemia*, 31 July 1970; *International Herald Tribune*, 2 June 1970; *Le Monde*, 24 June 1970 and 13 January 1971; Charles Van Hecke, "Cuba: de l'utopie aux realités," *Le Monde*, 17–19 March 1971.
40. Bettelheim, "La Révolution.'
41. Van Hecke, "Cuba: de l'utopie," 4.
42. Fidel Castro, speech of 12 June 1971, in *Granma*, 7 September 1972.
43. "Para que el hombre libre prodúzca mas que cuando era esclavo," *Granma*, 7 September 1972, p. 2.
44. Haitian writer and theorist René Depestre, was a staunch defender of the "racial integrity" of the Cuban leadership until the early 1980s when, disenchanted and heartbroken, he left Cuba forever. He summed it all up by saying that Cuban whites were incapable of dealing with a black person as any but a subordinate or someone to manipulate (conversation with author, Paris, 16 January 1985).

CHAPTER 20

1. Fidel Castro to Simon Malley, in "Vingt heures d'entrétiens avec Fidel Castro," *Afrique-Asie*, 16–29 May 1977, p. 13.
2. Barbara Walters, "Interview with Fidel Castro," *Foreign Policy* 28 (1977):37–38.
3. Juán Benemelis, former Cuban diplomat, interview with author, Los Angeles, 2 March 1985.
4. M. D. Yusufu, inspector general of the federal police and secret service of Nigeria, interview with author, Lagos, 9 October 1975. See Barron, *KGB*," 29–30, 200–208, 209–212, 222. Also Juán Benemelis, former Cuban diplomat, interview with author.
5. See Jorge I. Domínguez, "Racial and Ethnic Relations in the Cuban Armed Forces. A Non-Topic," *Armed Forces and Society* 2, no. 2 (February 1976). Dominguez must be given well-deserved credit for having been the first, and to my knowledge the only, analyst to have drawn attention to the racial balance of Cuba's military establishment.
6. Benemelis, interview with author. The official who was present when Castro made that statement, and who repeated it to Benemelis, must remain anonymous, at the request of my informant, since the person in question is still at his post in Cuba.
7. See *Statement by the Prime Minister Dr. Eric Williams in the House of Representatives* (18 December 1975), press release 578, Office of the Prime Minister.
8. See Nelson P. Valdés, "Revolutionary Solidarity in Angola," in Blasier and Mesa-Lago, *Cuba in the World*, 93.
9. Onesimo Silveira, interview with author.
10. See "Appel à tous les militants et à tous les cadres du MPLA," 11 May 1974 (document).
11. For some Africans' reactions to Cuba's military interventionist role on their continent, and their views on the Cuban revolution in general, see Appendix 4.

12. Pamela S. Falk, *Cuban Foreign Policy* (Massachusetts-Toronto: Lexington Books, 1986), 83. Cuba's long-standing involvement in African affairs is also treated by William LeoGrande, "Cuba's Policy in Africa 1959–1980," Berkeley, California, Institute of International Affairs, 1980); William J. Durch, "The Cuban Military in Africa and the Middle East: From Algeria to Angola?" (Center for Naval Analyses, Professional Paper No. 201, Alexandria, Arlington, Va., 1977). For a comprehensive panoramic view of Cuba's current Africa policy, see Pamela S. Falk, "Cuba in Africa" (*Foreign Affairs*, 65, No. 5, (1987) and Carmelo Mesa-Lago and June Belkin, eds., *Cuba in Africa*. (Pittsburgh: University of Pittsburgh Press, 1982).

13. See Barbara Walters, "An Interview with Fidel Castro," *Foreign Policy*, No. 28 (1977):39.

14. Raúl Roa García, *Sechaba* (London) 10 (1976).

15. Isidoro Malmierca Peoli, "La Conference de Belgrade," *Le Monde*, 30–31 July 1978, p. 3. My parentheses.

16. Isidoro Malmierca Peoli (See *Reuters*, London, dispatch No. WAF-989-990, 1 February 1977).

17. The author, himself a Cuban exile living in Senegal at the time of the intervention in Angola and Ethiopia, had strongly supported the first and opposed the second.

18. See Colin Legum and Tony Hodges, *After Angola: The War in Southern Africa* (London: Rex Collins, 1976), 20. The MPLA's envoy to Nigeria, Joaquim de Lemus, told Nigeria's Chief of Intelligence M. D. Yusufu, in the presence of this author, that the proportion of black Cubans among the incoming troops was between 60 percent and 70 percent. (The conversation took place at the Ikoyi residence of the Nigerian official, then a member of the ruling Supreme Military Council, in February 1976).

19. Ziegler, *Les Rebelles*, 355. My parenthesis.

20. Gilberto Aldama, interview with author. Then serving a thirty-year sentence in prison for having organized the all-black *Movimiento de Liberación Nacional*, he recalled the feeling of pride he and other imprisoned black opponents of the regime felt when they heard and read about "Operation Carlota", an emotion they kept to themselves.

21. Tidiani Guissé, Malian Ambassador to Senegal, interview with the author, Dakar, Senegal, 14 November 1979.

22. Ayalew Kanno, Ethiopian ambassador to Senegal (thereafter appointed minister of state), interview with the author, Dakar, Senegal, 5 April 1979.

23. Joaquim de Lemus, MPLA special envoy to Nigeria (1975-1976), to M. D. Yusufu, Nigerian chief of intelligence, in the presence of the author. Lagos, Nigeria, February 1976. Kenyan scholar Ali A. Mazrui told of an Angolan delegate to the Second General Meeting of the African Association of Political Science (Lagos, Nigeria, April 1976) who "also attempted to legitimize Cuba's participation in an African civil war on the grounds that Cuba was an 'Afro-Caribbean country'."

24. M. D. Yusufu, chief of Nigerian intelligence, inspector general of the police, supreme military council member from 1975 to October 1979, interviews with the author, Lagos, Nigeria, 8 November 1978 and 23 February 1981.

25. Fidel Castro (New York: Venceremos Brigade, 1976), as quoted in Falk, *Cuban Foreign Policy*, 106. My italics.

26. See Jeffrey M. Elliot and Mervyn M. Dymally, *Fidel Castro. Nothing Can Stop the Course of History*. (New York: Pathfinder Press, 1986), 177. My parenthesis.

27. Abbas Sykes, Tanzanian ambassador to France, interview with the author, Paris, 19 January 1978. Alioune Cissé, Senegalese ambassador to Mauritania, told the

author that Somalia's move toward the Arab world destroyed whatever goodwill there was for that country in black Africa. (Interview, Nuakchott, Mauritania, 18 December 1978). During a visit to Somalia in February 1981, the author repeatedly heard from Somalian officials themselves of the greater kinship Somalians felt with the Arab world. Mohamed Samantar, chief political advisor to President Mohamed Syad Barre, expressed similar feelings during an interview with the author, Geneva, 10 April 1981.

28. See W. R. Scott, "The American Negro and the Italo- Ethiopian Crisis, 1934-36," (Ph.D. dissertation, Howard University, 1966).

29. Abdulahi Conteh, foreign minister of Sierra Leone, interview with the author, Paris, 13 April 1981.

30. Andrew Young, former U.S. ambassador to the United Nations, interview with author, Atlanta, Ga., 23 November 1982.

31. Donald Eassum, interview with the author, New York, 9 October 1986. The affable Eassum, one of the most liberal-minded American policy makers to have been in charge of African affairs, had also had to withstand accusations of being too African-minded during his tenure.

32. Seydou Badian Kouyaté, interview with author, Dakar, 4 February 1979.

33. Mario de Andrade, interview with author, Dakar, 14 January 1977. At the time, de Andrade was Guinea-Bissau's minister for culture.

34. Practically all Afro-Cubans, for or against the Revolution, living in Cuba or abroad, whom the author has been able to question on the subject concur in that regard.

35. Glenn Jackman, interview with author, Kingston, 13 May 1986. Professor of Spanish at the University of the West Indies (Mona), Jackman, a Jamaican, lived and worked in Cuba through the 1960s and until 1979.

36. An in-depth study of changing patterns of political and cultural thought among Afro-Cubans since 1959 will reveal that these subjective mutations are often attributable, *involuntarily*, to the Castro regime's *Afrocentric* initiatives starting with President Sékou Touré's visit to Cuba in 1960.

37. Barroso, interview with the author. That view was subsequently corroborated by Glenn Jackman (interview with the author, Kingston, 13 May 1986) and other Afro-Cubans who came to the U.S. as a result of the 1980 Mariel boatlift, during interviews with the author in Miami, in September and October 1986.

38. Natividad Tórres, thirty-two-year-old Mariel exile, interview with the author, Miami, 18 September 1986.

39. Manuél Casanovas, interview with author, Miami, 3 October 1986.

40. Aldama, interview with author.

41. Domínguez, "Racial and Ethnic Relations," 273-290.

42. I am greatly indebted to Jean Huteau, director of information of *Agence France-Presse*, and to the AFP bureau chief in Havana, who supplied the racial data on diplomatic, ministerial, National Assembly and Party leadership posts (Paris, 20 March 1980). See Ezzedine Mestiri, *Les Cubains en Afrique*, (Paris: Khartala, 1980), 66-70; Carlos Moore, "Cuba: Ces Noirs qui partent," *Jeune Afrique*, No. 1027, September 10, 1980, pp. 38-39.

43. Edward Gonzalez and David Ronfeldt, *Castro, Cuba, and the World*, (The Rand Corporation, Santa Monica, Report No. R-3420, June 1986), 6-7ff.

44. See *Los Angeles Times* (6 December 1986, p. 16). As quoted by Gonzalez and Ronfeldt, *Castro, Cuba and the World*, 64 ff.

45. Domínguez, *Cuba: Order*, 354.

46. Natividad Tórres, interview with author. Mongo Santamaría, the U.S.-based Afro-Cuban jazz drummer, told the author about the restlessness he had found among

Blacks during his trip there in the late 1970s. (Conversation, Paris, April 1981.)

47. Esteban Cárdenas, interview with author, Miami, 26 December 1986. Osvaldo Cardenas, disgraced as a result of events in Grenada in September-October 1983, was rumored to have been appointed ambassador to France in 1986.

48. See Appendix 2.

49. The joke actually emerged from a paraphrasing of the oldest and most commonly used popular saying regarding black Cubans who claim to be whites and whites who claim to be pure: "Y tu abuela, donde está?" (And where is your grandma?)

50. Gonzalez and Ronfeldt, *Castro, Cuba and the World*, 70 ff.

51. See Ali Mazrui, "Cuba's Castro and Africa's Castration: A Case Study in Micro-Dependency" (in association with Lemuel Johnson and Rovan Locke). Unpublished paper presented to the International Conference on "Latin America: The Middle Class of Nations" (Lake Llanquihue, Chile, November 25–30, 1978), p. 23 (mimeo). I am grateful to Professor Mazrui for having allowed me to use this fascinating study.

CHAPTER 21

1. As Gonzalez and Ronfeldt pointed out, "Castro sees that the Gorbachev regime is shifting priorities to domestic economic issues and demanding better economic performance from its clients, including Cuba. Gorbachev appears intent on stabilizing superpower relations and less inclined to launch a new expansionist drive into the Third World . . . Castro must find this apparent Soviet deemphasis on the Third World disquieting, because this is where he has been able to fulfill his maximalist ambitions . . .", *Castro, Cuba and the World*, xii.

2. Manuel Sanchez Perez, the Cuban vice minister who defected in Spain in December 1985, reported Castro was warned by one of his military aides that more than two million Cubans would flee unless he stopped the outflow. See Gonzalez and Ronfeldt, *Castro, Cuba and the World*, 79 ff.

3. Wayne Smith, interview with the author, Washington, D.C., May 20, 1986. See Wayne Smith, *The Closest of Enemies* (New York: Norton and Norton, 1987), 197–235. Smith was chief of the U.S. interests section in Havana at the time of the Mariel exodus.

4. I am indebted to Jorge I. Domínguez for having provided that information. The report was one among tons of top secret and confidential documents seized by the U.S. forces in Grenada. See Paul Seabury and Walter A. McDougall, eds., *The Grenada Papers* (San Francisco: Institute of Contemporary Studies, 1984) and Michael Ledeen and Herbert Romerstain, eds., *Grenada Documents: An Overview and Selection* (Washington, D.C.: Department of State and the Department of Defense, September 1984).

5. Afro-Cubans accounted for an estimated 3.5% of the nearly one million Cubans who left the island between 1959 and 1979. See Appendix 2.

6. Gonzalez and Ronfeldt, *Castro, Cuba and the World*, 69.

7. Tad Szulc, *Fidel. A Critical Portrait* (New York: William Morrow, 1986), 649.

8. In June 1987, Cuba's tourist office (Cubatour) conducted its third yearly "International Folklore Workshop" for tourists. This two-week "course," costing the tourist $1,200 U.S., is designed "to teach the secrets of Cuban folklore dances of African and Hispanic origin . . ." *Granma Weekly Review*. 10 May 1987, p. 10. The workshops, conducted in Spanish, English, and French, include a sight-seeing visit to a *toque de santo* (Afro-Cuban invocation ceremony). These "courses" are

conducted chiefly by the Afro-Cuban ethnologists and musicologists, Rogelio Martínez Furé, Pedro Deschamps Chapeaux and Odilio Urfé.

9. Babalawo Eugenio Muñóz, 58-year old Mariel escapee, gave the author a detailed account of the repression of Afro-Cuban religions underwent throughout the 1960s and 1970s, interviews with author, Miami, 26 September 1986 and 17 March 1987.

10. That issue surfaced at the "Third International Congress on Orisha Tradition and Culture," New York, October 6–10, 1986, attended by the author. The Congress brought together Afro religious leaders from Africa and the diaspora.

11. Pedro Serviat, "La discriminación racial en Cuba, su orígen, desarrollo y terminación definitiva," *Islas*, No. 66, (May–August, 1980), 20.

12. See "René Depestre on Culture, Politics and Race in Cuba," *Socialism*, (Kingston), 3, No. 5 (May 1976), 29, 33. In this as well as other interviews, Depestre stated flatly: "There is no longer a racial question . . . so that one could say that racism belongs to the past in Cuba."

13. Proceedings of the conference, *José Martí and the Cuban Revolution Retraced*, 1–2 March 1985 (Los Angeles: UCLA Latin American Center Publications, Vol. 2, 1986), 71.

14. Mervyn M. Dymally, interview with author, Washington, D.C., 17 April 1984. After our forty-minute discussion, I handed Congressman Dymally two papers I'd just delivered at a one-day workshop at Harvard University on "Racial Factors in Cuba's Domestic and Foreign Policies" (Boston, 17 February 1984).

15. A'Lelia Bundles, NBC field producer, interview with the author, Knoxville, Tenn., 25 April 1987. Ms. Bundles was part of the press contingent covering Rev. Jesse Jackson's visit to Cuba.

16. Private information to the author from inside of Cuba.

17. Private information to the author from inside of Cuba.

18. *Granma Weekly Review*, 29 June 1987, p. 1.

19. Monsignor Carlos Manuel de Céspedes, interview with the author, Washington, D.C., 21 May 1986.

20. Gonzalez and Ronfeldt, *Castro, Cuba and the World*, 80.

21. Monsignor Carlos Manuel de Céspedes, interview with the author. Miami-based Monsignor Bryan O. Walsh, who has been involved in Cuban affairs for more than twenty years, also speculated that Castro's "reconciliation" bid with Catholicism might stem chiefly from a tactical need to combat Afro-Cuban religions rather than from a change of heart towards the church. (Interview with the author, Port-au-Prince, 15 November 1986). Miami-based *Time* Caribbean bureau chief, Bernard Diederich, who monitored the tug-of-war between the authorities and Afro-Cuban religions over the years, also believed the regime had changed tactics but not its ultimate aim. (Interview with the author, Miami, 12 March 1987).

22. *Granma Resúmen Semanal*, 27 April 1986, pp. 8–10. As quoted by Gonazalez and Ronfeldt, *Castro, Cuba and the World*, 85.

23. Gonzalez and Ronfeldt, *Castro, Cuba and the World*, 67.

24. Three-hour videotape of Fidel Castro's closing speech to the Third Congress of the Communist Party of Cuba.

25. Gonzalez and Ronfeldt, *Castro, Cuba and the World*, 69–70.

26. *Granma Weekly Review*, 10 February 1986, p. 15.

27. Proceedings of the conference *José Martí and the Cuban Revolution Retraced*, 12.

28. See Falk, *Cuban Foreign Policy*, 83–91.

29. Szulc, *Fidel*, 637. My italics.

30. Elliot and Dymally, *Fidel Castro*, 173. My italics.

31. See *The Observer*, (London, 24 November 1985). As quoted in Gonzalez and Ronfeldt, *Castro, Cuba and the World*, 132 ff.
32. See *The Observer*.
33. Gonzalez and Ronfeldt, *Castro, Cuba and the World*, 132.
34. See *The Observer*.
35. Gonzalez and Ronfeldt, *Castro, Cuba and the World*, 132 ff.
36. Cheikh Anta Diop, interview with the author, London, 15 January 1985. Also see Carlos Moore, "Interview with Professor Cheikh Anta Diop," *Afriscope* (Lagos) 7, No. 2 (February 1977), 9–15.
37. Oliver Tambo, interview with author, Paris, 25 May 1981.
38. *Granma Weekly Review*, 14 September 1986, p. 9.
39. *Granma Weekly Review*, 21 September 1986, p. 10. My italics.
40. *Granma Weekly Review*, 24 November 1985), p. 3.
41. Falk, "Cuba in Africa," 1092, 1095.
42. Gonzalez and Ronfeldt, *Castro, Cuba and the World*, 30.
43. *Granma Weekly Review*, 16 June 1985), p. 6. As quoted in Gonzalez and Ronfeldt, *Castro, Cuba and the World*, 30.
44. *Granma Weekly Review*, 9 June 1985, p. 3. As quoted in Gonzalez and Ronfeldt, *Castro, Cuba and the World*, 30.
45. See Barbara Walters, "An Interview," 38.
46. Mario da Souza Clington, Angolan sociologist, interview with the author, Paris, 15 October 1983. The Cubans, particularly the white ones, he said, displayed contemptuous attitudes towards Angolans and were resented by many. Da Souza Clington's *Angola Libre?* focuses on the nineteenth-century background to the current Angolan civil strife.
47. M. D. Yusufu, interview with author, Lagos.
48. Edem Kodjo, interview with author, Paris, 15 April 1981.
49. Edem Kodjo's *Et Demain l'Afrique* (Paris: Stock, 1985), is compulsory reading for an understanding of the outlook of Africa's new breed of security-conscious pan-Africanists.
50. Mario de Andrade, interview with author, Paris, 18 October 1983.
51. Cheikh Anta Diop, interview with author, London.
52. Mazrui, "Cuba's Castro."

APPENDIX 1

1. Gilberto Freyre, *O mundo que o portugues criou* (Rio de Janeiro: José Olympio, 1940).
2. Eugene D. Genovese, *Roll, Jordan, Roll: The World the Slaves Made* (New York: Pantheon Books, 1974), 5–6.

APPENDIX 2

1. Kenneth F. Kiple, *Blacks in Colonial Cuba* (Gainesville, Florida: University of Florida Press, 1976), 3.
2. Raymond T. Buell et al., *Problems of the New Cuba* (New York: Foreign Policy Association, 1935), 28–30.
3. Gustavo E. Urrútia, "El prejuicio en Cuba," in *Negro Anthology*, ed. Nancy Cunard, 476, 477.

4. W. E. B. Du Bois, *Black Folk, Then and Now* (New York: Henry Holt and Co., 1939), 190.

5. Carleton Beals, *America South* (New York and Philadelphia: J. B. Lippincott Co., 1937), 55.

6. *Cuba, Oficina Nacionál de los Censos Demográfico y Electoral*, and *Censos de Población, Viviendas y Electoral*, Enero 28 de 1953. Informe General (Havana: P. Fernández and Co., 1955); Informe Generál del Censo de 1943, Dirección General del Censo.

7. *Encyclopedia Americana*, vol. 3, "Cuba," p. 279.

8. Donald W. Bray and Timothy F. Harding, "Cuba," in *Latin America*, ed. Chilcote and Edelstein, 733.

9. Wyatt McGaffey and Clifford R. Barnett, *Cuba, Its People, Its Society, Its Culture* (New Haven, Conn.: Human Relations Area Files Press, 1962).

10. William R. Bascom, "Yoruba Acculturation in Cuba," *Les Afro-Américains* (Dakar) IFAN, no. 27 (1953): 163.

11. Thomas, *Cuba*, 1117.

12. Irving L. Horowitz, "Authenticity," 210.

13. Boris Goldenberg, *The Cuban Revolution and Latin America* (New York: Praeger, 1965), 131.

14. *Encyclopedia Britannica*, vol. 6, p. 843 (London, 1962).

15. Booth, "Cuba, Color, 140.

16. Walterio Carbonell, conversation with author, Havana, September 1963.

17. See *Obra revolucionária*, 26 May 1964.

18. *Le Monde*, 30–31 January 1966, p. 2; *Al Ahram*, 29 January 1966.

19. Petit, *Castro, Debray*, 119.

20. See R. J. Probias and Lourdes Casal, *The Cuban Minority in the United States. Preliminary Report on Need Identification and Program Evaluation* (Boca Ratón, Fla.: Atlantic University, 1973); *La población de Cuba* (Havana: Instituto Cubano del Libro, 1974), 80, 194; Benigno Aguirre, "Differential Migration of Cuban Social Races," *Latin American Research Review* 2, no. 1:103–104; Richard R. Fagen, Richard A. Brody, and Thomas J. O'Leary, *Cubans in Exile. Disaffection and the Revolution* (Stanford, Cal.: Stanford University Press, 1968), 145–146; George Volsky, "Cuban Negro Refugees in Miami Find 'Open Doors' to Prosperity,' *New York Times*, 8 June 1969.

21. *Granma*, 4 September 1983, p. 9.

22. Juán Pérez de la Riva, "La population de Cuba et ses problèmes," *Population* 22, no. 1:102.

23. *International Herald Tribune*, 23-24 July 1977, p. 6.

24. Black et al., *Area Handbook for Cuba*, 2d ed., 100.

25. See República de Cuba JUCEPLAN, *Censo de Población y Viviendas 1970* (Havana: Edicion Orbe, 1975); *La población de Cuba* (Havana: Editorial de Ciencias Sociales, Centro de Estudios Demográficos, 1976).

26. Casal, "Race Relations," 22.

27. As told to Carmelo Mesa-Lago by Lourdes Casal, information from Mesa-Lago to author 2 March 1985, Los Angeles.

28. See *Granma*, 19 September 1983.

29. See Chilcote and Edelstein, eds., *Latin America*, 699, 732.

30. Joseph North, *Cuba: Hope of a Hemisphere* (New York: International Publishers, 1961), 59.

31. Daniel Guerin, *Cuba-Paris* (Paris: Imp. des Gondoles, 1968), 3–4.
32. As reported to the author by journalist Michel Legré, conversation, Paris, 15 March 1978.
33. Information to the author by Reinaldo Barroso, who was classified as "mulatto," rather than Black, against his will. Taped interview, Paris.
34. Information to author by former Cuban official Juán Benemelis, 2 March 1985, Los Angeles.
35. *Le Monde Diplomatique*, June 1984, p. 25.
36. *Quid 1983* (Paris: Robert Laffont, 1983), 1085.
37. Benemelis, interview with author, 2 March 1985.
38. *Miami Herald*, 21 January 1985, p. 7.
39. Ziegler, *Les Rebelles*, 337.
40. (Paris: Unesco, 1970), 14.
41. Giorgio Mortara, "Evaluación de la información censal para América Latina," *América Latina* 2 (April–June 1964):50–51.
42. *América Latina* 2 (April–June 1964): 60, 61, 62.
43. "Negros y blancos en América Latina," *Revista de la Universidad de Buenos Aires* 3, 4 (July–December 1963).
44. "Problemas raciales en América Latina," *Courier de l'Unesco*, October 1960.
45. "Las relaciones inter-étnicas en algunas áreas de América indigena," *América Latina* 3 (July–September 1964): 104.
46. See *Le Monde*, 6–7 September 1970.

APPENDIX 3

1. After leaving the Congo, Guevara expressed such opinions to a number of people, among them, Ange Diawara, Ciro Bustos, and Anicet Kashamura.
2. See Rojo, *My Friend Ché*, 184.
3. Ché Guevara, in *Tricontinental*.
4. Bula Nyati, interview with author. See also, Andrew Sinclair, *Guevara* (London: Fontana/Collins, 1970), 79. When Havana carried out its spectacular "internationalist" operation in Angola in 1975 and 1976, one of its unfounded charges against the pro-western foes of the MPLA was that the FNLA/UNITA soldiers engaged in cannibalism (see García Marquez, "Opération Charlotte," 8).
5. García Marquez, "Opération Charlotte," 8.

APPENDIX 4

1. This survey was conducted clandestinely by the author in 1978 and 1979. I polled four hundred African students in a random sample (40 percent Malians, 35 percent from Ivory Coast, 15 percent Guineans, 7.5 percent from Upper Volta, and 2.5 percent Beninese) at the Ecole Normale Supérieure, Bamako, Mali, and the University of Abidjan and Cocody High School, Ivory Coast. The conclusions presented here are based on the two hundred completed questionnaires that were returned to me.

ABBREVIATIONS

DGI	Dirección General de Inteligencia (General Intelligence Directorate)
FAR	Fuerzas Armadas Revolucionárias (Revolutionary Armed Forces)
FEANF	Fédération des Etudiants d'Afrique Noire en France (Black African Students Federation in France)
FPCC	Fair Play for Cuba Committee
ICAIC	Instituto Cubano de Arte e Indústria Cinematográfica (Cuban Institute of Cinematographic Art and Industry)
ICAP	Instituto Cubano de Amistad con los Pueblos (Cuban Institute of Friendship with the Peoples of the World)
INEF	Instituto Nacional de Etnología y Folklore (National Institute of Ethnology and Folklore)
MPLA	Movimento Popular de Libertação de Angola (Popular Movement for the Liberation of Angola)
NAACP	National Association for the Advancement of Colored People
OAS	Organization of American States
ORI	Organizaciones Revolucionarías Integradas (Integrated Revolutionary Organizations)
OSPAAAL	Organización de Solidaridad de los Pueblos de Africa, Asia y América Latina (African, Asian, and Latin American Peoples Solidarity Organization)
PDG	Parti Démocratique de Guinée (Guinean Democratic Party)
PIC	Partido Independiente de Color (Independent Colored Party)
PSP	Partido Socialista Popular (Popular Socialist Party)
PURSC	Partido Unido de la Revolución Socialista Cubana (United Party of the Cuban Socialist Revolution)
UNDP	United Nations Development Program
UNEAC	Unión Nacional de Escritores y Artistas Cubanos (National Union of Cuban Writers and Artists)

SELECTED BIBLIOGRAPHY

1. Books and Pamphlets

Abel, Elie. *The Missile Crisis*. Philadelphia and New York: J. B. Lippincott Co., 1966.

Aguero, Luis Conte. *Fidel Castro: Psiquiatría y política*. Mexico City: Editorial Jus, 1968.

———. *Los dos rostros de Fidel Castro*. Mexico City: Editorial Jus, 1960.

———. *Fidel Castro, Vida y obra*. Havana: Editorial LEX, 1959.

Aguero, Sixto Gastón. *El materialismo explica el espiritismo y la santería*. Havana: Orbe, 1961.

Aiyh, Michel. *Ein Afrikaner in Moskau*. Cologne: Verlag Wissenschaft und Politik, 1961.

Ajao, Aderogba. *On the Tiger's Back*. London: Allen & Unicorn, 1962.

Alliluyeva, Svetlana. *Only One Year*. New York: Harper & Row, 1969.

Alvarez Ríos, Baldomero, ed. *Cuba: Revolución e imperialismo*. Havana: Instituto del Libro, 1969.

Amar, Andrew R. *A Student in Moscow*. London: Ampersand, Ltd., 1961.

Amaro Victoria, Nelson. "Mass and Class in the Origins of the Cuban Revolution." In *Cuban Communism*. See Horowitz, ed.

Attwood, William. *The Reds and the Blacks*. New York: Harper & Row, 1967.

Auroi, Claude. *La nouvelle agriculture cubaine*. Paris: Editions Anthropos, 1975.

Avineri, Shlomo, ed. *Karl Marx on Colonialism and Modernization*. New York: Doubleday, 1968.

Barron, John. *KGB: The Secret Work of Soviet Secret Agents*. London/New York: Bantam Books, 1974.

Bascom, William R. "The African Heritage and Its Religious Manifestations." In *Background to Revolution*. See Robert Freeman Smith, ed.

Bass, Robert and Elizabeth. "Eastern Europe." In *Africa and the Communist World*. See Brzezinski, ed.

Bastide, Roger, ed. *La femme de couleur en Amérique latine*. Paris: Editions Anthropos, 1974.

Beals, Carleton. *America South*. Philadelphia and New York: J. B. Lippincott Company, 1937.

Bebel-Gisler, Dany, and Laennec Hurbon. *Cultures et pouvoir dans la Caraibe. Langue créole, vaudou, sectes réligieuses en Guadeloupe et en Haiti*. Paris: l'Harmattan, 1975.

Betancourt Bencomo, Juán René. *Doctrina Negra. La única teoría certera contra la discriminación racial en Cuba*. Havana: P. Fernández, 1958.

——. *Prelúdios de la libertad. La tragedia del negro y la tactica del partido comunista*. Havana: n.p., 1950.

——. *El Negro: Ciudadano del futuro*. Havana: Talleres Tipográficos de Cárdenas, 1959.

Betto, Frei. *Fidel y la Religion: Conversaciones con Frei Betto*. Havana: Oficina de Publicaciones del Consejo de Estado, 1985.

Beyhaut, Gustavo. *Raíces de América Latina*. Buenos Aires: Eudeba Editorial Universitaria de Buenos Aires, 1964.

Black, Jan Knippers et al. *Area Handbook for Cuba*, 2d ed. Washington, D.C.: The American University Foreign Area Studies, 1976.

Blasier, Cole, and Carmelo Mesa-Lago, eds. *Cuba in the World*. Pittsburgh: University of Pittsburgh Press, 1979.

Blutstein, Howard I. et al. *Area Handbook for Cuba*. Washington, D.C.: The American University Foreign Area Studies, 1971.

Bonachea, Rolando E., and Nelson P. Valdes, eds. *Revolutionary Struggle 1947–1958. The Selected Works of Fidel Castro, vol. 1*. Cambridge, Mass.: M.I.T. Press, 1972.

Bray, Donald W., and Timothy F. Harding. "Cuba." In *Latin America*. See Chilcote and Edelstein, eds.

Breitman, George, ed. *Malcolm X Speaks, Selected Speeches and Statements*. New York: Merit Publishers, 1965.

——. *The Last Year of Malcolm X*. New York: Merit Publishers, 1967.

Brzezinski, Zbigniew, ed. *Africa and the Communist World*. Stanford: Stanford University, 1963.

Bell, Raymond L. et al. *Problems of the New Cuba*. New York: Foreign Policy Association, 1935.

Bueno, Salvador. *Figuras cubanas*. Havana: Comisión Nacional Cubana de la Unesco, 1964.

Bustos, Ciro Roberto. "Account by Ciro Bustos of His Stay with Guevara's Guerrillas in Bolivia." In *"Ché" Guevara*. See Mallin, ed.

Cabral, Amilcar. *Unité et lutte 1: L'Armée de la theorie.* Paris: Maspero, 1975.

Cabrera, Lydia. *La sociedad secreta Abacuá,* 2d ed. Havana: Ediciones C.R., 1958.

Cannon, Terry, and Johnnetta Cole. *Free and Equal. The End of Racial Discrimination in Cuba.* New York: Venceremos Brigade, 1978, pamphlet.

Carbonell, Walterio. *Crítica: Cómo surgió la cultura nacional.* Havana: Ediciones Yaka, 1961.

Carew, Jan. *Moscow Is not my Mecca.* London: Secker and Warburg, 1964.

Carrère d'Encausse, Hélène. *La politique soviétique au Moyen Orient, 1955-1975.* Paris: Presses de la Fondation Nationale des Sciences Politiques, 1975.

Carrere d'Encausse, Hélène, and Stuart R. Schram. *L'URSS et la Chine devant les révolutions dans les societés pré-industrielles.* Paris: Presses de la Fondation Nationale des Sciences Politiques, 1970.

Carrillo, Santiago. *'Eurocommunisme'' et l'etat.* Paris: Flammarion, 1977.

Casteyger, Curt. "Political and Strategic Implications of Soviet Naval Presence in the Caribbean." In *Soviet Seapower.* See Thebergue, ed.

Castro, Fidel. *Angola girón africain.* Havana: Editorial de Ciencias Sociales, 1976.

——. *Bilan de la révolution cubaine.* Paris: Maspero, 1963.

——. *Cuba et la crise des Caraibes.* Paris: Maspero, 1976.

—— and José Martí. "Declaración de la Habana." In *De Martí a Castro,* Mexico City: Editorial Grijalbo, 1970.

——. *Discursos para la história.* Havana: Imprenta Emilio Gall, 1959.

——. *Le gouvernement chinois a trahi la bonne foi du peuple cubain.* Havana: n.p., 6 February 1966 (pamphlet).

——. "La história me absolvera." In *De Martí a Castro.* Mexico: Editorial Grijalbo, 1970, 31-112.

——. *Nuestro partido representa la história reciente de la patria.* Havana: Editor en Colores, 1966 (brochure).

——. *Nuestro templo: la patria. Nuestro culto: la justicia.* Havana: Editorial En Marcha, 1961 (pamphlet).

——. *Pan sin terror.* Havana: Ediciones Movimiento, 1959.

——. *Pensamiento político, económico y social de Fidel Castro.* Havana: Editorial LEX, 1959.

——. *Playa girón*. Havana: Comisión Nacional del Monumento a los Caidos en Playa Girón, 1961.

Casuso, Teresa. *Cuba and Castro*. New York: Random House, 1961.

Cervenka, Znedek. *The Organization of African Unity and Its Charter*. London: C. Hurst, 1968.

Césaire, Aimé. *Letter to Maurice Thorez*. Paris: Présence Africaine, 1957 (pamphlet).

Challiand, Gerard. *L'Algérie est-elle Socialiste?* Paris: Maspero, 1964.

——. *Mythes révolutionnaires du Tièrs Monde*. Paris: Seuil, 1976.

Chilcote, Ronald H., and Joel C. Edelstein, eds. *Latin America: The Struggle with Dependency and Beyond*. New York: John Wiley & Sons, 1974.

Clarke, John Henrik, ed. *Malcolm X. The Man and His Times*. New York: Macmillan, 1969.

Cleaver, Eldridge. *Soul on Fire*. Waco, Texas: Word Books, 1976.

Clissold, Stephen. *Soviet Relations with Latin America, 1918–68*. London/New York: Oxford University Press, 1970.

Clytus, John. *Black Man in Red Cuba*. Coral Gables, Fla.: University of Miami Press, 1970.

Cohen, Robert Carl. *Black Crusader: A Biography of Robert Franklin Williams*. Secaucus, N.J.: Lyle Stuart, 1972.

Constant, Louis, ed. *Fidel Castro. Révolution cubaine*, vol. 1. Paris: Maspero, 1968.

Crankshaw, Edward, ed. *Khrushchev Remembers*. Boston: Little, Brown & Co., 1970.

Cruse, Harold. *The Crisis of the Negro Intellectual*. New York: William Morrow, 1967.

——. *Rebellion or Revolution?* New York: William Morrow, 1968.

Cunard, Nancy, ed. *Negro Anthology*. London: Nancy Cunard at Wishart & Co., 1934.

Dallin, Alexander. "The Soviet Union: Political Activity." In *Africa and the Communist World*. See Brzezinski, ed.

Daniel, Jean. *L'Aventure du vrai*. Paris: Albin Michel, 1979.

da Sousa Clington, Mario. *Angola Libre?* Paris: Gallimard, 1976.

Débray, Régis. *Revolution in the Revolution?* New York: Monthly Review Press, 1967.

Dépestre, René. "Carta de Cuba sobre el imperialismo de la mala fe." In *Por la Revolución, por la Poésia*. Havana: Instituto del Libro, 1969.

Dewart, Leslie. *Christianity and Revolution: The Lesson of Cuba*. New York: Herder & Herder, 1963.

Dinerstein, Herbert S. *The Making of a Missile Crisis: October 1962.* Baltimore: Johns Hopkins University Press, 1976.

Domínguez, Jorge I. *Cuba: Order and Revolution.* Cambridge, Mass.: Belknap Press of Harvard University Press, 1978.

Draper, Theodore. *Castro's Revolution: Myths and Realities.* New York: Praeger, 1962.

Du Bois, W. E. B. *Black Folk, Then and Now.* New York: Henry Holt, 1939.

Dumont, René. *Cuba est-il Socialiste?* Paris: Seuil, 1972.

——. *Is Cuba Socialist?* London: Andre Deutsch, 1974.

Duncan, W. Raymond. "Problems of Cuban Foreign Policy." In *Cuban Communism.* See Horowitz, ed.

Echanove, Carlos A. *La "Santería" cubana.* Havana: Imprenta de la Universidad de La Habana, 1959 (separata).

Edmonds, Robin. *Soviet Foreign Policy 1962–73.* London: Oxford University Press, 1975.

Edwards, Jorge. *Persona Non Grata.* London: Bodley Head, 1973.

Elliot, Jeffrey M., and Mervyn M. Dymally. *Fidel Castro: Nothing Can Stop the Course of History.* New York: Pathfinder Press, 1986.

Entralgo, José Elias. *La liberación étnica cubana.* Havana: Imprenta de la Universidad de la Habana, 1953.

Erlich, Alexander, and Christian R. Sonne, "The Soviet Union: Economic Activity." In *Africa and the Communist World.* See Brzezinski, ed.

Fagen, Richard R. "Revolution: For Internal Consumption Only." In *Cuban Communism.* See Horowitz, ed.

——, Richard A. Brody and Thomas J. O'Leary. *Cubans in Exile. Disaffection and the Revolution* Stanford, California: Stanford Univeristy Press, 1968.

Falk, Pamela. *Cuban Foreign Policy.* Mass.-Toronto: Lexington Books, 1986.

Fanon, Frantz. *The Wretched of the Earth.* Harmondsworth: Penguin, 1967.

Fontaine, Andre. *Un seul lit pour deux rêves.* Paris: Fayard, 1981.

Fox, Geoffrey E. "Race and Class in Contemporary Cuba." In *Cuban Communism.* See Horowitz, ed.

Franco, Victor. *The Morning After.* London: Pall Mall Press, 1963.

Franqui, Carlos. *Diario de la Revolución cubana.* Paris: Ruedo Ibérico, 1976.

——. *Retrato de Fidel con Familia.* Madrid: Editorial Seix Barreal, 1981.

Free, Lloyd A., and Hadley Cantrill. *Attitudes of the Cuban People toward the Castro Regime in the Late Spring of 1960.* Princeton, N.J.: Institute for International Social Research, 1960.

Freeman-Grenville, G.S.P. *Chronology of African History.* London: Oxford University Press, 1971.

Freyre, Gilberto. *O mundo que o portugues criou.* Rio de Janeiro: José Olympio, 1940.

Genovese, Eugene D. *Roll, Jordan, Roll. The World the Slaves Made.* New York: Pantheon Books, 1974.

Glucksmann, André. *Le discours de la guerre.* Paris: Union Générale d'Editions. (Col. 10/18), 1974.

Glucksmann, Christine, ed. *Fidel Castro: Discours de la Révolution.* Paris: Union Generale d'Editions, Col. 10/18, 1966.

Goldenberg, Boris. *The Cuban Revolution and Latin America.* New York: Praeger, 1965.

Golendorf, Pierre. *Sept ans à Cuba.* Paris: Belfont, 1976.

Gonzalez, Edward. *Cuba under Castro: The Limits of Charisma.* Boston: Houghton Mifflin Co., 1974.

—— and David Ronfeldt. *Castro, Cuba, and the World.* Santa Monica, California: The Rand Corporation, Paper R-3420, June 1986.

Goodsell, James Nelson, ed. *Fidel Castro's Personal Revolution in Cuba: 1959–1973.* New York: Knopf, 1975.

Goure, Leon. "Cuba's Military Dependence on the U.S.S.R." In *Soviet Seapower.* See Thebergue, ed.

Granádos, Manuel. *Adire y el tiempo roto.* Havana: CASA, 1967.

Grignon-Dumoulin, Jacques, ed. *Fidel Castro parle.* Paris: Maspero, 1961.

Guérin, Daniel. *Cuba-Paris.* Paris: Imp. des Gondoles, 1968.

Guevara, Ernesto Ché. *Reminiscences of the Revolutionary War.* New York: Monthly Review Press, 1968.

——. *Oeuvres révolutionnaires: 1959–1967,* vol. 2. Paris: Maspero, 1968.

Guilbert, Yves. *Castro l'Infidel.* Paris: La Table Ronde, 1961.

Guillén, Nicolás. *El son entero. Cantos para soldados y sones para turístas.* Buenos Aires: Editorial Losada, 1963.

——. *Sóngoro cosongo. Motivos de son. West Indies Ltd.* Buenos Aires: Editorial Losada, 1963.

Guttelman, Michel. *L'Agriculture socialisée a Cuba.* Paris: Maspero, 1967.

Hageman, Alice, and Phillip Wheaton, eds. *Religion in Cuba Today.* New York: Associated Press, 1971.

Halperin, Ernst. *Fidel Castro's Road to Power*, vol. 1, *Cuban Politics from Machado to Moncada*. Cambridge, Mass.: Center for International Studies, M.I.T., December 1970.

Halperin, Maurice. *The Rise and Decline of Fidel Castro*. Berkeley: University of California Press, 1972.

Hamrell, Sven, and Carl Gosta Widstrand, eds. *The Soviet Bloc, China and Africa*. Uppsala: The Scandinavian Institute of African Studies, 1964.

Heikal, Mohammed Hassanein. *Nasser. The Cairo Documents*. London: New English Library, 1972.

Hernton, Calvin C. *Sex and Racism*. London: Paladin, 1970.

Herrera, María Cristina, and Leonel Antonio de la Cuesta, eds. *Itinerario Ideológico. Antología de Lourdes Casal*. Miami: Instituto de Estúdios Cubanos, 1982.

Horowitz, Irving Louis. "Authenticity and Autonomy in Cuban Communism." In *Cuban Communism*. See Horowitz, ed.

———. "The Military Origins of the Cuban Revolution." In *Cuban Communism*. See Horowitz, ed.

———. "The Political Sociology of Cuban Communism." In *Cuban Communism*. See Horowitz, ed.

——— , ed. *Cuban Communism*, 3d ed. New Brunswick, N.J.: Transaction Books, 1977.

Hoskyns, Catherine. *The Congo Since Independence, January 1960–December 1961*. London: Oxford University Press, 1965.

Isaacs, Harold R. *The New World of Negro Americans*. New York: Viking Press, 1963.

Ismael, Tareq Y. *The U.A.R. in Africa. Egypt's Policy under Nasser*. Evanston, Ill.: Northwestern University Press, 1971.

James, Daniel. *Cuba: The First Soviet Satellite in the Americas*. New York: Avon Books, 1961.

Jaulin, Robert, ed. *Le livre blanc de l'ethnocide en Amérique*. Paris: Fayard, 1972.

Johnson, Haynes. *The Bay of Pigs*. New York: Norton, 1964.

Jones, Leroi, and Larry Neal, eds. *Black Fire*. New York: William Morrow, 1968.

Jones, Ronald E. "Cuba and the English-Speaking Caribbean." In *Cuba and the World*. See Blasier and Mesa-Lago, eds.

Joxe, Alain. *Socialism et crise nucléaire*. Paris: Editions de l'Herne, 1973.

Kanza, Thomas. *Conflict in the Congo*. London: Penguin Books, 1972.

Karol, K. S. *Guerrillas in Power*. New York: Hill & Wang, 1970.

———. "The Reckoning: Cuba and the U.S.S.R." In *Cuban Communism*. See Horowitz, ed.

Kennedy, Robert F. *Thirteen Days. A Memoir of the Cuban Missile Crisis*. New York: W. Norton, 1969.

Kenner, Martin, and James Petras, eds. *Fidel Castro Speaks*. Harmondsworth: Penguin Books, 1972.

Kiple, Kenneth F. *Blacks in Colonial Cuba, 1774–1899*. Gainesville, Fla.: University of Florida Press, 1976.

Kodjo, Edem. *Et Demain l'Afrique*. Paris: Stock, 1985.

Krushchev, Nikita. *Nikita Krushchev Remembers*. London: Andre Deutsch, 1971.

Lacy, Leslie Alexander. "African Responses to Malcolm X." In *Black Fire*. See Leroi Jones and Larry Neal, eds.

———. "Malcolm X in Ghana." In *Malcolm X. The Man and His Times*. See Clarke, ed.

Larkin, Bruce D. *China and Africa*. Uppsala: The Scandinavian Institute of African Studies, 1964.

Ledeen, Michael, and Herbert Romerstain, eds. *Grenada Documents: An Overview and Selection*. Washington, D.C.: Department of State and the Department of Defense, September 1984.

Lederer, Ivo, ed. *Conference on a Century of Russian Foreign Policy*. New Haven, Conn.: Yale University Press, 1962.

Legum, Colin, and Tony Hodges. *After Angola: The War in Southern Africa*. London: Rex Collins, 1976.

Leiris, Michel. "Folklore et culture vivante." In *Le livre blanc*. See Jaulin, ed.

Levesque, Jacques. *L'URSS et la Révolution Cubaine*. Paris: Presses de la Fondation Nationale des Sciences Politiques, 1976.

Levgold, Robert. *Soviet Policy in West Africa*. Cambridge, Mass.: Harvard University Press, 1970.

Leymarie, Philipe. *Océan Indien. Le nouveau coêur du monde*. Paris: Karthala, 1981.

Lightfoot, Claude M. *Ghetto Rebellion to Black Liberation*. New York: International Publishers, 1969.

Lockwood, Lee. *Castro's Cuba, Cuba's Fidel*. New York: Vintage Books, 1969.

———. *Conversations with Eldridge Cleaver*. New York: McGraw-Hill, 1970. Lofchie, Michael. *Zanzibar: Background to Revolution*. Princeton: Princeton University Press, 1965.

Loney, Marin. "Social Control in Cuba." In *Politics and Deviance*. See Taylor.

López Fresquet, Rufo. *My Fourteen Months with Castro*. Cleveland: The World, 1966.

López Valdez, Rafaél. "La sociedad secreta Abacuá y los procesos de cámbio en los obreros manuales del puerto de la Habana." In *VII Congrès International des Sciences Anthropologiques et Ethnologiques*, vol. 2. Moscow: Nauka, 1971.

Lowenthal, Richard. "The Sino-Soviet Split and its Repercussions in Africa." In *The Soviet Bloc, China and Africa*. See Sven Hamrell and Carl Gosta Widstrand, eds.

Makonnen, Ras. *Pan-Africanism from Within*. London: Oxford University Press, 1973.

Mallin, Jay, ed. *"Ché" Guevera on Revolution*. New York: Delta Books, 1969.

Manigat, Leslie. *Evolution et révolutions. L'Amérique latine au XXème siecle 1889–1929*. Paris: Editions Richelieu, 1973.

Mankiewicz, Frank, and Kirby Jones. *With Fidel: A Portrait of Castro and Cuba*. New York: Ballantine Books, 1976.

Martinet, Gilles. *Les cinq communismes*. Paris: Seuil, 1971.

Martínez-Alier, Juán, and Verena Martínez-Alier. *Cuba: Economía y sociedad*. Paris: Ruedo Iberico, 1972.

Martínez Furé, Rogelio. *Poesía yoruba*. Havana: Ediciones El Puente, 1963.

Marx, Karl, and Friedrich Engels. *On Colonialism*. Moscow: Progress Publishers, 1965.

Matthews, Herbert L. *Fidel Castro*. New York: Simon & Schuster, 1969.

Mayal, James. *Africa: The Cold War and After*. London: Elek Books, 1971.

McDougall, Walter A. Proceedings of the conference *José Martí and the Cuban Revolution*. Los Angeles: UCLA Latin American Center Publications, vol. 62, 1986.

McGaffey, Wyatt, and Clifford R. Barnett. *Cuba, Its People, Its Society, Its Culture*. New Haven, Conn.: Human Relations Area Files Press, 1962.

Melady, Thomas P. *The Revolution of Color*. New York: Hawthorn Books, 1966.

Merle, Robert. *Moncada, Premier combat de Fidel Castro*. Paris: Laffont, 1955.

Mesa-Lago, Carmelo. *Cuba in the 1970s*. Albuquerque: University of New Mexico Press, 1976.

—— and June Belkin, eds. *Cuba in Africa*. Pittsburgh: University of Pittsburgh Press, 1982.

Mestiri, Ezzédine. *Les Cubains en Afrique*. Paris: Karthala, 1980.

Middleton, John, and Jane Campbell. *Zanzibar: Its Society and Politics*. London: Oxford University Press, 1965.

Morales y Morales, Vidal. *Iniciadores y primeros mártires de la revolución cubana*, vols. 1 and 2. Havana: Consejo Nacional de Cultura, 1963.

Neuhauser, Charles. *Third World Politics: China and the Afro-Asian Peoples Solidarity Organization, 1957–1967*. Cambridge, Mass.: Harvard University East Asian Research Center, 1968 (monograph).

Nixon, Richard. *Six Crises*. New York: Doubleday, 1962.

Nkrumah, Kwame. *Challenge of the Congo*. New York: International Publishers, 1969.

North, Joseph. *Cuba: Hope of a Hemisphere*. New York: International Publishers, 1961.

Obiden, K.M. "Kuba v bor 'be za svobudo i nezavisimost." In *L'URSS et la Chine*. See Carrère d'Encausse and Schram, eds.

Okello, John. *Revolution in Zanzibar*. Nairobi: East African Publishing House, 1967.

Otero, Lisandro, and Francisco Hinojosa Martínez. *Política cultural de Cuba*. Paris: Unesco, 1971.

Ottaway, David, and Marina Ottaway. *Algeria: The Politics of a Socialist Revolution*. Berkeley and Los Angeles: University of California Press, 1970.

Petit, Antoine G. *Castro, Debray contre le Marxisme-Léninisme*. Paris: Laffont, 1968.

Pinos Sántos, Oscar. *História de Cuba. Aspéctos fundamentales*, 2d ed. Havana: Editorial Universitaria, 1963.

Portuondo Lináres, Serafín. *Los independientes de color. História del Partido Independiente de Color*. Havana: Publicaciones del Ministerio de Educación (Dirección de Cultura), 1950.

Prohias, R. J., and Lourdes Casal. *The Cuban Minority in the United States. Preliminary Report on Need Identification and Program Evaluation*. Boca Ratón, Fla.: Florida Atlantic University, 1973.

Reckord, Barry. *Does Fidel Eat More Than Your Father?* London: Andre Deutsch, 1971.

Ring, Harry. *How Cuba Uprooted Race Discrimination*. New York: Pioneer Publishers, 1961 (Pamphlet).

Rodney, Walter. *The Groundings with My Brothers*. London: Bogle-L'Ouverture Publications, 1969 (booklet).

Rodríguez Morejón, Gerardo. *Fidel Castro, biografía*. Havana: P. Fernandez, 1959.

Rojas, Marta. *La generación del centenario en el Moncada*. Havana, Ediciones R, 1965.

Rojo, Ricardo. *My Friend Ché*. New York: Dial Press, 1968.

Ruiz, Ramón Eduardo. *Cuba: The Making of a Revolution*. Amherst: University of Massachusetts Press, 1968.

Saco, José Antonio. *Contra la anexión*, vol. 1. Havana: 1928.

Salkey, Andrew. *Havana Journal*. London: Pelican Books, 1971.

San Martín, Marta, and Ramón L. Bonachea. "The Military Dimension of the Cuban Revolution." In *Cuban Communism*. See Horowitz, ed.

Sardinha, Dennis. *The Poetry of Nicolás Guillén*. London: New Beacon Books, 1976.

Scheer, Robert, and Maurice Zeitlin, eds. *Cuba, An American Tragedy*. Harmondsworth: Penguin, 1964.

Schlesinger, Jr., Arthur. *A Thousand Days. John F. Kennedy in the White House*. New York: Fawcett World Library, 1967.

Seabury, Paul, and Walter A. McDougall, eds. *The Grenada Papers*. San Francisco, California: Institute of Contemporary Studies, 1984.

Segal, Ronald. *The Race War*. London: Jonathan Cape, 1966.

Semidei, Manuela. *Les Etats-Unis et la Révolution cubaine*. Paris: Presses de la Fondation Nationale des Sciences Politiques, 1968.

Sinclair, Andrew. *Guevara*. London: Fontana/Collins, 1970.

Slusser, Robert M. *The Berlin Crisis of 1961*. Baltimore, Md.: Johns Hopkins University Press, 1973.

Smith, Robert Freeman, ed. *Background to Revolution: The Development of Modern Cuba*. New York: Alfred Knopf, 1966.

Smith, Wayne. *The Closest of Enemies*. New York: William Morrow, 1986.

Smith, William Gardner. *L'Amérique noire*. Paris: Casterman Col. PH, 1972.

Sobel, Lester A., ed. *Cuba, the U.S., and Russia, 1960-1963*. New York: Facts on File, 1964.

Stevens, Christopher. *The Soviet Union and Black Africa*. London: Macmillan Press, 1976.

Suárez, Andrés. *Cuba: Castroism and Communism, 1959-1966*. Cambridge, Mass.: M.I.T. Press, 1967.

Szulc, Tad. *Fidel. A Critical Portrait*. New York: William Morrow, 1986.

Suchlicki, Jaime. *University Students and Revolution in Cuba, 1920-1968*. Coral Gables, Fla.: University of Miami Press, 1969.

Sutherland, Elizabeth. *The Youngest Revolution*. New York: Dial Press, 1969.

Taylor, Ian, and Laurie Taylor, eds. *Politics and Deviance*. Harmondsworth: Penguin, 1973.

Tetlow, Edwin. *Eye on Cuba*. New York: Harcourt, Brace and World, Inc., 1966.

Thebergue, James D., ed. *Soviet Seapower in the Caribbean: Political and Strategic Implications*. New York: Praeger, 1972.

Thomas, Hugh. *Cuba, or the Pursuit of Freedom*. London: Eyre & Spottiswoode, 1971.

Tórres Ramírez, Blanca. *Las relaciones cubano-soviéticas (1959-1968)*. Mexico City: El Colegio de Mexico, 1969.

Tretiak, Daniel. *Cuban Relations with the Communist System: The Politics of a Communist Independent, 1967-1970*. Waltham, Mass.: Advanced Studies Group, June 1970 (monograph 4).

――. "Cuba's Integration into the Communist System." In *The World Communist System: International and Comparative Studies*, edited by J.F. Triska. New York: Bobbs-Merrill, 1960.

Tucker, Frank. *The White Conscience*. New York: Ungar, 1968.

Tutino, Saverio. *L'Octobre cubain*. Paris: Maspero, 1969.

Unesco. *Introducción a la cultura Africana en América Latina*. Paris: Unesco, 1970.

United States Department of State. *U.S. Policy Toward Cuba*. Washington, D.C., 1964.

Urrútia, Gustavo E. "El prejuicio en Cuba." In *Negro Anthology*. See Cunard.

Valdés, Nelson P. "Revolutionary Solidarity in Angola." in *Cuba in the World*. See Blasier and Mesa-Lago.

Vives, Juán. *Les maîtres de Cuba*. Paris: Laffont, 1981.

Walters, Robert S. "Soviet Economic Aid to Cuba." In *Fidel Castro's Personal Revolution in Cuba: 1959-1973*. See Goodsell, ed.

Wilkerson, Loree. *Fidel Castro's Political Program from Reformism to "Marxism-Leninism."* Gainesville, Fla.: University of Florida Press, 1965.

Williams, Robert F. *Negroes with Guns*. Chicago: Third World Press, 1973.

Wilson, Edward T. *Russia and Black Africa Before World War II*. New York and London: Holmes and Meir Pulblishers, 1974.

Wolpin, Miles D. *Cuban Foreign Policy and Chilean Politics*. Toronto: Lexington Books, 1972.

X, Malcolm, with Alex Haley. *The Autobiography of Malcolm X*. New York: Grove Press, 1966.

Yacobson, Serguis. "Russia and Africa." In *Conference on a Century of Russian Foreign Policy*, edited by Ivo Lederer. New Haven, Conn.: Yale University Press, 1962.

Ying-Hsiang, Cheng. *Idylle sino-cubaine, brouille sino-soviétique.* Paris: Armand Colin/Fondation Nationale des Sciences Politiques, 1973.

Zeitlin, Maurice. *Revolutionary Politics and the Cuban Working Class.* New York: Harper & Row, 1970.

———. "Cuba: Revolution Without a Blueprint." In *Cuban Communism.* See Horowitz, ed.

Ziegler, Jean. *Les rebelles.* Paris: Seuil, 1983.

2. Articles

Abir, Mordecai. "The Contentious Horn of Africa." *Conflict Studies* (London) 24 (June 1972).

Acosta, Teófilo. "Pierre Mulele: Un traître qui fit confiance à d'autres traîtres." *Granma* (Havana, weekly in French), 7 October 1968.

Aguirre, Benigno. "Differential Migration of Cuban Social Races." *Latin American Research Review* 2, no. 1.

Arnes, David. "Negro Family Types in a Cuban Solar." *Phylon* 2, no. 2 (1950).

Bascom, William R. "Yoruba Acculturation in Cuba." *Les Afro-Américains* (Dakar) IFAN, no. 27 (1953).

Betancourt Bencomo, Juán René. "Castro and the Cuban Negro." *Crisis* 68, no. 5 (1961).

———. "Fidel Castro y la integración nacional." In "Recuento de la grán mentira comunista," recopilación de la revista *Bohemia* 1, no. 2:36.

Booth, David. "Cuba, Color and the Revolution." *Science and Society* 40, no. 2 (1976).

Brito, Eloy G. Merino. "Racial Discrimination and the Policy of Apartheid." *Politica Internacional* 2, no. 8 (1964):19–35.

Burg, David. "The People's Friendship University." *Problems of Communism* (November-December 1961).

Cabral, Amilcar. "Decidés à résister." *Tricontinental* 8 (1968).

Carbonell, Walterio. "A propósito de las causas de la revolución de 1895." *Lunes de Revolución* 37 (30 November 1959):12–14.

———. "Africa y Cuba." *Lunes de Revolución* 83 (24 October 1960):15.

———. "Congreso mundial de países sub-desarrollados." *Revolución,* 5 December 1959, p. 2.

Carneado, José F. "La discriminación racial en Cuba no volvera jamás." *Cuba Socialista* 2, no. 5 (1962):54–67.

Carrère d'Encausse, Hélène. "Problème interne, instrument politique: pouvoir communiste et Islam en Union Soviétique." *Le Monde Diplomatique* 281 (August 1977).

Casal, Lourdes. "Race Relations in Contemporary Cuba." *Minority Rights Group* report no. 7 (1979).

Cattell, David T. "Communism and the African Negro." *Problems of Communism* (September–October 1959).

Cepeda, Rafaél. "Fidel Castro y el reino de Diós." *Bohemia*, 17 July 1960.

Cleaver, Eldridge. "Fidel Castro's African Gambit." *Newsweek* (International Edition), 3 May 1976.

Costa Pinto, L. A. "Negros y blancos en América Latina." *Revista de la Universidad de Buenos Aires* 3, no. 4 (July–December 1963).

Crimi, Bruno. "L'Afrique et la tentation cubaine." *Jeune Afrique* (Paris) 16 April 1976, p. 11.

Cruse, Harold. "Cuba y el Negro norteamericano." *Casa de las Américas* (August–September, 1960).

de Benoist, Joseph Roger. "Cuba-Afrique. Cubains avant tout." *Afrique* 29 (November 1979).

Dépestre, René. "El que no tiene de Congo." *Unión* (April–June 1965).

———. "Lèttre de Cuba." *Présence Africaine*, 4, no. 56 (1965).

———. "On Culture, Politics and Race in Cuba." *Socialism* (Kingston), 3, no. 5 (May 1986).

———. "Problemas de la identidad del hombre negro en las literatures antillanas." *CASA* 53 (March–April 1969).

Diagne, Pathé. "Langues africaines, dévéloppement économique et culture nationale." *Notes Africaines* (Dakar) IFAN no. 129 (1971):2–19.

———. "Pour une politique des langues nationales." *Famille et Dévéloppement* (Dakar) 6 (1976):39–43.

Díaz, Alberto Pedro. "Guanamaca: Una comunidad haitiana." *Etnología y Folklore* 1 (January–June 1966).

Dominguez, Jorge I. "Racial and Ethnic Relations in the Cuban Armed Forces: A Non Topic." *Armed Forces and Society* 2, no. 2 (February 1976).

dos Santos, Marcelino. "Une guerre internationale." *Tricontinental* (Havana) March–April 1971, p. 9.

Durch, William J. "The Cuban Military in Africa and the Middle East: From Algeria to Angola." Professional Paper no. 201, Arlington, Virginia: Center for Naval Analyses, September 1977.

Eggington, Joyce. "Racial Hatred Invades the U.N." *London Observer*, 13 December 1964, p. 2.

Entralgo, José Elías. "La mulatización cubana." *CASA* 36–37 (May–August 1966).

Fagen, Richard R. "Charismatic Authority and the Leadership of Fidel Castro." *Western Political Quarterly* (June 1965).

Falk, Pamela. "Cuba in Africa." *Foreign Affairs* 65, no. 5. (Summer 1987).

Fall, Babacar. "La croisade cubaine." *Afrique* (London) 12 (1978).

Fernández Retamar, Roberto. "Debunking the 'Black Legend.' A Hard Look at the Historical Role of Spain in Latin America." *The Unesco Courier* (Paris) (August–September 1977).

Fontaine, Andre. "Great Temptation." *Survival* 11, no. 11 (November 1969).

Franco, José Luciano. "Preséncia de Africa en América." *Triconti-nental* 14 (1969).

Franqui, Carlos. "Las prisiones de Ben Bella." *Cambio 16* (Madrid) 326 (5 March 1978).

Gaete Darbo, Adolfo. "Evaluación de las estadísticas vitales en América Latina." *America Latina* 2 (April–June 1964).

Galich, Manuel. "El Indio y el Negro, ahora y antes." *CASA* 36–37 (May–August 1966).

García Aguero, Salvador. "Preséncia africana en la música nacional." *Estúdios afrocubanos* (Havana) (1937).

García Marquez, Gabriel. "En Afrique: Les mois de ténèbres." *Afrique-Asie* (Paris) 147 (1977).

———. "Opération Charlotte." *Libération*, 27 January 1977.

Gibert, Stephen P. "Wars of Liberation and Soviet Military Policy." *Orbis* (Philadelphia) 10, no. 3 (Fall 1966):147.

Gilly, Adolfo. "A Conferecne without Glory and without Program." *Monthly Review* 17, no. 11 (April 1966).

Gonzalez, Edward. "Castro's Revolution, Cuban Communist Appeals and the Soviet Response." *World Politics* 21, no. 1 (1968):39–68.

———. "Complexities of Cuban Foreign Policy." *Problems of Communism* (Washington, D.C.) 26, no. 6 (November–December 1977).

Guevara, Ernesto Ché. "Notas para el estúdio de la ideología de la revolución cubana." *Verde Olivo*, 8 October 1960.

Hernández Artigas, J. "¡Negros no . . . ciudadanos!" *Revolución*, 20 February 1959.

Hountondji, Paulin. "Charabia et mauvaise conscience." *Présence Africaine* (Paris) 1, no. 61 (1967).

Howard, Charles P., Sr. "What's the Real Story on Cuba?" *Muhammad Speaks* (Chicago), 13 September 1963.

———. "The Afro-Cubans." *Freedomways* 4, no. 3.

Huberman, Leo and Paul Sweezy. "The Tricontinental and After." *Monthly Review* 17, no. 11 (April 1966).

Ivanov, K. "Present-day Colonialsm: Its Socioeconomic Aspects." *International Affairs* (Moscow) 10 (1960).

Johnson, Priscilla. "Apartheid U." *Harper's Magazine*, December 1960.

Jones, Leroi. "Cuba Libre." *Evergreen Review*, November–December 1960.

Julien, Claude. "Un prototype de révolution contre l'impérialisme économique." *Esprit* (Paris) 4 (April 1961).

——. "Sept heures avec M. Fidel Castro." *Le Monde*, 22–23 March 1963.

Karol, K. S. "Where Castro Went Wrong." *New Statesman*, 7 (August 1970).

King, Lloyd. "Mr. Black in Cuba." *African Studies Association of The West Indies* (Kingston) Bulletin no. 5 (December 1972).

Krief, Claude. "De Gaulle à Moscou." *Nouvel observateur*, 15 June 1966.

Kudryavtsev, V. "Problems of Afro-Asian Solidarity." *International Affairs* (Moscow) 5 (1963).

Kyle, Keith. "Coup in Zanzibar." *Africa Report* (February 1964).

——. "How It Happened." *The Spectator*, 4 February 1964, pp. 202–203.

Lacoste, Yves. "Fidel Castro et la Sierra Maestra." *Hérodote* 1, no. 5 (January–March 1977).

Legré, Michel. "Les africains a Cuba." *Jeune Afrique*, 18 January 1978.

LeoGrande, William. "Cuba's Policy in Africa 1959–1980." Berkeley, California: Institute of International Affairs, 1980.

Lopez Moráles, Humberto. "El supuesto 'Africanismo' del español en Cuba," *Archivus* (Madrid) 4, nos. 1,2 (January–December 1964).

Lopez Valdéz, Rafaél, and Pedro Deschamps. "La sociedad secreta 'Abakuá' en un grupo de obreros portuarios." Etnologiá y folklore 2 (July–December 1966): 5–26.

MacFarquar, Roderick. "Brinkmanship." *Survival* 11, no. 11.

Malick, S. Max Madher. "La conféssion d'un membre du P.A.I." *L'Unité Africaine* (Dakar), 11 March 1965, p. 5.

Malley, Simon. "Vingt heures d'entrétiens avec Fidel Castro." *Afrique-Asie*, 16–29 May 1977, p. 13.

Marti, Jorge L. "La cuestión racial en la evolución constitucional cubana." *Política* (Carácas) 33 (April 1964).

McGrath, Tom. "Robert Williams: Racism in Cuba?" *Los Angeles Free Press*, 17 February 1967, p. 9.

Moore, Carlos. "Cuba: The Untold Story." *Présence Africaine* 24, no. 52:177–229.

———. "Cuba: Ces noirs qui partent." *Jeune Afrique* no. 1027 (September 1980):38–39.

———. "Interview with Professor Cheikh Anta Diop." *Afriscope* (Lagos) 7, no. 2 (February 1977):9–15.

———. "Le peuple noir a-t-il sa place dans la révolution cubaine?" *Présence Africaine* 52 (1964).

Mortara, Georgio. "Evaluación de la información censal para América Latina." *América Latina* 2 (April–June 1964).

Nadle, Marlene. "Régis Debray Speaks from Prison." *Ramparts* (New York), 24 August 1968.

Nicot, Carlos, and Vicente Cubillas. "Relátos inéditos sobre la acción revolucionária del lider Frank País." *Revolución*, 30 July 1963.

Norden, Eric. "The Murder of Malcolm X." *The Realist* (New York) 73 (1967).

North, Joseph. "Negro and White in Cuba." *Political Affairs* (New York) (July 1963).

Perez de la Riva, Juán de la. "Cuadro sinóptico de la esclavitud en Cuba y de la cultura occidental." *Actas del folklore* 1, no. 5 (May 1961).

———. "La population de Cuba et ses problèmes," *Population* 22, no. 1.

Price, D.L. "Setbacks for the USSR in the Middle East." *Soviet Analyst* 5, no. 22 (28 October 1976).

Rodríguez, Carlos Rafaél. "Lenin y la cuestión colonial." *CASA*, 59 (March–April 1970).

Sauldie, Madan. "Moscow's New Hopes in Africa." *Africa* (London) 66 (February 1977).

Serviat, Pedro. "La discriminación racial en Cuba, su orígen, desarrollo y terminación definitiva." *Islas* (La Habana) 66 (May–August 1980).

Stavenhagen, Rodolfo. "Problemas raciales en América Latina." *Courrier de l'Unesco* (Paris), October 1960.

Sulzberger, C.L. "Race and Revolution." *International Herald Tribune*, 20 September 1967, p. 5.

Talbot, Strobe. "Curious Contrasts in Communism." *Time International*, 10 November 1975.

Tretiak, Daniel. "Cuba and the Soviet Union: The Growing Accommodation." *Orbis* (Philadelphia) 11, no. 2 (Summer 1967).

Tse-tung, Mao. "Statement Supporting the Afro-Americans in their Just Struggle Against Racial Discrimination by U.S. Imperialism." *Peking Review* 34 (18 August 1967).

Walters, Barbara. "An Interview with Fidel Castro." *Foreign Policy*, no. 28 (Fall 1977).

Wauthier, Claude. "Les études africaines en Union Soviétique. Une interpretation du colonialisme, du racisme et du développement." *Le Monde Diplomatique*, May 1976.

Werth, Alexander. "Fifty Years After: A Portrait of the Soviet Union in Jubilee Year, 1967." *New Statesman*, 19 September 1967.

Will, George F. "The Durability of Castro." *International Herald Tribune*, 12–13 March 1977.

Williams, Robert F. "USA: The Potential of a Minority Revolution." *The Crusader* (Havana) 6 and 7 (Summer 1965).

———. "Cuba: The Tragedy of No Proletarian Cultural Revolution." *The Crusader Newsletter* (Peking) 8, no. 3 (March 1967).

Worthy, William. "You Can't Come Home Anymore." *Revolution* (Lausanne) 4–5 (1963).

3. Unpublished Papers

Mancuso Edwards, Flora. "The Theater of the Black Diaspora: A Comparative Study of Black Drama in Brazil, Cuba and the United States." Ph.D. diss., New York University, 1975.

Mazrui, Ali, in association with Lemuel Johnson and Rovan Locke. "Cuba's Castro and Africa's Castration: A Case Study in Micro-Dependency." Paper presented to the International Conference on "Latin America: The Middle Class of Nations," in Lake Llanquihue, Chile, November 25–30, 1978.

Nascimento, Abdias do. "Afro-Brazilian Ethnicity and International Policy." Paper presented to first Congress on Black Cultures in the Americas, Cali, Colombia, 24–28 August 1977.

Scott, W. R. "The American Negro and the Italo-Ethiopian risis, 1934–36." Ph.D diss., Howard University, 1966.

Williams, Robert F. "Open Letter to Fidel Castro." Roneotyped, 28 August 1966.

4. Newspapers and Magazines

Actas del Folklore (Havana), October–December 1961.

Afriscope (Lagos), vol. 7, no. 2, February 1977.

Afrique 19 (November 1979).

Bohemia (Havana) 27 (5 July 1968); 31 January 1964; 31 July 1964; 30 July 1965.

La Calle (Havana), 30 May 1955.

Current Digest and the Soviet Press, 10 August 1960.

Diário de la Marina (Havana), 2 August 1933–21 April 1959.

Granma (Havana), 9 May 1971 (English weekly summary); 27 July 1967; 4 February 1968; 11 February 1968; 24 August 1968; 7 September 1972.

Granma (French weekly edition), 16 January 1966; 7 October 1968; 24 August 1969; 2 May 1971; 4 May 1972; 14 May 1972; 20 August 1972; 3 July 1983.

Hoy (Havana), 23 May 1959; 7 January 1960.

Jeune Afrique, 16 April 1976.

Libération, 27 January 1977.

Los Angeles Times (Los Angeles), December 6, 1985.

Lunes de Revolución (Havana), 24 October 1960.

Miami Herald, 21 January 1985.

Le Monde, 2 October 1960–1 November 1960; 12–13 May 1963; 17 October 1963; 8 November 1963; 6 August 1968; 20 March 1969; 17–19 March 1971; 12 May 1971; 4 December 1971; 23 June 1977.

Le Monde Diplomatique, June 1984.

El Mundo (Havana), 3 April 1959.

New York Times, 19 June 1960.

Obra Revoluciónaria (Havana) 12 (25 July 1960); 27 July 1963; 9 October 1963; 9 January 1964; 6 February 1964.

The Observer (London), November 24, 1985.

Pensamiento Crítico (Havana) 21 (1968).

Política Internacional (Havana).

Pravda, 9 July 1960.

Présence Africaine (Paris) 26(54).

Ramparts (New York), 24 August 1968.

Renmin Ribao (Peking), 15 December 1962.

Revolución (Havana), 23 January 1959–15 January 1963; 2 May 1963; 9 May 1963; 15 October 1983.

Revolution Africaine (Algiers), 26 December 1964; 23 October 1965.

Sechaba (London), vol. 10, 4th Quarter, 1976.

Tricontinental.

5. Interviews and Consultations

Adotevi, Stanislas S. Dakar. 21 December 1979.

Akuete, Ebenezer. Havana. July 1962.

Aldama, Gilberto. Paris. May 5, 1981.

Alméndros, Nestor. Paris. April 18, 1983.

Andrade, Mario de. Dakar. January 14, 1977; Paris, October 18, 1983.

Anta Diop, Cheikh. Dakar. February 21, 1981; Paris, March 14, 1982.

Aziz Iss-Hak, Mohammed Abdel. Cairo. December 1964.

Balin, Alix. Paris. February 14, 1978.
Bangoura, Salifou, and Abdelaziz Hadiri. Paris. March 14, 1977.
Barroso, Reinaldo. Paris. May 5, 1981.
Benemelis, Juán. Los Angeles. 2 March 1985.
Blanco, Orlando. Geneva. 18 March 1977.
Bula Nyati, Mandungu. Paris. February 10, 1971.
Bundles, A'Lelia. Knoxville, Tennessee. April 25, 1987.
Carbonell, Walterio. Havana. September, 1963.
Cárdenas, Esteban. Miami. August 28, 1985 and December 26, 1985.
Carmichael, Stokely. Geneva. March 23, 1972.
Casanovas, Manuél. Miami. October 13, 1986.
Céspedes, Carlos Manuel de. Washington, D.C. May 21, 1986.
Cissé, Alioune. Nouakchott. December 20, 1978.
Clington, Mario da Souza. Paris. October 15, 1983.
Conteh, Abdulahi. Paris. April 13, 1981.
Da Crúz, Viriato. Paris. November, 1965.
Darcier, Sabine. Paris. August 3, 1973.
Dépestre, René. Paris. 16 January 1985.
Diallo, Seydou. Bamako, Mali. December 27, 1976.
Díaz Cartaya, Agustín. Havana. September, 1963.
Diederich, Bernard. Miami. March 12, 1987.
Dymally, Mervyn M. Washington, D.C. April 17, 1984.
Eassum, Donald. New York. October 9, 1986.
Franqui, Carlos. Geneva. 17–18 March 1977; Montecatini, Italy, 15–17 April 1977.
Guissé, Tidiani. Dakar. 14 November 1979.
Howard, Sr., Charles P. Havana. July 1963.
Huteau, Jean. Paris. March 20, 1980.
Jackman, Glenn. Kingston. May 13, 1986.
Kane, Oumar. Paris. October 18, 1977.
Kanno, Ayalew. Dakar. April 5, 1979.
Kashamura, Anicet. Paris. 28 February and March 1977.
Kassongo, Kasmarlot. Lagos. 21–22 September 1979.
Keita, Karamoko. Bamako. 28 December 1978.
Kodjo, Edem. Paris. April 15, 1981; October 18, 1983.
Kouyaté, Mami. Rome. January 29, 1985.
Kouyaté, Seydou Badian. Dakar. February 4, 1979.
Lacy, Leslie Alexander. Havana. July–August 1963.
Lemus, Joaquim de. Lagos. October 1975 and February 1976.
Lopo, Castro. Paris. January 3, 1974.
Luke, Desmond. Lagos. October 16, 1976.
Makeba, Miriam. Lagos. October 1974.

Marof, Akhbar. New York. April 1961.

Medina, Julio. Havana. September 1963.

Melgar, Alfredo. Geneva. March 18, 1977.

Ming Huan, Chin. Paris. October 1966.

Mulele, Hygin. Paris. 8–10 March 1979.

Muñóz, Eugenio. Miami. September 26, 1986; March 17, 1987.

Naby Issa, Soumah. Havana. September 1962.

Nyerere, Julius. Dar es Salaam. 20 July 1974.

Otero, Juán. Havana. September 1963.

Ricardou, Vincent. Dakar. 5 June 1979.

Samantar, Mohamed. Geneva. April 10, 1981.

Savimbi, Jonas. Cairo. July 1964.

Signaté, Ibrahima. Dakar. 14 January 1976.

Silveira, Onesimo. Dakar. August 14, 1976.

Smith, William Gardner. Paris. October 1970.

Sykes, Abbas K. Paris. January 19, 1978 and 14–18 March 1978.

Tambo, Oliver. Paris. May 25, 1981.

Tchibindat, Felicité. Paris. 10 April 1981.

Tórres, Natividad. Miami. September 18, 1986.

Walsh, Bryan. Port-au-Prince. November 15, 1986.

Williams, Robert F. Havana. 1961–1963.

X, Malcolm. Paris. 23–24 November 1964.

Yerodia, Abdulay. Paris. 16 March 1983.

Young, Andrew. Atlanta, Georgia. November 23, 1982.

Yusufu, M. D. Lagos. October 9, 1975; November 8, 1978; February 23, 1981.

Carlos Moore was born in Cuba in 1942 of Jamaican-Barbadian immigrant, working-class parents. He left Cuba in 1963, in exile. An ethnologist, he holds two doctoral degrees from the University of Paris-7 (France) and specializes in the study of the impact of racial and ethnic dynamics on national and international politics.

Moore lived and worked in Africa for seven years (Egypt, Nigeria and Senegal), and for ten years in France. He has traveled extensively throughout Africa, Europe, the Pacific and Caribbean either as a news reporter or accomplishing field projects. His journalistic career involved working for *Agence-France-Presse* and *Jeune Afrique*, both in Paris.

He is the author of *This Bitch of a Life* (London: Allison and Busby and Paris: Karthala, 1982), a spicy first biography of the controversial, antiestablishment Nigerian musician, Fela Anikulapo-Kuti. His *Castro, The Blacks, and Africa* (Los Angeles: UCLA/CAAS, 1988), is the first comprehensive study on race relations in Socialist Cuba and of its impact on Fidel Castro's African-oriented foreign policy.

Moore makes his home in the French West Indies with his family. Currently, he divides his time between lectures at American campuses and writing his next book, *Growing Up With The Revolution*, a personal account of Castro's rise to power, seen through the eyes of a black youngster in a small sugar-producing town.

Other Titles of Interest

IMAGES OF BLACKS

Black Characters in the Brazilian Novel, Giorgio Marotti

Marotti describes the development of the depiction of Blacks from the beginnings of the Brazilian novel up to the present day, and analyzes how Brazil's greatest novelists, ranging from men like Jose Lins do Rego, a bitter white elitist, to Jorge Amado, the enlightened yet complex Bahian, came to their respective ideas of Blacks and black culture.
480 pages, 6 x 9", bibliography, glossary, illustrations, index
Clothbound **$50.95**   *ISBN 0-934934-24-X*   *Paperback* **$28.95**   *I SBN 0-934934-25-8*

Black Folk Here and There, St. Clair Drake

Volume I of a two volume work, *Black Folk Here and There* is an unusual blending of anthropology, intellectual history, the sociology of knowledge and Egyptology. While giving readers a remarkable intellectual history of Egypt, Drake manages to make old arguments astonishingly immediate by revealing both their intellectual and their political implications. No other study tackles the nature, development and impact of color prejudice with such force, clarity and relevance for contemporary times. A must read!
425 pages, 6 x 9", bibliography, illustrations, index.
Clothbound **$38.95**   *ISBN 0-934934-20-7*   *Paperback* **$22.95**   *ISBN 0-934934-21-5*

RACIAL INEQUALITY

Race, Class and Power in Brazil, Pierre-Michel Fontaine, ed.

New ground is broken in this book by some of the foremost scholars in the field of Brazilian race relations. In taking on the myth of the Brazilian"racial democracy," the authors examine various aspects of the Black Brazilian's changing racial attitudes and the struggle for parit and power. Contributors include Thomas Skidmore and Lelia Gonzalez.
160 pages, 6 x 9", glossary.
Clothbound **$19.95**   *ISBN 0-934934-22-3*   *Paperback* **$11.95**   *ISBN 0-934934-23-1*

Plantations, Peasants and State, Clive Thomas

Thomas's study demonstrates how the story of a developing nation is often the story of a single commodity and those who control it. He shows that sugar production was at the heart of colonial penetration, capitalist consolidation, and the subsequent underdevelopment of the Guyanese economy, while creating a solid basis for the analysis of other agrarian systems.
233 pages, 6 x 9", index. Co-published with University of the West Indies, Mona, Jamaica.
Clothbound **$26.00**   *ISBN 0-934934-18-5*   *Paperback* **$13.95**   *ISBN 0-934934-19-3*

The Other American Revolution, Vincent Harding

This is the story of the *"Other American Revolution,"* the centuries-old fight for freedom waged by black people in America. Beginning with African origins and concluding with perspectives on the period since the assassination of Martin Luther King, Jr., in 1968, Harding tells the story of the people, the movements, and the ideas that have given substance to one of the longest struggles for liberation in the modern world.
272 pages, 6 x 9"
Clothbound **$14.50**   *ISBN 0-934934-10-X*   *Paperback* **$ 8.50**   *ISBN 0-934934-06-1*

CAAS PUBLICATIONS ORDER FORM

	Circle one: clothbound/paperback	
Indicate number desired		
____ **Black Characters in the Brazilian Novel,** Marotti	$50.95	$28.95
____ **Black Folk Here and There, Volume 1,** Drake	$38.95	$22.95
____ **Race, Class, and Power in Brazil,** Fontaine	$19.95	$11.95
____ **Plantations, Peasants, and State,** Thomas	$26.00	$13.95
____ **The Other American Revolution,** Harding	$14.50	$ 8.50

Mail to:

UCLA Center for Afro-American Studies
Attention: Publication Unit
160 Haines Hall,
405 Hilgard Avenue
Los Angeles, CA 90024-1545

All orders MUST include payment in full. Please make checks payable to: The Regents of the University of California. Add $1.25 postage and handling for the first book, $.75 for each additional. California residents add 6.5% sales tax. For discounts on text book sales and multiple orders, call (213) 206-8080.

Name_____

Address_____

City_____ State_____ Zip_____